Model-Based Development and Evolution of Information Systems

John Krogstie

Model-Based Development and Evolution of Information Systems

A Quality Approach

 Springer

John Krogstie
Norwegian University
   of Science & Technology
Sem Sælandsvei 7-9
Trondheim, Norway

ISBN 978-1-4471-2935-6   ISBN 978-1-4471-2936-3 (eBook)
DOI 10.1007/978-1-4471-2936-3
Springer London Heidelberg New York Dordrecht

British Library Cataloguing in Publication Data
A catalogue record for this book is available from the British Library

Library of Congress Control Number: 2012939064

Printed on acid-free paper

Springer is part of Springer Science+Business Media (www.springer.com)

Preface

The work presented in this book is rooted many years back, both directly through own work over the last 20 years, and obviously indirectly, since this work has been done in a tradition of conceptual modelling going back additionally 20 years or more.

When I did my Master Thesis at NTH (now NTNU) in 1990, the 'five year plan' was to work 2 years in a consulting company to get more practical experience, before going back to do a Ph.D. in an area related to conceptual modelling. I still remember the interview with my later employer (Andersen Consulting) when being given the 'what do you do in 5 years' question. I obviously did not mention the Ph.D. plans.

Anyway, after 18 months in the trenches with Andersen Consulting, I was back at NTH as a Ph.D. student, with Arne Sølvberg as supervisor. At this time Arne had around ten Ph.D. students, all highly qualified. I had met several of them as a master student (as lecturers, supervisors and co-students), and quickly started to discuss. I remember in particular discussions with Odd Ivar Lindland on aspects of quality of models, discussion later followed up by many in the group, including my current colleagues at NTNU Jon Atle Gulla and Guttorm Sindre. In one particular group meeting, Odd Ivar described his early ideas on quality of models. Jon Atle, also having a masters in linguistics, suggested that he should look at the differentiation between syntax, semantics, and pragmatics found in linguistics and semiotics. The seed of the most important structuring principles you find in this book, the SEQUAL framework, was planted in these discussions almost 20 years ago.

So why this focus on (conceptual) modelling?

One can argue that the main reason why humans have excelled as species is our ability to represent, reuse and transfer knowledge across time and space. Whereas in most areas of human conduct, one-dimensional natural language is used to express and share knowledge, we see the need for and use of two and many-dimensional representational forms to be on the rise. One such representational form is called *conceptual modelling*. A *conceptual model* is traditionally defined as a description of the phenomena in a domain at some level of abstraction, which is expressed in a semi-formal or formal diagrammatical language.

Modelling is an important part of both information systems development and evolution, and organisational development in general (e.g. used in enterprise modelling/ enterprise architecture). The field includes numerous evolving modelling methods, notations and approaches. Even with some attempts to standardise (e.g. UML for object-oriented design), new modelling methods are being introduced regularly.

Whereas modelling techniques traditionally were used to create intermediate artefacts in systems analysis and design, more and more modelling methodologies take a more active approach to the exploitation of this particular form of knowledge representation. In approaches such as business process management (BPM), model driven architecture (MDA) and domain specific modelling/domain specific modelling languages (DSM/DSL). In enterprise architecture (EA) and active knowledge modelling (AKM), the models are used directly to form the information system of the organisation. At the same time, similar techniques are used also for sense-making and communication, model simulation, quality assurance and requirements specification in connection to more traditional forms of information systems development.

Given that modelling techniques are used in such a large variety of tasks with very different goals, it is important for appropriate use of the techniques to have a proper overview of different uses of modelling, and guidelines for what make a model sufficiently *good* to achieve the decided goals. An important aspect of this book is to discuss the quality of models and modelling languages in this setting. To help us in this process, a framework for understanding quality of models and modelling languages (SEQUAL) has been developed, and its use is described in detail in the book. Although we have been working relative to this framework over a long period, the book will provide many new developments and applications of the framework.

A number of books exist on particular approaches to modelling. There exist a number of standard system analysis and design books (dealing with ER-modelling, DFD, UML etc.), generally using these as tools to be learnt as part of software development. In our book we will look more broadly at the topic of modelling, making it easier when needing to use a new modelling approach to identify the type of approach and its strength and weaknesses.

What characterises existing books is that they look in particular on a given technique (and is often overly positive relative to this approach), without giving sufficient basis for judging the appropriateness of this technique relative to other available techniques for a given situation. There is no approach to modelling and model-based systems development that is best for all types of situations, thus a high-level overview to make it possible to evaluate the appropriateness of different approaches is called for.

The book has two intended audiences:

- It is primarily for computer science, software engineering and information system students on the post-graduate level (master's/Ph.D.), after they have had an introduction to information system analysis and design (for example, UML for systems design or process modelling-based using e.g. BPMN), and databases, that want to know more about conceptual modelling in their preparation for professional practice.
- Professionals with detailed experience and responsibilities related to development and evolution of information systems and information systems methodology including enterprise modelling and enterprise architecture that need to formalise

and structure their practical experiences or to update their knowledge, as a way to improve their professional activity.

At this level, many students have learnt modelling as a predefined tool, and have limited training in evaluating the appropriateness of models and modelling languages for a certain task. They also have limited practical experience with more than a few notations, and seldom real-life experiences with large-scale modelling and systems development. Many of the concepts and principles underlying the concrete modelling notation easily get abstract, and there is a need to exemplify the points and bridge the theoretical parts of the course to how it can address problems in practice.

Courses of this type often are a mix of general material and presentation of the favourite approaches of the lecturer. Thus I foresee the book to be a possible basis for many such courses, but where the syllabi in addition to material from the textbook can contain a number of recent articles and more detailed descriptions of selected techniques.

Acknowledgements

A large number of people deserve to be mentioned relative to the content of this book as collaborators and co-writers of projects and research work bringing us to the point we are today. Whereas many of our debts in this regard is visible through the references in the text, also many people have contributed in a more subtle way, bringing inspiration or roadblocks to be overcome.

When I started working in this field in the early 1990s, the research group around Arne Sølvberg was very important. I have already mentioned Arne, Odd Ivar, Jon Atle and Guttorm. Other collaborators at the time were Anne Helga Seltveit, Gunnar Brattås, Rudolf Andersen, Geir Willumsen, Mingwei Yang and Harald Rønneberg. In the Tempora project, I worked also with Benkt Wangler, Peter McBrien, and Richard Owens. The international collaboration led me into the IFIP WG 8.1 community and the CAiSE conference, which I have followed over the years collaborating with among others Wil van der Aalst, Jan Recker, Michael Rosemann, Andreas Opdahl, Sjaak Brinkkemper, Kalle Lyytinen, Barbara Pernici, Keng Siau, Terry Halpin, Antoni Olive, Oscar Pastor, Erik Proper, Janis Bubenko, Colette Rolland, Peri Loucopoulos, Janis Stirna, Anne Persson, Peter Fettke, Peter Loos and Constantin Houy.

After doing my Ph.D. I was again over in Andersen Consulting, and want to thank in particular Bjørn Ivar Danielsen, Nils Øveraas and Lars Henriksen for making it possible to keep in contact with the academic community also when working as a consultant. After this I worked in SINTEF, in particular on a number of Norwegian and EU projects where modelling of information systems was central. In particular I would like to thank Steinar Carlsen, Håvard Jørgensen, Dag Karlsen, Frank Lillehagen, Oddrun Ohren, Svein Johnsen, Heidi Brovold, Vibeke Dalberg, Siri Moe Jensen, Rolf Kenneth Rolfsen, Arne Jørgen Berre, Asbjørn Følstad, Reidar Gjersvik and Bjørn Skjellaug on the national front and Joerg Haake, Weigang Wang, Jessica Rubart, Michael Petit, Kurt Kosanke, Martin Zelm, Nacer Boudlidja, Herve Panetto, Guy Doumeingts and Thomas Knothe on the international front.

Also in the years connected to NTH and NTNU, I have had the pleasure to collaborate with a number of master's and Ph.D. students and postdocs, including Babak Amin Farschchian, Sofie de Flon Arnesen, Maria Rygge, Anna Gunnhild Nysetvold, Alexander Nossum, Yun Lin, Csaba Veres, Jennifer Sampson, Eirik Berg, Shang Gao, Sundar Gopalakrishnan, Gustav Aagesen and Lillian Hella.

A number of people at NTNU have also been influential through the normal scientific discourse, including Hallvard Trætteberg, Reidar Conradi, Monica Divitini, Dag Svanæs, Eric Monteiro, Agnar Aamodt, Pieter Toussaint, Letizia Jaccheri, Alf Inge Wang, Kjetil Nørvåg, Arild Faxvaag, Rolv Bræk, Sobah Abbas Petersen, Peter Herrmann, Frank Kraemer and Tor Stålhane.

Finally, I should mention my wife, Birgit Rognebakke Krogstie. Birgit also has a Ph.D. in Computer Science. Although it is in a somewhat different field, we often meet on various arenas including at home, making the dinner table discussions at times quite abstract and conceptual, to our children's irritation and at times (I hope) inspiration.

John Krogstie

Outline of the Book

In the first chapter we introduce the topic area and the most important concepts, including overall philosophy underlying the thinking on quality of models. This includes social constructivism, knowledge creation in organisations, semiotics and model monopoly. We also give a high-level overview of the most important goals of modelling and techniques for model-based development such as MDSD, DSM/DSL, BPM, MDA and AKM. The case studies used throughout the book both for illustrations in the book itself, and as cases for the exercises are briefly described (the actual case studies being provided in Appendix C).

Chapter 2. Methodology for Computerised Information Systems support in Organisation: Present the generic tasks and model types found in information systems development and evolution, and main methodologies for mixing different phases of information system development. In particular we describe in more detail the main approaches to model-based development presented on a high level in Chap. 1, but also provide a historical account of the development of methodologies in the area. Methodologies are classified relative to goal, process, product, capabilities needed, stakeholder participation, organisation and location of the tasks to be done.

Chapter 3. Modelling languages: Perspectives and abstraction mechanisms: Present main abstraction mechanisms used in modelling languages (generalisation, aggregation, classification, association), and survey well-known modelling approaches according to the perspective of modelling (behavioural, functional, structural, goal and rule, object-oriented, communicational, actor and role and topological). Process modelling is discussed relative to all perspectives. In addition, we present examples of multi-perspective modelling languages such as UML, EEML and GEMAL.

Chapter 4. Quality of models: Present the framework for quality of models (SEQUAL), including examples of means to achieve model quality of different levels (such as tool functionality and modelling techniques being appropriate for the development of models of high quality). Quality is discussed on seven levels: physical, empirical, syntactic, semantic, pragmatic, social and deontic.

Chapter 5. Quality of modelling languages: One important mean for making good models is the use of an appropriate modelling language. We describe here six facets of quality of a modelling language: domain appropriateness, comprehensibility appropriateness, participant appropriateness, modeller appropriateness, tool appropriateness and organisational appropriateness. The use of this part of the framework for the choice and guidance of development of new languages is further described in Chap. 7.

Chapter 6. Specialisation of SEQUAL: Whereas a strength of SEQUAL is that it is applicable on a large range of model types, this can also be a limitation since different types of models have their different characteristics and limitations. We have through practical needs devised a number of specialisations of the framework for different types of models, including for business process models, requirements models, data models, ontologies and interactive process models. We also see how we can apply SEQUAL for understanding data quality and the quality of maps, a different form of two-dimensional representation of knowledge.

Chapter 7. Applications of SEQUAL: Illustrates how to apply SEQUAL in connection to support modelling, but also in the assessment of existing and new models, modelling languages, modelling methodologies and modelling tools. Examples are provided from the application of SEQUAL in both industrial and governmental settings.

Chapter 8. Summary and outlook: Discusses the potential for model-based techniques in the future in the light of future developments in the business and IT world.

Each chapter ends with a summary of main aspects, and include a number of possible tasks. Whereas some of these are review question, where the answers can be found more or less directly in the text, the exercises are more demanding. The exercises are divided in three categories.

1. Smaller tasks that can be done alone
2. Pair exercises that for instance can be used during class in small breakout sessions
3. Group task, which are larger tasks, often including a more thorough investigation or modelling assignment to be done

Many tasks are to some extent open relative to for instance the modelling notations and tools that are used, to make it easier to adjust them to the interests and focus of concrete modelling courses using the book as a basis.

Contents

Introduction

In this chapter, we introduce the topic area and the most important concepts, including the overall philosophy underlying the thinking on quality of models. This includes social constructivism, knowledge creation in organisations, semiotics and model monopoly. We also give a high-level overview of the most important goals of modelling and techniques for model-based development, such as MDSD, DSM/DSL, BPM, MDA and AKM. This includes sense-making and communication, analysis and simulation, quality assurance, model deployment and activation and requirements specification. The case studies used throughout the book both for illustrations in the book itself and as cases for the exercises are described briefly.

One can argue that the main reason why humans have excelled as a species is because of our ability to represent, reuse and transfer knowledge across time and space. Based on mental models, we grow our knowledge and wisdom through experiences and participative learning. Whereas in most areas of human conduct, one-dimensional natural language is used to express and share knowledge, we see the need for and use of two- and many-dimensional representational forms to be on the rise. One such representational form is called *conceptual modelling*.

A *conceptual model* is traditionally defined as a description of the phenomena in a domain at some level of abstraction, which is expressed in a semi-formal or formal visual (diagrammatical) language.

In this text, we apply the following limitations when we talk about conceptual models:

- The languages for conceptual modelling are primarily diagrammatic having a limited vocabulary. The main symbols of the languages represent *concepts* such as states, processes, entities and objects. We prefer to use the terms '*phenomena*' and '*phenomena classes*' instead of '*concepts*' in this text since the word 'concept' is used in many different meanings in natural language. The diagrams typically consist of general (often directed) graphs containing nodes and edges between nodes and edges representing the different phenomena and phenomena classes.

J. Krogstie, *Model-Based Development and Evolution of Information Systems:*
A Quality Approach, DOI 10.1007/978-1-4471-2936-3_1,
© Springer-Verlag London 2012

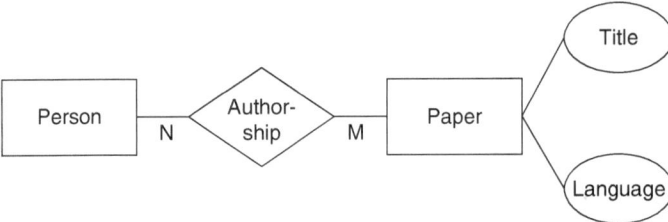

Fig. 1.1 Simple ER model

- Conceptual models are used either as an intermediate or directly used representation in the process of development and evolution of information systems. We recognise that conceptual modelling languages may be useful also for other purposes such as enterprise modelling when there is no immediate system implementation in mind, but focus particularly on use of models where the knowledge represented in the model is integrated as an active part of the information system supporting an organisation.
- The conceptual modelling languages presented in this text are meant to have general applicability; that is, they are not made specifically for the modelling of a limited area. We realise that the interest in and application of so-called domain-specific languages (DSM; Kelly and Tolvanen 2008) has increased over the last decade, but will in this book concentrate on generally applicable languages which obviously can be tailored to specific usage areas if it is called for.

A well-known language for conceptual modelling that can be used to illustrate the kind of models we are focusing on is the ER-modelling language (Chen 1976). A simple example is depicted in Fig. 1.1 where the relationship between persons and (scientific) papers is depicted. A paper has some attributes (title and language in the example) and can have more than one person as author. A person on the other hand can write more than one paper. Although we in this example have shown a data model, we use the term *conceptual modelling* much more broadly than data modelling, including process modelling, enterprise modelling, object-oriented modelling, rule modelling, organisational modelling and business modelling.

It is possible to track conceptual modelling back to the late 1950s, with the work of (Young et al. 1958). Modelling approaches as we know them today within the information system field were introduced on a large scale around 30 years ago, with the developments and take up of such techniques as DFDs (Demarco 1979) and ER diagrams (Chen 1976). In the beginning, focus was on developing conceptual modelling languages that would highlight *the* important concepts of the world, typically containing a few, generic concepts, depicted with simple and abstract visual icons. The languages were developed for IT experts to do the model building, although intended for use as a communication-artefact towards different 'domain experts'. In the 1980s, there were a large number of proposals for *the* right modelling notation. An understanding that language appropriateness depends on the objectives of modelling grew in the late 1980s. To address this situation, meta-modelling approaches started to appear around 1990 (Kelly et al. 1996), making it possible for projects and organisations to extend existing modelling languages and notations or to create entirely new modelling languages from scratch.

Model denotations are *signs*, and thus many in the field (Krogstie 2001; Price et al. 2004; Stamper 1987) base work on modelling on theories from semiotics. The study of signs has been associated with philosophical and linguistic enquiry into language and communication from the time of the Greek philosophers. Modern semiotics, as proposed by Pierce (1931–1935) and later developed by Morris (1938), describes the study of signs in terms of its logical components. These are the sign's actual *representation,* its *referent* or intended meaning and its *interpretation* or received meaning. Relations between these three aspects of a sign were further described by Morris as syntactic (between sign representations), semantic (between a representation and its referent) and pragmatic (between the representation and the interpretation) semiotic levels. The process of interpretation, called semiosis, at the pragmatic level necessarily results from and depends on the use of the sign. This process can be viewed in terms of its potential influence on the interpreter's subsequent actions or in cases where the sign representation was deliberately generated by a sender, as a means of communication. In either case, the actual interpretation of the sign depends both on the interpreter's general sociolinguistic context (e.g. societal and linguistic norms) and on their individual circumstances (e.g. personal experience or knowledge).

In the FRISCO report (Falkenberg et al. 1996), the key aspects to take into account in information systems models are:

1. Physical: Use of various media for modelling – documents, wall charts, computer-based CASE tools and so on; physical size and amount and effort to manipulate them
2. Empirical: Variety of elements distinguished, error frequencies when being written and read by different users, coding (shapes of boxes), ergonomics of computer-human interaction (CHI) for documentation and modelling tools
3. Syntactic: Languages, natural, constrained or formal, logical and mathematical methods for modelling
4. Semantic: Interpretation of the elements of the model in terms of the real world, ontological assumptions, operations for arriving at values of elements, justification of external validity
5. Pragmatic: Roles played by models – hypothesis, directive, description, expectation; responsibility for making and using the model; conversations needed to develop and use the model
6. Social: Communities of users, the norms governing use for different purposes, organisational framework for using the model

These lists are indicative rather than exhaustive, and we will return to how these influence our thinking on quality of models and modelling languages in more detail in Chaps. 4, 5, 6 and 7.

These six layers can be divided into two groups in order to reveal the technical vs. the social aspect. Physics, empirics and syntactic aspects comprise an area where technical and formal methods are adequate. However, semantics, pragmatics and the social sphere cannot be explored using those methods unmodified. This underpin than one has to include human judgment when discussing on the higher semiotic layers (layers 4–6). An issue when discussing a problem area such as modelling is that people, when using multilayer-related terms, frequently fail to mention the layer they are focusing on, which may result in severe misunderstandings.

It can be argued that the three additional levels not discussed by Morris (social, empirical and physical) have limited theoretical foundation in traditional semiotics. According to Price et al. (2004), the concepts described by these additional levels are already covered by the original three levels. With respect to the social level, the social context can be said to be addressed in the context of semiosis – the process of interpretation – at the pragmatic level in traditional semiotics. The physical and empirical levels have to do with the actual generation and transmission of signs. Although not an explicit focus of Piercean semiotics, sign generation and transmission are according to Price and Shanks implicitly included in the original syntactic level since they describe the process of sign representation in the same way that semiosis describes the process of interpretation at the pragmatic level. On the other hand, later critique of Morris (Nöth 1990) has pointed to that he includes a very large number of aspects in the pragmatics category. Newer work in organisational semiotics has also found it useful with a more fine-grained distinction when looking upon quality of information systems and information systems models. We will return to this in more detail in Chap. 4.

Another important distinction discussed in FRISCO was the scope of the term 'Information System'. There one describes two usages of the term:
• IS in the small
• IS in the large

When we use the term *IS* in this book, it is in the meaning of IS in the large, i.e. to describe large integrated human-machine systems that provide information to support the operational, managerial, analytic and decision-making functions of an organisation. IS in the small will be designated CIS – computerised information systems – in this book.

Because of the importance of the human actor and his or her judgement, we combine the use of conceptual models with the philosophical outlook that reality is socially constructed. Most traditional modelling approaches were consciously or unconsciously based on an objectivistic ontology, exemplified by statements such as 'the real world consists of entities and relationships' (Chen 1976; Klein and Lyytinen 1991). However, this assumption is not universally shared. In Sølvberg (1980) for instance, it is emphasised that what is modelled is one person's subjective *perception* of the 'real world' rather than the real world itself.

The practice of modelling inherently includes a large element of subjectivity (Lewis 1993). This subjectivity exists whether or not the approaches use 'things', 'entities', 'objects' or 'phenomena' as main concepts. If the phenomena are taken to have real-world existence, then the participants in the modelling effort must choose from the infinitely large number of phenomena that exist, only those that are relevant and suitable for inclusion in the model. Consequently, the process of creating such a model is not objective and value-free and the resulting conceptual model is not unbiased. If real-world existence of the relevant phenomena is not assumed, then the entities are, by definition, created subjectively by the participants in the modelling effort in order to make sense of the situation at hand. In either case, the conceptual model serves only as an interpretation of 'reality'.

Thus, in both cases, it will be useful to admit to this subjectivity and allow several models to co-exist, even if only one of them will be used in a prescriptive sense to govern the building of a computerised information system. There are several IS approaches that acknowledge the existence of several realities. Some approaches are grounded in object orientation (Harrison et al. 1993; Reenskaug et al. 1995). Another approach is Multiview (Avison and Wood-Harper 1990), which has a constructivistic worldview and uses traditional conceptual languages as an important part of the methodology. A similar attempt based on the integration of Soft Systems Methodology (SSM) (Checkland 1981) and software engineering approaches is reported in Doyle et al. (1993). In work on emergent and interactive workflow (Krogstie and Jørgensen 2004) and Active Knowledge Modelling (AKM) (Lillehagen and Krogstie 2008), there is an underlying premise that different people that at first sight seem to perform the same process need specialised solutions to support what is the best way of working for them.

Even if traditional conceptual modelling languages may be used in a way supporting a constructivistic worldview, they usually do not have explicit constructs for *capturing* differing views (and potential conflicts) directly in the model and making these available to those who use the model. They neither have the possibility to differentiate between the rules of necessity and deontic rules (rules that can be violated, although newer standards for business rules such as SBVR (OMG 2006) acknowledge this). Some exceptions exist (e.g. Bellström 2009), emphasising the importance of retaining different terms for the 'same' concept as long as possible.

Any conceptual modelling language is biased towards a particular way of perceiving the world:

- The languages have constructs that force both analysts, domain experts and users to emphasise some aspects of the world and neglect others.
- The more the analysts and users work with one particular language, the more their thinking will be influenced by this, and their awareness of those aspects of the world that do not fit in may consequently be diminished. This is a similar phenomena as the one presented in the Sapir-Whorf hypothesis, which states that a person's understanding of the world is influenced by the (natural) language he or she uses (Stamper 1987).
- For the types of problems that fit well with the particular language used, neglecting features that are not covered may have a positive effect, because it becomes easier to concentrate on the relevant issues. However, it is often hard to know what issues are relevant in the given case. In addition, different issues may be relevant for different people at the same time.

1.1 Philosophical Backdrop

Information systems development and evolution in organisations are closely related to organisational change. Organisational change and thus information systems development may be viewed from different philosophical points of view. Two common sets of assumptions are the objectivistic belief system and the constructivistic belief system (Guba and Lincoln 1989). They may be distinguished through differences in *ontology* (what exists that can be known), *epistemology* (what relationship is there between the knower and the known) and *methodology* (what are the ways of achieving knowledge).

Organisations are made up of individuals who perceive the world differently from each other. The constructivistic view stresses that an organisation develops through a process of social construction, based on its individuals' constantly changing perception of the world. In the objectivistic view (Guba and Lincoln 1989), there exists only one reality, which is measurable and essentially the same for all. According to Guba and Lincoln, the objectivistic belief system can somewhat simplistically be said to have the following characteristics:

- Ontology: Realism, asserting that there exist a single reality which is independent of any observer's interest in it and which operates according to immutable natural laws. Truth is defined as that set of statements whose model is isomorphic to reality.
- Epistemology: Dualistic objectivism, asserting that it is possible, indeed mandatory, for an observer to exteriorise the phenomenon studied, remaining detached and distant from it and excluding any value considerations from influencing it.
- Methodology: Interventionism, stripping context of its contaminating influences so that the inquiry can converge on truth and explain the things studied as they really are and really work, leading to the capability to predict and to control.

The constructivistic belief system has the following characteristics (still according to Guba and Lincoln 1989):

- Ontology: Relativism, asserting that there exist multiple socially constructed realities ungoverned by any natural laws, causal or otherwise. 'Truth' is defined as the best-informed and most sophisticated construction on which there is agreement.
- Epistemology: Subjectivism, asserting that the inquirer and the inquired-into are interlocked in such a way that the findings of an investigation are the literal creation of the inquiry process.
- Methodology: Hermeneutical, involving a continuing dialectic of iteration, analysis, critique, reiteration, reanalysis, and so on, leading to the emergence of a joint construction and understanding among all the stakeholders.

Many features of the constructivistic world-view have emerged from natural sciences such as physics and chemistry. The argument for this world-view can be made even more persuasively when the phenomena being studied involve human beings, as in the social sciences or information systems in organisation. Much theoretical discussion in the social sciences is dedicated to analysing constructivism and its consequences (Dahlbom 1991). The idea of reality construction has been a central topic for philosophical debate during the last three to four decades and has been approached differently by French, American and German philosophers. Many different approaches to constructivistic thinking have appeared, although probably the most influential one is that of Berger and Luckmann (1966).

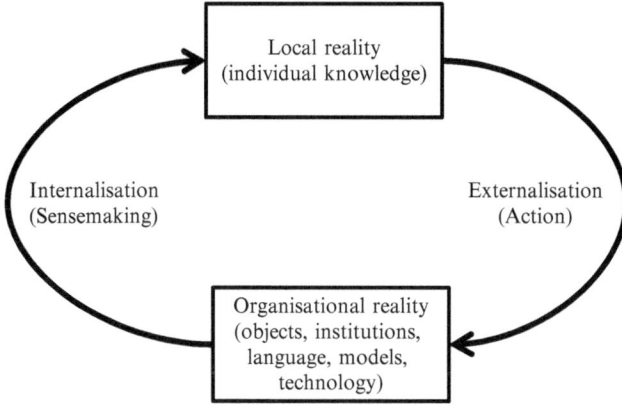

Fig. 1.2 Social construction in an organisation

Their insights will be used as our starting point. Their view of the social construction of reality is based on Husserl's phenomenology. Whereas Husserl was primarily a philosopher, Schutz (1962) took phenomenology into the social sciences. From there on it branched into two directions: ethnomethodology, primarily developed by (Garfinkel 1967), and the social constructivism of Berger and Luckmann. Whereas ethnomethodology is focused on questioning what individuals take as given in different cultures, Berger and Luckmann developed their approach to investigate how these presumptions are constructed.

Organisations can be looked upon as realities constructed socially through the joint actions of the social actors in the organisation (Gjersvik 1993), as illustrated in Fig. 1.2.

An organisation consists of individuals who view the world in their own specific way, because each of them has different experiences arising both from work and other arenas. The local reality depicted in the top of Fig. 1.2 refers to the way an individual perceives the world in which he or she acts. The local reality is the way the world is for the individual; it is the everyday perceived reality of the individual social actor. Some of this local reality may be made explicit and talked about. However, a lot of what we know is tacit. The distinction between explicit and tacit knowledge follows from Polanyi (1966). Explicit or codified knowledge is transmittable in a formal systematic language, while tacit knowledge has a personal quality that makes it hard to formalise and communicate. When the social actors of an organisation act, they externalise their local reality. The most important ways in which social actors externalise their local reality are by speaking and constructing languages, artefacts (including models) and institutions. What they do is to construct organisational reality by making something that other actors have to relate to by being part of the organisation. This organisational reality may consist of different things, such as institutions, language, models, artefacts and technology (including computerised information systems). Finally, internalisation is the process of making sense out of the actions, institutions, models, artefacts, etc., in the organisation, making this organisational reality part of the individual's local reality. This linear presentation does not mean that the processes of externalisation and internalisation occur in a strict sequence. Externalisation and internalisation may be performed simultaneously. In addition, it does not mean that only organisational reality is internalised by individuals. Other externalisations (e.g. from other organisations and social settings which people participate in) also influence the construction of the local reality of an individual.

Since knowledge creation and representation is such an important aspect of modelling, we will look into this in more detail below.

1.1.1 Background on Knowledge Creation in Organisations

Nonaka and Takeuchi's theory on organisational knowledge creation (Nonaka 1994) uses the following definition: *'knowledge is justified true belief'*. It can be argued that this definition only applies to some aspects of human knowledge. Nonaka and Takeuchi tightly link knowledge to human activity. Central to their theory is that organisational knowledge (or reality in the vocabulary of Gjersvik) is created through a continuous dialogue between tacit and explicit knowledge[1] performed by organisational 'communities of interaction' that contribute to the amplification and development of new knowledge. Thus, their theory of knowledge creation is based on two dimensions:

Nonaka and Takeuchi identify four patterns of interaction between tacit and explicit knowledge, commonly called *modes of knowledge conversion*:
1. Socialisation: Creating tacit knowledge from existing tacit knowledge through shared experience
2. Externalisation: Conversion from tacit to explicit knowledge
3. Combination: Creation of new explicit knowledge from existing explicit knowledge
4. Internalisation: Conversion of explicit knowledge to tacit knowledge

The internalisation mode of knowledge creation is closely related to 'learning by doing'; hence, the internalisation process is deeply related to action. Nonaka and Takeuchi criticise traditional theories on organisational learning for not addressing the notion of externalisation and having paid little attention to the importance of socialisation. They also argue that a double-loop learning ability (cf. Argyris and Schön 1978) is implicitly built into the knowledge creation model, since organisations continuously make new knowledge by reconstructing existing perspectives, frameworks or premises on a day-to-day basis.

In much knowledge management literature, inspired by Nonaka (1994), a model of, e.g. business process would be considered externalised knowledge about the organisation. Some might interpret this such that the model is the actual knowledge.

---

[1] Or more precisely knowledge externalisation, since we chose to restrain the term *knowledge* to humans. When we below use the terminology of Nonaka, 'explicit knowledge' should be interpreted as representation of knowledge, not the actual knowledge.

However, this 'knowledge-as-object' view has been criticised by Walsham (2004, 2005), maintaining that Nonaka misinterpreted the distinction between explicit and tacit knowledge (Polanyi 1966), and that *knowledge* is something within the human mind, so that the term should not be used for passive representations of information in writing or in a computer system. Other researchers are in line with this view, furthermore stressing that an essential quality of knowledge lies in its ability to support action (Braf 2004). Hence, knowledge is not only *about* action, but *for* action, or even *part of* action (Cook and Brown 1999). The same view pertains to information systems, which can be seen as (partial) automations of conceptual models of the problem domain. IS Actability Theory (Goldkuhl and Ågerfalk 2002; Ågerfalk 2003) stresses that information systems are action systems used in a social action context (Ågerfalk and Eriksson 2003).

We support the criticism of the 'knowledge-as-object' view; hence, in this book a model (e.g. of a business process) is not as such considered to *be* knowledge, but it may *contribute to knowledge* when interpreted (and acted upon) by a human or other intelligent agent.

1.2   Use of Modelling in the Development and Evolution of Information Systems

Changing the computerised information system (CIS) support in an organisation – for instance by introducing new application systems – may, as any organisational development, be looked upon as a process of social construction. This outlook is adopted in this book, especially when focusing on the creation and evolution of conceptual models in connection with improving the computerised information system support of an organisation. This does not mean that we are ignorant of the more technical aspects of computerised information systems support. Constructed realities are often related to, and also often inseparable from, tangible phenomena. On the other hand, as discussed in the above paragraph on semiotics, technical computer science approach alone is not sufficient to explain the development, implementation and evolution of a CIS.

The development of a conceptual model of 'reality' as it is perceived by someone is partly a process of externalisation of parts of this person's internal reality (knowledge) and will in the first place act as a potential organisational reality for the audience of the model. This model can then be used in the sense-making process by the other stakeholders, internalising the views of the others if they are found appropriate. This internalisation is based on pre-understanding, which includes assumptions implicit in the languages used for modelling. The language in turn is learned through internalisation. After reaching a sufficiently stable shared model, one might wish to externalise this in a more tangible way, transferring it to the organisation in the form of computer technology. Here a new need for internalisation of the technology is needed for the CIS to be useful for the part of the organisation that is influenced by it. Also here, it should be possible to utilise the conceptual models for the users to understand what the CIS does, and even more importantly, why it does it.

Making sense of the technology is important to be able to change it, and the conceptual models already developed can act as a starting point for additional maintenance and evolution efforts on the CIS when deemed necessary. Some newer approaches also provide the models themselves as part of the computerised information systems, so that these so-called emergent or interactive models can be changed at run-time immediately influencing the organisation (Lillehagen and Krogstie 2008).

The abilities and opportunities for the different persons in the organisation to externalise their local reality (through modelling or through other forms) will differ. Since the languages and particularly types of languages used in conceptual modelling are often predefined when a decision to create an information system is made, persons with long experience in using these kinds of languages will have an advantage in the modelling process. Within the areas of enterprise modelling and domain-specific modelling (DSM), this is often addressed by specialising the modelling language being used to the knowledge of the main stakeholders. This is often more difficult to do in a traditional system development setting. This in-balance is not necessarily bad, for if the IT people did not have this knowledge, it would not be interesting to include them in the development process in the first place. Rather, it is important to be aware of this difference to avoid the most apparent dangers of model (and language) monopoly and model power as discussed by Bråten (1973, 1983). The theory of model power is based on the assumption that understanding takes place on either own or on the premises of others. Bråten works with the understanding of 'model strong' participants who are rich in their understandings, ideas and language on a certain subject area (e.g. systems analysis and design) and 'model weak' participants who are poor on relevant knowledge, ideas and language. He lists the rules in the theory of model power in the following way:

1. If participant A is to be able to control x, it is necessary that x is developed on the premises of A.
2. If two participants, A and B, are to be able to communicate, it is necessary that they have access to models on the subject area.
3. Following this, a trade or conversation between a model strong A and a model weak B means that the model weak B will try to acquire the models of the model strong A.
4. Following 1 and 3, the better the model weak B succeeds in acquiring A's models, which are developed on the premises of A, the more B will be under A's control.

What is also apparent is that some persons in the organisation have a greater possibility to externalise their reality than others, both generally (the financiers of an endeavour will for instance usually be in a position to bias a solution in their perceived favour) and specifically, by the use of certain modelling techniques. Gjersvik (1993) has, for instance, investigated how the way management perceives the world could be more easily externalised in a CIS than the way shop-floor workers perceive the world (Gjersvik 1993).

Abstractly as illustrated in Fig. 1.3, one can look upon an organisation and its information system to be in a current state (often looked upon as a descriptive 'as-is') that are to be evolved to some future wanted state (often looked upon as a prescriptive 'to be').

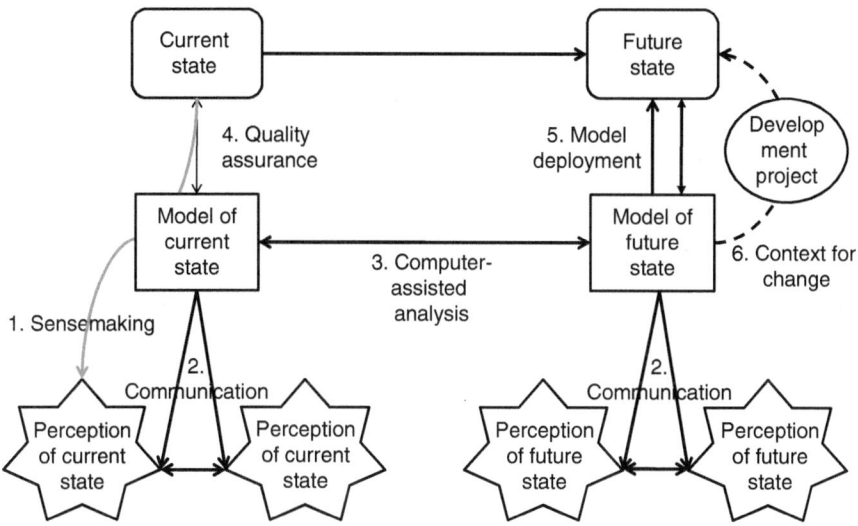

Fig. 1.3 Application of conceptual modelling

Obviously, changes will happen in an organisation no matter what is actually planned, thus one might in practice have the use for many different models and scenarios of possible future states (e.g. what happens if we do nothing), but we simplify the number of possible futures in the discussion below.

The state includes the existing processes, organisation and computer systems. These states are often modelled, and the state of the organisation is perceived (differently) by different persons through these models. This opens up for different usage areas of conceptual models as described in Nysetvold and Krogstie (2006):

- Human sense-making: The model of the current state can be useful for people to make sense of the current situation, models being (perceived as) organisational reality.
- Communication between people in the organisation: As emphasised by Bråten, models are important for communication. Thus, in addition to support the sense-making process for the individual, a model can also act as a common framework supporting communication between people. This relates both to communication relative to the existing state, and relative to a possible future state. A conceptual model can give insight into the problems motivating a development project and can help the systems developers and users understand the application system to be built. By hopefully helping to bridge the realm of the end-users and the CIS, it facilitates a more reliable and constructive exchange of opinions between users and the developers of the CIS, and between different users. The models both help (but also restrict) the communication by establishing a nomenclature and a definition of phenomena in the modelling domain. Effects such as language and model-monopoly discussed above can hamper the communicational value of the model.

- Computer-assisted analysis: To gain knowledge about the organisation through simulation or deduction, often by comparing a model of the current state and a model of a future, potentially better state. Moreover, by analysing the model instead of the business area itself, one might deduce properties that are difficult if not impossible to perceive directly since the model enables one to concentrate on just a few aspects at a time.
- Quality assurance: To ensure, e.g. that the organisation acts according to a certified process achieved, e.g. through an ISO-certification process modelled in a process model.
- Model deployment and activation: To integrate the model of the future state in an information system directly and thereby make it actively take part in the actions of the organisation. Models can be activated in three ways:
  1. Through people guided by process 'maps', where the system offers no active support.
  2. Automatically, where the system plays an active role, as in most automated workflow systems.
  3. Interactively, where the computer and the users co-operate in interpreting the model. The computer makes decisions about prescribed parts of the model, while the users resolve ambiguities.
- To give the context for a traditional system development project, without being directly activated. This is the traditional usage of conceptual models, where the model represents the wanted future and act as a prescriptive model including requirements as a basis for design and implementation, acting in the end as documentation of the developed system that can be useful in the future evolution of the system if one manage to keep it up to date.

With the introduction of more extensible methodologies and tool support, conceptual models are also likely to be used in reverse engineering and re-engineering, and when reusing artefacts constructed in connection with other application systems. Summing up, a conceptual model can be used both for communication and representation, and faces demands from both social and technical actors. As a consequence of this duality, requirements for conceptual modelling languages and modelling techniques will pull in opposite directions, and as we shall see, it is not possible to develop a perfect modelling language, as there are always trade-offs that must be made. The different uses of a conceptual model listed above put different demands on the modelling languages, tools and methods used to create and maintain the models, which can be particularly challenging since (parts of) conceptual models often are used for many of the above purposes in the same project.

An important aspect of this book is to discuss the quality of models and modelling languages in this setting. To help us in this process, a framework for understanding quality of models (SEQUAL) has been developed. This framework will be discussed in more detail in Chaps. 4 and 5, and applied further in Chaps. 6 and 7.

Whereas usage area 6 above has been the traditional usage area of conceptual models, the direct activation of models as indicated in usage area 5 is of increasing interest, and we will in the next section briefly mention the different approaches to such model-based development.

1.3   Approaches to Model-Based Development and Evolution of Information Systems

Although most software developers are aware of modelling-oriented methodologies such as data, process and object-oriented modelling, they are often not followed in detail in practice, and mostly only in initial development stages. What differentiates model-based development from using models in this fashion are:
- Models are in some sense activated, being utilised throughout development, use and evolution of the systems.
- Models are made both of the system, and of the environment of the system.

MBSE, also often termed Model-Driven Software Development (MDSD (Stahl and Völter 2006)), include such approaches as Model-Driven Architecture (MDA), Microsoft Software Factory (applying domain-specific languages – DSL) and Domain-Specific Modelling (DSM (Kelly and Tolvanen 2008), and Eclipse. According to Stahl and Völter (2006), the goals of MDSD are:
- Increased development speed through automated system-generation
- Improved software quality through the use of automated transformations and formally defined modelling languages
- The possibility to change cross-cutting implementation in one place
- Higher level of reusability of software engineering knowledge
- Improved manageability of complexity through abstraction
- Interoperability and portability of software systems

However, this is a bit limiting. To approach this problem area, one needs to attack and integrate aspects of a number of different research traditions: Ontologies, Model-Driven Architecture (MDA) (Pastor and Molina 2007), Business Process Modelling/Management and Workflow (BPM) (Havey 2005), Enterprise Modelling (EM) (Vernadat 1996) and Active Knowledge Modelling (AKM) (Lillehagen and Krogstie 2008) are important parts of the puzzle, addressing different parts of the problem. These approaches will be described in Sect. 2.3 in more detail.

The different approaches to model-based development are appropriate for supporting different types of processes, from static, to very dynamic, even emergent processes. Whereas a standard process might be automated, more knowledge-intensive processes are hard to pre-define, but has to emerge and change in unforeseen ways due to the knowledge developed throughout the process. Certain work processes are in addition emotionally intensive (e.g. in health care); thus, parts of the process need to be adapted in the interaction between people there and then. This indicates that parts of the process need be kept implicit. We can exemplify processes according to the spectrum with the university course example:
- When a student registers for the course, this will automatically produce a confirmation to the student that this has taken place.
- When the course is set up and planned, one can based on the wishes from the lecturer set up the plan for the whole semester as for when and where lectures and assignments are to take place, providing the potential for workflow support.

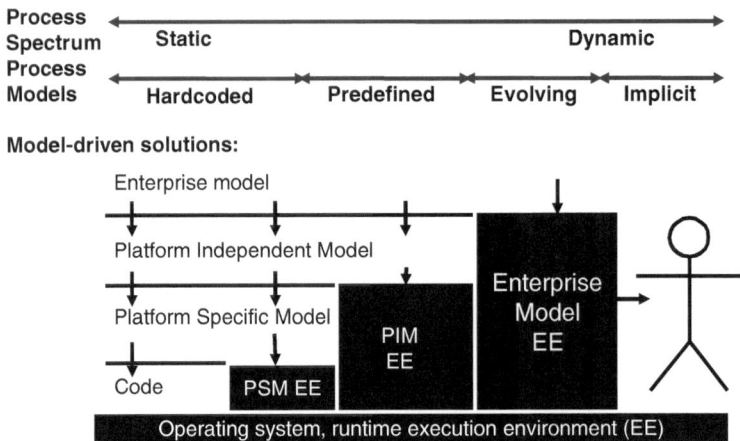

Fig. 1.4 Overview of different execution environments for different process models (from Krogstie (2004))

- On the other hand, this schedule often needs to be adapted due to unexpected events, such as travel and illness.
- Assignments in a course might be meant to be performed in groups and act as a portfolio. Here, due to the knowledge that is developed in the group throughout the course, one needs an even higher level of adaptation.
- When parts of the grade in the course are based on group work, there can be emotionally sensitive aspects. For instance, some group members feel that other group members do not contribute. How to address such issues is hard to prescribe at all, since it is dependent a lot on the situation, e.g. communication patterns in the group, physical and psychological illness, etc., and thus can be hard to describe.

As illustrated above, within the same domain, you often have to deal with process across the process spectrum. Also note that the same process instance can move either to the left (as a process is better understood, and thus possible to formalise to a larger degree) or to the right (when there is a breakdown in the assumptions behind a formalised process).

The different process types decide the extent to which the underlying technology can be based on hard-coded, predefined, evolving or only implicit process models. This gives a number of development approaches as illustrated in Fig. 1.4. On one extreme, systems are manually coded on top of a traditional runtime environment, and on the other, enterprise models are used directly to generate and evolve solutions. In between these, we have the approaches typically described in MDA, namely, the development of PIMs for code-generation (e.g. on top of a UML Virtual Machine) or for platform-specific models (PSMs) for more traditional code-generation. The use of BPM and Workflow technology is typically based on an existing platform-independent model (PIM) EE for execution of a process-oriented solution.

1.4   Outline of the Book

In Chap. 2 we give a more detailed overview of different methodological frameworks for different types of model-based development. In Chap. 3 we give an overview of the different abstraction mechanisms and perspectives used in conceptual modelling. Quality of models and modelling languages as defined in SEQUAL will then be discussed in detail in Chaps. 4 (Model Quality) and 5 (Quality of Modelling Languages). Specialisations of the framework addressing particular types of models are found in Chap. 6. Chapter 7 presents in more detail the different usage areas of SEQUAL relative to different tasks within preparing for and conducting model-driven development and evolution. Chapter 8 wraps up the book and discusses the future possible developments of model-based methods given the general trends in IT and organisational developments. Each chapter contains a summary, review questions, larger problems and exercises.

In Appendix A, we present a brief overview of important terms as used by us in the book. Note that when describing existing approaches developed by others, we might deviate a bit from this terminology since we will in this case try to follow the terminology of the developer of the approach when that is important. Important abbreviations are found in Appendix B. The different approaches to modelling will be illustrated through examples from primarily two cases:

- Teaching at the university (both on the study-program and course level)
- Arrangement of international conferences and events

A comprehensive description of the cases is given in Appendix C. Whereas the first is meant to be easy to understand both for lecturers and students, the second is an extension of the exemplar conference case – an example (and a setting) well known to most academics. The appendix also contains a list of relevant websites and an index.

1.5   Summary

We have in this chapter discussed on a high level the main characteristics of conceptual modelling. We have described the philosophical outlook guiding our thinking as for how modelling can be used in relation to information systems development and evolution. The constructivistic stance influences to a large degree the practical approach to modelling, as will become evident when discussing the quality of models and modelling languages throughout the book.

Conceptual modelling techniques are used for many purposes:

- Human sense-making
- Supporting human communication
- Computer-assisted analysis
- Quality assurance
- Model deployment and activation
- To give the context for a traditional system development project

Whereas conceptual modelling traditionally has been used in the sixth setting, more active use of the models is getting increased interest. To approach this problem area, one needs to attack and integrate the aspects of a number of different research traditions, including Model-Driven Architecture (MDA), Business Process Modelling and Workflow (BPM), Enterprise Modelling (EM) and Active Knowledge Modelling (AKM).

Review Questions

1. What characterises a conceptual model?
2. Describe the different goals of modelling.
3. How is interactive activation different from traditional workflow?
4. Give a short description of MBSE.
5. Give an overview of different model execution environments.

Problems and Exercises

Individual Exercises
1. Select one or more modelling languages you are familiar with.
   - What are the most important concepts of this modelling language?
   - Which goals listed under Sect. 1.2 is the language most appropriate to be used for addressing? Why do you think so?

Pair Exercises
1. Model monopoly in practice: This task can be done in class following the following steps:
   - Pair up two and two.
   - Choose an area of interest (domain) where you have particularly much knowledge (e.g. a hobby you have).
   - Choose a modelling language you are familiar with.
   - Model the main parts of the chosen domain with the modelling language of choice.
   - Explain your model to your neighbour (and vice versa).
   - When all have done this, the lecturer should choose one person and ask him to tell about the domain chosen by his neighbour.
   - Discuss how the model influenced the last part in the light of model monopoly.

Group Exercises
1. Choose a modelling methodology (e.g. UML, BPMN or ARIS) that you are familiar with. Based on the method description, try to establish if the methodology has an objectivistic or constructivistic world-view.

References

Argyris, C., Schön, D.: Organizational Learning: A Theory of Action Perspective. Addison Wesley, Reading (1978)

Avison, D.E., Wood-Harper, A.T.: Multiview: An Exploration in Information Systems Development. Blackwell, Oxford (1990)

Ågerfalk, P.J.: Information systems actability: understanding Information Technology as a tool for business action and communication. PhD thesis, Dept of Computer and Information Science, Univ. Linköping, Sweden (2003)

Ågerfalk, P.J., Eriksson, O.: Usability in social action: reinterpreting effectiveness, efficiency, and satisfaction. In: Proceedings of the European Conference on Information Systems (ECIS'03), Naples, Italy, 19–21 June (2003)

Bellström, P.: On the problem of semantic loss in view integration. In: Barry, C., Conboy, K., Lang, M., Wojtkowski, G., Wojtkowski, W. (eds.) Information Systems Development Challenges in Practice, Theory, and Education, pp. 963–974. Springer Science, New York (2009)

Berger, P., Luckmann, T.: The Social Construction of Reality: A Treatise in the Sociology of Knowledge. Penguin, London (1966)

Braf, E.: Knowledge demanded for action: studies on knowledge mediation in organizations. PhD thesis (Linköping Studies in Information Science, Dissertation no.10), Department of Computer and Information Science, Linköping University, Sweden (2004)

Bråten, S.: Model monopoly and communications: systems theoretical notes on democratization. Acta Sociol. J. Scand. Social. Assoc. **16**(2), 98–107 (1973)

Bråten, S.: Dialogens vilkår i datasamfunnet (In Norwegian). Universitetsforlaget (1983)

Checkland, P.B.: Systems Thinking, Systems Practice. Wiley, Chichester (1981)

Chen, P.P.: The entity-relationship model: towards a unified view of data. ACM Trans. Database Syst. **1**(1), 9–36 (1976)

Cook, S.D.N., Brown, J.S.: Bridging epistemologies: the generic dance between knowledge and knowing. Organ. Sci. **10**(4), 381–400 (1999)

Dahlbom, B.: The idea that reality is socially constructed. In: Floyd, C., Zullighoven, H., Budde, R., Keil-Slawik, R. (eds.) Software Development and Reality Construction, pp. 101–126. Springer, Secaucus (1991)

DeMarco, T.: Structured Analysis and System Specification. Prentice Hall, Upper Saddle River (1979)

Doyle, K.G., Wood, J.R.G., Wood-Harper, A.T.: Soft systems and systems engineering: on the use of conceptual models in information system development. J. Inform. Syst. **3**(3), 187–198 (1993)

Falkenberg, E.D., Hesse, W., Lindgreen, P., Nilsson, B.E., Oei, J.L.H., Rolland, C., Stamper, R.K., Assche, F.J.M.V., Verrijn-Stuart, A.A., Voss, K.: A framework of information system concepts – the FRISCO Report, IFIP WG 8.1 Task Group FRISCO. http://home.dei.polimi.it/pernici/ifip81/publications.html (1996). Cited Dec 2011

Garfinkel, H.: Studies in Ethnomethodology. Prentice Hall, Englewood Cliffs (1967)

Gjersvik, R.: The construction of information systems in organization: an action research project on technology, organizational closure, reflection, and change. PhD thesis, ORAL, NTH, Trondheim, Norway (1993)

Goldkuhl, G., Ågerfalk, P.: Actability: a way to understand information system pragmatics. In: Liu, K., et al. (eds.) Coordination and Communication Using Signs, pp. 85–114. Kluwer Academic Publishers, Dordrecht (2002)

Guba, E.G., Lincoln, Y.S.: Fourth Generation Evaluation. Sage, Newbury Park (1989)

Harrison, W., Ossher, H.: Subject-oriented programming (a critique of pure objects). In: Proceedings of the Conference on Object-Oriented Programming Systems, Languages, and Applications (OOPSLA'93), pp. 411–428 (1993)

Havey, M.: Essential Business Process Modelling. O'Reilly, Sebastopol (2005)

Kelly, S., Tolvanen, J.-P.: Domain Specific Modeling. Wiley, Hoboken (2008)

Kelly, S., Lyytinen, K., Rossi, M.: MetaEdit+: a fully configurable multi-user and multi-tool CASE and CAME environment. In: Constantopoulos P., Mylopoulos J., Vassiliou Y. (eds.) Lecture Notes in Computer Science, vol. 1080. Springer, Berlin/Heidelberg/New York (1996)

Klein, H., Lyytinen, K.: Towards a new understanding of data modelling. In: Floyd, C., Zullighoven, H., Budde, R., Keil-Slawik, R. (eds.) Software Development and Reality Construction, pp. 203–217. Springer, Secaucus (1991)

Krogstie, J.: A semiotic approach to quality in requirements specifications. IFIP 8.1. Working Conference on Organizational Semiotics (2001)

Krogstie, J.: Integrating enterprise and IS-development using a Model-Driven Approach. In: Proceedings of the 13th International Conference on Information Systems Development (ISD 2004) (2004)

Krogstie, J., Jørgensen, H.: Interactive models for supporting networked organisations. In: 16th Conference on Advanced Information Systems Engineering. Riga, Latvia: Springer, Berlin/Heidelberg/New York (2004)

Lewis, P.J.: Linking soft systems methodology with data-focused information systems development. J. Inform. Syst. 3, 169–186 (1993)

Lillehagen, F., Krogstie, J.: Active Knowledge Modeling of Enterprises. Springer, Berlin (2008)

Morris, C.: Foundations of the Theory of Signs, in International Encyclopedia of Unified Science, vol. 1. University of Chicago Press, London (1938)

Nonaka, I.: A dynamic theory of organizational knowledge creation. Organ. Sci. 5(1), 14–37 (1994)

Nöth, W.: Handbook of Semiotics. Indiana University Press, Bloomington (1990)

Nysetvold, A.G., Krogstie, J.: Assessing business process modeling languages using a generic quality framework. In: Advanced Topics in Database Research, Idea Group (2006)

OMG: SBVR: Semantics of Business Vocabulary and Rules Interim Specification. http://www.omg.org/spec/SBVR/1.0/ (2006). Cited Dec 2011

Pastor, O., Molina, J.C.: Model-Driven Architecture in Practice: A Software Production Environment Based On Conceptual Modeling. Springer, New York (2007)

Pierce, C.S.: Collected Papers. Harvard University Press, Cambridge, MA (1931–1935)

Polanyi, M.: The Tacit Dimension. Routledge, London (1966)

Price, R., Shanks, G.: A Semiotic Information Quality Framework, IFIP WG8.3 International Conference on Decision Support Systems (DSS2004), Prato, Italy, 1–3 July, 2004, pp. 658–672 (2004)

Reenskaug, T., Wold, P., Lehne, O.A.: Working with Objects. Manning/Prentice Hall, Upper Saddle River (1995)

Schutz, A.: Collected Papers. Njiho (1962), Njihoff Publishers, Dordrecht, The Netherlands

Sølvberg, A.: A contribution to the definition of concepts for expressing users' information systems requirements. In: Chen, P.P. (ed.) Entity-Relationship Approach to Systems Analysis and Design. North-Holland, Amsterdam (1980)

Stahl, T., Völter, M.: Model-Driven Software Development: Technology, Engineering, Management. Wiley, Chichester (2006)

Stamper, R.: Semantics. In: Boland Jr., T.J., Hirschheim, R.A. (eds.) Critical Issues in Information Systems Research, pp. 43–78. Wiley, Chichester (1987)

Vernadat, F.B.: Enterprise Modelling and Integration: Principles and Applications. Chapman & Hall, London (1996)

Walsham, G.: Knowledge management systems: action and representation. In: Proceedings ALOIS*2004, 17–18 Mar, Linköping, Sweden (2004)

Walsham, G.: Knowledge management systems: representation and communication in context. Syst. Signs Actions 1(1), 6–18 (2005)

Young, J.W., Kent, H.K.: Abstract formulation of data processing problems. J. Indust. Eng. (Nov. Dec.), 9(6), 471–479 (1958)

Methodologies for Computerised Information Systems Support in Organisations

In this chapter, we present the generic tasks and model types found in information systems development and evolution, and the main methodologies for mixing different phases of information systems development. In particular, we describe in more detail the main approaches to model-based development presented on a high level in Chap. 1, but also provide a historical account of the development of methodologies in the area of information systems development and evolution. Methodologies are classified relative to goal, process, product, capabilities needed, stakeholder participation, organisation and location of the tasks to be done. The last section focuses on stakeholder involvement, in particular, participatory development of models.

2.1   A Framework for IS Methodologies

Several frameworks for classifications of methodologies have been developed through the years (Abrahamsson et al. 2010; Berente and Lyytinen 2007; Blum 1994; Davis 1988; Lyytinen 1987). A weakness of these is, in our view, their limited scope, primarily looking upon the development of a single application system in a comparatively stable environment. IT has, over the last 30 years, gone from obscure to infrastructure. All organisations are dependent on an application systems portfolio supporting its current and future tasks, and newcomers in any area are dependent on establishing such new application portfolios quickly in a way that can evolve with changed business needs, technological affordances and expectations among co-operators, competitors and customers. Also, all people interacting with the organisation are expected to be able to do this by means of IT applications.

Over these 30 years, researchers have regularly investigated how IT systems are developed, used and evolved. In (Lientz et al. 1978), results from a 1977 survey on distribution of work on IT in organisations were published. Surprisingly at that time, it was found that almost half of the time was used on maintenance (i.e. changing systems that were already in production). We have done similar investigations in Norway in 1993, 1998, 2003 and 2008. For some areas, there are large differences

J. Krogstie, *Model-Based Development and Evolution of Information Systems:*
A Quality Approach, DOI 10.1007/978-1-4471-2936-3_2,
© Springer-Verlag London 2012

Table 2.1 Percentages of systems developed using different programming languages

	2008	2003	1998	1993	NS90	LS77
COBOL	4.5	0.5	32.6	49	51	52
4GL	12	13.5	16.9	24	8	
C	2.4	12.5	15.4	4	3	
C++	17.5	23.1	15.1			
C#	4.9					
RPG/Scripts	6.7	NA	12.9	4	10	22
Java	22.6	29.8	2			
Ass.	0.4		0.9	3		12
Fortran			0.6	4	7	2.4
PASCAL			0.3	2		
PL/1			0.3	2		3.2
Other	28.9	20.2	2.6	6	21	7.7

Table 2.2 Comparisons of maintenance figures in percent across investigations

Category	2008	2003	1998	1993	NP 90	LS 77
Development	21	22	17	30	35	43
Maintenance	35	37	41	40	58	49
Other work	44	41	42	30	7	8
Disregarding other work						
Development	34	34	27	41	38	47
Maintenance	66	66	73	59	62	53

between the results of investigations. In this section and in the subsequent, we will particularly look at the results from the 2008 investigation (Davidsen and Krogstie 2010) and compare some of the results with the results of similar investigations. The most important of these are the investigations carried out by:

1. Krogstie, Jahr and Sjøberg in 2003 reported in Krogstie et al. (2006).
2. Holgeid, Krogstie and Sjøberg in 1998 reported in Holgeid et al. (2000).
3. Krogstie in 1993 reported in Krogstie and Sølvberg (1994), Krogstie (1995, 1996).
4. Lientz and Swanson (LS) (Lientz et al. 1978): This investigation was carried out in 1977, with responses from 487 American organisations on 487 application systems.
5. Nosek and Palvia (NP) (Nosek and Palvia 1990): A follow-up study to Lientz/ Swanson performed in 1990 asking many of the same questions as those of Lientz and Swanson. Their results are based on responses from 52 American organisations.

As an example, Table 2.1 illustrates the developments in the main programming languages being used. The use of underlying technical platform (e.g. the database technologies used) has also changed a lot.

Other areas are remarkably stable. As illustrated in Table 2.2, the split of the time used for development vs. maintenance is still as it was 30 years ago. (In absolute terms, less time is used for both development and maintenance, since most of the time used by IT departments these days are on user-support and systems operations.) Over the last 20 years, the percentage of the so-called new systems that are in fact replacement systems, being installed basically to replace old systems, has stayed above 50%, rising slowly.

On the other hand, most research on the use of IT to support organisations, information systems and software engineering has focused on the development of new systems, even if this kind of work is actually no longer typical for most IT-related activities. As different actors support organisations with IT in what can be looked upon as a flexible ecosystem of solution providers, the actors being supported are more diverse. There are still a number of stable organisations (local municipalities comes to mind), but these also and (parts of) other organisations participate in an increasingly wider spectrum of organisational forms (e.g. virtual enterprises, value chain networks, extended enterprises, dynamic networked organisation, etc.), a trend that we look upon as likely to continue.

Organisations are continuously under the pressure of change from both internal and external forces. All organisations of some size are supported by and depend upon a portfolio of application systems that likewise has to be changed, often rapidly, for the organisation to be able to keep up and extend their activities. In addition to be integrated internally, more and more systems are integrated with systems outside the control of the organisation and have to adhere to different standards and common components that are also potentially changing. Change, thus, is the norm, not the exception for an organisation's application portfolios and their individual information systems. A first step towards facing this is to accept change as a way of life, rather than as an annoying exception.

With this backdrop, and our worldview of social construction of reality described in Chap. 1, we have classified methodologies according to the following areas:

- What is the *goal* of the methodology, and why do we attack the overall problem area in the way we do? This last aspect is covered by the 'Weltanschauung', i.e. the underlying philosophical view of the methodology, whereas the first relates to the value one expects to achieve.
- When is the methodology applied? We have termed this aspect coverage in *process*, meaning the main tasks that are covered by the methodology.
- What part of the application portfolio of information systems is supported by the methodology? We have termed this aspect coverage in *product*.
- What are the *capabilities* needed to make the methodology work.
- *Who* is involved? This is discussed under the area of stakeholder participation.
- How is the work *organised* (i.e. what organisational actors are involved)?
- Where are the changes done? This is covered under the aspect of *location*.

2.1.1 Goal of the Methodology

IT is normally seen as a means to achieve results in another sphere (e.g. achieve business results, better public services) rather than a goal in itself. What this external goal is will naturally vary, but it is normally to achieve some sort of *value*. Based on the goals of those using resources to perform the change we can briefly highlight these as to:

- Ensure economic gain
- Ensure personal gain
- Ensure organisational (business) gain
- Ensure societal gain

Personal and societal gain might be linked to economic gain, but they can raise a number of goals in addition, which are not purely economical.

Economical value is highly tangible and can be viewed from different stakeholder perspectives. Business value is somewhat less tangible that includes all forms of value that determine the health and well-being of an organisation in the long run. Business value expands the concept of economical value to include other forms of value such as employee value, customer value, supplier value, managerial value and potentially also societal value (related to corporate responsibility). Business value also often embraces intangible assets not necessarily attributable to any stakeholder group such as intellectual capital and a firm's business model and public opinion.

For an organisation, IT can be looked upon as a service. According to Kuusisto (2008), the concept of value-adding services or products imply that value is contained in the product or the service. Another perspective is the value-in-use concept that focuses on the experience of a user interacting with products or services in use situations. This concept implies that the user is always a co-creator of the value. According to this concept, the user experience and perception are essential to be able to determine the value (Kuusisto 2008).

In all cases, one can differentiate three stages to achieve the value using IT:

1. Plan for value achievement. In a business setting this would often be termed 'develop business case and value realisation plan'.
2. Perform change (and manage the business case on the way, some of the basis for the original business case might change, and new opportunities might arise). Additional value can be explicit and easy to grasp, but some additional value is also tacit. Tacit value, e.g. the improved understanding of a work process for those involved in the installation of a work process support system, is often not explicitly captured in traditional project documentation, but may still affect decisions before or during a project, or the perceived value of the project in retrospect. Future reuse of results from the change can be a benefit of the current project, especially if this potential is taken into account at an early stage.
3. Implement change. First at this stage it is possible to achieve the expected value, and a focus on benefit realisation is necessary to assure that the value will be achieved over time.

The broadest set of issues to address is found relative to eGovernment solutions, and we will discuss briefly realisation of the benefits in this setting, based on Flak et al. (2009).

Calculating costs and benefits in the public sector is a major challenge. The reason for this is that there are difficulties in calculating tangible long-term benefits to offset clear, often apparently high, short-term costs that can severely hamper the speed and scope of eGovernment progress (Eynon 2007). A key challenge is to find ways of calculating benefits while also recognising the true costs and risks. Such calculations must be based on public sector value models. In contrast to the business sector, the public sector has to increase not only economic values but also societal (e.g. equality and rule of law) and democratic (e.g. openness and transparency) ones. Not only does this add to the list of goals to be strived for, there are typically conflicts between goals (Irani et al. 2005). Public sector activities also involve a wide variety of target stakeholders (Flak and Rose 2005; Scholl 2005) and hence require trade-offs that are not easily decided.

To meet this complex situation, there are a number of models developed to measure benefits in the public sector in general and for eGovernment projects in particular. Two such models are one developed by the OECD and another by the EU (Lonti and Woods 2008; Codagnone and Boccardelli 2006). Both models address three categories of benefits, (internal) efficiency, (external) effectiveness and democracy/openness. While there is no single universally used standard model for measuring values produced in the public sector, the examples given above show that there are at least good candidates.

Measuring benefits is not just a matter of having assessment models. There is also a need for implementing the measurement criteria of such models as structured ways of working. This is commonly called Benefits Management, a term comprised of Benefits Realisation and Change Management (Ward and Daniel 2006). While still an emerging field, there are lessons to be learned from existing experiences with benefits management methodologies. Such approaches generally address issues related to realising and managing benefits in organisations and are thus considered relevant in this context.

It can also be argued that benefits management is too restricted, being focused on the benefits within an individual organisation. All complex eGovernment systems involve interaction of several different public and private services. To achieve higher value levels, it is necessary to depart from pursuing only traditional strategies (efficiency) and aim at value innovation. To accomplish this, collaboration needs to be developed and reinforced. This requires changes not only in the information systems and business processes inside the different organisations, but also calls for process innovation across traditional public and private organisations (Flak et al. 2009) as they constitute ecosystems for service delivery.

No matter how value is defined, the overarching world-view that is applied influences the more concrete method of achieving this value. FRISCO (Falkenberg et al. 1996) distinguishes between three different views of the world:
1. Objectivistic: 'Reality' exists independently of any observer and merely needs to be mapped to an adequate description. For the objectivist, the relationship between reality and models thereof is trivial or obvious.
2. Constructivistic: 'Reality' exists independently of any observer, but what each person possesses is a restricted mental model only. For the constructivist, the relationship between 'reality' and models of this reality is subject to negotiations among the community of observers and may be adapted from time to time.
3. Mentalistic. To talk about 'reality' as such does not make sense because we can only form mental constructions of our perceptions. For the mentalist, what people usually call 'reality' as well as its relationship to any model of is totally dependent on the observer.

Methodologies can be categorised as being either objectivistic or constructivistic. The 'Weltanschauung' of a methodology is often not explicitly stated, but often appears only indirectly. Since different underlying philosophies may lead to radically different approaches, it is important to establish the underlying Weltanschauung. The distinction between objectivistic and constructivistic stated above is parallel to the distinction between objectivistic and subjectivistic in the overview of Hirschheim and Klein (1989). Hirschheim and Klein also distinguish these along the order-conflict dimension. In this dimension, the order or integration view emphasises a social world characterised by order, stability, integration, consensus and functional coordination. The conflict or coercion view stresses change, conflict, disintegration and coercion. These two dimensions were originally identified by Burrel and Morgan (1979) in the context of organisational and social research.

Based on the discussion in Chap. 1, it should come as no surprise that we find it beneficial to adapt a constructivistic world-view. Note, however, that we have a somewhat different approach to constructivism than the one described in the FRISCO report.

2.1.2   Coverage in Process

Looking at the introduction of this chapter, we see a differentiation between the four major types of tasks in IT support in organisations:

Does the methodology address the following?
- Development of application systems
- Use of application systems in production
- Operation of application systems in production
- Maintenance and evolution of application systems in production

One or more of the above four areas can be covered more or less completely and in varying degrees of detail. More detailed specifications of dimensions of development methodologies are given by Blum (1994) and Davis (1988). Whereas Davis classifies a methodology according to the way it is able to address varying user-needs over time, Blum classifies development methodologies in two dimensions: if they are product or problem-oriented and if they are conceptual or formal. The product vs. problem-oriented dimension, as discussed by Blum, is in our view a distinction on the part of development that is covered. The differentiation in abstraction level (analysis, requirements, design, implementation) is a useful, detailed breakdown of this. In some methodologies (e.g. agile methodologies), one apparently collapses these abstraction levels, but it is important to differentiate between these as illustrated by Davis (1995), looking upon the differences between analysis (OOA), requirements (OOR) and design (OOD) when working with object-oriented systems:
- There are different (but probably overlapping) sets of objects in OOR and OOD. Is the object important in the problem domain (OOR) vs. can the object be constructed in a way that makes efficient use of data abstractions (OOD)?
- There are different reasons for not having a System-object. In OOA, the domain does not contain the system; in OOD, the object model is the system.

- There are different reasons for using aggregation. At design time, it is important to record whole-part relationship to achieve optimal packaging.
- The focus on instantiation is different. At analysis time, one does not care about creation and destruction of instances.
- At analysis time, one does not focus on the detailed algorithms and behaviour of the object.
- Whereas generalisation is used in analysis for improved understanding, in design it aids delegation, productivity and encapsulation.
- Verification and validation are done towards different models; in design, it is primarily to find that the design satisfies the requirements, whereas in analysis, one needs to find if the requirements satisfy the human and organisational needs.

Thus, even if one uses the same concepts in analysis and design, the models are fundamentally different, since one can say that the domains one model are fundamentally different.

We claim that a comprehensive methodology should cover all the four areas such as development, use, operations and maintenance in an integrated manner. The emphasis in this book will be put on development and maintenance/evolution, but also the usage aspect is important, enabling the different end-users to make sense of the existing applications system in the organisation, to both be able to use them more efficiently and to be able to come up with constructive change-request and ideas for more revolutionary changes in the IT-support of the organisation when the environment of the organisation is changing. To have an integrated view of development and operations is important for getting the value out of the IT-investments (Iden et al. 2011).

We also claim that it is beneficial not to differentiate between development and maintenance as distinctly as is done in many approaches.

Maintenance was earlier looked upon as a more boring and less challenging task than development. According to our discussion in the introduction of this chapter, it is both natural and desirable for information systems to change. As shown both in our own and other surveys, approximately half of the work that is normally termed maintenance is in fact further development of the information systems portfolio and should be given credit as such. On the other hand, almost half of the new systems being developed are replacement systems, being application portfolio upkeep not enhancing the functional coverage of the portfolio or in other words, what the users can do with the system. Thus, seen from the end-users' point of view, a better assessment of information system support efficiency seems to be found by blurring the old temporal distinction between maintenance and development, and instead focus on the percentage of application portfolio development (Davidsen and Krogstie 2010; Krogstie 1996). This is difficult to achieve when there is a large mental and organisational gap between development and maintenance, even though the actual tasks being done have many similarities.

Swanson and Beath (1989) recognise the similarities of the tasks of development and maintenance, but still argue for keeping the old distinction based on the following perceived differences:

- A large proportion of traditional maintenance work is to perform reverse engineering of existing systems, finding out what the system does. We will argue that with

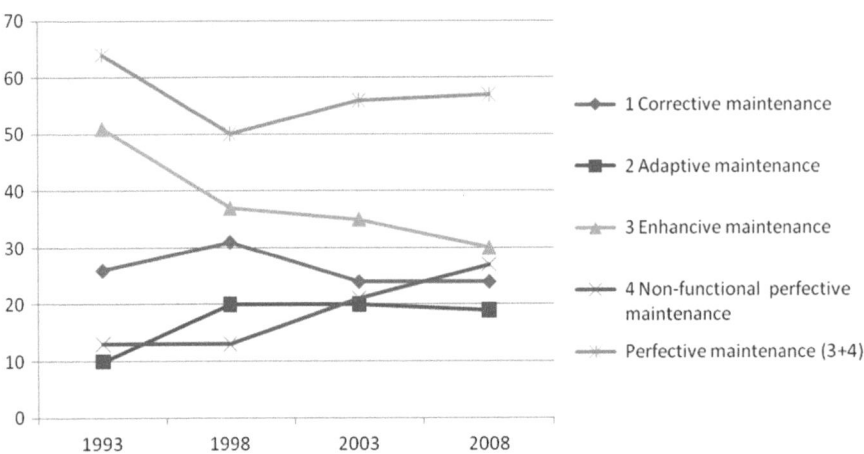

Fig. 2.1 Comparisons of distribution on maintenance tasks, percentage

modern development approaches where as much as possible of the work should take place on a specification and design level, the difference will be smaller. Another thing is that, when developing new systems, they have to be integrated with the existing systems; thus, reverse engineering is also an important activity in these cases. We also note that because of the large amount of replacement work of often poorly documented application systems, code understanding problems are often just as important when developing 'new' systems as when maintaining old systems today. Code and design understanding will also often be a problem when reusing the products from other projects, and during traditional development, when due to changing work load, developers have to work on other peoples' code, for instance, during system-test, or because developers are transferred to other projects.

- It is generally believed that 'Maintenance of systems is characterised by problems of unpredictable urgency and significant consequent fire-fighting. In difference to new systems development, which is buffered from the day to day tasks of the users, the systems in production is much more visible' (Swanson and Beath 1989). Looking in detail on the distribution of maintenance activities, as reported in Benestad et al. (2009); and Gupta (2009), it appears that very large differences reported in different studies. Whereas Lientz and Swanson (1980) reported 60% perfective, 18% adaptive and 17% corrective maintenance when asking about selected systems from a large number of organisations (one per organisation), Sousa and Moreira (1998) reported (based on a number of systems in one organisation) 49% adaptive, 36% corrective and 14% perfective maintenance. Mohagheghi and Conradi (2004) reported 53% corrective, 36% perfective and 4% adaptive maintenance, based on data on three open source products. Lee and Jefferson (2005) reported 62% perfective, 32% corrective and 6% adaptive maintenance based on data from one application in production. Figure 2.1 summarises the results from our own investigations, where we look upon the complete portfolio of a number of organisations (i.e. a more aggregated view that is less influenced on where the system is its lifecycle). Most interesting for comparison with other surveys is looking at corrective, adaptive and perfective maintenance, which appears to be much more stable than the numbers reported from others above. Jørgensen (1994) indicates that the assessed corrective percentage of the work used on maintenance often might be exaggerated since these kinds of problems are more visible for management. They found in their investigation of individual maintenance tasks that even if 38% of the changes were corrective, this only took up 9% of the time used for maintenance. Management assessed the percentage of corrective maintenance to be 19%. Those managers who based their answers on good data had a result of 9% corrective maintenance. Also, in our investigations, we found a similar tendency, on the data of the maintenance task of the individual systems, those reporting to have good data, reported that only 8% of the work effort was corrective maintenance, 4% being emergency fixes.

The effect of this would then probably decrease the total amount of functional maintenance even further, thus indicating an even better situation regarding the average functional maintenance. Related to this are the results of a survey reported in Dekleva (1992), which gave no conclusive evidence that organisations using modern development methods used less time on maintenance activities. On the other hand, time spent on emergency error corrections as well as the number of system failures decrease significantly with the use of modern development methods. Systems developed with modern methodologies seemed to facilitate making greater changes in functionality as the systems aged, and the request from users seemed more reasonable, based on a more complete understanding of the system.

The problem of many small maintenance tasks done more or less continuously seems to be increased by how maintenance is often done in an event-driven manner. In Jørgensen's investigation (Jørgensen 1994), where 38% of the tasks were of a corrective nature, as much as two-thirds of the tasks were classified to have high importance by the maintainers themselves.

Even if the problem of emergency fixes seems to be smaller than that perceived earlier, a methodology uniting development and maintenance must take into account that one has to be able to perform rapid changes to software artefacts in production, but it has been shown to be possible to reduce this by good development practice (Krogstie 2000). Another aspect here is that with shorter turnaround time and agile development, the visibility of development changes are increasing.

2.1.3 Coverage of Product

This is the method concerned with the development, use, operations and maintenance of

- One single application system
- A family of application systems
- The whole portfolio of application systems in an organisation
- The whole organisation (developing and maintaining so-called enterprise architectures)
- A cluster of cooperating organisations in combined digital content and software ecosystems (Krogstie 2011)

We can argue that it is beneficial for a methodology to be able to consider the whole portfolio and not only the single application system, although being able to concentrate on different areas at different times.

For the end-users of information systems, it is not important which concrete application system has changed. What is important is that their perceived needs are supported by the complete portfolio of available systems.

Application systems are not developed in a vacuum. They are related to old systems, by inheriting data and functionality; and they are integrated to other systems by data, control, presentation philosophy and process. They need to adhere to de facto and de jure standards as the applications in different companies are more and more integrated, utilising common resources and components. On a national level, countries such as Norway are developing common national components (Aagesen et al. 2011).

In our investigation from 2008 (Davidsen and Krogstie 2010), 94 new systems were currently being developed, and as many as 60 of these systems (64%) were regarded as replacement systems (in 2003 – 60%; in 1998 – 57%; in 1993 – 48%). The portfolio of the organisations responding to this question contained 446 systems, meaning that 13% of the current portfolio was being replaced (in 2003 – 13%; in 1998 – 9%; in 1993 – 11%). The average age of systems to be replaced was 7 years (in 2003 – 5.5 years; in 1998 – 7.7 years; in 1993 – 8.5 years).

More detailed reasons for the replacements are reported in Davidsen and Krogstie (2010). Here one sees that the main motivation for replacement has changed slightly from earlier investigations. The most important reasons for replacement in the 2008 investigations are partly a need for integration and the burden to maintain and operate, which appear to become more important again, a bit surprising given the relatively young age of the systems that are replaced. On the other hand, the web-systems developed over the last 10 years relates to much more demanding and volatile operating environments than the primarily in-house systems developed earlier.

Often when doing system integration, it can be useful to collect the functionality of several existing application systems into a new application system, something that is not well-supported when having strict borders for what is inside and outside of an application system.

As noted already in (Swanson and Beath 1989), the CISs of an organisation tend to congregate and develop as families. By original design or not, they come to rely upon each other for their data. In Swanson/Beath, 56% of the systems were connected to other systems through data integration. In our survey, we found that 73% of the main information systems in the organisations surveyed were dependent on data produced by other systems.

Over time, newer application systems originate in niches provided by older ones, and identifiable families of systems come to exist. Relationships among families are further established. In the long run, an organisation is served more by its CISs as a whole than by the application systems taken individually.

In addition to the core systems used by the organisation, a number of supporting systems are used to develop and operate these. A normal differentiation is between execution architecture (what applications run on), operating architecture (systems needed in addition for efficient operation and user-support) and development architecture (systems used to develop, evolve and maintain all the other systems).

2.1.4 Capabilities for CIS-Portfolio Evolution

For the different tasks within a methodology, and for the different products as part of the systems portfolio, a number of skills need to be available on the personal and organisational level to ensure that value is achieved.

A good source in relation to development is the person-roles described in Rational Unified Process (RUP) (Kruchten 2000); although the descriptions are written specific to the development of object-oriented systems, RUP role definitions are consistent with the notion of separating breadth and depth. Personality types for breadth workers and depth workers are very different. Breadth work is quick, inexact and resilient. Depth work takes much more time, requires attention to detail and must be of significantly better (syntactic) quality. Each of the RUP's disciplines has one role that focuses on breadth for that discipline and a different role that focuses on depth for the same discipline. Table 2.3 lists each RUP discipline along with its corresponding breadth and depth roles, and briefly explains the roles' functions, being generalised to be applicable also in other methodologies than RUP.

In simpler methods, such as Scrum (Schwaber and Beedle 2002), the number of roles are smaller. Scrum also illustrates the concept of organisational role, and the related capability of the role. Scrum has three roles: product owner, ScrumMaster and team (consisting of individual team members).

Product Owner: The product owner decides what will be built and in which order.
- Defines the features of the product or desired outcomes of the project
- Chooses release date and content
- Ensures profitability (ROI)
- Prioritises features/outcomes
- Adjusts features/outcomes and priority as needed
- Accepts or rejects work results
- Facilitates scrum planning ceremony

Scrum Master: The Scrum Master is a facilitative team leader who ensures that the team adheres to its chosen process and removes blocking issues.
- Ensures that the team is fully functional and productive
- Enables close cooperation across all roles and functions
- Removes barriers
- Shields the team from external interferences
- Ensures that the process is followed, including issuing invitations to daily scrums, sprint reviews and sprint planning
- Facilitates the daily scrums

Table 2.3 Breadth and depth roles relative to methodology disciplines

Discipline	Breadth role	Depth role
Analysis	*Business Analyst*: Discovers and analyse all business requirements.	*Business Designer*: Details a single set of business requirements.
Requirements	*Systems Analyst*: Discovers all system requirements.	*Requirements Specifier*: Details a single set of system requirement.
Design	*Software Architect*: Decides on technologies for the whole solution.	*Designer*: Details the design for a part of the solution (e.g. in RUP relative to a single use case).
Implementation	*Integrator*: Owns the build plan that shows what system components will integrate with one another.	*Implementer*: Codes a single set of system components
Test	*Test Manager*: Ensures that testing is complete and conducted for the right motivators.	*Test Designer*: Implements automated portions of the test design for the iteration.
	Test Analyst: Selects what to test based on the motivators.	*Tester*: Runs a specific test.
	Test Designer: Decides what tests should be automated vs. manual and creates automations.	
Deployment	*Deployment Manager*: Oversees deployment for all deployment units.	*Tech Writer, Course Developer, Graphic Artist*: Create detailed materials to ensure a successful deployment.
Project management	*Project Manager*: Creates the business case and a coarse-grained plan; makes go/no go decisions.	*Project Manager*: Plans, tracks, and manages risk for a single iteration. (Note that this discipline has only one role. Assigning the depth view to a project coordinator can provide relief for project managers.)
Environment	*Process Engineer*: Owns the process for the project.	*Tool Specialist*: Creates guidelines for using a specific tool.
Configuration and change management	*Configuration Manager*: Sets up the configuration management environment, policies, and plan.	*Configuration Manager*: Creates a deployment unit, reports on configuration status, performs audits, and so forth.
	Change Control Manager: Establishes a change control process.	*Change Control Manager*: Reviews and manages change requests.

The team:
- Is cross-functional
- Is right-sized (the ideal size is seven (plus/minus two) members)
- Selects the sprint goal and specifies work results
- Has the right to do everything within the boundaries of the project guidelines to reach the sprint goal
- Organises itself and its work
- Demonstrates work results to the product owner and any other interested parties

When extending the coverage of the product to be the whole organisation, not only the IT-systems, the need for participatory enterprise modelling and enterprise architecture skills as well as knowledge get more pronounced. The following lists the needed competences in this regard (Persson and Stirna 2010), distinguishing between modelling competence and management competence.

Competences related to modelling are as follows:
- Ability to model: This is making use of the chosen modelling language to create and refine enterprise models. Knowing how to use modelling tools for documenting and analysing the modelling result is also included in this capability.
- Ability to facilitate a modelling session: This capability is very much based on knowledge about the effects of modelling, the principles of human communication and socialisation (especially in groups) as well as the conditions of human learning and problem solving (cognition).

Competences related to managing enterprise modelling projects are as follows:
- Ability to select an appropriate EM approach and tailor it in order to fit the situation at hand
- Ability to interview involved domain experts
- Ability to define a relevant problem
- Ability to define requirements on the results
- Ability to establish a modelling project
- Ability to adjust a presentation of project results
- Ability to navigate between the wishes of various stakeholders
- Ability to assess the impact of the modelling result and the modelling process

We will return to how these skills are used in different modelling tasks in Sect. 2.4—the section on participatory modelling.

2.1.5   Stakeholder Participation

A large number of persons are playing different roles in connection to IS-development and evolution. In general, stakeholders in information systems implementation can be divided into the following groups (Macauley 1993):
- Those who are responsible for its design, development, introduction and maintenance, e.g. the project manager, system developers, communications experts, technical authors, training and user support staff and their managers.

- Those with financial interest, responsible for the application systems sale or purchase. These are typically termed the 'customer' of the system.
- Those who have an interest in its use, e.g. direct or indirect users and user's managers. Direct users are often called end-users.

In relation to the last group, in particular, different methods differentiate between how they take part in activities related to making or evolving the information system. The term 'participation' means to take part in something, most typically to take part in and influence a change of some sort that again influences the different stakeholders of the change. The change is typically done in some organisational or societal context, where someone uses resources to perform the change, to achieve some sort of value (cf. Sect. 2.1.1).

There exist different forms of participation:

- Direct participation: Every stakeholder has an opportunity to participate.
- Indirect participation: Every stakeholder participates more or less through representatives that are supposed to look after their interests. The representatives can either be:
  - Selected: The representatives are picked out by somebody, e.g. the management
  - Elected: The representatives are chosen from among their peers

Based on the discussion in Mumford (1983, 1986), there are a number of different reasons for participation, partly based on the power position of the stakeholders.

1. Morally right: The classical reasoning behind participation, based on a vision of a common good (e.g. justice and freedom) and how universal involvement in decision-making could help ensure this.
2. Educational: Involvement might provide understanding and knowledge among those participating that can assist an organisation to more effectively realise its objectives.
3. Improved ownership/motivation among stakeholders, resulting in better effect of the change. Focus on that by being involved in the process that the stakeholders will be more willing to accept the changes produced in use.
4. Leveraging of power: Unions, for instance, may encourage participation because they see it as a lever for increasing workers' control over the work situation and contribute to industrial democracy.
5. Protect against unwanted solutions: In a company, employees might see participation as a way to prevent things that they believe to be undesirable from happening (i.e. being made redundant or deskilled).
6. Transparency: Ensure that the decision-making process behind the changed solution is (perceived to be) open and trustworthy (i.e. not based on hidden agendas).
7. Emancipation: Enables those participating to feel free, be their own masters and in control of their own destinies.
8. Character-building: It assists people to develop active, non-servile characters and democratic personalities, and also enables them to broaden their horizons and appreciate the viewpoints and perspectives of others.
9. Improved solution: Through participation, more relevant knowledge is available and thus a better solution can be provided.

Whereas the above points indicate positive reasons for participations, there might also be negative reasons, e.g. to involve people as 'hostages', persuading people to accept changes that otherwise might be rejected or having possible scapegoats if a change is not successful.

Based on the reason for participation, the value to be achieved from participation is obviously varying. Often in a systems development setting, the primary reasoning for having participation is the last point in the above list (to have an improved solution), but you can also have variants of the others by ensuring stakeholder *influence*. A key aspect of the influence principle is to view 'users' as active and competent partners and domain experts. Equally important is to base these innovations on the needs and desires of potential users and to realise that these users often represent a heterogeneous group.

In information systems' literature, user participation is basically motivated applying a cost-benefit-perspective through achieving a better solution. Since all stakeholders have their individual local reality, everyone have a potential useful view of how the current situation can be improved. Including more people in the process will ideally increase the possibility of keeping up with the evermore rapidly changing environment of the organisation. Added to this is the general argument of including those who are believed to have relevant knowledge in the area and who are influenced by the solution.

We thus focus here specifically on participation of (potential) end-users of the information system. Note that a lot of the user involvement literature, related to the so-called Scandinavian School and Participatory Design (Bjerknes and Bratteteig 1995; Schuler and Namioka 1993), have a different outset with a focus on democratic participation, where the empowerment of employees through participation is often regarded a goal in itself.

According to Heller (1991), participation is sharing power and influence. One can classify the influence by the stakeholder of a change on the following levels (Arnstein 1969; Heller 1991):

0. Manipulation by giving wrong or biased information
1. No information to stakeholders
2. Information to stakeholders provided
3. Consultation with stakeholders (e.g. hearings)
4. Advice of stakeholders taken into account
5. Common decision between stakeholder (problem owners) and developers
6. Delegated authority to stakeholders
7. The problem-owners have full control

Note that the higher on this scale one is, the *responsibilities* laid on the stakeholders also increases.

Due to the large number of potential stakeholders in IS development and evolution, in most cases, representative participation will be the only practical possibility. From the point of view of social construction (Berger and Luckmann 1966), it is doubtful that a user representative can truly represent anyone else than himself or herself. Different perspectives and views on the reality are also often mentioned reasons for why it is crucial to involve users as well as many different types of stakeholders in the development process. The reality aspect is also considered by focusing on involving real users, not basing on personas (Grudin and Pruitt 2002) or other user representative theories. On the other hand, even if the internal reality of each individual will always differ to a certain degree, the explicit knowledge concerning a constrained area might be more or less equal, especially within groups of social actors (Orlikowski and Gash 1994).

Another factor is the scope of participation, i.e. when does participation take place. Usually one would expect that user-participation would take place heavily in analysis/requirements and in acceptance testing, more lightly in technical design, and very little in implementation, but this will often depend on the chosen methodology. For instance, in agile development (Abrahamsson et al. 2010), the main point is to try to also have user participation in the implementation, to ensure short turnaround time from changes in the technical solutions to feedback on these changes.

When it comes to suggesting improvements and evolutions of the current information system of the organisation, direct participation should be made possible to a larger degree, e.g. as illustrated in the use of Active Knowledge Modelling (AKM). Also in the project establishment, a larger proportion of the stakeholders should be able to participate.

Practices and methods of user involvement include a multitude of different traditions and approaches. One useful way to analyse this multitude relative to for instance the governmental systems is to differentiate between (1) methods and practices designed to fit information systems development processes and (2) government participation practices (Følstad et al. 2004).

The field of Human-Computer Interaction (HCI) is an example of an approach developed to conduct user involvement in software development projects. This field covers methods and practices suited for the development phases of analyses, requirement specification, design and evaluation. HCI methods for analyses include analyses of users and stakeholders, user tasks and context of use; methods for requirements elicitation and description include workshops, interviews, field studies, personas and use cases; methods for design include rapid prototyping, design patterns, card sorting and story boarding; and methods for evaluation include analytical methods like cognitive walkthrough and heuristic evaluation as well as empirical methods like user tests and field evaluations (Maguire 2001).

Within, in particular, the governmental sector, a different form of user involvement has evolved. Government user involvement practices typically include: user reference groups following the development project for a substantial period of time, user representatives in the project team, user and stakeholder representatives in project steering committees, formal and semi-formal audits of project plans and system specifications, workshops with user and stakeholder representatives, involvement of user interest organisations, public meetings and public information activities.

2.1.6   Organisation of Development and Evolution of Information Systems

A number of organisations can be involved in IS development and evolution, and these can be organised in different manners.

Early on IT was interleaved with other activities in the organisation, but as the importance of IT increased, a separate organisation appeared, taking care of development, maintenance (application management), systems operation, user support and management. Slowly, this has been divided in distinct organisational units. Actually, since one has always based internal IT-systems on the existing technology, one has had to deal with external vendors of equipment and systems. As more and more packaged systems have appeared, both with large and small adaptations, the number of external partners developing and maintaining the information system support of organisations have gradually increased. The increasing use of open source and the new development of governmental common components (Aagesen et al. 2011) illustrate this development. For instance, within OSS (Fitzgerald 2001) hundred thousands of co-developed software components are freely available, often via portals like http://sourceForge.net. The quality is variable and often poorly documented.

The following illustrates one way of dividing the tasks in different organisational units from a Norwegian organisation after outsourcing parts of the tasks, primarily to organisation NN (Krogstie 2000).

Application management (AM) includes the development of new releases of existing systems, error corrections and handling change requests to the existing application portfolio of the organisation. New releases are typically developed through small projects, having all the normal tasks of a systems development project such as analysis, requirement specification, design, programming, testing, deployment and project management. IT operations were outsourced to a third company, and also several other companies were responsible for the maintenance/evolution and further development of selected packaged systems. The IT-steering model in the organisation is illustrated in Fig. 2.2. The company retained some people in the IT-function to have the overall control of the IT-strategy and vendor agreements and to ensure sufficient in-house knowledge to use IR in a strategic manner. The different company divisions and steering groups were decision-makers on overall IT-spending and project-direction. Two coordination bodies were established: Program management, coordinating dependencies across all larger ongoing projects and application management releases, and Service Management, controlling the overall IT-service levels, SLAs, requests, errors, etc. The system developers in the AM unit were divided into seven groups, each supporting a separate part of the highly interrelated application portfolio supporting the activities of organisation.

Earlier, some work was done to investigate the pros and cons of differentiating development and maintenance activities. Already, Chapin (1987) investigated into this area and concluded that no differences in the nature and characteristics of the demand for or performance of software maintenance work was found between the two types of departmentalisation. What those organisations adopting a separate

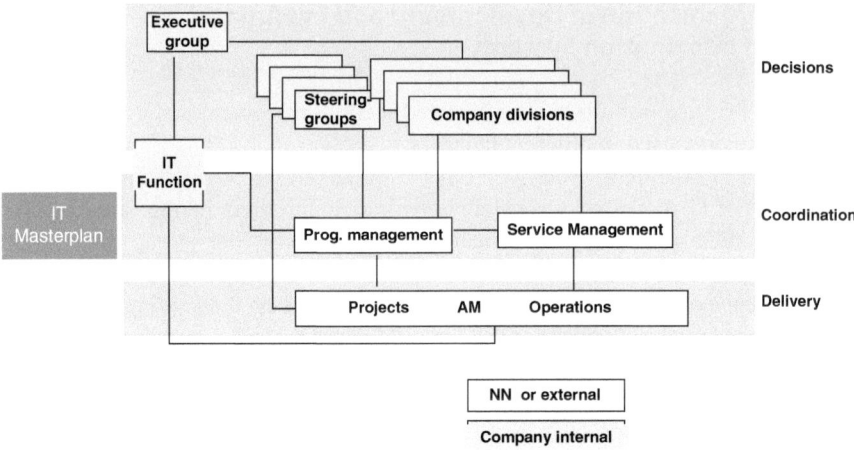

Fig. 2.2 An example of an IT-Steering Model

organisational place for software maintenance had achieved was fewer management problems and a more positive attitude towards software maintenance by those managing it—something we believe that can also be achieved by not differentiating between development and maintenance projects in the first place.

As for system operations, it is more usual to have this in a separate organisation (Iden et al. 2011) than systems development and evolution.

2.1.7   Location: Where the Work Takes Place

This is often looked upon in connection with the organisation, but is actually another dimension. A lot of the focus of agile development is that people involved in the development project should be co-located, no matter if they actually worked in different parts of the same organisations or were external consultants. Similarly, in the model presented in Fig. 2.2, most of the workers in the different organisational units were actually co-located even if working for different organisations.

One example of a notable change from our survey investigations mentioned in the introduction of this chapter is where systems are developed, maintained, and operate compared to 15 years ago. In 1993, 58% of the systems were developed by the IS-organisation, and only 1% was developed *in* the user organisation. In 1998, however, 27% of the systems were developed by the IS-organisation and 27% as custom systems *in* the user organisation. In 2003, 23% of the systems were developed in the IS-organisation, whereas in 2008 only 12% were developed in the IS organisation. The percentage of systems developed by outside firms is higher in 2008 (40% vs. 35% in 2003, vs. 22% in 1998, vs. 12% in 1993, vs. 15% in Swanson/ Beath). The percentage of systems developed based on packages with small or large adjustments is also comparatively high (41% in 2008 vs. 39% in 2003, vs. 24% in

1998, vs. 28% in 1993, vs. 2% in Swanson/Beath). The new category we introduced in 1998, component-based development (renamed 'use of external web services' in 2008) is still small (5% in 2008), although increasing (1.0% in 2003, 0.4% in 1998).

Whereas earlier the main way of developing systems was to do it in-house or using temporary consultants (potentially based on adapting packages), outsourcing of all type of IT-activities has been on the rise over the last 10 years, although you also find examples lately on in-sourcing (were earlier outsourced tasks that are taken back into the organisation). In the 2008 investigation, around a third of the IT-activity was outsourced (32.9% in private sector, 24.1 in public sector (Krogstie 2010)). Whereas only two of the respondents reported to have outsourced all the IT-activities, as many as 84% of the organisations had outsourced parts of their IT-activity. Whereas the public organisations have outsourced more of the development (40% in public, 29% in private) and maintenance (34% in public, 30% in private) work than the private organisations, they have outsourced less of the operations (31% in public, 41% in private) and user support (21% in public, 29% in private). Other important aspects to take into account are the rise of new delivery models (e.g. OSS) not only for infrastructure applications, but also business applications. It is reported that 50% of Norwegian IT companies now integrate OSS components into their own applications, and 10% also contribute back to the OSS community (Hauge et al. 2010).

Another trend is towards using cloud infrastructures for the operations of IT-solutions.

The conceptual idea underlying cloud computing started its development as early as the 1960s, when John McCarthy expressed that 'computation may someday be organised as a public utility'. This thought was further developed in Parkhill (1966), where he compared the supply of computational power to the supply of electrical power. This analogy is oversimplified, i.e. the data transferred over the network represent symbol structures, electrons in electric power do not, but it gives a basic idea of the concept. Cloud computing is relatively new term within the IT-field. The National Institute of Standards and Technology (NIST) defines cloud computing as (Mell and Grance 2009):

> A model for enabling convenient, on-demand network access to a shared pool of configurable computing resources (e.g., networks, servers, storage, applications, and services) that can be rapidly provisioned and released with minimal management effort or service provider interac.tion.

The NIST definition describes five essential characteristics of cloud computing. On-demand self-service, broad network access, resource pooling, rapid elasticity and measured service.

1. On-demand self-service: Clouds offer automatic scaling of resources without human interaction.
2. Broad network access: Applications hosted in the cloud are often available from thin-clients like mobile devices and web browsers, thereby offering great flexibility in the choice of end-user device.
3. Resource pooling: The cloud uses virtualisation of resources and, therefore, appears as one large pool of resources. These resources are dynamically assigned

to the users of the cloud. The users of cloud services generally do not know the exact location of the resources being provided, but can in some cases define a location at a higher level of abstraction (e.g. country, continent).

4. Rapid elasticity: Demanded resources in the cloud can be quickly allocated to the customer. The cloud's resources often appear as unlimited from the customer's point of view.

5. Measured service: The system automatically monitors and controls the resources used by each customer. The most used method of payment is a pay-per-use model, where the customer pays for the resources used. This requires monitoring and control of resources.

The NIST definition describes three different service models. The three levels offer different levels of abstraction.

1. Cloud Software as a Service (SaaS): A customer can rent an application running in the cloud. The application is often accessed via thin clients like web browsers. The customer does not control the underlying cloud structure and not even the application capabilities except for limited configuration settings for the application. Examples of SaaS providers are Salesforce.com and Service-now.com. The model has been available for quite some time, and was earlier marketed under the term Application Service Provider (ASP).

2. Cloud Platform as a Service (PaaS): The customer is offered a platform where customer-created applications can be deployed using APIs offered by and programming languages supported by the service provider. The customer does not control the underlying structure (i.e. operating system, network or storage). An example of this is Microsoft's Windows Azure platform.

3. Cloud Infrastructure as a Service (IaaS): The cloud infrastructure, usually a platform virtualisation environment, is delivered as a service. The customer can control a large part of the platform (i.e. operating system and storage).

Customers using cloud computing have different needs when it comes to data privacy and data security. Some have data that they will not risk being accessed by others, some organisations share privacy concerns and can use the same cloud (e.g. different governmental agencies needing to store data on the citizens), while others do not have any concerns with sharing computational resources with others. The NIST definition of cloud computing describes four deployment methods for clouds. A deployment method describes who has access to the cloud.

1. Private Cloud: A private cloud is as the name says private. Private clouds are typical for organisations that have sensitive data that they do not want to risk unauthorised access to, but still need the other characteristics of cloud computing.

2. Community Cloud: A community cloud is a private cloud for a larger group of organisations. This may be organisations that require the same type of security. They may also use the same type of data in their applications.

3. Public Cloud: A public cloud is a cloud infrastructure that is available to everyone (the public). Applications and data can coexist independently.

4. Hybrid Cloud: A hybrid cloud is a combination of the previously mentioned cloud types. An organisation can run a private or community cloud and utilise the resources of a public cloud if it is needed for restricted parts of their applications.

For organisations as large as national governments, a private cloud does not differ very much from community cloud.

As providers of software through open source and mash-ups get more professional, one has started to talk about software ecosystems (Messerschmitt and Szyperski 2003). A *software ecosystem* (Jansen et al. 2009) is

> a set of businesses functioning as a unit and interacting with a shared market for software and services, together with relationships among them. These relationships are frequently underpinned by a common technological platform and operate through the exchange of information, resources, and artefacts

We will return to software ecosystems in and other new organisational forms in Chap. 8.

2.2   A Short History of IS Methodologies

Although we find a large number of methodologies, we can recognise back to the work in the 1960s (Langefors 1967), a differentiation according to abstractions levels. Crudely, as discussed in Sect. 2.1.2, the following abstraction levels are found in most methodologies:

- Analysis
- Requirements specification
- Design
- Implemented systems

The main differentiation between different methodologies is how we organise the work on the different abstraction levels, relative to scope, time and persons involved, and iterations between these (Berente and Lyytinen 2007). In Sect. 2.1, we presented a framework for IS methodologies meant to clarify facets of this. Here we will briefly describe some important methodology developments. Particular model-based approaches are discussed in Sect. 2.3.

There is a common understanding that one in the early years of computing (1950s and 1960s) was basically following a naive approach of code-and-test. Actually, already in the 1960s, a number of theoretical notions differentiating the different levels of abstractions for information systems were described by Langefors (Bubenko 2007). They appeared when Langefors was at the Swedish SAAB aircraft company (e.g. (Langefors 1963)). In 1967, many of these reports were compiled in Langefors (1967).

Langefors introduced a number of concepts related to modelling for information systems, among others the partitioning of the systems development life-cycle in four important *method areas.*

- Methods for management and control of organisations
- Methods for analysis and description of information systems at an elementary, 'problem-oriented' level (the 'infological' realm)
- Methods for design and analysis of computerised information systems on a 'product-oriented' level (the 'datalogical' realm)
- Methods for implementation of the information system on computer hardware and choice of hardware

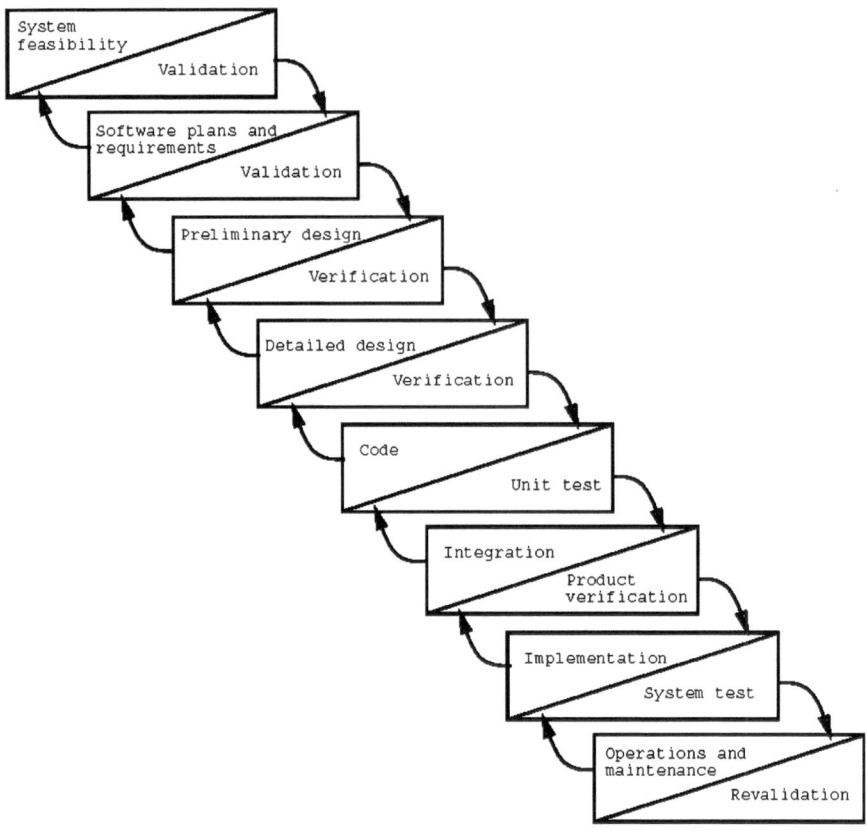

Fig. 2.3 An example of steps in a waterfall methodology

2.2.1   The Waterfall Methodology

An important contribution of the 1960s was the confirmation of the significance of the infological realm, i.e. the realm where data processing problems were expressed formally, but in a machine-independent way. This laid the basis for a number of new modelling notions during the next decade. The differentiation also made its way into mainstream systems development methodology, first in the form of the so-called waterfall model. The waterfall model, illustrated in Fig. 2.3, is usually attributed to (Royce 1970).

The waterfall methodology organises CIS projects as a linear sequence of phases, where each phase is completed by documenting its achievements. In addition, there are feedback loops between successive phases that enable the modification of the documents from the previous phase.

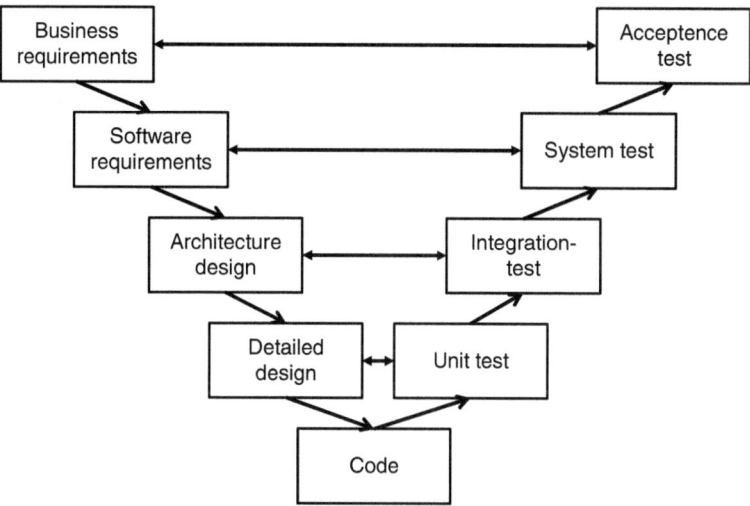

Fig. 2.4   The V-Model relating development and testing activities

The perceived benefits of using the waterfall model can be summarised as follows (Davis et al. 1988):

- It instructs the developers to specify the system prior to the construction of it.
- It encourages one to design the system components before they are actually coded.
- By viewing the project as a sequence of phases, the managers can more easily control the progress of the work and use the defined milestones as a tool for deciding if the project is to continue or not. It will also help the managers to set up a structured and manageable project-organisation.
- One is required to write documents that will ease the testing and documentation of the system, and that will reduce maintenance costs.

Every project starts out with a feasibility study. The main problems are identified and the pursuit of a new CIS is justified in terms of unfulfilled needs and wishes in the organisation to be supported by the information system.

The purpose of the requirements specification is to define and document all the stakeholder's needs. The specification is supposed to contain a complete description of what the system will do from a user's point of view. How the system will do it, is deliberately ignored. This is meant to be addressed during design.

Most early 'standard' methodologies for commercial organisations, government contractors and governmental organisations followed some basic variation of this model, even if the number of phases and the names of the phases often varied (Davis 1988).

In was soon realised that the traditional depiction of the waterfall could be improved by linking the test activities (on different abstraction levels) closer to the 'downstream' development levels. The V-model (Beizer 1990) (as shown in Fig. 2.4) builds a logical V shape sequence where the system and acceptance testing are tightly associated with the requirements.

The (conventional) waterfall model received much criticism already in the beginning of the 1980s (McCracken and Jackson 1982; Swartout and Balzer 1982):

- The phases are artificial constructs, 'one specific kind of project management strategy imposed on software development' (McCracken and Jackson 1982). It is in practice often difficult to separate specification completely from design and implementation.
- An executing system is presented first at the end of the project. This is unfortunate for several reasons:
  - Errors made in the specification will be more difficult and thus more costly to remove when they are not discovered before the end of the project.
  - The customer and end-users may get impatient and press for premature results or lose interest in the project because they do not see any result of the work that has been done.
  - The communication gap between the users and the developers arising because of their different realities not being attacked.
  - Systems developed using the conventional methodology is often difficult to change, resulting in poor support for system evolution.

Similar critiques have been raised in the last decade in connection to the introduction of so-called agile development methods (Abrahamsson et al. 2010; Beck 2002), but has been attempted to be attacked by a number of works already in the 1980s, classical work on alternative approaches, which we will discuss first.

2.2.2 Prototyping

A prototype can be defined as 'an executable model of (parts of) an information system, which emphasises specific aspects of that system' (Vonk 1990).

Prototyping as a *technique* is usually seen as a supplement to conventional application systems development methodologies (Taylor and Standish 1982; Vonk 1990). It emphasises on high user participation and tangible representations of selected user requirements at an early stage. The iterative generation and validation of executable models makes the approach particularly useful when the requirements are unstable or uncertain. Another usage is a technically oriented proof-of-concept prototyping, which focuses on making sure that the attempted approach is technically possible at all.

Prototyping as *methodology* is a highly iterative process, which is characterised by extensive use of prototypes (Carey 1990; Vonk 1990). The objective is to clarify certain characteristics of an application system by constructing an artefact that can be executed. On the basis of user feedback the prototype is revised and new knowledge and new insights are gained. After a series of revisions, the prototype is acceptable to the users, which indicates that it reflects the user requirements in some specific aspects.

According to Vonk (1990), prototyping differs from a traditional (waterfall) methodology on the following areas:

- The users can validate the requirements by testing a corresponding executable model. The communication between users and developers is improved in that the users can directly experience the consequences of the specified requirements.

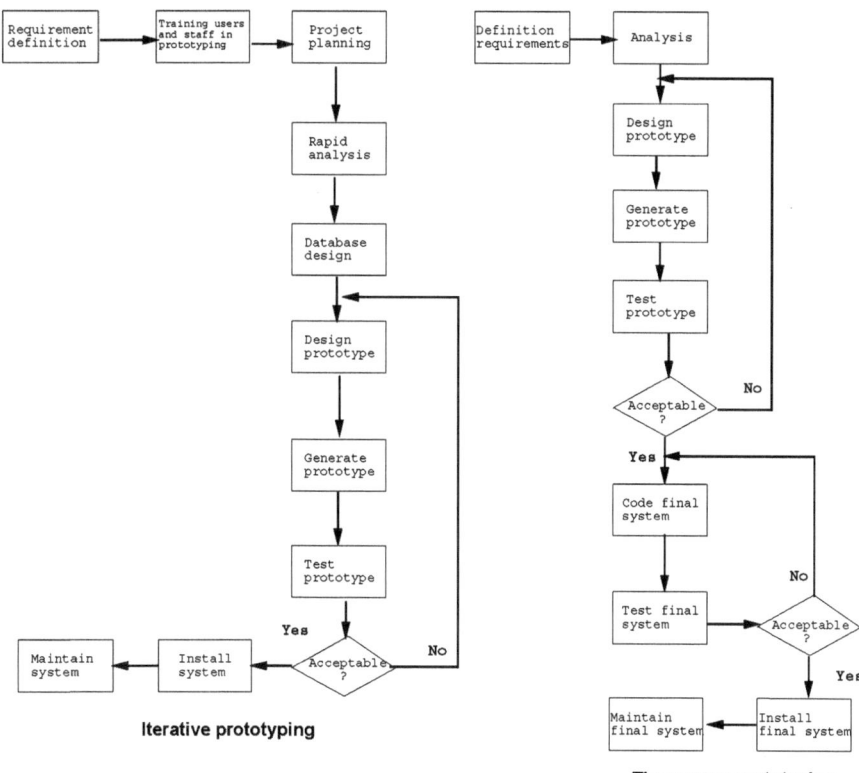

Fig. 2.5 Different forms of prototyping methodologies

- Traditional tool-support for these methodologies has been unable to focus on the user interface aspects. Prototypes exploit the execution of (simplified) user interfaces to improve the externalisation of user requirements.
- The requirements tend to change as the project is carried out. Instability of functional requirements is easily handled through the interactive generation and validation of functional prototypes.

In Vonk's opinion, its main benefit is the reduction of uncertainty. The choice of development strategy, thus, should be based on the judgement of project uncertainty.

Carey (1990) sees the following advantages with prototyping: faster development time, easier end-use and learning, less labour to develop systems, decreased backlogs and enhanced user/analyst communication. Some disadvantages include: the fostering of undue expectations on the part of the users, what the users see may not be what the users get and the availability of application generator software may encourage unduly end-user computing.

There are two main types of prototyping as illustrated in Fig. 2.5: In iterative prototyping, also called evolutionary prototyping, the prototype evolves into the final application system after a series of evolutionary user-initiated changes.

In throwaway prototyping, the prototype is only used to help to establish the user's requirements to the application system. As soon as the process is finished, the prototype is discarded and the real application system is implemented.

Another classification of prototypes is based on the particular aspects that are included, i.e. the focus.

- Functional prototypes include some functionality of the system, and will often contain simple algorithms and data structures.
- User interface prototypes are used to design both the presentational and the behavioural part of human-computer interfaces, simulating the core functionality of the system.
- Performance prototypes concentrate on workload and hardware characteristics.

2.2.3   Transformational and Operational Development

The transformational approach, which was originally also often termed automatic software synthesis (Lowry and McCartney 1991), assumes the existence of formal specification languages and tools for automatic transformations.

Its main philosophy, gradually transforming formal requirements specifications into target code, has proved to be a very ambitious goal, but still a goal-pursued in current approaches such as MDA (described in Sect. 2.3.2).

As shown in Fig. 2.6a, the formal specification is the crucial element. It is used as a starting point for the transformation process, but is at the same time the main document for stakeholder validation. This illustrates the main problem using transformational techniques: on the one hand, formality is necessary to apply automatic transformations; on the other hand, the formality normally makes specifications more difficult to understand for end-users.

A series of transformations are applied to reach the final target code. During these transformations, additional details are added to the specification. Not all of these details can be automatically added, and a developer is needed to guide the transformation process.

The sequence of transformations and decisions is kept in a development record. Using this record, one can maintain and re-implement the formal specification.

The operational approach was first described in detail already by Zave (1984). Its main characteristics are (1) the separation of problem-oriented and implementation-oriented system features and (2) the provision of executable system models early in the development process. It is claimed that the approach will enhance the validation process as prototypes are immediately available. The approach is illustrated in Fig. 2.6b.

The approach rests on the use of an operational specification language. This language is defined as a suitable interpreter making the models available through prototyping or symbolic evaluation or both (Harel 1992) for validation.

The specification model is rarely suited as the final program code. It is a functional model, although ideas to include non-functional requirements have been explored. Resource management and resource allocation strategies are usually omitted, and

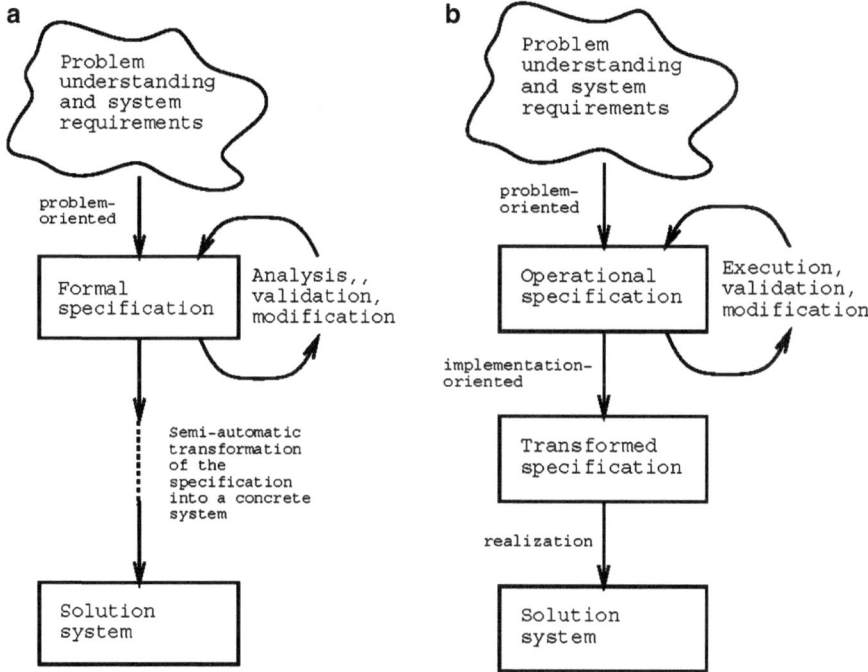

Fig. 2.6 (**a**) Transformational and (**b**) operational life cycle models

characteristics of the target environment are deliberately ignored. As stated by Agresti (1986), the operational paradigm violates the traditional distinction between 'what' and 'how' considerations. Instead, the development process is separated on the basis of problem-oriented versus product-oriented concerns.

As soon as the operational model is finished, a series of transformations are carried out. The goal of these transformations is to reach another specification, which is directly interpretable by the target processor. In order to do so, decisions concerning performance and implementation resources are made.

The approach is claimed to have several advantages to conventional waterfall life cycle models (Zave 1984).

- It exploits the advantages of formality (e.g. for formal analysis).
- Rapid prototypes or symbolically executable units are available all away from the start.
- Since the transformations preserve correctness, it is not necessary to verify the final code.
- All functional modifications are done at the specification level.

In addition, in Zave's opinion the separation of problem-oriented and implementation-oriented issues is useful to improve the system's maintainability. Operational specifications are constructed with maintenance in mind, while transformations try to take care of requirements concerning performance and efficiency. Conventional techniques, on the other hand, support only one decomposition principle. The conflicting issue of efficiency and ease of maintenance must be addressed in the same process, which tends to result in more or less unconscious compromises.

Among the disadvantages of the operational approach are the danger for premature design decisions, the difficulties of comprehending the formal specifications for end-user and the problems of guiding the transformations. An early approach in this area based on the use of conceptual modelling techniques, TEMPORA, is described in further detail in Sect. 3.3.5.

2.2.4 The Spiral Model

The spiral model was introduced by Boehm (1988). It may be perceived as a framework for systems development, in which risk analysis governs the choice of more specific methodologies as the project progresses. The spiral model potentially subsumes both the prototyping (both iterative and throwaway), operational/transformational and waterfall methodology.

As shown in Fig. 2.7, the project is intended to iterate through a number of basic steps. Each iteration encompasses some objectives to be solved, and is comprised of the following steps:

- Determine objectives, alternatives and constraints.
- Evaluate the alternatives and identify risks connected to central components or features.
- Develop product to resolve the most critical risks and evaluate the results. Prototyping, reuse techniques and requirement and design specifications are all means of reducing risks.
- Plan the next iteration and review the achievements of the current one.
  According to Boehm, the strengths of the spiral model are:
- It focuses early attention on options involving the reuse of existing software.
- It accommodates for life-cycle evolution, growth and changes of the software product.
- It provides a mechanism for incorporating software quality objectives into software product development.
- It focuses on eliminating errors and unattractive alternatives early.
- For each of the sources of project activity and resource expenditure, it answers the key question 'how much is enough'.
- It does not involve separate techniques for software development and maintenance.
- It provides a viable framework for integrated hardware-software systems development.

Its major weakness is connected to the availability of proper risk analysis techniques. As long as risk determination is more an art than an engineering discipline, the model will give a rather theoretical and superficial impression. Moreover, the iterated reviewing of current objectives may impose some troubles to the specification of contracts between customers and developers. As presented in Boehm (1988), it is merely a framework for development and maintenance that will be difficult to apply directly by inexperienced developers.

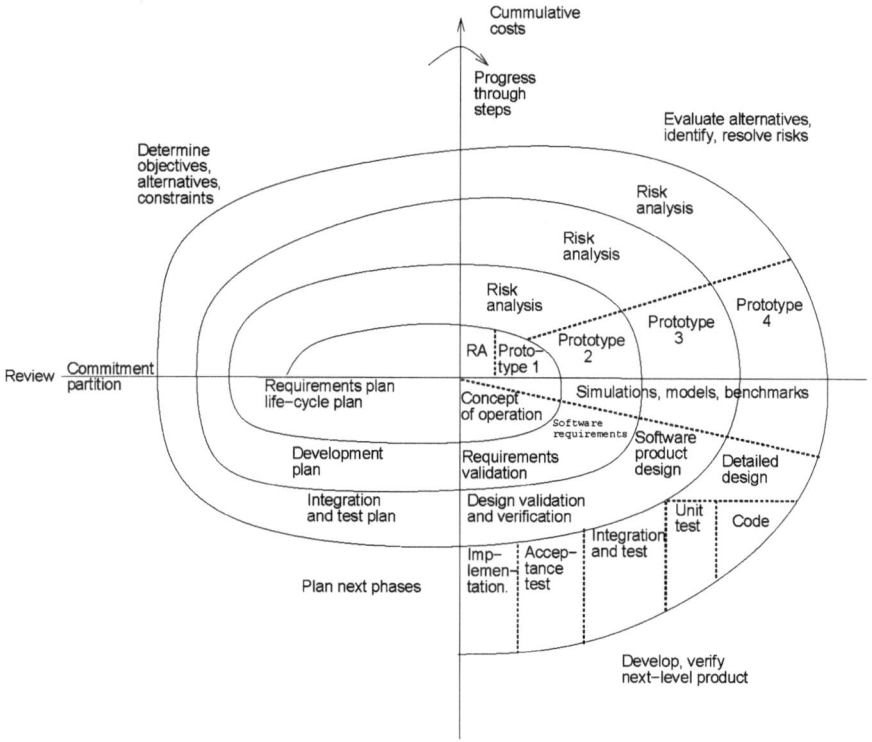

Fig. 2.7 The spiral model (Adapted from Boehm 1988)

2.2.5   Object-Oriented Systems Development and the Rational Unified Process

As object-oriented development (including object-oriented analysis and design) became increasingly popular throughout the 1990s, object-oriented development methods also became more popular, especially as UML emerged as a standard for modelling of object-oriented systems. The Unified Process and RUP are examples of methodological frameworks for systems development that arose in this period. These methods exist in several variants. The activity view of the development process is exemplified in Fig. 2.8 in the form of a 'whale-diagram'. This view shows the main activities performed during a systems development process.

There are four phases in the development process: the inception phase, the elaboration phase, the construction phase and the transition phase. The completion of a phase means that the product under development has reached a certain degree of completeness and, thus, represents a major milestone of the project. The milestones are shown at the bottom of Fig. 2.8.

There are two kinds of activities: *process activities* and *supporting activities*. Process activities are activities that are directly related to the systems development tasks. They are requirements capture, analysis and design, implementation and test.

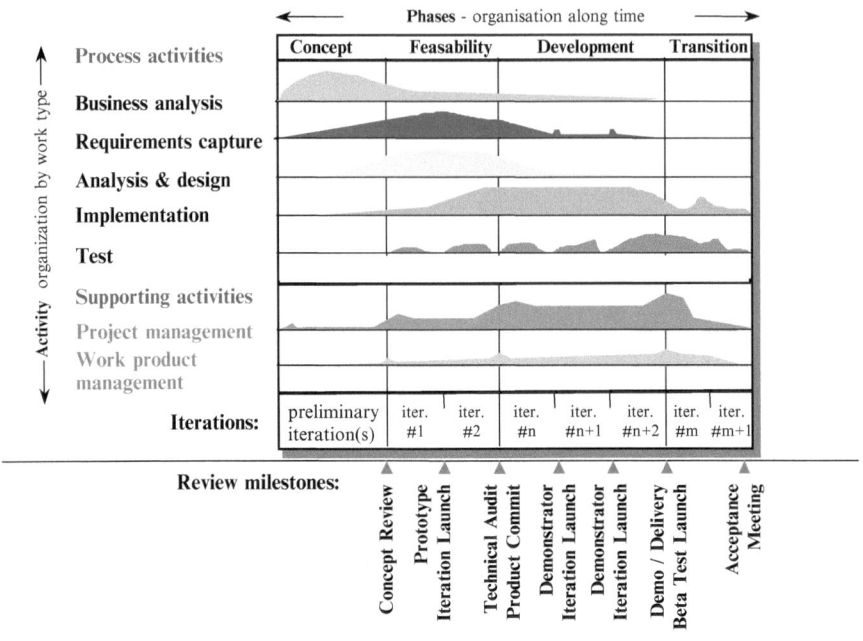

Fig. 2.8 The activity view of a development process following RUP

Supporting activities are activities that support the process activities to ensure that they are carried out effectively and efficiently. They are project management and work product management.

The relative importance of the process activities varies during the life cycle of a development project. In early phases, analysis and architecture level design tend to dominate, while in later phases the majority of the work is on class level design, implementation and testing. This is illustrated in Fig. 2.8 where the curves indicate the effort on each activity as a function of time.

Note that the figure shows an example. Exactly how these curves will look depends on the type of project. In more explorative projects for instance, where the requirements and architecture is difficult to stabilise early, significant effort on requirements analysis and architectural design may persist all the way to the end of the project. In more straightforward projects, on the other hand, these activities will be more or less completed after the first two phases.

The Rational Unified Process captures many of software development's best practices in a form suitable for a wide range of projects and organisations:

- Develop software iteratively
- Manage requirements
- Use component-based architectures
- Model software with visual languages
- Continuously verify software quality
- Control changes to software

2.2.6   Incremental Development and Agile Development

Incremental development (Davis 1988) is the process of constructing a partial implementation of a total system and slowly adding increased functionality or performance. When the increments are released to the production environment one by one, one often talks about stage-wise development. This is meant to reduce the costs incurred before an initial capability is achieved. It also produces an operational system more quickly, and it thus reduces the possibility that the user needs will change during development. It also enables rapid feedback from the use of the systems to inform the work in later increments. Originally, incremental development presupposed that most of the requirements were understood up front, and one chose to implement only a subset of the requirements at a time. Note how this differs from evolutionary prototyping, even if these techniques could be integrated.

Modern approaches to incremental development practices are labelled 'agile' or lightweight methodologies (Abrahamsson et al. 2010; Cockburn 2002). Agile methodologies are based on the assumption that communication is necessarily imperfect (Cockburn 2002), and that software development is a social, communication-intensive activity among multiple developers and users of the system. According to proponents of agile methods, increased documentation is not necessarily the answer to the weaknesses of evolutionary development practices. Rather, certain complementary activities must be in place to augment evolutionary development and to increase the quality or scope of iterations, such as pair programming, time-boxing, test-first development (Beck 2002).

The agile alliance defined the Agile Manifesto in 2001. The four agile values are specified as follows (Beck et al. 2001):
- Individuals and interactions over processes and tools
- Working software over comprehensive documentation
- Customer collaboration over contract negotiation
- Responding to change over following a plan

Note that this does not mean that one does not maintain any documentation at all, just that the focus is rather on working software.

A number of agile methods and approaches have been developed, including:
- Extreme Programming (XP) (Beck 2002)
- Scrum (Schwaber and Beedle 2002)
- Dynamic Systems Development Method – DSDM (Stapleton 1997)
- Feature-Driven Development – FDD (Palmer and Felsing 2002)
- Adaptive Software Development – ASD (Highsmith 2000)
- Agile Modelling – AM (Ambler and Jeffries 2002)
- Crystal (Cockburn 2002)
- Internet Speed Development – ISD (Baskerville et al. 2001)
- Pragmatic Programming – PP (Hunt and Thomas 2000)
- Test-Driven Development – TDD (Janzen and Saiedian 2005)

Often one thinks about agile methods primarily looking on coding and testing. As Fig. 2.9 from Abrahamsson et al. (2010) illustrates, the scope and coverage of the methods differ quite a bit, although we will not go into detail on this here. One thing

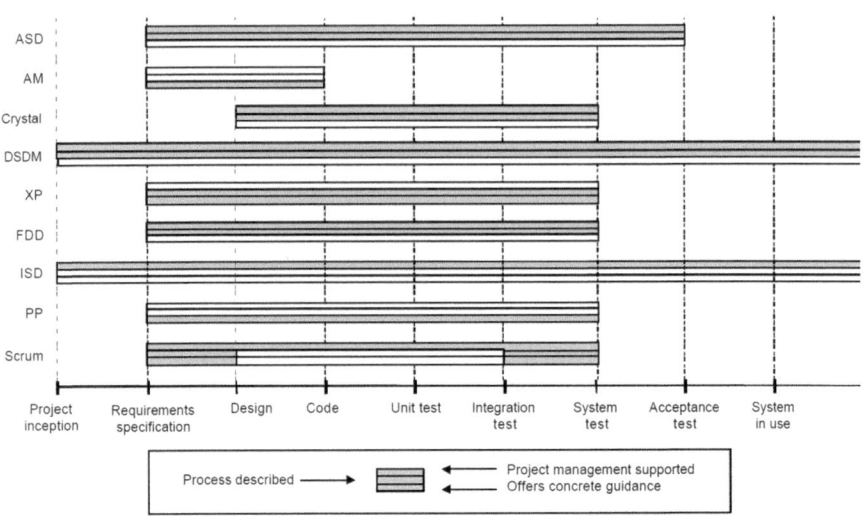

Fig. 2.9 Comparing project management, life-cycle and guidance support in agile development methods (From Abrahamsson et al. 2010)

Table 2.4 Comparing agile and plan-driven development

Aspect	Agile	Traditional/plan-driven
Developers	Agile, knowledgeable, collocated, and collaborative	Plan-oriented, adequate skills, access to external knowledge
Customers	Dedicated, knowledgeable, collocated, collaborative, representative, and empowered customers	Access to knowledgeable, collaborative, representative, and empowered customers
Requirements	Largely emergent, rapid change	Knowable early, largely stable
Architecture	Designed for current requirements	Designed for current and foreseeable requirements
Size	Smaller teams and products	Larger teams and products
Primary objective	Rapid value	High assurance

worth to mention though is that even if focus is being close to the end-user (or rather customer), few agile development methods relate directly to systems in use.

Table 2.4 based on discussions in Boehm (2002); Nerur et al. (2005) indicates some differences between more traditional development and agile development.

One problem with strict incremental design, however, is the lack of 'iterative' planning for each increment. Starting with a poor initial increment could turn users away; the focus on the main increment can contribute to a short-term, myopic focus for the project; and 'developing a suboptimal system' could necessitate a great deal of rework in later phases (Boehm 1981). The output of incremental development might often resemble unmanageable 'spaghetti code' that is difficult to maintain and integrate, similar to the 'code and fix' problems that Waterfall was originally intended to correct (Boehm 1988). Also, by using the software code itself to guide discussions of requirements, conversations tend to focus mainly on detail, rather than business principles associated with the information system. Many continuing problems associated with incremental development include 'ad hoc requirements management; ambiguous and imprecise communication; brittle architectures; overwhelming complexity; undetected inconsistencies in requirements, designs, and implementation; insufficient testing; subjective assessment of project status; failure to attack risk; uncontrolled change propagation; insufficient automation' (Kruchten 2000).

To address this, several approaches have looked upon dividing the methodology into two: one phase where the long-term architecture is developed, and one with many iterations where functionality is developed (so-called RAAD – Rapid Architected Application Development). Both in incremental/agile approaches and RUP, the focus is on bundling requirement into iterations/increments. As a basis for this, one often looks upon the priority of the requirements. Another way of structuring requirements is according to the Kano model (Kano 1984). According to this, software requirements can be classified into three categories: normal, exciting and expected.

Whereas many of the traditional methodologies are oriented primarily towards the development of the IT-system, a number of methodologies take a broader view, looking upon the development of the overall organisation. An early example of this was Multiview.

2.2.7   Multiview

This methodology was based on several existing methodologies (Avison and Wood-Harper 1990). Multiview addresses the following areas:
1. How is the application system supposed to further the aims of the organisation using it?
2. How can it be fitted into the working lives of the stakeholders in the organisation?
3. How can the stakeholders best relate to the application system in terms of operating it and using the output from it?
4. What information processing functions are the application system to perform?
5. What is the technical specification of an application system that will come close enough to addressing the above questions?

Multiview largely addresses problems associated with the analysis and design activities in application systems development. It tries to take into account the different views of the stakeholders.

The methodology sees information systems as social system that relies to an increasing extent on computer technology. Multiview includes phases for addressing both human/social and technical aspects.

The methodology is based on five main phases (Fig. 2.10):
1. Analysis of human activity (answer to question 1)
2. Analysis of information (answer to question 4)
3. Analysis and design of socio-technical aspects (answer to question 2)

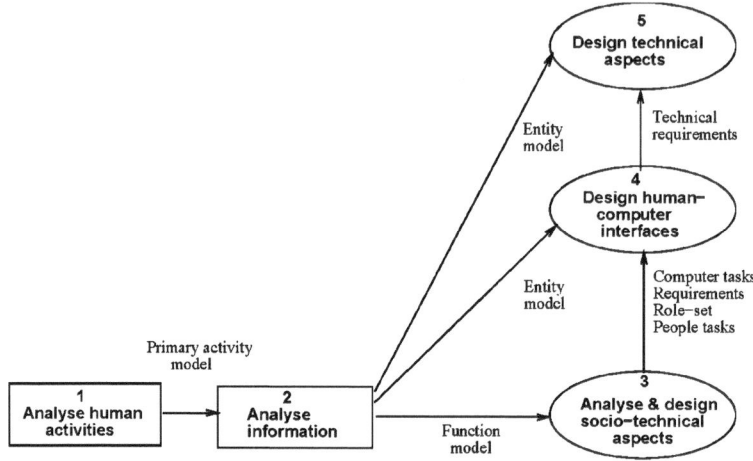

Fig. 2.10 The phases and interdependencies in Multiview

4. Design of the human-computer interface (answer to question 3)
5. Design of technical aspects (answer to question 5)

Not all development projects go through the same phases since the surroundings and particular circumstances differ from case to case. Multiview forms a flexible framework since different tools are available and are adjusted to different situations.

Analysis of human activity is based on the work of Checkland (1981), Checkland and Scholes (1990) on Soft Systems Methodology (SSM). It focuses on finding the different stakeholders view of the world.

Developers will with help from the users form a *rich picture* of the problem situation. Based on the rich picture, the problems to be investigated in more detail may be extracted. The developers imagine and name systems that might help revealing the cause of the problem. Among suggested systems, the developers and the users have to decide on a relevant system that is appropriate for the actual situation. Rich pictures are based on root definitions. A root definition is a concise verbal description of the system, which captures its essential nature. One technique to help come up with the root definitions is the 'CATWOE' technique that answers the following question:

Who is doing *what* for *whom*, and to whom are they *answerable*, what *assumptions* are being made, and in what *environment* is this happening?

- *C*ostumer is the 'whom'
- *A*ctor is 'who'
- *T*ransformation is 'what'
- *W*eltanschauung is 'assumptions'
- *O*wner is the 'answerable'
- *E*nvironment is the environment

1. An activity model shows how the various activities are related to each other temporally. The activity model is a semi-formal conceptual model with some similarities to a DFD.

2. In information analysis, the three main tasks are development of a functional model, a data model and interacting functions and entities and verifying the models.
3. Analysis and design of socio-technical aspects is concerned with the people using the IS. In order to develop a successful system, the system must be fitted into the working live of the users. The socio-technical methodology means that the technical and social aspects must fit each other in order to construct the best system. This phase is based on ETHICS (Mumford 1983).
4. Design of human-computer interfaces is concerned with the way users communicate with the CIS. Prototyping of user interfaces (described above) is supported.
5. In the design of technical aspects, a technical solution is created in accordance with the requirements specified in early phases. What is considered is the entity model (phase 2), computer tasks (phase 3) and the human-computer interfaces (phase 4).

2.2.8 Methodologies for Maintenance and Evolution of IS

Whereas most methodologies focus on development of new systems, some also focus on maintenance and application management. An early example was the CONFORM method. CONFORM (Configuration Management Formalisation for Maintenance) (Capretz and Munro 1994) is a method that provides guidelines for carrying out a variety of activities performed during maintenance. The method accommodates a change control framework around which software configuration management (SCM) is applied. The aim is to exert control over an existing application system while simultaneously incrementally re-documenting it. In order to enforce software quality, a change control framework has been established within CONFORM called the software maintenance model (SMM).

Below is an overview of the individual phases of SMM:

- Change request: If the proposed change is corrective, a description of the error situation is included. For other types, a requirements specification is submitted.
- Change evaluation: Whereas a rejected proposed change is abandoned, a change approval form is created for an approved change. This together with the corresponding change proposal is the basic tool of the change management. By documenting new requirements, these forms become the contract between the requester of the change and the maintainers. The approved changes are ranked and selected for the next release. Changes are batched by system releases. The work required is classified as perfective, adaptive, corrective or preventive. The inadequacies described in the change proposal are identified in the application system.
- Maintenance design phase: The result of this phase is the maintenance specification form. The design of a modification requires an examination of side-effects of changes. The maintainer must consider the software components affected and ensure that component properties are kept consistent. The integration and system test need to be planned and updated. Additionally, if the changes require the development of new functionality, these are specified.

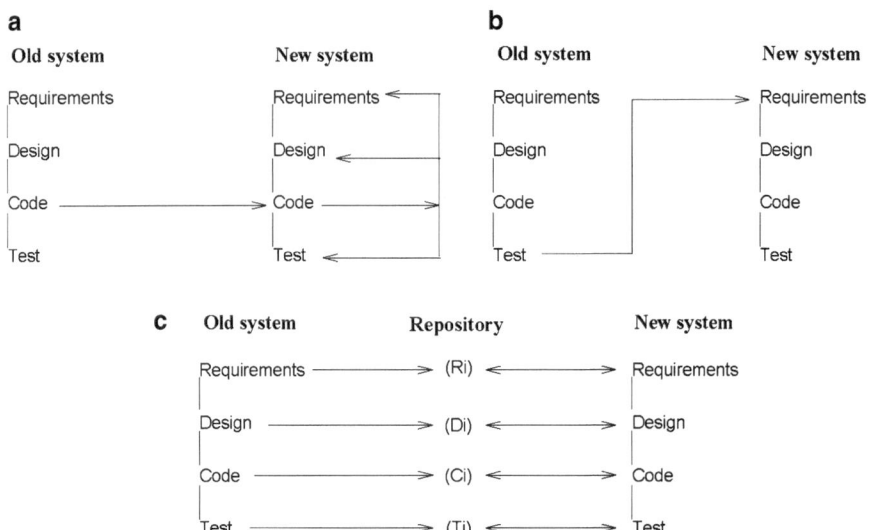

Fig. 2.11 Maintenance process models. (**a**) Quick fix methodology, (**b**) iterative enhancement methodology, and (**c**) full-reuse methodology model

- Maintenance design re-documentation: This phase, along with the next, facilitates system comprehension by incremental re-documentation. The forms associated with these phases aim at documenting the software components of an existing application system.
- Maintenance implementation.
- System release: Validation of the overall system is achieved by performing integration and system test. The configuration release form contains details of the new application.

Basili (1990) illustrates how development and maintenance can be merged in a methodology.

According to Basili, all maintenance is in a sense reuse. One can view a new version of an application system as a modification of the old or a new system that reuses much of the old system. Basili describes three maintenance models (Fig. 2.11).

Quick fix methodology: The existing application system, usually just the source code, is taken as outset. The code and accompanying documentation is changed, and a re-compilation gives a new version. Figure 2.11a demonstrates the change of the old system's source code to the new version's source code.

Iterative-enhancement methodology: Although this was originally proposed for development, it is well-suited for maintenance. It assumes a complete and consistent set of documents describing the application system and:
- Starts with the existing requirements, design, code and test documents
- Modifies the set of documents, starting with the highest level document affected by the changes, propagating the changes down through the full set of documents

- At each step let one redesign the application system, based on the analysis of the existing system – an environment that supports the iterative-enhancement methodology
- Also supports the quick-fix methodology

Full-reuse methodology: A full reuse methodology starts with the requirements analysis and design of the new application system and reuses the appropriate requirements, design and code from any earlier versions of the old system. It assumes a repository of artefacts defining earlier versions of the current application system and similar systems.

An environment that supports the full-reuse methodology also supports the two other methodologies. According to Basili, one can consider development as a subset of maintenance. Maintenance environments differ from development environments in the constraints on the solution, customer demand, timeliness of response and organisation. Traditionally, most maintenance organisations were set up for the quick-fix methodology, but not for the iterative enhancement or full reuse methodology, since they are responding to timeliness. This is best used when there is little chance the system will be modified again. Its weaknesses are that the modification is usually a patch that is not well-documented, the structure of the application system has partly been destroyed, making future evolution of the system difficult and error-ridden, and it is not compatible with development. The iterative-enhancement methodology allows redesign that lets the application system evolve, making future modifications easier. It is compatible with traditional development methodologies. It is a good methodology to use when the product will have a long life and evolve over time. In this case, if timeliness is also a constraint, one can use the quick-fix technique for patches and the iterative-enhancement methodology for long-term change. The drawbacks are that it is a more costly and possibly less timely technique in the short run and provides little support for generic artefacts or future similar systems.

The full-reuse methodology gives the maintainer the greatest degree of freedom for change, focusing on long range development for a set of application systems, which has the side effect of creating reusable artefacts of all kinds for future developments. It is compatible with development, and is, according to Basili, the way methodology should evolve. It is best used when you have multi-product environments or generic development where the portfolio has a long life. Its drawback is that it is more costly in the short run and is not appropriate for small modifications, although you can combine it with other models for such changes.

In practice, large organisations have a number of applications that will follow different approaches according to the stage the application is in the life-cycle (development, evolution, servicing, phase-out, closed (Rajlich and Bennett 2000).

Over the last years, standard approaches such as Information Technology Infrastructure Library (ITIL) (Hochstein et al. 2005) have become popular supporting not only application management, but also service management more generally when providing IT-services. ITIL is a framework of best practices to manage IT operations and services. The Government of Commerce, UK, defined ITIL in the mid-1980s. ITIL's main objective is to align business and Information

Technology. ITIL's IT Service Support process helps organisations to manage software, hardware and human resource services to ensure continued and uninterrupted business. ITIL defines that the core function of IT Service is to offer 'uninterrupted and best possible service' to all users. It defines five processes: Incident Management, Problem Management, Configuration Management, Change Management and Release Management. ITIL does not mandate enterprises and organisations to implement all the framework specifications. This freedom to choose is one of the prime reasons why ITIL is still very relevant even today to enterprises of all sizes.

2.2.9   Enterprise Architecture

Whereas most methodologies described so far relate to development and evolution of IT-systems, other methodologies take a wider approach, looking on the whole enterprise. This is often discussed under the heading of enterprise architecture.

A number of enterprise architectures approaches exist, including:
1. The Zachman Framework from the Zachman Institute for Architecture (Sowa and Zachman 1992; Zachman 1987)
2. The GERAM Framework from The University of Brisbane (Bernus and Nemes 1996)
3. Archimate (Lankhorst 2005)
4. ARIS (Architecture of Integrated Information Systems) from IDS Scheer (1999)
5. The CIMOSA Framework from CIMOSA GmbH (Zelm 1995)
6. The DoDAF Architecture Methodology from the FEAC Institute (DoD 2003)
7. TOGAF Architecture Methodology from the Open Group (TOGAF 2011)

We briefly describe two of these, Zachman and TOGAF. A short description of the others can be found in Lillehagen and Krogstie (2008).

2.2.9.1 The Zachman Framework for Enterprise Architecture

The Zachman framework as it applies to enterprises is simply a logical structure for classifying and organising the descriptive representations of an enterprise that are significant to the management of the enterprise as well as to the development of the enterprise's systems.

The framework graphic in its most simplistic form depicts the design artefacts that constitute the intersection between the roles in the design process, i.e. owner, designer and builder; and the product abstractions, i.e. what (material) it is made of, how (process) it works and where (geometry) the components are, relative to one another. These roles are somewhat arbitrarily labelled planner and sub-contractor and are included in the framework graphic that is commonly exhibited.

From the very inception of the framework, some other product abstractions were known to exist because it was obvious that in addition to what, how and where, a complete description would necessarily have to include the remaining primitive interrogatives: who, when and why. These three additional interrogatives would be manifest as three additional columns of models that, in the case of enterprises, would depict:

- Who does what work
- When do things happen
- Why are various choices made

A balance between the holistic, contextual view and the pragmatic, implementation view can be facilitated by a framework that has the characteristics of any good classification scheme, i.e. it allows for abstractions intended to:

- Simplify for understanding and communication
- Clearly focus on independent variables for analytical purposes, but at the same time
- Maintain a disciplined awareness of contextual relationships that are significant to preserve the integrity of the object

  In summary, the framework is meant to be:
- Simple, i.e. it is easy to understand. It is not technical, but purely logical. Anybody (technical or non-technical) can understand it.
- Comprehensive, i.e. it addresses the enterprise in its entirety. Any issues can be mapped against it to understand where they fit within the context of the enterprise as a whole.
- A language: It helps one think about complex concepts and communicate them precisely with few, non-technical words.
- A planning tool: It helps one make better choices as it is never done in a vacuum. One can position issues in the context of the enterprise and see a total range of alternatives.
- A problem solving tool: It enables to work with abstractions, to simplify, to isolate simple variables without losing sense of the complexity of the enterprise as a whole.
- Neutral: It is defined independently of tools or methodologies and, therefore, any tool or any methodology can be mapped against it to understand their implicit trade-offs, i.e. what they are doing and what they are not doing.

2.2.9.2 TOGAF Architecture Methodology

TOGAF (The Open Group Architecture Framework) has from its early days, 1997, been developed and owned by the Open Group, an international interest organisation. It now has a strong position with private industry in the United States, Great Britain and Japan.

The present version of TOGAF being offered is version 9. TOGAF has had a good certification and training services in place since version 7. Most enterprise architecture tool vendors are members and have access to these versions, and to services helping them to qualify as authorised and certified TOGAF-compliant providers of the methodology and to get access to other services like training, consulting and events participation.

TOGAF has itself an interesting architecture. It offers an Architecture Development Methodology (ADM) as a separate model following the steps depicted in Fig. 2.12. Popkin System Architect has the most comprehensive model of the

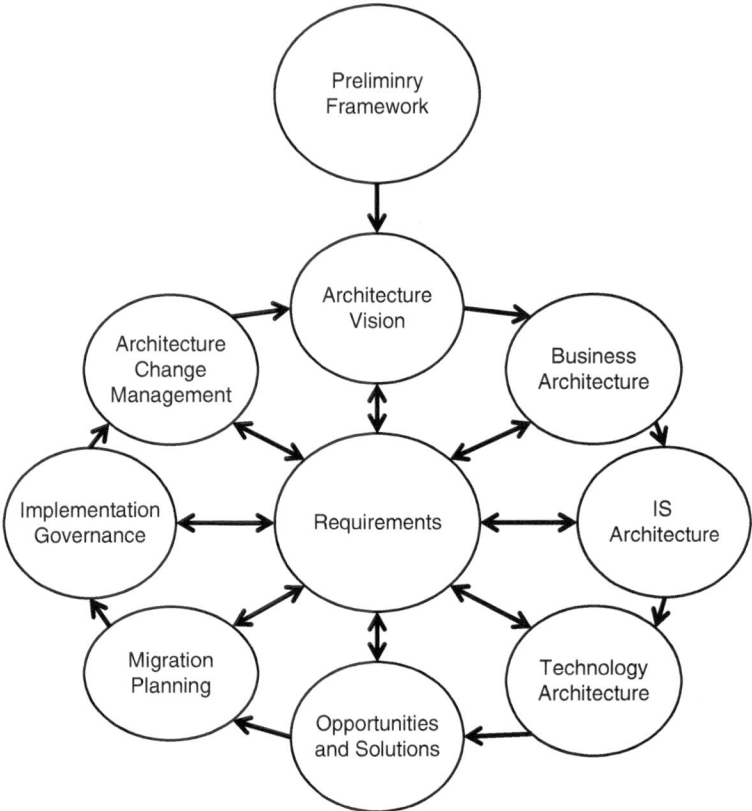

Fig. 2.12 Main steps in a TOGAF architecture development project

TOGAF methodology, allowing visual navigation of all core domains and their constructs and relationships to other constructs and domains, such as: strategies, proposed initiatives, present IT portfolio, present systems and their use, users and vendors, all systems, their capabilities and use and support for searching, view-generation, reporting and 'what-if' analysis.

Most leading Enterprise Architecture vendors are supporting TOGAF, such as Troux Architect from Troux, System Architect from Popkin and Mega.

2.2.10 Complete Methodological Framework

With a complete framework, we refer to methods with a full coverage of product and process. As focus has shifted from developing technical application to providing value for organisations, also methodologies have gone from to encompass changes across the whole enterprise architecture to ensure the delivery and evolution of solutions in a managed way. Towards the end of the 1990s, consultancy companies had developed integrated frameworks that had to be adapted from project to project. As an example, we provide some highlights of BIM – Business Integration Methodology.

BIM looked at the development of strategy, organisational structure, process and technology in an integrated manner, involving:

- Management
  - Change management
  - Program management
  - Project management
- Planning
  - Strategic diagnosis
  - Strategy development
  - Operating strategy
  - Enterprise architecture
- Delivery
  - Analysis
  - Design
  - Implementation
  - Deployment
- Operations
  - Service management
  - Application management (including maintenance)

2.3   Examples of Model-Based Methodologies

A number of artefacts are developed in different methodologies for developing and evolving information systems. These will differ, including informal natural language, semi-formal and formal two-dimensional (conceptual) models and operational code. Given the theme of the book, we focus in particular on the role of conceptual models, both in development, use and evolution.

2.3.1   Traditional Use of Modelling in Analysis, Requirements Specification and Design

Modelling has traditionally been used in analysis, requirements and design as a documentation method to be used as input for further development.

In a structured analysis (Yourdon 1988), one follows a traditional waterfall approach, enriching this with a set of graphical documentation/modelling techniques to specify the functional requirements in a top-down manner:

- Data flow diagrams (DFDs) (Gane and Sarson 1979) document the overall functional properties of the system. DFDs are described in more detail in Sect. 3.3.3.
- Entity relationship (ER) diagrams (Chen 1976) or models in a similar semantical data modelling language model entities and the relationship between these entities. ER-diagrams are described in more detail in Sect. 3.3.4.

- A data dictionary is used to record definitions of data elements.
- State transition diagrams (STD) may be used to specify the time-dependent behaviour (control structures) of the system. Behavioural modelling of this type is described in more detail in Sect. 3.3.2.
- Process specifications can be written in a variety of ways: decision tables, flowcharts, graphs, 'pre' and 'post' conditions (rules) and structured English.

Structured design is defined as 'the determination of which modules, interconnected in which way, will best solve some well-defined problem' (Yourdon 1988). It is assumed that structured design has been preceded by structured analysis. The design process is guided by design evaluation criteria and design heuristics, resulting in a set of structure charts.

A number of text-books exist in this area (e.g. (Avison and Fitzgerald 2006; Hawryszkiewycz 2001; Marakas 2006; Lejk and Deeks 2002; Valacich et al. 2012), and we expect this material to be well-known by those reading this book and do not use more space on it here. We will return to the main modelling languages from this tradition in Chap. 3.

2.3.2   MDA: Model-Driven Architecture

Model-Driven Architecture™ (MDA) has become OMG's notion of doing model-driven development and has gained a lot of interest (Miller et al. 2003). MDA has for some time being used in some practical case studies in industry, also on the enterprise level (Günther and Steenbergen 2004).

Model-driven architecture (MDA) can be looked upon as a variant of model-driven development (MDD), which represents an approach to system engineering where models are used in the understanding, design, construction, deployment, operation, maintenance and modification of software systems. Model transformation tools and services are used to align the different models, ensuring that they are consistent across different refinement levels, and such that it resembles the transformational approach described in Sect. 2.2.3.

MDD in this view represents a business-driven approach to software systems development that starts as illustrated in (Fig. 2.13) with a computation independent model (CIM), describing the business context and business requirements. The CIM is refined to a platform independent model (PIM), which specifies services and interfaces that the software systems must provide to the business, independent of software technology platforms. The PIM is further refined to a platform-specific model (PSM), which describes the realisation of the software systems with respect to the chosen software technology platforms. In addition to the business-driven approach, a model-driven framework should also address how to integrate and modernise existing legacy systems according to new business needs. This approach is known as architecture-driven modernisation (ADM) in the OMG.

The three primary goals of MDA are portability, interoperability and reusability. The MDA starts with the well-known and long-established idea of separating the specification of the operation of the system from the details of the way the system

Fig. 2.13 Levels of models
in MDA

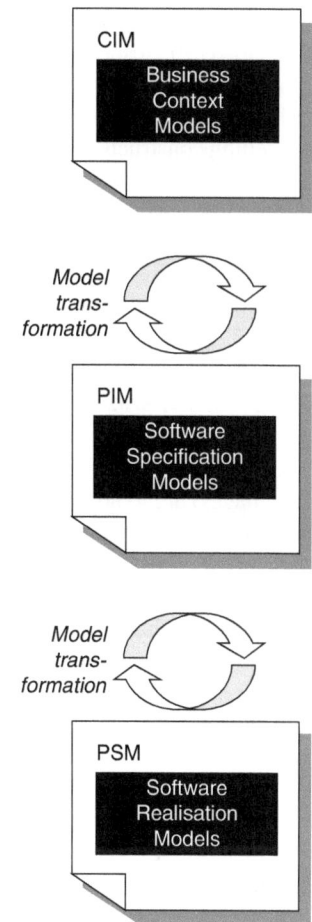

uses the capabilities of its software execution platform (e.g. J2EE, CORBA, Microsoft .NET and web services).

MDA provides an approach for:

- Specifying a system independently of the software execution platform that supports it
- Specifying software execution platforms
- Choosing a particular software execution platform for the system
- Transforming the system specification into one for a particular software execution platform

MDD is concerned with using the appropriate set of models and modelling techniques, supported by the appropriate tools, to provide sufficient help for reasoning about systems. In MDA, one takes as a outset that one is using UML for modelling, although different parts of UML are relevant at different levels. One also often needs to adapt UML, especially for the representation of PSMs. MDA defines a meta-model hierarchy for modelling a system. A system is described by a model (at the M1 level). A model conforms to a meta-model (at the M2 level), which defines the modelling constructs used in the model. The meta-model itself is described in a common meta-meta-model language (at the M3 level). The meta-meta-model language in the OMG MDA is MOF. MOF defines the core modelling constructs needed to describe all meta-models of interest to model-driven development. MOF can, e.g. be used to describe the UML meta-model and adaptations of this for supporting specialisations of UML. Meta-model levels are further discussed in Sect. 3.1.3.

2.3.3   DSM and DSL

The essence of DSM (Domain-Specific Modelling) and DSL (Domain-Specific Languages) are to adapt the modelling language used to the domain to be modelled and the stakeholders' knowledge of this domain including the important concepts in the domain. Early tools enabling meta-modelling was developed already in the late 1980s and early 1990s (e.g. the Ramatic – tool). Later, a number of environments for DSM/DSL have appeared, including Troux Architect (earlier METIS), MetaEdit (Kelly et al. 1996; Kelly and Tolvanen 2008), Eclipse (EMP), GME and Microsoft's DSL Tools for Software Factories (Bézivin et al. 2005).

Generally, two areas have been supported with DSM-tools:
- Enterprise modelling, primarily supporting sense-making and communication of the enterprise level
- Software development, support code-generation for new software systems

The term DSL (Domain-Specific Languages) is traditionally used relative to the second use. In both cases, a main difference from more traditional use of modelling is that rather than using a standard modelling language, the one adapted to the particular domain should be used. Since there is an additional cost of building the modelling language to be used, one finds most examples of this approach in case where there are a number of similar products to be developed (e.g. the case study reported for Nokia by MetaEdit+ (Kelly and Tolvanen 2008). With the right domain, the following advantages have been reported for this type of approach (Kelly and Pohjonen 2003).
- Increased productivity (when the DSL has been developed). Productivity increases by as much as a factor of 5–10 have been reported.
- Better flexibility and responsiveness to change.
- Sharing domain expertise with the whole theme, reducing training time needed before being productive.

In connection to work on MetaEdit+, e.g. they devise the following generic methodology for developing a DSL:
- Develop the domain concepts: Define the concepts and relationships between concepts that are important in the chosen domain. Concentrate in this stage on the semantics of the concepts, not how to represent them in the language. Wait

with necessary aspects relative to make the language usable for code-generation. The meta-modelling in MetaEdit uses a language particularly developed for the task (GOPRR). Approaches for meta-modelling (language modelling) are described more generally in Sect. 3.1.3).

- Define domain rules, i.e. the rules for how relationships can link concepts, rules for decomposition, etc.
- Create the notation, i.e. which symbols to use to represent concepts and relationships between symbols.
- Implement generators: This includes both code generators and other generators, e.g. for documentation.

Although one in principle can start from scratch at developing a new language, one often takes as an outset (a subset of) an existing language, which gives some constraints, e.g. on how the notation can be developed.

When the language is developed, it can be used as part of software production. One should be aware that the practical usage of the approach often will necessitate further development of the language, which again will necessitate a formal version control and configuration management approach.

Newer versions of, e.g. MetaEdit include functionality to deal with this situation, including Tolvanen et al. (2007).

- Graphical and form-based meta-modelling not needing programming of the meta-model environment to implement the DSL
- WYSIWYG symbol editor with conditional and generated elements
- Integrated, incremental meta-modelling and modelling: Models update automatically yet non-destructively when the meta-model changes
- Support for handling multiple integrated modelling languages
- Support for multiple simultaneous language developers (meta-modellers) when developing and maintaining the DSL
- Generator editor and debugger integrated with meta-model and models
- Straight model-to-code transformations not needing to go through intermediate formats
- Generator that can map freely between multiple models and multiple files
- Support for multiple simultaneous modellers, enabling free reuse across models
- Being able to run on all major platforms, and integrate with any IDE
- Live relations between code and models, being able to click generated code to see the original model element

In Sect. 7.4, we look upon how one can use general knowledge about quality of models and modelling language (described in Chaps. 4 and 5) for developing new or adapted modelling languages.

2.3.4 Business Process Modelling (BPM) and Workflow Modelling

Business Process Modelling is the activity of representing both the current ('as is') and future ('to be') processes of an enterprise, so that the current process may be analysed and improved. It focuses on business processes as a sequence/three of executions in a business context, based on the purpose of creating goods and services (Scheer 1999). BPM is typically performed by business analysts and managers who are seeking to improve process efficiency and quality. The process improvements identified by BPM may or may not require IT involvement, although that is a common driver for the need to model a business process.

Business Process Modelling plays an important role in the business process management (BPM) discipline, a more wide-ranging method of aligning an organisation with the wants and needs of clients.

Modelling language standards that are used for BPM include Business Process Modelling Notation (BPMN), Business Process Execution Language (BPEL) and Web Services Choreography Description Language (WS-CDL). BPM addresses (as one of many possible approaches) the process aspects of an Enterprise Architecture (see below).

BPM solutions are built on and extend the idea of workflow. WfMC (Workflow Management Coalition, a non-profit, international organisation of workflow vendors, users, analysts and university/research groups) was founded already in 1993 to develop and promote workflow integration capability. A Workflow Management System is a system that defines, manages and executes 'workflows' through the execution of software whose order of execution is driven by a computer representation of the workflow logic.

Three functional areas are supported by WfMC:

- The build-time functions, concerned with defining, and possibly modelling, the workflow process and its constituent activities
- The runtime control functions concerned with managing the workflow processes in an operational environment and sequencing the various activities to be handled as part of each process (the workflow engine)
- The runtime interactions with human users and other IT applications for processing the various tasks

In BPM, different aspects of this are typically replaced by specific technologies and modelling approaches (Havey 2005). The only part in his conceptualisation that is purely modelling-oriented is BPMN, which are described in more detail in Sect. 3.3.3.

According to (Havey 2005), a difference between workflow and BPM is that instead of sending messages between processes based on process IDs, using, e.g. BPEL a process knows to accept a message intended for it based on some aspect of the message. In addition, process flow is decentralised, not dependent on a central workflow engine. BPM is often integrated with the application of SOA – Service Oriented Architecture. SOA aims to break up monolithic applications into reusable component services that can be put together in new ways to support emerging business needs.

Many projects are concerned with the development of service-oriented solutions that can be more easily planned and then later customised when they are being deployed. This is intended to provide better industry focused solutions that can be adapted better for deployment into client environments. This is to directly counter the problem of high costs of customisation and integration of highly generic industry solutions.

There are two basic approaches to BPM and process improvement: (1) Business Process Reengineering (BPR) as a radical redesign of business processes by a singular transformation (Hammer and Champy 1993) and (2) evolutionary improvement of business processes by continuous transformation. Today the latter is the most important for practical BPM efforts (Weske 2007). Models are important in all phases, since the models used in definition and modelling typically are implemented through semi-automatic or automatic transformation to the executional level. In Weske (2007), an overall approach is provided, with the following steps:

- Strategy and organisation
- Survey: Define project goals, establish project team, gather information on the business environment
- Design: Represent information as business process models
- Platform selection
- Implementation and test
- Deployment
- Operations, monitoring and control

Results from operations often are used in connection to continuous improvement and eventually for further strategy work. This continuous improvement approach is typically conceptualised by a BPM Life Cycle (Houy et al. 2010).

More agile approaches to process modelling exist. The limited success of traditional WfMS in supporting knowledge intensive and cooperative work has partly been attributed to lack of flexibility (Agostini and Michelis 2000). Most work within the area of flexible workflow looks at how conventional systems can be extended and enhanced, how static workflow systems can be made *adaptive*. Research challenges for adaptive workflow include:

- Controlled handling of exceptions
- The dynamic change problem: Migration of instances from an old workflow model to a new one
- Late modelling during enactment and local adaptation of particular workflow instances

Most researchers in this area recognise that change is a way of life in organisations, but a basic premise is still that work is repetitive and can be relatively completely prescribed.

Within the community, an understanding seems to have emerged that change requires process definition and process enactment to be intertwined. Still, most research on adaptive workflow is based on the premise that the enactment engine is solely responsible for interpreting the workflow model. In other words, users contribute by making alterations to the model, not by interpreting any part of the model. Thus, the model must be formally complete to prevent ambiguity and deadlock from paralysing the process. Jørgensen (2001) and Weber et al. (2009) identify a range of issues related to more dynamic provisioning of process support than usually found in BPM solutions. This involves:

- Providing good usability and pragmatic quality of models and user interfaces
- Validation and activation of ad-hoc changes to models

- Support for changes at a high-abstraction level and creating change patterns updating several parts of the model
- Process schema evolution, version control and migrating process instances
- Providing coordination support (enactment, awareness)
- Making changes made to process instances reusable
- Resolving access control to different parts of the model, handling concurrency control for conflicting changes performed by different users, as well as resolving ambiguities and exception handling
- Model maintenance and administration of model repositories
- Enterprise resource management and horizontal resource allocation
- Supporting communication between actors in virtual organisations
- Allowing for local variants and domain-specific models at the agency-level synchronised to the service process
- Diagnosing and mining based on process instance variants
- Traceability of changes and monitoring of dynamic processes (transparency and trust)
- Orchestration of multithreaded cross-agency process instances

In interactive workflow, one tries to address some of these issues, and we will describe this relative to how it is supported in AKM in Sect. 2.3.6.

2.3.5 Enterprise Modelling

Enterprise modelling (Fox and Grüninger 2000; Vernadat 1996) is used for externalising, making and sharing enterprise knowledge, which is again vital to support enterprise systems evolution. Enterprise modelling has been defined as the art of externalising enterprise knowledge, i.e. representing the core knowledge of the enterprise (Vernadat 1996). A crucial problem for the successful evolution of enterprise systems (and thereby of enterprises) is that the management has a limited understanding of their own business processes (Dalal et al. 2004), and it is argued that this can be helped by making processes and other parts of the organisation explicit in models. The importance of EM is also evident in the increasing interest for *enterprise architecture*, e.g. (Pereira and Sousa 2004), which has revitalised past research on information systems architecture (Zachman 1987). Some examples of approaches to Enterprise Architecture were provided in Sect. 2.2.8 and will not be reiterated here. Another framework, GERAM, will be described in some more detail.

GERAM (Generalized Enterprise Reference Architecture and Methodology) encompasses knowledge needed for enterprise engineering/integration. GERAM is describing the components needed in enterprise engineering/enterprise integration processes, such as:

- Major enterprise engineering/enterprise integration efforts (green field installation, complete re-engineering, merger, reorganisation, formation of virtual enterprise or consortium, value chain or supply chain integration, etc.)
- Incremental changes of various sorts for continuous improvement and adaptation

GERAM is intended to facilitate the unification of methods of several disciplines used in the change process, such as methods of industrial engineering, management science, control engineering, communication and information technology, i.e. to allow their combined use, as opposed to segregated application.

Previous research carried out by the AMICE Consortium on CIMOSA, by the GRAI Laboratory on GRAI and GIM and by the Purdue Consortium on PERA (as well as similar methodologies by others) has produced reference architectures that were meant to be organising all enterprise integration knowledge and serve as a guide in enterprise integration programs. Starting from the evaluation of existing enterprise integration architectures (CIMOSA, GRAI/GIM and PERA), the IFAC/IFIP Task Force on Architectures for Enterprise Integration has developed an overall definition of a generalised architecture (GERAM). GERAM is about those methods, models and tools that are needed to build and maintain the integrated enterprise, be it a part of an enterprise, a single enterprise or a network of enterprises (virtual enterprise or extended enterprise).

Figure 2.14 depicts the main components of GERAM, which are further described below.

GERA (Generalized Enterprise Reference Architecture) defines the generic concepts recommended for use in enterprise engineering and integration projects. These concepts can be classified as:

1. Human-oriented concepts: They cover human aspects such as capabilities, skills, know-how and competencies as well as roles of humans in the enterprise. The organisation-related aspects have to do with decision level, responsibilities and authorities, the operational ones relate to the capabilities and qualities of humans as enterprise resource elements. In addition, the communication aspects of humans have to be recognised to cover interoperation with other humans and with technology elements when realising enterprise operations.
2. Process-oriented concepts: They deal with enterprise operations (functionality and behaviour) and cover enterprise entity life-cycle and activities in various life-cycle phases; life history, enterprise entity types, enterprise modelling with integrated model representation and model views.
3. Technology-oriented concepts: They deal with various infrastructures used to support processes and include, e.g. resource models (information technology, manufacturing technology, office automation and others), facility layout models, information system models, communication system models and logistics models.

2.3.5.1 Modelling Framework of GERA

GERA provides an analysis and modelling framework that is based on the life-cycle concept and identifies three dimensions for defining the scope and content of enterprise modelling.

1. *Life-cycle dimension*: Providing for the controlled modelling process of enterprise entities according to the life-cycle activities
2. *Genericity dimension*: Providing for the controlled particularisation (instantiation) process from generic and partial to particular
3. *View dimension*: Providing for the controlled visualisation of specific views of the enterprise entity

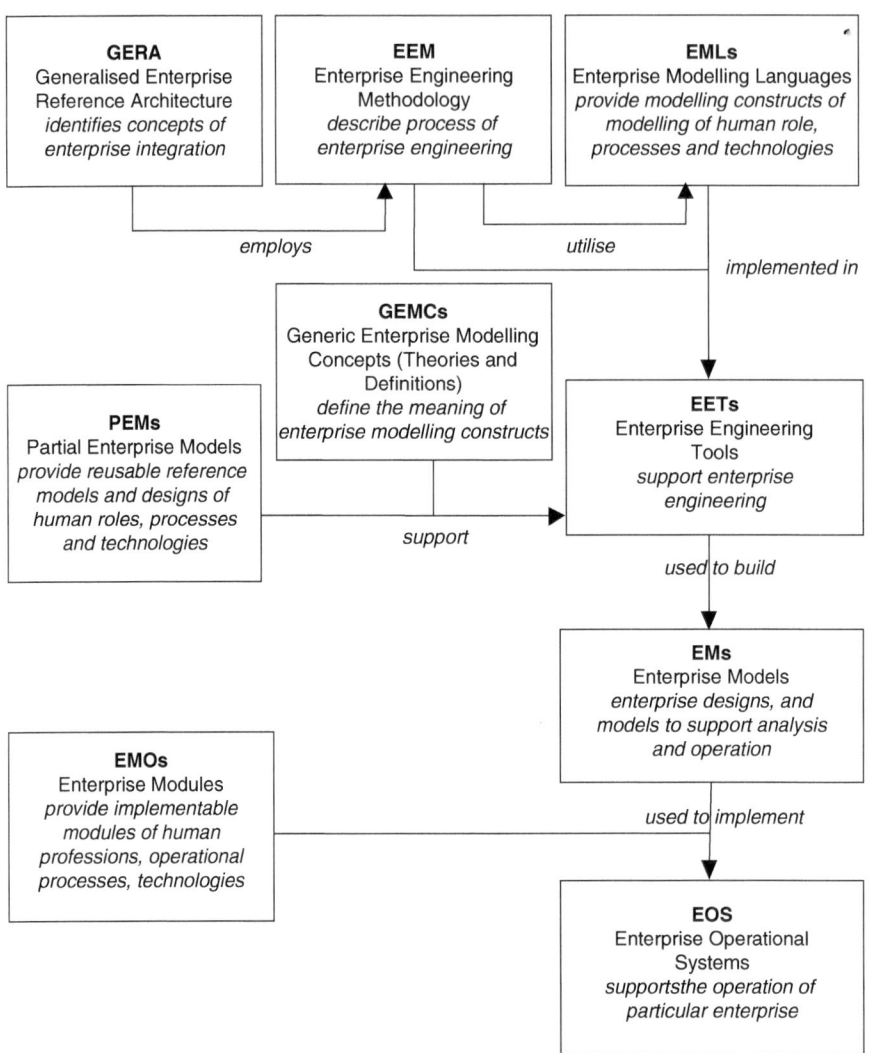

Fig. 2.14 GERAM framework components

Figure 2.15 shows the three-dimensional structure identified above, which represents the modelling framework. The reference part of the modelling framework consists of the generic and the partial levels only. These two levels organise into a structure the definitions of concepts, basic and macro level constructs (the modelling languages), defined and utilised for the description of the given area. The particular level represents the results of the modelling process – which is the model or description of the enterprise entity at the state of the modelling process corresponding to the particular set of life-cycle activities. However, it is intended that the modelling languages should support the two-way relationship between

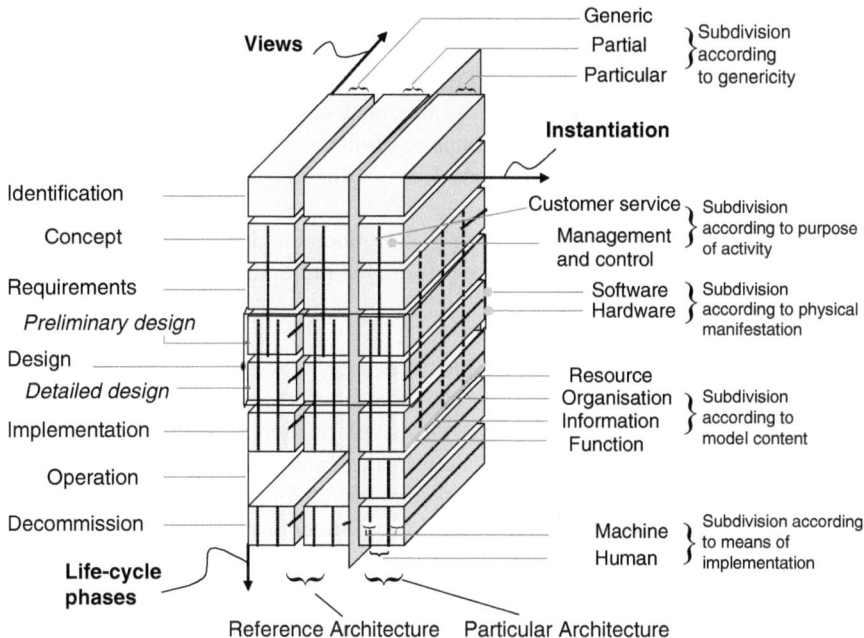

Fig. 2.15 GERA Modelling Framework with Modelling Views

models of adjacent life-cycle phases, i.e. the derivation of models from an upper to a lower state or the abstraction of lower models to an upper state, rather than having to create different models for the different sets of life-cycle activities.

2.3.5.2 EEMs: Enterprise Engineering Methodology

Enterprise engineering methodologies describe the processes of enterprise integration. A generalised methodology like generalised architectures is applicable to any enterprise regardless of the industry involved. An EEM will help the user in the process of the enterprise engineering of integration projects whether the overall integration of a new or revitalised enterprise or in management of on-going change. It provides methods of progression for every type of life-cycle activity. The upper two sets of these activities (identification and concept) are partly management and partly engineering analysis and description (modelling) tasks.

2.3.5.3 EMLs: Enterprise Modelling Languages

Enterprise modelling language define the generic modelling constructs for enterprise modelling adapted to the needs of people creating and using enterprise models. In particular, enterprise modelling languages will provide constructs to describe and model human roles, operational processes and their functional contents as well as the supporting information, tools, office and production technologies.

2.3.5.4 GEMCs: Generic Enterprise Modelling Concepts

Generic enterprise modelling concepts are the most generically used concepts and definitions of enterprise integration and modelling. Three forms of concept definition are, in increasing order of formality: Glossaries, meta-models and ontological theories.

Some requirements that must be met are as follows:

- Concepts defined in more than one form of the above must be defined in a consistent way.
- Those concepts that are used in an enterprise modelling language must also have at least a definition in the meta-model form, but preferably the definition should appear in an ontological theory.

2.3.5.5 PEMs: Partial Enterprise Models

Partial enterprise models (reusable reference models) are models that capture concepts common to many enterprises. PEMs will be used in enterprise modelling to increase modelling process efficiency. In the enterprise engineering process, these partial models can be used as tested components for building particular enterprise models (EMs). However, in general, such models still need to be adapted (completed) to the particular enterprise entity.

2.3.5.6 EETs: Enterprise Engineering Tools

Enterprise engineering tools support the processes of enterprise engineering and integration by implementing an enterprise engineering methodology and supporting modelling languages. Engineering tools should provide for analysis, design and use of enterprise models.

2.3.5.7 EMOs: Enterprise Modules

Enterprise modules are implemented building blocks or systems (products, or families of products), which can be utilised as common resources in enterprise engineering and enterprise integration. As physical entities (systems, subsystems, software, hardware and available human resources/professions), such modules are accessible in the enterprise, or can be made easily available from the marketplace. In general, EMOs are implementations of partial models identified in the field as the basis of commonly required products for which there is a market.

2.3.5.8 EMs: Enterprise Models

The goal of enterprise modelling is to create and continuously maintain a model of a particular enterprise entity. A model should represent the reality of the enterprise operation according to the requirements of the user and his application. This means the granularity of the model has to be adapted to the particular needs, but still allow interoperability with models of other enterprises. Enterprise models include all those descriptions, designs and formal models of the enterprise, which are prepared in the course of the enterprise's life history.

2.3.5.9 EOSs: Enterprise Operational Systems

Enterprise operational systems support the operation of a particular enterprise. They consist of all the hardware and software needed to fulfil the enterprise objective and goals.

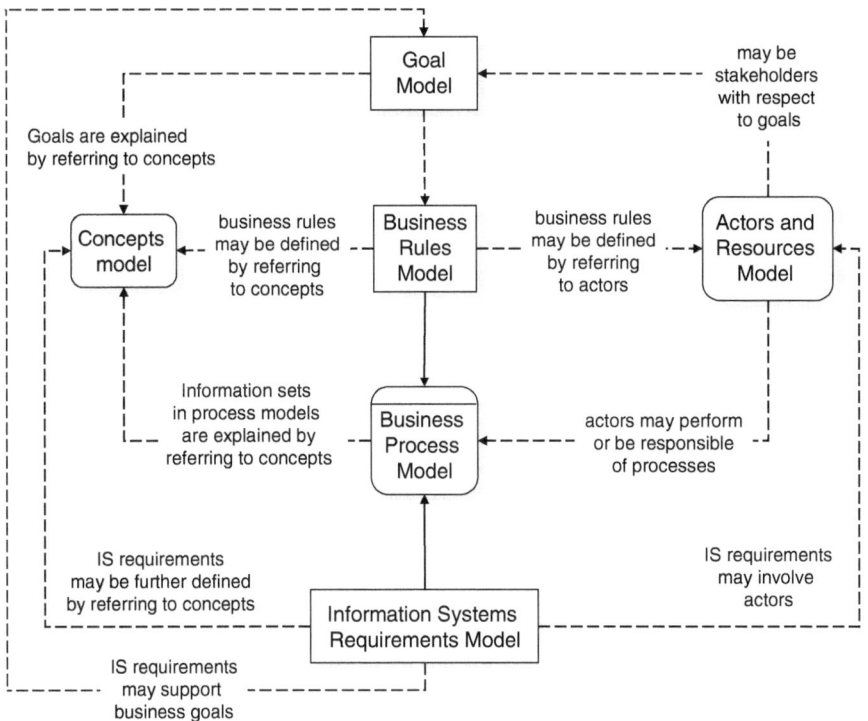

Fig. 2.16 A top view of the multi-model approach EKD (From Bubenko 2007)

Their contents are derived from enterprise requirements and their implementation is guided by the design models, which provide the system specifications and identify the enterprise modules used in the system implementation.

A number of other approaches to enterprise modelling have been developed over the last 10–15 years. We present briefly one here, Enterprise Knowledge Development (EKD), indicating the scope of modelling. Other approaches will be described in more detail in later chapters. EKD builds of Tempora (described in Sect. 3.3.5) and F³ (Bubenko et al. 1994), and then further elaborated in the ELEKTRA project (22927) (Bubenko et al. 1998; Persson and Stirna 2002). EKD is an approach strongly based on involvement and participation of stakeholders (users, managers, owners, …). This means that an EKD model is gradually built by its stakeholders in participatory modelling seminars, led by one or more facilitators, an approach to modelling described in Sect. 3.4. Second, it is a multi-model approach involving not only a model for conceptual structures but also interlinked sub-models for goals, actors, business rules, business processes and requirements to be stated for the information system, if such is developed. All these models are interlinked, for instance, a goal in a goal model may refer to a concept in the concepts model, if the concept is used in the goal description (see Fig. 2.16). The EKD approach, or other multi-model, participatory approaches similar to EKD, are now in frequent use in a wide range of practical applications and are having a spectrum of purposes. We find uses of this kind of approach not only for information systems development, but also for organisational development, business process analysis, knowledge management studies and many more.

Although enterprise modelling, as described here, is useful both in sense-making and systems development, for modelling and model-based approaches to have a more profound effect, we propose a shift in modelling approaches and methodologies. Model-based approaches and methods must enable *regular users to be active modellers*, both when performing their work, expressing and sharing their results and values created, and when adapting and composing the services they are using to support their work. This is described below as AKM – Active Knowledge Modelling.

2.3.6   Interactive Models and Active Knowledge Modelling

For the support of knowledge workers, who need more flexible support than what can be given by traditional workflow systems, it is important that emergent and interactive work processes can be captured and supported (Jørgensen 2001; Krogstie and Jørgensen 2004; Lillehagen and Krogstie 2008). The most comprehensive theoretical approach in this field is Peter Wegner's interaction framework (Wegner 1997; Wegner and Goldin 1999). The primary characteristic of an *interaction machine* is that it can pose questions to users during its computation. The process can be a multi-step conversation between the user and the machine, each being able to take the initiative.

The Active Knowledge Modelling (AKM) (Lillehagen and Krogstie 2008) technology is about discovering, externalising, expressing, representing, sharing, exploring, configuring, activating, growing and managing enterprise knowledge. Active and work-centric knowledge has some very important intrinsic properties found in mental models of the human mind, such as reflective views, repetitive flows, recursive tasks and replicable knowledge architecture elements. One approach to benefit from these intrinsic properties is by enabling users to perform enterprise modelling using the AKM platform services to model methods, and execute work using role-specific, model-generated and configured workplaces (MGWP). Visual knowledge modelling must become as easy for designers and engineers as scribbling in order for them to express their knowledge while performing work, learning and excelling in their roles. This will also enable users to capture contextual dependencies between roles, tasks, information elements and the views required for performing work.

To be active, a visual model using an appropriate representation must be available to the users of the underlying information system at execution time. Second, the model must influence the behaviour of the computerised work support system. Third, the model must be dynamically extended and adapted, users must be supported in changing the model to fit their local needs, enabling tailoring of the system's behaviour. Industrial users should, therefore, be able to manipulate and use active knowledge models as part of their day-to-day work (Jørgensen 2001; Krogstie 2007).

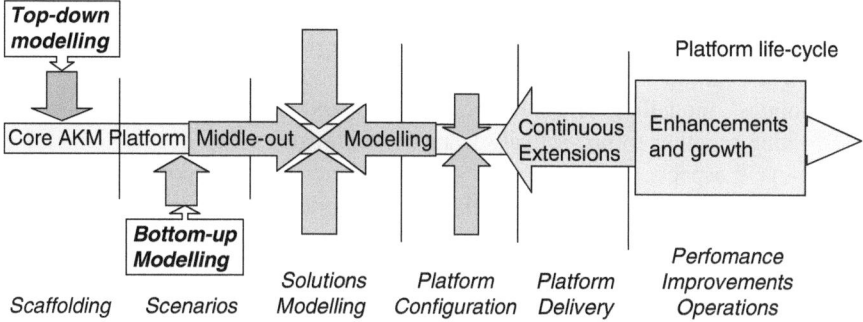

Fig. 2.17 The steps of the customer delivery process (From Lillehagen and Krogstie 2008)

Recent platform developments support integrated modelling and execution in one common platform, enabling what in cognitive psychology is denoted as 'closing the learning cycle'. The AKM approach has at its core a customer delivery process with seven steps (C3S3P – see below). The first time an enterprise applies AKM technology, it is recommended that these steps are closely followed in the sequence indicated to establish a platform for evolution. However, second and third time around work processes and tasks from the last five steps can be re-iterated and executed in any order necessary to achieve the desired results.

The AKM approach is also about mutual learning, discovering, externalising and sharing new knowledge with partners and colleagues. Tacit knowledge of the type that actually can be externalised is most vividly externalised by letting people that contribute to the same end-product work together, all the time exchanging, capturing and synthesising their views, methods, properties, parameters and values and validating their solutions. Common views of critical resources and performance parameters provide a sense of holism and are important instruments in achieving consensus in working towards common goals. The seven steps of the approach are shown in Fig. 2.17. The steps are denoted C3S3P and have briefly been described in Stirna et al. (2007).

Concept testing (the C in C3S3P), performing a proof-of-concept at the customer site, is not included in the figure. The solutions modelling stage is vital for creating holistic, multiple role-views supporting work across multi-dimensional knowledge spaces, which in turn yield high-quality solution models.

Description of Steps in the C3S3P Methodology

1. Concept testing is about creating customer interest and motivation for applying the AKM technology. This is done by running pilots and by assessing value propositions and benefits from applying the AKM approach.

2. Scaffolding is about expressing stakeholder information structures and views, and relating them to roles, activities and systems to provide a model to raise the customer's understanding for modelling and inspire motivation and belief in the benefits and values of the AKM approach.

3. Scenario modelling is about modelling 'best-practice' work processes. The focus is on capturing the steps and routines that are or should be adhered to when performing

the work they describe. This is the core competence of the enterprise, and capturing these work-processes is vital to perform work, support execution and perform several kinds of analyses in the solutions modelling step.

4. Solutions' modelling is about cross-disciplinary and cross-functional teams working together to pro-actively learn and improve quality in most enterprise life-cycle aspects. The purpose is creating a coherent and consistent holistic model or rather structures of models and sub-models meeting a well-articulated purpose. Solutions' modelling involves top-down, bottom-up and middle-out multi-dimensional modelling for reflective behaviour and execution.

5. Platform configuration is about integrating other systems and tools by modelling other systems data models and other aspects often found as, e.g. UML models. These are created as integral sub-models of the customised AKM platform, and their functionality will complement the CPPD methodology (see below) with PLM (Product Lifecycle Management) system functions, linking the required web-services with available software components.

6. Platform delivery and practicing adapts services to continuous growth and change by providing services to keep consistency and compliance across platforms and networks as the user community and project networking expands, involving dynamic deployment of model-designed and configured workplace solutions and services.

7. Performance improvement and operations is continuously performing adaptations, or providing services to semi-automatically re-iterate structures and solution models, adjusting platform models and re-generating model-configured and -generated workplaces and services and tuning solutions to produce the desired effects and results.

Collaborative Product and Process Design (CPPD), as mentioned above, is anchored in pragmatic product logic, open data definitions and practical work processes, capturing local innovations and packaging them for repetition and reuse. Actually, most of the components of the AKM platform, such as the Configurable Product Components – CPC and the Configurable Visual Workplaces – CVW, are based on documented industrial methodologies. CPPD mostly re-implements them, applying the principles, concepts and services of the AKM platform. CVW, in particular, is the workplace for configuring workplaces. This includes functionality to:

- Define the design methodology tasks and processes
- Define the roles participating in the design methodology
- Define the product information structures
- Define the views on product information structures needed for each task
- Perform the work in role-specific workplaces
- Extend, adapt and customise when needed

Industrial users need freedom to develop and adapt their own methodologies, knowledge structures and architectures and to manage their own workplaces, services and the meaning and use of data. The AKM approach and the CPPD methodology support these capabilities, enabling collaborative product and process design and concurrent engineering.

2.4   Participatory Modelling

An important aspect of modelling is to be able to represent the knowledge as held by people as directly as possible. A practical limitation earlier was that the techniques and tools used were hard to use, thus often necessitating by design or by chance the involvement of an intermediary analyst. Newer approaches have shown the possibility of involving stakeholders more directly, often with the guidance of modelling facilitators.

One approach to the involvement of users is modelling conferences (Gjersvik et al. 2004). A number of other approaches exist, e.g. the use of DSL and AKM, as described above, and EKD and later use as described in Persson and Stirna (2010).

2.4.1   The Modelling Conference Technique

The Modelling Conference is a method for participatory construction and development of enterprise models. In this, it takes as a starting point business process modelling to understanding how organisations work. However, while most approaches to the mapping and 're-engineering' of business processes tend to be expert and management focused, the Modelling Conference technique focuses on participation from all stakeholder groups, and on the link between organisational learning and process institutionalisation through the use of technology.

The core of the Modelling Conference method has been adopted from the Search Conference method (Emery and Purser 1996). The Search Conference is a method for participatory, strategic planning in turbulent and uncertain environments. It has been used in various setting, including community development, organisation development, and the creation of research initiatives. It has also been done with a number of different designs. The method is based on a few basic ideas:

- Open systems thinking
- Active adaptation
- Genuine participation
- Learning

The concrete result of a Search Conference is a set of action plans, addressing various challenges that the conference have prioritised, and which people at the conference have committed themselves to implement. The plans may not always be congruent or coordinated, but there is a shared understanding among the participants on why each of the plans is important for parts of the system. This may be summed up in two core points:

- Action plans. '(…) multiple action plans focused on different parallel initiatives stand a better chance of diffusion than those that concentrate all their resources on one big hit.' (ibid., p. 63)
- Shared frame of reference. '(…) the Search Conference does not just result in more information and data about the environment. Rather, the Search Conference process also yields a shared view of the environment as conflicts or perceptual

disagreements are made rational, data and information are integrated, and common ground is discovered.' (ibid., p. 67)

The Modelling Conference combines process modelling and search conferences, by doing process modelling in a structured conference setting, promoting broad participation. The argument for participation is discussed under Sect. 2.1.5.

A set of principles guides the Modelling Conference. The core of these principles is the ones listed for the Search Conference above, but a few are added due to the special purpose and techniques of the Modelling Conference:

- *Open systems thinking*: The unit of development (organisation, community, enterprise) is viewed as an open system, interacting with its environment. At the Modelling Conference, both the whole system itself and the main parts of the environment should be modelled. In the Modelling Conference, this might be called 'open process thinking'. The process is always in a context, interlinked with other processes and the rest of the contextual environment.
- *Active adaptation*: A further consequence of the open systems view is that the system needs to adapt to the environment. However, in a turbulent environment, passive adaptation is not enough. The organisation needs to influence and inter-act with its environment, to actively create a context in which it can develop. The participants are encouraged to think not only about both how they might develop the process to adapt to the demands of the customers and the context, but also what demands they might want to put on other processes and actors, including customers.
- *Genuine participation*: As in a search conference, the Modelling Conference is based on the belief that all who are part of the system or process are experts on how the system/process works as seen from their point of view. All local realities are both valid and important in constructing the common model. Given a suitable structure, the participants are themselves jointly able to analyse and understand the situation, and create suitable action plans.
- *Simplicity*: Modelling languages, methods and concepts should be simple so that it is possible for actors with various local realities to express themselves, and thus make real participation possible (Gjersvik and and Hepsø 1998)
- *Pragmatism*: An important issue in the design of the conference is to find a structure and a mix of methods that will work for all participants, and which is useful in order to produce a satisfactory outcome for the actors in the organisation (Greenwood and Levin 1998).
- *The use of the process model as a communicative and reflective device*: The models are, in addition to being the product of the conference, the main device driving the conference process. The use of large physical process visualisations encourages dialogue among the participants within a common frame of reference (Gjersvik and Hepsø 1998).
- *Learning*: The conference should create conditions under which the participants can learn from each other, but also from the way, they work at the conference. We emphasise that the learning should not only be about the process model, but also about how to lead a discussion about the process, and about what constitutes knowledge and truth about the process and the organisation. We have used the

ideas of triple loop learning (Flood and Romm 1996), stressing that the conference is only one event in a continuous, multi-level learning process.

A Modelling Conference is performed according to the following guidelines:

- The whole process is performed in one room (or a set closely positioned rooms when parallel group-work is performed). All relevant actors in the process should be present or represented during the modelling tasks. In many cases, this also includes outside actors, like users, owners, customers, and public authorities.
- The tasks alternate between group work and plenary work.
- The participants primarily represent themselves, but are jointly responsible for the content and result of the conference.
- The staff facilitates the work, and is responsible for the method used during the conference (but not the result).
- The modelling language, tools, and the overall method must be simple so that the participants may focus on the content.
- The main outcome of the conference is a process model, which names the key processes, products, and roles. Additional results are related to this process model.

The modelling language used has the following concepts and notation:

Process: A series of tasks that produce a specific product. An example is 'Draw technical installations'.

Product. The result of a process, and in demand by a customer. An example is the product 'Drawings of technical installations', which is a product of the process mentioned above. A process may have several products; the process above may, e.g., also have 'Documentation' as a product. We distinguish between *end products (open circle)* and *intermediate products (filled circle)*.

Customer. Someone who demands and uses the product of a process. Often, the customer is another process. For instance, the process 'Install technical applications' is a customer of the process 'Draw technical installations' and demands the product 'Drawings of technical installations'.

The conference preferably lasts at least one and a half days. Every group has a large sheet of paper on the wall, on which they work. All symbols are pre-cut, and can be attached to the sheet of paper. Through these simple symbols and physical way of working together, one gets great flexibility and intensive learning, but they also limit the form of work. The results of the group work are presented in plenary sessions for discussion and joint construction of consolidated models.

The documentation from a Modelling Conference is a report and a process model. The most important outcome of the conference is the ownership that the participants develop through the construction process, which makes the model an important common reference for further more detailed development.

The conference agenda is designed so that the actors of the conference should develop models based on their own local reality before they enter a discussion with actors having (presumably) different local realities. One always starts with homogenous groups, where people with the same background develop their process models. After this, the participants are more comfortable with the modelling language and tools, and have more self-confidence about their own point of view. This is especially important in organisations where there is a high risk of some groups of actors (i.e., management, experts) having model power over other participants through having a previously developed model available (Bråten 1973). One subsequently mixes the participants in heterogeneous groups, where the whole modelling starts all over again.

The difficult part of the agenda is after the second modelling task, where the models of several groups are to be merged into one. This is done in a plenary session. The conference leader needs to be very attentive to the logic of the different groups, so that he or she is able to combine the elements from different models into one coherent whole. It is important that this plenary session is allowed to take the time it needs to obtain a consensus about the model.

This participatory technique has some commonalties with what is found within the field of Participatory Design (Schuler and Namioka 1993), but focuses as we have seen primarily on enterprise modelling and not the design of technical information systems.

2.4.2   Tasks and Roles in Participatory Modelling

In Persson and Stirna (2010), the authors describe in more detail the processes, roles and needed competencies for a (participatory) enterprise modelling practitioner, which often is the basis for further projects including IS implementation:

The core processes and needed abilities defined (described in Sect. 2.1.5) are (Persson and Stirna 2010):

- Define the modelling process:
  - Ability to select an appropriate EM approach and tailor it in order to fit the situation at hand
- Ability to define scope and objectives of the EM project
  - Ability to define a relevant problem
  - Ability to define requirements on the results
  - Ability to establish a modelling project
  - Ability to navigate between the wishes of various stakeholders
  - Ability to assess the impact of the modelling result and the modelling process

More about assessing the organisation and the problem at hand is available in, e.g., Nilsson et al. (1999); and Stirna et al. (2007).

- Plan project activities and resources.
  - Ability to define requirements on the results
  - Ability to navigate between the wishes of various stakeholders
  - Ability to assess the impact of the modelling result and the modelling process
- Plan modelling sessions.
  - Ability to define a relevant problem
  - Ability to define requirements on the results
- Gather and analyse background information.
  - Interview modelling participants
  - Ability to interview involved domain experts
  - Ability to navigate between the wishes of various stakeholders
- Prepare modelling session.
  - Ability to define a relevant problem
  - Ability to adjust a presentation of project results
  - Ability to assess the impact of the modelling result and the modelling process
- Conduct modelling sessions.
  - Ability to model
  - Ability to facilitate a modelling session
  - Ability to navigate between the wishes of various stakeholders

More detailed recommendations of what to do and what not to do during a modelling session are available, e.g., in Jørgensen (2009); Sandkuhl and Lillehagen (2008); Stirna et al. (2007); and Stirna and Persson (2009).

- Write meeting minutes. At this stage, the models should not be more refined because the main purpose of this activity is to send notes to the participants that might also serve as a reminder of the actions that they have agreed to be responsible for.
- Analyse and refine models.
  - Ability to model
  - Ability to define a relevant problem
  - Ability to assess the impact of the modelling result and the modelling process
- Present the results to stakeholders.
  - Ability to adjust a presentation of project results
  - Ability to navigate between the wishes of various stakeholders
  - Ability to assess the impact of the modelling result and the modelling process

2.5 Summary

In this chapter, we have looked at IS-methodology more generally providing a general classification according to:
- Goal of the methodology
- Coverage of process (development, use, operations, maintenance)

- Coverage of product (from a single application to a set of co-operating organisations)
- Capabilities needed
- Stakeholder participation
- Organisation
- Location

The historical development of IS-methodologies from the first methods in the late 1960s is described briefly, before we discuss in more detail some of the current modelling-oriented approaches to IS development and evolution including

- Model-driven architecture (MDA)
- Domain-specific modelling (DSM) and domain-specific languages (DSL)
- Business process modelling/Management (BPM)
- Enterprise modelling (EM) and Enterprise Architecture (EA)
- Active Knowledge Modelling (AKM)

Review Questions

1. What are the eight areas in the framework for IS methodologies?
2. We describe four main abstraction levels in IS development. What are these?
3. Describe the roles in Scrum.
4. Describe competencies necessary in an enterprise modelling project.
5. Mention some goals for stakeholder participation.
6. List the levels of participation.
7. What are the characteristics of cloud computing?
8. What is the difference between the waterfall-model and the V-model?
9. What is the difference between iterative prototyping and throwaway prototyping?
10. What is the difference between the transformational and operational life-cycle model?
11. What are the three levels of models in MDA?
12. List two different approaches to DSM.
13. What is the difference between workflow and BPM?
14. What are the main differences between a traditional enterprise model and an active model?
15. Describe the steps in CS3P3.
16. Describe the modelling conference technique.

Problems and Exercises

Individual Exercises

1. What are the differences and similarities between Agile Modelling and Incremental and iterative development?
2. How can the work of Gjersvik et al. (2004) and Persson and Stirna (2010) on participatory modelling be combined?
3. Select one of the model-based approaches described in Sect. 2.3. At what level(s) of abstraction relative to Fig. 1.4 is modelling performed on?

Pair Exercises

1. Discuss in pairs your own experiences with working in a project using a methodology. Classify the methodology according to level of participation.
2. Discuss in pairs your own experiences with working in a project using a methodology. Classify the methodology according to coverage in process and product.
3. Discuss in pairs your own experiences with working in a project using a methodology. Classify the methodology relative to organisation and location.
4. Discuss in pairs your own experiences with working in a project using a methodology. Classify the methodology according to needed capabilities.

Group Exercises

1. Select a number of the methodologies described in Sects. 2.2 and 2.3 and describe them relative to the eight dimensions of methodologies presented in Sect. 2.1.
2. Select one of the model-based approaches described in Sect. 2.3. Look upon this approach relative to the framework on types of modelling in Fig. 1.3, deciding what kind of modelling tasks it focuses on. You must check out some of the references or other external material to do this.
3. In connection with a modelling task (e.g. some of the later modelling tasks suggested in this book), arrange a modelling conference involving relevant stakeholders.
4. Choose one of the modelling methodologies described in this chapter. Find out if the methodology is described in Wikipedia. If it is, update the description based on the material provided in this chapter and on other reputable sources. If not make an entry in Wikipedia on the topic.
5. Develop a 10–15 page state-of-the-art paper on a modelling methodology mentioned in this chapter.

References

Aagesen, G., van Veenstra, A.F., Janssen, M., Krogstie, J.: The entanglement of enterprise architecture and IT-governance: the cases of Norway and the Netherlands. In: Paper presented at the HICCS, Koloa (2011)

Abrahamsson, P., Oza, N., Siponen, M.T.: Agile software development methods: a comparative review. In: Dingsøyr, T., et al. (eds.) Agile Software Development, pp. 31–59. Springer, Berlin/Heidelberg (2010)

Agostini, A., Michelis, G.D.: Improving flexibility of workflow management systems. In Aalst, W.V.D., Desel, J., Oberweis, A. (eds.) Business Process Management. LNCS 1806. Springer, Berlin (2000)

Agresti, W.W.: What are the new paradigms? In: New Paradigms for Software Development, pp. 6–10. IEEE, Washington, D.C. (1986)

Ambler, S., Jeffries, R.: Agile Modelling: Effective Practices for Extreme Programming and the Unified Process. Wiley, New York (2002)

Arnstein, S.R.: A ladder of citizen participation. JAIP **35**(4), 216–224 (1969)

Avison, D.E., Fitzgerald, G.: Information Systems Development: Methodologies, Techniques and Tools, 4th edn. McGraw Hill, New York (2006)

Avison, D.E., Wood-Harper, A.T.: Multiview: An Exploration in Information Systems Development. Blackwell, Oxford (1990)

Basili, V.R.: Viewing maintenance as reuse-oriented software development. IEEE Softw. **7**(1), 19–25 (1990), January

Baskerville, R., Levine, L., Pries-Heje, J., Ramesh, B., Slaughter, S.: How internet companies negotiate quality. IEEE Comput. **34**(5), 51–57 (2001)

Beck, K.: Extreme Programming Explained: Embrace Change. Addison-Wesley, Boston (2002). The Agile Software Development Series

Beck, K., et al.: The Agile Manifesto. http://www.agileAlliance.org, 20/4-2012 (2001)

Beizer, B.: Software Testing Techniques, 2nd edn. International Thomson Computer Press, Boston (1990)

Benestad, H.C., Anda, B.C.D., Arisholm, E.: Understanding software maintenance and evolution by analyzing individual changes: a literature review. J. Softw. Maint. Evol. Res. Pract. **21**(6), 349–378 (2009)

Berente, N., Lyytinen, K.: What is being iterated? reflections on iteration in information system engineering processes. In: Krogstie, J., Opdahl, A., Brinkkemper, S. (eds.) Conceptual Modelling in Information Systems Engineering. Springer, New York (2007)

Berger, P., Luckmann, T.: The Social Construction of Reality: A Treatise in the Sociology of Knowledge. Penguin, London (1966)

Bernus, P., Nemes, L.: A framework to define a generic enterprise reference architecture and methodology. Comput. Integr. Manufac. Syst. **9**(3), 179–191 (1996)

Bézivin, J., Hillairet, G., Jouault, F., Kurtev, I., Piers, W.: Bridging MS/DSL tools and the eclipse modelling framework OOPSLA 2005. In: International Workshop on Software Factories, San Diego (2005)

Bjerknes, G., Bratteteig, T.: User participation and democracy: a discussion of Scandinavian research on system development. Scand. J. Inform. Syst. **7**(1), 73–98 (1995)

Blum, B.: A taxonomy of software development methods. Commun. ACM **37**(11), 82–94 (1994). November

Boehm, B.W.: Software Engineering Economics. Prentice-Hall, Saddle River (1981)

Boehm, B.W.: A spiral model of software development and enhancement. IEEE Comput. **21**(5), 61–72 (1988). May

Boehm, B.W.: Get ready for agile methods with care. Computer **35**, 64–69 (2002)

Bråten, S.: Model monopoly and communications: systems theoretical notes on democratization. Acta Sociol. J. Scand. Social. Assoc. **16**(2), 98–107 (1973)

Bubenko Jr., J.A.: From information algebra to enterprise modelling and ontologies – a historical perspective on modelling for information systems. In: Krogstie, J., Opdahl, A., Brinkkemper, S. (eds.) Conceptual Modelling in Information Systems Engineering. Springer, Berlin (2007)

Bubenko, Jr. J.A., Brash, D., Stirna, J. EKD user guide, Department of Computer and Systems Science, KTH and Stockholm University, Kista (1988)

Bubenko, Jr. J.A., Rolland, C., Loucopoulos, P., DeAntonellis, V.: Facilitating fuzzy to formal requirements modelling. In: Proceedings of the First International Conference on Requirements Engineering (ICRE94), Colorado Springs, 18–22 Apr 1994, pp. 154–157. IEEE Computer Society Press, New York (1994)

Burrel, G., Morgan, G.: Sociological Paradigms and Organizational Analysis. Heinemann, London (1979)

Capretz, M.A.M., Munro, M.: Software configuration management issues in the maintenance of existing system. J. Softw. Maint. **6**, 1–14 (1994)

Carey, J.M.: Prototyping: alternative systems development methodology. Inform. Softw. Technol. **32**(2), 119–126 (1990). March

Chapin, N.: Evidence on seperately organizing for software maintenance. In: Proceedings of the National Computer Conference, pp. 517–522. AFIPS Press, Chicago (1987)

Checkland, P.B.: Systems Thinking, Systems Practice. Wiley, New York (1981)

Checkland, P.B., Scholes, J.: Soft Systems Methodology in Action. Wiley, New York (1990)

Chen, P.P.: The entity-relationship model: towards a unified view of data. ACM Trans. Database Syst. **1**(1), 9–36 (1976), March

Cockburn, A.: Agile Software Development. Addison-Wesley, Boston (2002)

Codagnone, C., Boccardelli, P.: eGovernment Economics Project (eGEP): Measurement Framework, Final Version. In: European Commission (ed.) Egovernment Unit, D. I. S. A. M. (2006), http://www.umic.pt/images/stories/publicacoes200709/D.2.4_Measurement_Framework_final_version.pdf, Accessed 20 Apr 2012

Dalal, N.P., Kamath, M., Kolarik, W.J., Sivaraman, E.: Toward an integrated framework for modelling enterprise processes. Commun. ACM **47**(3), 83–87 (2004), March

Davidsen, M.K., Krogstie, J.: A longitudinal study of development and maintenance. Inform. Softw. Technol. **52**, 707–719 (2010)

Davis, A.M.: A comparison of techniques for the specification of external system behaviour. Commun. ACM **31**(9), 1098–1115 (1988). September

Davis, A.M.: Object-oriented requirements to object-oriented design: an easy transition? J. Syst. Softw. **30**(1–2), 151–159 (1995). July-August

Davis, A.M., Bersoff, E.H., Comer, E.R.: A strategy for comparing alternative software development life cycle models. IEEE Trans. Softw. Eng. **14**(8), 1453–1461 (1988). October

Dekleva, S.M.: Software maintenance: 1990 status. J. Softw. Maint. **4**, 233–247 (1992)

Department of Defence (DoD): DoD architecture framework. Version 1.0. Volume I: Definitions and Guidelines. Office of the DoD Chief Information Officer, Department of Defense, Washington, D.C. (2003)

Emery, M., Purser, R.E.: The Search Conference. A Powerful Method for Planning Organizational Change and Community Action. Jossey-Bass Publishers, San Francisco (1996)

Eynon, R.: Breaking Barriers to eGovernment: Overcoming obstacles to improving European public services. DG Information Society and Media. European Commission (2007)

Falkenberg, E.D., Hesse, W., Lindgreen, P., Nilsson, B.E., Oei, J.L.H., Rolland, C., Stamper, R.K., Assche, F.J.M.V., Verrijn-Stuart, A.A., Voss, K.: A framework of information system concepts – The FRISCO Report, IFIP WG 8.1 Task Group FRISCO http://home.dei.polimi.it/pernici/ifip81/publications.html (1996). Cited Dec 2011

Fitzgerald, B.: The transformation of open source software. MIS Q. **30**(3), 587–598 (2001)

Flak, L.S., Rose, J.: Stakeholder governance: adapting stakeholder theory to the e-Government field. Commun. Assoc. Inform. Syst. **16**, 642–664 (2005)

Flak, L.S., Dertz, W., Jansen, A., Krogstie, J., Ølnes, S., Spjelkavik, I.: What is the value of eGovernment – and how can we actually realize it. Transforming Gov. People Process Policy **3**(3), 220–226 (2009)

Flood, R.L., Romm, N.R.A.: Diversity Management. Triple Loop Learning. Wiley, Chichester (1996)

Følstad, A., Jørgensen, H., Krogstie, J.: User involvement in e-Government development projects. In: Paper presented at the NordiChi'2004, Tampere (2004)

Fox, M.S., Gruninger, M.: Enterprise modeling. AI Mag. **19**(3), 109–121 (2000)

Gane, C., Sarson, T.: Structured Systems Analysis: Tools and Techniques. Prentice Hall, Englewood Cliffs (1979)

Gjersvik, R., Hepsø, V.: Using models of work practice as reflective and communicative devices: two cases from the Norwegian Offshore Industry. In: Paper presented at the Participatory Design Conference, Seattle (1998)

Gjersvik, R., Krogstie, J., Følstad, A.: Participatory development of enterprise process models. In: Krogstie, J., Siau, K., Halpin, T. (eds.) Information Modelling Methods and Methodologies. Idea Group Publishers, Hershey (2004)

Greenwood, D., Levin, M.: Introduction to Action Research: Social Research for Social Change. Sage, Thousand Oaks (1998)

Grudin, J., Pruitt, J.: Personas, participatory design and product development: an infrastructure for engagement. In: Paper presented at Participatory Design Conference 2002, Malmø, Sweden, June 2002

Günther, J., Steenbergen, C.: Application of MDA for the development of the DATOS billing and customer care system (Case study on the use of MDA for the development of a larger J2EE System). In: Proceedings of the First European Workshop on Model Driven Architecture with Emphasis on Industrial Application, University of Twente, Enschede, the Netherlands, 17–18 Mar 2004.

Gupta, A.: The profile of software changes in reused vs. non-reused industrial software systems, Doctoral thesis, 2009:90 (2009)

Hammer, M., Champy, J.: Reengineering the Corporation: A Manifesto for Business Revolution. Harper Business, New York (1993)

Harel, D.: Biting the silver bullet: toward a brighter future for system development. IEEE Comput. **25**, 8–20 (1992), January

Hauge, Ø., Ayala, C., Conradi, R.: Adoption of open source software in software-intensive industry – a systematic literature review. Inform. Softw. Technol. **52**(11), 1133–1154 (2010)

Havey, M.: Essential Business Process Modelling. O'Reilly, Sebastopol (2005)

Hawryszkiewycz, I.: Introduction to Systems Analysis and Design. Prentice Hall, Frenchs Forest (2001)

Heller, F.: Participation and competence: a necessary relationship. In: Russell, R., Rus, V. (eds.) International Handbook of Participation in Organizations, pp. 265–281. Oxford University Press, Oxford (1991)

Highsmith, J.: Adaptive Software Development: A Collaborative Approach to Managing Complex Systems. Dorset House Publishing Co., Inc, New York (2000)

Hirschheim, R.A., Klein, H.K.: Four paradigms of information systems development. Commun. ACM **32**(10), 1199–1216 (1989). October

Hochstein, A., Zarnekow, R., Brenner, W.: ITIL as common practice reference model for IT service management: formal assessment and implications for practice proceedings. In: The 2005 IEEE International Conference on e-Technology, e-Commerce and e-Service, Hong Kong (2005)

Holgeid, K.K., Krogstie, J., Sjøberg, D.I.K.: A study of development and maintenance in Norway: assessing the efficiency of information systems support using functional maintenance. Inform. Softw. Technol. **42**, 687–700 (2000)

Houy, C., Fettke, P., Loos, P.: Empirical research in business process management – analysis of an emerging field of research. Bus. Process Manage. J. **16**(4), 619–661 (2010)

Hunt, A., Thomas, D.: The Pragmatic Programmer. Addison Wesley, Reading (2000)

Iden, J., Tessem, B., Päivärinta, T.: The alignment of IS development and IT-operations in system development projects: a multi – method research. In: Proceeding NOKOBIT 2011, Tromsø, Norway (2011)

Irani, Z., Love, P.E.D., Elliman, T., Jones, S., Themistocleous, M.: Evaluating e-government: learning from the experiences of two UK local authorities. Inform. Syst. J. **15**, 61–82 (2005)

Jansen, S., Finkelstein, A., Brinkkemper, S.: A sense of community: a research agenda for software ecosystems. In: Proceedings of the 31st International Conference on Software Engineering (ICSE), New and Emerging Research Track – Companion Volume, Vancouver, 16–24 May 2009, pp. 187–190

Janzen, D., Saiedian, H.: Test-driven development: concepts, taxonomy, and future direction. Computer **38**(9), 43–50 (2005)

Jørgensen, H.D.: Enterprise modelling – what we have learned, and what we have not. In Proceedings of PoEM 2009, Wuhan, 2009. LNBIP 39. Springer, Berlin (2009)

Jørgensen, H.D.: Interaction as a framework for flexible workflow modelling. In: Proceedings of the 2001 International ACM SIGGROUP Conference on Supporting Group Work, Boulder, 2001, pp. 33–41. ACM Press, New York (2001)

Jørgensen, M.: Empirical studies of software maintenance, Ph.D. thesis, University of Oslo, Oslo, Research Report 188, ISBN 82-7368-098-3 (1994)

Kano, N.: Attractive quality and must-be quality. J. Jpn. Soc. Qual. Control **14**, 39–48 (1984), April

Kelly, S., Tolvanen, J.-P.: Domain-Specific Modelling: Enabling Full Code Generation. Wiley, Hoboken (2008)

Kelly, S., Lyytinen, K., Rossi, M.: MetaEdit+: A fully configurable multi-user and multi-tool CASE environment. In: Proceedings of CAiSE'96, 8th International Conference on Advanced Information Systems Engineering, Herakleion, 1996. Lecture Notes in Computer Science 1080, pp. 1–21. Springer, Berlin (1996)

Kelly, S., Pohjonen, R.: Domain-specific modelling for cross-platform product families. In: Olive, A., et al. (eds.) ER 2002 Ws, LNCS 2784, pp. 182–194. Springer, Berlin (2003)

Krogstie, J.: On the distinction between functional development and functional maintenance. J. Softw. Maint. **7**, 383–403 (1995)

Krogstie, J.: Use of methods and CASE-tools in Norway: results from a survey. J. Autom. Softw. Eng. **3**, 347–367 (1996)

Krogstie, J.: Modelling of the people, by the people, for the people. In: Krogstie, J., Opdahl, A., Brinkkemper, S. (eds.) Conceptual Modelling in Information Systems Engineering. Springer, Berlin (2007)

Krogstie, J.: Information systems development and maintenance in Norway: comparing private and public sector. In: Paper presented at the NOKOBIT 2010, Gjøvik, Norway (2010)

Krogstie, J., Sølvberg, A.: Software maintenance in Norway: a survey investigation. In: Paper presented at the International Conference of Software Maintenance (ICSM'94), Victoria, 19–23 Sept 1994

Krogstie, J.: Process improvement as organizational development: A case study on the introduction and improvement of information system processes in a Norwegian organization. In: Paper presented at the NOKOBIT'2000, Bodø, Norway (2000)

Krogstie, J., Jahr, A., Sjøberg, D.I.K.: A longitudinal study of development and maintenance in Norway. Report from the 2003 investigation Information and Software Technology 48, pp. 993–1005 (2006)

Krogstie, J., Jørgensen, H.: Interactive models for supporting networked organisations. In: 16th Conference on Advanced Information Systems Engineering, Riga, Latvia, 2004. Springer, Berlin/Heidelberg/New York (2004)

Krogstie, J.: Business information systems utilizing the future internet. In: Perspectives in Business Informatics Research, Riga, Latvia, 6–8 Oct 2011. Springer, Heidelberg (2011)

Kruchten, P.: The Rational Unified Process: An Introduction, 2nd edn. Addison-Wesley, Boston (2000)

Kuusisto, A.: Customer roles in business service production – implications for involving the customer in service innovation. Research report 195. Lappeenranta University of Technology, Lappeenranta (2008)

Langefors, B.: Some approaches to the theory of information systems. BIT **3**(34), 229–254 (1963)

Langefors, B.: Theoretical Analysis of Information Systems. Studentlitteratur, Lund (1967)

Lankhorst, M.: Enterprise Archoitecture at Work. Springer, Berlin (2005)

Lee, M.-G.T., Jefferson, T.L.: An empirical study of software maintenance of a web-based Java application. In: Proceedings ICSM'05, Herakleion (2005)

Lejk, M., Deeks, D.: An Introduction to Systems Analysis Techniques. Pearson, London (2002)

Lientz, B.P., Swanson, E.B.: Software Maintenance Management. Addison Wesley, Reading (1980)

Lientz, B.P., Swanson, E.B., Tompkins, G.E.: Characteristics of application software maintenance. Commun. ACM **21**(6), 466–471 (1978)

Lillehagen, F., Krogstie, J.: Active Knowledge Modelling of Enterprises. Springer, Berlin (2008)

Lonti, Z., Woods, M.: Towards Government at a glance: identification of core data and issues related to public sector efficiency. In: OECD Working Papers on Public Governance. OECD, Brisbane, Paris, see http://www.oecd.org/dataoecd/52/34/40209928.pdf (2008)

Lowry, M.R., McCartney, R.D. (eds.): Automating Software Design. The MIT Press, California (1991)

Lyytinen, K.: A taxonomic perspective of information systems development: Theoretical constructs and recommendations, Chapter 1. In: Boland Jr., R.J., Hirschheim, R.A. (eds.) Critical Issues in Information Systems Research, pp. 3–41. Wiley, New York (1987)

Macauley, L.: Requirements capture as a cooperative activity. In: Proceedings of the First Symposium on Requirements Engineering (RE'93), San Diego, 1993, pp. 174–181

Maguire, M.: Methods to support human-centred design. Int. J. Hum.-Comput. Stud. **55**(4), 587–634 (2001)

Marakas, G.M.: System Analysis & Design: An Active Approach. McGraw-Hill, New York (2006)

McCracken, D., Jackson, M.: Life cycle concept considered harmful. ACM SIGSOFT Softw. Eng. Notes **7**(2), 29–32 (1982). April

Mell, P., Grance, T.: The NIST Definition of Cloud Computing (2009), http://csrc.nist.gov/publications/nistpubs/800-145/SP800-145.pdf, Accessed 20 Apr 2012

Messerschmitt, D.G., Szyperski, C.: Software Ecosystems: Understanding an Indispensable Technology and Industry. MIT Press, Cambridge (2003)

Miller, G., et al.: Model driven architecture: how far have we come, how far can we go? In: Panel at OOPSLA'03, Anaheim, October 2003

Mohagheghi, P., Conradi, R.: An empirical study of software change: origin, acceptance rate, and functionality vs. quality attributes, empirical software engineering. In: International Symposium on Empirical Software Engineering (ISESE'04), Redondo Beach, 2004, pp. 7–16

Mumford, E.: Designing Human Systems for new technology: The ETHICS Method. Manchester Busines School, Manchester (1983)

Mumford, E.: Participation: from Aristotle to today. In: Langefors, B., Verrijn-Stuart, A.A., Bracchi, G. (eds.) Trends in information systems North-Holland an Anthology of Papers from Conferences of the IFIP Technical Committee, vol. 8, pp. 303–312. North-Holland Publishing Co., Amsterdam (1986)

Nerur, S., Mahapatra, R., Mangalaraj, G.: Challenges of migrating to agile methodologies. Commun. ACM **48**, 72–78 (2005)

Nilsson, A.G., Tolis, C., Nellborn, C. (eds.): Perspectives on Business Modelling: Understanding and Changing Organisations. Springer, Berlin (1999)

Nosek, J.T., Palvia, P.: Software maintenance management: changes in the last decade. J. Softw. Maint. **2**, 157–174 (1990)

Orlikowski, J.W., Gash, D.C.: Technological frames: making sense of information technology in organizations. ACM Trans. Inform. Syst. **12**(2), 174–207 (1994)

Palmer, S., Felsing, J.: A Practical Guide to Feature-Driven Development (The Coad Series). Prentice Hall PTR, Upper Saddle River (2002)

Parkhill, D.H.: Challenge of the Computer Utility. Addison-Wesley, Reading (1966)

Pereira, C.M., Sousa, P.: A method to define an enterprise architecture using the Zachman framework. In: Proceedings of the ACM SAC'04, Nicosia, Cyprus, 14–17 Mar 2004.

Persson, A., Stirna, J.: Why enterprise modelling – an explorative study into current practice. In: The 13th International Conference on Advanced Information Systems Engineering, CAiSE '02, Interlaken, Switzerland, 2002. Springer, Berlin (2002)

Persson, A., Stirna, J.: Towards defining a competence profile for the enterprise modelling practitioner the practice of enterprise modelling. In: PoEM 2010, Delft, 2010. Springer, Berlin (2010)

Rajlich, V.T., Bennett, K.H.: A staged model for the software life cycle. IEEE Comput. **33**, 66–71 (2000)

Royce, W.W.: Managing the development of large software systems: concepts and techniques. In: Proceedings WESCON, Los Angeles, August 1970

Sandkuhl, K., Lillehagen, F.: The early phases of enterprise knowledge modelling: practices and experiences from scaffolding and scoping. In: Proceedings of PoEM 2008, Stockholm, 2008. LNBIP 15. Springer, Berlin (2008)

Scheer, A.W.: ARIS, Business Process Framework, 3rd edn. Springer, Berlin (1999)

Scholl, H.J.: Involving Salient Stakeholders: Beyond the Technocratic View on Change. *Action Research* (AR), **2**, 281–308 (2005)

Schuler, D., Namioka, A.: Participatory design: Principles and Practices. Lawrence Erlbaum, Hillsdale (1993)

Schwaber, K., Beedle, M.: Agile Software Development with SCRUM. Prentice Hall, Saddle River (2002)

Sousa, H., Moreira, H.: A survey of the software maintenance process. In: Proceedings of ICSM'98, Bethesda, 1998, pp. 268–274. IEEE CS Press, Washington D.C. (1998)

Sowa, J.F., Zachman, J.A.: Extending and formalizing the framework for information systems architecture. IBM Syst. J. **31**(3), 590–616 (1992)

Stapleton, J.: Dynamic Systems Development Method. Addison Wesley, Reading (1997)

Stirna, J., Persson, A., Sandkuhl, K.: Participative enterprise modelling: experiences and recommendations. In: Krogstie, J., Opdahl, A.L., Sindre, G. (eds.) Proceedings of the 19th International

Conference on Advanced Information Systems Engineering, CAiSE 2007, Trondheim, Norway, 11–15 June 2007. Lecture Notes in Computer Science 4495. Springer, Berlin (2007)

Stirna, J., Persson, A.: Anti-patterns as a means of focusing on critical quality aspects in enterprise modelling. In: Proceedings of the BPMDS/EMMSAD 2009, Amsterdam. LNBIP 29. Springer, Berlin (2009)

Swanson, E.B., Beath, C.M.: Maintaining Information Systems in Organizations. Wiley Series in Information Systems. Wiley, New York (1989)

Swartout, W.R., Balzer, R.: On the inevitable intertwining of specification and implementation. Commun. ACM **25**(7), 438–440 (1982), July

Taylor, T., Standish, T.A.: Initial thoughts on rapid prototyping techniques. ACM SIGSOFT Softw. Eng. Notes **7**(5), 160–166 (1982), December

The Open Group architectural framework (TOGAF) http://www.opengroup.org/togaf/ (2011). Cited Dec 2011

Tolvanen, J.-P., Pohjonen, R., Kelly, S.: Advanced tooling for domain specific modelling: Metaedit+. In: The 7th OOPSLA Workshop on Domain-Specific Modelling DSM'07, Montreal (2007)

Valacich, J.S., George, J.F., Hoffer, J.A.: Essentials of Systems Analysis & Design, 5th edn. Pearson, Englewood Cliffs (2012)

Vernadat, F.B.: Enterprise Modelling and Integration: Principles and Applications. Chapman & Hall, London (1996)

Vonk, R.: Prototyping: The Effective Use of CASE Technology. Prentice Hall, Upper Saddle River (1990)

Ward, J., Daniel, E.: Benefits Management. Delivering Value from IT Investments. Wiley, Chichester (2006)

Weber, B., Sadiq, S., Reichert, M.: Beyond rigidity – dynamic process lifecycle support. Comput. Sci. Res. Dev. **23**(2), 47–65 (2009), Springer

Wegner, P.: Why interaction is more powerful than algorithms. Commun. ACM **40**(5), 80–91 (1997)

Wegner, P., Goldin, D.: Interaction as a framework for modelling. In: Chen, P.P., Akoka, J., Kangassalo, H., Thalheim, B. (eds.) Conceptual Modelling, Paris, 1999. Lecture Notes in Computer Science, Springer, Berlin/Heidelberg/New York (1999)

Weske, M.: Business Process Management: Concepts, Languages, Architectures. Springer, Berlin (2007)

Yourdon, E.: Managing the System Life Cycle. Prentice-Hall, New York (1988)

Zachman, J.A.: A framework for information systems architecture. IBM Syst. J. **26**(3), 276–291 (1987)

Zave, P.: The operational versus the conventional approach to software development. Commun. ACM **27**(2), 104–117 (1984), February

Zelm, M. (ed.): CIMOSA: a primer on key concepts, purpose, and business value (Technical Report), Stuttgart (1995)

Modelling Languages: Perspectives and Abstraction Mechanisms

In this chapter, we will give an overview of general mechanisms and perspectives used in conceptual modelling. We will first look upon modelling as a type of hierarchical abstraction. We present main abstraction mechanisms used in modelling languages (generalisation, aggregation, classification, association). Meta-modelling as a type of classification is discussed specifically, as is influence of philosophical ontology through BWW and UEML. We survey different modelling languages according to the main phenomena they describe, what we call the main modelling *perspective* of a modelling language. We have identified eight perspectives (behavioural, functional, structural, goal and rule, object-oriented, communicational, actor and role and topological). We discuss process modelling according to these perspectives before finally we discuss how to apply several such perspectives at the same time in an integrated manner, including examples of different approaches for integrating different perspectives in one language both for design modelling (UML) and enterprise modelling (EEML).

3.1   Abstraction Mechanisms in Modelling

A model is an abstraction. One mechanism for abstraction used in many of the existing languages for conceptual modelling is the use of hierarchies. The importance of hierarchical abstractions is based on the following assumptions:

- Hierarchies are essential for human understanding of complex systems.
- Thinking in terms of hierarchical constructs such as aggregation and generalisation appears to be very natural. At least such mechanisms are applied in a number of domains of human thinking.
- Information systems are complex systems because they must reflect the part of the world they process information about which tend to be increasingly complex,
- A proper support for hierarchical constructs is an essential requirement throughout the entire information system development and evolution process.

We will get back to these issues, and appropriate hierarchical mechanisms after defining the term 'Hierarchy' in more detail.

J. Krogstie, *Model-Based Development and Evolution of Information Systems:*
A Quality Approach, DOI 10.1007/978-1-4471-2936-3_3,
© Springer-Verlag London 2012

3.1.1   Hierarchical Abstraction

Here we will discuss what a *hierarchy* is in more detail. The first subsection discusses the possibilities for arriving at a precise definition of the term in terms of graph theory. As will be seen, however, it is difficult to come up with a definition that is precise and at the same time satisfactory in the sense that it is sufficiently broad to capture what we intuitively regard as a hierarchy. The second subsection thus argues that being hierarchical is very much a question of degree.

In Grobstein (1973) and Simon (1973), a hierarchy is defined rather vaguely as any collection of Chinese boxes (where each box can contain several smaller boxes). Mesarović et al. (1970) refrains from giving any exact definition of what a hierarchy is, but lists some properties that all hierarchies should have, namely 'vertical arrangement of subsystems which comprise the overall system, priority of action or right of intervention of the higher level subsystems, and dependence of the higher level subsystems upon the actual performance of the lower levels'. More precise definitions are given in Baas (1976) and Bunge (1969).

Some works distinguish between different kinds of hierarchical systems. Baas (1976) distinguishes formally between division hierarchies and control hierarchies. Mesarović et al. (1970) operates with three notions of hierarchical levels, namely strata (levels of description or abstraction), layers (levels of decision complexity), and echelons (organisational levels). All in all it seems that the word 'hierarchy' may be used in quite different ways by different authors – as stated in Sowa (1983) some use it indiscriminately for any partial ordering, whereas the above definitions require something more. Since it is important to make clear what we are talking about, we need some kind of definition. To this end, it is illuminating to look at the definition presented by Bunge (1969):

H is a hierarchy if and only if it is an ordered triple H=<S, b, D> where S is a non-empty set, b a distinguished element of S and D a binary relation in S such that

1. S has a single beginner, b. (That is, H has one and only one supreme commander.)
2. b stands in some power of D to every other member of S. (That is, no matter how low in the hierarchy an element of S may stand, it is still under the command of the beginner.)
3. For any given element y of S except b, there is exactly one other element x of S such that Dxy. (That is, every member has a single direct boss.)
4. D is transitive and antisymmetric.
5. D represents (mirrors) domination or power. (That is, S is not merely a partially ordered set with a first element: the behaviour of each element of S, save its beginner, is ultimately determined by its superiors.)

Figure 3.1 illustrates a possible hierarchy according to this definition. As pointed out by Bunge, this definition does two things:

- The first four points state what a hierarchy is in a graph-theoretic sense, namely a strict tree-structure (To be precise, it is an open-ended directed graph whose underlying graph, i.e. the undirected parallel of a directed graph, is a tree, since trees, graph-theoretically, are undirected graphs). For an introduction to graph theory, including definitions of graphs (directed and undirected), trees and underlying graphs, see for instance Wilson (1985).

Fig. 3.1 Example on hierarchy according to Bunge's definition

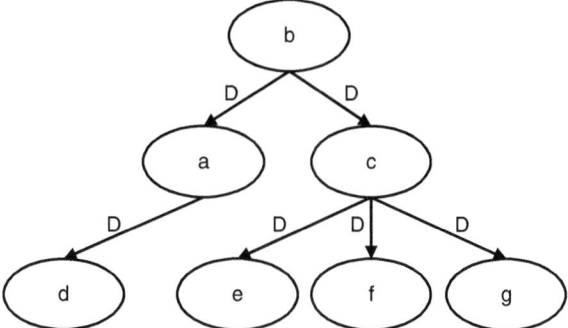

- The fifth point introduces an extra requirement on the nature of the relation D (i.e. edges) between the nodes, namely that they represent domination or power.
  Thus, Bunge makes the important point that whether something is a hierarchy or not cannot be determined by graph-theoretic considerations alone.
  However, Bunge's definition might be too strict:
- The graph-theoretic demands are very limiting. In real life, it often happens that a node can have more than one boss, or even that there are cycles in the graph, and still many people might consider the system to be of a hierarchical nature.
- The requirement that nodes are related by domination severely limits the scope of hierarchical systems. As stated by Bunge himself reciprocal action, rather than unidirectional action, seems to be the rule in nature (which leads Bunge to the conclusion that it is misleading to speak of hierarchies in nature: 'Hierarchical structures are found in society, e.g. in armies and in old-fashioned universities; but there are no cases of hierarchy in physics or in biology'). Since one might want to be able to model practically anything, we have to recognise other kinds of hierarchical relations in addition to domination or power.
  To achieve more generality, we will allow more general graphs to be considered as hierarchical. It will also be useful to have a specific term for those systems that satisfy the rather restrictive requirements stated above.
  Below we will use the following terminology:
- Strictly hierarchical graph: a digraph whose underlying graph is a tree, and for which there is one specific element b from which all other vertices can be reached (this is the distinguished element of Bunge's definition, as exemplified in Fig. 3.1).
- Weakly hierarchical graph: a connected acyclic digraph which deviates from the former in that there is no distinguished element and/or in that it's underlying graph is cyclic. Mathematically, this class of graphs is called DAGs (directed acyclic graphs).
- Cyclic hierarchical graph: a cyclic digraph.
  Obviously, the latter two notions should be used carefully – there is no point in calling any graph a hierarchy. Thus, even if we allow some DAGs, and maybe even some cycles, we should still require that a graph is pretty close to being a strict hierarchy if we call it hierarchical.

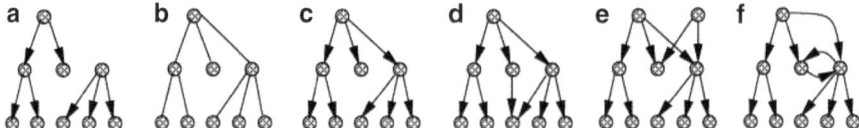

Fig. 3.2 Six graphs illustrating the nature of hierarchies

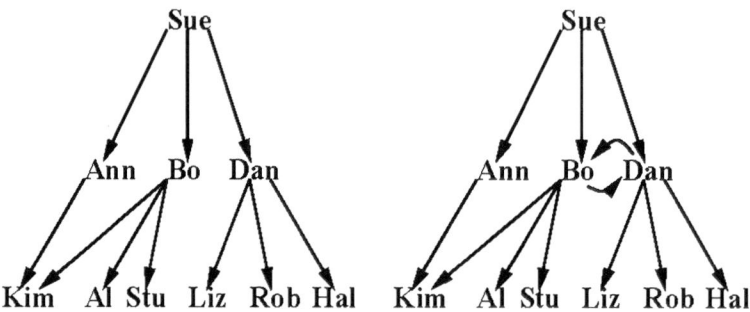

Fig. 3.3 Two graphs with hierarchical tendencies

The meaning of our suggested terminology can be visualised by Fig. 3.2. Of these graphs (a) would not be a hierarchy because it is not connected (but it might be two hierarchies), and (b) would not be a hierarchy because the edges are not directed. (c) On the other hand, is the kind of graph that satisfies Bunge's requirements, i.e. it is a strict hierarchy. The graph marked (d) would not be accepted as a hierarchy according to Bunge's definition because the underlying graph has a cycle (i.e. the middle element at the lowest level has two bosses), but we might call it a weak hierarchy. Similarly, (e) does not have one distinguished element – there are two elements on top that do not control each other. This could also be a weak hierarchy in our terminology. Finally, (f) contains a cycle and is thus clearly excluded by Bunge's definition, whereas we could call it a cyclic hierarchy (because although containing a cycle, the graph is not very far from being a strict hierarchy).

The motivation for removing some of the restrictions of Bunge's definition is that we want to be as general as possible, and clearly many people might feel that systems are hierarchical even when they are not strictly hierarchical.

This is exemplified by the two graphs of Fig. 3.3, where (a) breaks the single boss requirement, and (b) breaks the anti-symmetry requirement. If the edges denote the relation like 'is the boss of', it is still likely that both systems will be considered as hierarchical. Moreover, our definition has not required that the relations denoted by the edges be transitive. Clearly, most hierarchical relations are transitive (e.g. if A is the boss of B, and B the boss of C, it is also true that A is the boss of C), but there is no point in rejecting cases where this does not apply (e.g. if A is the parent of B, and B the parent of C, it will not be true to say based on this that A is the parent of C, and still people might feel that 'parent of' is a typically hierarchical relation).

Having loosened up Bunge's graph-theoretic restrictions, it might seem that we may end up calling any kind of directed graph a hierarchy. However, this is not our intention. We still need some requirement corresponding to the fifth point of Bunge's definition. Dominance or power is too narrow. Still, one needs to make some restriction on the semantics of the relation denoted by the edges. This is not easy, but we will refrain from discussing this in general terms, and rather move to certain hierarchical relations that have been found particularly useful in connection to IT development.

3.1.2 Standard Hierarchical Abstraction Mechanisms

There are a vast number of hierarchies that one might want to model, and these have rather diverse properties. Imagine, for example, organisation hierarchies, definition hierarchies, goal hierarchies, process decompositions, file system hierarchies and operating system process hierarchies.

Work in the field of semantic data modelling (Hull and King 1987; Peckham and Maryanski 1988; Potter and Trueblood 1988), ontologies (Leppänen 2005) and semantic networks (Findler 1979) has lead to the identification of four standard hierarchical relations:

- Classification
- Aggregation
- Generalisation
- Association
  We define the following abbreviations:
- CAGA (classification, aggregation, generalisation and association)
- AGA (aggregation, generalisation and association)
  The four constructs have the following definitions, going back to the definitions provided in Potter and Trueblood (1988):
- Classification: specific instances are considered as a higher level object type (a class) via the *is-instance-of* relationship (e.g. 'Rod Stewart' and 'Mick Jagger' are specific instances of 'male singer', 'CAiSE'2012' is an instance of 'Conference').
- Aggregation: an object is related to the components that make it up via the *is-part-of* relationship (e.g. a bicycle has wheels, a seat, a frame, handlebars etc.; a conference might have keynote sessions, paper sessions, workshops, tutorials, panels etc.). Leppänen (2005) calls this relation composition.
- Generalisation: similar object types are abstracted into a higher level object type via the *is-a* relationship (e.g. an employee is a person, a male singer is a singer, a conference is an event).
- Association: several object types are considered as a higher level set object-type via the *is-a-member-of* relationship (e.g. the sets 'men' and 'women' are members of the set 'sex-groups', CAiSE'1989…CAiSE'2012 are members of the set 'CAiSE conferences'). Association can also be found under the names of membership (e.g. Potter and Trueblood 1988), grouping (e.g. Hull and King 1987; Leppänen 2005) or collection (e.g. Hagelstein and Rifaut 1987).
  We will describe the four relations in more detail below.

3.1.2.1 Classification

Classification can be regarded as orthogonal to the other three – whereas the others construct bigger things from smaller things (on the same meta-level), classification results in a shift of meta-level, in accordance with the philosophical notions of intension and extension (Carnap 1947; Dowty et al. 1981). The intension of 'man' is the property of being a man, whereas the extension of 'man' (in any specific world, at any specific time) will be the set of all existing men (in that specific world, at that specific time). Going one meta-level higher from 'man', one can get to 'species', of whose extension 'man' is a member (in this particular world, at this particular time). One does not have to go much higher until there are only very abstract notions like 'words' and 'phenomena', so it is of limited interest to use many meta-levels in modelling. For the other three constructs, the complicated notions of intension and extension are unnecessary, and rather straightforward set-theoretic definitions can be provided as will be described below.

Thus classification is the principle of abstractions where a concept, called the class, is generated from other concepts, called instances. When performing classification, features special to individual things are ignored to uncover features common to all the things of interest. Classification should not be confused with set-theoretic membership, nor the notion of class with that of set, although there are clearly similarities in both cases. A class can be viewed as a collection of its instances. Moreover, each instance can be thought of as 'a member of' a class. However, a set is an extensional notion whose identity is determined by its membership. Thus, two sets A and B are equal if they have the same members, unlike classes where equality cannot be decided by simply comparing their instances. A thing is an instance of the class if it has all the predicates defined for the class. Consider the example of Person and John. Person is a class characterised by the predicates hasName, hasAddress and isMarriedTo. John is the instance of the class Person, and is characterised by the predicates hasName:John and hasAddress: MainStreet3. Often the term 'type' is used in the same sense as we use the term 'class' here, although in an object-oriented programming language, you would find differences between the terms, talking about basic types such as integer etc., that are not classes. Here a type is the non-empty set of properties which together characterise certain phenomena, whereas the class in the set of all phenomena of a certain type.

The principle inverse to classification is called instantiation.

Turning to cognitive psychology, one has identified three types of theories to explain how people develop and use categories (Ellis and Hunt 1993):

1. Attribute theory: Contends that one think of a list of defining attributes or features. For example, fish swim and have gills. We have above defined classification according to this theory. There are some deficiencies of this approach. It is not always possible to specify defining features, and it does not take into account goodness-of-examples effects; that some instances are more *typical* and *representative* than others. Thus among cognitive psychologists, the next two theories are the main contenders as humans are actually performing classification in the brain.

2. Prototype theory. States that when persons are presented a set of stimuli, they abstract the commonalties among the stimulus set and the abstracted representation is stored in memory. A prototype is the best representation of a class. For example, a prototypical fish might be the size of a trout, have scales and fins, swim in an ocean, lake or river and so forth. We have a general or abstract conception of fish that somehow is typical or representative of the variety of examples with which we are familiar. When given a particular example, we compare it to the abstract prototype of the class. If it is sufficiently similar to the prototype, we then judge it to be an instance of the class.

3. Exemplar theory: Assumes that all instances are stored in memory. New instances encountered are then compared with the set of exemplars already known. This theory does not assume the abstraction of a prototype, a best example as the prototype theory.

Parsons and Wand (1997a, b) present some guidelines for how to decide upon classes and class structure based on the cognitive economy and inference, which are regarded as the primary function of classification (Rosch 1978; Smith 1988). Cognitive economy means that, by viewing many things as instances of the same class, classification provides maximum information with the least cognitive effort. Inference means that identifying an instance as a member of a class makes it possible to draw conclusions. To decide upon potential classes, two principles are discussed:

1. Abstraction from instances: A class can be defined only if there are instances in the relevant domain possessing all properties of the type that defines the class.

2. Maximal abstraction: A property possessed by all instances of a class should be included in the class definition.

They propose two additional principles that apply to collections of classes:

1. Completeness, which requires that all properties from the relevant domain be used in classification

2. Non-redundancy, which ensures that there are no redundant classes

There can be variants of the relation between a class and an instance. There may be one or more instances that apply to the intentional definition of a certain class. A thing can be an instance of one or more classes. In some approaches, one would like to postpone classification, thus dealing with instances that are not yet assigned a class. These aspects relates to the view of a person at a specific time, i.e. the number of instances of a class can vary over time (and by perceiver), and the class (es) of an instance can also vary over time, either because of changes of the instance (e.g. a person growing older, changes class from children, to teenager, to adult) or because of changes in the class definition (e.g. when legislation is changed such as changing the age of adulthood). Based on this, Leppänen (2005) distinguishes the following cases:

• Objective vs. subjective classification (or better, inter-subjective vs. subjective classification). Do all classify the instances in the same way at all times?

• Permanent vs. evolving classification: Is the instance always of the same class (es) or not?

• Strict vs. non-strict classification. Do instances exist that are not of a class? Are there instances that can be of more than one class at the same time? Obviously one can also imagine classes without instances (e.g. the president of Norway).

3.1.2.2 Aggregation

Aggregation corresponds to the Cartesian product: If the set A is said to be an aggregation of the sets $A_1, ..., A_N$ this means that $A \subseteq A_1 \times ... \times A_N$, i.e. each element of A consists of one element from each of $A_1, ..., A_N$.

Some languages (like, for instance, SDM (Hammer and Mcleod 1981) and TAXIS (Mylopoulos et al. 1980) represent aggregations by means of attributes (instead of cross product type construction). The part-of relation can be looked upon as a special case of aggregation. Essential to a whole is that the parts are interrelated, in contrast to a group whose elements can be considered to be unrelated. Parts can be characterised by Motschnig-Pitrik and Kaasbøll (1999):

- Spatial and/or temporal proximity with respect to one another and/or the whole
- Propagation of some structural and behavioural properties from the part to the whole
- Propagation of some structural and behavioural properties from the whole to the part
- Particular ordering or constellation of parts

Based on work on object-oriented databases, this relation is further specialised (Motschnig-Pitrik and Kaasbøll 1999) according to two dimensions:

1. Degree of sharing indicates to which extent a part can be shared by more than one whole.
2. Degree of dependence indicates how mandatory and persistent is the relationship between the part and the whole.

Based on the degree of sharing, we can distinguish between two extremes, namely total exclusiveness and arbitrary sharing. The part-of relationship is total exclusive if a thing can be part of only one whole. For example a Motor can be part of only one Car (at a certain time). The part-of relationship is arbitrary shared if a thing can be part in arbitrary many wholes (at the same time). For example, a figure can be part of a book-chapter, an article and a document at the same time. Within the dimension degree of dependence, we have two extremes. The part-of relationship can bind a part to the whole with a lifetime dependence. In another case, there may be things of certain part class that are related to things not of the whole class. This kind of part-of relationship is called optional. Related to the degree of dependence is the notion of essentiality. The part-of relationship between a part class and a whole class is essential (or mandatory) if each part instance must be interconnected to at least one arbitrary whole instance of that class.

Until now, we have considered the part-of relationship from the viewpoint of the part. Similarly we can look upon this from the viewpoint of the whole. One can recognise the following kind of wholes:

- A homogeneous whole is a thing that is composed of parts of one class (e.g. a puzzle).
- A heterogeneous whole is a thing composed of parts of several classes.
- A single-part whole is a thing that contains only one thing of a certain class (a Train has one engine)
- A multi-part whole is a thing that contains several things of a certain class

- A flexible-structure whole is a thing in which parts of some class can be missing
- A fixed-structure whole is a thing which must be composed of one or more parts of all the defined part classes.

3.1.2.3 Generalisation

Generalisation corresponds to union: If the set A is a generalisation of the sets $A_1, ..., A_N$, this means that $A_1 \cup ... \cup A_N \subseteq A$.

The relationship between the subclass and superclass is called the isA relationship. The isA relationship is reflexive, non-symmetric and transitive. The opposite of generalisation is called specialisation. A class that is a subclass of several other classes should be defined by at least one property not in any of its superclasses. The principle of specialisation itself can be specialised based on the criteria for the specialisation

- Factual predicates (called discriminators in UML Booch et al. 2005). A particular type of this is when a subclass is derived from the population of the superclass excluding those instances that belong also to the extension of some subclass. For instance, unmarried may be defined as a subtype of person excluding those that are married
- Specification given by users (e.g. Accepted-paper, Gray-paper, Rejected-paper)
- Operators used in the specialisation. Is established by set-operations over the population of the type (e.g. papers_written_by_PC_member)

Some languages have identified several kinds of generalisation. The following types of generalisations are defined by Kung (1990).

- A set of subclasses of a class *cover* the class if all members of the class are members of at least one of the subclasses.
- A set of subclasses of a class are *disjoint* if no members of a subclass are members of any of the other subclasses of the class.
- A set of subclasses that are both disjoint and cover the class is called a *partition* of the class.

Normally the things of a subclass inherit all the properties of the things in the superclass. Likewise, things in a subclass inherit the relationships of the superclass (e.g. if a person can only be married to one other person, the same applies to all subclasses of person). This is also called strict derivation. In reality, some exceptions always appear (cf. the well-known examples about Birds and Penguins, a penguin is a bird but it does not fly). A way to manage this is to take the derivation as a default, and allow some properties to be overridden. This is called the default derivation. A special case of this is the way in which a predicate is refined during derivation. For example, a person will have an age between 0 and 120, whereas the subclass Adult has a property age between 18 and 120. In object-orientation one will also inherit the behaviour of the superclass.

When a subclass can have more than one superclass one derives properties etc. from several superclasses. Using the AND-strategy, a subclass inherits all properties and relationships from each superclass. In some cases, there might be inconsistencies between what is inherited from the different superclasses, and some sort of choice must be done between the candidates.

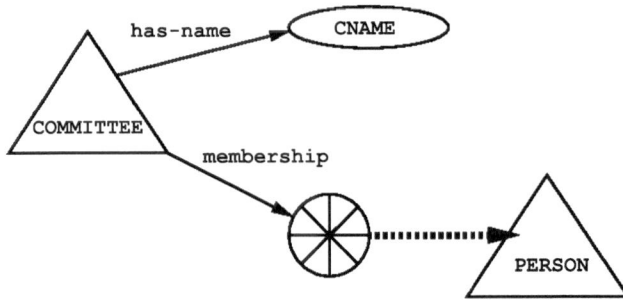

Fig. 3.4 Association with a single child

3.1.2.4 Association

Association corresponds to membership (i.e. embracing by set brackets): If the set A is an association of the sets $A_1, ..., A_N$ this means that $A = \{A_1, ..., A_N\}$.

There is a subtle difference between an association and a set. If two sets have the same members, they are equal; two associations having the same members may differ in their internal identifiers or by some characterising property. Association is an intransitive relationship.

It is often useful to define association in terms of the powerset operator. As suggested both by Hull and King (1987) and Peckham and Maryanski (1988), association is commonly used for constructing sets of objects of the same type. Consider the example of Fig. 3.4 (taken from Hull and King (1987), the SDM language is described further in Sect. 3.3.4), where the *-node denotes the association of the 'person' node, meaning that the former is a subset of the powerset of the set of persons (i.e. each program committee will have some group of members taken from the set of persons). Since we do not want to express at an abstract level the exact members of each program committee, and since all members are persons, the association operator will have only one child in this case (whereas the example with 'men' and 'women' being members of 'sex-groups' earlier in this section signalled a use of association with several children).

The principle inverse to association is called individualisation by which a member (class) is distinguished from a group (class).

You can identify different kinds of associations. On the class-level, you can have:

- In homogeneous association, there is only one member class (as in the example in Fig. 3.4 above).
- In heterogeneous association, several member classes can be involved.
- In a categorical association, a member class is related to one association class at the time.
- In shared associations, a thing can be member of several associations at the same time.

3.1.2.5 Evaluation of the Standard Hierarchical Relations

We will here briefly discuss the strength and weaknesses of the suggested constructs.

Strengths: As illustrated by Hull and King (1987), Peckham and Maryanski (1988), Potter and Trueblood (1988) and Leppänen (2005), many modelling languages provide at least some of the CAGA constructs, and the effects of introducing such constructs are positively described. Peckham and Maryanski (1988) reports improvements in expressive economy, integrity maintenance, modelling flexibility and modelling efficiency. Several examples of the use of these relations in language design, and how they present important evolutions in languages of different perspectives is given in Sect. 3.3. Why is it that languages tend to predefine exactly CAGA and not any other hierarchical relations (like 'is the boss of')? The main reason is their generality and intuitivity.

The generality of CAGA can be accounted for by the fact that they are a-substantial. Whereas relations like 'is-the-father-of' and 'is-the-boss-of' contain nouns 'father' and 'boss', whose semantics clearly limit the applicability of the relations, 'is-part-of' uses the semantically very anonymous noun 'part'. Anything can be a 'part' of something – the set of potential fathers is much more limited. The nouns 'instance', 'sub-set' and 'member' are similarly weak in semantic specificity. Defined in terms of sets, with no commitment as to what these sets contain, these abstraction mechanisms should be able to cover any application area. Thus, as will be illustrated in Sect. 3.3 they can be useful in organisational modelling, state modelling, process modelling, data modelling etc.

Moreover, CAGA are apparently very intuitive abstraction mechanisms, which must be why they have become so popular in the first place. We seem to find it natural to think of things as being put together from smaller parts (aggregation), as being of a specific class (classification), as being members of groups (association) which can have smaller subgroups (generalisation). This might partly be because we are being trained in using such hierarchies in school, for instance learning languages (aggregation: assembling words from letters, sentences from words, etc., classification: distinguishing between word classes, identifying phrases as subject, predicate, direct object, indirect object etc., generalisation: different kinds of sentences, nouns, verbs etc., association: memorising lists of prepositions demanding a certain case in German), learning biology, learning mathematics etc.

Weaknesses: However, there are also some weaknesses relative to CAGA as defined here that should be mentioned:

- The set-oriented definition of CAGA causes some limitations on their use.
- There are hierarchies that are certainly of interest in conceptual modelling which are not covered by the CAGA scheme.

As can be seen from the definitions given in this chapter, classification means to move up one meta-level, from an instance to a type. As discussed above, there are certain limitations in the way we think about classification relative to how this is done by humans, and we will not repeat these here. The other three are set-level constructs. Thus, there are two problems:

1. What to do about instances?
2. What to do about masses?

1. *Instances*: Instances are not necessarily a big problem. The association construct is trivially applicable, since it can produce a set of instances just as easily as a set of sets ('Peter, Patricia, and Joey are members of the Party Committee'). Moreover, if we treat instances like sets with only one member (like in Quine 1963), the definition of aggregation just presented is also trivially applicable ('The car # 346 was constructed from the chassis # 9213, the body# 2134, and the engine #905'), and so is generalisation (with the limitation that it only seems to be useful in situations where the general notion is a variable: 'Joey's murderer must have been either Peter or Patricia', in which case 'Joey's murderer' can be said to be a generalisation of 'Peter' and 'Patricia'). We can also look at more specific relationships when using the relationships on the instance level. For instance for association we have the following types:

   • Disjoint association: An instance is only member of one association.
   • Overlapping association: An instance can be member of several associations.
   • Mandatory association: All instances are members of one (or more) groups.
   • Optional association: There might be instances not being member of an association.

   Another question is hierarchical relations between instances (like 'father-of', 'boss-of'). We see in certain languages (e.g. EEML described in Sect. 3.5.2) generic relations like 'supervision' being defined by that one phenomenon govern the behaviour of another phenomena (cf. the power aspect of the original hierarchy-definition of Bunge above). We will not discuss here to what extent this is another possibly generally applicable hierarchical relation on the same level as CAGA.

2. *Mass Concepts*. As Sowa (1983) points out the set-oriented way of thinking work well for things that are countable, whereas there are problems for so-called mass nouns, like water and money. Again it appears that the notions of AGA are applicable ('Chocolate is made of cocoa, sugar and milk (in certain quantities)' (aggregation), 'Milk and water are both liquids' (generalisation), 'Milk and Water are members of the set Liquids' (association)). However, the problem is that we cannot use the set-based definitions presented earlier in this chapter. There are two possible ways out of this:

   • One can go for a more general definition of AGA that is not at all based on sets (but for instance on types).
   • One can use the definitions already suggested and add some special tactics for dealing with masses. In Sindre (1990), masses are considered as virtual sets of sets. This means that a mass that can be measured in one or more dimension can be split up in any partitioning of continuous intervals in these dimensions. Since this means that there will be an infinite number of possible sets for the mass, we cannot store the mass as such, but for any partitioning we can check if it is within the given limits (thus '5 l of water' is part of '9 l of water' although we have not stored explicitly the fact that '9 l of water' is an aggregation of 4 l of water and 5 l of water). In OntoUML (Guizzardi 2005; Guizzardi et al. 2010) address these problems by defining a modelling primitive 'quantity'. In OntoUML, a type stereotyped as 'quantity' represents a type whose instances represent portions of amounts of matter, which are

maximal under the relation of topological self-connectedness (Guizzardi 2005). If A is self-connected, any part of A is connected to any other part of A. If B is part of A then B is connected to all parts of A. Connection is transitive.

3.1.3 Levels of Models

There have for a long-time been approaches to support the development of new modelling languages (so-called meta-modelling) rather than the use of existing already defined languages. In particular, in DSM/DSL discussed in Sect. 2.3.3 this is exploited. You also find the use of meta-modelling in MDA and in enterprise modelling. The term 'meta' indicates that something is after something, i.e. a meta-model is a model after (of) a model. This meta-level-discussion use the classification abstraction described in Sect. 3.1.2.1 above. It can be argued that the term meta-model is most correctly used when it is the model used for designing the database structure of a model repository (i.e. so that the instances in the meta-model constitutes a model). Often, the term is also used for the related (but at times somewhat different) model that you get when describing the modelling concepts and relationships of a modelling language (below termed language model). The meta-model for defining the storage of the model, and the language model usually are quite similar, but the meta-model typically covers additional technically oriented aspects. We will use both terms below, and distinguish them according to how we have defined the difference here.

In principle, it is possible to apply an infinite number of meta-levels. In practice, one normally looks at this at (maximum) four levels. Generally accepted conceptual framework for meta-modelling explains the relationships between meta-meta-model, meta-model, model and (not somewhat misleading) 'user data'. Together they form four layers on top of each other, illustrated in Meta-object facility (MOF) in OMG (which again is based on the work on CDIF in the 1980s) as depicted in Fig. 3.5:

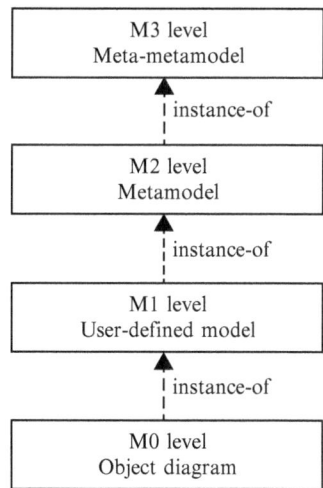

Fig. 3.5 Meta-levels as defined in OMG MOF

- M0: The user object layer is comprised of the information that we wish to describe. This information is what one in a database-world typically referred to as 'data', but this is just as much a model as what we find on the other levels. More precisely, it is a model on the *instance* level. Whereas instance level modelling is quite common within enterprise modelling, software modelling is typically done only on the next layer (M1). Note that contrary to the figure a M0 model can also be an instance of an M2 concept (when the language includes instance level concepts in addition to type-level concepts, something often found in enterprise modelling for instance).
- M1: The model layer is comprised of the meta-data that describes information. Meta-data are informally aggregated as models.
- M2: The meta-model layer is comprised of the descriptions (i.e. meta-meta-data) that define the structure and semantics of meta-data. Meta-meta-data is informally aggregated as meta-models. A meta-model can also be thought of as a 'language' for describing different kinds of data.
- M3: The meta-meta-model layer is comprised of the description of the structure and semantics of meta-meta-data. In other words, it is the 'language' for defining different kinds of meta-data (modelling languages).

In EXTERNAL (Lillehagen and Krogstie 2008), another four level model was proposed. This can be said to bifurcate the two lowest levels (object/data and model) in CDIF/MOF as for the specific or general applicability of the model. Even if the terms below refer to process modelling in particular, these levels can be used for discussion of levels for all sorts of modelling.

The four levels identified in EXTERNAL are:

- Layer 1 – Describe process logic: At this layer, one identifies the constituent activities of generic, repetitive processes and the logical dependencies between these activities. A process model at this layer should be transferable across time and space to a mixture of execution environments.
- Layer 2 – Engineer activities: Here process models are expanded and elaborated to facilitate particular business solutions. Elaboration includes concretisation, decomposition and specialisation. Integration with local execution environment is achieved, e.g. by describing resources required for actual performance.
- Layer 3 – Manage work: The more abstract layers of process logic and of activity description provide constraints, but also useful resources (in the form of process templates) to the planning and performance of each process instance. At layer 3, more detailed decisions are taken regarding the performance of work in the *actual work environment* with its organisational, information and tool resources; the scope is narrowed down to an actual process instance. *Concrete* resources increasingly are intertwined in the model, leading to the introduction of more dependencies. Management of activities may be said to consist of detailed planning, co-ordination and preparation for resource allocation.
- Layer 4 – Perform work: This lowest layer of the model covers the actual execution of tasks according to the determined granularity of work breakdown, which in practice is coupled to issues of empowerment and decentralisation. When a

group or person performs the task, whether to supply a further decomposition may be left to their discretion, or alternative candidate decompositions might be provided as advisory resources. At this layer resources are utilised or consumed, in an exclusive or shared manner.

To illustrate the differences between these four layers, we use the example of a project model:

- Describe process logic: General methodologies are typically written at this level. This includes project management methodologies such as PMBOK, and software development methodologies such as RUP described in Sect. 2.2.5
- Engineer activities: When an organisation decides to standardise their project methodology, e.g. based on PMBOK, they will typically select the relevant parts of this and extend this, and link it with tools and techniques in their current operating environment, such as their standard project management tool.
- Manage work: A project manager for a specific project will typically operate with a model at this level, taking the company project management model, specialising it and allocating concrete resources to specific tasks.
- Perform work: The different workers of the project will relate to a model at this level, as they are doing their day-to-day tasks in the project.

Combining the CDIF/MOF and the EXTERNAL approach gives a framework of eight levels (two at each instantiation-level). The lower four is described above, whereas we below describe and exemplify the higher four.

- Meta-meta model for all types of modelling approaches. Meta-meta modelling will generally be on this level. The meta-meta model in for instance OMG (MOF) is meant to be of this type.
- Meta-meta model for specific types of modelling approaches. At this level, you take the specific possibilities of a certain environment into account (such as the METIS modelling environment).
- Meta-model meant for all modelling tasks. UML for instance is stated to be (Booch et al. 2005) 'a language for specifying, visualising, constructing, and document the artefacts of software systems, as well as for business modelling and other non-software systems'. In other words, UML is meant to be used in analysis of business and information, requirements specification and design. UML is designed to support the modelling of transaction systems, real-time and safety critical systems. The meta-model of such a language thus easily get very large and complex due to its extensive scope.
- Meta-model meant for a specific modelling task. For example, a language made in connection to one task (or a set of specific tasks, i.e. so-called domain-specific modelling as described in Chap. 2 (DSM/DSL Kelly and Tolvanen (2008))).

Note that these levels are conceptual, i.e. a technical system implementing these levels does not have to strictly follow them. Often we also see approaches that mix aspects of the two sub-levels at the same level. We will return to how to represent modelling languages in a meta-model in Sect. 4.4 when discussing means for supporting the syntactic quality of a model, i.e. that it adheres to the rules of the modelling language used.

3.2   Impact on Philosophical Ontologies on Modelling

In Chap. 1, we argued for approaching modelling from a constructivistic rather than an objectivistic point of view. Much of the work relating to finding the central parts of modelling and modelling languages has traditionally taken a more objectivistic outlook, building on an objectivistic ontology. Even if it can be argued that this outlook has fundamental flaws, we will mention the most influential work of this kind, the Bunge-Wand-Weber (BWW) model. We do this since it in addition to have influenced a lot of modelling languages (explicitly or implicitly), it has been shown to be pragmatically useful for supporting the development of models and modelling languages of high quality when used in the right way, when it is combined with more context-specific considerations.

3.2.1   BWW – Bunge-Wand-Weber

The development of the *representation theory* that is known as the Bunge-Wand-Weber model stemmed from the perception that, in their essence, computerised information systems are representations of real-world systems. Wand and Weber (1990, 1993, 1995) suggest that the use of philosophical ontology may help define and build information systems that faithfully represent real-world systems. Ontology is a well-established theoretical domain within philosophy that deals with identifying and understanding elements of the real world (Bunge 2003). Wand and Weber adopted an ontology defined by Bunge (1977) and from this derived a theory of representation for the Information Systems discipline that has become widely known as the Bunge-Wand-Weber (BWW) representation model. Following Wand and Weber's arguments, models of information systems and thus their underlying modelling language should contain the necessary representations of real-world constructs including their properties and interactions. The BWW representation model contains four clusters of constructs that are deemed necessary to faithfully model and thus represent information systems (Rosemann and Green 2002).

1. Things including properties and types of things
2. States assumed by things
3. Events and transformations occurring on things
4. Systems structured around things

Wand and Weber's work based on Bunge's theory is not the only case of ontology-based research on conceptual modelling. The approaches of Milton and Kazmierczak (2004) and Guizzardi (2005) are closest to the ideas of Wand and Weber. These so-called upper-level ontologies (in contrast to more particular domain-specific ontologies) have been built for similar purposes and appear to be equally expressive (Davies et al. 2005), but have not yet achieved the popularity and dissemination of the BWW model.

As demonstrated in many papers, the BWW model (Recker et al. 2007; Wand and Weber 1993, 1995; Weber and Zhang 1996) can be used to analyse the meaning of modelling constructs used in information systems development and to evaluate

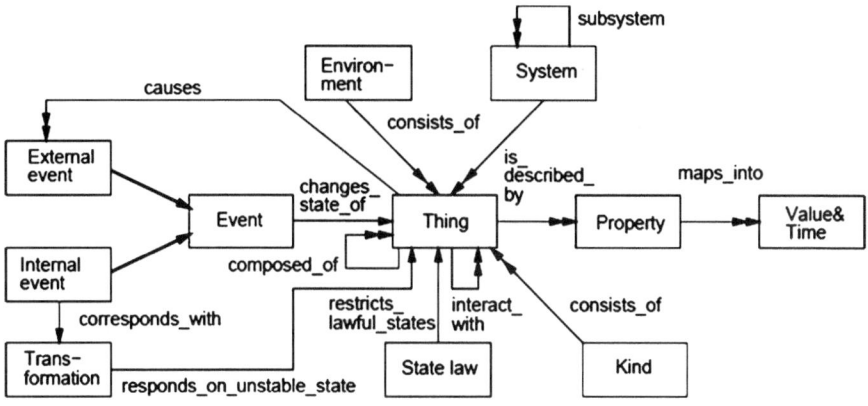

Fig. 3.6 Main concepts in BWW

whether the constructs provided by single IS modelling languages and by integrated IS development methodologies are appropriate or not. A meta-model for the BWW model has been presented in Rosemann and Green (2002). The BWW model has been applied to the analysis and evaluation of IS-design methods in general (Wand 1988), BPMN (Recker et al. 2007), dataflow diagrams (Wand and Weber 1993), ER diagrams (Wand and Weber 1989; Weber 1997), NIAM (Weber and Zhang 1996), nine languages supported by the Excelerator-toolset (Green 1996), four languages supported the ARIS-toolset for business modelling (Green and Rosemann 1999), and the OPEN Modelling Language (OML) (Opdahl and Henderson-Sellers 2001b) and UML (Opdahl and Henderson-Sellers 2002). The BWW model has also been used to analyse optional properties in conceptual modelling (Bodart et al. 2001) and whole-part relationships discussed in Sect. 3.1.2 (like UML's aggregation and composition constructs) in OO models (Opdahl and Henderson Sellers 2001a).

A more detailed overview of the main concepts is found in Fig. 3.6. The most central phenomena in the ontological model are *thing*, *property*, *state* and *transformation*. From these, all other constructs can be derived. Things are what the world is made up of. Things may be composite, consisting of other things. Things are described by properties, which map them into values. A kind is a set of things with two or more common properties. The state of a thing at a particular point in time is the vector of values of its properties. A state law restricts the states of a thing to a set of states that are deemed lawful in some sense. A system is a set of things that interact, i.e. their states affect the states of other things in the system. A system can be decomposed into subsystems. The environment consists of things that interact with the things in the system, in the way that they may directly change the state of a thing through an external event. Such an event may lead the system to an unstable state, to which transformations respond by bringing the system back to a stable state. A more detailed overview of the main concepts can be found in Opdahl and Henderson-Sellers (2002), based on Bunge (1977), Green (1996), Parsons and Wand (1997a, b), Wand and Weber (1995), Weber (1997) and Weber and Zhang (1996).

It can be argued that Bunge's ontology is primarily concerned with representing the material world – the world of material objects that possess physical properties existing independently from human perception. Although later versions of BWW include social notions such as human laws, it has limited place for human intentions, interpretations, creations or meaning. It is not particularly focused on institutional reality – the world of conceptual objects and attributes created by human intentions and for human purposes. Examples of such conceptual objects are enterprises (real and virtual), government agencies, educational institutions, contracts, money and transactions. None of these are material objects about which Bunge's ontology is concerned yet they are at the core of business organisations. Lacking constructs for such objects, Bunge's ontology is an inappropriate foundation alone for conceptual modelling in the context of (organisational) information systems. A discussion on the usage possibilities and problems with BWW is found in Kautz (2006). That said, we will return in Chap. 7 with the examples of the use of BWW in combination with other aspects for the evaluation of domain appropriateness of modelling languages.

The Unified Enterprise Modelling Language (UEML) (Anaya et al. 2010) aims at supporting *integrated use of enterprise and IS models* expressed using different languages and took BWW as an outset.

The following illustrate the goal of UEML:

• *Exchanging information contained in enterprise and IS models* across modelling language boundaries. This is the central motivation behind UEML, which explains its focus on *interoperability between modelling languages* as a prerequisite for integrated use of the models that are expressed in those languages.
• *Creating new problem- and/or domain-specific methods* by combining elements from existing modelling techniques.
• Systematic, quality-driven, reuse of existing enterprise and IS modelling languages.
• Defining a core language for enterprise and IS modelling. As UEML stabilises, it may become possible to extract a core set of modelling construct to use as the starting point for a new enterprise/IS modelling language.
• Facilitating a web of languages and of models is another long-term objective.

The UEML ontology was first populated with a set of initial classes, properties, states and transformations derived directly from the BWW model. Since then, it has evolved and grown as new constructs have been added. Currently, UEML incorporates a selection of academic and industrial modelling languages, such as ARIS (Dossogne and Jeanmart 2007), BMM (Tu 2007), BPMN (Dossogne and Jeanmart 2007), coloured Petri nets, GRL (Dallons et al. 2005; Heymans et al. 2005; Matulevičius et al. 2006, 2007a; Tu 2007), IDEF3 (Harzallah et al. 2007), ISO/DIS 19440, KAOS (Matulevičius et al. 2006, 2007a, b).

3.3   Perspectives to Modelling

In this section, we survey the state of the art of modelling languages, including those that have been applied in mature methodologies for system development and evolution and some that are still on the research level. We also draw the lines from the original modelling approach to today's practice. The overview will concentrate on the basic components and features of the languages to illustrate different ways of abstracting human perception of reality.

Modelling languages can be divided into classes according to the core phenomena (concepts) that are represented and focused on in the language. We have called this the *perspective* of the language. Another term that can be used, is *structuring principle*. Generally, we can define a structuring principle to be some rule or assumption concerning how information should be structured. This is a very vague definition. We observe that

- A structuring principle can be more or less detailed: on a high level one for instance has the choice between structuring the information hierarchically, or in a general network. Most approaches take a far more detailed attitude towards structuring: deciding what is going to be decomposed, and how. For instance, structured analysis implies that the things primarily to be decomposed are processes, and an additional suggestion might be that the hierarchy of processes should not be deeper than four levels, and the maximum number of processes in one model is seven.
- A structuring principle might be more or less rigid: In some approaches, one can override the standard structuring principle if one wants to, in others this is impossible.

We will here start with a discussion on what we call aggregation principles. As stated in Sect. 3.1.2, aggregation means to build larger components of a system by assembling smaller ones. Selecting a certain aggregation principle thus implies decision concerning:

- What kind of components to aggregate.
- How other kinds of components (if any) will be connected to the hierarchical structure.

Discussions between the supporters of different aggregation principles can often be rather heated. As we will show, the aggregation principle is a very important feature of a modelling approach, so this is understandable. Some possible aggregation principles are:

- Object orientation
- Process orientation
- Actor orientation
- Goal orientation

Objects are the things subject to processing, processes are the actions performed, and actors are the ones who perform the actions. Goals are why we do the actions in the first place. Clearly, these four approaches concentrate on different aspects of the perceived reality, but it is easy to be mistaken about the difference. It is not which aspects they are able to represent that are relevant. Instead, the difference is one of focus, representation, dedication, visualisation and sequence, in that an oriented language typically prescribes that (Opdahl and Sindre 1997):

- Some aspects are promoted as fundamental for modelling, whereas other aspects are covered mainly to set the context of the promoted ones (focus).
- Some aspects are represented explicitly, others only implicitly (representation).
- Some aspects are covered by dedicated modelling constructs, whereas others are less accurately covered by general ones (dedication).

- Some aspects are visualised in diagrams; others only recorded textually (visualisation).
- Some aspects are captured before others during modelling (sequence).
  Below we will investigate the characteristics of such perspectives in more detail.

3.3.1 An Overview of Modelling Perspectives

A classic distinction regarding modelling perspectives is between the structural, functional and behavioural perspective (Olle et al. 1988). Yang (1993), based on Falkenberg et al. (1996) and Wand and Weber (1993), identifies the following perspectives:
- Data perspective. This is parallel to the structural perspective.
- Process perspective. This is parallel to a functional perspective.
- Event/behaviour perspective. The conditions by which the processes are invoked or triggered. This is covered by the behavioural perspective.
- Role perspective. The roles of various actors carrying out the processes of a system.
  Curtis et al. (1992) identified at the same time the following perspectives relevant in process modelling:
- Functional: What elements are performed (functional perspective)
- Behavioural: When and how elements are performed (behavioural perspective)
- Organisational: Where and by whom elements are performed
- Informational: Represent informational entities (structural perspective)
  In F^3 (Bubenko et al. 1994), it was recognised that a requirement specification should answer the following questions:
- Why is the system built?
- Which are the processes to be supported by the system?
- Which are the actors of the organisation performing the processes?
- What data or material are they processing or talking about?
- Which initial objectives and requirements can be stated regarding the system to be developed?
  This indicates a need to support what we will term the goal and rule-perspective, in addition to the other perspectives mentioned by Yang.
  In the NATURE project (Jarke et al. 1993), one distinguished between four worlds: Usage, subject, system and development. Conceptual modelling as we use it here applies to the subject and usage world for which NATURE propose data models, functional models and behaviour models; and organisation models, business models, speech act models and actor models respectively. As discussed in Sect. 2.2.9, the Zachman Framework for enterprise modelling (Sowa and Zachman 1992) highlight the intersection between the roles in the design process, that is, Owner, Designer and Builder; and the product abstractions, that is, What (material) it is made of, How (process) it works and Where (geometry) the components are, relative to one another. From the very inception of the framework, some other product abstractions were known to exist because in addition to What, How and Where, a complete description would necessarily have to include the remaining primitive interrogatives: Who, When and Why.

- Who does what work,
- When do things happen (and in what order) and
- Why are various choices made?

In addition to perspectives indicated above, this highlight the topological/geographical dimension which have increased in the last decade also due to the proliferation of mobile and multi-channel solutions, and location-based services in general.

Based on the above, to give a broad overview of the different perspectives state-of-the-art conceptual modelling approaches accommodate, we have focused on the following eight perspectives:

1. Behavioural perspective
2. Functional perspective
3. Structural perspective
4. Goal and rule perspective
5. Object perspective
6. Communication perspective
7. Actor and role perspective
8. Topological perspective

This is only one way of classifying modelling approaches, and in many cases it will be difficult to classify a specific approach solely according to one perspective within this scheme since they are related. On the other hand, we have experienced this as a useful way of ordering the presentation of modelling approaches due to the similarities found between different languages sharing the main perspective.

Another way of classifying modelling languages is according to their time-perspective (Sølvberg and Kung 1993):

- Static perspective: Provide facilities for describing a snapshot of the perceived reality, thus only considering one state. Languages of the structural perspective are usually of this kind
- Dynamic perspective: Provide facilities for modelling state transitions, considering two states, and how the transition between the states takes place. Languages of the behavioural perspective are often of this type
- Temporal perspective: Allow the specification of time-dependant constraints. In general, sequences of states are explicitly considered. Some rule-oriented approaches are of this type.
- Full-time perspective: Emphasise the important role and particular treatment of time in modelling. The number of states explicitly considered at a time is indefinite.

Yet another way of classifying languages is according to their level of formality. Conceptual modelling languages can be classified as semi-formal (having a formal syntax, but no formal semantics) or formal, having a logical and/or executional semantics. The logical semantics used can vary (e.g. first-order logic, description logic, modal logic etc.). Executional or operational semantics indicate that a model in the language can be executed on a computing machine if it is complete relative to this need. They can in addition be used together with descriptions in informal (natural) languages and non-linguistic representations, such as audio and video recordings.

Finally, it is important to differentiate the level of modelling; are we modelling types or instances? In traditional conceptual modelling, one is normally only modelling

Fig. 3.7 Symbols in the state transition modelling language

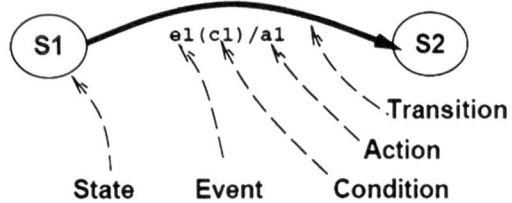

on the type level, whereas in enterprise modelling it is also usual to model on the instance level, often combining concepts on the type and instance level, including process-types and process instances in the same model.

We will below present some languages within the main perspectives, and also indicate their temporal expressiveness and level of formality. Many of the languages presented here are often used together with other languages in so-called combined approaches. Some examples of such combined approaches will also be given later in the chapter.

3.3.2 The Behavioural Perspective

Languages in this perspective go back to at least the early 1960s, with the introduction of Petri nets. In most languages with a behavioural perspective the main phenomena are states and transitions between states. State transitions are triggered by events (Davis 1988). A finite state machine (FSM) is a hypothetical machine that can be in only one of a given number of states at any specific time. In response to an input, the machine generates an output, and changes state. There are two language-types commonly used to model FSM's: State transition diagrams (STD) and state transition matrices (STM). The vocabulary of state transition diagrams is illustrated in Fig. 3.7 and is described below:

- State: A system is always in one of the states in the lawful state space for the system. A state is defined by the set of transitions leading to that state, the set of transitions leading out of that state and the set of values assigned to attributes of the system while the system resides in that state.
- Event: An event is a message from the environment or from system itself to the system. The system can react to a set of predefined events.
- Condition: A condition for reacting to an event. Another term used for this is 'guard'.
- Action: The system can perform an action in response to an event in addition to perform the transition to a new state.
- Transition: Receiving an event will cause a transition to a new state if the event is defined for the current state, and if the condition assigned to the event (if any) evaluates to true.

A simple example that models the state of a paper during the preparation of a professional conference is depicted in Fig. 3.8. The double circles indicate end states. In state *0:Non-existent*, the paper is under development. When it is finished, it is submitted and received by the conference organisers, it is in state *1:Received*. Usually a confirmation of the reception of paper is sent, putting the paper in state

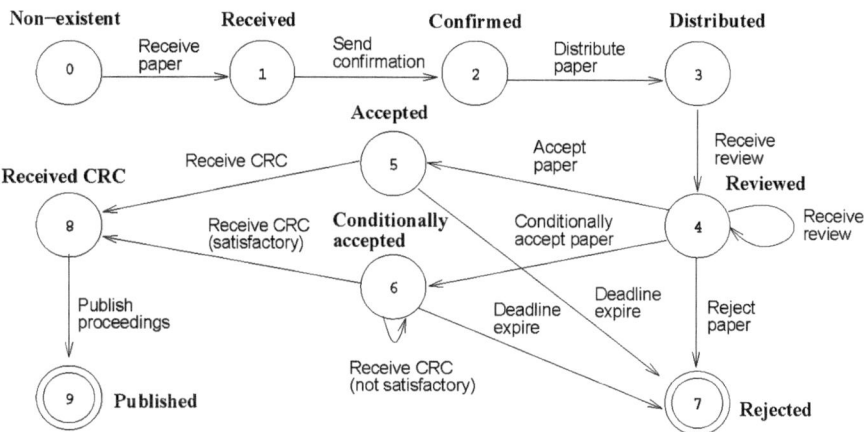

Fig. 3.8 Example of a state transition model for the review process

2:Confirmed. The paper is sent to a number of reviewers. First it is decide who are to review which paper, providing an even work-load. Then the papers are distributed to the reviewers entering state *3:Distributed.* As each review is received the paper is in state *4:Reviewed.* Often there would be additional rules relating to the minimum number of reviews that should be received before making a verdict. This is not included in this model. Before a certain time, decisions are made if the paper is accepted, conditionally accepted or rejected, entering state *5:Accepted,* *6:Conditionally accepted* or *7:Rejected.* A conditionally accepted paper needs to be reworked to be finally accepted. All accepted papers have to be sent in following the appropriate format (so-called CRC – Camera Ready Copy). When this is received, the paper is in state *8:Received CRC.* When all accepted papers are received in a CRC format, the proceedings are put together and then eventually published, made available to the larger audience (state *9:Published).*

In an STM, a table is drawn with all the possible states labelling the rows and all possible stimuli labelling the columns. The next state and the required system response appear at each intersection (Davis 1990). In basic finite state, machine one assumes that the system response is a function of the transition. This is the Mealy model of a finite state machine. An alternative is the Moore model in which system responses are associated with the state rather than the transitions between states. Moore and Mealy machines are identical with respect to their expressiveness. SDL (Specification and Description Language) developed originally in the telecommunications area was in its original form focused on Extended Finite State Machines, extended among others in the possibilities to send explicit messages as part of transitions.

It is generally acknowledged that a complex system cannot be beneficially described in the fashion depicted in Fig. 3.8, because of the unmanageable, exponentially growing multitude of states, all of which have to be arranged in a 'flat' model. Hierarchical abstraction mechanisms where added to traditional STD in Statecharts (Harel 1987) to provide the language with modularity and hierarchical construct as illustrated in Fig. 3.9.

Fig. 3.9 Decomposition
mechanisms in Statecharts

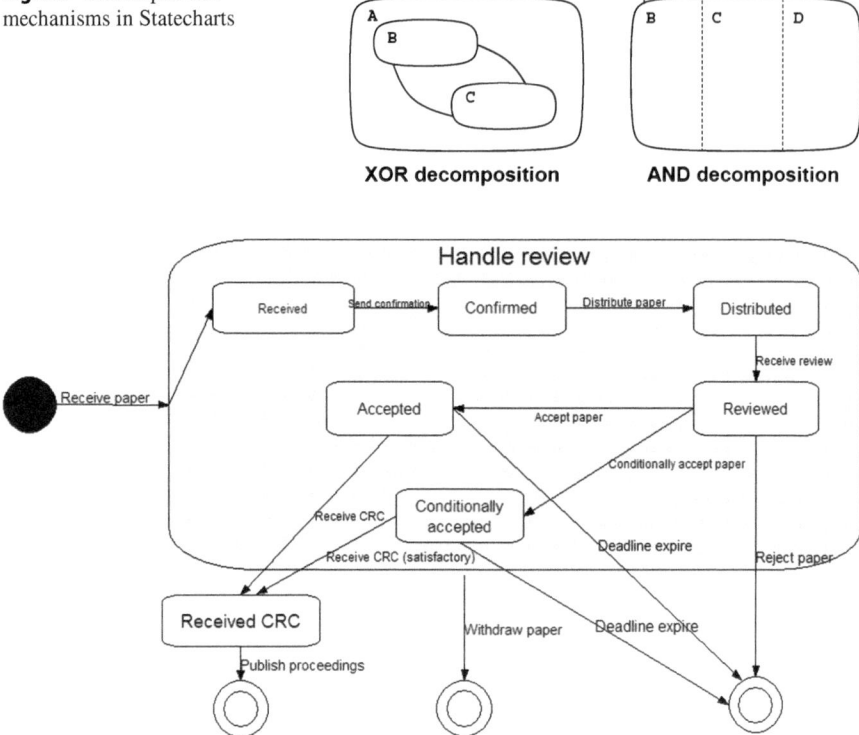

XOR decomposition   **AND decomposition**

Fig. 3.10 Statechart of paper review process

- XOR decomposition: A state is decomposed into several states. An event entering
  this state (A) will have to enter one and only one of its sub-states (B or C). In this
  way generalisation is supported.
- AND decomposition: A state is divided into several states. The system resides in
  all these states (B, C and D) when entering the decomposed state (A). In this way
  aggregation is supported.

In Fig. 3.10 we illustrate the usefulness for such mechanisms. If we want to
introduce the possibility of withdrawing the paper before the CRC is submitted, we
would in the standard STD depicted in Fig. 3.8 have to introduce six new edges
(from state 1 to 6 to the new withdrawn state). In Fig. 3.10, one new edge is provided
to cater for the same by being able to decompose states.

One has introduced a number of additional mechanisms to be used with these
abstractions in Statecharts:

- History: When entering the history of an XOR decomposed state, the sub-state
  that was visited last will be chosen.
- Deep history: The semantics of history repeated all the way down the hierarchy
  of XOR decomposed states.
- Condition: When entering a condition inside a XOR decomposed state, one of the
  sub-states will be chosen to be activated depending on the value of the condition.

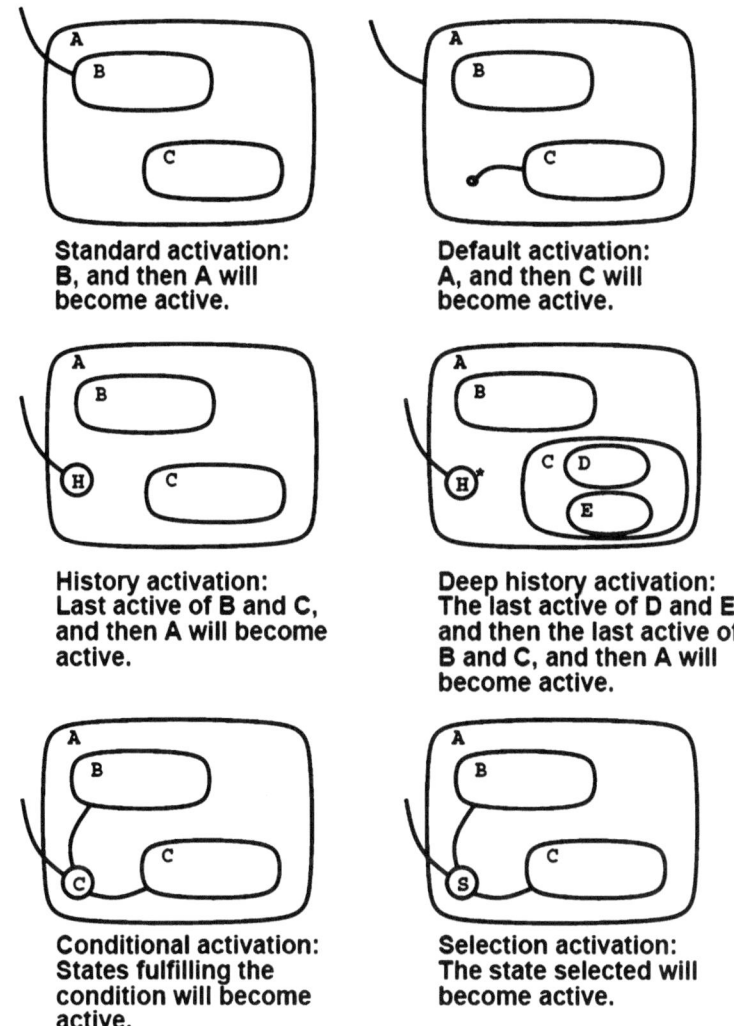

Fig. 3.11   Activation mechanisms in Statecharts

- Selection: When entering a selection in a state, the sub-state selected by the user will be activated.

  In addition support for the modelling of delays and time-outs is included.

  Figure 3.11 shows the semantics behind these concepts and various activating methods available.

  Statecharts are integrated with functional modelling (described below) in Harel et al. (1990). Later extensions of Statecharts for object-oriented modelling are found in Coleman et al. (1992), Harel and Gery (1996) and Rumbaugh et al. (1991), and Statecharts is also the basis for the state transitions diagrams in UML as described in Sect. 3.5.1 (Fig. 3.11).

Fig. 3.12 Modelling
control-flow in Petri nets

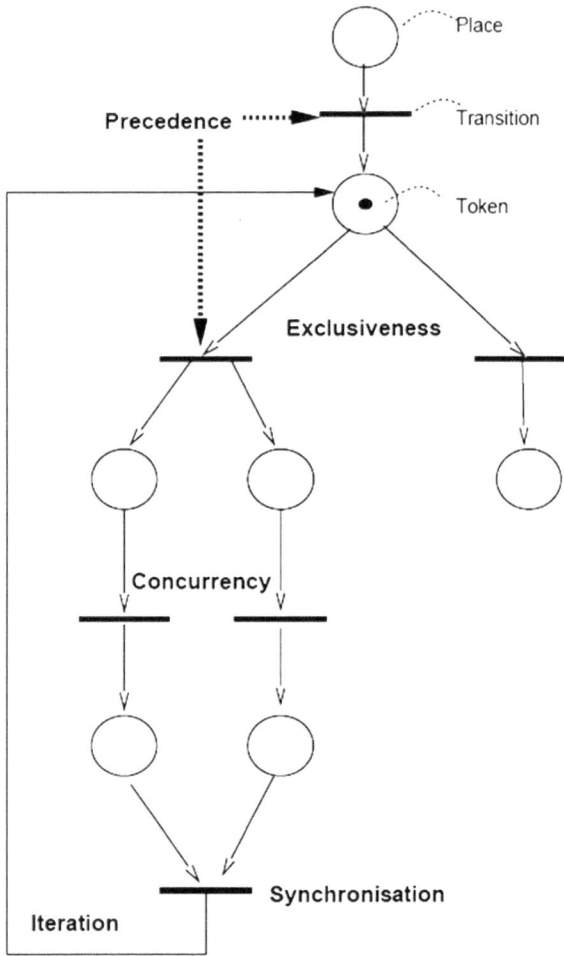

Petri nets (Petri 1962) are another well-known behaviourally oriented modelling language. A model in the original Petri net language is shown in Fig. 3.12. Here, *places* indicate a system state space, and a combination of *tokens* included in the places determines the specific system state. State transitions are regulated by firing rules: A transition is enabled if each of its input places contains a token. A transition can fire at any time after it is enabled. The transition takes zero time. After the firing of a transition, a token is removed from each of its input places and a token is produced in all output places.

Figure 3.12 shows how dynamic properties like precedence, concurrency, synchronisation, exclusiveness and iteration can be modelled in a Petri net.

The associated model patterns along with the firing rule above establish the execution semantics of a Petri net. A weakness in the traditional state-transition

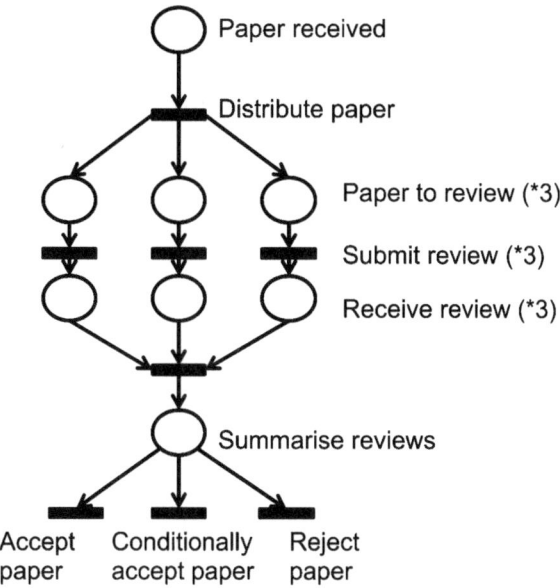

Fig. 3.13 Petri net modelling parallel paper reviews

depicted in Fig. 3.8 is that one do not represent that one will wait for all reviews to be submitted. Figure 3.13 below is part of a Petri net that models this.

The classical Petri net cannot be decomposed. This is inevitable by the fact that transitions are instantaneous, which makes it impossible to compose more complex networks (whose execution is bound to take time) into higher level transitions. However, there exists several dialects of the Petri net language (for instance (Marsan 1985)) where the transitions are allowed to take time, and these approaches provide decomposition in a way not very different from that of a data flow diagram (see next section). Timed Petri Nets (Marsan 1985) also provide probability distributions that can be assigned to the time consumption of each transition and is particularly suited to performance modelling.

Another type of behavioural modelling is based on System dynamics. Holistic systems thinking (Senge 1990) regards causal relations as mutual, circular and non-linear, hence the straightforward sequences in transformational process models is seen as an idealisation that hides important facts. This perspective is also reflected in mathematical models of interaction (Wegner and Goldin 1999). System dynamics have been utilised for analysis of complex relationships in cooperative work arrangements (Abdel-Hamid and Madnick 1989). A simple example is depicted in Fig. 3.14 It shows one aspect of the interdependencies between design and implementation in a system development project. The more time you spend designing, the less time you have for coding and testing, hence you better get the design right the first time. This creates a positive feedback loop similar to 'analysis paralysis' that must be balanced by some means, in our example iterative development.

System dynamic process models can be used for analysis and simulation, but not for deployment. Most importantly, system dynamics shows the complex

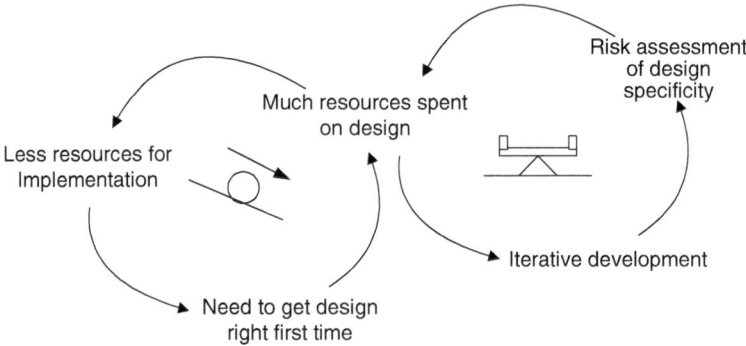

Fig. 3.14 A simple system dynamic model

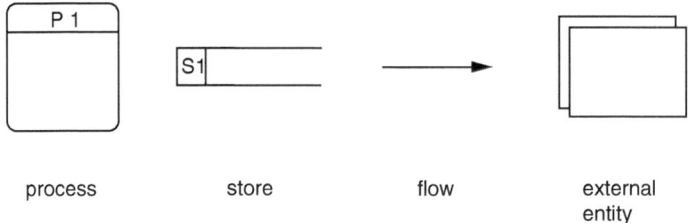

Fig. 3.15 Symbols in the DFD language

interdependencies that are so often ignored in conventional notations, illustrating the need for articulating more relations between tasks, beyond simple sequencing. A challenge with these models is that it can be difficult to find data for the parameters needed to run simulations.

3.3.3   The Functional Perspective

The main phenomena class in the functional perspective is the transformation: A transformation is defined as an activity, which based on a set of phenomena transforms them to another (possibly empty) set of phenomena. Other terms used for the main concept are function, process, activity and task.

The best known conceptual modelling language with a functional perspective is data flow diagrams (DFD) (Gane and Sarson 1979) which describes a situation using the symbols illustrated in Fig. 3.15:

- Process. Illustrates a part of a system that transforms a set of inputs to a set of outputs.
- Store. A collection of data or material.
- Flow. A movement of data or material within the system, from one system component (process, store or external entity) to another.
- External entity. An individual or organisational actor, or a technical actor that is outside the boundaries of the system to be modelled, which interact with the system.

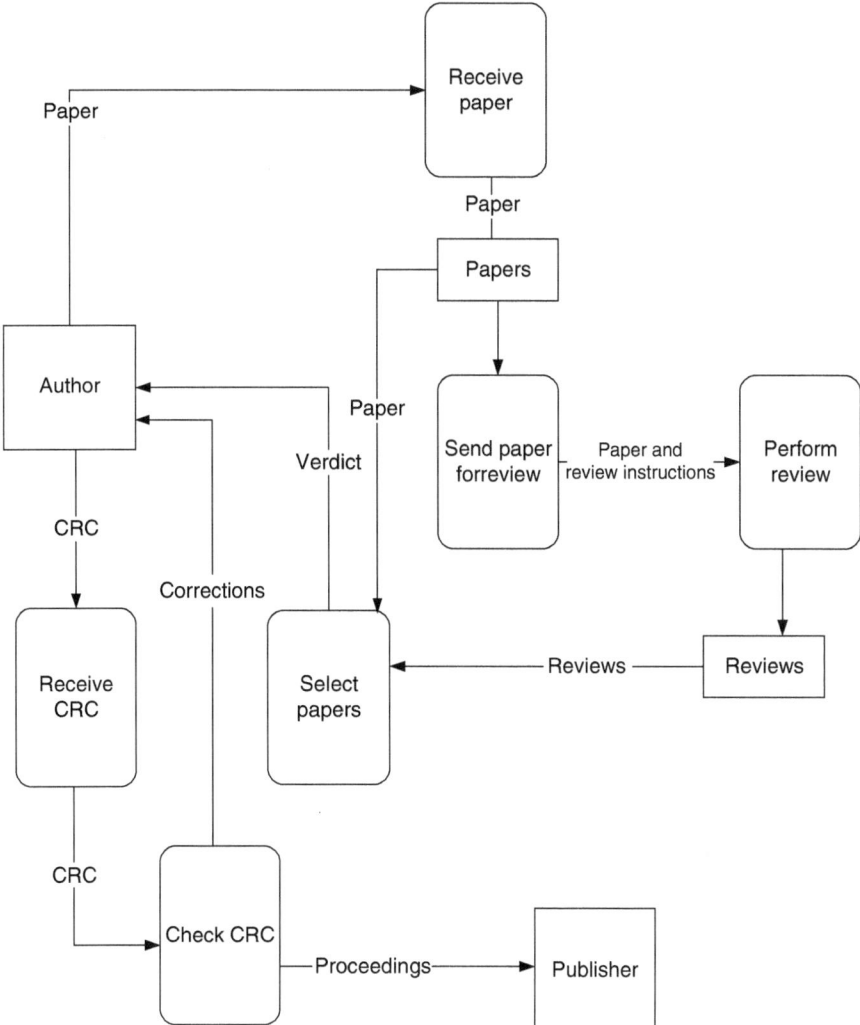

Fig. 3.16 DFD of paper submission and selection

With these symbols, a system can be represented as a network of processes, stores and external entities linked by flows. A process can be decomposed into a new DFD. When the description of the process is considered to have reached a detailed level where no further decomposition is needed, 'process logic' can be defined in forms of, e.g. structured English, decision tables and decision trees.

An example from the conference domain is provided in Fig. 3.16, where one depicts the main external actors and task relative to the review and evaluation of scientific papers at a conference (cf. Fig. 3.8).

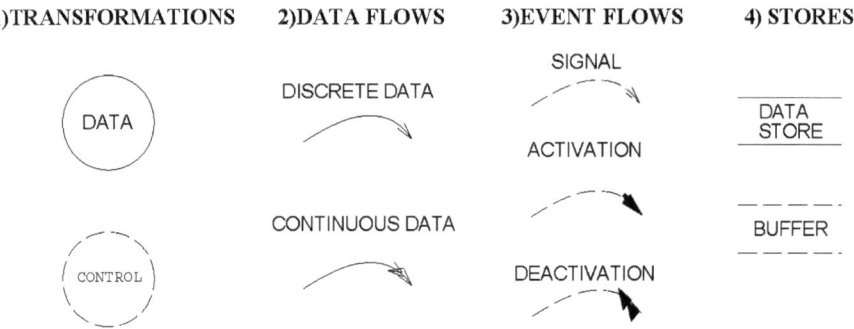

Fig. 3.17 Symbols in the transformation schema language

When a process is decomposed into a set of sub-processes, the sub-processes are grouped around the higher level process, and are co-operating to fulfil the higher-level function. This view on DFDs has resulted in the 'context diagram' that regards the whole system as a process which receives and sends all inputs and outputs to and from the system. A context diagram determines the boundary of a system. Every activity of the system is seen as the result of a stimulus by the arrival of a data flow across some boundary. If no external data flow arrives, then the system will remain in a stable state. Therefore, a DFD is basically able to model reactive systems.

DFD is a semi-formal language. Some of the short-comings of DFD regarding formality are addressed in the transformation schema presented by Ward (1986). The main symbols of his language are illustrated in Fig. 3.17

There are four main classes of symbols:

1. Transformations: A solid circle represents a data transformation, which is used approximately as a process in DFD. A dotted circle represents a control transformation that controls the behaviour of data transformations by activating or deactivating them, thus being an abstraction on some portion of the systems' control logic.

2. Data flows: A discrete data flow is associated with a set of variable values that is defined at discrete points in time. Continuous data flows are associated with a value or a set of values defined continuously over a time-interval.

3. Event flows: These report a happening or give a command at a discrete point in time. A signal shows the sender's intention to report that something has happened, and the absence of any knowledge on the sender's part of the use to which the signal is put. Activations show the sender's intention to cause a receiver to produce some output. A deactivation shows the sender's intention to prevent a receiver from producing some output.

4. Stores: A store acts as a repository for data that is subject to a storage delay. A buffer is a special kind of store in which flows produced by one or more transformations are subject to a delay before being consumed by one or more transformations. It is an abstraction of a stack or a queue.

Both process and flow decomposition are supported.

Table 3.1   A data flow diagram taxonomy of real-world dynamics

Phenomena class	Process	Flow	Store
Activity	Transformation	Transportation	Preservation
Aspect	Matter	Location	Time

Whereas Ward had a goal of formalising DFD's and adding more possibilities of representing control-flow, Opdahl and Sindre (1994, 1995) tried to adapt data flow diagrams to what they term 'real-world modelling'.

Problems they note with DFD in this respect are as follows:

- 'Flows' are semantically overloaded: Sometimes a flow means transportation, other times it merely connects the output of one process to the input of the next.
- Parallelism often has to be modelled by duplicating data on several flows. This is all right for data, but material cannot be duplicated in the same way January 2,
- Whereas processes can be decomposed to contain flows and stores in addition to sub-processes, decomposition of flows and stores is not allowed. This makes it hard to deal sensibly with flows at high levels of abstraction.

These problems have been addressed by unifying the traditional DFD vocabulary with a taxonomy of real-world activity, shown in Table 3.1: The three DFD phenomena 'process', 'flow', and 'store' correspond to the physical activities of 'transformation', 'transportation', and 'preservation' respectively. Furthermore, these three activities correspond to the three fundamental aspects of our perception of the physical world: matter, location and time. Hence, e.g. an ideal flow changes the location of items in zero time and without modifying them.

Since these ideal phenomena classes are too restricted for high level modelling, real phenomena classes are introduced. Real processes, flows and stores are actually one and the same, since they all can change all three physical aspects, i.e. these are fully inter-decomposable. The difference is only subjective, i.e. a real-world process is mainly perceived as a transformation activity, although it may also use time and move the items being processed. Additionally, the problem with the overloading of 'flow' is addressed by introducing a link, for cases where there is no transportation. Links go between ports located on various processes, stores and flows and may be associated with spatial coordinates. Opdahl and Sindre (1995) also provide some definitions relating to the items to be processed, including proper distinctions between data and material. Items have attributes that represent the properties of data and materials, and they belong to item classes. Furthermore, classes are related by the conventional abstraction relations aggregation, generalisation and association. Hence the specification of item classes constitute a static model that complements the dynamic models comprising processes, flows, stores and links.

The symbols in the language are shown in Fig. 3.18. The traditional DFD notation for processes and flows are retained, however, to facilitate the visualisation of decomposition, it is also possible to depict the flow as an enlarged kind of box-arrow. Similarly, to facilitate the illustration of decomposed stores, full rectangles instead of open-ended ones are used. Links are shown as dotted arrows.

Fig. 3.18 Symbols in the real-world modelling language

A number of the recent process modelling notations typically add control-flow aspects of the sort depicted in Fig. 3.12, i.e. can be said to somehow combine expressiveness from the transformational and behavioural perspectives. Some examples of this are ARIS EPC, UML Activity Diagrams, YAWL (ter Hofstede et al. 2010), and BPMN.

An Event-driven Process Chain (EPC) (Keller et al. 1992) is a graphical modelling language used for business process modelling. EPC was developed within the framework of Architecture of Integrated Information System (ARIS) (Scheer and Nüttgens 2000) to model business processes. The language is targeted to describe processes on the level of their business logic, not necessarily on the formal specification level. EPC are supported in tools such as ARIS and Microsoft Visio.

An event-driven process chain consists of the following elements: Functions; Event; Organisation unit; Information, material or resource object; Logical connectors; Logical relationships (i.e. Branch/Merge, Fork/Join, OR); Control flow; Information flow; Organisation unit assignment and Process path.

The strength of EPC lies on its easy-to-understand notation that is capable of portraying business information system while at the same time incorporating other important features such as functions, data, organisational structure and information resources. However the semantics of an event-driven process chain are not well-defined, and it is not possible to check the model for consistency and completeness. As demonstrated in van der Aalst (1999), these problems can be tackled by mapping EPC to Petri nets since Petri nets have formal semantics and a number of analysis techniques are provided. In addition, in order to support data and model interchange among heterogeneous BPM tools, an XML-based EPC–EPML (Event-driven Process Chain Markup Language) has been proposed by Mendling and Nüttgens (2006).

In 2004, the Business Process Modelling Notation (BPMN) was presented as the standard business process modelling notation (White 2004). Since then, BPMN has been evaluated in different ways by the academic community and has become widely supported industry.

There is a large number of implementation of BPMN . The tool support in industry has increased with the awareness of Business Process Management (BPM).

The Business Process Modelling Notation (BPMN version 1.0) was proposed adopted by OMG for ratification in February 2006. The current version is BPMN 2.0 (OMG 2011). BPMN is based on the revision of other notations and methodologies, especially UML Activity Diagram, UML EDOC Business Process, IDEF, ebXML BPSS, Activity-Decision Flow (ADF) Diagram, RosettaNet, LOVeM and Event-Process Chains.

The primary goal of BPMN is to provide a notation that is readily understandable by all business users, from the business analysts who create the initial draft of the processes, to the technical developers responsible for implementing the technology that will support the performance of those processes, and, finally to the business people who will manage and monitor those processes (White 2004).

Another factor that drove the development of BPMN is that, historically, business process models developed by business people have been technically separated from the process representations required by systems designed to implement and execute those processes. Thus, it was a need to manually translate the original process models to execution models. Such translations are subject to errors and make it difficult for the process owners to understand the evolution and the performance of the processes they have developed. To address this, a key goal in the development of BPMN was to create a bridge from notation to execution languages. BPMN models are thus designed to be activated through the mapping to BPEL.

BPMN allows the creation of end-to-end business processes and is designed to cover many types of modelling tasks constrained to business processes. The structuring elements of BPMN will allow the viewer to be able to differentiate between sections of a BPMN Diagram using groups, pools or lanes. Basic types of sub-models found within a BPMN model can be *private business processes* (internal), *abstract processes* (public) and *collaboration processes* (global).

- *Private business processes* are those internal to a specific organisation and are the types of processes that have been generally called workflow or BPM processes.
- *Abstract Processes* represents the interactions between a private business process and another process or participant. Abstract processes are contained within a Pool and can be modelled separately or within a larger BPMN Diagram to show the Message Flow between the abstract process activities and other entities.
- *Collaboration processes* depicts the interactions between two or more business entities. These interactions are defined as a sequence of activities that represent the message exchange patterns between the entities involved.

3.3.3.1 Language Constructs and Properties of BPMN

The Business Process Diagram (BPD) is the graphical representation of the BPMN. Its language constructs are grouped in four basic categories of elements: Flow Objects, Connecting Objects, Swimlanes and Artefacts. The notation is further divided into a core element set and an extended element set. The intention of the core element set is to support the requirements of simple notations and most business processes should be modelled adequately with the core set. The extended set provides additional graphical notations for the modelling of more complex processes.

The four basic categories of elements of BPMN are (White 2004):

- Flow Objects
- Connecting Objects
- Swimlanes
- Artefacts

Flow Objects

This category contains the three core elements used to create BPDs:

Event	There are three event-types: *Start, Intermediate* and *End* respectively, as shown in the figure to the right.	○ ◎ ⬤
Activity	Activities contain work that is performed, and can be either a *Task* (atomic) or a *Sub-Process* (non-atomic/compound).	▢
Gateway	Gateways are used for decision-making, forking and merging of paths.	◇

Connecting Objects

Connecting Objects are used to connect Flow Objects to each other:

Sequence Flow	This is used to show the order in which activities are performed in a Process.	──────▶
Message Flow	This represents a flow of messages between two Process Participants (business entities or business roles).	o─────▷
Association	Associations are used to associate data, text and other Artefacts with Flow Objects.	·········▷

Swimlanes

Swimlanes are used to group activities into separate categories for different functional capabilities or responsibilities (e.g. a role/participant):

Pool	A Pool represents a Participant in a Process, and partitions a set of activities from other Pools by acting as a graphical container.	Name
Lane	Pools can be divided into Lanes, which are used to organise and categorise activities	Name Name / Name

Artefacts (not illustrated) are data objects, groups and annotations. *Data Objects* are not considered as having any other effect on the process than information on resources required or produced by activities. The *Group* construct is a visual aid used for documentation or analysis purposes while the *Text Annotation* is used to add additional information about certain aspects of the model.

Figure 3.19 shows an example BPMN process summoning participants for a workshop. The workshop organiser sends out the invitations, which are received by the potential participants. The participants evaluate the relevance of the workshop and decide whether they will participate or not. Those who want to participate, sign up for the workshop by informing the organiser.

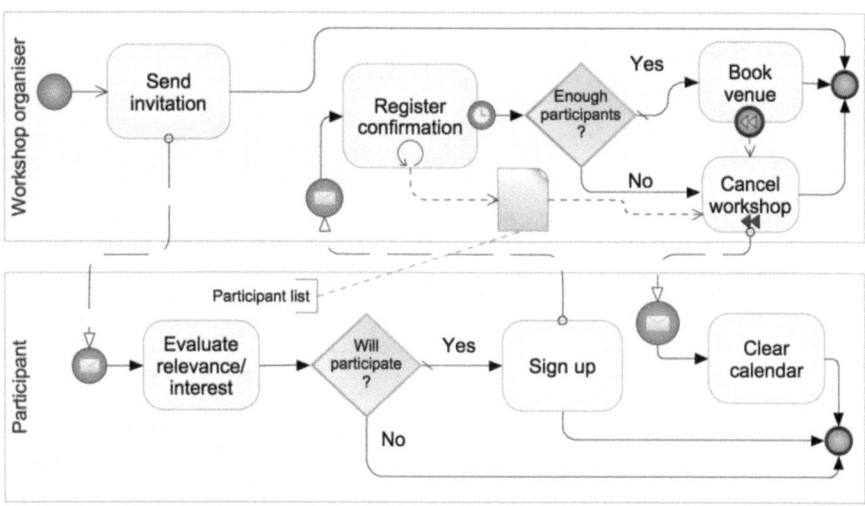

Fig. 3.19 BPMN model showing the summons for a workshop (From Aagesen and Krogstie 2010)

The organiser registers the confirmations from the participants until the deadline for registering, making a list of participants. When the deadline is reached (indicated by the timer event on the looping register confirmation activity), the organiser will see if there are enough participants to conduct the workshop. If there are too few participants, the organiser will inform those participants who signed up that the workshop is cancelled, and the registered participants will clear their calendar for the day. If there are sufficient participants registered for the workshop, the organiser will try to book a venue. If there is no venue available, the workshop will have to be cancelled by informing registered participants. This is shown using the compensation and undo activity.

3.3.4   The Structural Perspective

Approaches within the structural perspective concentrate on describing the static structure of a system. The main construct of such languages is the 'entity'. Other terms used for this phenomenon with some differences in semantics are object, concept, thing and phenomena. Objects as used in object-oriented approaches are discussed further under the description of the object-perspective in Sect. 3.3.6.

The structural perspective has traditionally been handled by languages for data modelling. Whereas the first data modelling language was published in 1974 (Hull and King 1987), the first having major impact was the entity-relationship language of (Chen 1976). The basic components of ER are:

- Entities. An entity is a phenomenon that can be distinctly identified. Entities can be classified into entity classes.

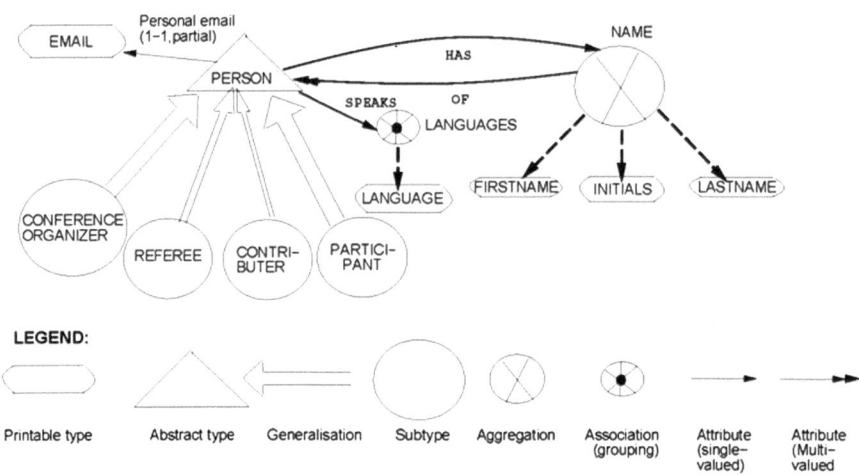

Fig. 3.20 Example of a GSM model

- Relationships. A relationship is an association between entities. Relationships can be classified into relationship classes which can be looked upon as an aggregation between the related entity-classes cf. Sect. 3.1
- Attributes and data values. A value is used to give value to a property of an entity or relationship. Values are grouped into value classes by their types. An attribute is a function which maps from an entity class or relationship class to a value class; thus the property of an entity or a relationship can be expressed by an attribute-value pair

An ER-model contains a set of entity classes, relationship classes and attributes. An example of a simple ER-model was given in Fig. 1.1.

Several extensions have later been proposed for so-called semantic data modelling languages (Hull and King 1987; Peckham and Maryanski 1988) with specific focus on the addition of mechanisms for hierarchical abstraction. In Hull and King's overview a generic semantic modelling language (GSM) is presented. Figure 3.20 illustrates the vocabulary of GSM:

- Primitive types. The data types in GSM are classified into two kinds: the printable data types, that are used to specify some visible values, and the abstract types that represent some entities. In the example, the following printable types can be identified: *Email address, language, firstname, initials* and *lastname*.
- Constructed types built by means of abstraction. The most often used constructors for building abstractions (as discussed in Sect. 3.1.1) are generalisation, aggregation and association. In the example we find Person as an abstract type, with specialisations conference organiser, referee, contributor and participant. Name is an aggregation of firstname, initials and lastname, whereas languages is an association of a set of language
- Attributes

In addition it is possible to specify derived classes in GSM.

Relationships between instances of types may be defined in different ways. We see in Fig. 3.20 that a relationship in GSM is defined by a two-way attribute (an attribute and its inverse). In the ER modelling language, a relationship is represented as an explicit type. The definition of relationship types provides the possibility of specifying such relationships among the instances of more than two types (n-ary relationship classes) as well as that of defining attributes of such relationship types.

Many other approaches have been developed over the years: The NIAM language (Nijssen and Halpin 1989) is a binary relationship language, which means that relationships that involve three or more entities are not allowed. Relationships with more than two involved parts will thus have to be objectified (i.e. modelled as entity sets instead). In other respects, the NIAM language has many similarities with ER, although often being classified as a form of object-role modelling. The distinction between entities and printable values is reflected in NIAM through the concepts of lexical and non-lexical object types, where the former denote printable values and the latter abstract entities. Aggregation is provided by the relationship construct just like in ER, but NIAM also provides generalisation through the sub-object-type construct. The diagrammatic notation is rather different from ER, and we describe a successor of NIAM, ORM in more detail to illustrate this. ORM (Object Role Modelling) is arguably one of the most expressive languages of this type. ORM includes graphical and textual notations for specifying structural models, as well as procedures for creating, transforming, mapping and querying structural models.

For space considerations, we limit our attention to the ORM 2 notation (Halpin 2007), as supported by the NORMA tool. Figure 3.21 presents the main graphical symbols, numbered for easy reference, which are now briefly explained.

An *entity type* (e.g. Person) is depicted as a named, soft rectangle (symbol 1). As a configuration option, the soft rectangle may be replaced by an ellipse (symbol 2), which was commonly used in earlier versions of ORM, or a hard rectangle (symbol 3). A *value type* (e.g. PersonName) is a lexical object type (instances are typically character strings or numbers) and is shown as a named, dotted soft rectangle (symbol 4). Each entity type has a *reference scheme*, indicating how each instance of the entity type may be mapped via predicates to a combination of one or more values.

A simple injective (1:1 into) reference scheme maps entities to single values. For example, countries may be identified by country codes (e.g. 'NO'). In such cases the reference scheme may be abbreviated as in symbol 5 by displaying the *reference mode* in parentheses, e.g. Country (.code). The reference mode indicates how values relate to the entities. Values are constants with a known denotation, so require no reference scheme.

Typically each entity type has a *preferred* reference scheme. Relationships used for preferred reference are called *existential facts* (e.g. there exists a country that has the country code 'NO'). The other relationships are *elementary facts* (e.g. The country with country code 'NO' has a population of 5,000,000). In symbol 6, an exclamation mark declares that an object type is *independent*. This means that instances of that type may exist without participating in any elementary facts. By default, this is not so.

A fact type results from applying a logical *predicate* a sequence of one or more object types. Each predicate comprises a named sequence of one or more *roles*

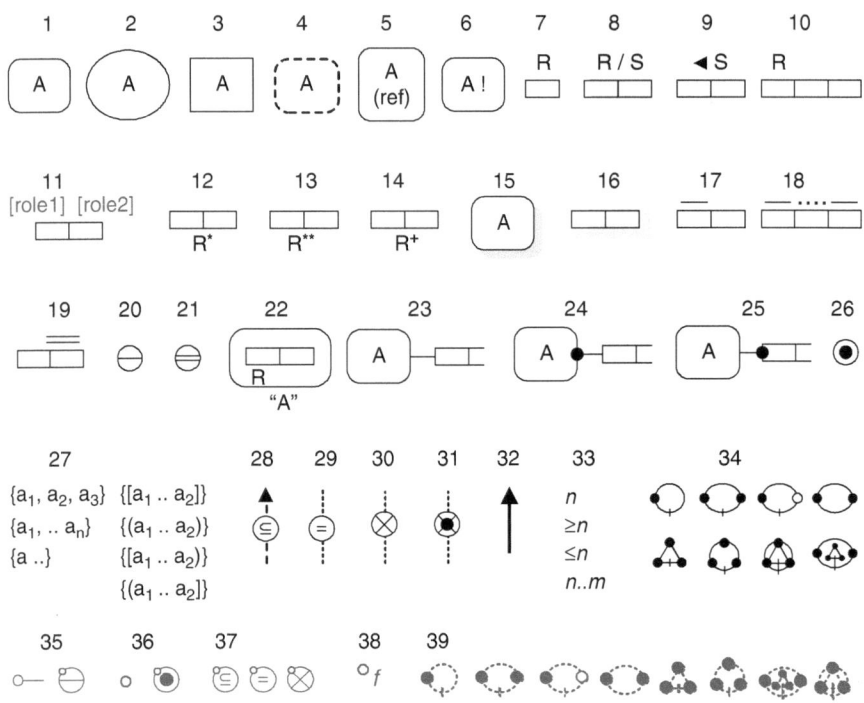

Fig. 3.21 ORM graphic symbols (From Halpin 2007)

(parts played in the relationship). A predicate is basically a sentence with object roles in it, one for each role, which each role depicted as a box and played by exactly one object type. Symbol 7 shows a unary predicate (e.g. … smokes), symbols 8 and 9 depict binary predicates (e.g. … was born in …), and symbol 10 shows a ternary predicate. Predicates of higher *arity* (number of roles) are allowed. Each predicate has at least one *predicate reading*. ORM uses *mixfix* predicates, so objects may be placed at any position in the predicate (e.g. the fact type Person introduced Person to Person uses the predicate '… introduced … to …'). Mixfix predicates allow natural verbalisation of n-ary relationships, as well as non-infix binary relationships (e.g. in Japanese, verbs are at the end).

Forward readings traverse the predicate from left to right (if displayed horizontally) or top to bottom (if displayed vertically). Inverse readings reverse the reading direction, as indicated by a reverse arrow-tip (symbol 9). For binaries, forward and inverse readings may be separated by a slash (symbol 8). Optionally, forward arrow tips may be used for forward readings. Optionally, roles may be given *role names*, displayed in square brackets (symbol 11). An asterisk after a predicate reading indicates that the fact type is *derived* from other fact types (symbol 12). If the fact type is both derived and stored, a double asterisk is used (symbol 13). Fact types that are only partly derived are marked '+' (symbol 14). Object types and predicates displayed in multiple places are shadowed (symbols 15, 16).

Internal uniqueness constraints are depicted as bars over one or more roles in a predicate to declare that instances for that role (combination) in the fact type population must be unique (e.g. symbols 17, 18). For example, adding a uniqueness constraint over the first role of Person was born in Country declares that each person was born in at most one country. If the constrained roles are not contiguous, a dotted line separates the parts of the uniqueness bar that do constrain roles (symbol 18). A predicate may have one or more uniqueness constraints, at most one of which may be declared preferred by using a double-bar (symbol 19).

An *external uniqueness constraint* shown as a circled uniqueness bar (symbol 20) may be applied to two or more roles from different predicates by connecting to them with dotted lines. This indicates that instances of the combination of those roles in the join of those predicates are unique. For example, if a state is identified by combining its state code and country, we add an external uniqueness constraint to the roles played by Statecode and Country in: State has Statecode; State is in Country. To declare an external uniqueness constraint preferred, a circled double-bar is used (symbol 21).

If we want to talk about a relationship, we may *objectify* it (make an object out of it) so that it can play roles. Graphically, the objectified predicate (a.k.a. *nested predicate*) is enclosed in a soft rectangle, with its name in quotes (symbol 22). Roles are connected to their players by a line segment (symbol 23). A *mandatory role constraint* declares that every instance in the population of the role's object type must play that role. This is shown as a large dot placed either at the object type end (symbol 24) or the role end (symbol 25). An *inclusive-or (disjunctive mandatory)* constraint may be applied to two or more roles to indicate that all instances of the object type population must play at least one of those roles. This is shown by connecting the roles by dotted lines to a circled dot (symbol 26).

To restrict the population of an object type or role, the relevant values may be listed in braces connected by a dotted line to the object type or role (symbol 27). For ordered values, a range is declared using '…' between the first and last values. For continuous ranges, a square or round bracket indicates the end value is respectively included or excluded. For example, '(0…10]' denotes a range of positive (hence excluding 0) real numbers up to and including 10. These constraints are called *value constraints*.

Symbols 28–30 denote *set comparison constraints*, which apply only between compatible role sequences (i.e. sequences of one or more roles, where the corresponding roles have the same host object type). A dotted arrow with a circled subset symbol from one role sequence to another depicts a *subset constraint*, restricting the population of the first sequence to be a subset of the second (symbol 28). A dotted line with a circled '=' symbol depicts an *equality constraint*, indicating the populations must be equal (symbol 29). A circled 'X' (symbol 30) depicts an *exclusion constraint*, indicating the populations are mutually exclusive. Exclusion and equality constraints may be applied between two or more sequences. Combining an inclusive-or constraint with an exclusion constraint yields an *exclusive-or constraint* (symbol 31).

A solid arrow (symbol 32) from one object type to another indicates that the first object type is a (proper) *subtype* of the other. For example, Woman is a subtype of

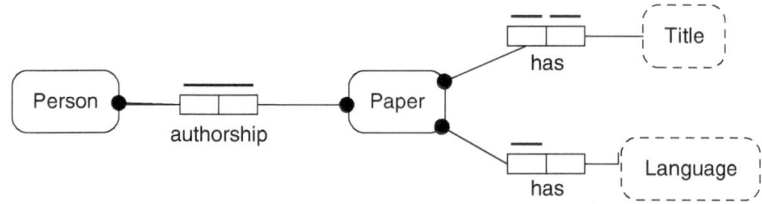

Fig. 3.22 A simple ORM-model

Person. Mandatory (circled dot) and exclusion (circled 'X') constraints may also be displayed between subtypes, but are implied by other constraints if the subtypes are given formal definitions.

Symbol 33 shows four kinds of *frequency constraint*. Applied to a sequence of one or more roles, these indicate that instances that play those roles must do so *exactly n* times, *at least n and at most m* times, *at most n* times, or *at least n* times.

Symbol 34 shows eight kinds of *ring constraint* that may be applied to a pair of roles played by the same host type. Read left to right and top row first, these indicate that the binary relation formed by the role population must respectively be irreflexive, asymmetric, antisymmetric, reflexive, intransitive, acyclic, intransitive and acyclic or intransitive and asymmetric.

All the constraints so far considered are *alethic* (necessary, so cannot be violated) and are coloured violet. ORM 2 also supports *deontic* versions (obligatory, but can be violated) of these constraints. These are coloured blue, and either add an 'o' for obligatory, or soften lines to dashed lines. Displayed here are the deontic symbols for uniqueness (symbol 35), mandatory (symbol 36), set-comparison (symbol 37), frequency (symbol 38) and ring (symbol 39) constraints.

You very seldom need all the above aspects. A simple model, expressing the same as Fig. 1.1 and Fig. 3.20 is found in Fig. 3.22 below.

Another type of structural modelling languages also used a lot in the AI-world is semantic networks (Sølvberg and Kung 1993). A semantic network is a graph where the nodes are objects, situations or lower level semantic networks, and the edges are binary relations between the nodes. Semantic networks constitute a large family of languages with very diverse expressive power, but often including the standard hierarchical abstraction mechanisms cf. Sect. 3.1.2. In connection to this, we can also mention Sowa's conceptual graphs (Sowa 1983).

3.3.5 The Goal and Rule Perspective

Goal-oriented modelling focuses on goals and rules. A *rule* is something that influences the actions of a set of actors. A rule is either a rule of necessity or a deontic rule (Wieringa 1989). A rule of necessity (alethic rule) is a rule that must always be satisfied. A deontic rule is a rule which is only socially agreed among a set of persons and organisations. A deontic rule can thus be violated without redefining the terms in the rule. We found this differentiation between deontic and alethic rules also in ORM above (Halpin 2007). A deontic rule can be classified as being an obligation, a recommendation, permission, a discouragement or a prohibition (Krogstie and Sindre 1996).

The general structure of a rule is

if condition then expression

where *condition* is descriptive, indicating the scope of the rule by designating the conditions in which the rule apply, and the *expression* is prescriptive. According to (Twining and Miers 1982) any rule, however expressed, can be analysed and restated as a compound conditional statement of this form.

Representing knowledge by means of rules is an old idea. According to Davis and King (1977), production systems were first proposed as a general computational mechanism by Post in 1943. Today, goals and rules are used for knowledge representation in a wide variety of applications.

Several advantages have been experienced with a declarative, rule-based approach to information systems modelling (Krogstie and Sindre 1996):

- Problem-orientation. The representation of business rules declaratively is independent of what they are used for and how they will be implemented. With an explicit specification of assumptions, rules and constraints, the analyst has freedom from technical considerations to reason about application problems. This freedom is even more important for the communication with the stakeholders with a non-technical background.
- Evolution: A declarative approach makes possible a one place representation of the rules, which is a great advantage when it comes to the maintainability of the specification and system.
- Knowledge enhancement: The rules used in an organisation, and as such in a supporting computerised information system (CIS), are not always explicitly given. In the words of Stamper (1987) 'Every organisation, in as far as it is organised, acts as though its members were confronting to a set of rules only a *few of which may be explicit*'. This has inspired certain researchers to look upon CIS specification as a process of rule reconstruction, i.e. the goal is not only to represent and support rules that are already known, but also to uncover de facto and implicit rules which are not yet part of a shared organisational reality, in addition to the construction of new, possibly more appropriate ones.

On the other hand, several problems have been observed when using a simple rule-format.

- Every statement must be either true or false, there is nothing in between.
- It traditional rule-based approaches it is not possible to distinguish between rules of necessity and deontic rules
- In many goal and rule modelling languages, it is not possible to specify for whom the rules apply.
- Formal rule languages have the advantage of eliminating ambiguity. However, this does not mean that rule-based models are easy to understand. There are two problems with the comprehension of such models, both the comprehension of single rules, and the comprehension of the whole rule base. Whereas the traditional

operational models (e.g. process models) have decomposition and modularisation facilities that make it possible to view a system at various levels of abstraction and to navigate in a hierarchical structure, rule models are usually flat. With many rules, such a model soon becomes difficult to grasp, even if each rule should be understandable in itself. They are also seldom linked to other models of the organisation used to understand and develop the information systems, such as structural, functional and behavioural models.

- A general problem is that a set of rules is either consistent or inconsistent. On the other hand, human organisations may often have contradictory rules, and have to be able to deal with this.

An early example of rule-based systems was the so-called expert-systems, which received great interest in the 1980s (Parsaye and Chignell 1988). Unfortunately, these systems did not scale sufficiently well for large-scale general industrial applications. Lately, these approaches has reappeared under the term rule-based systems and are in fact now able to deal with the processing of large databases (e.g. experiences with tools like Blaze Advisor, which is an extension of the Nexpert Object system that goes back to the late 1980s have shown this. See http:// www.brcommunity.org for an overview of current industrial solutions on this marked). Although being an improvement as for efficiency, they still have limited internal structuring among rules, and few explicit links to the other models underlying large industrial information systems. They seldom differentiate between deontic rules and rules of necessity, although this might be changing after the development of the OMG SVBR-standard that includes deontic operators (OMG 2006b). On the other hand, since the way of representing deontic notions in SVBR is not executable, it is possible that theses aspects will be ignored by vendors of rule-based solutions such as Blaze Advisor since these largely focus on the execution of formal rules, and not the representation of more high-level strategic and tactical aspects of the organisation.

On the other hand, high-level rules *are* the focus on application of goal-oriented modelling in the field of requirements specification. Over the last 15 years, a large number of these approaches have been developed, as summarised in Kavakli and Loucopoulos (2005). They focus on different parts of requirements specification work, including:

- Understanding the current organisational situation
- Understanding the need for change
- Providing the deliberation context of the RE process
- Relating business goals to functional and non-functional system components
- Validating system specifications against stakeholder goals

An area which combines structural entities and rules is so-called ontologies, appearing from people both in the data modelling and AI world. There is a great deal of debate about what an ontology is and is not, although the standard definition is an 'explicit specification of a conceptualisation' (Gruber 1995). We will not pursue this here. Instead we look at a number of concepts related to ontology, and try to build an understanding from considering the related terms, associated problems and technologies.

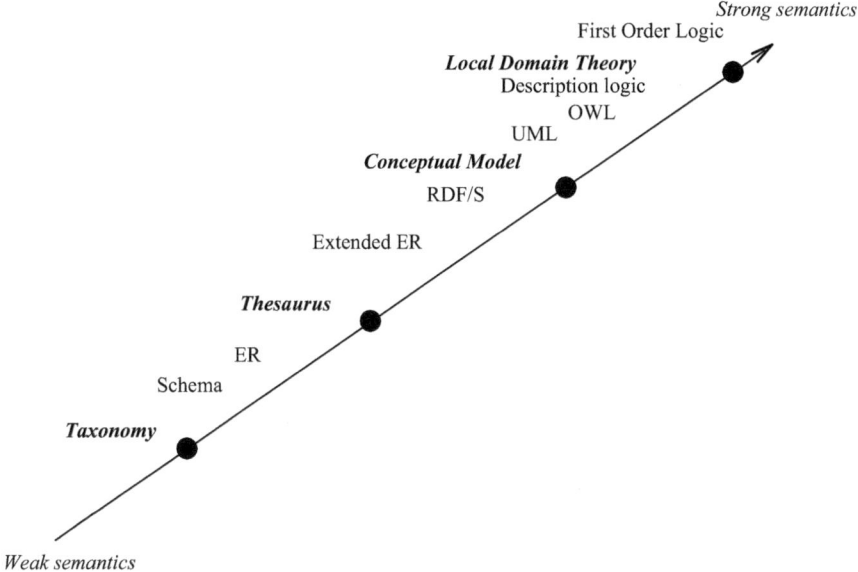

Fig. 3.23   The ontology spectrum

A good starting point is to consider Fig. 3.23, adopted from Daconta et al. (2003), which places a number of structurally oriented models on a scale relative to expressiveness. This is shown on the right of the arrow with some typical expressions that have some sort of defined semantics for the particular model. It is also important to note that all of the terms on the left hand side have been called 'ontology' by at least some authors, which is part of the source for confusion about the word.

Representational models on the various points along the ontology spectrum have different uses (McGuinnes 2003). In the simplest case, a group of users can agree to use a controlled vocabulary for their domain. This of course does not guarantee that they will use the terms in the same way all the time, but if all the users including database designers chose their terms from an accepted set, then the chances of mutual understanding are enhanced.

Perhaps the most publicly visible use for simple ontologies is the taxonomies used for site organisation on the World Wide Web.

Structured ontologies provide more sophisticated usage scenarios. For instance, they can provide simple consistency and completeness checks. If all *products* must have a *price*, then websites can automatically be checked for missing or conflicting information. Such ontologies can also provide completion where partially specified information can be expanded automatically by reference to the terms in the ontology. This expanded information could also be used for refining search, for instance.

Ontologies can also be used to facilitate interoperability, in the first instance, by aligning different terms that might be used in different applications. For example an ontology in one application might include a definition that a NTNUEmployee is a

Person whose employer property is filled with the individual NTNU. If another application does not understand NTNUEmployee or employee but does understand Person, employer and NTNU, then it is possible to make the two applications talk to each other if the second application can intelligently interpret the ontology of the first (McGuinnes 2003).

The ontologies on the most formal end of the spectrum are often taken as the default interpretation in the context of the semantic web, where ontologies provide the conceptual underpinning for '… making the semantics of metadata machine interpretable' (Staab and Studer 2004).

For the semantics of a domain model to be machine interpretable in any interesting way, it must be in a format that allows automated reasoning in a flexible way. Obviously, taxonomies can specify very little in this sense. Database schemas are more powerful, but they limit the interpretation to a single model, that is interpreted by the database designer. The only automated reasoning that can be performed is what is allowed by the relational model, and the semantics can only be understood through complex inferences supplied by the database designer, or any other human that deals with the model. Formal logic based ontologies provide multiple possible models that are specified in a way that allows machine based inferences, but still limits the set of formal models to the set of intended meanings. They are at the same time more formally constrained and more semantically flexible than database schemas. Ontologies based on different logical models can support different kinds of inference, but a minimal set of services should include reasoning about class membership, class equivalence, consistency and classification (Antoniou and van Harmelen 2004).

The representational language adopted by the Web Ontology Working Group of the W3C for ontologies is the Web Ontology Language (OWL). OWL is a response to a number of requirements (OWL 2004) including the need for a language with formal semantics that enables automated reasoning, and to address the previously discussed, inherent limitations of other representation forms on the web.

According to the original design goal, OWL was to be a straightforward extension of RDF/S, guaranteeing downward compatibility such that an OWL aware processor could also understand RDF/S documents without modification. Unfortunately this did not turn out to be the case because the generality of some RDF/S elements (e.g. the semantics of *class* as '*the class of all classes*') does not make RDF/S expressions tractable in the general case. In order to maintain computational tractability, OWL processors include restrictions that prevent the interpretation of some RDF/S expressions. OWL comes in three flavours: OWL Full, OWL DL and OWL Lite. OWL Full is upward and downward compatible with RDF, whereas OWL DL and OWL Lite are not. In each sub language, however, some constructors are specialisations of their RDF counterparts

The three sub languages of OWL describe the expressiveness of the languages, keeping in mind a fundamental trade-off between expressiveness and efficiency of reasoning. OWL Full already has constructs that make the language undecidable. Developers should therefore only use OWL Full if the other two sub languages are inadequate for modelling the relevant domain. Similarly, OWL DL should be used if OWL Lite is not sufficient. The layering of the OWL sub languages can be summarised as follows (Grigoris and van Harmelen 2004):

- Every legal OWL Lite ontology is a legal OWL DL ontology.
- Every legal OWL DL ontology is a legal OWL Full ontology.
- Every valid OWL Lite conclusion is a valid OWL DL conclusion.
- Every valid OWL DL conclusion is a valid OWL Full conclusion.

Apart from the computational properties inherent with various levels of expressiveness, the layering of OWL also has certain advantages for software applications intended for use with ontologies.

The following quote from the OWL language guide provides a brief description of the capabilities of the three sublanguages (OWL 2004).

The OWL language provides three increasingly expressive sublanguages designed for use by specific communities of implementers and users.

- *OWL Lite* supports those users primarily needing a classification hierarchy and simple constraint features. For example, while OWL Lite supports cardinality constraints, it only permits cardinality values of 0 or 1.
- *OWL DL* supports those users who want the maximum expressiveness without losing computational completeness (all entailments are guaranteed to be computed) and decidability (all computations will finish in finite time) of reasoning systems. OWL DL includes all OWL language constructs with restrictions such as type separation (a class cannot also be an individual or property, a property cannot also be an individual or class). OWL DL is so named due to its correspondence with *description logics* a field of research that has studied a particular decidable fragment of first order logic. OWL DL was designed to support the existing Description Logic business segment and has desirable computational properties for reasoning systems.
- *OWL Full* is meant for users who want maximum expressiveness with no computational guarantees. For example, in OWL Full a class can be treated simultaneously as a collection of individuals and as an individual in its own right. OWL Full allows an ontology to augment the meaning of the pre-defined vocabulary. It is unlikely that any reasoning software will be able to support every feature of OWL Full.

Details of the syntax and semantics can be obtained from the technical documentation web site of the W3C, http://www.w3.org/TR/

Some approaches also link rules to other models, but with limited support of following up these links in the running system. An early example of such an approach was Tempora (Loucopoulos et al. 1991) which was an ESPRIT-3 project that finished in 1994. It aimed at creating an environment for the development of complex application systems. The underlying idea was that development of a CIS should be viewed as the task of developing the rule-base of an organisation, which is used throughout development and into maintenance.

Tempora had three closely interrelated languages for conceptual modelling. ERT (McBrien et al. 1992), being an extension of the ER language, PID (Gulla et al.. 1991), being an extension of the DFD in the SA/RT-tradition, and ERL (McBrien et al. 1991), a formal language for expressing the rules of an organisation. These are briefly described below.

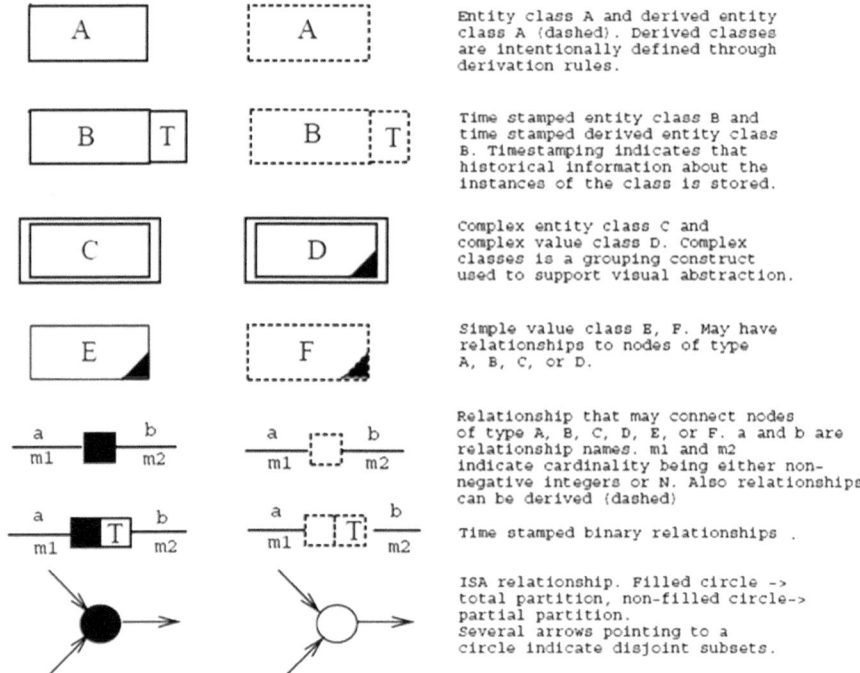

Fig. 3.24 Symbols in the ERT languages

The ERT Language. The basic modelling constructs of ERT are entity classes, relationship classes and value classes. The language also contains the most usual constructs from semantic data modelling such as generalisation and aggregation, and derived entities and relationships, as well as some extensions for temporal aspects particular for ERT. It also has a grouping mechanism to enhance the visual abstraction possibilities of ERT models. The graphical symbols of ERT are shown in Fig. 3.24.

The PID Language. This language is used to specify processes and their interaction in a formal way. The basic modelling constructs are processes, ERT-views being links to an ERT-model, external agents, flows (both control and data flows), ports and timers, acting as either clocks or delays. The graphical symbols of PID's are shown in Fig. 3.25.

The External Rule Language (ERL). The ERL is based on first-order temporal logic, with the addition of syntax for querying the ERT model. The general structure of an ERL rule is as follows:

when *trigger* if *condition*, then *consequence* else *consequence*.

- *trigger* is optional. It refers to a state change, i.e. the rule will only be enabled in cases where the trigger part becomes true, after having been previously false. The trigger is expressed in a limited form of first order temporal logic.

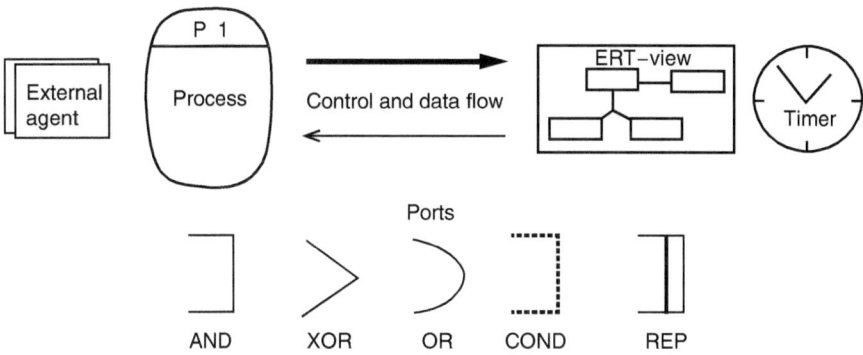

Fig. 3.25 Symbols in the PID language

- *condition* is an optional condition in first order temporal logic.
- *consequence* is an action or state that should hold given the trigger and condition. The consequence is expressed in a limited form of first order temporal logic. The 'else' clause indicates the consequence when the condition is not true, given the same trigger.

ERL-rules have both declarative and procedural semantics. To give procedural semantics to an ERL-rule, it must be categorised as being a constraint, a derivation rule or an action rule. In addition, it is possible to define predicates to simplify complex rules by splitting them up into several rules.

The rule can be expressed on several levels of details ranging from a natural language form to rules that can be executed.

- Constraints express conditions on the ERT model that must not be violated.
- Derivation rules express how data can be automatically derived from data that already exist.
- Action rules express which actions to perform under what conditions. Action rules are typically linked to atomic processes in the process model giving the execution semantics for the processes as illustrated in Fig. 3.26. A detailed treatment of the relationship between processed and rules is given in (McBrien and Seltveit 1995).

The main extension in ERL compared to earlier rule-languages was the temporal expressiveness. At any time during execution, the temporal database will have stored facts not only about the present time, but also about the past and the future. This is viewed as a sequence of databases, each associated with some tick, and one may query any of these databases. ERL rules are always evaluated with respect to the database that corresponds to the real time the query is posed.

In addition to linking PID to ERT-models and ERL-rules to ERT-models and PIDs, one have the possibility of relating rules in rule hierarchies. The relationships available for this in Tempora were (Seltveit 1993; Sindre 1990):

- Refers to: Used to link rules where definitions or the introduction of a necessary situation can be found in another rule.
- Necessitates and motivates: Used to create goal hierarchies.

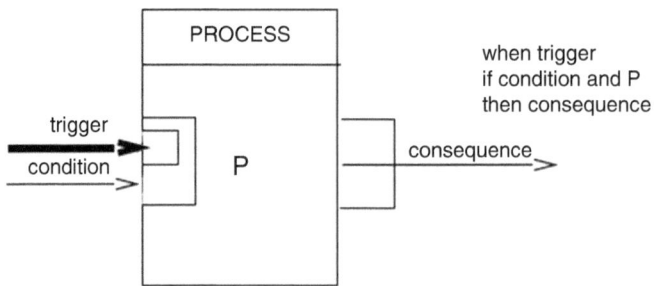

Fig. 3.26 Relationship between the PID and ERL languages (From Krogstie et al. 1991)

- Overrules and suspends: These relationships deal with exceptions. If an action is over-ruled by another rule, then it will not be performed at all, whereas an action that is suspended, can be performed when the condition of the suspending rule no longer holds. With these two relations, exceptions can be stated separately and then be connected to the rules they apply to. This provides a facility for hiding details, while obtaining the necessary exceptional behaviour when it is needed.

Tempora is one of many goal-oriented approaches that have appeared in the nineties and after the millennium; other such approaches are described below. In the ABC method developed by SISU (Willars 1988) a goal-model is supported, where goals can be said to obstruct, contribute to or imply other goals. A similar model is part of the F3 modelling languages (Bubenko et al. 1994), which were taken further in EKD briefly described in Sect. 2.3.5. Other examples of goal-oriented requirement approaches are reported by Feather (1993) where the possible relations between goals and policies are Supports, Impedes and Augments. Goals can also be sub-goals i.e. decompositions of other goals. Sutcliffe and Maiden (1993) and Mylopoulos et al. (1992) who use a rule-hierarchy for the representation of non-functional requirements are other examples.

Sutcliffe and Maiden (1993) differentiate between six classes of goals:
- Positive state goals: Indicate states that must be achieved.
- Negative state goals: Express a state to be avoided.
- Alternative state goal: The choice of which state applies depends on input during run-time.
- Exception repair goal: In these cases nothing can be done about the state an object achieves, even if it is unsatisfactory and therefore must be corrected in some way.
- Feedback goals: These are associated with a desired state and a range of exceptions that can be tolerated.
- Mixed state goals: A mixture of several of the above.

For each goal-type there is defined heuristics to help refine the different goal-types. Most parent nodes in the hierarchy will have 'and' relations with the child nodes, as two or more sub-goals will support the achievement of a higher level goal, however there may be occasions when 'or' relations are required for alternatives. Goals are divided into policies, functional goals and domain goals. The policy level describes statements of what should be done. The functionally level has linguistic expressions containing some information about how the policy might be achieved. Further relationship types may be added to show goal conflicts, such as 'inhibits', 'promotes' and 'enables' to create an argumentation structure. On the domain level templates are used to encourage addition of facts linking the functional view of aims and purpose to a model in terms of objects, agents and processes.

Chung (1993) and Mylopoulos et al. (1992) describes a similar language for representing non-functional requirements, e.g. requirements for efficiency, integrity, reliability, usability, maintainability and portability of a CIS. The framework consists of five major components:

1. A set of goals for representing non-functional requirements, design decisions and arguments in support of or against other goals.
2. A set of link types for relating goals and goal relationships.
3. A set of generic methods for refining goals into other goals.
4. A collection of correlation rules for inferring potential interaction among goals.
5. A labelling procedure that determines the degree to which any given non-functional requirement is being addressed by a set of design decisions.

Goals are organised into a graph-structure in the spirit of and/or-trees, where goals are stated in the nodes. The goal structure represents design steps, alternatives and decisions with respect to non-functional requirements. Goals are of three classes:

- Non-functional requirements goals: This includes requirements for accuracy, security, development, operating and hardware costs and performance.
- Satisficing goals: Design decisions that might be adopted in order to satisfice one or more non-functional requirement goal.
- Arguments: Represent formally or informally stated evidence or counter-evidence for other goals or goal-refinements.

Nodes are labelled as undetermined (U), satisficed (S) and denied (D). The following link types are supported describing how the satisficing of the offspring or failure thereof relates to the satisficing of the parent goal:

- sub: The satisficing of the offspring contributes to the satisficing of the parent.
- sup: The satisficing of the offspring is a sufficient evidence for the satisficing of the parent.
- -sub: The satisficing of the offspring contributes to the denial of the parent
- -sup: The satisficing of the offspring is a sufficient evidence for the denial of the parent.
- und: There is a link between the goal and the offspring, but the effect is as yet undetermined.

Links can relate goals, but also links between links and arguments are possible. Links can be induced by a method or by a correlation rule (see below). Goals may be refined by the modeller, who is then responsible for satisficing not only the goal's offspring, but also the refinement itself represented as a link. Alternatively, the framework provides goal refinement methods that represent generic procedures for refining a goal into one or more offspring. These are of different kinds: Goal decomposition methods, goal satisficing methods and argumentation methods.

As indicated above, the non-functional requirements set down for a particular system may be contradictory. Guidance is needed in discovering such implicit relationship and in selecting the satisficing goals that best meet the need of the non-functional goals. This is achieved either through external input by the designer or through generic correlation rules. When describing multi-perspective language in Sect. 3.5 we will provide some examples of such mechanisms, using the goal-oriented aspects of the EEML language. Newer approaches to goal-based engineering are also treated in van Lamsweerde (2009).

3.3.6   The Object Perspective

The basic phenomena of object-oriented modelling languages are similar to those found in most object-oriented programming languages:

- Object: An object is an 'entity' which has a unique and unchangeable identifier and a local state consisting of a collection of attributes with assignable values. The state can only be manipulated with a set of methods defined on the object. The value of the state can only be accessed by sending a message to the object to call on one of its methods. The details of the methods may not be known, except through their interfaces. The happening of an operation being triggered by receiving a message, is called an event.
- Process: The process of an object, also called the object's life cycle, is the trace of the events during the existence of the object.
- Class: A set of objects that share the same definitions of attributes and operations compose an object class. A subset of a class, called subclass, may have its special attribute and operation definitions, but still share all definitions of its superclass through inheritance.

According to Wilkie (1993), object-oriented analysis should provide several representations of a system to fully specify it including:

- Class relationship models: These are similar to ER models.
- Class inheritance models: Similar to generalisation hierarchies in semantic data-models.
- Object interaction models: Show message passing between objects
- Object state tables (or models): Follow a state-transition idea as found in the behavioural perspective.
- User access diagrams: User interface specification.

A general overview of phenomena represented in object-modelling languages is given in Fig. 3.27. These break down into structural, behavioural and rules, cf. Sects. 3.3.4, 3.3.2, and 3.3.5 with a particular focus on structure and behaviour.

Static phenomena break down into type-related and class-related. In object-oriented systems, a type represents a definition of some set of phenomena with similar behaviour. A class is a description of a group of phenomena with similar properties. A class represents a particular implementation of a type. The same hierarchical abstraction mechanisms found in semantic data models and discussed in Sect. 3.1.1 is also found here.

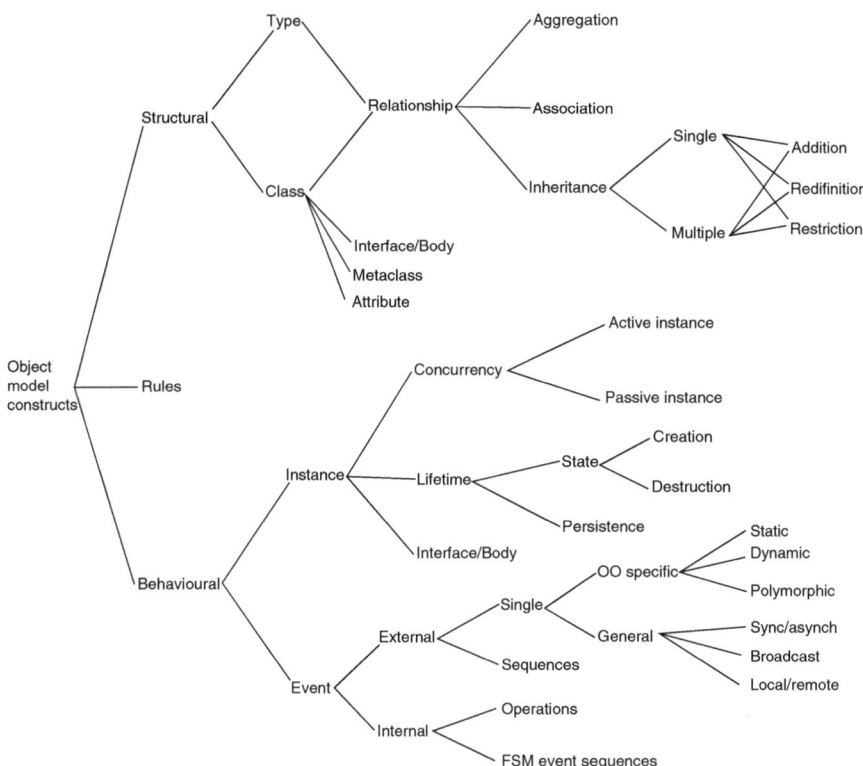

Fig. 3.27 Concepts in object-oriented modelling

Inheritance is indicated as a generalisation of the 'generalisation'-mechanism. Classes or types bound by this kind of relationship share attributes and operations. Inheritance can be either single (where a class or type can have no more than one parent), or multiple (where a class or type can have more than one parent). Inheritance in a class hierarchy can exhibit more features than that of a type hierarchy. Class inheritance may exhibit addition (where the subclass merely adds some extra properties (attributes and methods) over what is inherited from its superclass(es)). Class inheritance can also involve redefinition (where some of the inherited properties are redefined). Class in-heritance may finally exhibit restriction (where only some properties of the superclass are inherited by the subclass). Inheritance is described in more detail in Taivalsaari (1996).

A metaclass is a higher-order class, responsible for describing other classes.

Rules within object-oriented modelling language are basically static rules (similar to constraints in semantic data modelling).

Behavioural phenomena describe the dynamics of a system. Dynamic phenomena relates to instances of classes and the events or messages that pass between such instances. An instance has a definite lifetime from when it is created to when it is destroyed. In between these two events, an instance may spend time in a number of interim states. If the lifetime of an instance can exceed the lifetime of the application or process that created it, the instance is said to be persistent. Instances can execute in parallel (active) or serially (passive) with others. Events are stimuli within instances. An external event is an event received by an instance. An internal event is an event generated internally within an instance which may cause a state change (through an FSM (see Sect. 3.3.2) or similar) or other action (defined by an internal operation) to be taken within the instance. Such actions may involve generating messages to be sent to other instances whereby a sequence of events (or messages) may ensue. Various mechanisms may be used to deliver a message to its destination, depending on the capabilities of the implementation language. For example, a message may employ static binding – where the destination is known at application compile time. Conversely, a message may employ dynamic binding, where the message destination cannot be resolved until application run-time. In this case, message-sending polymorphism may result, where the same message may be sent to more than one type or class of instances. Messages may be categorised as either asynchronous where the message is sent from originator to receiver and the originator continues processing, or synchronous where the thread of control passes from the originating instance to the receiving instance. Messages may also be sent in broadcast mode where there are multiple destinations. Where an overall system is distributed among several processes, messages may be either local or remote. Many of these detailed aspects of modelling of behaviour are first relevant during design of a system.

One early example of the object perspective covering both structural and behavioural aspects of objects is the Object Modeling Technique (OMT), although being primarily focused on the structural perspective (Rosenberg 1999). OMT was one of the precursors of UML, which will be presented as a multi-perspective technique in Sect. 3.5.1 and is presented here to illustrate the link between structural, functional and behavioural modelling perspectives with the object-oriented perspective. OMT (Rumbaugh et al. 1991) had three modelling languages: the object modelling language, the dynamic modelling language and the functional modelling language.

3.3.6.1 OMT Object Modelling Language

This describes the static structure of the objects and their relationships. It is a semantic data modelling language. The vocabulary and grammar of the language are illustrated in Fig. 3.28.

Figure 3.28a Illustrates a class, including attributes (aka properties) and operations (aka methods). For attributes, it is possible to specify both data type and an initial value. Derived attributes can be described, and also class attributes and operations. For operations, it is possible to specify an argument list and the type of the return value. It is also possible to specify rules regarding objects of a class, for instance by limiting the values of an attribute.

Figure 3.28b Illustrates generalisation, being non-disjoint (shaded triangle) or disjoint. Multiple inheritances can be expressed. The dots beneath superclass2 indicate that there exist more subclasses than what is modelled. It is also possible to

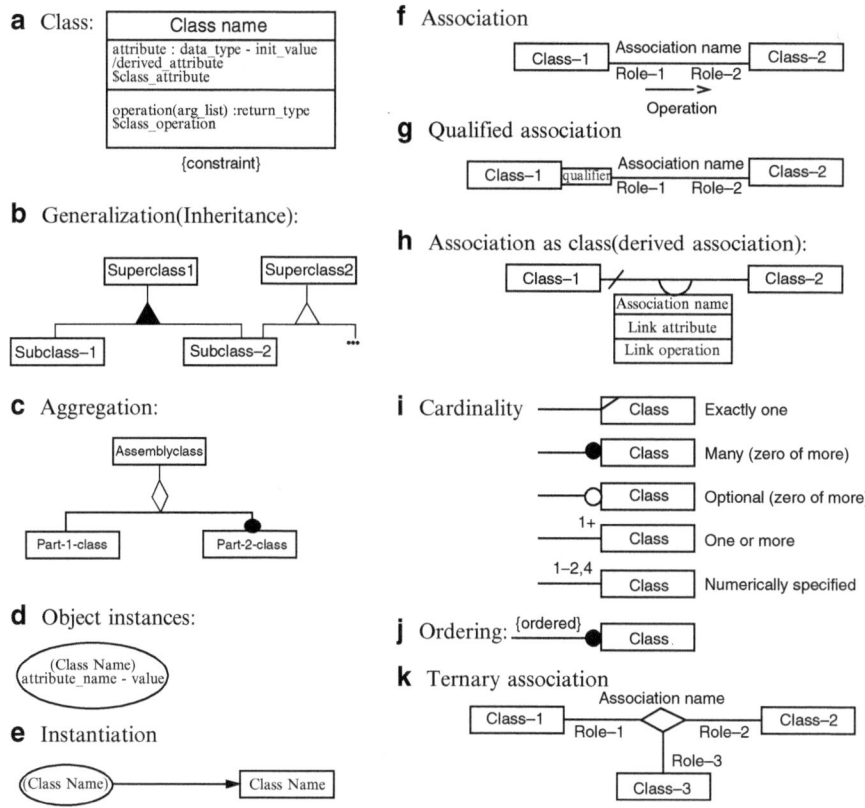

Fig. 3.28 Symbols in the OMT object modelling language

indicate a discriminator (not shown). A discriminator is an attribute whose value differentiates between subclasses.

Figure 3.28c Illustrates aggregation, i.e. part-of relationship on objects.

Figure 3.28d Illustrates an instance of an object and indicates the class and the value of attributes for the object.

Figure 3.28e Illustrates instantiation of a class.

Figure 3.28f Illustrates relationships (associations in OMT-terms) between classes. In addition to the relationship name, it is possible to indicate a role name on each side, which uniquely identifies one end of a relationship. The figure also illustrates propagation of operations. This is the automatic application of an operation to a network of objects when the operation is applied to some starting object.

Figure 3.28g Illustrates a qualified relationship. The qualifier is a special attribute that reduces the effective cardinality of a relationship. One-to-many and many-to-many relationships may be qualified. The qualifier distinguishes among the set of objects at the many end of a relationship.

Figure 3.28h Illustrates that also relationships can have attributes and operations. This figure also shows an example of a derived relationship (through the use of the slanted line).

Figure 3.28i Illustrates cardinality constraints on relationships. Not shown in any of the figures is the possibility to define constraints between relationships, e.g. that one relationship is a subset of another.

Figure 3.28j Illustrates that the elements of the many-end of a relationship are ordered.

Figure 3.28k Illustrates the possibility of specifying n-ary relationships (here a ternary relationship).

An example that illustrates the use of main parts of the languages is given in Fig. 3.29 indicating parts of a structural model for a conference system. A Person is related to one or more Organisation through the Affiliation relationship. A Person is specialised into among others Conference organiser, Referee, Contributor and Participant. A person can fill one or more of these roles. A conference organiser can be either a OC (organising committee) member or a PC (program committee) member or both. A Referee is creating a Review being an evaluation of a Paper. A PC member is responsible for the Review, but is not necessarily the Referee. The Review contains a set of Comments, being of a Commenttype. Two of the possible instances of this class 'Comments to the author' and 'Main contributor' are also depicted. A Review has a set of Scores being Values on a Scale measuring different Dimensions such as contribution, presentation, suitability to the conference and significance.

3.3.6.2 OMT Behavioural Modelling Language

This describes the state transitions of the objects being modelled. It consists of a set of concurrent state transition diagrams. The vocabulary and grammar of the language is illustrated in Fig. 3.30. The standard state transition diagram functionality is illustrated in Fig. 3.30a and partly Fig. 3.30b, but this figure also illustrates the possibility of capturing events that do not result in a state transition. This also includes entry and exit events for states. Figure 3.30c illustrates an event on event situation, whereas Fig. 3.30d illustrates sending this event to objects of another class.

Figure 3.30e–g shows hierarchical constructs similar to those found in Statecharts to address the combinatorial explosion in traditional state transition diagrams. See Sect. 3.3.3 for a more detailed overview of Statecharts, where we have also depicted some examples from the conference case. Not shown in the figure are so-called automatic transitions.

Frequently, the only purpose of a state is in this language to perform a sequential activity. When the activity is completed, a transition to another state fires. This procedural way of using a state transition diagram is somewhat different from the traditional use.

3.3.6.3 OMT Functional Modelling Language

This describes the transformations of data values within a system. It is described using data flow diagrams. The notation used is similar to traditional DFD as

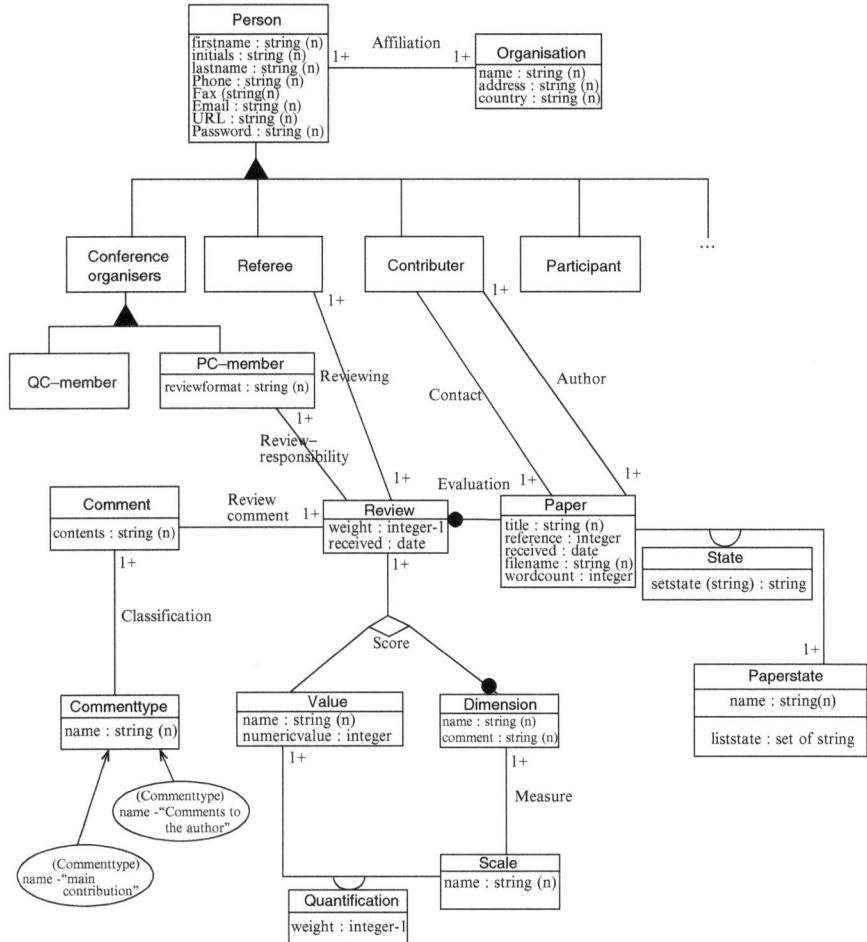

Fig. 3.29 Example of an OMT object model for the conference case

described in Sect. 3.3.3, with the exception of the possibility of sending control flows between processes, being signals only. External agents correspond to objects as sources or sinks of data.

OORASS (Reenskaug et al. 1995) is another object-oriented method, but with more focus on the role the objects are taking during their lifetime. A role model is a model of object interaction described by means of message passing between roles. It focuses on describing patterns of interaction without connecting the interaction to particular objects.

The main parts of a role model are described in Fig. 3.31. A role is defined as the why-abstraction. Why is an object included in the structure of collaborating objects? What is its position in the organisation, what are the responsibilities and duties? All objects having the same position in the structure of objects play the same role. A

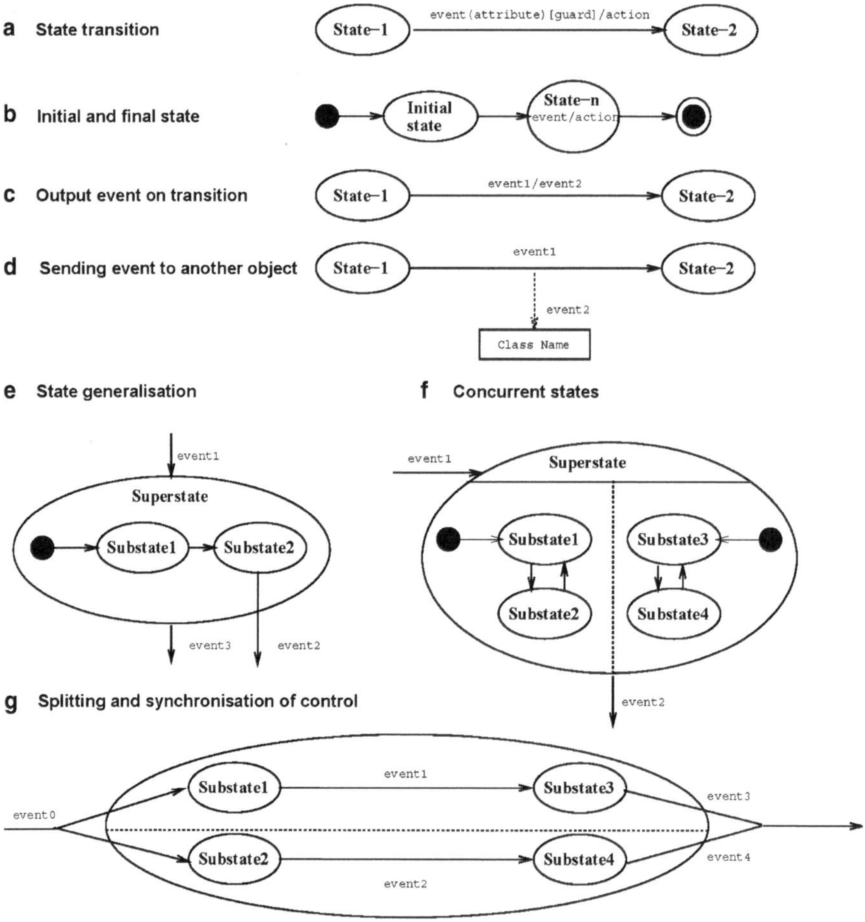

a State transition

State–1 ——— event(attribute) [guard]/action ——— State–2

b Initial and final state

● → Initial state → State–n event/action → ◉

c Output event on transition

State–1 ——— event1/event2 ——→ State–2

d Sending event to another object

State–1 ——— event1 ——————→ State–2
                            ┊ event2
                            ▼
                      Class Name

e State generalisation   **f** Concurrent states

g Splitting and synchronisation of control

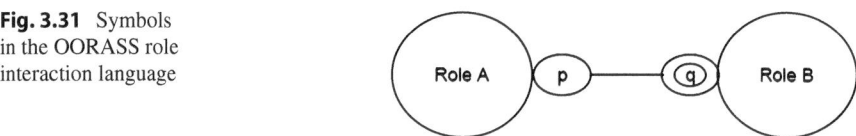

Fig. 3.30 Symbols in the OMT dynamic modelling language

Fig. 3.31 Symbols
in the OORASS role
interaction language

Role A p ——— q Role B

role only has meaning as a part of some structure. This makes the role different from objects which are entities existing 'in their own right'. An object has identity and is thus unique, a role may be played by any number of objects (of any type). An object is also able to play many different roles. In the figure there are two roles A and B. A path between two roles means that a role may 'know about' the other role so that it can send messages to it. A path is terminated by a port symbol at both ends. A port symbol may be a single small circle, a double circle or nothing. *Nothing* means that the near role do not know about the far role. A single circle (p) indicates that an instance of the near role (A) knows about none or one instance of the far role (B). A double circle (q) indicates that an instance of the near role knows about none, one or more instances of the far role. In the figure 'p' is a reference to some object playing the role B. Which object this is may change during the lifetime of A. If some object is present, we are always assured that it is capable of playing the role B. For a port, one can define an associated set of operations called a contract. These operations are the ones that the near role requires from the far role, not what the near role implements. The signatures offered must be deduced from what is required in the other end. Role models may be viewed through different views.

- Environment view: The observer can observe the system interact with its environment.
- External view: The observer can observe the messages owing between the roles.
- Internal view: The observer can observe the implementation

Other views are given in OORASS using additional languages with structural, functional and behavioural perspectives.

A large number of other object-oriented modelling languages have appeared in the literature, e.g. Anderl and Raßler (2008), Bailin (1989), Booch (1991), Coad and Yourdon (1990), Coleman et al. (1992), Embley et al. (1995), Henderson-Sellers et al. (1999), Jacobson et al. (1992), Rubin and Goldberg (1992), Shlaer and Mellor (1991) and Wirfs-Brock et al. (1990). The situation in the mid-1990s was according to Slonim (1994) 'OO methodologies for analysis and design are a mess. There are over 150 contenders out there with no clear leader of the pack. Each methodology boasts their own theory, their own terminology, and their own diagramming techniques'. With the teaming of Rumbaugh, Booch and Jacobson on the development of UML (Unified Modeling Language) this situation is very different now. We will present UML in more detail as a multi-perspective approach in Sect. 3.5.1.

3.3.7 The Communication Perspective

Much of the work within this perspective is based on language/action theory from philosophical linguistics. The basic assumption of language/action theory is that persons cooperate within work processes through their conversations and through mutual commitments taken within them. Speech act theory, which has mainly been developed by Austin (1962) and Searle (1969, 1979) starts from the assumption that the minimal unit of human communication is not a sentence or other expression, but rather the performance of certain types of language acts. Illocutionary logic (Searle and Vanderveken 1985) is a logical formalisation of the theory and can be used to formally describe the communication structure. The main parts of illocutionary logic are the illocutionary act consisting of three parts, illocutionary context, illocutionary force and propositional context.

The context of an illocutionary act consists of five elements: speaker (S), hearer (H), time, location and circumstances.

The illocutionary force determines the reasons and the goal of the communication. The central element of the illocutionary force is the illocutionary point, and the other elements depend on this. Five illocutionary points are distinguished (Searle 1979):

- Assertives: Commit S to the truth of the expressed proposition (e.g. 'A conference will take place in Gdansk in June 2012').
- Directives: Attempts by S to get H to do something (e.g. 'Write the article according to these guidelines').
- Commissives: Commit S to some future course of action (e.g. 'If you send us a paper before a certain date, it will be reviewed').
- Declaratives: The successful performance guarantees the correspondence between the proposition p and the world (e.g. 'your paper is accepted' (stated by the program committee)).
- Expressives: Express the psychological state about a state of affairs specified in the proposition. (e.g. 'Congratulations!').
   These distinctions are directly related to the 'direction of fit' of speech acts.
   We can distinguish four directions of fit.

1. Word-to-world: The propositional content of the speech act has to fit with an existing state of affairs in the world (assertive)
2. World-to-word: The world is altered to fit the propositional content of the speech act (directive and commissive)
3. Double direction fit: The world is altered by uttering the speech act to conform to the propositional content of the speech act (declaratives)
4. Empty direction of fit: There is no relation between the propositional content of the speech act and the world (expressives).

In addition to the illocutionary point, the illocutionary force contains six elements:

- Degree of strength of the illocutionary point: Indicates the strength of the direction of fit.
- Mode of achievement: Indicates that some conditions must hold for the illocutionary act to be performed in that way.
- Propositional content conditions: For example, if a speaker makes a promise, the propositional content must be that the speaker will cause some condition to be true in the future.
- Preparatory condition: There are basically two types of preparatory conditions, those dependant on the illocutionary point and those dependant on the propositional content.
- Sincerity conditions: Every illocutionary act expresses a certain psychological state. If the propositional content of the speech act conforms with the psychological state of the speaker, we say that the illocutionary force is sincere.
- Degree of strength of sincerity condition: Often related to the degree of strength of the illocutionary point.

Speech acts are elements within larger conversational structures that define the possible courses of action within a conversation between two actors. One class of conversational structures is what (Winograd and Flores 1986) calls 'conversation for action'. Graphs similar to state transition diagrams have been used to plot the

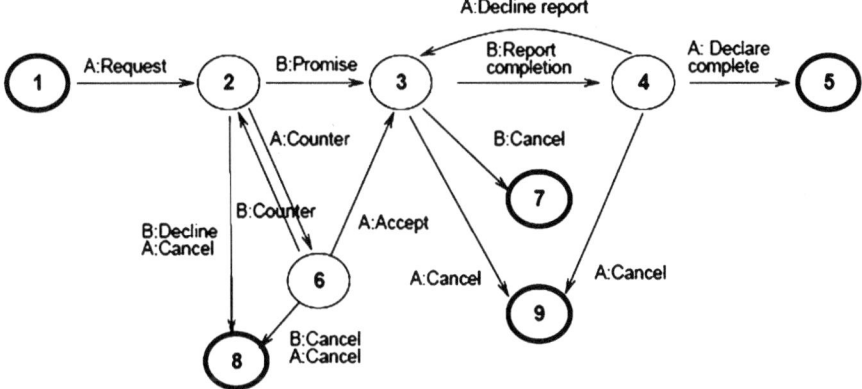

Fig. 3.32 Conversation for action

basic course of such a conversation (see Fig. 3.32). The conversation starts with that part A comes with a request (a directive) going from state 1 to state 2. Part B might then promise to fulfil this request performing a commissive act, sending the conversation to state 3. Alternatively, B might the decline the request, sending the conversation to the end state 8, or counter the request with an alternative request, sending the conversation into state 6. In a normal conversation, when in state 3, B reports completion, performing an assertive act, the conversation is sent to state 4. If A accepts this, performing the appropriate declarative act, the conversation is ended in state 5. Alternatively, the conversation is returned to state 3.

This is only one form of conversation. Several others are distinguished, including conversations for clarification, possibilities and orientation.

This application of speech act-theory forms the basis for several computer systems. An early example was the Coordinator (Flores et al. 1988).

Speech act theory is often labelled as a 'meaning in use theory' together with the philosophy of the later Wittgenstein. Both associate the meaning of an expression with how it is used. However, it is also important to see the differences between the two. Searle associated meaning with a limited set of rules for how an expression should be used to perform certain actions. With this as a basis, he created a taxonomy of different types of speech acts. For Wittgenstein, on the other hand, meaning is related to the whole context of use and not only a limited set of rules. According to Wittgenstein, meaning can never be fully described in a theory or by means of systematic philosophy.

Speech act theory is also the basis for modelling of workflow as coordination among people in Action Workflow (Medina-mora et al. 1992). The basic structure is shown in Fig. 3.33. Two major roles, customer and supplier, are modelled. Workflow is defined as coordination between actors having these roles, and is represented by a conversation pattern with four phases. In the first phase, the customer makes a request for work, or the supplier makes an offer to the customer. In the second phase, the customer and supplier aim at reaching a mutual agreement about

Fig. 3.33 Main phases of action workflow

what is to be accomplished. This is reflected in the contract conditions of satisfaction. In the third phase, after the performer has performed what has been agreed upon and completed the work, completion is declared for the customer. In the fourth and final phase the customer assesses the work according to the conditions of satisfaction and declares satisfaction or dissatisfaction. The ultimate goal of the loop is customer satisfaction. This implies that the workflow loop have to be closed. It is possible to decompose steps into other loops. The specific activities carried out in order to meet the contract are not modelled. The four phases in Fig. 3.33 corresponds to the 'normal path' 1–5 in Fig. 3.32.

Habermas built on Searle's theory for his theory of communicative action (Habermas 1984). Central to Habermas is the distinction between strategic and communicative action. When involved in strategic action, the participants strive after their own private goals. When they cooperate, they try to maximise their own profit or minimise their own losses. When involved in communicative action on the other hand, the participants are oriented towards mutual agreement. The motivation for co-operation is thus rational. In any speech act the speaker S raises three claims: a claim to truth, a claim to justice and a claim to sincerity. The claim to truth refers to the object world, the claim to justice refers to the social world of the participants, and the claim to sincerity refers to the subjective world of the speaker. This leads to a different classification of speech acts (Dietz and Widdershoven 1992):

- Imperativa: S aims at a change of the state in the objective world and attempts to let H act in such a way that this change is brought about. The dominant claim is the power claim. Example; 'You must pay the cost of registration to attend the conference'
- Constativa: S asserts something about the state of affairs in the objective world. The dominate claim is the claim to truth. Example: 'The conference starts tomorrow'
- Regulative: S refers to a common social world, in such a way that he tries to establish an interpersonal relation that is considered to be legitimate. The dominant claim is the claim to justice. Example: 'Write the article according to these guidelines', 'If you send us a paper according to the deadline at a certain date, it will be reviewed'.
- Expressiva: S refers to his subjective world in such a way that he discloses publicly a lived experience: The dominant claim is the claim to sincerity. Example: 'Congratulations'.

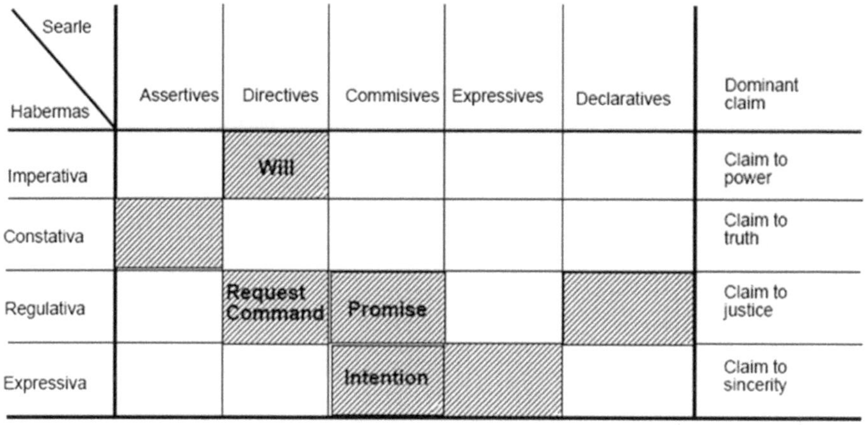

Searle ⟍ Habermas	Assertives	Directives	Commisives	Expressives	Declaratives	Dominant claim
Imperativa		Will				Claim to power
Constativa						Claim to truth
Regulativa		Request Command	Promise			Claim to justice
Expressiva			Intention			Claim to sincerity

Fig. 3.34 Comparing communicative action in Habermas and Searle

A comparisons between Habermas' and Searle's classifications is given in Fig. 3.34.

To illustrate this mix in practice we have in Fig. 3.35 indicated the interaction between a conference organiser and an IS-professional in connection to the paper process. We have only indicated the role, and not the processes involved, although modelling according to a role-based perspective is included in our approach. This is in addition an example on the connection between deontic rules and speech acts (Dignum and Weigand 1995). There are normally no power-relations between these parties, thus all claims will be either to truth, justice or sincerity. The presentation is based on the sending of items. The illocutionary acts are then presented as a triplet <illocutionary point, propositional content, dominant claim> and implied rules are listed after this triplet if any, followed by a comment. Rules are written semi-formally for clarity and brevity. Only the speech acts in the main loop for getting papers for the scientific program of the conference are described.

- Organiser distributes CFP to IS-professional

  <dir, paper, truth>

  If before CFP-deadline it is permitted for IS-professionals to issue a paper to the conference

  <ass,conference,truth>

  If issuing a paper to the conference, it is recommended for the issuer to write within the areas of interest indicated in the CFP

- IS-professional (*Person*) sends a letter of intent to the conference organiser.

  <com, paper,sincerity>

  When letterofintent (Person,Conference) if before CFP-deadline and Paper written by Person has not been issued to Conference, it is recommended for Person to issue Paper to Conference within the CFP-deadline.

  Note that in most cases where an offer is accepted, this will result in that an *obligation* is established.

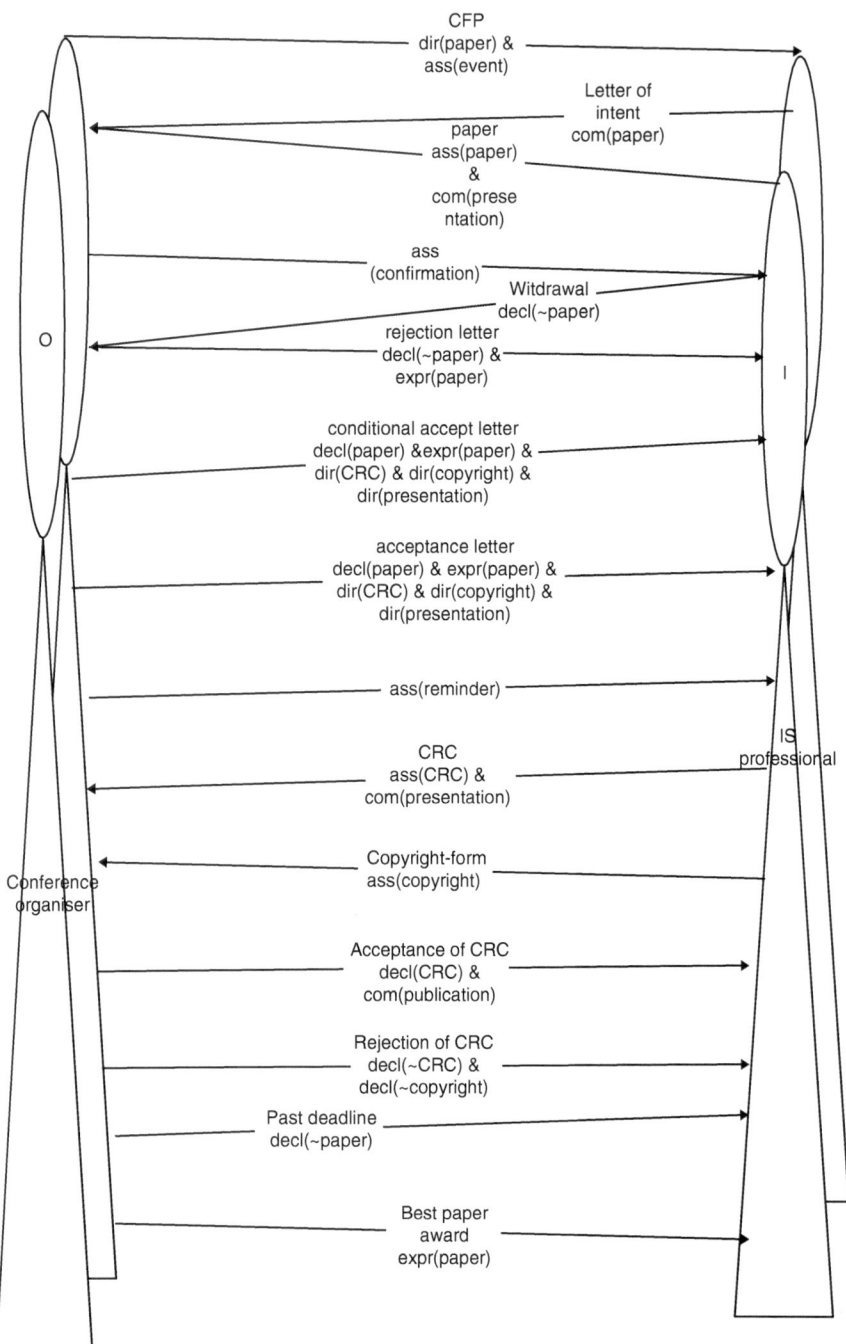

Fig. 3.35 Speech acts in paper-process

A letter of intent is requested in some conferences, but not in all, indicating an example of a conversation not having all the four major speech act-steps.

- IS-professional issues a paper to the conference
  <ass, paper, justice>

     By doing this, the person is no longer recommended to issue a paper to the conference if he had issued a letter of intent. The retraction of the recommendation is already covered by the above rule.
  <com, presentation,justice>

     When issuepaper(Authors,Paper,Conference) if paper accepted, it is obligatory for at least one of Authors to attend Conference and present Paper there.

     When issuepaper(Paper,Conference) if not withdraw(Paper) after issuepaper (Paper,Conference), it is obligatory for the Conference organisers of Conference to ensure fair review of Paper
- The conference organiser issues a confirmation on the paper being received:
  <ass, confirmation,truth>
- The IS-professional withdraws his paper from the conference:
  <decl, not paper,justice>

     When withdrawal(Paper) if Paper distributed to Reviewer, it is obligatory to notice Reviewer of new situation and update overview of reviews to be expected.
- The conference organiser issues a rejection letter, including the review forms.
  <decl, not paper,justice>

  <expr,paper ± reviews,sincerity> (the actual reviews)
- The information about conditional acceptance of the paper, including review-forms, copyright-form and style-guidelines are sent to the IS-professional.
  <decl, paper,justice>

  <expr,paper,sincerity> (the actual reviews)

  <dir, CRC,justice>

     If Paper is to be printed in the proceedings, it is obligatory for the Authors to make and issue a CRC following the style-guide and taking the review comments into account before the CRC-deadline.
  <dir,copyright,justice>

     If Paper is to be printed in the proceedings, it is obligatory for the authors to pass over copyright to the publishers.
  <dir,presentation,justice>

     It is obligatory for at least one of the authors to attend the conference and present the paper. Note that this is already promised by the authors above, thus here the commissive act in fact precede the directive act. One possible situation here is that the authors feel that some of the comments by the reviewers are impossible to adhere to and thus might come with a counter-offer based on truth, where they indicate what they will be able to change.
  < dir,CRC,truth>

     If this is accepted, it is indicated through an acceptance letter <com,CRC,justice> from the conference organisers.

For non-conditional acceptance, the pattern is equal to the above one, with the difference that here changing the paper according to the reviewer's comments would

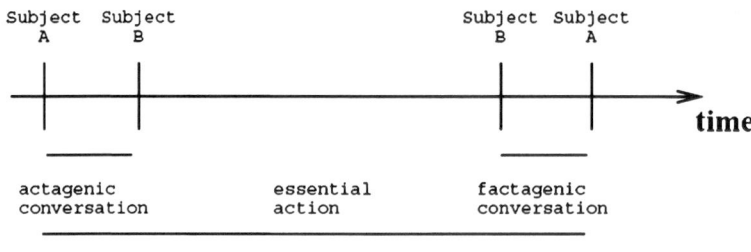

Fig. 3.36 The pattern of transaction in ABC/DEMO

only be a recommendation, whereas the change according to the style guide still would be an obligation.

In addition to the approaches to workflow-modelling described above, several other approaches to conceptual modelling are inspired by the theories of Habermas and Searle such as SAMPO (Auramäki et al. 1992), and ABC/DEMO. We will describe one of these, ABC (in later versions this is named DEMO (Dietz 2006)). Dietz (1994) differentiates between two kinds of conversations:

- Actagenic, where the result of the conversation is the creation of something to be done (agendum), consisting of a directive and a commissive speech act.
- Factagenic, which are conversations that are aimed at the creation of facts typically consisting of an assertive and a declarative act.

Actagenic and factagenic conversations are both called performative conversations. Opposed to these are informative conversations where the outcome is a production of already created data. This includes the deduction of data using e.g. derivation rules. A transaction is a sequence of three steps (see Fig. 3.36): carrying out an actagenic conversation, executing an essential action and carrying out a factagenic conversation.

In the actagenic conversation initiated by subject A, the plan or agreement for the execution of the essential action by subject B is achieved. The actagenic conversation is successful if B commits himself to execute the essential action. The result then is an agendum for B. An agendum is a pair <a;p>where a is the action to be executed and p the period in which this execution has to take place.

In the factagenic conversation, the result of the execution is stated by the supplier. It is successful if the customer accepts these results. Note the similarities between this and the workflow-loop in action workflow.

In order to concentrate on the functions performed by the subjects while abstracting from the particular subjects that perform a function, the notion of actor is introduced. An actor is defined by the set of actions and communications it is able to perform.

The actor that initiates the actagenic conversation and consequently terminates the factagenic one of transactions of type T, is called the initiator of transaction type T. Subject B in Fig. 3.36 is called the executor of transaction T.

An actor that is element of the composition of the subject system is called an internal actor, whereas an actor that belongs to the environment is called an external actor. Transaction types of which the initiator as well as the executor is an internal actor is called an internal transaction. If both are external, the transaction is called

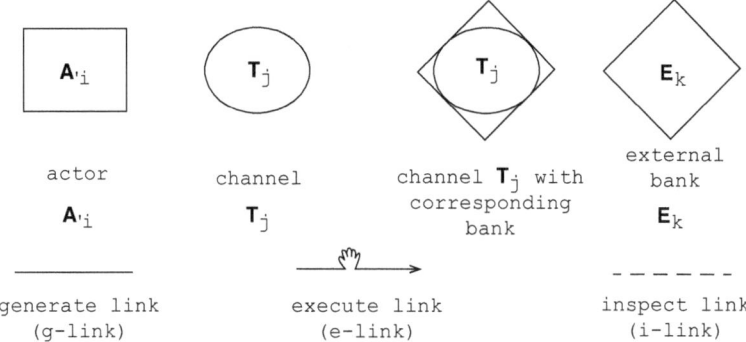

Fig. 3.37 The symbols of the ABC-language

external. If only one of the actors is external it is called an interface transaction type. Interaction between two actors takes place if one of them is the initiator and the other one is the executor of the same transaction type. *Interstriction* takes place when already created data or status values of current transactions are taken into account in carrying out a transaction.

In order to represent interaction and interstriction between the actors of a system, Dietz introduce ABC diagrams. The graphical elements in this language are shown in Fig. 3.37.

An actor is represented by a box, identified by a number. A transaction type is represented by a disk (circle). The operational interpretation of a disk is a store for the statuses through which the transaction of that type passes in the course of time. The disk symbol is called a channel.

The diamond symbol is called a bank, (circle and contain the data created through the transaction). The actor who is the initiator of a transaction type is connected to the transaction channel by a generate link (g-link) symbolised by a plain link. The actor who is the executor is connected to the transaction by an execute link (e-link). Informative conversations are represented by inspect links (i-links), symbolised by dashed lines.

Finally, we notice the use of Language action theory in so-called agent communication languages. *Knowledge Query and Manipulation Language* (KQML) (Finin et al. 1994) as an agent communication language provides a set of performatives which can be used by the agents, it also introduces the concept of communication facilitator that provides different service to the agents who communicate with each other. Agent Communication Language (ACL) (FIPA-ACL 2002) allows associating meta-data information to the content of the message. It also provides a set of performatives with predefined semantics.

3.3.8   The Actor and Role Perspective

The main phenomena of languages within this perspective are actor (alternatively agent) and role. The background for modelling of the kind described here comes both from organisational science, work on programming languages (e.g. actor-languages

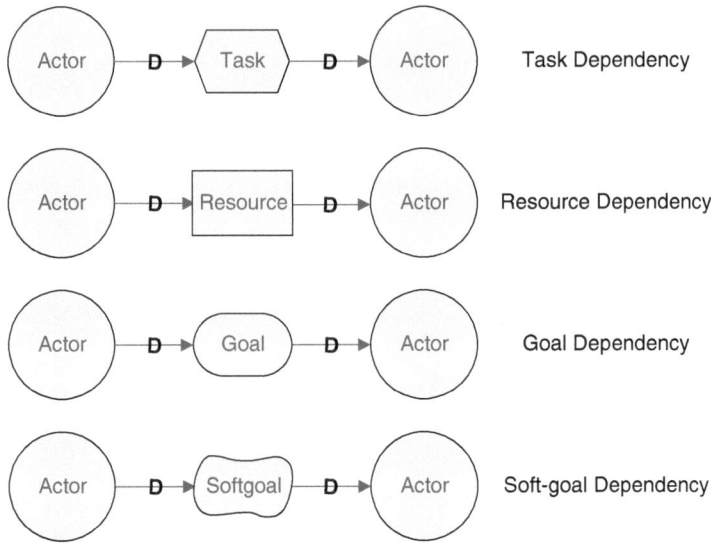

Fig. 3.38 Notation of the actor dependency model

Tomlinson and Scheevel 1989), and work on intelligent agents in artificial intelligence (e.g. Shoham 1994). For our purpose, visual, organisational modelling is of most interest.

Yu and Mylopoulos (1994) proposed a set of integrated languages to be used for organisational modelling known as i*:

- The Actor Dependency modelling language (ADM)
- The Agents-Roles-Positions modelling language
- The Issue-Argumentation modelling language also known as GRL – (Goal-oriented Requirements Language)

The Issue-Argumentation modelling language is an application of a subset of the non-functional framework presented in Sect. 3.3.5. The two other modelling languages are presented below.

In actor dependency models each node represents a social actor/role. Figure 3.38 depicts the main part of the language. Each link between the nodes indicates that a social actor depends on the other to achieve a goal. The depending actor is called the depender, and the actor that is depended upon is called the dependee. The object assigned to each link is called a dependum. It is distinguished between four types of dependencies:

- Goal dependency: The depender depends on the dependee to bring about a certain situation. The dependee is expected to make whatever decisions are necessary to achieve the goal.
- Task dependency: The depender depends on the dependee to carry out an activity. A task dependency specifies how, and not why the task is performed.
- Resource dependency: The depender depends on the dependee for the availability of some resources (material or data).

- Soft-goal dependencies: Similar to a goal dependency, except that the condition to be attained is not precisely defined.

The language allows dependencies of different strength: Open, Committed and Critical. An activity description, with attributes as input and output, sub-activities and pre and post-conditions expresses the rules of the situation. In addition to this, goal attributes are added to activities. Several activities might match a goal, thus sub-goals are allowed.

An example is depicted below in Fig. 3.39, based on the following part of the conference example in Appendix C:

'An organisation arranging a scientific conference depends on a number of other people and organisations for the practical arrangement of the conference. Whereas the organising and program committees are typically recruited from the research community and do the work relating to securing the quality of the scientific program for free, there need to be facilities for holding the conference, housing the participants, supporting their trip to the conference, taking care of payments and money matters, publishing information on the web, arranging social events part of the social program, perform registration at the start of the conference, and publish proceedings. Many of these tasks can be supported by a conference arrangement organisation, whereas others are supported by organisations such as travel arrangers, local tourist offices (e.g. for arranging the social program), conference venues, hotels and publishers (for the proceedings). All these services cost money, which have to be balanced by the income mainly through the participant fee and from sponsors. Thus a budget needs to be developed to guide the choices of the organising committee'.

The Agents-Roles-Positions modelling language consists of a set nodes and links as illustrated in Fig. 3.40. An actor is here as above used to refer to any unit to which intentional dependencies can be ascribed. The term social actor is used to emphasise that the actor is made up of a complex network of associated agents, roles and positions. A role is an abstract characterisation of the behaviour of a social actor within some specialised context or domain. A position is an abstract place-holder that mediates between agents and roles. It is a collection of roles that are to be played by the same agent. An agent refers to those aspects of a social actor that are closely tied to its being a concrete, physically embodied individual.

Agents, roles and positions are associated to each other via links: An agent (e.g. John Krogstie) can occupy a position (e.g. program coordinator), a position is said to cover a role (e.g. program coordinator covers delegation of papers to reviewers), and an agent is said to play a role. In general these associations may be many-to-many. An interdependency is a less detailed way of indicating the dependency between two actors. Each of the three kinds of actors- agents, roles and positions, can have sub-parts.

e³value (Gordijn et al. 2006) is a actor/role-oriented modelling language for inter-organisational modelling The purpose of this modelling language focus on representing how actors of a system create, exchange and consume objects of economic value. The modelling language focus on communicate about the key points of a business model, and to get an understanding of business operations and systems

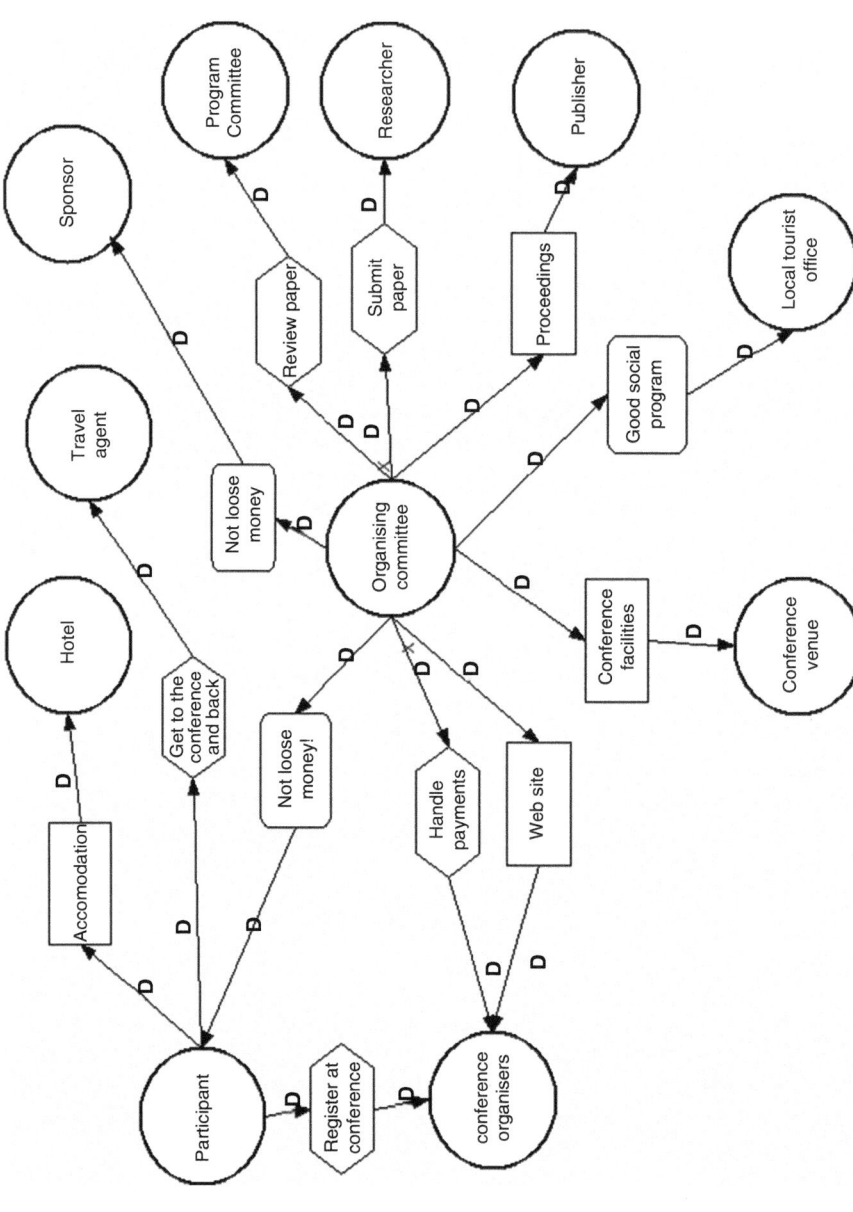

Fig. 3.39 I*ADM model of part of the conference example

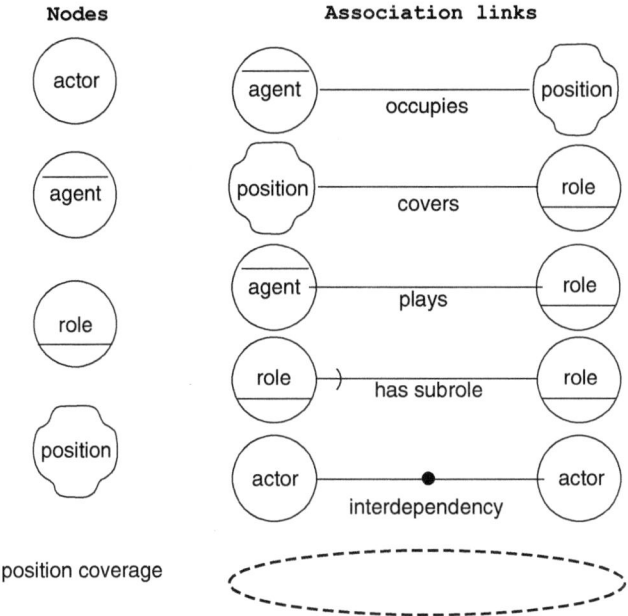

Fig. 3.40 Symbols in agents-role-position modelling language

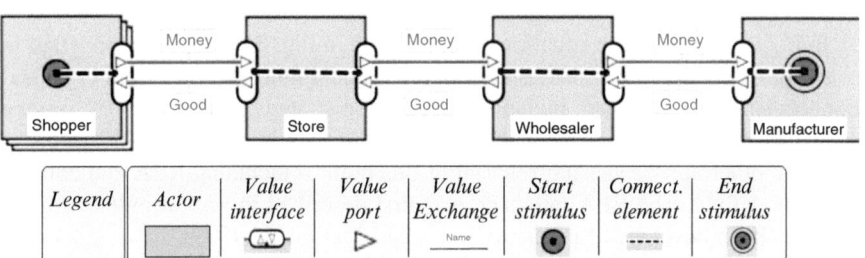

Fig. 3.41 Symbols in e³value modelling language

requirements through scenario analysis and evaluation. Through an evaluation, the purpose of e³value is to determine whether if a business idea is profitable or not, that is to say by analysing for each actor involved in the system whether if the idea is profitable for them or not.

e³value models give a representation of actors, exchanges, value objects of a business system (Fig. 3.41).

- Actor: Entity that is economically independent in its environment, that is to say supposed to be profitable (for different kind of value, e.g. intellectual, economical, etc.). An actor is identified by its name. *Example: organising committee, Travel agent, Publisher, etc.*

- Value object A value object can be of many types: services, product, knowledge, etc. It is exchanged by actors who consider it has an economic value. The value object is defined by its name, which is representative of the kind of object it is. *Example: money, facilities, manuscript.*
- Value Port: It belongs to an actor, and allows it to request value objects to the others actors, and so to create an interconnection. Moreover, it is representatives of the external view of e^3value, by focusing on external trades and not on internal process. The value port is characterised by its direction ('in' or 'out').
- Value interface: It belongs to an actor, and usually groups one 'ingoing' value port, and one 'outgoing' value port. It introduces the notion of 'fair trade' or 'reciprocity' in the trade: one offering against one request.
- Value exchange: It connects two value ports with each other, that is to say it establish a connection between two actors for potential exchange of value object. Because value port is represented by a direction, value exchange is represented by both the *has in* and the *has out* relation.
- Value Transaction: A value transaction links two or more values exchanges to conceptualise the fair-trade exchange between actors. If a value exchange appears in more than one transaction, we call it a multi-party transaction
- Market segment: A market segment group together value interfaces of actors that assign economic value to object equally. It is a simplification for systems where actors have similar value interfaces. An important point is that an actor can be a member of different market segments, because we consider only the value interface. The market segment is identified by the name and a count of the number of members. Example: travel agencies

In Fig. 3.42 below, the situation depicted in i* in Fig. 3.39 above is modelled in e^3 value. A number of extensions taking into account other theories from organisational science is developed, including e^3control, e^3strategy, e^3boardroom, e^3service and e^3alignment (http://www.e3value.com/).

Some other approaches are relevant at this point – including REA and competency modelling. The REA language was first described in McCarthy (1982) and then has been developed further in Geerts and McCarthy (1999). REA was originally intended as a basis for accounting information systems and focuses on representing increases and decreases of value in an organisation. REA has subsequently been extended to apply to enterprise architectures (Hruby 2006) and e-commerce frameworks (UMM 2007).

The core concepts in the REA language are *resource*, *event* and *agent*. The intuition behind this language is that every business transaction can be described as an event where two agents exchange resources. In order to acquire a resource from other agents, an agent has to give up some of its own resource. It never happens that one agent simply gives away a resource to another without expecting another resource back as compensation. Basically, there are two types of events: *exchange* and *conversion* (Hruby 2006). An exchange occurs when an agent receives economic resources from another agent and gives resource back to that agent. A conversion occurs when an agent consumes resources to produce other resources. REA has influence the electronic commerce standard ebXML, with McCarthy actively involved in the standards committee.

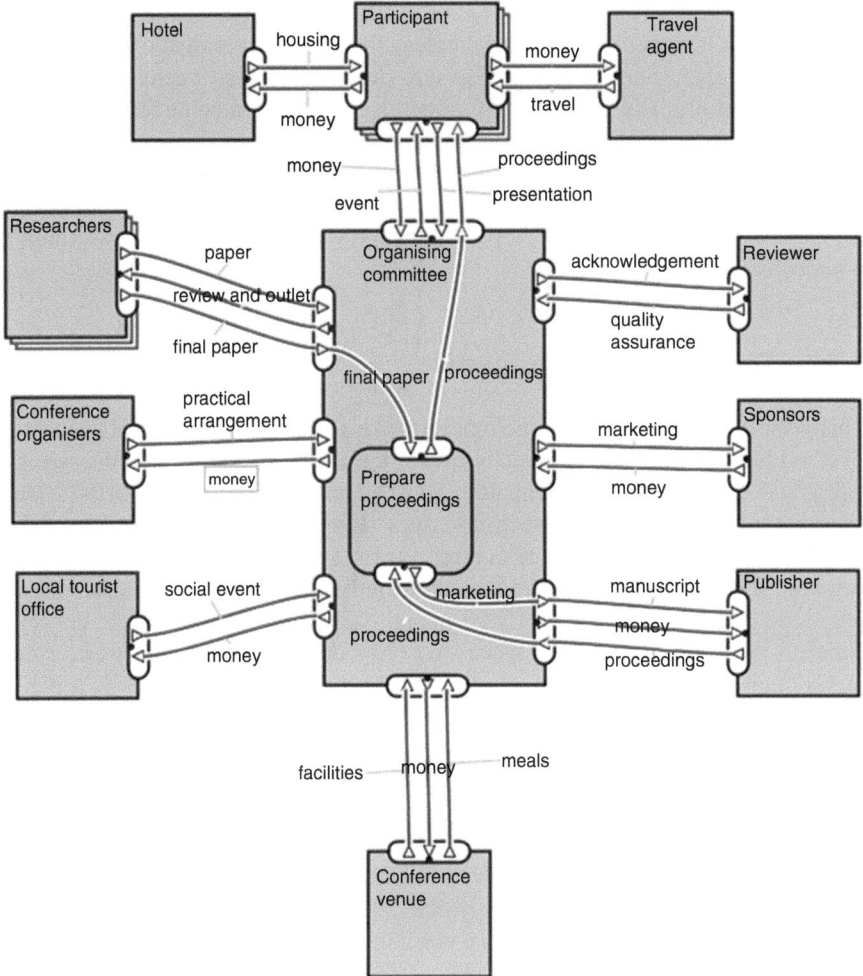

Fig. 3.42 e³value example form the conference case

Finally, competency modelling (Albertsen et al. 2010) relates to the capabilities of typically persons (but also groups and organisations e.g. when specifying so-called business capabilities). Although different sub-fields define competence differently, (Cheetham and Chivers 2005) applies the following definition: '*effective performance within a domain/context at different levels of proficiency*'. According to Albertsen et al. (2010) several approaches for competency modelling has been developed:

- Berio and Harzallah (2007) provide the CRAI model (competence, resource, aspect, individual) associated with axioms based on set theory. The approach aims at describing formal competence in order to provide a mapping between required and existing competence in an enterprise.

- Pepiot et al. (2008) use fuzzy logic for the evaluation of competencies. A competence indicator is constructed by a fuzzy aggregation of several evaluation criteria.
- In OntoProPer (Sure 2000), profiles are described by flat vectors containing weighted skills. The system mainly focuses on profile matching and introduces an automated way of building and maintaining profiles based on ontologies.

Very few results concerning evaluation of collective competences have been reported to date, although there are several examples of techniques that try to model the members of teams to find if they will function well (e.g. Belbin analysis (http://www.belbin.com))

3.3.9   The Topological Perspective

This perspective relates to the topological ordering between the different concepts. The best background for conceptualisation of these aspects comes from the cartography and CSCW field, differentiating between space and place (Dourish 2006; Harrison and Dourish 1996). 'Space' describes geometrical arrangements that might structure, constrain and enable certain forms of movement and interaction, 'place' denotes the ways in which settings acquire recognisable and persistent social meaning in the course of interaction. Different approaches looks at the 'place'-concept either to be a classification of 'space' (e.g. My office (room 116 IT-west at the IT-building of Gløshaugen)) as a space, whereas the concept 'office' is a place (where one normal perform certain kinds of work) or as an instantiation of space (My office today from my point of view). Casey as a philosopher discusses *Place* (Casey 1993, 1998) in this latter view as an emergent concept based on how individuals experience it. From this standpoint *Place*s evolve over time and have no static attributes. As different activities occur in a *Place,* its understanding among its occupants is renegotiated and redefined. In the view of Tuan (1975) *'Place is a centre of meaning constructed by experience'*. The debate provided by Tuan strongly suggests that the experience of a *Place* is not only based on the sensory input such as touch, seeing etc.… but is more abstract such as thoughts and feelings. Four main dimensions characterise according to Tuan (1975) *Place.*

1 *Physical dimension*: relates to the physical characteristics of the *Place.*
2 *Personal dimension:* is related to the personal beliefs, thoughts, emotions and feelings.
3 *Social dimension:* is the presence of others within a given *Place*
4 *Cultural dimension:* is the code of conduct, rule and norms prevalent in the *Place.*

In our view, dimension 4, the cultural dimension point to the need for class-level kind of concept, and due to our focus on modelling in this book, we use the term 'place' in this meaning here. Another possible term for this concept is habitat or 'type of space'.

Some approaches letting you take this type of the place-oriented aspects into account exist, e.g. work on extending UML activity diagrams with place-oriented aspects (Gopalakrishnan et al. 2010).

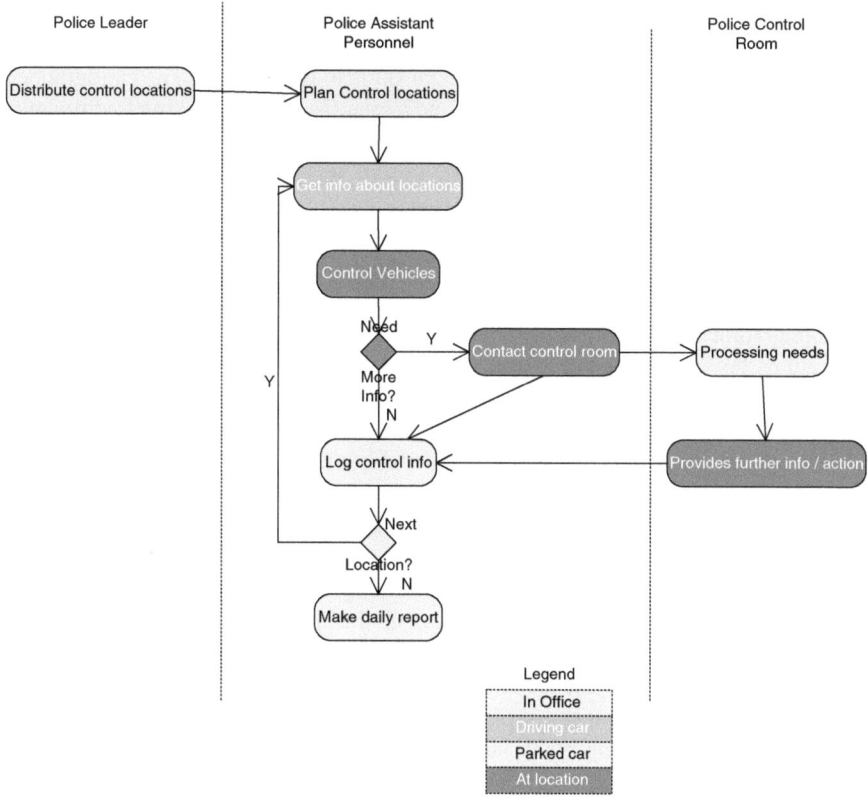

Fig. 3.43 Place-oriented modelling (From Gopalakrishnan et al. 2010)

A specific notations based on UML Activity Diagrams extended using colours to differentiate place-oriented aspects is presented in Fig. 3.43. The model is based on a simple task in a police traffic control case. The leader of the police allots control locations for each police assistant personnel for controlling the vehicles through those locations. Controlling includes following up things such as driver license, speeding, drunk driving etc. Police Assistant Personnel (PAP) receives info about control locations at the office from the leader. PAP plans and gets information about the control locations while driving the car. After reaching the control location, PAP controls the drivers and vehicles. If he decides he needs more info/personnel he contacts through mobile/radio/hand held devices the Police control room. The control room provides necessary info/further actions to PAP at control locations. PAP completes the scheduled task for scheduled hour at particular locations and logs all the information from the car while parked. He repeats the task until PAP finishes all control locations for the day. After completion, PAP returns to the office and make a daily report. An even more topologically oriented approach is to group concepts at the same location relative to areas on the diagram (Gopalakrishnan and Sindre 2011).

As for the representation of space, the classical area to address this is cartography, the study and science of creating and using geographic maps. Traditionally, maps have been designed by cartographers with special skills in map design. The cartographer was often considered to be both an artist and a scientist, as map making traditionally was a difficult and time consuming task. It is possible to look at a map of this sort as a model on the instance level. How quality of such models can be evaluated is discussed in Sect. 6.7, quality of maps. Geographical maps are traditionally designed for general-purpose use. In addition there exist thematic maps, which are made with a specific purpose and intent in mind, often including some specific concepts. You can also differentiate between topographic and topological maps.

- Topographical maps primarily focus on the shape and surface of geographical features. As such topographic maps can be said to have a strong focus on depicting information accurately, in adherence to physical reality.
- Topological maps focus primarily on topological aspects of the available information, depicting only the spatial relationship of the geographical information. A standard example of the latter is metro-maps.

Traditional representations of space such as a map have only to a limited degree been oriented towards representation of conceptual knowledge. Some recent approaches do take these aspects more consciously into account, as exemplified by Nossum and Krogstie (2009). We will illustrate the approach with an application to provide process support/decision support in the medical domain. Work in the medical domain is often highly dependent on the spatial properties of concepts, such as the same time location of tasks, equipment, staff and patients. Additionally the conceptual properties are important, such as staffs relation to tasks (e.g. scheduled tasks), doctors responsibilities for specific patients and similar.

One particular complex task in medical work is the self-coordination each staff member needs to undertake. At any given day, a doctor has a set of tasks that needs to be performed. These tasks may be scheduled in advance, or they may occur spontaneously (i.e. emergencies). The doctor needs to coordinate himself by deciding what tasks he performs, and when he performs them. This decision can potentially be a complex task, involving elements like:

- Most effective sequence of tasks based on
  - Location of task (e.g. nearness from current position)
  - Importance of tasks
  - Magnitude of task
- When the task is to be performed (i.e. present or future)
  - Involved patients
  - State (health status of patients)
  - Location (if they are at the task location)
- Involved actors (other staff members)
  - Location (if they are at (or near) the task location)
  - State (availability etc.)

Research, mainly from the field of CSCW, suggests that providing awareness of the hospital environment is one means to lower the complexity of the decision-making. Both a focus towards the spatial dimension (i.e. location), but also the

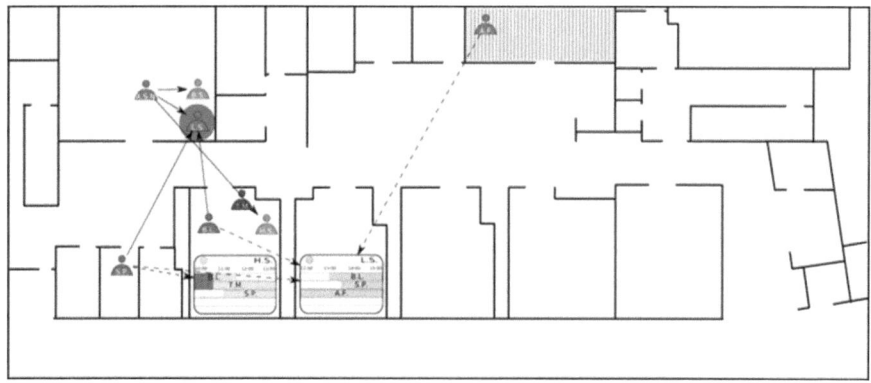

Fig. 3.44 Floor plan visualisation of operating ward (From Nossum and Krogstie 2009)

conceptual dimension (i.e. state, relationship etc.) is needed (Bardram and Bossen 2005; Bardram et al. 2006).

The spatial dimension in indoor environments is commonly visualised either directly in a floor-plan (i.e. an indoor map) (McCarty and Meidel 1999) or as an attribute in a diagram-like fashion (Bardram et al. 2006). Both approaches aim at visualising the spatial dimension as well as the conceptual dimension including relationships, state and similar – which is an instance level conceptual model of the environment in question. However, both approaches focus the visualisation towards their respective field (i.e. floor map on spatial dimension, traditional diagrams on the conceptual dimension) without successfully obtaining a good representation of both dimensions at the same time.

The following will illustrate two distinctly different ways of representing a situation which is directly associated with a typical situation at a hospital. The scenario is based in an operating ward. Several different actors (patients, doctors, surgeons, nurses etc.) are working in the environment each having their respective relations to activities (tasks) and other actors. Two activities (surgeries) are included, one that is in progression and one that is scheduled. Additionally a patient (L.S.) is having an emergency. The main user is intended to be the surgeon 'B.L.'. Combined this provides an illustrative model which can be visualised in different ways. The following two different visualisations illustrate the necessity of developing guidelines for understanding of quality of such mixed representations.

Figure 3.44 illustrates a floor plan visualisation of the model. Concepts are placed absolute in the floor plan and relationships are visualised by traditional arrows. The temporal nearness of the environment is communicated, although not explicitly. Taken into account that the scenario is situated only in one floor minimises the complexity the visualisation has to deal with. When incorporating several floors and buildings (as was the case in e.g. Bardram et al. 2006) will increase this complexity to a potentially unworkable state.

Figure 3.45 positions the concepts according to their relative temporal nearness (i.e. temporal topology). The temporal nearness is communicated using scaled circles.

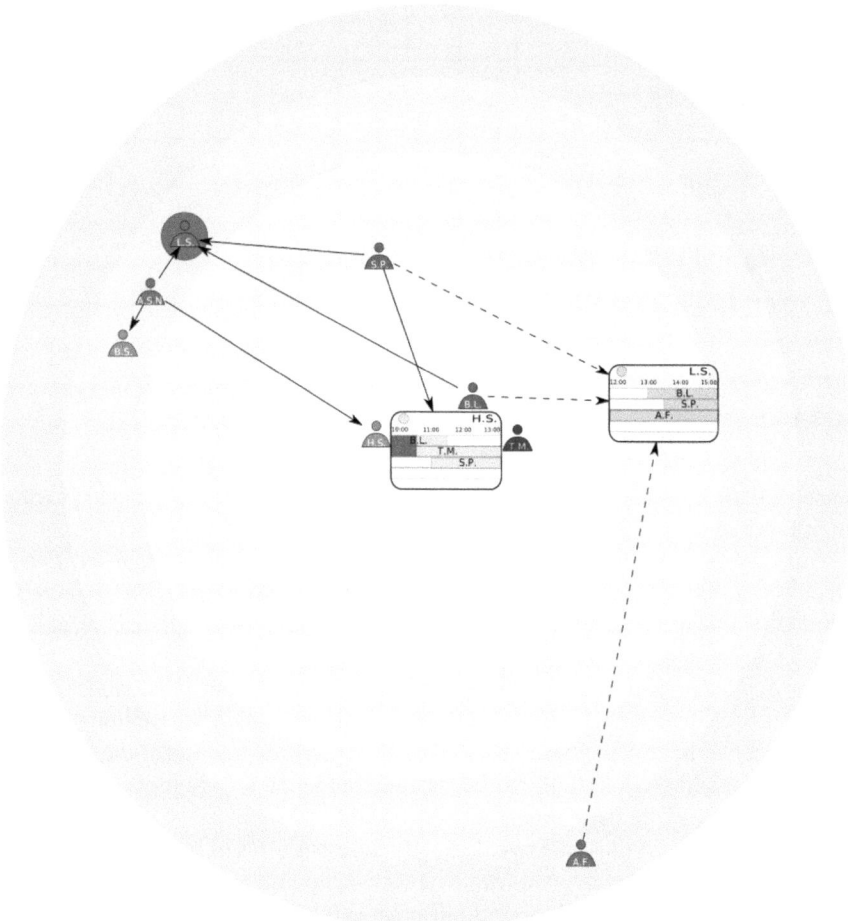

Fig. 3.45 Visualisation of operating wards emphasising the temporal nearness (From Nossum and Krogstie 2009)

Relative nearness is conveyed by using the same scaled circles approach on the different actors. It is believed this visualisation is better suited at visualising the model when the actors know the spatial environment of the model, which is the case for the scenario.

3.4   Process Modelling According to Different Modelling Perspectives

A *process* is a collection of related, structured tasks that produce a specific service or product to address a certain goal for a particular actor or set of actors. Process modelling has been performed relative to IT and organisational development at least since the 1970s. The interest has going through phases with the introduction of different approaches, including Structured Analysis in the 1970s (Gane and Sarson 1979), Business Process Reengineering in the late 1980s/early 1990s (Hammer and Champy 1993), and Workflow Management in the 1990s (WfMC 2001). Lately, with the proliferation of BPM (Business process management) (Havey 2005), interest and use of process modelling has increased even further, although focusing primarily on a selected number of modelling perspectives.

Models of work processes have long been utilised to learn about, guide and support practice also in other areas. In software process improvement (Derniame 1998), enterprise modelling (Fox and Gruninger 2000) and quality management, process models describe methods and standard working procedures. Simulation and quantitative analyses are also performed to improve efficiency (Abdel-Hamid and Madnick 1989; Kuntz et al. 1998). In process centric software engineering environments (Ambriola et al. 1997) and workflow systems (WfMC 2001), model execution is automated. This wide range of applications is reflected in current notations, which emphasise different aspects of work.

The archetypical way to look on processes is as a function or transformation, according to an IPO (input-process-output) functional perspective. Whereas early process modelling approaches had this as a base approach, as process modelling have been integrated with other types of conceptual modelling, also variants of this have appeared, also for modelling of the core processes, as different approaches to modelling is beneficial for achieving different goals. Carlsen (1998) identifies five categories of process modelling languages: transformational (functional perspective), conversational (communicational perspective), role-oriented, constraint-based (rule and goal perspective), and system dynamics (coverage aspects of the behavioural perspective). In Lillehagen and Krogstie (2008) we looked upon these, but also included the OO-perspective due to increased interest in UML. Lately, also other approaches have appeared making it important to provide a more comprehensive overview of perspectives to process modelling.

We will here give a brief overview of modelling languages used for process modelling according to the different perspectives presented in Sect. 3.3. In the last section we summarise how modelling according to the different perspectives is beneficial to achieve the various goals (presented in Chap. 1).

3.4.1 Process Modelling According to the Behavioural Perspective

As indicated in Sect. 3.3.2, states (of systems, products, entities, processes) and transformation between states are the central aspect in this perspective, and the approaches described in that section has been used for process modelling for a number of years. We do not reiterate the description of these here.

3.4.2 Process Modelling According to the Functional Perspective

As described above, most process modelling languages take a functional (or transformational/input-process-output) approach, although some of the most popular process modelling languages from the last decade also include behavioural aspects as was discussed towards the end of Sect. 3.3.3. Processes are divided into activities, which may be divided further into sub-activities. Each activity takes inputs, which it transforms to outputs. Input and output relations thus define the sequence of work. This perspective is chosen for the standards of the Workflow Management Coalition (WfMC 2001), the Internet Engineering Task Force (IETF) (Bolcer and Kaiser 1999), as well as most commercial systems.

An approach not described in Sect. 3.3.3 is found in the eScience area in data-oriented workflow models (e.g. Scufl Hull et al. 2006) where the existence of required data determines the activation of activities.

Given the extensive use of transformational languages, a number of analyses focus on this category (Conradi and Jaccheri 1998; Curtis et al. 1992; Green and Rosemann 1999). The expressiveness of these languages typically includes decomposition, and data flow, while organisational modelling and roles often are integrated (see also role-oriented modelling below). In approaches that integrate behavioural and functional aspects, we see also a support for control flow. Aspects like timing and quantification, products and communication or commitments are better supported by other paradigms. User-orientedness is a major advantage of transformational languages. Partitioning the process into steps, match well the descriptions that people use elsewhere. Graphical input-process-output models are comprehensible given some training, but you can also build models by simply listing the tasks in plain text, or in a hierarchical work breakdown structure (in approaches for HTA – Hierarchical Task Analysis). Hence, the models can be quite simple, provided that incomplete ordering of steps is allowed.

3.4.3 Process Modelling According to the Structural Perspective

Usually one look upon structural modelling to be fundamentally different from functional (process) modelling, since the structural perspective focus on the static aspects, whereas process modelling focus on dynamics. It is possible to look at processes and tasks as entities though (like one have done in OO-process modelling discussed below, looking at the processes as the objects) in which case one can model the situation in a similar way as when doing more traditional data-modelling. Figure 3.46 shows part of a traditional data-model for a conference organisation case, relative to involved roles and products in connection to the paper submission, review and selection. Figure 3.47 describes parts of the conference case where the focus is on tasks performed in connection to this, and one notice many similarity (but also some differences) from when the entities are data/structural constructs and processes, i.e. the inclusion of task outside the scope of the database system, and the possibility of expressing additional rules.

One finds very few attempts for this type of modelling in practice. We look more on such approaches below when discussing OO process models in Sect. 3.4.5 below.

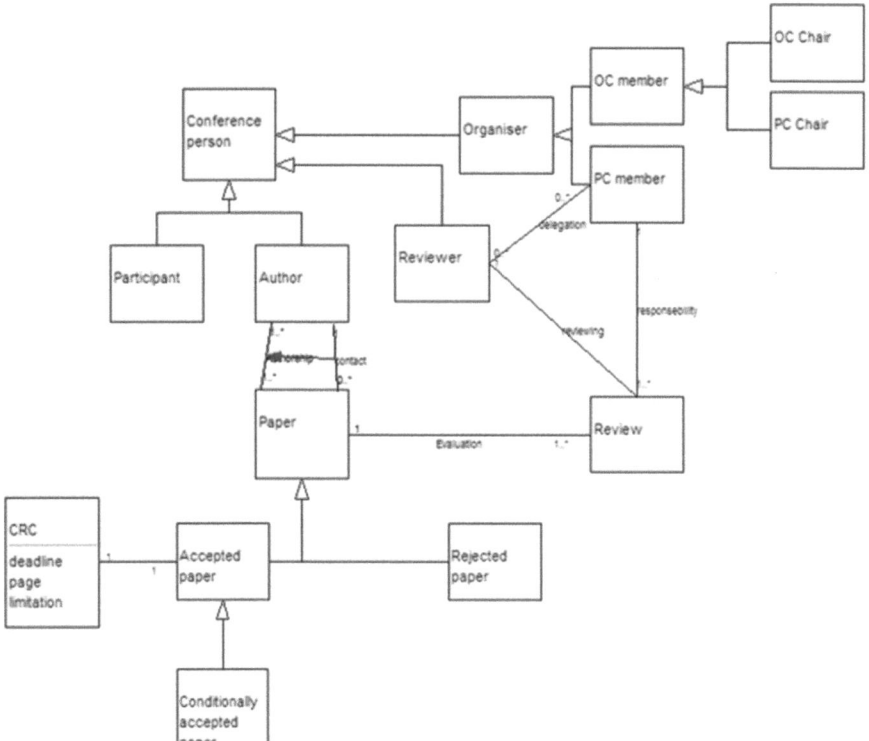

Fig. 3.46 Traditional data model of the conference case

3.4.4   Process Modelling According to the Goal and Rule Perspective

In the workflow area, this is often termed declarative workflow. Constraint based languages (Dourish et al. 1996; Glance et al. 1996) do not prescribe a course of events, rather they capture the boundaries within which the process must be performed, leaving the actors to control the internal details. Instead of telling people what to do, these systems warn about rule violations and enforce constraints. Thus, common problems with over-serialisation can be avoided (Glance et al. 1996).

A wide variety of declarative modelling approaches has been specified in business process management, from the use of basic event-condition-action (ECA) rules (Kappel et al. 1998) to declarative process modelling languages such as DecSerFlow (van der Aalst and Pesic 2006), BPCN (Lu et al. 2009) and ConDec (Pesic and van der Aalst 2006). Goedertier and Vanthienen (2009) present an overview of the most common declarative process modelling languages.

Languages representing rule-based process modelling can potentially provide a higher expressiveness than diagrammatic languages (e.g. the ability to specify

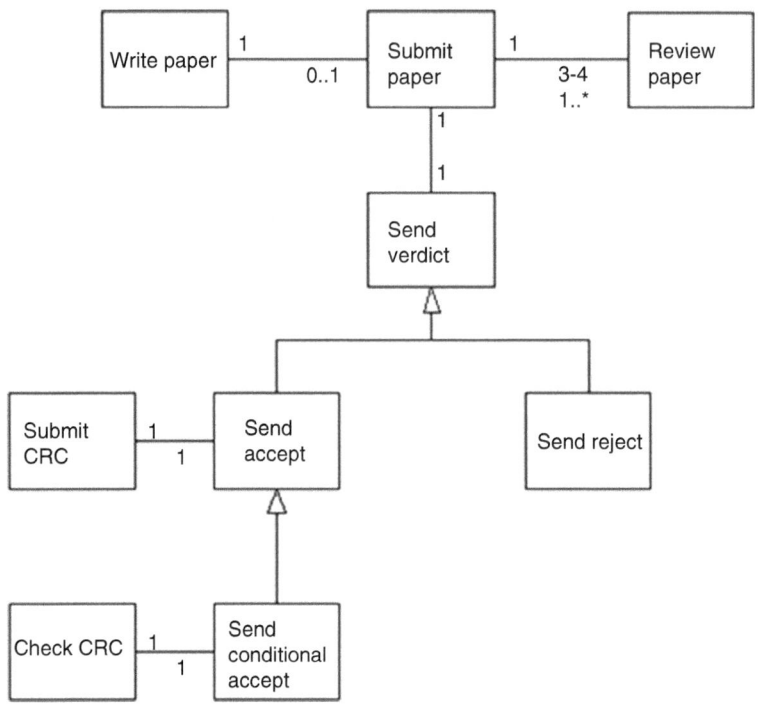

Fig. 3.47 Structural process model of conference case

temporal requirements) (Lu and Sadiq 2007), but this might result in process models which are less comprehensible (Fickas 1989) due to large rule-based as discussed in Sect. 3.3.5.

Declarative process enactment guarantees run-time flexibility for declarative process specifications that contain only the strictly required mandatory constraints. An individual execution path that satisfies the set of mandatory constraints can be dynamically built for a specific process instance. Process compliance is assured when all mandatory rules are correctly mapped onto mandatory business constraints. During the construction of a suitable execution path, little support is provided to the end user (Weske 2007), which could affect the process effectiveness. In Krogstie and Sindre (1996), the idea of differentiating constraints by modality was proposed, recommendations would guide the user, whereas mandatory constraints would ensure compliant behaviour. The guidance provided by the deontic constraints might depend on explicit domain knowledge or can be learned through process mining (Schonenberg et al. 2008). Lastly, the increased size and complexity of contemporary process models might decrease the potential for process automation since current declarative workflow management systems might have limited efficiency in these cases according to van der Aalst et al. (2009).

A graphic depiction is difficult since it would correspond to a visualisation of several possible solutions to the set of constraint equations constituting the model.

The support for articulation of planned and ongoing tasks is limited. Consequently, constraints are often combined with transformational models (Bernstein 2000; Dourish et al. 1996). Alternatively one can have the operational rules also linked to goal hierarchies as in EEML (Krogstie 2008) (see Sect. 3.5.2) and other approaches for goal-oriented modelling. Constraints mainly capture external control on the workflow, not articulation inside the process.

3.4.5   Process Modelling According to the Object Perspective

UML (Booch et al. 2005) has become the official and de facto standard for object-oriented analysis and design. Consequently, people also apply UML to model business processes. Object orientation offers a number of useful modelling techniques like encapsulation, polymorphism, subtyping and inheritance (Loos and Allweyer 1998; zur Muehlen and Becker 1999). UML integrates these capabilities with e.g. requirements capture in use case descriptions and behaviour modelling in state, activity and sequence diagrams. On the other hand, UML is designed for software developers, not for end users. A core challenge thus remains in mapping system-oriented UML constructs to user- and process-oriented concepts (Hommes and Reijswoud 1999). To this problem no general solution exists (Loos and Allweyer 1998; Störle 2001). UML process languages utilise associations, classes, operations, use cases, interaction sequence or activity diagrams. The lack of a standardised approach reflects the wide range of process modelling approaches in business and software engineering. Many of these are already covered above. One approach that is somewhat similar to how one can use structural modelling for process modelling is PML (Anderl and Raßler 2008). They describe an approach for a process modelling language which uses object-oriented techniques based on looking upon classes in a particular way. Whereas a class is defined by classname, attributes and methods, one in this approach define this as processname, methods and resources. The PML process class describes the process in a generic way. It allows one to define all methods with assurances and resources needed for the process. The instantiation of a process is a project. This means, the instance of a process defines the current occurrence of resources, used data models etc. Regarding to connections and dependencies between single process classes, PML features the standard UML-concepts of inheritance and associations. Although with intriguing possibilities, it is safe to say to OO process modelling has yet to be taken into use in large scale in practice.

3.4.6   Process Modelling According to the Communicational Perspective

As discussed in Sect. 3.3.7, the communication perspective was brought into the workflow arena through the COORDINATOR prototype (Winograd and Flores 1986), later succeeded by the Action Workflow system (Medina-Mora et al. 1992).

The main strength of this approach relative to process modelling is that it facilitates analysis of the communicative aspects of the process, something we will return to in the next perspective. It highlights that each process is an interaction between a customer and a performer, represented as a cycle with four phases: preparation, negotiation, performance and acceptance. The dual role constellation is a basis for work breakdown, e.g. the performer can delegate parts of the work to other people. Process models may thus spread out. This explicit representation of communication and negotiation, and especially the structuring of the conversation into predefined speech act steps, has also been criticised (Button 1995; De Michelis and Grasso 1994; King 1995; Suchman 1994). Minimal support for situated conversations, the danger that explication leads to increased external control of the work and a simplistic one-to-one mapping between utterances and actions are among the weaknesses. On the other hand, it has been reported that the Action Workflow approach is useful when people act pragmatically and do not always follow the encoded rules of behaviour (De Michelis and Grasso 1994), i.e. when the communication models are interactively activated.

Some later approaches to workflow modelling include aspects of both the functional (see Sect. 3.3.3) and language action modelling. In WooRKS (Ader et al. 1994) functional modelling is used for representing the main processes and language action modelling for representing exceptions thus not using these perspectives in combination. TeamWare Flow (Swenson et al. 1994) and Obligations (Bogia 1995) on the other hand can be said to be hybrid approaches, but using very different concepts from those found in traditional conceptual modelling. The interest for language action modelling has been less in the workflow/BPM area in this decade though, even if you find some approaches such as DEMO described in Sect. 3.3.7 still being applied.

3.4.7 Process Modelling According to the Actor and Role Perspective

Role-centric process modelling languages have been applied for work flow analysis and implementation. Role Interaction Nets (RIN) (Singh and Rein 1992) and Role Activity Diagrams (RAD) (Ould 1995) use roles as their main structuring concept. The activities performed by a role are grouped together in the diagram, either in swim-lanes (RIN), or inside boxes (RAD). The use of roles as a structuring concept makes it very clear who is responsible for what. RAD has also been merged with speech acts for interaction between roles (Benson et al. 2000). A newer approach in this direction is S-BPM (subject-oriented business process management (Fleischmann 2010)).

The role-based approach also has limitations, e.g. making it difficult to change the organisational distribution of work. It primarily targets analysis of administrative procedures, where formal roles are important. The use of swimlanes in BPMN and UML Activity Diagrams as described in Sect. 3.3.3 might also have this effect. Some other relevant approaches that were presented in Sect. 3.3.8 were REA and e^{3}Value, although the description of e^{3}Value emphasise that the approach focus is on value exchange, not process modelling.

Table 3.2 Appropriateness of different perspectives for process modelling

	1+2	3	4	5a	5b	5c	6
Area	S&C	Sim	QA	Man Act	Work-flow	Inter-active	Req
Behavioural	–/OK	+/OK	–/–	–/–	+/OK	–/–	OK/–
Functional	+/+	–/–	+/OK	+/OK	–/–	OK/–	+/OK
Beha+Func	+/OK	+/OK	OK/–	OK/–	+/+	+/OK	OK/OK
Structural	OK/–	–/–	–/–	–/–	–/–	–/–	OK/–
Rule/Goal	–/–	OK/–	OK/–	–/–	OK/–	OK/–	OK/OK
Object	–/–	OK/–	–/–	–/–	–/–	–/–	OK/–
LAP	OK/–	–/–	–/–	–/–	OK/–	OK/–	–/–
Actor	+/OK	OK/–	OK/–	OK/–	–/–	–/–	OK/OK
Geographical	OK/–	–/–	–/–	OK/–	–/–	OK/–	OK/–

3.4.8   Process Modelling According to the Topological Perspective

The concept of place in the sense it is defined in Sect. 3.3.9 can be related to for instance a process, given that one focus on the typical behaviour in a certain setting (a meeting-room or a lecture room say) rather than where this is physically. Whereas some processes is closely related to a concrete space (e.g. what can be done in a certain, specialised factory), more and more tasks can be done in more or less any setting due to the mobile information infrastructure that has been established over the last decade, thus making it useful to be able to differentiate geographic from functionally oriented modelling. In certain representations, aspects of space and place is closely interlinked (e.g. in the representation of the agenda of a conference, also taking time into account). Example of process modelling according to place and space is described in Sect. 3.3.9, although it is primarily the space-oriented depictions of Figs. 3.45 and 3.46 that can be said to be primarily topologically oriented.

3.4.9   Summary on Process Modelling

We have summarised the results below of this high-level overview of the field, looking upon approaches according to different perspectives relative to the different usage areas for process modelling, and also indicated the amount of actual use of the perspective to achieve the different goals of modelling described in Chap. 1 (Table 3.2):

The legend indicates the applicability of the approach/the actual use of the approach (relative to the usage of modelling for this task), + indicates good applicability or high use, 'OK' is some applicability and use, whereas '–' indicates poor applicability and limited use. Obviously different approaches according to the same perspective can be more or less applicable as partly discussed above, and different languages of a certain perspective would score differently based on the concrete expressiveness and level of formality of the language and modelling approach. We do not here provide more concrete evaluations of all approaches that we mentioned in the previous section. From the table, we see that functional and combinations of functional and behavioural approaches are used the most. All other perspectives have potential for use for certain areas, although this often varies relative to concrete needs in the domain for representing particular aspects (such as topological aspects which in many cases might not be relevant). In particular, some of the less traditional approaches appear to have large untapped potential for a richer more appropriate representation of what we term processes and business processes.

3.5   Applying Several Modelling Perspectives in Concert

We have above presented different perspectives towards conceptual modelling. If we follow a social construction theory, we cannot claim that the general features of the world to exist a priori. According to this belief one might wish to go to the other extreme; an approach without any presumptions at all. However, this is impossible. Any methodology and any language imply some presumptions. Thus, having an approach totally free of presumptions would mean to have no approach at all, inventing a new one fit for the specific problem for every new development and maintenance task. For philosophers this might be acceptable, but engineers are expected to adapt to certain demands for efficiency. Inventing a new approach for every development and evolution effort would not give us that efficiency, neither is it likely that it will give better CIS-support for the organisation. Developing and maintaining a CIS without any fixed ideas about how it should be done would be tedious and unsystematic and make communication difficult between those involved in the work. As stated by Boehm (1988), the ad hoc methods used in the earliest days of software development were much worse than those used today. So clearly one needs to make some presumptions. What is necessary is to find a point of balance: making enough presumptions for the approach to be systematic and efficient, but not so many that its flexibility and applicability is severely reduced. We can become aware of some of our presumptions, and in that way emancipate ourselves from some of the limits they place on our thinking, but we can never free us from all presumptions.

As we have illustrated in this chapter, there are a number of different approaches to conceptual modelling, each emphasising different aspects of the perceived reality. Towards the end of the 1980s and early 1990s several researchers claimed that one perspective is better, or more natural, than others:

- Sowa (1983) bases his language for conceptual graphs on work on human perception and thinking done in cognitive psychology, and uses this to motivate the use of the language. It seems safe to say that even with his convincing discussion, his approach applying conceptual graphs have had a very limited influence on conceptual modelling practices and the development and evolution of CISs in most organisations, even if it has received much attention within computer science research.
- Many authors have advocated object-oriented modelling partly based on the claim that it is a more natural way to perceive the world (Loy 1990; Wilkie 1993). The view that object-orientation is a suitable perspective for all situations

have been criticised by many; see e.g. Bryant and Evans (1994), Høydalsvik and Sindre (1993) and Jacobs et al. (1994). The report on the First International Symposium on Requirements Engineering (Jacobs et al. 1994) said it so strongly that 'requirements are not object-oriented. Panellists reported that users do not find it natural to express their requirements in object-oriented fashion'. Even if there are cases where a purely object-oriented perspective is beneficial, it does not seem to be an appropriate way of describing all sorts of problems, as discussed in Høydalsvik and Sindre (1993). As stated by Meyer (1996), 'Object technology is not about modelling the real world. Object technology is about producing quality software, and the way to obtain this is to devise the right abstractions, whether or not they model what someone sees as the reality'.

- In Tempora (1988), rules were originally given a similar role in that it was claimed, 'end users perceive large parts of a business in terms of policies or rules'. This is a truth with modification. Even if people may act according to rules, they are not necessarily looking upon it as they are as discussed by Stamper (1987). Rule-based approaches also have to deal with several deficiencies, as discussed earlier in the chapter.

- Much of the early work on conceptual modelling that has been based on a constructivistic world-view has suggested language/action modelling as a possible cornerstone of conceptual modelling (Goldkuhl and Lyytinen 1982; Klein and Lyytinen 1991; Winograd and Flores 1986), claiming that it is more suitable than traditional 'objectivistic' conceptual modelling. On the other hand, the use of this perspective has also been criticised, also from people sharing a basic constructivistic outlook. An overview of the critique is given in De Michelis and Grasso (1994):

  - Speech act theory is wrong in that it assumes a one-to-one mapping between utterances and illocutionary acts, which is not recognisable in real life conversations.
  - The normative use of the illocutionary force of utterances is the basis for developing tools for the discipline and control over organisations
  - Member's actions and not supporting cooperative work among equals.
  - The language/action perspective does not recognise that embedded in any conversation is a process of negotiating the agreement of meaning.
  - The language/action perspective misses the locality and situatedness of conversations, because it proposes a set of fixed models of conversations for any group without supporting its ability to design its own conversation models.
  - The language/action perspective offers only a partial insight; it has to be integrated with other theories.

- As discussed earlier in this chapter, also functionally and structurally oriented approaches have been criticised in the literature (Opdahl and Sindre 1994).

Although the use of a single perspective has been criticised, this does not mean that modelling according to a perspective should be abandoned, as long as we do not limit ourselves to one single perspective. A given language according to a specific perspective emphasise a specific way of ordering and abstracting ones internal reality. One model in a given language will thus seldom be sufficient. With this in mind, more and more approaches are based on the combination of several modelling languages. There are four general ways of attacking this:

1. Use existing single-perspective languages as they are defined, without trying to integrate them further. This is the approach followed in many existing modelling tools.
2. Refine common approaches to make a set of formally integrated, but still partly independent set of languages.
3. Develop a set of entirely new integrated conceptual modelling languages.
4. Create frameworks that can be used for creating the modelling languages that are deemed necessary in any given situation.

A consequence of a combined approach is that it requires much better tool support than a single-perspective approach to be practical. Due to the increased possibilities of consistency checking and traceability across models, in addition to better possibilities for the conceptual models to serve as input for code-generation, and to support validation techniques such as execution, explanation generation and animation the second of these approaches has been receiving increased interest, especially in the academic world. Basing integrated modelling languages on well-known modelling languages also have advantages with respect to perceptibility, and because of the existing practical experience with these languages. Also, many examples of the third and fourth solution exist, together with work on so-called meta-modelling systems supporting domain specific modelling e.g. (Kelly and Tolvanen 2008). Work based on language-modelling might also be used to improve the applicability of approaches of all the other types

Having discussed the weaknesses of fixed orientation above, the fundamental goals for a modelling approach that attempts to avoid orientation can be identified:

- Perspective freedom: It should enable the modeller to choose to capture any *kind of aspect* of a problem-domain phenomenon, and any *kind of dependency* between aspects. To the extent possible, *the choice of what to* represent *and when to* represent *it should be left to the modeller* contingent on the problem domain and the problems at hand.
- Perspective co-representation: Whenever several aspects of the same phenomenon are relevant to describe the problem domain, it should be possible to capture them *simultaneously as* well as structurally and semantically close *to* one *another in the model* instead of having to use several isolated modelling constructs and several isolated partial models.
- Perspective integration: If several aspects of the same phenomenon are *semantically related,* this should be reflected in the problem domain model.
- Perspective extensibility: As new kinds of aspects are recognised as relevant to the problems at hand during analysis, it should be possible to *extend* the modelling language to account for them. Also, it should be possible to visualise perspectives freely based on the already recognised kinds of aspects that are represented in a model.

These are the four main characteristics of what in Opdahl and Sindre (1995) was introduced as the *facet-modelling ap*proach. We will present another language of this sort (GEMAL) later in this section. We will also look at other multi-perspective languages made according to approach 2, UML being rooted in object-orientation, but also found useful for modelling according to other perspectives, and EEML, rooted on transformations, but also able to cover the other perspectives for the use in enterprise modelling with a focus on process modelling in particular.

3.5.1   Description of UML

The use of object-oriented modelling in analysis and design started to become popular in the late 1980s, producing a large number of different languages and approaches. Over the last 15 years, UML has taken a leading position in this area, partly through the standardisation of the language within the Object Management Group (OMG).

According to OMG (2006a), UML is a language for specifying, visualising, constructing and documenting the artefacts of software systems, as well as for business modelling and modelling of other non-software systems. In other words, UML is meant to be used in the analysis of business and information, requirement specification and design. This said, UML has its main strength for object-oriented design. UML is meant to support the modelling of (object-oriented) transaction systems, real-time and safety critical systems. As illustrated in e.g. Favre (2003), UML is used and adapted for a number of different specific areas. As described in Sect. 3.3.6 the use of object-oriented modelling in analysis and design started to become popular in the late 1980s, producing a large number of different languages and approaches. Over the last 15 years, UML (OMG 2006a) has taken a leading position in this area.

The development of UML began in late 1994 when Grady Booch and Jim Rumbaugh of Rational Software Corporation began their work on unifying the Booch and OMT (Object Modeling Technique) methods. In the autumn of 1995, Ivar Jacobson joined this unification effort, merging in the OOSE (Object-Oriented Software Engineering) method.

As the primary authors of the Booch, OMT and OOSE methods, Booch, Rumbaugh and Jacobson were motivated to create a unified modelling language for three reasons. First, these methods were already evolving toward each other independently. The methods had different strengths and one started to see people combining them in different ways (Rosenberg 1999). Second, by unifying the semantics and notation, they wanted to bring some stability to the object-oriented modelling and development marketplace, allowing projects to settle on one modelling language and letting tool builders focus on delivering more useful features. Third, they expected that their collaboration would yield improvements in all three earlier methods, helping them to capture lessons learned and to address problems that none of their methods previously handled well.http://atlas.kennesaw.edu/~dbraun/csis4650/A&D/UML_tutorial/history_of_uml.htm – 1

UML 0.9 and 0.91 documents were released in June and October of 1996. During 1996, the UML authors invited and received feedback from the object-oriented modelling community. They incorporated this feedback, but it was clear that additional focused work was still required.http://atlas.kennesaw.edu/~dbraun/csis4650/A&D/ UML_tutorial/history_of_uml.htm – 1

While Rational was bringing UML together, efforts were being made on achieving the broader goal of an industry standard OO-modelling language. In early 1995, Ivar Jacobson and Richard Soley (then Chief Technology Officer of OMG – Object Management Group) decided to push harder to achieve standardisation in the OO-modelling area. In June 1995, an OMG-hosted meeting of all major methodologists (or their representatives) resulted in the first worldwide agreement to seek methodology standards in this area utilising the OMG process.

During 1996, it became clear that several organisations saw UML as strategic to their business. A Request for Proposal (RFP) issued by OMG provided the means for these organisations to join forces around producing a joint response. Rational established the UML Partners consortium with several organisations. This collaboration produced UML 1.0 submitted to the OMG in January 1997 as an initial response to the RFP. http://atlas.kennesaw.edu/~dbraun/csis4650/A&D/UML_tutorial/history_of_uml.htm – 1

In January 1997 a number of other companies joined the UML partners to contribute their ideas, and together the partners produced the revised UML 1.1. The focus of the UML 1.1 release was to improve the clarity of the UML 1.0 semantics and to incorporate contributions from the new partners. It was submitted to the OMG for their consideration and adopted in the fall of 1997. http://atlas.kennesaw. edu/~dbraun/csis4650/A&D/UML_tutorial/history_of_uml.htm – 1 Several minor revisions (UML 1.3, 1.4 and 1.5) fixed shortcomings and bugs with the first version of UML, followed by the UML 2.0 major revision that was adopted by the OMG in 2005. http://en.wikipedia.org/wiki/Unified_Modeling_Language – cite_note-5 Although UML 2.1 was never released as a formal specification, versions 2.1.1 and 2.1.2 appeared in 2007, followed by UML 2.2 in February 2009. UML 2.3 was formally released in May 2010. http://en.wikipedia.org/wiki/Unified_Modeling_Language – cite_note-6 UML 2.4 is in the beta stage as of March 2011.

There are now two documents available that describe UML:

- UML 2.0 Infrastructure defines the basic constructs of the language on which UML is based. This section is not directly relevant to the users of UML. This is directed more towards the developers of modelling tools.
- UML 2.0 Superstructure defines the user constructs of UML 2.0. It means those elements of UML that users will use for modelling.

This revision of UML was created to fulfil a goal to restructure and refine UML so that usability was improved and implementation and adaptation were simplified.

The UML infrastructure is used to:

- Provide a reusable meta-language core. This is used to define UML itself.
- Provide mechanisms to adjustment the language.

The UML superstructure is used to:

- Provide better support for component-based development.
- Improve constructs for the specification of architecture
- Provide better options for the modelling of behaviour.

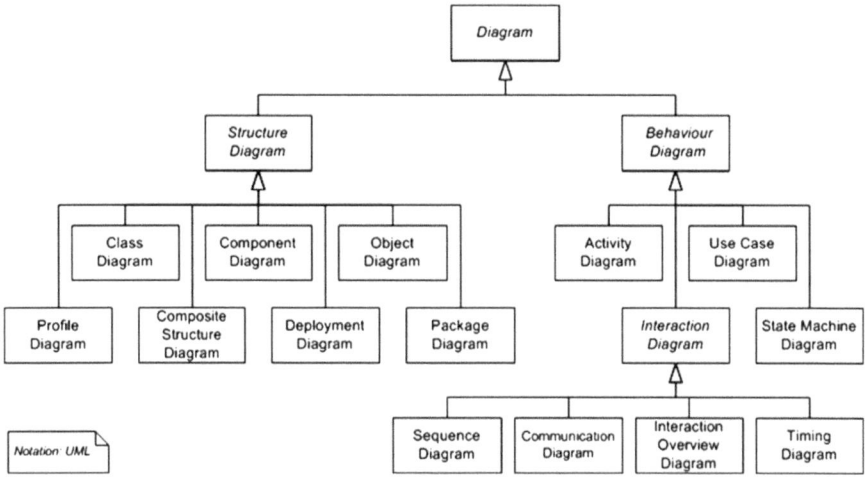

Fig. 3.48 Overview of UML diagrams in UML 2.2

UML 2.2 has 14 types illustrated in Fig. 3.48 of defined sub-models to be depicted in separate diagrams. The diagrams are divided into two categories. http://en.wikipedia. org/wiki/Unified_Modeling_Language – cite_note-10 Seven diagram types represent *structural* information, and the other seven represent general types of *behaviour*, including four that represent different aspects of *interactions*. These diagrams can be categorised hierarchically as shown in the following class diagram:

UML does only partly restrict UML element types to a certain diagram type. In general, every UML element may appear on almost all types of diagrams; this flexibility has been partially restricted in UML 2.0. UML profiles may define additional diagram types or extend existing diagrams with additional concepts. We will present the main parts of the language briefly here; see Booch (2005) for a full description of the different diagrams and modelling concepts typically found in these. In addition to the books by Booch, Jacobson and Rumbaugh UML is also described in detail in a number of books e.g. Fowler (2003), Larman (2004) and Rosenberg (1999). We give a high level overview of the diagrams below.

3.5.1.1 Structure diagrams
Structure diagrams emphasise the things that must be present in the system being modelled. Since structure diagrams represent the structure, they are used extensively in documenting the software architecture of software systems, but are also used for modelling the static structure and concepts of the domain, as a kind of structural (data) modelling.

• Class diagram: describes the structure of a system by showing the system's classes, their attributes and the relationships among the classes. Figure 3.49

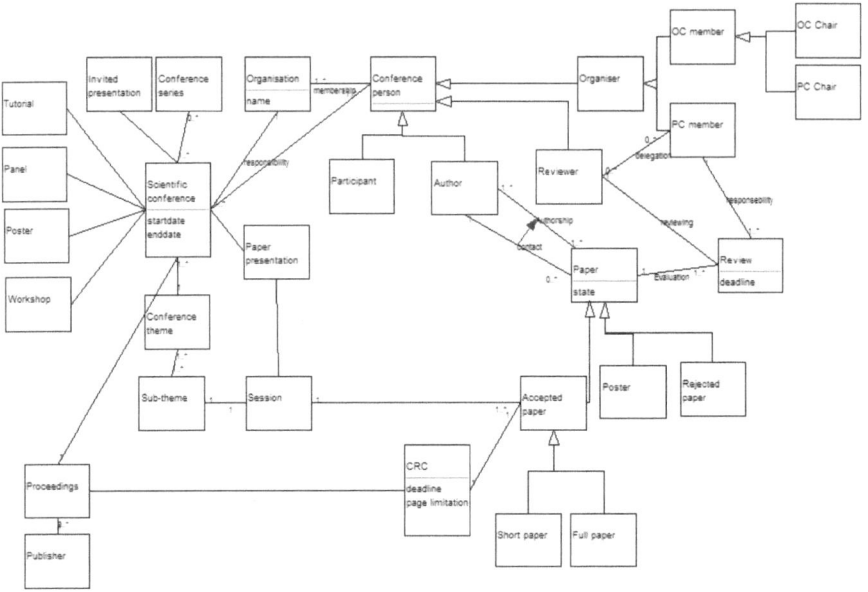

Fig. 3.49 Example of UML class diagram on the conceptual level

shows a UML class diagram on the conceptual level relative to the conference
case. When used for OO-design, the class diagram will typically contain more
attributes, and also a specification of the methods (which do not have a role on
the conceptual level), see for instance the OMT-class diagram in Sect. 3.3.6

- Component diagram: describes how a software system is split up into components and shows the dependencies among these components.
- Composite structure diagram: describes the internal structure of a class and the
  collaborations that this structure makes possible.
- Deployment diagram: describes the hardware used in system implementations
  and the execution environments and artefacts deployed on the hardware.
- Object diagram: shows a complete or partial view of the structure of a modelled
  system at a specific time.
- Package diagram: describes how a system is split up into logical groupings by
  showing the dependencies among these groupings.
- Profile diagram: operates at the meta-model level to show stereotypes as classes
  with the <<stereotype>> stereotype, and profiles as packages with the <<profile>>
  stereotype. The extension relation (solid line with closed, filled arrowhead) indicates what meta-model element a given stereotype is extending.

3.5.1.2 Behaviour Diagrams

Behaviour diagrams emphasise the dynamics of the system being modelled. Since
behaviour diagrams illustrate the behaviour of a system, they are used extensively
to describe the functionality of software systems.

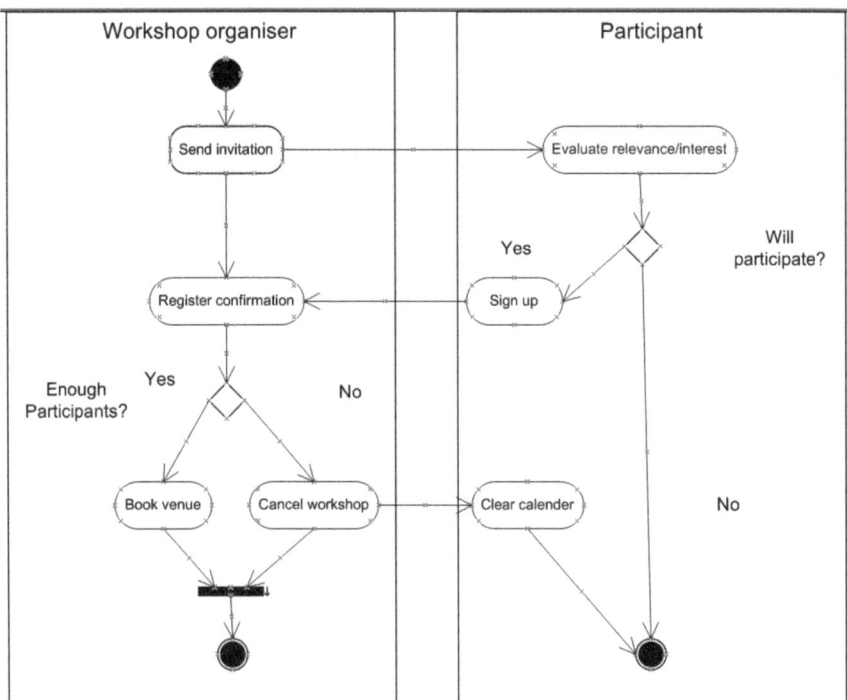

Fig. 3.50 Example of activity diagram

- Activity diagram: describes the business and operational step-by-step workflows of components in a system. An activity diagram shows the overall flow of control, and is quite similar when it comes to usage pattern and expressiveness as BPMN (see Sect. 3.3.3).

  The most important concepts in the UML activity diagram are as follows:
- *Rounded rectangles* represent activities
- *Diamonds* represent decisions
- *Bars* represent the start (split) or end (join) of concurrent activities
- *Black circle* represents the start (initial state) of the workflow
- *Encircled black circle* represents the end (final state)

  In Fig. 3.50, we see an example of a simple activity diagram of the same part of the case that we had for illustrating BPMN in Sect. 3.3.3 relative to the registration to a workshop.
- UML state machine diagram: describes the states and state transitions of the system. These are quite similar to the state machines developed originally by Harel described in Sect. 3.3.2, see the section for an example
- Use case diagram: describes the functionality provided by a system in terms of actors, their goals represented as use cases, and any dependencies among those use cases. Figure 3.51 illustrates the main actors relative to conference and main functionality relative to the submission of papers and registrations.

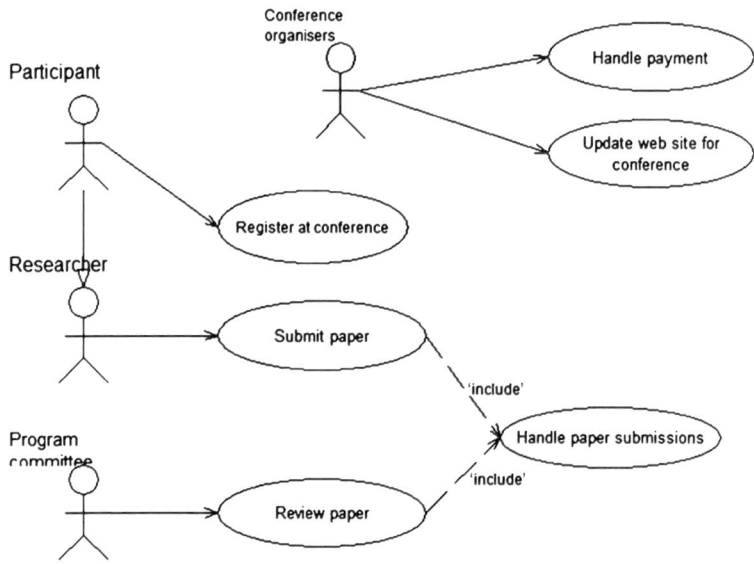

Fig. 3.51   Example of a Use Case diagram

3.5.1.3 Interaction Diagrams

Interaction diagrams, a subset of behaviour diagrams, emphasise the flow of control and data among the things in the system being modelled:

- Communication diagram: shows the interactions between objects or parts in terms of sequenced messages. They represent a combination of information taken from Class, Sequence and Use Case Diagrams describing both the static structure and dynamic behaviour of a system.
- Interaction overview diagram: provides an overview in which the nodes represent communication diagrams.
- Sequence diagram: shows how objects communicate with each other in terms of a sequence of messages. It also indicates the lifespan of objects relative to those messages.
- Timing diagrams: a specific type of interaction diagram where the focus is on timing constraints.

A modelling project seldom uses all these diagrams. Somewhat depended on the type of systems, you find use-case diagrams, sequence diagrams, class diagrams and state diagrams to be used the most (Erickson and Siau 2007). After the change of the semantics of activity diagrams in UML 2.0 to be closer to business process modelling languages such as BPMN, this has also seen increased use in particular relative to enterprise modelling and enterprise systems development.

Looking upon UML relative to the different modelling perspectives we can observe the following:

- Structural
  - Class diagram (when modelling without using methods) covers this perspective quite well

- Object oriented
  - Object and Class diagrams (with methods)
  - Sequence and collaboration diagrams
- Functional
  - Use cases
  - Activity diagrams
- Behavioural
  - State diagrams
- Rule oriented
  - OCL (a rule language not directly part of UML for individual rules). No support of rule and goal hierarchies
- Actor/role oriented
  - Limited coverage (in the sense of modelling social actors)
  - Actors in use case diagrams, swimlanes in activity diagrams
- (Social) communication
  - Not covered
- Topological
  - Not covered

A more thorough evaluation of UML is provided in Sect. 7.3.1, after we have introduced our approach for evaluating quality of modelling languages in Chap. 5.

3.5.2   Description of EEML

We have over the last 10 years been developing a model-based approach to be able to quickly support the development of model-based solutions primarily supporting interactive activation (vs. Sect. 2.3.6) both within single organisations and across networked organisation (Krogstie and Jørgensen 2004). Although geared towards generation of process support environment, it is also possible to use EEML for more general enterprise modelling, focus on usage areas 1 and 2 from Chap. 1.

The kernel EEML-concepts are shown in Fig. 3.52 as a simplified conceptual meta-model (i.e. using the actual symbols of the language also in the meta-model, and not as in a logical meta-model modelling the concepts more abstractly using a structural modelling language such as UML class diagrams).

The language is divided into four sub-languages, with well-defined links across these languages:

- Process modelling
- Data modelling
- Resource modelling
- Goal modelling

Process modelling support the modelling of process logic, which is mainly expressed through nested structures of *tasks* and *decision points*. The sequencing of the tasks is expressed by the *flow* relation between decision points. Each task has minimum an input port and an output port being decision points for modelling process logic, *Resource roles* are used to connect resources of various kinds (persons, organisations, information, material objects, software tools and manual tools) to the

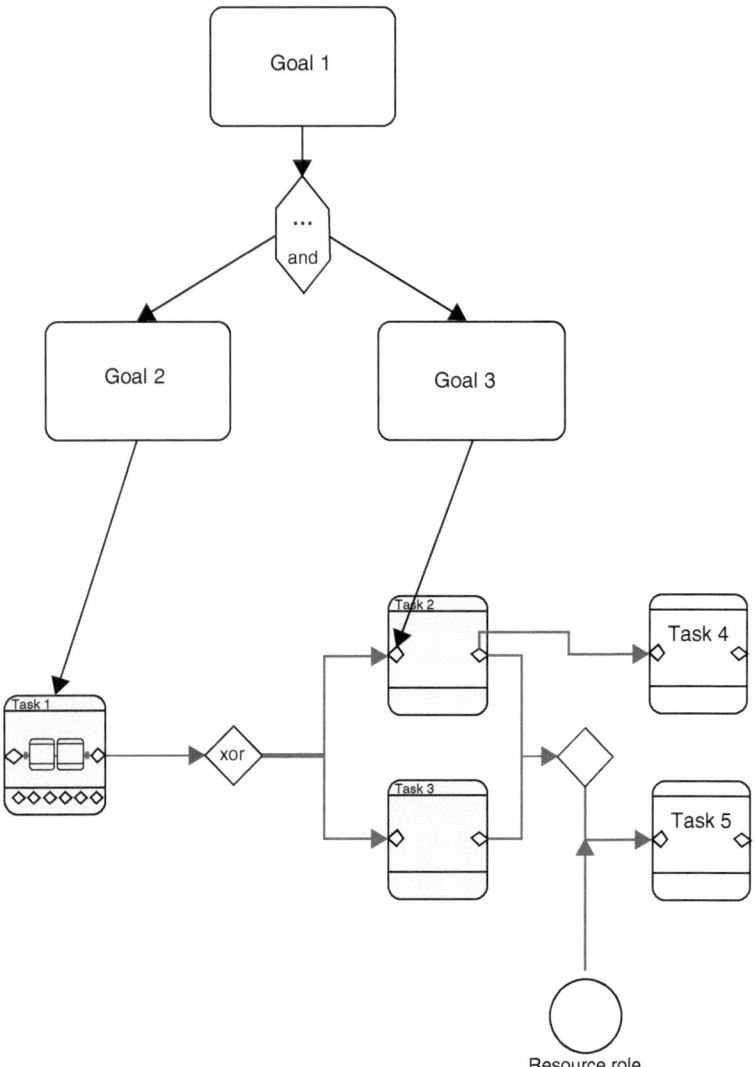

Fig. 3.52 Conceptual meta-model of process and goal modelling parts of EEML

tasks, see Fig. 3.54. In addition, data modelling (using UML class diagrams, see Fig. 3.49), goal modelling and competency modelling (skill requirements and skills possessed) can be integrated with the process models. We will discuss specifically the goal modelling in more detail below.

An example of high-level process modelling from the conference case is illustrated in Fig. 3.53.

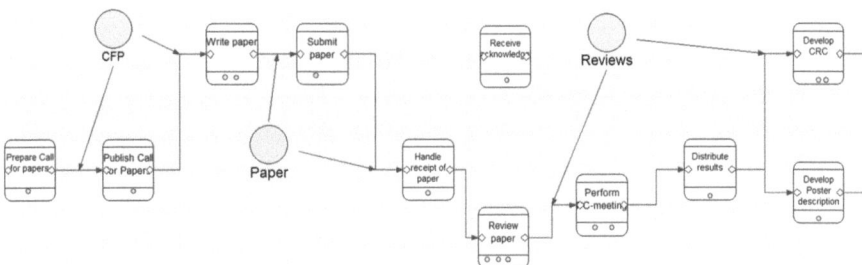

Fig. 3.53 The paper review process modelled in EEML

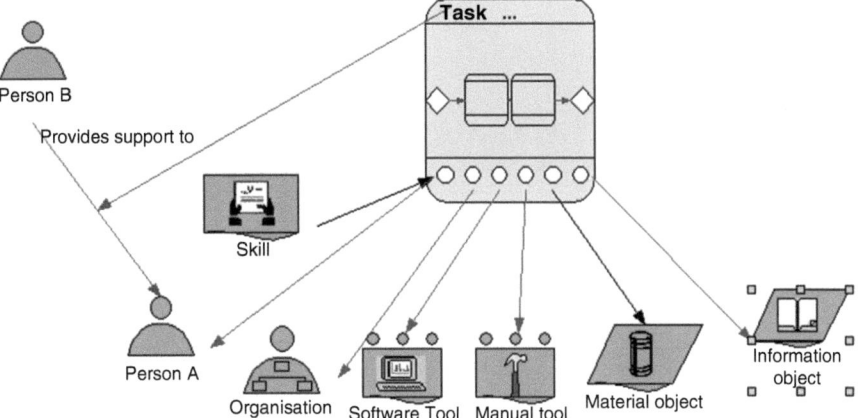

Fig. 3.54 Conceptual meta-model of EEML resource types

Figure 3.54 provides further detail on the resource modelling. A number of resource types and construct related to resources can be defined:

- Person
- Organisation
- Information object/material object
- Software tool/Manual tool
- Skill
- Physical location

A number of relationships exist between resources and resource roles to support e.g. organisational modelling such as

- Resourcerole is filled by resourcerole|resource
- Resourcerole is candidate for resourcerole|resource
- Resourcerole|resource communicates with resourcerole|resource
- Resourcerole|resource has supervision over resourcerole|resource
- Resourcerole|resource provides support to resourcerole|resource
- Organisation has members

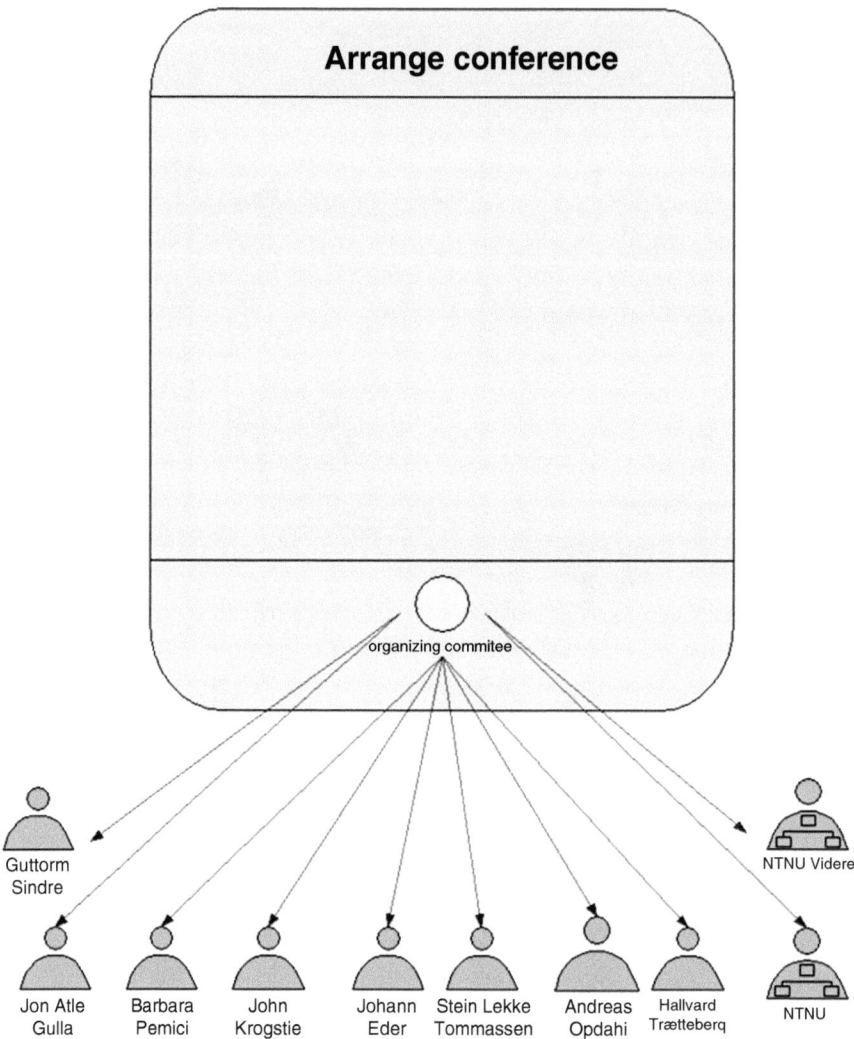

Fig. 3.55 An example of modelling of concrete resources in EEML

In Fig. 3.55, we see an example (depicting some of the actors of a particular conference, the CAiSE 2007 conference) how different people and organisations acted as important resources in relation to the organisation of the conference.

Goals in the goal modelling are inspired by Krogstie and Sindre (1996) represented as

If context then deontic operator achieve state

Where the deontic operators possible are: necessitate, obligate, recommend, permit, discourage, forbid and contradict.

There are a number of relationships between goals and other modelling constructs:

- Goal applies to task/milestone/resourcerole/resource
- Goal is action rule for task

Fig. 3.56 Mechanisms for modelling complex rule-hierarchies in EEML

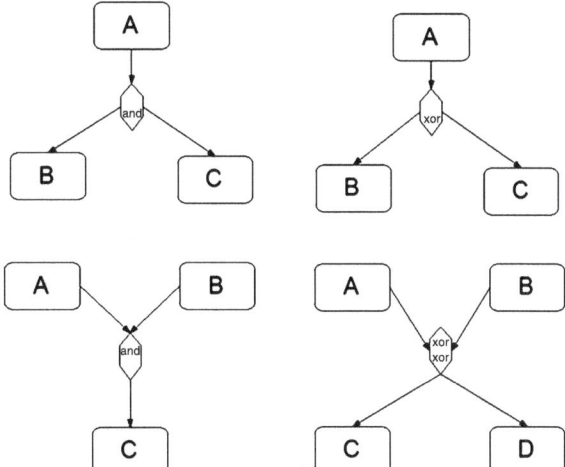

- Goal is precondition/decision rule/postcondition for task
- Role/resource is the source of a goal
  Finally, goals can be related in mean end hierarchies in the format
- Goal deontic operator goal (argument)
  where deontic operator can be chosen from the same list as for the use of deontic operators above. A model G1 obligatory G2 can be read as that to achieve G1 it is obligatory to achieve G2. G1 forbidden G2 on the other hand indicates that if you achieve G2, you are forbidden to achieve G1 (this is similar to the positive and negative contributions of goals in Yu and Mylopoulos (1994). Also as in GRL Yu and Mylopoulos (1994), we provide a way to model and/or graphs in the goal hierarchy (as shown in Fig. 3.56).

  Figure 3.57 provides high-level goals of the conference case.

  Finally, we illustrate how some of the more detailed goals interrelate with some of the tasks relative to the paper review process in Fig. 3.58.

  Looking upon EEML relative to the different modelling perspectives we can conclude the following.
- Structural
  – Class diagram (when modelling without using methods) covers this perspective quite well
- Object oriented
  – Not really covered (even if UML Class diagrams are included)
- Functional
  – Process modelling
- Behavioural
  – Possible to represent to traditional control structures through the process modelling
- Rule oriented
  – Both deontic and alethic rules and goal-hierarchies
- Actor/role oriented
  – Through the modelling of resources and resource roles, and relations between these

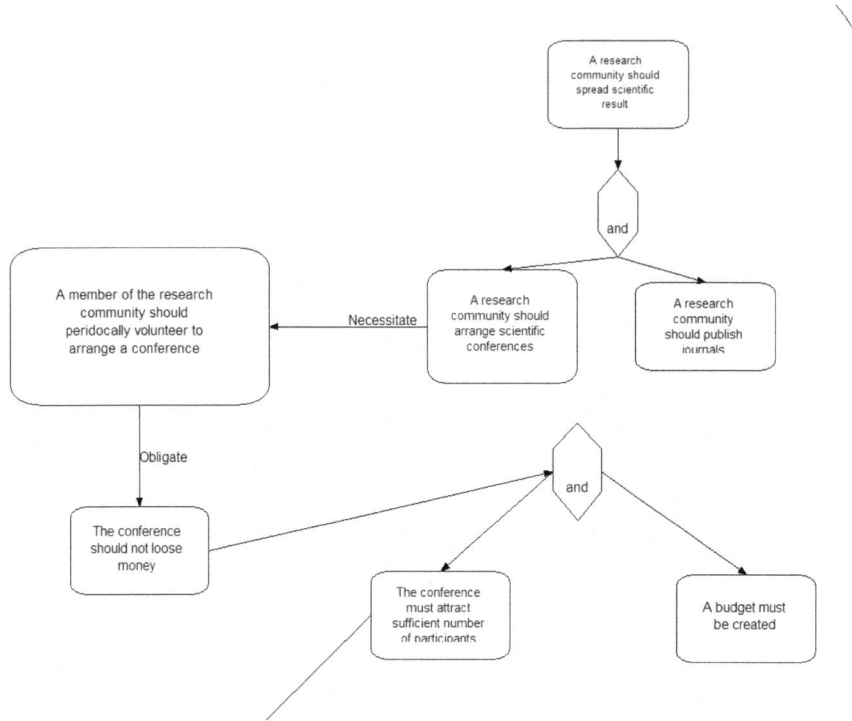

Fig. 3.57 Top-level goals in the conference case

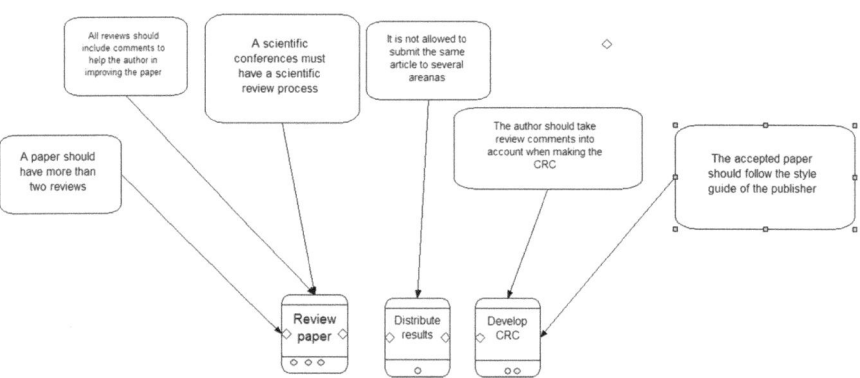

Fig. 3.58 Relationships between goals and tasks in EEML

- (Social) communication
  - Not directly covered
- Topological
  - Covered on a high level by modelling of geographical locations

3.5.3   Description of GEMAL

A guideline in modelling language design is that the number of concepts should be reasonable, something we will return to in Chap. 5 on language quality. For a generic modelling language, there are an infinite number of statements that we might want to make, and these have to be dealt with through a limited number of concepts. This means that

- The core concepts must be general rather than specialised.
- The concepts must be composable, which means that we can group and combine related statements in a natural way.
- The language must be flexible in precision.

If the number of constructs has to be large, the phenomena should be organised hierarchically and/or in sub-languages of reasonable size linked to specific modelling tasks, making it possible to approach the modelling language at different levels of abstraction or from different perspectives and usage areas. UML for instance can be argued to be a complex language, with a total of 233 different concepts (Castellani 1999). An approach to address such a problem is to go for a holistic or molecular modelling language. (Kangassalo 1999) distinguishes between holistic, molecular and atomic semantics of modelling languages. With atomic semantics, the meaning of a model element is completely specified by that element, while with holistic semantics the meaning depends on every other element in the model. Molecular semantics offer a compromise, where meaning is given by some parts of the model. A language with atomic semantics requires a lot of specific constructs, while holism allows meaning to be constructed by combining a number of elements, like words in a sentence. In its extreme this provides a large number of senseless statements, thus we approach this using a molecular approach.

The following contains a brief, informal overview over core concepts in an enterprise modelling multi-perspective language (similar to a facet-language (Opdahl and Sindre 1997)), adhering to molecular principles, which we have named GEMAL – General Enterprise Modelling and Activation Language. To illustrate some of the aspects we use examples from the conference case.

In GEMAL, all concepts can exist both on a type level and an instance level. Any instance can have a type, but do not have to. There is one basic concept: Thing: As in Wand and Weber (1993), a thing is the elementary unit. The physical and social world is perceived to be made up of things. Two or more things can be associated into a composite thing. A system is a set of things if, for any bi-partition of the set, couplings exist among things in the two subsets.

Things possess properties. A property is modelled via a function that maps the thing into some value. A class is a set of things that can be defined via their possessing a single property. The state of a thing is the vector of all values for all property functions of the thing. A transformation is a mapping from one state to another state. The history is the trajectory of states of the thing. All things possess at least the following properties

- ID, Name, Description, Start-time, End-time, Instantiation level (type or instance showed visually on the concept), Concept specialisations (the possible specialisations of a thing), Modality (necessity, obligation, recommendation, permission, discouragement, prohibition, contradiction), Current state (from a set of possible states of a thing).

Relationships between things have the same properties except instantiation levels. All other concepts are a specialisation of a thing. There are seven types of things defined:

- Goal: A state that one wants to achieve in some context. Generic goals apply for a type concept (Get paper accepted), and concrete goals apply to instances (Get this paper accepted for the CAiSE conference).
- Process: A process is a transformation. Either it transforms things into other things, or changes the state of a thing: Both process types (write paper) and process instances (write the paper on GEMAL to send to CAiSE 2013) exist.
- Product: A thing produced through a process. Products also exist on type (a scientific paper) and instance level (this concrete book).
- Capability: A generic capability (the skill needed to write of a scientific paper) is something useful for achieving a generic goal. A concrete capability (writing CAiSE papers) makes it possible to change the state of the world in order to reach a goal.
- Person: Type of person (person-role e.g. author) or concrete person (me)
- Organisation: A set of persons (more than one) where goal-oriented processes takes place. Type of organisation (role e.g. program committee) and concrete organisations (CAiSE 2013 Program Committee)
- Location: A type of location (place – e.g. a conference venue) or a concrete (physical) location (space – The conference venue for CAiSE 2013), where the state-changes actually take place.

One can freely describe sub-concepts of the above concepts (e.g. constraint as a specialised sub-concept of goal) if necessary. All concepts are decomposable (except concrete persons), and all have a meta-construct (which is related to the creation/development of itself). This is exemplified below.

Process-centric: When looking upon this relative to a process, all other aspects are resources to be used or produced in the process. For a process-type (e. g. arrange a conference), we have the following specific meanings.

- Process: A process needed to create the process:
  - Type: The process to set up the schedule relative to conference arrangement
  - Instance: The process setting up the schedule for paper process for CAiSE 2013
- Organisation: As actor or resource in the process
  - Type: Program management board (PMB)
  - Instance: CAiSE PMB
- Person: An actor or resource in the process
  - Type: Program Chair
  - Instance: Colette Rolland

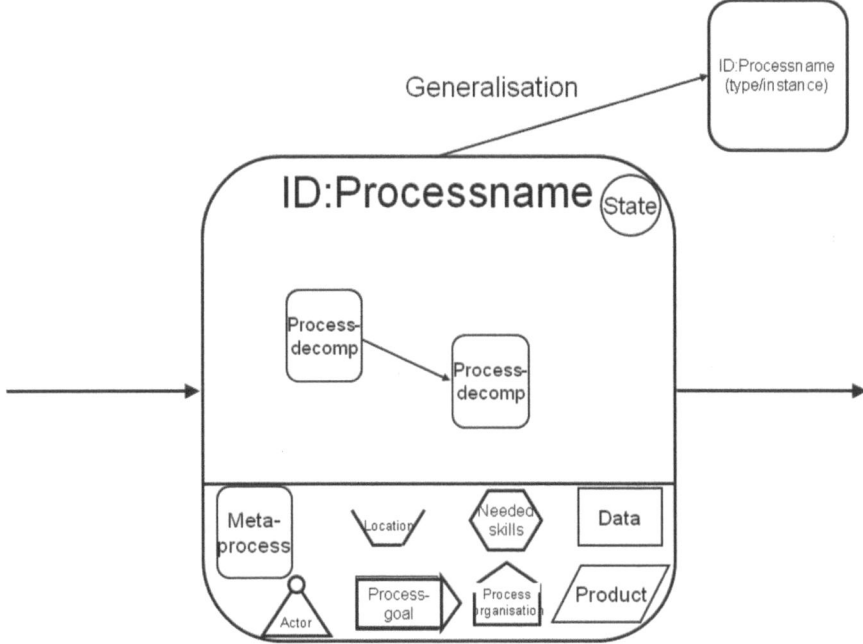

Fig. 3.59 Visualisation of processes in GEMAL

- Product: A resource (including data) used or produced in the process
  - Type: Proceedings
  - Instance CAiSE forum proceedings
- Goal: The goal of the process (what should be achieved)
  - Type: Control budget of conference
  - Instance: CAiSE 2013 should have a small surplus
- Capability: The capabilities needed to perform the process
  - Type: Conference arrangement skill
  - Instance: Set up easy chair for accepting and reviewing CAiSE forum papers
- Location: Space and place where the process takes place
  - Type: Meeting venue, meeting rooms
  - Instance: The room where the CAiSE forum is arranged
- Aggregation: Sub-processes within the process. For example, for the conference paper process, there are sub-processes on spreading the CFP, accepting paper, reviewing paper, selecting paper etc.

    The Fig. 3.59 illustrate the way we visualise the different concepts, being inspired by EEML-visualisations of processes as illustrated in Sect. 3.5.2.

Product-centric:
- Process: The production and usage processes (Product life-cycle)
- Organisation: Organisation making, selling or using the product

- Person: Persons producing, selling or using the product: The market of a product is those organisations and users that has/can buy the permission to use the product
- Product: A product needed to create the product (i.e. not a sub-product, but for instance a tool)
- Goal: The goal of the product (i.e. what is meant to be possible to do with the product)
- Capability: The capabilities needed to produce or use the product
- Location; Space/place where the product is developed or used
- Aggregation: Part of product

Organisation-centric:
- Process: The core processes of the organisation
- Organisation: One or more organisation necessary to create the organisation
- Person: Persons in the organisations (person-role in the context of a position)
- Product: Product used or developed by the organisation
- Goal: The goal of the organisation e.g. vision, mission and strategic goals
- Capability: The capabilities needed or developed in the organisation
- Location; Space/place occupied by the organisation
- Aggregation: Sub-organisation

Person centric:
- Process: The processes that a person performs
- Organisation: The organisations that the person is part of
- Person: Persons to develop persons, e.g. those hiring and training other people in an organisation.
- Product: Product used or made by the person
- Goal: The goal of a person or goal applicable to the person
- Capability: The current or needed capabilities of the person
- Location; Space/place occupied by the person
- Aggregation: Only applicable for person-roles, not individual persons

Goal centric:
- Process: How goals are developed and maintained (governance process)
- Organisation: Those developing or being subject to goals
- Person: Persons developing or being subject to goals
- Product: The product influenced by the goal
- Goal: meta-goal: Goal to govern the creation and evolution of goals
- Capability: The needed capability to develop or fulfil a goal
- Location; The space/place where the goal applies
- Aggregation: Sub-goals

Capability centric: This focus on the development and evolution of what is termed business capabilities:
- Process: The process needed to ensure the capabilities needed (e.g. training, career planning)
- Organisation: Those being involved in developing or using the capability
- Person : The persons being involved in developing or using the capability

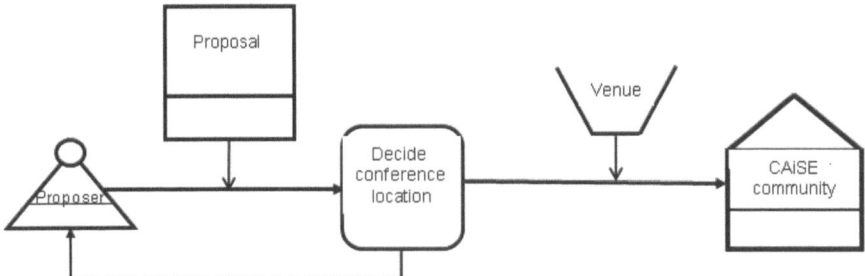

Fig. 3.60 Modelling 'Decide conference Location' in GEMAL

- Product: System to ensure the development or correct use of the capability
- Goal: The goal for developing capability
- Capability: meta-capability: Needed capability to use or produce the capability (e.g. training skills)
- Location; Space/place where capabilities are developed
- Aggregation: Sub-capabilities

Location-centric:

- Process: The process needed to develop and maintain the space/place
- Organisation: The organisation residing at the space/place
- Person: Those individuals residing in the space/place
- Product: Products developed, used or consumed in the space/place
- Goal: What is to be achieved in the space/place?
- Capability: The capabilities being developed or used in the space/place
- Location; Space/place where the space/place is developed (e.g. a factory making parts of a house)
- Aggregation: sub-space/place
  Generalisation-hierarchies can exist between all main concepts (on type-level). Generic relationships between things includes
- Relationship (There is a relationship between the things, so far undecided)
- Precede (A thing precede another thing in time (e.g. process flow))
- Support (A thing support that another thing achieve a state (a goal))
- Govern (A thing restrict and thus influence the state of another thing)
- Communicate (A thing informs another thing)

All relationships can be annotated with things or relationships indicating the context of the relationship, annotations can be to the relationship in general, or to any end of the relationship. Annotations can again be annotated. Relationships can in addition to go between things be connected to build up generic logical relationships (such as gateways for modelling process logic).

An early implementation is made available in the modelling environment METIS (now Troux Architect). When a concept is added as a sub-concept in one place, it is included as a first-level concept from this perspective. As an example in Fig. 3.60 we see the high-level process, where proposers (role), send a proposal (product),

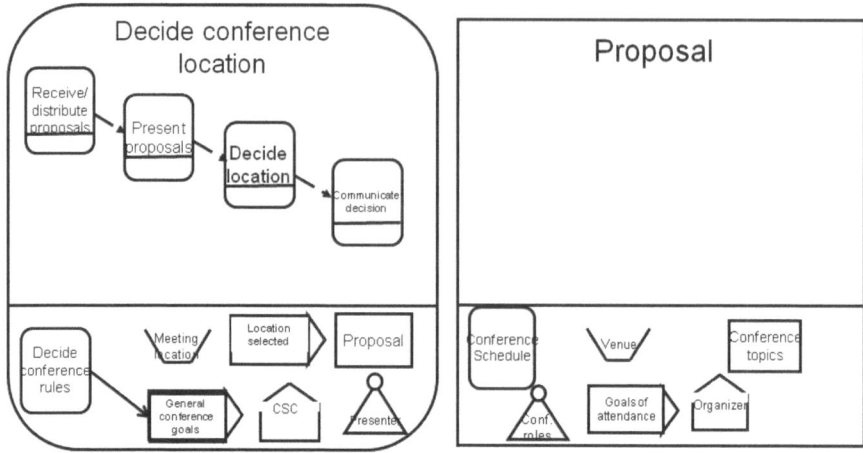

Fig. 3.61 Decomposition of main process and product in GEMAL

which is used in the process 'Decide Conference Location'. The chosen venue (location) is communicated to the CAiSE Community (an organisation instance)

When looking at the modelling of 'Proposal' (product) and 'Decide conference location' (process) in more detail in Fig. 3.61, some of the more particular aspects are illustrated:

How the process is to be done, is actually decided in another process (Decide conference rules). One concrete organisation is modelled (CSC – CAiSE Steering Committee). The proposal (product) contains as we see also other aspects e.g. the conference schedule (process), venue (location) etc., and when a proposal is selected, these aspects can be used as basis for the detailed model that will later be developed for the concrete conference.

3.6   Summary

In this chapter we have discussed mechanisms for modelling languages. We started looking at modelling as hierarchical abstraction, identifying the following generally applied abstraction mechanisms:
- Classification
- Aggregation
- Generalisation
- Association

The use of classification in relation to the level of models and their relationships where discussed. Modelling languages were described according to the perspectives they supported. Eight modelling perspectives were described:
- Behavioural
- Functional

- Structural
- Goal/rule oriented
- Object oriented
- Communicational
- Actor and role oriented
- Topological

We discussed how process modelling could be approached according to all these perspectives. Modern modelling languages in both analysis and design combine traits from several perspectives. We concluded the chapter with three examples of such combined languages: UML, EEML and GEMAL.

Review Questions

1. List the four main abstraction mechanisms used in conceptual modelling
2. What is a modelling perspective?
3. List the eight main modelling perspectives.
4. What four ways are there to combine modelling perspectives?
5. List two functionally oriented modelling languages.
6. List three behaviourally oriented modelling languages.
7. List two object-oriented modelling languages.
8. List three different structurally oriented modelling languages.
9. List three different organisational modelling languages.
10. List two modelling languages following the communicational perspective.
11. List two modelling languages supporting a goal-oriented modelling perspective.
12. Describe the difference between place and space.
13. Describe the main sub-languages of EEML.
14. Describe the main sub-languages of UML.
15. What are the main perspectives found to be used in most process modelling languages?

Problems and Exercises

Individual Exercises

The modelling exercises mentioned below can also be combined into larger assignments fit for a group exercise where you should also indicate the relationships between the different sub-models. The language to use on the different sub-exercises can be varied according to available tool support.

1. Based on the case description on course-arrangement in Appendix C (alternatively how you arrange courses at your university)
   (a) Model the structural aspects in a structurally oriented modelling language of choice (e.g. ER, ORM, UML Class Diagrams)
   (b) Model the high-level functionality in a support system for course-administration using e.g. DFD or UML Use Cases

(c) Model the processes in a language combining functional and behavioural aspects (e.g. BPMN, UML Activity diagrams, EPC, YAWL)
(d) Model goals and goal-relationships using the goal-oriented modelling language in EEML
(e) Model actor dependencies using i*
(f) Model value-exchange using e³value

Pair Exercises

1. Discuss a modelling language you are familiar with. What modelling perspective(s) does the language cover? If it covers more than one perspective, what would you say is the main perspective of the language?
2. Why has there been developed so many modelling languages?
3. We have in this chapter classified modelling languages according to eight different modelling perspectives. Are there other perspectives that might be envisaged to emerge in the next 10 years?

Group Exercises

1. Choose one of the modelling languages described in this chapter. Find if the modelling language is described in Wikipedia. If it is, update the description based on material in this chapter and on other reputable sources. If not make an entry in Wikipedia on the topic.
2. Develop a 10–15 page state-of-the-art paper on a modelling language or a modelling perspective mentioned in this chapter.

References

Aagesen, G., Krogstie, J.: Analysis and design of business processes using BPMN. In: vom Brocke, J., Rosemann, M. (eds.) Handbook on Business Process Management. International Handbooks of Information Systems. Springer, Berlin (2010)

Abdel-Hamid, T.K., Madnick, S.E.: Lessons learned from modeling the dynamics of software development. Commun. ACM **32**(12), 1426–1428 (1989)

Ader, M., Lu, G., Pons, P., Monguio, J., Lopez, L., De Michelis, G., Grasso, M.A., Vlondakis, G.: WOOrks, an object-oriented workflow system for offices. Technical report, ITHACA technical report (1994)

Albertsen, T., Sandkuhl, K., Seigerroth, U., Tarasov, V.: The practice of competence modelling. In: van Bommel, P. (ed.) PoEM 2010. LNBIP 68, pp. 106–120. Springer, Berlin/Heidelberg (2010)

Ambriola, V., Conradi, R., Fuggetta, A.: Assessing process-centered software engineering environments. ACM Trans. Softw. Eng. Methodol. **6**(3), 283–328 (1997)

Anaya, V., Berio, G., Harzallah, M., Heymans, P., Matulevičius, R., Opdahl, A.L., Panetto, H., Verdecho, M.J.: The unified enterprise modelling language – overview and further work. Comput. Ind. **61**, 99–111 (2010)

Anderl, R., Raßler, J.: PML, an object-oriented process modelling language. In: Computer-Aided Innovation (CAI); Gaetano Cascini, vol. 277, pp. 145–156. Springer, Boston (2008)

Antoniou, G., van Harmelen, F.: Web ontology language: OWL. In: Handbook on Ontologies, pp. 67–92. Springer, Berlin (2004)

Auramäki, E., Hirschheim, R., Lyytinen, K.: Modelling offices through discourse analysis: the SAMPO approach. Comput. J. **35**(4), 342–352 (1992)

Austin, J.L.: How to Do Things with Words. Harvard University Press, Cambrige, MA (1962)

Baas, N.A.: Hierarchical systems. Foundations of a mathematical theory and application. Technical report, Department of mathematics, The University of Trondheim, Norway (1976)

Bailin, S.C.: An object-oriented requirements specification method. Commun. ACM **32**(5), 608–623 (1989)

Bardram, J., Bossen, C.: Mobility work: the spatial dimension of collaboration at a hospital. Comput. Support. Cooper. Work **14**, 131–160 (2005)

Bardram, J., Hansen, T.R., Soegaard, M.: AwareMedia – a shared interactive display supporting social, temporal, and spatial awareness in surgery. In: Proceedings of CSCW'06, 4–8 Nov, Banff, Alberta (2006)

Benson et al.: (2000) Mathematical structure for reasoning about emergent organizations, CSCW2000 Workshop: Beyond Workflow Management: Supporting Dynamic Organizational Processes, Philadelphia, USA (2000)

Berio, G., Harzallah, M.: Towards an integrating architecture for competence management. Comput. Ind. **58**, 199–209 (2007)

Bernstein, A.: How can cooperative work tools support dynamic group processes? Bridging the specificity frontier. In: ACM CSCW Conference, Philadelphia (2000)

Bodart, F., Patel, A., Sim, M., Weber, R.: Should optional properties be used in conceptual modelling? A theory and three empirical tests. Inf. Syst. Res. **12**(4), 384–405 (2001)

Boehm, B.W.: A spiral model of software development and enhancement. IEEE Comput. **21**(5), 61–72 (1988)

Bogia, D.P.: Supporting flexible, extensible task descriptions in and among tasks. PhD thesis, University of Illinois, Urbana-Champaign (1995)

Bolcer, G., Kaiser, G.: SWAP: leveraging the web to manage workflow. IEEE Internet Comput. **3**(1), 85–88 (1999)

Booch, G.: Object Oriented Design with Applications. Benjamin/Cummings, Redwood City (1991)

Booch, G., Rumbaugh, J., Jacobson, I.: The Unified Modeling Language: User Guide, Secondth edn. Addison-Wesley, Reading (2005)

Bryant, T., Evans, A.: OO oversold: those objects of obscure desire. Inf. Softw. Technol. **36**(1), 35–42 (1994)

Bubenko, J.A., Jr., Rolland, C., Loucopoulos, P., DeAntonellis, V.: Facilitating fuzzy to formal requirements modelling. In: Proceedings of the First International Conference on Requirements Engineering (ICRE94), pp. 154–157, Colorado Springs, 18–22 April. IEEE Computer Society Press (1994), http://www.computer.org/portal/web/cspress/home

Bunge, M.A.: The Metaphysics, Epistemology, and Methodology of Levels. Elsevier, New York (1969)

Bunge, M.A.: Treatise on Basic Philosophy. Ontology I – The Furniture of the World, vol. 3. Kluwer Academic Publishers, Dordrecht (1977)

Bunge, M.A.: Philosophical Dictionary. Prometheus Books, New York (2003)

Button, G.: What's wrong with speach act theory. Comput. Support. Cooper. Work **3**(1), 39–42 (1995)

Carlsen, S.: Action port model: a mixed paradigm conceptual workflow modeling language. In: Third IFCIS Conference on Cooperative Information Systems (CoopIS'98), New York (1998)

Carnap, R.: Meaning and Necessity: A study in Semantics and Model Logic. University of Chicago Press, Chicago (1947)

Casey, E.S.: Getting Back into Place: Toward a Renewed Understanding of the Place-World. Indiana University Press, Bloomington (1993)

Casey, E.S.: The Fate of Place: A Philosophical History. University of California Press, Berkeley (1998)

Castellani, X.: Overview of models defined with charts of concepts. In: Falkenberg, E., Lyytinen, K., Verrijn-Stuart, A.A. (eds.) Proceedings of the IFIP8.1 Working Conference on Information Systems Concepts (ISCO4); An Integrated Discipline Emerging, 20–22 Sept 20–22, Leiden, pp. 235–256 (1999)

Cheetham, G., Chivers, G.E.: Professions, Competence and Informal Learning. Edgard Elgar Publishing Limited, Cheltenham (2005)

Chen, P.P.: The entity-relationship model: towards a unified view of data. ACM Trans. Database Syst. 1(1), 9–36 (1976)

Chung, L.: Dealing with security requirements during the development of information systems. In: Rolland, C., Bodart, F., Cauvet, C. (eds.) Proceedings of the 5th International Conference on Advanced Information Systems Engineering (CAiSE'93), Paris, France, 8–11 June 1993, pp. 234–251. Springer, Berlin (1993)

Coad, P., Yourdon, E.: Object-Oriented Analysis, 1st edn. Prentice-Hall, Englewood Cliffs (1990)

Coleman, D., Hayes, F., Bear, S.: Introducing objectcharts or how to use statecharts in object-oriented design. IEEE Trans. Softw. Eng. 18(1), 9–18 (1992)

Conradi, R., Jaccheri, M.L.: Process modelling languages. In: Software Process: Principles, Methodology and Technology. Lecture Notes in Computer Science 1500. Springer, Berlin (1998)

Curtis, B., Kellner, M.I., Over, J.: Process modeling. Commun. ACM 35(9), 75–90 (1992)

Daconta, M., Orbst, L., Smith, K.: The Semantic Web: A Guide to the Future of XML, Web Services and Knowledge Management. Wiley, London (2003)

Dallons, G., Heymans, P., Pollet, I.: A template-based analysis of GRL. In: Proceedings of EMMSAD'05 (CAiSE*05), Tenth International Workshop on Exploring Modeling Methods in Systems Analysis and Design, pp. 493–504 (2005)

Davies, I.P., Green, S., Milton, K., Rosemann, M.: Analysing and comparing ontologies with meta models. In: Krogstie, J., Halpin, T., Siau, K. (eds.) Information Modeling Methods and Methodologies, pp. 1–16. Idea Group, Hershey (2005)

Davis, A.M.: A comparison of techniques for the specification of external system behaviour. Commun. ACM 31(9), 1098–1115 (1988)

Davis, A.M.: Software Requirements Analysis and Specification. Prentice-Hall, Upper Saddle River (1990)

Davis, R., King, J.: An overview of production systems. In: Elcock, E.W., Mitchie, D. (eds.) Machine Intelligence, pp. 300–332. Wiley, New York (1977)

De Michelis, G., Grasso, M.A.: Situating conversations within the language/action perspective: the Milan conversation model. In: Proceedings of the ACM 1994 Conference on Computer Supported Cooperative Work (CSCW'94), pp. 89–100, Chapel Hill, NC, 22–26 Oct (1994)

Derniame, J.C. (ed.): Software Process: Principles, Methodology and Technology. Lecture Notes in Computer Science 1500. Springer, New York (1998)

Dietz, J.L.G.: Integrating management of human and computer resources in task processing organizations: a conceptual view. In: Nunamaker, J.F., Sprague, R.H. (eds.) Proceedings of the Twenty-seventh Annual Hawaii International Conference on Systems Sciences (HICCS'27), pp. 723–733 Maui, Hawaii, 4–7 Jan. IEEE Computer Society Press (1994)

Dietz, J.L.G.: Enterprise Ontology – Theory and Methodology. Springer, Berlin/Heidelberg/New York (2006)

Dietz, J.L.G., Widdershoven, G.A.M.: A comparison of the linguistic theories of Searle and Habermas as a basis for communication supporting systems. In: van Riet, R.P., Meersman, R.A. (eds.) Linguistic Instruments in Knowledge Engineering, pp. 121–130. Elsevier, Amsterdam (1992)

Dignum, F., Weigand, H.: Modelling communication between cooperative systems. In: Iivari, J., Lyytinen, K., Rossi, M. (eds.) Proceedings of the 7th International Conference on Advanced Information Systems Engineering (CAiSE'95), Jyväskylä, Finland, 12–16 June 1995, pp. 140–153. Springer, Berlin (1995)

Dossogne, A., Jeanmart, C.: Evaluation of ARIS and BPMN using the UEML approach. Master thesis, University of Namur (2007)

Dourish, P.: Re-space-ing place: "place" and "space" ten years on proceedings of ACM conference. In: Computer-Supported Cooperative Work CSCW'06, Banff, Canada, pp. 299–308. ACM, New York (2006)

Dourish, P., Holmes, J., MacLean, A., Marqvardsen, P., Zbyslaw, A.: A freeflow: mediating between representation and action in workflow systems. In: ACM CSCW Conference, Boston (1996)

Dowty, D.R., et al.: Introduction to Montague Semantic. Reidel, Dordrecht (1981)

Ellis, H.C., Hunt, R.R.: Fundamentals of Cognitive Psychology, 5th edn. Brown and Benchmark, Madiso (1993)

Embley, D.W., Jackson, R.B., Woodfield, S.N.: OO system analysis: is it or isn't it? IEEE Softw. **12**(3), 19–33 (1995)

Erickson, J., Siau, K.: Can UML be simplified? Practitioner use of UML in separate domains. In: proceedings EMMSAD 2007. Proceedings of Twelfth International Workshop on Exploring Modeling Methods in System Analysis and Design, Trondheim, Norway, pp. 89–98 (2007)

Falkenberg, E.D., Hesse, W., Lindgreen, P., Nilsson, B.E., Oei, J.L.H., Rolland, C., Stamper, R.K., Assche, F.J.M.V., Verrijn-Stuart, A.A., Voss. K.: A Framework of information system concepts – the FRISCO report, IFIP WG 8.1 Task Group FRISCO. http://home.dei.polimi.it/pernici/ifip81/publications.html (1996). Cited Dec 2011

Favre, L. (ed.): UML and the Unified Process. IRM Press, Hershey (2003)

Feather, M.S.: Requirement reconnoitering at the juncture of domain and instance. In: Proceedings of the IEEE International Symposium on Requirements Engineering (RE'93), pp. 73–76, San Diego, 4–6 Jan (1993)

Fickas, S.: Design issues in a rule-based system. J. Syst. Softw. **10**(2), 113–123 (1989)

Findler, N.V. (ed.): Associative Networks: Representation and Use of Knowledge by Computer. Academic, New York (1979)

Finin, T., Fritzson, R., McKay, D., McEntire, R.: KQML as an agent communication language. In: Proceedings of the Third International Conference on Information and Knowledge Management, CIKM'94, pp. 456–463. ACM, NewYork (1994)

FIPA-ACL: FIPA ACL message structure specification. Retrieved from http://www.fipa.org/specs/fipa00061/SC00061G.html (2002)

Fleischmann, A.: What is S-BPM? In: Buchwald, H., Fleischmann, A., Seese, S., Stary, C. (eds.) S-BPM. CICS Band 85. Springer, Berlin (2010)

Flores, F., Graves, M., Hartfield, B., Winograd, T.: Computer systems and the design of organizational interaction. ACM Trans. Off. Inf. Syst. **6**(2), 153–172 (1988)

Fowler, M.: UML Distilled: A Brief Guide to the Standard Object Modeling Language, 3rd edn. Addison-Wesley, Boston (2003)

Fox, M.S., Gruninger, M.: Enterprise modeling. AI Mag. **19**(3), 109–121 (2000)

Gane, C., Sarson, T.: Structured Systems Analysis: Tools and Techniques. Prentice Hall, Englewood Cliffs (1979)

Geerts, G.L., McCarthy, W.E.: An accounting object infrastructure for knowledge-based enterprise models. IEEE Intell. Syst. **14**, 89–94 (1999)

Glance, N.S., Pagani, D.S., Pareschi, R.: Generalized process structure grammars (GPSG) for flexible representation of work. In: ACM CSCW Conference, Boston (1996)

Goedertier, S., Vanthienen, J.: An overview of declarative process modeling principles and languages. Commun. Syst. Inf. World Netw. **6**, 51–58 (2009)

Goldkuhl, G., Lyytinen, K.: A language action view of information systems. In: Proceedings of the International Conference on Information Systems (ICIS'82), pp. 13–29, Ann Arbor, MI (1982)

Gopalakrishnan, S., Sindre, G.: Diagram notations for mobile work processes. Presented at PoEM 2011, Oslo, Norway, 2–3 Nov (2011)

Gopalakrishnan, S., Krogstie, J., Sindre, G.: Adapting UML activity diagrams for mobile work process modelling: experimental comparison of two notation alternatives. In: Proceedings of PoEM 2010. Springer, Berlin/Heidelberg (2010)

Gordijn, J., Yu, E., van der Raadt, B.: e-service design using i* and e³value. IEEE Softw. **23**(3), 23–33 (2006)

Green, P.F.: An ontological analysis of information systems analysis and design (ISAD) grammars in Upper CASE tools. PhD thesis, Department of Commerce, University of Queensland (1996)

Green, P.F., Rosemann, M.: An ontological evaluation of integrated process modelling, 1999. In: Proceedings of CAiSE'99, the 11th Conference on Advanced information Systems Engineering, Heidelberg/Germany, 14–18 June (1999)

Grigoris, A. & v. Harmelen, F. Web Ontology Language: OWL, in Handbook On Ontologies, Eds. International Handbooks on Information Systems, Springer, 2004, Berlin, Germany

Grobstein, C.: Hierarchical order and neogenesis. In: Pattee, H.H. (ed.) Hierarchy Theory. Braziller, New York (1973)

Gruber, T.R.: Toward principles for the design of ontologies used for knowledge sharing. Int. J. Hum. Comput. Stud. **43**(5–6), 907–928 (1995)

Guizzardi, G.: Ontological Foundations for Structural Conceptual Models, vol. 015. Telematica Instituut, Enschede (2005)

Guizzardi, G., Baião, F.A., Lopes, M., de Almeida, F.R.: The role of foundational ontologies for domain ontology engineering: an industrial case study in the domain of oil and gas exploration and production. IJISMD **1**(2), 1–22 (2010)

Gulla, J.A., Lindland, O.I., Willumsen, G.: PPP – an integrated CASE environment. In: Andersen, R., Bubenko, J.A., Jr., Sølvberg, A. (eds.) Proceedings of the Third International Conference on Advanced Information Systems Engineering (CAiSE'91), Trondheim, pp. 194–221 (1991)

Habermas, J.: The Theory of Communicative Action. Beacon, Boston (1984)

Hagelstein, J., Rifaut, A.: A comparison of semantic models for collections. Technical report, Philips Research Lab, Brussels, Belgium (1987)

Halpin, T.: Fact-oriented modeling: past, present and future. In: Krogstie, J., Opdahl, A., Brinkkemper, S. (eds.) Conceptual Modelling in Information Systems Engineering. Springer, Berlin (2007)

Hammer, M., Champy, J.: Reengineering the Corporation: A Manifesto for Business Revolution. Harper Business, New York (1993)

Hammer, M., McLeod, D.: Database description with SDM: a semantic database model. ACM Trans. Database Syst. **6**(3), 351–386 (1981)

Harel, D.: Statecharts: a visual formalism for complex systems. Sci. Comput. Progr. **8**, 231–274 (1987)

Harel, D., Gery, E.: Executable object modelling with statecharts. In: 18th International Conference on Software Engineering (ICSE'96), pp. 246–257, Berlin, Germany, 25–29 March (1996)

Harel, D., Lachover, H., Naamed, A., Pnueli, A., Politi, M., Sherman, R., Shtull-Trauring, A., Trakhtenbrot, M.: STATEMATE: a working environment for the development of complex reactive systems. IEEE Trans. Softw. Eng. **16**(4), 403–414 (1990)

Harrison, S., Dourish, P.: Re-place-ing space: the roles of space and place in collaborative systems. In: Proceedings of ACM Conference on Computer-Supported Cooperative Work CSCW'96, Boston, MA, pp. 67–76. ACM, New York (1996)

Harzallah, M., Berio, G., Opdahl. A.L.: Incorporating IDEF3 into the Unified Enterprise Modelling Language (UEML). In: Proceedings of the VORTE 2007, joint with EDOC07 (2007)

Havey, M.: Essential Business Process Modelling. O'Reilly, Cambridge (2005)

Henderson-Sellers, B., Atkinson, C., Firesmith, D.G.: Viewing the OML as a variant of the UML. In: Rumpe, B., France, R. (eds.) Proceedings of the Second International Conference on the UML'99, Fort Collins, CO. Lecture Notes in Computer Science, vol. 1723, pp. 49–66. Springer, Berlin (1999)

Heymans, P., Saval, G., Dallons, G., Pollet, I.: A template-based analysis of GRL. In: Advanced Topic in Database Research, vol. 5. Idea Group Publishing, Hershey (2005)

Hommes, B.-J., van Reijswoud, V.: The quality of business process modelling techniques, In: Conference on Information Systems Concepts (ISCO), Leiden. Kluwer (1999)

Høydalsvik, G.M., Sindre, G.: On the purpose of object-oriented analysis. In: Paepcke, A. (ed.) Proceedings of the Conference on Object-Oriented Programming Systems, Languages, and Applications (OOPSLA'93), pp. 240–255. ACM Press, New York (1993)

Hruby, P.: Model-Driven Design Using Business Patterns. Springer, New York (2006)

Hull, R., King, R.: Semantic database modeling: survey, applications, and research issues. ACM Comput. Surv. **19**(3), 201–260 (1987)

Hull, D., Wolstencroft, K., Stevens, R., Goble, C.A., Pocock, M.R., Li, P., Oinn, T.: Taverna: a tool for building and running workflows of services. Nucleic Acids Res. **34**(Web-Server-Issue), 729–732 (2006)

Jacobs, S., Jarke, M., Pohl, K.: Report on the first international IEEE symposium on requirements engineering (RE'93) San Diego, 4–6 Jan 1993. Autom. Softw. Eng. **1**(1), 129–132 (1994)

Jacobson, I., Christerson, M., Jonsson, P., Övergaard, G.: Object-Oriented Software Engineering: A Use Case Driven Approach. Addison-Wesley, Reading (1992)

Jarke, M., Bubenko, J.A., Jr., Rolland, C., Sutcliffe, A., Vassiliou, Y.: Theories underlying requirements engineering: an overview of NATURE at genesis. In: Proceedings of the IEEE International Symposium on Requirements Engineering (RE'93), pp. 19–31, San Diego (1993)

Kangassalo, H.: Are global understanding, communication and information management in information systems possible? In: Chen, P.P., Akoka, J., Kangassalo, H., Thalheim, B. (eds.) Conceptual Modeling. Current Issues and Future Directions. LNCS 1565. Springer, Berlin (1999)

Kappel, G., Rausch-Schott, S., Retschitzegger, W.: Coordination in workflow management systems: a rule-based approach. In: Coordination Technology for Collaborative Applications, pp. 99–119. Springer, Berlin/New York (1998)

Kautz, K.: Debate forum editorial. Scand. J. Inf. Syst. 18(1), 61–62 (2006)

Kavakli, E., Loucopoulos, P.: Goal modeling in requirements engineering: analysis and critique of current methods in information modeling methods and methodologies. In: Krogstie, J., Siau, K., Halpin, T. (eds.) Information Modeling Methods and Methodologies. Idea Group Publishing, Hershey (2005)

Keller, G., Nüttgens, M., Scheer, A.W.: Semantische Prozeßmodellierung auf der Grundlage Ereignisgesteuerter Prozeßketten (EPK). Wirtschaftsinformatik 89 (1992), http://www.wiso. uni-hamburg.de/fileadmin/wiso_fs_wi/Team/Mitarbeiter/Prof._Dr._Markus_Nuettgens/ Publikationen/heft089.pdf

Kelly, S., Tolvanen, J.-P.: Domain-Specific Modelling: Enabling Full Code Generation. Wiley, Hoboken (2008)

King, J.L.: SimLanguage. Comput. Support. Cooper. Work 3(1), 51–54 (1995)

Klein, H., Lyytinen, K.: Towards a new understanding of data modelling. In: Floyd, F.C., Züllighoven, H., Budde, R., Keil-Slawik, R. (eds.) Software Development and Reality Construction, pp. 203–217. Springer, New York (1991)

Krogstie, J.: Integrated goal, data and process modeling: from TEMPORA to model-generated work-places. In: Johannesson, P., Söderstrøm, E. (eds.) Information Systems Engineering From Data Analysis to Process Networks, pp. 43–65. IGI, Hershey (2008)

Krogstie, J., Jørgensen, H.: Interactive models for supporting networked organisations. Paper presented at the 16th conference on advanced information systems engineering (CAiSE 2004), Riga, Latvia, 9–11 June 2004

Krogstie, J., Sindre, G.: Utilizing deontic operators in information systems specifications. Requir. Eng. J. 1, 210–237 (1996)

Krogstie, J., McBrien, P., Owens, R., Seltveit, A.H.: Information systems development using a combination of process and rule based approaches. Paper presented at the third international conference on advanced information systems engineering (CAiSE'91), Trondheim, Norway, 1991

Kung, C.H.: Object subclass hierarchy in SQL: a simple approach. Commun. ACM 33(7), 117–125 (1990)

Kuntz, J.C., Christiansen, T.R., Cohen, G.P., Jin, Y., Levitt, R.E.: The virtual design team: a computational simulation model of project organizations. Commun. ACM 41(11), 84–91 (1998)

Larman, C.: Applying UML AND Patterns: An Introduction to Object-Oriented Analysis and Design and Iterative Development. Prentice Hall, Upper Saddle River (2004)

Leppänen, M.: An ontological framework and a methodocal skeleton for method engineering: a contextual approach. PhD thesis, University of Jyväskylä (2005)

Lillehagen, F., Krogstie, J.: Active Knowledge Modeling of Enterprises. Springer, Berlin (2008)

Loos, P., Allweyer, T.: Process orientation and object-orientation – an approach for integrating UML with event-driven process chains (EPC), University of Saarland, Homburg (1998)

Loucopoulos, P., McBrien, P., Schumacker, F., Theodoulidis, B., Kopanas, V., Wangler, B.: Integrating database technology, rule-based systems and temporal reasoning for effective information systems: the TEMPORA paradigm. J. Inf. Syst. 1, 129–152 (1991)

Loy, P.H.: A comparison of object-oriented and structured development methods. ACM SIGSOFT Softw. Eng. Notes 15(1), 44–48 (1990)

Lu, R., Sadiq, S.: A survey of comparative business process modeling approaches. In: Business Information Systems, pp. 82–94. Springer, Heidelberg (2007)

Lu, R., Sadiq, S., Governatori, G.: On managing business processes variants. Data Knowl. Eng. 68(7), 642–664 (2009)

Marsan, M.A., et al. (eds.): Proceeding of the International workshop on Timed Petri Nets, Torino, Italy, 1985. IEEE Computer Society Press (1985)

Matulevičius, R., Heymans, P., Opdahl, A.L.: Comparison of goal-oriented languages using the UEML approach. In: Panetto, H., Boudjlida, N. (eds.) Interoperability for Enterprise Software Applications, pp. 37–48. ISTE, London (2006)

Matulevičius, R., Heymans, P., Opdahl, A.L.: Comparing GRL and KAOS using the UEML approach. In: Concalves, R.J., Muller, J.P., Mertins, K., Zelm, M. (eds.) Enterprise Interoperability II. New Challenges and Approaches, pp. 77–88. Springer, London (2007a)

Matulevičius, R., Heymans, P., Opdahl, A.L.: Ontological analysis of KAOS using separation of reference. In: Siau, K. (ed.) Contemporary Issues in Database Design and Information Systems Development, pp. 37–51. IGI Publishing, Hershey (2007b)

McBrien, P., Seltveit, A.H.: Coupling process models and business rules. In: Sølvberg, A., Krogstie, J., Seltveit, A.H. (eds.) Proceedings of the IFIP8.1 WC on Information Systems Development for Decentralized Organizations (ISDO'95), pp. 201–217, Trondheim, Norway, 21–23 Aug 1995. Chapman & Hall (1995)

McBrien, P., Niezette, M., Pantazis, D., Seltveit, A.H., Sundin, U., Theodoulidis, B., Tziallas, G., Wohed, R.: A rule language to capture and model business policy specifications. In: Andersen, R., Bubenko, J.A. Jr., Sølvberg, A. (eds.) Proceedings of the Third International Conference on Advanced Information Systems Engineering (CAiSE'91), Trondheim, pp. 307–318 (1991)

McBrien, P., Seltveit, A.H., Wangler, B.: An entity-relationship model extended to describe historical information. In: Proceedings of CISMOD'92, Bangalore, India, July (1992)

McCarthy, W.E.: The REA accounting model: a generalized framework for accounting systems in a shared data environment. Account. Rev. 57, 554–578 (1982)

McCarty, J.F., Meidel, E.S.: ActiveMap: a visualization tool for location awareness to support informal interactions. In: Handheld and Ubiquitous Computing (HUC'99), 27–29 Sept 1999, Karlsruhe (1999)

McGuinness, D.L.: Ontologies come of age. In: Fensel, D., Hendler, J., Lieberman, H., Wahlster, W. (eds.) Spinning the Semantic Web. MIT Press, Cambridge, MA (2003)

Medina-Mora, R., Winograd, T., Flores, R., Flores, F.: The action workflow approach to work flow management technology. In: Proceedings of CSCW'92, Toronto (1992)

Mendling, J., Nüttgens, M.: EPC markup language (EPML): an XML-based interchange format for event-driven process chains (EPC). Inf. Syst. E-Bus. Manag. 4, 245–263 (2006)

Mesarović, M.D., et al.: Theory of Hierarchical, Multilevel, Systems. Academic, New York (1970)

Meyer, B.: Reality: a cousin twice removed. IEEE Comput. 29(7), 96–97 (1996)

Milton, S., Kazmierczak, E.: An ontology of data modelling languages: a study using a common-sense realistic ontology. J. Database Manag. 15(2), 19–38 (2004)

Motschnig-Pitrik, R., Kaasbøll, J.: Part-whole relationship categories and their application in object-oriented analysis. IEEE Trans. Knowl. Data Eng. 11(5), 779–797 (1999)

Mylopoulos, J., et al.: A language facility for designing database intensive applications. ACM Trans. Database Syst. 5(2), 185–207 (1980)

Mylopoulos, J., Chung, L., Nixon, B.: Representing and using nonfunctional requirements: a process-oriented approach. IEEE Trans. Softw. Eng. 18(6), 483–497 (1992)

Nijssen, G.M., Halpin, T.A.: Conceptual Schema and Relational Database Design. Prentice Hall, New York (1989)

Nossum, A., Krogstie, J.: Integrated quality of models and quality of maps. Paper presented at the EMMSAD (2009)

Olle, T.W., Hagelstein, J., MacDonald, I.G., Rolland, C., Sol, H.G., van Assche, F.J.M., Verrijn-Stuart, A.A.: Information Systems Methodologies. Addison-Wesley, Reading (1988)

OMG: Unified modeling language v 2.0 OMG web site. http://www.omg.org (2006a)

OMG: Semantics of business vocabulary and rules interim specification. Retrieved 1 Jan 2006 from http://www.omg.org/cgi-bin/doc?dtc/06/03/02 (2006b)

OMG: BPMN v2 specification. Technical report, OMG. In: White, S.A (ed) Introduction to BPMN. IBM Cooperation. http://www.omg.org/, http://www.omg.org/spec/BPMN/2.0/ Jan (2011)

Opdahl, A.L., Henderson-Sellers, B.: Grounding the OML metamodel in ontology. J. Syst. Softw. **57**(2), 119–143 (2001)

Opdahl, A.L., Henderson-Sellers, B.: Ontological evaluation of the UML using the Bunge–Wand–Weber model. Softw. Syst. Model. **1**, 43–67 (2002)

Opdahl, A.L., Sindre, G.: A taxonomy for real-world modeling concepts. Inf. Syst. **19**(3), 229–241 (1994)

Opdahl, A.L., Sindre, G.: Facet models for problem analysis. In: Iivari, J., Lyytinen, K., Rossi, M. (eds.) Proceedings of the 7th International Conference on Advanced Information Systems Engineering (CAiSE'95), Jyväskylä, Finland, 12–16 June, pp. 54–67. Springer, Berlin (1995)

Opdahl, A.L., Sindre, G.: Facet modeling: an approach to flexible and integrated conceptual modeling. Inf. Syst. **22**(5), 291–323 (1997)

Opdahl, A.L., Henderson-Sellers, B., Barbier, F.: Ontological analysis of whole-part relationships in OO models. Inf. Softw. Technol. **43**(6), 387–399 (2001)

Ould, M.A.: Business Processes – Modeling and Analysis for Re-engineering and Improvement. Wiley, Beverly Hills (1995)

OWL: Web ontology language use cases and requirements. http://www.w3.org/TR/webont-req/ (2004)

Parsaye, K., Chignell, M.: Expert Systems for Experts. Wiley, New York (1988)

Parsons, J., Wand, Y.: Choosing classes in conceptual modeling. Commun. ACM **40**(6), 63–69 (1997a)

Parsons, J., Wand, Y.: Using objects for systems analysis. Commun. ACM **40**(12), 104–110 (1997b)

Peckham, J., Maryanski, F.: Semantic data models. ACM Comput. Surv. **20**(3), 153–190 (1988)

Pepiot, G., et al.: A fuzzy approach for the evaluation of competences. Int. J. Prod. Econ. **112**, 336–353 (2008)

Pesic, M., van der Aalst, W.M.P.: A declarative approach for flexible business processes management. In: Business Process Management Workshops. LNCS, vol. 4103, pp. 169–180. Springer, Heidelberg (2006)

Petri, C.A.: Kommunikation mit automaten (In German). Schriften des Rheinisch-Westfalischen Institut für Instrumentelle Mathematik an der Universität Bonn, (2) (1962)

Potter, W.D., Trueblood, R.P.: Traditional, semantic and hyper-semantic approaches to data modeling. IEEE Comput. **21**(6), 53–63 (1988)

Quine, W.: Set Theory and Its Logic. Belknap, Cambridge, MA (1963)

Recker, J., Rosemann, M., Krogstie, J.: Ontology- versus pattern-based evaluation of process modeling language: a comparison. Commun. Assoc. Inf. Syst. **20**, 774–799 (2007)

Reenskaug, T., Wold, P., Lehne, O.A.: Working with Objects. Manning/Prentice Hall, Greenwich (1995)

Rosch, E.: Principles of categorization. In: Rosch, E., Lloyd, B. (eds.) Cognition and Categorization. Erlbaum, Hillsdale (1978)

Rosemann, M., Green, P.: Developing a meta model for the Bunge-Wand-Weber ontological constructs. Inf. Syst. **27**(2), 75–91 (2002)

Rosenberg, D.: Use Case Driven Object Modeling with UML: A Practical Approach. Addison Wesley, Reading (1999)

Rubin, K.S., Goldberg, A.: Object behavior analysis. Commun. ACM **35**(9), 48–62 (1992)

Rumbaugh, J., Blaha, M., Premerlani, W., Eddy, F., Lorensen, W.: Object-Oriented Modeling and Design. Prentice-Hall, Englewood Cliffs (1991)

Scheer, A.-W., Nüttgens, M. (eds.): ARIS Architecture and Reference Models for Business Process Management, pp. 301–304. Springer, Berlin/Heidelberg (2000)

Schonenberg, H.B., Weber, B., van Dongen, B., van der Aalst, W.M.P.: Supporting flexible processes through recommendations based on history. In: Proceedings of the 6th International Conference on Business Process Management. Springer, Berlin (2008)

Searle, J.R.: Speech Acts. Cambridge University Press, Cambridge (1969)

Searle, J.R.: Expression and Meaning. Cambridge University Press, Cambridge (1979)

Searle, J.R., Vanderveken, D.: Foundations of Illocutionary Logic. Cambridge University Press, Cambridge (1985)

Seltveit, A.H.: An abstraction-based rule approach to large-scale information systems development. In: Proceedings of the 5th International Conference on Advanced Information Systems Engineering (CAiSE'93), Paris, France, 8–11 June 1993, pp. 328–351. Springer, Berlin (1993)

Senge, P.: The Fifth Discipline: The Art and Practice of the Learning Organization. Century Business Publishers, London (1990)

Shlaer, S., Mellor, S.J.: Object Lifecycles, Modeling the World in States. Yourdon Press, Englewood Cliffs (1991)

Shoham, Y.: Agent oriented programming: an overview of the framework and summary of recent research. In: Masuch, M., Polos, L. (eds.) Knowledge Representation and Reasoning under Uncertainty: Logic at Work, pp. 123–129. Springer, Berlin (1994)

Simon, H.A.: The organization of complex systems. In: Pattee, H.H. (ed.) Hierarchy Theory. Braziller, New York (1973)

Sindre, G.: HICONS: A general diagrammatic framework for hierarchical modelling. PhD thesis, IDT, NTH, Trondheim, Norway, 1990. NTH report 1990:44, IDT report 1990:31 (1990)

Singh, B., Rein, G.L.: Role Interaction Nets (RINs); a process description formalism. Technical Report CT-083-92, MCC, Austin (1992)

Slonim, J.: OO in the real world – success or latest fashion? In: Müller, H.A., Georges, M. (eds.) Proceedings of the International Conference on Software Maintenance (ICSM'94), pp. 440–441, 19–23 Sept 1994. IEEE Computer Society Press (1994)

Smith, W.: Concepts and thoughts. In: Sternberg, R., Smith, E. (eds.) The Psychology of Human Thought. Cambridge University Press, Cambridge/New York (1988)

Sølvberg, A., Kung, C.H.: Information Systems Engineering. Springer, Berlin (1993)

Sowa, J.: Conceptual Structures. Addison Wesley, Reading (1983)

Sowa, J.F., Zachman, J.A.: Extending and formalizing the framework for information systems architecture. IBM Syst. J. **31**(3), 590–616 (1992)

Staab, S., Studer, R.: Handbook on Ontologies, International Handbooks on Information Systems. Springer, Berlin (2004)

Stamper, R.: Semantics. In: Boland Jr., T.J., Hirschheim, R.A. (eds.) Critical Issues in Information Systems Research, pp. 43–78. Wiley, Englewood Cliffs (1987)

Störle, H.: Describing process patterns with UML. In: EWSPT 2001. Lecture Notes in Computer Science 2077. Springer, Berlin/Heidelberg/New York (2001)

Suchman, L.: Do categories have politics? Comput. Support. Cooper. Work **2**(3), 177–190 (1994)

Sure, Y.: Leveraging corporate skill knowledge – from ProPer to OntoProper. In: Proceedings of the Third International Conference on Practical Aspects of Knowledge Management, Basel, Switzerland (2000)

Sutcliffe, A.G., Maiden, N.A.M.: Bridging the requirements gap: policies, goals and domains. In: Proceedings of the Seventh International Workshop on Software Specification and Design (IWSSD-7), pp. 52–55, Redondo Beach, 6–7 Dec 1993

Swenson, K.D., Maxwell, R.J., Matsymoto, T., Saghari, B., Irwin, I.: A business process environment supporting collaborative planning. J. Collab. Comput. **1**(1), 15–34 (1994)

Taivalsaari, A.: On the notion of inheritance. ACM Comput. Surv. **28**(3), 438–479 (1996)

Tempora: Integrating database technology, rule-based systems and temporal reasoning for effective software. Technical report ESPRIT project 2469, Technical Annex, Tempora Consortium, 17 Oct (1988)

ter Hofstede, A.H.M., van der Aalst, W.M.P., Adams, M., Russell, N. (eds.): Modern Business Process Automation: YAWL and Its Support Environment. Springer, Berlin/Heidelberg (2010)

Tomlinson, C., Scheevel, M.: Concurrent programming. In: Kim, W., Lochovsky, F.H. (eds.) Object-Oriented Concepts, Databases and Applications. Addison-Wesley, New York (1989)

Tu, C.: Ontological evaluation of BMM and i* with the UEML approach. Master thesis, University of Namur (2007)

Tuan, Y.-F.: Place: an experiential perspective. Geogr. Rev. 65(2), 151–165 (1975)

Twining, W., Miers, D.: How to Do Things with Rules. Weidenfeld and Nicholson, London (1982)

UN/CEFACT: Modeling Methodology (UMM) User Guide (2007), Project report, available here http://www.unece.org/fileadmin/DAM/cefact/umm/UMM_userguide-nutshell.pdf

van der Aalst, W.M.P.: Formalization and verification of event-driven process chains. Inf. Softw. Technol. 41, 639–650 (1999)

van der Aalst, W.M.P., Pesic, M.: DecSerFlow: towards a truly declarative service flow language. Web Serv. Form. Method. 4814, 1–23 (2006)

van der Aalst, W.M.P., Pesic, M., Schonenberg, H.: Declarative workflows: balancing between flexibility and support. Comput. Sci. Res. Dev. 23(2), 99–113 (2009)

van Lamsweerde, A.: Requirements Engineering: From System Goals to UML Models to Software Specifications. Wiley, Chichester/Hoboken (2009)

Wand, Y.: An ontological foundation for information systems design theory. In: Pernici, B., Verrijn-Stuart, A.A. (eds.) Office Information Systems: The Design Process, May 1989; Proceedings of IFIP WG8.4 Working Conference on "Office Information Systems: The Design Process", Linz/Austria, August. Elsevier/North-Holland, Amsterdam (1988)

Wand, Y., Weber, R.: An ontological evaluation of systems analysis and design methods. In: Falkenberg, E., Lindgreen, P. (eds.) Proceedings of the IFIP WG8.1 Working Conferenceon Information Systems Concepts: An In-Depth Analysis, Namur/Belgium, Amsterdam/North-Holland, The Netherlands, Oct 1989, pp. 79–107 (1989)

Wand, Y., Weber, R.: An ontological model of an information system. IEEE Trans. Softw. Eng. 16(11), 1282–1292 (1990)

Wand, Y., Weber, R.: On the ontological expressiveness of information systems analysis and design grammars. J. Inf. Syst. 3(4), 217–237 (1993)

Wand, Y., Weber, R.: On the deep structure of information systems. Inf. Syst. J. 5(3), 203–223 (1995)

Ward, P.T.: The transformation schema: an extension of the dataflow diagram to represent control and timing. IEEE Trans. Softw. Eng. 12(2), 198–210 (1986)

Weber, R.: Ontological Foundations of Information Systems. Number 4 in Accounting Research Methodology Monograph series. Coopers & Lybrand, 333 Collins Street, Melbourne Vic 3000, Australia (1997)

Weber, R., Zhang, Y.: An analytical evaluation of NIAM's grammar for conceptual schema diagrams. Inf. Syst. J. 6, 147–170 (1996)

Wegner, P., Goldin, D.: Interaction as a framework for modeling. In: Chen, P.P., Akoka, J., Kangassalo, H., Thalheim, B. (eds.) Conceptual Modeling. Lecture Notes in Computer Science 1565. Springer, Berlin/Heidelberg/New York (1999)

Weske, M.: Business Process Management: Concepts, Languages, Architectures. Springer, New York (2007)

WfMC: Workflow Handbook. Workflow Management Coalition, Future Strategies Inc, Lighthouse Point (2001)

Wieringa, R.: Three roles of conceptual models in information systems design and use. In: Falkenberg, E., Lindgren, P. (eds.) Information Systems Concepts: An In-Depth Analysis, pp. 31–51. North-Holland, Amsterdam (1989)

Wilkie, G.: Object-Oriented Software Engineering – The Professional Developers's Guide. Addison-Wesley, Reading (1993)

Willars, H.: Handbok i ABC-metoden (In Swedish). Plandata Strategi, Stockholm, Sweden (1988)

Wilson, R.J.: Introduction to Graph Theory, 3rd edn. Longman, New York (1985)

Winograd, T., Flores, F.: Understanding Computers and Cognition. Addison-Wesley, Reading (1986)

Wirfs-Brock, R., Wilkerson, B., Wiener, L.: Designing Object-Oriented Software. Prentice-Hall, Englewood Cliffs (1990)

Yang, M.: COMIS – a conceptual model for information systems. PhD thesis, IDT, NTH, Trondheim, Norway (1993)

Yu, E.S.K., Mylopoulos, J.: Using goals, rules, and methods to support reasoning in business process reengineering. In: Nunamaker, J.F., Sprague, R.H. (eds.) Proceedings of the Twenty-seventh Annual Hawaii International Conference on Systems Sciences (HICCS'27), pp. 234–243, Maui, Hawaii, January 4-7 1994. IEEE Computer Society Press (1994)

zur Muehlen, M., Becker, J.: Workflow management and object-orientation – a matter of perspectives or why perspectives matter. In: OOPSLA Workshop on Object-Oriented Workflow Management, Denver (1999)

Quality of Models

In this chapter, we describe a framework for understanding quality in conceptual modelling (SEQUAL), including examples of means to achieve model quality of different levels (such as tool functionality and modelling techniques being appropriate for the development of models of high quality). Quality is discussed on seven levels: physical, empirical, syntactic, semantic, pragmatic, social, and deontic. How different quality types build upon each other is also indicated.

'Quality' is a difficult notion, and within the field of information systems, many approaches to quality have been proposed. Whereas some have a rather mystical approach to quality of models (e.g. (Rumbaugh et al. 1991) states: '*A good model feels right and does not appear to have extraneous detail*'), a standard approach to quality within the engineering community is to say that a product has high quality if it is according to its specification. For example, the ISO 9000 quality standard was originally developed according to this philosophy. ISO (2005) states that quality is the 'Degree to which a set of inherent characteristic fulfils requirements'. ISO-9000:2005 defines requirement as needs or expectations from a customer (and no longer as necessarily explicit *specifications* of such needs). In ISO-9000, one defines a number of quality characteristics, with sub-characteristics, and metrics to be able to measure the different sub-characteristics. The following quality characteristics are listed for software products in ISO/IEC 9126:

- Functionality: Does the software support all the required functions?
- Reliability: How reliable is the software?
- Efficiency: How efficiently does the software perform?
- Usability: How easy is the software to use?
- Portability: How easy is it to transfer the software to another (technical) environment?
- Maintainability: How easy is the software to modify?

ISO/IEC 9126 further divides these into 24 quality sub-characteristics, which are measured by 113 quality metrics. Denning (1992) goes beyond the original ISO 9000 thinking by viewing the fact that a product is 'accordance to the specification' as the first level of quality. A second level is achieved if there are no negative side effects of the installed information system. The highest (third) level of quality is achieved if in addition to achieving the first two levels, the information system enables additional information system support to its users not conceived in the first place, i.e. actually giving the users more of what they need than what was promised in the specification. It can be argued that the newest ISO definitions also take these levels into account. The three-level distinction is parallel to the differentiation of software requirements in the Kano model (Kano 1984; Krogstie 1999), where requirements are classified into three categories: normal, expected, and exciting.

1. Normal requirements are what the stakeholders communicate during traditional facilitated sessions or in interviews. They cover the basic functionality of the application. These requirements contribute proportionally to customer satisfaction and expectations.
2. Expected requirements are those aspects that the users assume the developers already know. Missing an expected requirement represents the greatest risk to user satisfaction. There is little benefit for implementing these requirements. However, there is a heavy price if they are omitted. Observation techniques represent one approach to addressing unstated and expected requirements. Studying the existing system and prototyping are other techniques often used.
3. Exciting requirements are aspects that the users do not expect. Often exciting requirements involve innovation of the business process or new ways of handling functionality. Stakeholder satisfaction with the application can be dramatically improved through the implementation of a few exciting requirements. Failure to implement these requirements does not adversely affect overall satisfaction. Exciting requirements can be identified through a number of techniques. These include observation, brainstorming, affinity analysis, relations diagramming, and causal loop diagramming.

Early proposals for a more fine-grained definition of quality goals for conceptual models and requirement specifications as summarised by Davis et al. (1993) included many useful aspects, but unfortunately in the form of unsystematic lists as pointed out already in Lindland et al. (1994). They are also often restricted in the kind of models they regard (e.g. requirements specifications (Davis et al. 1993)) or the modelling language (e.g. ER models, Moody and Shanks 1994). Over the last 10–15 years though, the thinking on quality of models has progressed a lot. Although many have worked on this area as summarised by Moody (2005), we will in this book focus on the application of SEQUAL, a framework based on semiotics for understanding the different facets of quality of conceptual models and modelling languages.

4.1   SEQUAL: A Framework for Quality of Models Based on Semiotic Theory

To have a scientific basis to create a more comprehensive framework, we have looked at the field of semiotic, the science of signs and what they refer to. The way we apply semiotic theory is very similar to what was described in the Framework for Information Systems Concepts (FRISCO) report (Falkenberg et al. 1996) which identifies that the means of communication and related areas can be examined in a semiotic framework, describing a number of levels in the form of a semiotic ladder. As described in Chap. 1, the FRISCO report describes different semiotic levels and on a high level describes the relevant aspect relative to modelling on each level. In SEQUAL, we describe in much more detail what the different levels entails, to be able to have a more precise understanding of the issues at stake at each level, and how deliberation on the different levels can be combined.

SEQUAL has three unique properties compared to the early work on quality of models:

- It distinguishes between quality characteristics (goals) and means to potentially achieve these goals by separating what you are trying to achieve from how to achieve it.
- It is based on a constructivistic world-view as discussed in Chap. 1, recognising that significant models are usually created as part of a dialogue between the many stakeholders involved in modelling, whose knowledge of the modelling domain changes as modelling takes place.
- It is closely linked to linguistic and semiotic concepts. In particular, the core of the framework including the discussion on syntax, semantics, and pragmatics is parallel to the use of these terms in the semiotic theory of Morris (see e.g. Nöth 1990 for an introduction). Also, the work in FRISCO on the semiotic ladder took the work of Morris as an outset, but has extended this with physical, empirical and social aspects. The differentiation between empirical quality (on comprehensibility) and pragmatic quality (on actual human comprehension) was motivated by empirical investigation on the applicability of the framework (Moody et al. 2002) and the utility to distinguish between technical and social aspects discussed in Chap. 1. The inclusion of the semiotic levels enables us to address quality at different levels. A term such as 'quality' is used on all the semiotic levels. We include physical, empirical, syntactical, semantical, pragmatic, social and deontic quality. The inclusion of deontic quality (earlier called organisational quality) is to be able to better take into account the overriding goals of modelling in a modelling task, often decided in a wider organisational setting. An overview of each level is given in this chapter in the following section in this chapter.

The main concepts and their relationships are shown in Fig. 4.1. Quality types for a conceptual model are indicated in the figure with solid lines, indicating relationships between sets, in Fig. 4.1 depicted as boxes. We take a set-theoretic approach to the discussion of the different quality types and characteristics. Sets are written using **SLANTED BOLDFACE UPPERCASE** letters, whereas elements of sets are written in normal UPPERCASE letters. The different sets are described first, whereas quality types, including goals and means to achieve quality at each level, are described next. Readers familiar with the field of logic programming should be aware of that we use several terms somewhat differently from how they are used in that field, since a slightly different terminology have been established in the field on conceptual modelling than in logic programming.

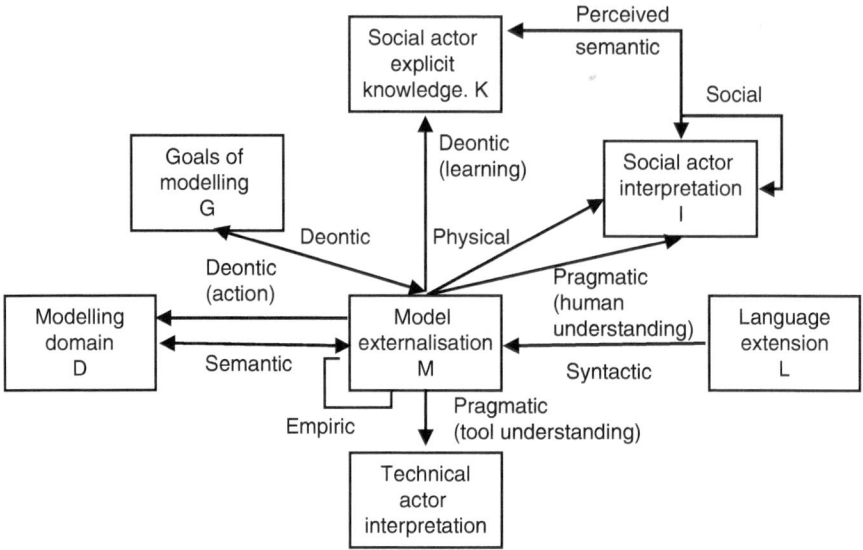

Fig. 4.1 SEQUAL framework for discussing quality of models

4.1.1   G, the Goals of the Modelling Task

What goals are meant to be fulfilled through the modelling? Whereas in simple cases, there is one well-defined goal, often (views and versions of) the same model is used to achieve many, often partly contradictory goals. As discussed in Chap. 1, conceptual models are used for a number of different purposes, and as seen from practice, even within the same project different stakeholders can have different goals. For example, in Krogstie et al. (2004) a number of different goals for modelling were identified for the same process model, roughly structured according to the usage areas of conceptual modelling depicted in Fig. 1.3:

- Communication and sense-making around models of the current state
  - The models developed should help sharing best practice between different units of the organisation.
  - The models developed should be helpful in the refining of the processes.
- Communication around models of the future state
  - The new work process should be documented through the models.
  - The models developed should help harmonise the current work processes across different parts of the organisation.
  - The models developed should be used to teach the software developers about the domain.
- Computer-assisted analysis
  - The models developed should help analyse the current work processes
- Model deployment
  - The models developed should be used as a procedural tool in everyday work.

  – The models developed should support the use of the software application
    developed for process-support.
- Context for change
  – The models developed should define the scope of the software application.

This case is described further in Chap. 7. Initial goals of modelling are normally
defined before the modelling starts, but can often be changed and extended during a
project, either in a planned or an emergent fashion (Krogstie et al. 2006). Goals also
include other organisational and economic issues, for instance, will a requirements
specification model be constrained through the fact that one wants to produce an
information system based on the software requirement specifications under given
time and resource constraints.

4.1.2   A, the Audience

The audience is not directly depicted in Fig. 4.1, but are indirectly captured through
their explicit knowledge (K) and interpretation of models (I). The audience is the
union of the set of individual actors $A_1, \ldots, A_k$ the set of organisational actors
(an organisational actor is typically consisting of a group of people with at least one
shared goal) $A_{k+1}, \ldots, A_n$, and the set of technical actors $A_{n+1}, \ldots, A_m$ who need to
relate to the model. The individuals being members of the audience are called the
participants of the modelling process. The participants P is a subset of the set of
stakeholders S of the process of creating the model. Types of stakeholders and
participants were discussed in Sect. 2.1.5.

Those actively creating models (modellers) are a subset of the participants.

A technical actor is typically a computer program e.g. a modelling tool, which
must 'understand' parts of the model at a certain level to automatically manipulate
it to, for instance, perform code generation, model layout or model analysis.

The audience often changes during the process of developing and evolving the
model, when people leave or enter the project or organisation.

4.1.3   L, the Language Extension

The language extension is the set of all statements that are possible to make according
to the vocabulary and syntax of the modelling languages used. Several languages
can be used in the same modelling effort, corresponding to the sets $L_1, \ldots, L_j$. One
example is the different diagrams defined in UML (described in Sect. 3.5.1). These
languages can be interrelated (usually by sharing concepts). Sub-languages are
related to the complete language by limitations on the vocabulary or on the set of
allowed grammar rules in the syntax of the overall language or (typically) both. The
statements in the language model of a formal or semi-formal language L_i are denoted
with $M(L_i)$. This model is often called the meta-model of the language, a term that
is appropriate only in connection to work on repositories for conceptual models as
discussed in Sect. 3.1.3.

The languages used in a modelling effort are often predefined, but it is more and more usual as discussed in Chap. 2 in both software modelling and enterprise modelling that one create specific modelling languages or extensions to existing languages using a meta-modelling environment for the modelling effort, in which case the syntax and semantics of the languages have to be intersubjectively agreed among the audience as part of modelling. If one is using an existing language, the 'correct' syntax and semantics of the language (to the extent that this is formally defined) can be regarded as predefined. Note that in, e.g. UML 2.0, there is a mechanism called semantic variation points (France et al. 2006), where it is indicated that the semantics of a certain part of the language is not standardised. One can choose to apply only parts of the predefined modelling languages for a given modelling effort, and change this subset during a project as appropriate (e.g. it is seldom that the whole of UML or BPMN is used within one project) (Erickson and Siau 2007; zur Muehlen and Recker 2008).

4.1.4   *M*, the Externalised Model

This is the set of all statements in someone's model of part of the perceived reality expressed in a modelling language. M_E is the set of explicit statements in a model, whereas M_I is the set of implicit statements, being the statements not made, but implied through the deduction rules of the modelling language. For example, assume that L is propositional logic and M_E contains the statements $A \rightarrow B$ and A. M_I will contain the derived statement B. A model written in language L_i is denoted M_{Li}. The meaning of M_{Li} is established through the intersubjectively agreed syntax and semantics of L_i.

For each participant, the part of the externalised model that is considered relevant can be seen as a projection of the total externalised model; hence, M can be divided into projections $M^1, \ldots, M^k$ corresponding to the participants $A_1, \ldots, A_k$. Generally, these projections will not be disjoint, but the union of the projections should cover M. M will obviously evolve during modelling as statements are inserted into and deleted from the model.

4.1.5   D, the Modelling Domain

The modelling domain is the set of all statements, which can be stated about the situation at hand. One can differentiate between domains along two orthogonal dimensions:

- Temporal: Is the model of a past, current (e.g. as-is) or future situation (e.g. to-be) as it is perceived by someone in the audience? Whereas the first two are descriptive models, the last type will typically be a prescriptive model, although it might also be a future unwanted situation.
- Scope: Examples of different scopes are (a subset of) the physical world, (a subset of) the social world, an organisation, an information system, a computerised information system (CIS).

During development of a CIS more specifically, several different although interrelated modelling domains, with accompanying models, are recognised as also discussed in Chap. 2:

- *The existing IS* as it is perceived, $M(EIS)$.
- *A future IS* as it is perceived, e.g. requirements to a future IS, $M(FIS)$.
- *The external behaviour of the future CIS* as it is perceived, e.g. requirements to a future CIS. This can be regarded as an extension of $M(FIS)$.
- *The internal behaviour of the future CIS* as it is perceived, e.g. design of a future CIS, $M(FCIS)$.
- *The implemented CIS*. Also the CIS can be regarded as a model, although usually not a conceptual model in the sense we use the term.

Note the similarity of these levels, with the Computation Independent Model (CIM), Platform Independent Model (PIM) and Platform Specific Model (PSM), described in OMG's MDA architecture (OMG 2006).

The domains evolves during modelling, both through external changes outside the control of the modelling activity and through the deployment and activation of the model itself. One can differentiate between the current domain D, and a perceived optimal domain D^O which one tries to achieve (e.g. through the information systems development). Any of the above domains can be divided into two parts, exemplified by looking at a software requirements specification (Davis et al. 1993):

- Everything the CIS is supposed to do (for the moment ignoring the different views the stakeholders have on the CIS to be produced). This is termed the *primary domain*.
- Constraints on the model because of earlier baseline models such as system level requirements specifications, enterprise architecture models, statements of work, and earlier versions of the requirement specification to which the new requirement specification model must be compatible. As another example, a design model ($M(FCIS)$) is (hopefully) constrained by the requirements model $M(FIS)$. This is termed the *modelling context*.

4.1.6   *K*, the Relevant Explicit Knowledge of the Audience

The relevant explicit knowledge is the union of the set of statements, $K_1,\ldots, K_k$, one for each participant. K_i is all possible statements that would be correct and relevant for addressing the problem at hand according to the knowledge of participant A_i. K_i is a subset of K^i, the part of internal reality of the social actor A_i that can be externalised. M_i is an externalisation of K_i and is a model made based on the knowledge of the individual or organisational actor. Even if the internal reality of each individual will always differ, the explicit internal reality concerning a constrained area might be equal for all practical purposes, especially within specific groups of participants (Gjersvik 1993; Orlikowski and Gash 1994). Thus, it can be useful to also speak about the explicit knowledge of an organisational actor. $M_i \setminus M^i = \varnothing$, whereas the opposite might not be true, i.e. more of the total externalised model than the part which is an externalisation of parts of an actor's internal reality is potentially relevant for this actor. K will and should change during modelling to achieve both personal

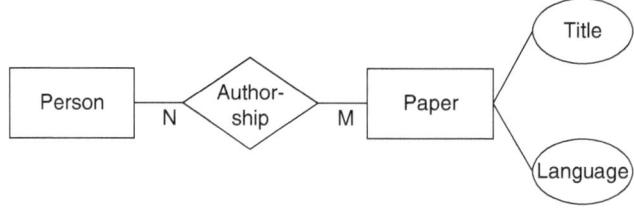

Fig. 4.2 A simple ER-model from the conference organising domain

and organisational learning. At a given point, the knowledge of different members of the audience on the domain might be different and inconsistent.

Representing knowledge as sets of statements is not to claim that this is how knowledge is actually stored in the human brain, since this would clash with advances in neuro-science (Churchland 1989). On the other hand, it is a useful abstraction for the kind of knowledge it is possible to represent explicitly by using a (modelling) language (e.g. in a conceptual model).

4.1.7   *I*, the Social Audience Interpretation

The social audience interpretation is the set of all statements that the social audience perceive that an externalised model consists of. Just like for the externalised model itself, its interpretation can be projected into $I_1, \ldots, I_n$ denoting the statements in the externalised model that are perceived by each social actor.

4.1.8   T, the Technical Audience Interpretation

Similar to above, $I_{n+1}, \ldots, I_m$ denote the statements in the conceptual model as they are interpreted by each individual technical actor in the audience.

Throughout this chapter, we will use part of an ER model from the domain of conference organising as depicted in Fig. 4.2 to illustrate the different types of model quality. The modelling goal in this case is the design of database-based solution to support conference organising. This figure (also used in Chap. 1) states that a paper is written by one or more persons, and a person can write one or more paper. A paper has a title and is written in a language.

In the next seven sections, we present each of the seven quality levels illustrated by relations between the sets in Fig. 4.1. For each quality level, there are one or more quality characteristics (i.e. goal to be achieved). We describe different means that can be beneficially used to reach these goals. Means can be of different types:

- Model properties, which are sub-characteristics of the high-level goal.
- Beneficial existing quality; i.e. other quality levels that you would normally try to address before addressing quality at the given level.
- Language properties; characteristics of the modelling language being used. Language quality in the SEQUAL framework is discussed in more detail in Chap. 5.

- Modelling methods and techniques.
- Modelling tool functionality (often in combination with a modelling technique, but some modelling techniques are not dependent on tool support).

Metrics for these quality characteristics and sub-characteristics are described. How to use these means and metrics as part of a modelling methodology is further discussed in Chap. 7.

4.2   Physical Quality

Although information system models are not usually of the physical (three-dimensional, tactile) kind, any model must be represented physically somehow, e.g. on disk, on paper or on a blackboard. In our example, it is represented on paper as Fig. 4.2 (and in the electronic source of the book of course, but in a version that cannot be edited). Originally, this model was made in Powerpoint, thus I do have access to also update this model. The basic quality features on the physical level is that the externalised model is persistent, current and available enabling the audience to make sense of it (and potentially for modellers to change it when necessary). This is not the same as participants actually internalise the model, and at the physical level we only look at how it is made available for possible interpretation by different actors.

- Persistence: How persistent is the model, how protected is it against loss or damage? For a model on disk, the physical quality will be higher if there is a backup copy, even higher if this backup is on another disk whose failure is independent of the original. Similarly, for models on paper, the amount and security of backup copies can be essential. The way of storing the model should be efficient, i.e. not using more space than necessary.

A simple metric for persistence is the proportion of model statements that are electronically stored in a model repository. This is particularly relevant in enterprise modelling and requirements modelling, where large part of the model statements are elicited through informal modelling techniques (e.g. participatory techniques using wall-charts as discussed in Sect. 2.4), and often need to be transferred into the model repository at a later stage to be made generally available.

- Currency: How long time ago is it that the model statements were included in the model (assuming the statements were current when entered)? Depending on the type of model, the age of the model statements is of differing importance. When the domain is changing rapidly (has high volatility), currency of the stored model is of more importance for the model to have appropriate timeliness. This is particularly urgent on models on the instance level (for instance data in a database, but also many enterprise models are partly on the instance level).

Metrics on currency can easily be devised and calculated if the model repository support time-stamping of statements. This area will relate to semantic quality, relative not only to the time of entering of a model statement, but also last time the model statement is validated.

- Availability: How available is the model to the audience? Clearly, this is dependent on that the model is externalised and made persistent in the first place.

Availability also depends on distributability, especially when members of the audience are geographically dispersed. A model which is in an electronically distributable format will be more easily distributed than one which must be printed on paper (or is only on paper in the first place) and sent by ordinary mail or fax. It may also matter exactly what is distributed, e.g. the model in an editable form or merely in an output format, or a format where you can add annotations, but cannot change the actual model.

A metric for availability is the proportion of model statements relevant for a member of the audience being available for that audience member. In connection to currency and availability, the term 'timeliness' is often used, i.e. the model is not only current, but are also available in time for events that corresponds to their usage. This relates directly to the goal of modelling, thus timeliness is set up as a deontic goal (see Sect. 4.8). A possible measurement of timeliness consists of (i) a currency measurement and (ii) a check that the model is available before the planned usage time.

Many of the modelling techniques and tool functionality in connection with physical quality are based on traditional database functionality using a model-repository-solution for the internal representation of the model. In addition, it is regarded necessary for advanced tools for conceptual modelling, enterprise architecture/modelling (Wesenberg 2011) and system development to include functionality such as version control and configuration management and advanced concurrency control mechanisms that are not normally found in conventional DBMSs.

A more detailed list of modelling tool mechanisms, most of them concerning availability, is presented below. The list is based on the needs identified in the ATHENA A1 EU-project for a complex modelling environment with combined access to the enterprise models from a number of different organisations and modelling tools and environments (ATHENA 2005). For simpler modelling environments, only some of these points will be relevant.

4.2.1 Model Repository

- The models should be stored in a repository, which can handle multiple users at multiple locations if necessary.
- The models should be made available over the web (for browsing and annotating).
- It should be possible to print (selected parts of) the models.
- It should be possible to work with and update both large and small model fragments (e.g. by sub-setting the model, not having to check out the whole model to do changes).
- In an integrated modelling environment comprising several modelling tools, a Single Sign-on Service should be available, meaning that one only should need to identify oneself once.

- The environment should support group definition to control access rights. One should allow flexible assignment of members to different groups, i.e. a person can be member of many groups. The assignment should be done based on the roles of each member.
- There should be possible to define single user and group access permission rights (reading, writing) on all entities, according to their role in the modelling group and according to the model content.
- Enterprises concurrently run a multitude of projects and the modelling services must be able to support these projects. That means that it should be possible to have several models stored and managed independently inside the repository.
- The modelling platform should inform the user about other users logged in to the platform. It should be possible to inform partners when a locked part of a model again becomes available (information about check in/check-out). A standard message handler should be able to send messages to certain people in order to inform about modelling and methodological issues (e.g. about critical repository management activities like model mismatch).
- It must be possible to define, modify and delete projects. Depending on the user's permission rights, new models may be defined, modified and deleted independent of other models and projects inside the repository.
- Different models will be stored in one repository. Sub-models will be exported and imported separately.
- The models and model parts will be versioned. The meta-model has to include standard attributes of every modelling element that has been updated automatically by the repository service.
- Dependency control in order to link or merge models must be supported. In case of merging and linking, one model to another, these activities has to be supported by defining a common reference architecture (model product structure) and re-linking instances to new enterprise structures. In case of changing structure in one model, the effects on the other model have to be identified automatically. Models will be linkable to different general models in different repositories.
- Check in and check-out functionality has also to support local repositories and (file) storage and later synchronisation to make it possible to work with models and sub-models off-line.
- Standard database backup and replication services have to be provided.
- Access control is required to distinguish between external (public) model information and internal private model information.

4.2.2   Model Interchange

- The environment should provide a standard platform for connection of enterprise models with execution-oriented standards and de facto standards. The platform should provide adaptable building blocks for easy definition of own exchange objects in the repository.

- The environment should help and allow an easy transferring of knowledge between business areas, company boundaries and geographical locations.
- The modelling services should provide a standard API for connecting modelling tools to the repository.
- One should provide interfaces to standard IT systems that will enable the enterprise models to support the configuration of software systems.
- Interfaces to information coming from corporate IT systems like ERP systems should be provided. Here, especially the import of the operational enterprise data stored in these systems should be supported in order to validate models or for simulation and further analysis.
- To ease the access to repository services for model management, one may have to provide services to the external world to simplify modelling and model management. This could mean that part of a model contains data automatically updated from legacy databases or XML or text files.

4.2.3 Support for Meta-Modelling

- The environment should allow the user to define the attributes required on each object type and each relationship type; so the system is not limited to a predefined set of attributes.
- More general meta-model adaptation should be available, both relative to adapting the concepts and the notation. See further services below for how to achieve this.
- Meta-modelling capabilities – e.g. for defining templates (sub-languages) – should be provided according to specific needs of the modelling independent from the modelling tool. Separate building blocks for modelling should be defined and linked to the actual meta-model.
- The kernel meta-model will be extendable by using a definition service, changes has to be tracked to the repository API to be used by other modelling tools.
- The ability to add new modelling concepts, to specialise and extend existing concepts, possibly including versioning of class definitions should be available.
- The ability to add, remove or modify features (properties or behaviour) of individual objects, independently of class definitions should be available. The ability to change the class of an object, explicitly through modelling, but also implicitly as an automatic effect of the object changing its properties (*dynamic objects*) should be supported.
- Class definitions and their interrelationships such as specialisation hierarchies, composition hierarchies and role relations must be manageable.
- Property definition, including attribute encodings, should be managed in a separate structure, and reusable property templates will be easy to add to existing classes or objects. Property structures such as specialisation, composition, symmetric and asymmetric relations, transformational and state properties will be captured and utilised. The used modelling tool has to provide the capabilities.
- Behavioural features, whether implemented by other services, process models, scripts or declarative tasks, will be defined and managed separately. Relationships

such as specialisation, replacement-alternative, roles/interfaces, dependencies, composition should be possible to represent.

- In order to simplify modelling and make the model-driven enterprise system automatically adaptable, inheritance should be user-controlled and allowed along any model relationship. Inheritance could be implemented as a propagation of features (properties and/or behaviours) from one element (object, process, class, property, behaviour, etc.) to another. The inheritance should be selective at various levels of granularity (e.g. it should be possible to inherit 'all behaviours', but also individual properties) from another element. Inheritance policies, defining who inherits what from whom, should also be inheritable. The handling of multiple-inheritance conflicts should be implemented as a set of alternative behaviours, enabling both to be automated by a service, controlled by rules or handled interactively in a prescribed process.

4.3 Empirical Quality

As described briefly in Chap. 1, empirical quality deals with the variety of elements distinguished, error frequencies when being written or read, coding (including shapes of boxes) and ergonomics for both documentation and modelling tools. The term relates to that this layer collects traits of visual or textual communication that has been shown empirically (e.g. through the work in cognitive psychology) to result in models that are easier to understand.

Changes to improve empirical quality of a model do not change the statements that are included in the model; thus, we have no set-theoretic definition of this quality characteristic.

A model consists of both graphics and text. Although the diagrammatical aspects are most focused in connection to conceptual models, there are also relevant aspects linked to the textual parts of the models. The text can be in the form of labels (naming the concepts) and longer descriptions. As for labels, there have for a long time existed simple guidelines for labelling of particular type of concepts. For example, in process modelling (using DFD in particular see Gane and Sarson 1979), there is a guideline that you should name a process in an 'active verb, noun' manner (i.e. 'register participant'). One reason for this is obviously to enforce that the process is actually named as a process (and not as an organisational unit for instance). As reported in Mendling and Recker (2008), it also has a positive effect as for the comprehension of the model. Hawryszkiewycz (2001) provides in addition more detailed guidelines for naming of processes, data stores and flows in DFDs. As we see, detailed metrics for labelling are very much dependant on the type of modelling language used (e.g. process modelling), and in certain cases for concrete modelling languages (e.g. DFD or BPMN). A general metric that can be specialised is the proportion of concepts that are labelled in way not conforming to the guidelines for the labelling of the concrete concept. Often, simple linguistic techniques can be utilised to calculate this automatically, although this is normally not supported in standard modelling tools. An aspect of labels that are easier to evaluate visually is that they fit the area assigned for labels on nodes, not crossing node boundaries (and that they are still readable when having this characteristic, i.e. not a too small font either on screen or printed out). We will return to further details on this in the next chapter when we discuss the quality of particular types of models.

For longer descriptions of concepts and informal textual models, several means for text readability have been devised, such as different types of readability indexes.

In the Flesch Reading Ease test (Flesch 1948), lower numbers mark more-difficult-to-read passages. The formula for the Flesch Reading Ease Score (FRES) test = 206.835 − 1.015*(total words/total sentences) − 84.6*(total syllables/total words).

Scores of 90.0–100.0 are considered easily understandable by an average 11-year-old pupil, 13–15-year-old pupil could easily understand passages with a score of 60–70 and passages with results of 0–30 are best understood by college graduates.

The use of this scale is supported in popular word processing programs and services such as KWord, Lotus WordPro, Microsoft Word and Google Docs.

In, e.g. Microsoft Word, you also find support for calculating the Flesch-Kincaid Grade Level (Kincaid et al. 1975) which can be interpreted to mean the number of years of education generally required to understand a text. The grade level is calculated with the following formula:

$$0.39 * (\text{total words} / \text{total sentences}) + 11.8 * (\text{total syllables} / \text{total words}) - 15.59$$

The result is a number that corresponds with a grade level. For example, a score of 8.2 would indicate that the text is expected to be understandable by an average student in eighth grade.

Another example, the 'Fog Index' is arrived at in four steps:

1. Select several 100-word samples from a text.
2. Calculate the average sentence length by dividing the number of words by the number of complete sentences.
3. Obtain the percentage of long words in the entire sample; count the number of words containing three or more syllables and divide this total by the number of 100-word samples.
4. Add the results from steps 2 and 3 and multiply with 0.4. The product is the (American) grade-level for which the text is appropriate, in terms of difficulty.

Several other such formulae have been proposed, of varying level of complexity. Most assume that difficulty can be measured simply in terms of the length of the words and/or sentences. Factors such as the complexity of sentence structure and the nature of word meaning are often found to be much more important, but these, the procedures usually ignore. Readability formulae have thus attracted a great deal of criticism, but in the absence of more sophisticated measures that can be easily calculated, they continue to attract widespread use as a reasonably convenient way of predicting (though not explaining) reading difficulty.

For computer-output specifically, many of the principles and tools used for improving human computer interfaces are relevant at the empirical level.

Other general guidelines regarding not mixing different fonts, colours, etc., (Shneiderman 1992) in a paragraph that is on the same level within the overall text can also be used.

Rules for colour-usage are also useful in connection to evaluating diagrammatical models (if different colours are used). Around 10% of the male population and 1% of the female population suffer from some form of colour vision deficiency (Ware 2000); thus, many modelling notations (e.g. UML) explicitly avoid the use of colours as a part of the notation to convey meaning. Use of colour in a modelling notation is discussed further in Chap. 5 on quality of modelling language. On the other hand, many modelling tools might give the modeller freedom to assign any colour both to the background, the symbols, the labels and the icon/shape used to represent the concept. Colour is an important differentiator in other visual representations that is meant to be widely used (e.g. maps, see Bertin 1983). Shneiderman (1992) has listed a number of guidelines for the usage of colour in visual displays in general.

- Use colour conservatively
- Limit the number of colours used. Many design guidelines suggest limiting the number of colours in a display to four, with a limit to seven colours. According to the opponent process theory (Ware 2000), there are six elementary colours, and these colours are arranged perceptually as opponent pair's long three axes: black-white, red-green and yellow-blue. There is both physiological and linguistic support for using these colours for differentiation. In a study of more than 100 languages from many different cultures, it was showed that primary colour terms are remarkably consistent across cultures. In languages with only two basic colour words, they are always black and white; if a third colour is present, it is always red; the fourth and the fifth are either yellow then green or green and then yellow; the sixth is always blue, the seventh is brown, followed by pink, purple, orange and grey in no particular order.
- Red attracts the eye more than other colours.
- Ensure that the use of colours supports your task.
- Have colour coding appear with minimal user effort.
- Place the application of colour coding under (guided) user control.
- Use colour to help in formatting.
- Be consistent in colour coding.
- Be aware of common expectations about colour codes. This can be dependent on the local culture.
- Be aware of problems with colour pairings. If saturated (pure) red and blue appear on a display at the same time, it may be difficult for users to absorb the information. Red and blue are on the opposite ends of the spectrum, and the muscles surrounding the human eye will be strained by attempts to produce a sharp focus for both colours simultaneously. Blue text on a red background would present an especially difficult challenge for users to read. Similarly, other combinations will appear difficult, such as yellow on purple and magenta on green. Too little contrast is also a problem (yellow letters on a white background or brown letters on a black background). Note that this might be different on different screens and projectors.

Fig. 4.3 Standard colours for differentiating between six concepts

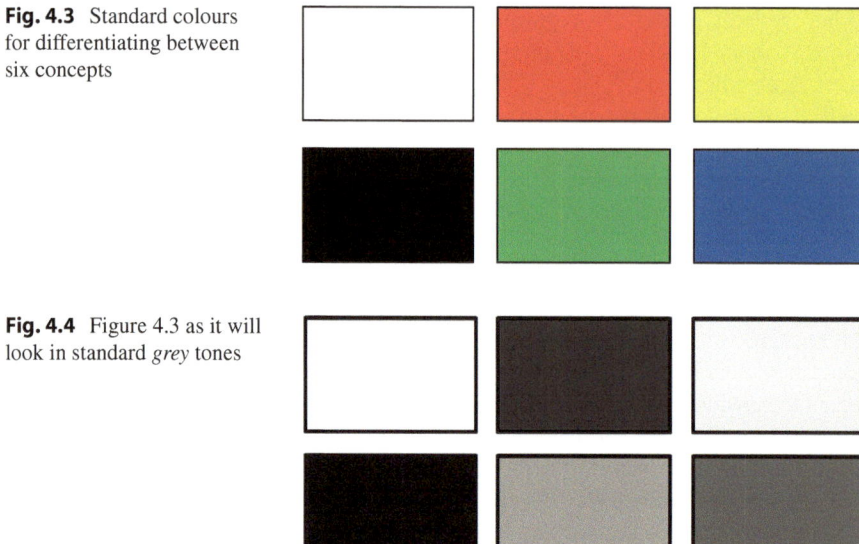

Fig. 4.4 Figure 4.3 as it will look in standard *grey* tones

- Use colour changes to indicate status changes.
- Use colour in graphic displays for greater information density.
- When using a colour coding, take into account that the model might need to be presented or distributed in greyscale (e.g. when printed).

As indicated above, colours that might differentiate well might not differentiate equally well when printed out in black and white. Figures 4.3 and 4.4 illustrate this issue.

Although there are techniques to assure differentiation also when transferring to a black and white print-out, normal printers do not necessarily use the best algorithms for this (Alsam 2009). As we see above, six colours also can look relatively different in greyscale, introducing more colours can be done, but one will then need to ensure that the difference introduced by the use of colours are retained in the greyscale print.

Overall, it might be better to have the use of colours under the control of the modelling language design (as will be discussed in Chap. 5) rather than let it be up to the individual modeller. The same is partly the case for other usage of emphasis. The use of emphasis can also be in accordance with the relative importance of the statements in a given model. Factors that have an important impact on visual emphasis are:

- Size (the big is more easily noticed than the small)
- Solidity (e.g. **bold** letters vs. ordinary letters, full lines vs. dotted lines, thick lines vs. thin lines, filled boxes vs. non-filled boxes)
- Difference from ordinary pattern (e.g. *slanted* letters will attract attention among a large number of ordinary ones)
- Foreground/background differences (if the background is white, things will be easier noticed the darker they are)

- Change (blinking or moving symbols attract attention)
- Position (looking at a diagram, people tend to start at its middle)
- Connectivity (objects that connect to many others (having a high degree) will attract attention compared to objects with few connections)

Many of these aspects are often controlled on the language level, in which case one must have this in mind when addressing modelling language quality (more precisely, comprehensibility appropriateness).

For diagrammatical models (diagrams), layout modification is a meaning-preserving transformation that can improve the comprehensibility of a model. A layout modification is a spatially different arrangement of the elements in the diagrammatical representation of the model.

Lists of guidelines for graph aesthetics are presented in Battista et al. (1994) and Tamassia et al. (1988). These are summarised below and can act as a starting point for automatic layout modification techniques or metrics to be calculated to support the manual improvement of the model layout. Note that a model that is optimal according to one of these aesthetics is not necessarily optimal for another.

- ANGLE: Angles between edges going out from the same node should not be too small.
- AREA: Minimise the area occupied by the drawing.
- BALAN: Balance the diagram with respect to the axis.
- BENDS: Minimise the number of bends along edges.
- CONVEX: Maximise the number of faces drawn as convex polygons.
- CROSS: Minimise the number of crossings between edges.
- DEGREE: Place nodes with high degree in the centre of the drawing.
- DIM: Minimise differences among nodes' dimensions (given nodes of the same type).
- LENGTH: Minimise the global length of edges.
- MAXCON: Minimise the length of the longest edge.
- SYMM: Have symmetry of sons in hierarchies.
- UNIDEN: Have uniform density of nodes in the drawing.
- VERT: Have verticality of hierarchical structures. This means that in a tree/hierarchy, nodes at the same level in the tree are placed along a horizontal line with a minimum distance in between.

A number of metrics can be produced relatively easily based on these guidelines, e.g. the number of crossing edges divided by the total number of edges in a model or compared with the minimum possible number of crossing as long as one does not duplicate symbols. Similar metrics can be devised for the other aesthetics and be used during modelling to assess the potential for improving empirical quality. Based on such metrics, one could easily assess that the quality of Fig. 4.5 is less than that of Fig. 4.2 on this account although it contains the same statements. In particular, we can observe a worsening of the aspects relative to guidelines ANGLE, AREA, BALAN, CROSS, DEGREE, DIM, LENGTH, MAXCON, SYMM, UNIDEN and VERT.

On the other hand, we should remember that aesthetics is a subjective issue; thus, familiarity with a diagram is often just as important for comprehension. As noted by

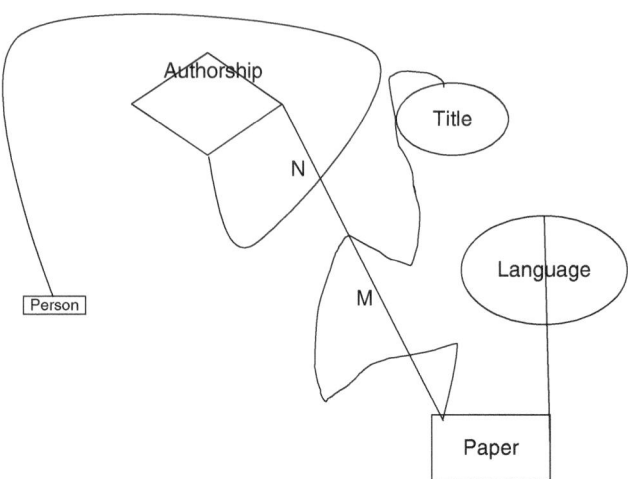

Fig. 4.5 Example on poor model aesthetics

Table 4.1 A taxonomy of constraints for graph layout

Aspects	Explanation
CENTRE	Place a set of given nodes in the centre of the drawing
DIMENSION	Assign the dimensions of symbols
EXTERNAL	Place specified nodes on the external boundary of the drawing
NEIGH	Place a group of nodes close
SHAPE	Draw a sub graph of selected nodes with a predefined shape
STREAM	Place a sequence of nodes along a straight line (a specialisation of SHAPE)

Petre (1995), one of the main advantages of diagrammatic modelling languages appears to be the use of so-called secondary notation, i.e. the use of layout and perceptual cues to improve comprehension of the model. Thus, one often needs to constrain automatic layout modifications. Although it would be more accurate to place this as a means for pragmatic quality (see below), we include it here since it is used in techniques for automatic graph layout which it is natural to cover as part of empirical quality. A list of constraints used in connection to automatic graph layout is given in Table 4.1. Also, manual diagram layout mechanisms should be available in a modelling tool to quickly make an existing model visually pleasing (including horizontal and vertical alignment, equal spacing when selecting more than two nodes, etc.). Tool functionality to make the size and font size of selected elements in the model equal is also useful.

Obviously, it should be easy to retain the aesthetically pleasing diagram when we have to update the model at a later point in time. This includes the possibility of selecting and moving a group of nodes as one, the moving of complete sub-trees as one in a hierarchical model, re-routing connections when changing the relative position of two interconnected nodes and tool functionality such as snap-to-grid. In advanced modelling tools, one finds all these mechanisms. In tools such as Troux Architect, you also can define layout strategies, so that you automatically keep, e.g. a collection of elements in a matrix format (compared to how cumbersome this is to do, e.g. in Powerpoint when you have six elements in a matrix and adds two more, changing a 3*2 to a 4*2 matrix with equal spacing).

Finally, there are structures that one have found beneficial in general (e.g. to limit the number of task on a decomposition level in a DFD). Techniques to keep the model in an adequate structure as the model develops are called model refactoring. In programming, refactoring is 'the process of changing a software system in such a way that it does not alter the external behaviour of the code yet improves the internal structure' (Fowler and Beck 1999). Similar information-preserving model transformations can be defined for models. Refactoring techniques are often special to a modelling perspective or modelling language (as the example with the number of tasks on a given decomposition level above for functional models).

Some other examples are:

- Combining attributes (e.g. from a day, a month and a year attribute into a date attribute).
- Collapsing generalisation hierarchies (if there is only one sub-class) in a structural model.
- Move relationship classes higher in a generalisation hierarchy.
- Remove unnecessary relationships in a structural model, given it can be deduced by other relationships.
- Normalisation of logical data models.
- Collapsing decompositions if there is only one sub-class.
- Remove, e.g. and gateways in a BPMN model if there is only one flow in and one flow out from it.

Refactoring will often support expressive economy, and through this indirectly improve many of the graph layout metrics. A comprehensive overview of model refactoring strategies is found in Conesa et al. (2011).

4.4   Syntactic Quality

Syntactic quality is the correspondence between the model M and the language extension L of the language in which the model is written. Referring to the discussion on meta-levels in Sect. 3.1.3, L is constrained by a model on a higher meta-level (the language-model).

There is only one syntactic quality characteristic, *syntactical correctness*, meaning that all statements in the model are according to the syntax and vocabulary of the language, i.e.

$$M_{\mathrm{E}} \setminus L = \varnothing$$

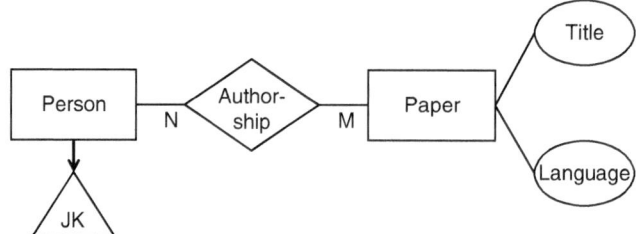

Fig. 4.6 Example of syntactic invalidity

Fig. 4.7 Example of
syntactic incompleteness

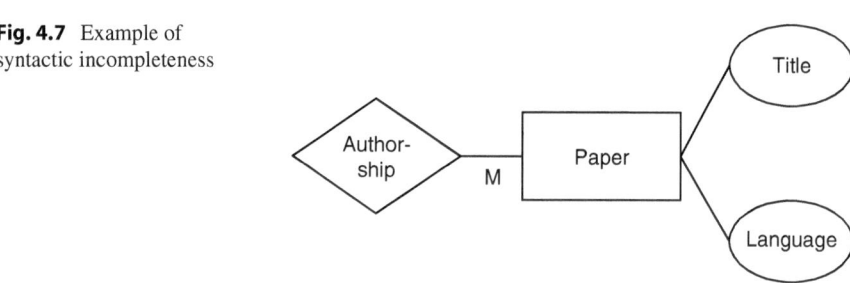

Syntax errors are of two kinds:

- *Syntactic invalidity*, in which words or graphemes not part of the language are used. An example of syntactic invalidity is given in Fig. 4.6, where an actor-symbol (with label JK) not being part of the chosen language (ER) is used.
- *Syntactic incompleteness*, in which the model lacks constructs or information to obey the language's grammar. An example of syntactic incompleteness is given in Fig. 4.7, where only one of the two mandatory entity classes that take part in the relationship is indicated.

The degree of syntactic quality can be measured as one minus the rate of errone-ous statements, i.e.

$$Syntactic\ quality\ =\ 1 - (\#\,M_{\mathrm{E}}\ \backslash\ L + M_{\mathrm{missing}})\ /\ \#\,M_{\mathrm{E}}$$

where M_{missing} is the number of statements that would be necessary to make the model syntactically complete.

To assure the syntactic quality of the model, syntax checks should be provided as an integral part of the modelling support of a modelling tool, either supported in the modelling tools or modelling techniques applied. The checks may be carried out along two main directions:

- Error prevention: This type of checks adapts the principles of *syntax-directed editors*. Thus, only modelling constructs that are defined in the language's vocab-ulary are available through the modelling tool. This includes having modelling pallets (the concepts available to choose for modelling) being limited to the allowed concepts of the language or sub-language used in the given diagram or decomposition, and limitations as for what kind of relationships can be made between two or more concepts. Also, when a modeller violates a syntax rule of the language, the modelling session should be temporarily interrupted in order to restore the illegal model. This type of checks is controlled by the tool.

- Error detection: During a modelling session, some syntactical errors – in particular errors related to *syntactic incompleteness* – should be allowed on a temporary basis. For instance, although a DFD requires that all processes are linked to a flow, it is difficult and/or inconvenient to draw a process and a flow simultaneously. Syntactical completeness has in this case to be checked upon user's request. One might also imagine cases where you want to allow syntactic invalidity for a moment to be able to capture insights during a modelling session that is at odds with the chosen language. So, in contrast to implicit checks where the tool is 'forcing' the user to follow the language syntax, explicit check can only detect and report on existing errors. The user has to make the corrections.

By distinguishing between these types of syntax checks, *modelling freedom* can be encouraged. Throughout the modelling process, the tool will accept some syntactical errors, but these can be detected upon the user's request. The developer is free to construct the model achieving semantic quality as discussed below unless syntax rules are directly violated. Although error-free models are the ultimate goal of model quality assurance, it can be advantageous to have some errors early in model development. Too much focus on syntax quality at this stage might hamper the creativity of the modelling process. This idea is summed up in what is termed 'The Heisenberg Uncertainty Principle of CASE' (Hewett and Durham 1989): 'High levels of inconsistency and incompleteness are permissible if they are confined to a small region of space and time'.

A third syntactic mean is error correction. Error correction – to replace a detected error with a correct statement – is more difficult to automate. When implemented, it usually works as a typical spell-checker found in a word processor, giving suggestions for the correct modelling structure, but leaving it up to the modeller to do the actual change.

All syntactic means are only meaningful to provide if the languages used have a well-defined syntax. There are several ways to describe the syntax of languages for conceptual modelling to, among other things, support error detection and prevention. Some of these are presented below.

- Backus-Naur Form (Gill 1976): This is a widely used language for specification of programming language syntax, but can also be used for specification of conceptual modelling languages. It exists in many variants, but common to these is that they can be used to specify a class of grammars called *context-free phrase grammars (CFG)*. This is a subtype of phrase-structure grammars, which generate sentences being built from hierarchies of phrases. CFGs are often used due to their simplicity, which makes parsing of sentences relatively easy. A weakness of CFG's is that they cannot express complex constraints.
- Data modelling languages: These provide a natural way of expressing basic language constructs and their interrelationships and properties. In the last years, UML

class diagrams have been used by many for this purpose (including OMG for the structural meta-modelling of UML itself). For some environments, specific meta-modelling notations have been devised (e.g. GOPRR in connection to the MetaEdit tool (Kelly et al. 1996)). The main difference between GOPRR and standard data modelling is the G (Graph), the possibility to specify links between entity classes and sub-structures of the overall model, which is specifically relevant for meta-modelling. An advantage of data modelling languages is the ease with which the language syntax is understood within the information system field, at least when the data model is graphical. Also, data models often provide straightforward mappings to database schemas, which mean that large parts of the model repository for the tool supporting conceptual modelling can be easily derived. On the other hand, most data modelling languages offer limited expressiveness for constraint specification. Another disadvantage is that, although possible, data modelling languages are not that well suited to specify languages with complex phrase structures.

- Predicate logic: Logic is a powerful language. Compared to data modelling languages, it allows also complex constraints to be specified. The capabilities of logic for meta-modelling are demonstrated by Brinkkemper (1990). An obvious drawback of predicate logic is that it is less understandable, and it is not well suited to specify phrase-structure grammars.
- Combined representation languages: Some of these languages combine the expressive power of data modelling languages, restricted versions of predicate logic and the possibility to model on the instance level. In the DAIDA project (Jarke et al. 1992), Telos (Mylopoulos et al. 1990) was used as a meta-language, offering necessary modelling constructs to be defined through meta-classes (i.e. classification mechanisms). Current projects in this area such as ConceptBase still use variants of Telos. Although these languages are very expressive, they are also unsuitable for specifying phrase-structure grammars.

Newer approaches to meta-modelling also focus on the modelling of behavioural aspects and constraints of the modelling language, including the use of state transition diagrams and sequence diagrams to represent a trace-based semantics. This is particularly important for the specification of languages from the functional and behavioural perspective such as languages for workflow, BPM and (interactive) process support. The executional semantics of the process modelling of EEML described in Sect. 3.5.2, for instance, used state-diagrams combined with the structural models to describe the task-concept in more detail. Figure 4.8 shows this interpretation. Each state gives the user access to a different set of services (causing transitions). So far, these states are defined:

- *New*, not yet started. These tasks are put in the 'New tasks' task-list.
- *Ongoing*, work is being done on this task. These items are put in the 'Ongoing tasks' task-list.
- *Suspended*, signalling that the work is pending some input flow in order to be resumed. At any time, the participants may restart the task.
- *Finished*, normal completion of the task.
- *Terminated*, representing abnormal termination or deletion of a task. Any task not already *finished* can be terminated.

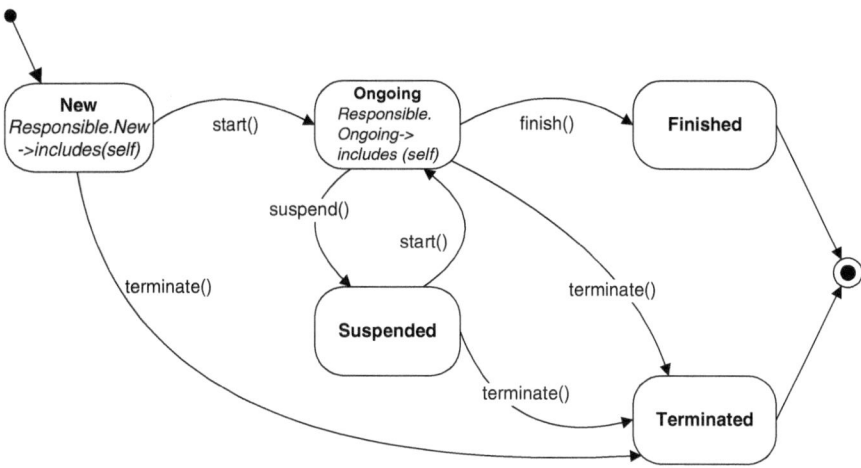

Fig. 4.8 Tasks interpreted by a task management system

4.5   Semantic and Perceived Semantic Quality

Semantic quality was originally defined as the correspondence between the model and the modelling domain (Lindland et al. 1994).

The framework contains two primary semantic quality characteristics: validity and completeness.

- Validity means that all statements made in the model are regarded as correct and relevant for the problem, i.e.

$$M \setminus D = \emptyset$$

A definition for the degree of validity could be

$$Validity = (1 - (\# M_E \setminus D)) / \# M_E$$

However, it can be questioned how useful such a metric might be, since it can usually not be measured automatically due to the intractability of the domain. An example of invalidity is given in Fig. 4.9 where the attribute 'max speed' is added to the entity 'paper', something we believe most persons would agree is invalid (in the sense that it is not a relevant property of a paper).

- Completeness means that the model contains all the statements which would be correct and relevant about the domain, i.e.

$$D \setminus M = \emptyset$$

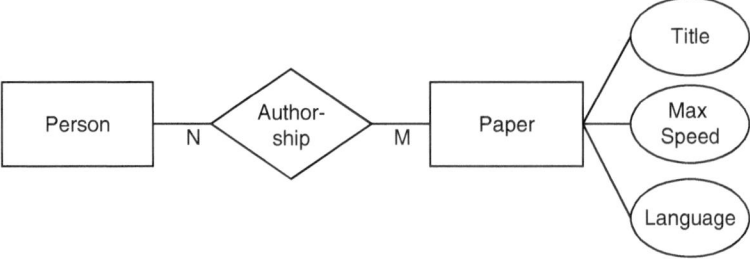

Fig. 4.9 Example of a model with semantic invalidity

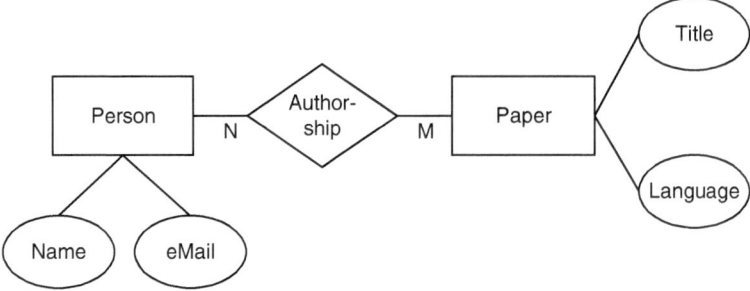

Fig. 4.10 Example of a more complete version of the model in Fig. 4.2

A definition for the degree of completeness could similarly be

$$Completeness = 1 - \big(\#\left(D \ \backslash \ M\right)\big)/ \# D$$

This would only be interesting in well-defined and limited domains, for instance, that it is temporarily decided upon a model of a new CIS. Then one would like to see all the statements in the model also being part of the implemented CIS. On the other hand, D is not completely represented in the previous model in this case, thus validity is also more relevant here. An example of incompleteness can be the original Fig. 4.2, i.e. missing 'name' and eMail as attributes of 'person', something we believe most persons would regard as important to represent in a conference system (see Fig. 4.10).

The primary goal for semantic quality is a correspondence between the externalised model and the domain, but this correspondence can neither be established nor checked directly: to build the model, one has to go through the participants' knowledge (K) regarding the domain, and to check the model one has to compare this with the participants' interpretation (I) of the externalised model. Hence, what we observe at quality control is not the actual semantic quality of the model, but what we term *perceived semantic quality* based on comparisons of the current knowledge with the current interpretation of the model.

Perceived validity and completeness related to the individual performing validation can be expressed as follows:

- *Perceived validity* of the model externalisation: $I_i \setminus K_i = \emptyset$
- *Perceived completeness* of the model externalisation: $K_i \setminus I_i = \emptyset$

Metrics for the degree of perceived validity and completeness can be defined by means of cardinalities in the same way as for semantic quality. Thus, we can define perceived validity in the following way:

$$Perceived\ validity = 1 - (\#(I_i \setminus K_i)) / \# I_i$$

That is, the number of invalid statements interpreted, divided by the total number of statements interpreted by the actor A_i, and similarly one can device a sum over all participants to get an overall number. An example of a model with a perceived invalid statement is the example in Fig. 4.2, where I (the author of this book playing the role of actor A_i), in the subjective role of an end-user of a conference system, might claim that the 'language' attribute is not necessary for 'paper' (normally, papers for scientific conferences in the information systems field are to be written in English). Note that for a conference system to also cater for local (national) conferences, one might actually need this property, thus indicating a lack of agreement between different participants. Agreement will be further discussed as part of social quality below.

Perceived completeness can be defined in the following way:

$$Perceived\ completeness = 1 - (\#(K_i \setminus I_i)) / \# K_i$$

That is, the number of relevant statements known, but not seen in the model, divided by the total number of relevant knowledge statements known by the actor A_i, and similarly a sum over all participants can be established to get an overall number. As on semantic quality, I (in the subjective role of an end-user of a conference system) miss among other things the name and email address of person in the model in Fig. 4.2 (as found in Fig. 4.10).

The perceived semantic quality of the model can change in many ways:

- A statement is added to M^i that A_i understands to be in accordance with K_i, thus increasing perceived completeness.
- A statement is added to M^i that A_i understands to not be in accordance with K_i, thus decreasing perceived validity.
- A statement is removed from M^i that earlier was understood not to be in accordance with K_i thus increasing perceived validity.
- A statement is removed from M^i that earlier was understood to be in accordance with K_i, thus decreasing perceived completeness.
- K_i changes, which can both increase and decrease perceived validity and completeness of the model. One way K_i can change is through the internalisation of another model made based on the knowledge of another actor.
- The actor's knowledge of the modelling language changes, potentially changing I_i which can both increase and decrease the perceived validity and completeness of the model.

Basic modelling activities for establishing higher semantic quality are statement insertion and deletion. An update can conceptually be looked upon as a deletion followed by an insertion. Statement insertions and deletions can obviously also result in lower semantic quality. Statement insertion and deletion can generally be looked upon as meaning updating transformations, which can be done either manually or automatically.

Of specific importance is model reuse (being a specific type of statement insertion). This can either be the reuse of a previous model of a similar domain (e.g. a reference process model of the domain) or might be a translation of a previously baseline model.

Consistency checking is another activity on the semantic level. Note that consistency is subsumed by the combination of validity and completeness since an inconsistency must be caused by at least one invalid statement or the lack of a statement that are to sort out the inconsistency. This is further illustrated in the section on quality of a software requirements specification in Chap. 6. To be able to do consistency checking, the model must be made in a formal, preferably logical language, and to enable and assess the impact of updates, the model should be modifiable. This includes properties such as structure, locality of changes and control of redundancy. Consistency checking can be looked upon as one of several types of model testing which is beneficial at this level. There are two main approaches for formal specifications as the basis for consistency verification:

1. The algebraic specification approach specifies a system as a set of abstract data types (ADTs). The theory of an ADT consists of a set of symbols (sorts and operators, the signature) and a collection of formula (the axioms of the theory); the interpretation of the theory is a many sorted algebra. The specification is a set of theories and the relationships between them.
2. The logical theory approach on the other hand treats the complete model (including both structural and behavioural parts) as a logical theory.

Of particular interest in models with decompositions is test for constructivity. The notion of constructivity was bought into the field of information systems by Langefors (1973). It entails that one can derive the properties of a system based on the properties of the sub-system, and check if the derived properties are the same as those specified for the system earlier (if any). Thus, constructivity is necessary when we want to check the consistency of a hierarchical model, i.e. to check whether decompositions are correct.

A wide range of conceptual modelling techniques start out by verbalising sample and cases. The verbalisations resulting from this step are then used for the development of the first version of the model. A technique for further elaboration on the model is the use of driving questions based on the already existing model as used, e.g. in Tempora (Wangler et al. 1993). Driving questions can be both intra-language and inter-language. A simple example of an inter-language driving question is to assure that what is depicted in a store in a data-flow diagram is also found in the accompanying data model. More concrete guidelines for this kind of technique will be linked to particular modelling languages and combination of modelling languages.

In the area of semantic quality, general automated tools are difficult to develop for the simple reason that the domain and audience are beyond automatic manipulation. The means for achieving a high perceived validity and completeness are similar to the ones for traditional validity and completeness, with the addition of participant training (in the modelling language). The actual checking of perceived semantic quality does as we understand involve the view of the participants, and cannot be totally automated, which is also why we put semantic quality into the social and not the technical realm in the discussion in Chap. 1.

Using a formal language, one can in a sense translate some semantic problems into syntactic problems, but this sets additional requirements to the domain appropriateness of the language used. In many cases, the modelling language chosen is not appropriate for representing the knowledge on the domain, thus making it very difficult to achieve completeness. One important activity to address this is the adaptation of the meta-model of the modelling language used to suit the domain, both by adding concepts, but also by removing concepts (temporarily) from the language if they are not relevant for the modelling of the particular domain. This is treated in more detail under the discussion on language quality in Chap. 5. Domain appropriateness, modeller appropriateness and participant appropriateness are all relevant dimensions in connection to this. A more detailed approach for doing meta-modelling in practice being supported by SEQUAL is presented in Sect. 7.4.2.

4.6 Pragmatic Quality

Pragmatic quality as we define it relates to the comprehension of the model by participants. Two aspects can be distinguished:

- That the interpretation by human stakeholders of the model is correct relative to what is meant to be expressed in the model. Note that a model only can be said to formally mean anything if the syntax and semantics of the language used is intersubjectively agreed, and is at least semiformal, but preferably formal; thus, one can trace or execute the model and experience the dynamic behaviour of the model. In addition, it will often be useful to have different meta-data of the models represented (such as who has made the model, when was it made). In particular, it can be useful to have the *intention* of making the model explicitly represented (since a model created to achieve one goal might often have little value in achieving a different goal). This is also important to take into account in model reuse as described briefly in Sect. 4.5 on semantic quality.
- That the tool interpretation is correct relative to what is meant to be expressed in the model.

Starting with the human comprehension part, pragmatic quality on this level is the correspondence between the model and the audience's interpretation of it. Not even the most brilliant model would be of any use if nobody was able to understand it. Moreover, it is not only important that the model has been understood, but also who has understood (the relevant parts of) it.

Individual comprehension is defined that the individual actor A_i understands the part of the model relevant to that actor, i.e. $I_i = M^i$.

The corresponding error class is *incomprehension*, meaning that the above formula does not hold.

It is important to note that the pragmatic goal is stated as *comprehension*, i.e. that the model has been understood, not as *comprehensibility*, i.e. the model's ability to be understood (which is what we treated under empirical quality in Sect. 4.3 above). There are several reasons for doing so. First, the ultimate goal is that the model is understood, not that it is understandable per se, although this can be an important mean to achieve comprehension. Moreover, comprehension is very dependent on the process by which it is developed, the way the participants communicates with each other and various kinds of tool support.

From the technical actors' point of view, that a model is understood means that all statements that are relevant to the technical actors to be able to perform, e.g. code generation or simulation are comprehended by the relevant technical actors (tools). In this sense, formality can be looked upon as being a pragmatic mean, formal syntax and formal (operational) semantics of the modelling language are means for achieving pragmatic quality. This illustrates that pragmatic quality is dependent on the different actors. This also applies to social actors. Whereas some individuals from the outset are familiar with formal languages, and a formal model will be best for them also for comprehension, other people will find a mix of formal and informal statements to be more comprehensive, even if the set of statements in the complete model is redundant.

A conceptual model can be difficult to comprehend due to the formality or unfamiliarity of the modelling language used, the complexity or size of the model or the effort needed to deduce important properties of it. A conceptual modelling environment may make use of certain techniques to enhance user's comprehension. Looking at the linguistic aspects of conceptual modelling, we can describe such strategies along the following four dimensions:

- *Language perception* concerns user's ability to understand the concepts of the modelling language. We look in more detail on this as part of language quality in the next chapter.
- *Content relevance* indicates the possibilities of separating between irrelevant and relevant model properties, so that at any time one is able to focus on just the relevant parts (for the individual actor or group in question).
- *Structure analysis* depends on the environment's abilities to analyse and expose structural properties of the conceptual model.
- *Behaviour experience* is related to the model execution facilities offered.

Some of the activities to achieve pragmatic quality are:

- Participant training: Educate the audience in the syntax and semantics of the modelling languages used or on aspects of the domain.
- Model inspection and walkthroughs: Manually reading a model, going through it in an orderly manner and potentially explaining it to others. Having stakeholders that have not developed the model themselves, but which need to understand the

Fig. 4.11 Example of the use of a language filter

model go through it and explain what it states aloud is often a very good way of testing the current comprehension of the model. Other techniques from code inspections have been adapted to (requirements) model inspection (van Lamsweerde 2009). Useful support for this in a modelling tool is support for navigation and browsing of the model. This also includes the possibility of scrolling the model, either incrementally (pan) or one page at a time (page), and zooming.

- Model transformations: Generally to transform a model into another model in the same language. This can generally be expressed as

$$T : M1_{Li} \rightarrow M2_{Li}$$

The need for transforming models arises for several reasons. First, models may be transformed to improve the efficiency. In several approaches, an initial operational specification gradually evolves into the final implementation by a continuous replacement of real-world modelling constructs with more efficient constructs from the programming world. Second, models or programs may achieve improved readability through use of transformations. This is discussed under layout modifications in Sect. 4.3 on empirical quality. As a final example, models or programs need to be changed if the underlying language changes.

- Model rephrasing is a meaning preserving transformation where some of the implicit statements of the model are made explicit. This is related to model refactoring discussed under empirical quality above.
- Model filtering is a meaning removing transformation, concentrating on and illuminating specific parts of a model. Filtering has been defined in (Seltveit 1993) based on the notion of a *views* **V**, which is a model containing a subset of the statements of another model in the same language, i.e. **V** is a subset of **M**.

Another way of specifying a filter is to say that it is a set of not necessarily syntactically complete *deletes* of statements. Filters can be classified into two major groups:

- Language/meta-model filters: Suppress details with respect to graphemes and symbols in the modelling language. An example is illustrated in Fig. 4.11 where all attributes are removed.
- Model/specification filters: Suppress details with respect to a particular model. An example is given in Fig. 4.12 where only the attributes and subclasses of a selected entity-class, in this case 'paper', are retained.

Other relevant aspects of filters include:

- Inclusiveness/exclusiveness: A filter can be defined by specifying the components to be included in the view or by specifying the components to be excluded in the view. This is referred to as inclusiveness and exclusiveness properties of the viewspecs, respectively.

Fig. 4.12 Example of the
use of a model filter

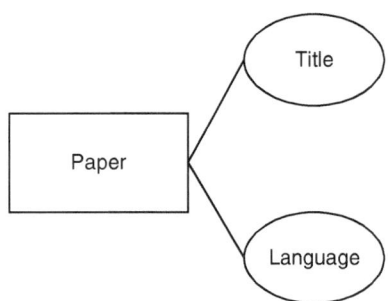

- Query: A filter can be defined as a query after elements having a certain attribute.
- Determinism/non-determinism: A filter is deterministic if the resulting views of performing the filter on a model **M** is the same each time, given that it operates on **M** each time. If the result is not predictable, the filter is non-deterministic.
- Global/local effects: We distinguish between two cases: (1) The scope of effects is local if there is no effect of the filter beyond the model upon which it operates, and (2) it is global if the scope of effect is beyond the model upon which it operates. A serious problem with filters with global effects is how to propagate changes to affected models.

Tools for dealing with large models (e.g. enterprise architecture models) such as METIS/Troux Architect, have good facilities for creating views of models, being filters of different types, where it is also possible to update the views, propagating changed values back to the main model.

- Model translation: A translation can generally be described as a mapping from a model in one language to a model containing all or some of the same statements in another language.

$$T : M_{L_i} \rightarrow M_{L_j}, \ i \neq j$$

In *paraphrasing*, both L_i and L_j are textual languages. Often this term is used more generally. In *visualisation*, L_i is a textual language whereas L_j is a diagrammatical language. FORML2 (Halpin 2010) is an example of a textual language where statements can be transferred to visual ORM data models.

Translations between different diagrammatical languages can also be useful for comprehension in case different persons are fluent in different related languages. For example, for those being familiar with GSM described in Sect. 3.3.4, the diagram in Fig. 4.13 might be better for comprehension than the diagram in Fig. 4.2.

Finally, one might want to translate a diagrammatical model into a textual language, for instance, a programming language so that the resulting model can be executed, or a natural language for improved comprehensibility. In this case, L_i is diagrammatical and L_j is textual. Again in the NORMA tool (Halpin 2010), ORM models can be translated into FORML2 statements to enhance validation activities.

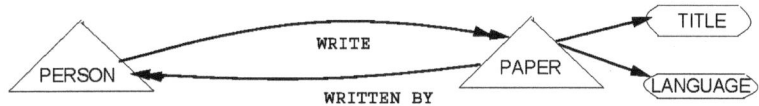

Fig. 4.13 The conference example written in the GSM language

Although most translations and transformations will be easier and faster to perform when having tool support, they can also be done manually. Manual translations and transformations can also be used as part of participant training. On the other hand, also participant training might be enhanced by using tool support. Several specific applications of translations and transformations and combinations of these exist. Some examples are:

- Model execution: Translate or transform the model to a model in an executable language, e.g. the languages used for the resulting CIS or some special execution language, and execute the model (Lindland and Krogstie 1993). When doing this translation manually, we speak about *prototyping* in the traditional sense.
- Animation: Make systems dynamics explicit by using moving pictures. This might take the form of icons such as a telephone ringing or a customer arriving at a registration desk, or it might apply the symbols of the modelling language. Recently, techniques applying virtual reality environments have been illustrated as a validation technique (Brown 2010).
- Explanation generation (Gulla 1996): This can be manual or tool-supported. An explanation generator can answer questions about a model and its behaviour.
- Simulation: Use statistical assumptions about the domain, such as arrival rate of customers and distributions of processing times, to anticipate how a system built according to the model would behave if implemented. Neither of these is practical without tool support for large models. Simulation can be combined with execution, animation and explanation.

The properties a model has and the languages it is made in must have to support these techniques including those for syntactic and semantic quality as well as executability (i.e. the execution of the model has to be efficient). Other beneficial characteristics are expressive economy, and aesthetics (empirical quality) as mentioned above.

4.7   Social Quality

The goal defined for social quality is *agreement*. Six kinds of agreement can be identified, according to the following dimensions:

- Agreement in knowledge vs. agreement in model interpretation. In the case where two models are made based on the view of two different actors, we can also talk about agreement in model.
- Relative agreement vs. absolute agreement.

Relative agreement means that the various sets to be compared are consistent – hence, there may be many statements in the model of one actor that are not present in that of another, as long as they do not contradict each other. Absolute agreement, on the other hand, means that all models are the same.

Agreement in model interpretation will usually be a more limited demand than agreement in knowledge, since the former one means that the actors agree about what is stated in the model, whereas there may still be much they disagree about which is not stated in the model so far, even if it might be regarded as relevant by one or both participants for the current modelling task. Agreement of models will be easier to check in practice especially if the languages have formal syntax or semantics, although this is limited to the situation described above. Hence, we can define

- Relative agreement in interpretation: all I_i are consistent
- Absolute agreement in interpretation: all I_i are equal
- Relative agreement in knowledge: all K_i are consistent
- Absolute agreement in knowledge: all K_i are equal
- Relative agreement in model: all M_i are consistent
- Absolute agreement in model: all M_i are equal

Metrics can be defined for the degree of agreement based on the number of inconsistent statements divided by the total number of statements perceived or by the number of non-corresponding statements divided by the total number of statements perceived.

Since different participants will have their expertise in different fields, relative agreement is regarded to be more useful than absolute agreement. On the other hand, the different actors must have the *possibility* to agree and disagree on something, i.e. the parts of the model that are relevant to them should overlap to some extent.

The pragmatic goal of comprehension is looked upon as a social mean. This is because agreement without comprehension is not very useful, at least not when having democratic ideals. Obviously if someone is trying to manipulate a situation, agreement without comprehension is 'useful'.

The area of *model monopoly* (Bråten 1973) as discussed in Chap. 1 is related to this; thus, one should be aware of the dangers of particularly modellers consciously or (more likely) unconsciously misleading other participants.

Tool support related to social quality is most easy to device on achieving agreement in models created based on the internal reality of the participants that are to agree. Based on this, main activities for investigating and hopefully achieving agreement are the use of model integration techniques with specific emphasis on conflict resolution in the integrated models.

The general model integration process has many similarities with view integration, which has been a topic of much research in the database community over the last 20+ years. The process can be considered as consisting of four sub-processes (Francalanci and Pernici 1993).

- Pre-integration: When more than two models are used as input to the process, one must decide on how many models should be considered at a time. A number of strategies have been developed such as binary ladder integration, N-ary integration, balanced binary strategy and mixed strategies. The strategy chosen will often be depending on the organisational setting for the modelling project.

For instance, in the case of participatory modelling described in Sect. 2.4 (Gjersvik et al. 2004), one first integrated the two or three individual models in the first four workshops, and then integrated all the resulting four models into a final model.

- Viewpoint comparison: Includes identifying correspondences and detecting conflicts among the viewpoints. Some types of conflict that may be detected are:
  - *Naming conflicts:* Problems based on the use of synonyms and homonyms.
  - *Type conflicts:* That the same statements are represented by different concepts in different models.
  - *Value conflicts:* An attribute has different domains in two models.
  - *Constraint conflicts:* Two models represent different constraints on the same phenomena.
- Viewpoint conforming: Aims at solving the previously detected conflicts. Representations of statements in two different models can be classified as follows: Identical, equivalent, compatible, and inconsistent. To deal with such conflicts traditional approaches are mostly based on either transformational equivalence or they entrust the skill of the participants by providing only examples valid for the particular model. According to Francalanci and Pernici (1993), few of the early approaches dealt with inconsistent statements. An exception is Leite and Freeman (1991). They describe a way of dealing with conflicting rules in the modelling process. Rules are described in the rule-language VPWI where data, actor and process aspects can be represented. A view consists of a set of rules. Mechanisms are provided to compare two different views of a given situation in order to identify, classify and evaluate discrepancies between the views, and integrate the solution into a single model.

  Other useful techniques in this respect is goal modelling as described in Chap. 3, in particular where you can explicitly represent conflicting goals such as in EEML, and the use of argumentation systems (Conklin and Begeman 1988; Conklin 2005; Hahn et al. 1990) for supporting the argumentation process. These use the IBIS (Issue Based Information Systems)-approach originally proposed by Rittel (1972) or extensions of this. IBIS focuses on the articulation of the key issues in the problem area. Each issue may have many *positions*, which are statements or assertions that resolve the issue. Each of the issue's positions in turn may have one or more *arguments* which either support or object to the position. Going from one node-type to another is done through so-called rhetorical moves.
- Merging and restructuring: The different models are merged into a joint model and then restructured. The latter involves checking the resulting model against criteria for empirical, semantic, pragmatic and social quality.

  Generally, it is not to be expected that matching, apart from syntactic matching, can be performed fully automatic, although several modelling tools have this kind of functionality (Rittgen 2011). Model merging can be supported in several ways, having computerised support for manual integration, possibly with the use of CSCW-techniques.
- Computerised support of manual integration: Manual merging may be supported in various ways by exploiting modern user-interface technology. Working styles

such as virtual paper, clipboards, cut and paste and active structures can be supported. It can be useful to provide facilities to track the transformations performed on a predecessor model, i.e. recording modelling history during updating and filtering. The changes can be recorded textually, or shown explicitly relative to the diagrams of the predecessor model by using special notation in the diagram. In the latter case, cut and paste facilities across windows between models greatly improve the merging process.

- Automatic integration support: The result of automatic merges are useful only in some cases, e.g. if all components of the different models have unique identifiers. However, the use of formal modelling techniques opens up for more extensive integration techniques where, e.g. structural conflicts may be resolved. This is useful in most modelling situations where different participants may have different perceptions on the area and a possible CIS-implementation to address the perceived problems.

- CSCW support: CSCW techniques can be applied to create new arenas for dialogue. In addition to face-to-face meetings, the integration effort can take place by applying more advanced workstation and networking technology in cooperative sessions. The negotiation session may be synchronous or asynchronous.
  - Synchronous negotiations: In the synchronous case, all candidate models are available to all involved participants in the session through a shared workspace for comments and comparisons. Several modes of working can be supported.
  - The public screen and public desktop allow all participants involved to view one participants screen or physical desktop. This mode implements multicasting of the changes made to one screen or desktop. Only the owner of the screen/desktop may update it.
  - Desktop on screen and desktop on desktop allow participants to draw sketches and comment the contents of other developer's screens or desktops, using overlays. Experimental evidence indicates that users easily differentiate up to three overlays.
  - The shared tool mode allows all participants to simultaneously view and edit the conceptual models.
  The usefulness of these modes is dependent on the presence of synchronised sound or video and the possibility of flexible switching between modes.

- Asynchronous negotiations: In this case, one relies on written communications in the form of comments and cut-and-paste versions, and multi-media annotations to the artefacts. The multimedia messages passed between participants are based on the candidate versions. The messages can contain annotations to one or several candidate versions in the form of synchronised pointing, drawing, writing and speaking. To annotate a local version of a model, one would add a transparent annotation layer to it, where the annotation is entered. This may be played back in synchronous mode, playing back voice comments, the cursor movements of a stylus, as well as hand-drawn and typed messages. For example, a tool like METIS has annotation facilities where different participants can annotate different model elements, where you can then get an aggregated view of all annotations received.

4.8 Deontic Quality

Modelling is (usually) not done for the fun of it, but to achieve some goal (termed the goals of modelling, G), which usually are linked to some business and organisational goals. This introduces the need of looking at both cost and benefit of modelling. Means here are related to the modelling of these goals, and checking their fulfilment (i.e. that all goals are achieved and that there are no goals that are not achieved). We will look at this more concretely when specialising the framework for different types of models in Chap. 6.

For anything but extremely simple and highly intersubjectively agreed domains, total validity, completeness, comprehension and agreement as described above cannot be achieved. Hence, for the goals on these areas to be realistic, they have to be somewhat relaxed, by introducing the idea of *feasibility*. Attempts at reaching a state of total validity, completeness, comprehension and agreement will potentially lead to unlimited spending of time and money on the modelling activity. The time to terminate a modelling activity is thus not when the model is 'perfect' (which will never happen), but when it has reached a state where further modelling is regarded to be less beneficial than applying the model in its current state. Accordingly, a relaxed kind of these human-related goals can be defined, which we term feasible validity, feasible completeness, feasible comprehension and feasible agreement.

- *Feasible validity*: $M \setminus D = R, R \neq \emptyset$, but there is no statement $r \in R$ such that the benefit of performing a syntactically valid delete of r from M exceeds the drawback eliminating the invalidity r.
- *Feasible perceived validity*: $I \setminus K = R, R \neq \emptyset$, but there is no statement $r \in R$ such that the benefit of performing a syntactically valid delete of r from M exceeds the drawback eliminating the invalidity r.
- *Feasible completeness*: $D \setminus M = S, S \neq \emptyset$, but there is no statement $s \in S$ such that the benefit of inserting s in M in a syntactically complete way exceeds the drawback of adding the statement s.
- *Feasible perceived completeness*: $K \setminus I = S, S \neq \emptyset$, but there is no statement $s \in S$ such that the benefit of inserting s in M in a syntactically complete way exceeds the drawback of adding the statement s.
- *Feasible comprehension* means that although the model may not have been correctly understood by all audience members, there is no statement in the model such that the benefit of rooting out the misunderstanding corresponding to a statement here exceeds the drawback of taking that effort.
- *Feasible agreement* is achieved if feasible perceived semantic quality and feasible comprehension are achieved and inconsistencies are resolved by choosing one of the alternatives when the benefits of doing this are greater than the drawbacks of working out an agreement.

Feasibility thus introduces a trade-off between the *value* and *drawbacks* for achieving a given model quality. We have used the term 'drawback' here instead of the more usual 'cost' to indicate that the discussion is not necessarily restricted to purely economical issues. Judging completeness with respect to some intersubjectively agreed standard as suggested by Pohl (1994) is one approach to feasibility. By making the standard a part of the language, one can in addition transfer this inherently semantic problem into a syntactic one to enable automatic checks for conformance to the standard. Note again that this is only workable if the standard is appropriate to achieve the goals of modelling in the first place. Another relevant issue on this level is how to decide the timeliness of model updates, as discussed in Sect. 4.2.

As we can see from the variety of goals of modelling, in addition to changing the models, these might also be meant to change other aspects, including

- That the participants learn based on the model (i.e. K is increased).
- That if the modelling is related to bring about change (e.g. an organisational improvement or a system development is taking place) the domain D is changed, preferably in a positive direction relative to the goal of modelling.

   These aspects can also be defined more precisely.

- *Overall learning*: Let ΔK^M be the increase of the set K (i.e., the current knowledge) facilitated by the model M. Then the overall learning gain of the model is $\Delta K^M \cap K^N$, i.e. the new knowledge acquired by the organisation that is also within the knowledge need (K^N). Similarly, let ΔK^m be the increase of the set K caused by the modelling *activity*, a similar knowledge gain $\Delta K^m \cap K^N$ may be associated with this.

- *Local learning*: Often, the goal of a modelling activity is knowledge transfer through communication and sense-making, i.e. there is one or a few persons in the organisation who know something, but there is a wish to make this knowledge available to more people: $((K_i \setminus K_j) \cap K_j^N)$, i.e. there is knowledge held by a person or group i in the organisation, but not by person/group j, although it is within the knowledge need of j. Similar to above, the improvement will be $\Delta K_j^M \cap K_j^N$, the added knowledge of j which was within j's knowledge need.

- *Overall domain improvement*: Let ΔD^M be the change of the domain D facilitated by the model, and ΔD^m similarly by the modelling activity. The improvement resulting from the model and modelling activity together will then be $(\Delta D^M \cup \Delta D^m) \cap D^O$, i.e. the alterations to the domain that were in line with some perceived optimal domain. Local domain improvement (i.e. for a particular person or group, but not necessarily for the entire organisation) could be defined in the same manner as local learning if relevant, e.g. when the specific work process for a particular group improves, even if this is not transferable to a larger context.

Table 4.2 shows an overview of the quality characteristics and means that have been identified on the different semiotic levels.

Language quality goals are looked upon as means in the framework. Six areas of language quality are differentiated:

1. Domain appropriateness: This relates the language and the domain. Ideally, the conceptual basis must be powerful enough to express anything in the domain, not having what Wand and Weber (1993) terms construct deficit. On the other hand, you should not be able to express things that are not in the domain, i.e. what is termed construct excess (Wand and Weber 1993). Domain appropriateness is primarily a mean to achieve semantic quality.

Table 4.2 Overview of SEQUAL quality levels, goals and means

Quality type and characteristics	Means	Model and language properties	Modelling techniques and tool-support
Physical – internaliseability	Beneficial existing quality	Persistence	Database activities
		Currency	Repository functionality
		Availability	
Empirical – minimal error frequency	Physical	Comprehensibility appropriateness	Diagram layout
		Aesthetics	Readability index
			Refactoring
Syntactic – syntactic correctness	Physical	Formal syntax	Structural metamodelling
			Error prevention
			Error detection
			Error correction
Semantic – validity	Physical	Domain appropriateness	Statement insertion
		Participant appropriateness	Statement deletion
		Modeller appropriateness	Behavioural meta-modelling
		Language extension mechanisms	Meta-model adaptation
		Formal semantics	
Completeness	Syntactic	Modifiability	Driving questions
		Analysability	Model reuse
			Model testing and consistency checking

(continued)

Table 4.2 (continued)

Quality type and characteristics	Means		
	Beneficial existing quality	Model and language properties	Modelling techniques and tool-support
Pragmatic – comprehension	Physical	Operational semantics	Inspection
	Empirical	Executability	Visualisation
	Syntactic	Modelling of intentions and other meta-data	Filtering
			Rephrasing
			Paraphrasing
			Explanation
			Execution
			Animation
			Simulation
Perceived semantic-perceived validity	Physical	Variety	Participant training
Perceived completeness	Empirical		
	Syntactic		
	Pragmatic		
Social – agreement	Physical	Inconsistency modelling	Model integration
	Perceived semantic		Conflict resolution
Deontic-goal validity	All	Traceability	
Goal completeness		Tracedness	
Feasibility		Adherence to standards	Based on the specific type of modelling and goals of modelling
Learning			
Action			

2. Comprehensibility appropriateness: This relates the language to the social actor interpretation. The goal is that the participants in the modelling effort using the language understand all the possible statements of the language. Comprehensibility appropriateness is primarily a mean to achieve empirical and pragmatic quality.
3. Participant appropriateness: This relates the social actors' explicit knowledge to the language (i.e. do the participants know the language being used). Participant appropriateness is primarily a mean to achieve semantic and pragmatic quality.
4. Modeller appropriateness: This area relates the language extension to the knowledge of the modeller. The goal is that there are no statements in the explicit knowledge of the modeller that cannot be expressed in the language. Modeller appropriateness is primarily a mean to achieve semantic quality.
5. Tool appropriateness: This relates the language to the technical audience interpretations. For tools interpretation, it is especially important that the language lend itself to automatic reasoning. This requires formality (i.e. both formal syntax and semantics being operational and/or logical), but formality is not necessarily enough, since the reasoning must also be efficient to be of practical use. This is covered by what we term analysability (to be able to exploit any mathematical semantics efficiently) and executability (to be able to exploit any operational semantics efficiently). Different aspects of technical actor interpretation appropriateness are a mean to achieve syntactic, semantic and pragmatic quality (through formal syntax, mathematical semantics and operational semantics).
6. Organisational appropriateness: This area relates the language to standards and other organisational needs within the organisational context of modelling. These are means to support deontic quality.

Language quality is discussed in more detail in Chap. 5. A specific technique or tool functionality is positioned as a mean in Table 4.2 in the category where it is believed to be of most importance, although closer analysis of a technique such as 'prototyping' will reveal potential usefulness of this technique on many levels. We have also indicated quality types that can be beneficial to achieve before attacking the relevant area, thus indirectly the means for achieving, e.g. empirical quality is also a potential means for achieving pragmatic quality. Methodological aspects relative to how to combine the deliberation on the different levels are discussed in more detail in Chap. 7. In Chap. 6, we will look at specialisations of SEQUAL relative to evaluation of quality of different types of models.

4.9 Summary

We have in this chapter described the main parts of SEQUAL, a framework for the understanding and assessment of quality of models. Inspired by earlier discussion on quality of conceptual models and requirement specifications, combined with semiotic theory, model quality has been divided into seven areas:

- Physical quality: The persistence, currency and availability of the model.
- Empirical quality: The relationship between the model and another model containing the same statements being somehow regarded as better through different arrangement or layout.

- Syntactic quality: The relationship between the model and the language used for modelling. Is the modelling language used correctly?
- Semantic quality: The relationship between the model and the domain of modelling. Perceived semantic quality is the parallel relationship between the knowledge of the participants and their interpretation of the model. Is the model complete (containing all valid statements) and valid (not containing invalid statement)?
- Pragmatic quality: The relationship between the model and the stakeholder's interpretation of the model. Do the audience understand the implications of the part of the model relevant to them?
- Social quality: The relationship between different model interpretations. Do the different participants of the modelling agree on the semantic quality of the model?
- Deontic quality: How the models contribute to fulfil the overall goals of modelling?

Review Questions

1. Describe the different levels of quality in SEQUAL
2. What does the beneficial existing quality column in Table 4.2 tell us relative to the order of looking at the different quality levels?
3. What is the main difference between empirical quality and pragmatic quality?
4. What are the most important means for achieving physical quality?
5. What are the most important means for achieving pragmatic quality?
6. What are the most important means for achieving deontic quality?
7. What are the most important means for achieving syntactic quality?
8. What are the most important means for achieving semantic quality?
9. What are the most important means for achieving social quality?
10. What are the most important means for achieving empirical quality?
11. What is the difference between semantic and perceived semantic quality?

Problems and Exercises

Individual Exercises
1. Prototyping is above looked upon as a mean for achieving pragmatic quality. Discuss the prototyping technique relative to aspects on all the different levels of quality in SEQUAL.
2. Based on any of the model done as part of any of the modelling tasks in Chap. 3, evaluate the empirical, syntactic, semantic quality of the models you have produced.

Pair Exercises
1. Model the process for the development and evaluation of exercises in one of your current courses in a process modelling language of choice. After you have both modelled this, evaluate the quality of the model of the other in turn, and see if you can come up with a common model you agree on.

Group Exercises

1. In connection to a modelling task in your course (e.g. relative to models made in exercises in Chap. 3), use the resources of the group in the best way to quickly evaluate the quality of the model (physical, empirical, syntactic, semantic, pragmatic, social) and come up with an improved model based on this.
2. Discuss how different goals of modelling as described in Chap. 1 influence the emphasis on model quality levels (i.e. what type of quality that is likely to be of most importance when having different goals of modelling).
3. Use SEQUAL to evaluate the quality of SEQUAL itself (as described in Fig. 4.1 and accompanying text in this chapter).

References

Alsam, A.: Contrast enhancing colour to grey. SCIA '09 Proceedings of the 16th Scandinavian Conference on Image Analysis, Oslo (2009)

ATHENA: Deliverable DA1.5.2: report on methodology description and guidelines definition. By Ohren, O.P., Chen, D., Grangel, R., Jaekel, F.-W., Karlsen, D., Knothe, T., Rolfsen, R.K., in ATHENA A1 deliverables. 2005, SINTEF, Oslo (2005)

Battista, G., Eades, P., Tamassia, R., Tollis, I.G.: Algorithms for drawing graphs: an annotated bibliography. Technical report, Brown University, June (1994)

Bertin, J.: Semiology of Graphics: Diagrams, Networks, Maps. University of Wisconsin Press, Madison (1983)

Bråten, S.: Model monopoly and communications: systems theoretical notes on democratization. Acta Sociol. J. Scand. Social. Assoc. **16**(2), 98–107 (1973)

Brinkkemper, S.: Formalisation of information systems modelling. PhD thesis, University of Nijmegen. Thesis Publishers (1990)

Brown, R.A.: Conceptual modelling in 3D virtual worlds for process communication. Proceedings of the 7th Asia-Pacific Conference on Conceptual Modelling (APCCM 2010), Brisbane (2010)

Churchland, P.M.: A Neurocomputational Perspective. MIT Press, Cambridge (1989)

Conesa, J., Olive, A., Caballé, S.: Semantic web personalization and context awareness information science reference. In: Refactoring and Its Application to Ontologies, pp. 107–136 (2011)

Conklin, J.: Dialogue Mapping: Building Shared Understanding of Wicked Problems. Wiley, New York (2005)

Conklin, J., Begeman, M.J.: gIBIS: a hypertext tool for exploratory policy discussion. ACM Trans. Inform. Syst. **6**(4), 303–331 (1988)

Davis, A.M., Overmeyer, S., Jordan, K., Caruso, J., Dandashi, F., Dinh, A., Kincaid, G., Ledeboer, G., Reynolds, P., Sitaram, P., Ta, A., Theofanos, M.: Identifying and measuring quality in a software requirements specification. In: Proceedings of the First International Software Metrics Symposium, Baltimore, pp. 141–152 (1993)

Denning, P.J.: What is software quality. Commun. ACM **35**(1), 13–15 (1992). January

Erickson, J., Siau, K.: Can UML be simplified? Practitioner use of UML in separate domains. In: proceedings EMMSAD 2007. Proceedings of Twelfth International Workshop on Exploring Modeling Methods in System Analysis and Design, Trondheim, Norway, pp. 89–98 (2007)

Falkenberg, E.D., Hesse, W., Lindgreen, P., Nilsson, B.E., Oei, J.L.H., Rolland, C., Stamper, R.K., Assche, F.J.M.V., Verrijn-Stuart, A.A., Voss, K.: A framework of information system concepts – The FRISCO Report, IFIP WG 8.1 Task Group FRISCO. http://home.dei.polimi.it/pernici/ifip81/publications.html (1996). Cited Dec 2011

Flesch, R.: A new readability yardstick. J. Appl. Psychol. **32**, 221–233 (1948)

Fowler, M., Beck, K.: Refactoring: Improving the Design of Existing Code. Addison-Wesley Professional, Reading (1999)

Francalanci, C., Pernici, B.: View integration: a survey of current developments. Technical Report 93–053, Politecnico de Milano, Milan (1993)

France, R.B., Ghosh, S., Dinh-Trong, T., Solberg, A.: Model-Driven Development Using UML2.0: promises and Pitfalls. IEEE Computer, February (2006)

Gane, C., Sarson, T.: Structured Systems Analysis: Tools and Techniques. Prentice Hall, Englewood Cliffs (1979)

Gill, A.: Applied Algebra for the Computer Sciences. Prentice-Hall, Englewood Cliffs (1976)

Gjersvik, R.: The construction of information systems in organizations. Unpublished PhD- thesis, Norwegian University of Science and Technology, Trondheim (1993)

Gjersvik, R., Krogstie, J., Følstad, A.: Participatory development of enterprise process models. In: Krogstie, J., Siau, K., Halpin, T. (eds.) Information Modelling Methods and Methodologies. Idea Group Publishers, Hershey (2004)

Gulla, J.A.: A general explanation component for conceptual modeling in CASE environments. ACM Trans. Inform. Syst. **14**(3), 297–329 (1996)

Hahn, U., Jarke, M., Rose, T.: Group work in software projects: integrated conceptual models and collaboration tools. In: Gibbs, S., Verrijn-Stuart, A.A. (eds.) Multi-User Interfaces and Applications: Proceedings of the IFIP WG 8.4 Conference on Multi-User Interfaces and Applications, pp. 83–102. North-Holland, Amsterdam (1990)

Halpin, T.: FORML 2. In: Bider, I., Halpin, T., Krogstie, J., Nurcan, S., Proper, E., Schmidt, R., et al. (eds.) (2010). Enterprise, business-process and information systems modeling. Lecture Notes in Business Information Processing **50**, 247–260. Springer (2010)

Hawryszkiewycz, I.: Introduction to Systems Analysis and Design. Prentice Hall, Upper Saddle River (2001)

Hewett, J., Durham, T.: CASE: the next steps. Technical report, OVUM (1989)

ISO 9000: Quality management systems – fundamentals and vocabulary. International Organization for Standardization (2005)

Jarke, M., Mylopoulos, J., Schmidt, J.W., Vassiliou, Y.: DAIDA: an environment for evolving information systems. ACM Trans. Inform. Syst. **10**(1), 1–50 (1992)

Kano, N: Attractive quality and must-be quality. J. Japanese Soc. Qual. Control, April, **14**(2), 39–48 (1984)

Kelly, S., Lyytinen, K., Rossi, M.: MetaEdit+: a fully configurable multi-user and multi-tool CASE and CAME environment. In: Constantopoulos, P., Mylopoulos, J., Vassiliou, Y. (eds.) Proceedings CAiSE'96 Lecture Notes in Computer Science, vol. 1080. Springer, Berlin/Heidelberg/New York (1996)

Kincaid, J.P., Fishburne, R.P. Jr., Rogers, R.L., Chissom, B.S.: Derivation of new readability formulas (Automated Readability Index, Fog Count and Flesch Reading Ease Formula) for Navy enlisted personnel, Research Branch Report 8–75, Millington, TN: Naval Technical Training, U.S. Naval Air Station, Memphis, TN (1975)

Krogstie, J.: Using quality function deployment in software requirements specification. Paper presented at the Fifth International Workshop on Requirements Engineering: Foundations for Software Quality (REFSQ'99), Heidelberg, Germany, June 14–15 (1999)

Krogstie, J., Dalberg, V., Jensen, S.M.: Harmonising Business Processes of Collaborative Networked Organization Using Process Modelling in PROVE'04 Toulouse, France (2004)

Krogstie, J., Dalberg, V., Jensen, S.M.: Increasing the value of process modelling. Paper presented at the 8th International Conference on Enterprise Information Systems ICEIS 2006, Cyprus (2006)

Langefors, B.: Theoretical Analysis of Information Systems, 1st edn. Studentliteratur, Auerbach, New York (1973)

Leite, J.C.S.P., Freeman, P.A.: Requirements validation through viewpoint resolution. IEEE Trans. Softw. Eng. **17**(12), 1253–1269 (1991). December

Lindland, O.I., Krogstie, J.: Validating conceptual models by transformational prototyping. Paper presented at the 5th International Conference on Advanced Information Systems Engineering (CAiSE'93), Paris, France, June 8–11 (1993)

Lindland, O.I., Sindre, G., Sølvberg, A.: Understanding quality in conceptual modeling. IEEE Softw. **11**(2), 42–49 (1994)

Mendling, J., Recker, J.: Towards systematic usage of labels and icons in business process models. In: Halpin, T., Proper, H.A., Krogstie, J. (eds.) 13th International Workshop on Exploring Modeling Methods in Systems Analysis and Design, CEUR Workshop Proceedings Series, Montpellier. See http://ceur-ws.org/ France (2008)

Moody, D.L.: Theoretical and practical issues in evaluating the quality of conceptual models: current state and future directions. Data Knowl. Eng. **55**, 243–276 (2005)

Moody, D.L., Shanks, G.G.: What makes a good data model? Evaluating the quality of entity relationship models. In: Proceedings of the 13th International Conference on the Entity-Relationship Approach (ER'94), pp. 94–111, Manchester, England (1994)

Moody, D.L., Sindre, G., Brasethvik, T., Sølvberg, A.: Evaluating the quality of process models: empirical analysis of a quality framework. In: Proceedings of the 21st International Conference on Conceptual Modeling (ER'2002), Tampere, Finland, 7–11 Oct (2002)

Mylopoulos, J., Borgida, A., Jarke, M., Koubarakis, M.: TELOS: representing knowledge about information systems. ACM Trans. Inform. Syst. **8**(4), 325–362 (1990). October

Nöth, W.: Handbook of Semiotics. Indiana University Press, Bloomington (1990)

OMG: Unified Modeling Language v 2.0 OMG Web site. http://www.omg.org (2006)

Orlikowski, J.W., Gash, D.C.: Technological frames: making sense of information technology in organizations. ACM Trans. Inform. Syst. **12**(2), 174–207 (1994)

Petre, M.: Why looking isn't always seeing. Readership skills and graphical programming. Commun. ACM **38**(6), 33–44 (1995). June

Pohl, K.: The three dimensions of requirements engineering: a framework and its applications. Inform. Syst. **19**(3), 243–258 (1994). April

Rittel, H.: On the planning crisis: systems analysis of the first and second generations. Bedriftsøkonomen **34**(8) (1972)

Rittgen, P.: Business process model similarity as a Proxy for Group Consensus. Paper presented at PoEM 2011, Oslo, Norway, 2–3 November (2011)

Rumbaugh, J., Blaha, M., Premerlani, W., Eddy, F., Lorensen, W.: Object-Oriented Modeling and Design. Prentice-Hall, Englewood Cliffs (1991)

Seltveit, A.H.: An abstraction-based rule approach to large-scale information systems development. In: Proceedings of the 5th International Conference on Advanced Information Systems Engineering (CAiSE'93), Paris, France, 8–11 June 1993, pp. 328–351. Springer, Berlin (1993)

Shneiderman, B.: Designing the User Interface: Strategies for Effective Human – Computer Interaction, 2nd edn. Addison Wesley, Reading (1992)

Tamassia, R., Di Battista, G., Batini, C.: Automatic graph drawing and readability of diagrams. IEEE Trans. Syst. Man Cybern. **18**(1), 61–79 (1988). January

van Lamsweerde, A.: Requirements Engineering: From System Goals to UML Models to Software Specifications. Wiley, Chichester (2009)

Wand, Y., Weber, R.: On the ontological expressiveness of information systems analysis and design grammars. J. Inform. Syst. **3**(4), 217–237 (1993)

Wangler, B., Wohed, R., Ohlund, S.-E.: Business modelling and rule capture in a CASE environment. In: Proceedings of the Fourth Workshop on the Next Generation of CASE Tools, Twente, (1993)

Ware, C.: Information Visualization. Morgan Kaufmann, San Francisco (2000)

Wesenberg, H.: Enterprise Modeling in an Agile World. In: Proceedings of the 4th conference on Practice of Enterprise Modeling, Oslo, November 2–3 (2011)

zur Muehlen, M., Recker, J.C.: How much language is enough? Theoretical and practical use of the business process modeling notation. In: Proceedings CAiSE'08 Montpellier France, Springer (2008)

Quality of Modelling Languages

Although the primary goal of modelling is to provide good models (as a trade-off between different quality types described in the previous chapter), an important *means* to achieve model quality is to use an appropriate modelling language for the modelling task at hand. As illustrated in the previous chapter, language quality goals are looked upon as means in the overall quality framework. A good language is useful, but not sufficient, to get a good model. It is obviously still possible to create a poor model in any language. In this chapter, we will first present the general guidelines for the quality of modelling languages according to six categories:

1. Domain appropriateness
2. Comprehensibility appropriateness
3. Participant appropriateness
4. Modeller appropriateness
5. Tool appropriateness
6. Organisational appropriateness

We then specialise these categories for certain type of modelling languages. Examples of concrete use of SEQUAL for evaluating and choosing between modelling languages in concrete organisational settings are found in Chap. 7.

When conceptual modelling started to become popular in the late 1970s, one quickly started to develop competing modelling languages, with a need to compare the different languages. In IFIP WG 8.1 this challenge was addressed through a number of conferences in the 1980s (the so-called CRIS conferences) (Olle et al. 1982, 1983), but primarily focusing on the expressiveness of the different languages. In some comparisons, there was also focus on necessary formality to have certain tool support.

Whereas early work on comparing expressiveness looked on this relative to some cases (and what certain modelling languages were able to represent or not), one has in later work developed baselines. As a baseline for needed expressiveness in general in conceptual modelling, a lot of work has been based on Bunge-Wand-Weber as described in Sect. 3.2.1. Formally, the relationships between what can be represented (the set of semantics, i.e. the constructs, of the modelling language) and what

Fig. 5.1 Example
of construct incompleteness

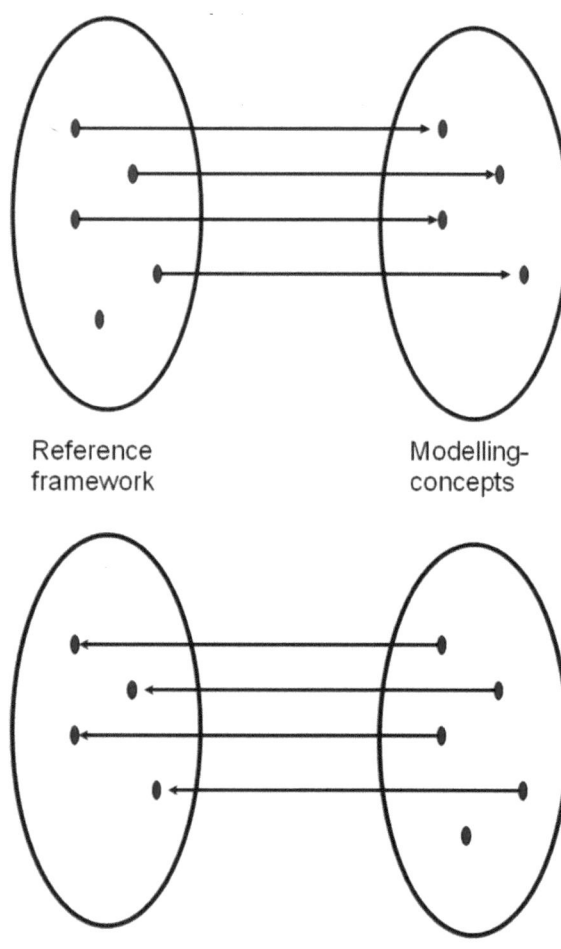

Reference   Modelling-
framework   concepts

Fig. 5.2 Example
of construct excess

Framework   Modelling-
concepts   concepts

is represented (the set of semantics, i.e. the concepts, of the reference framework as
a heuristic for the domain being modelled) can be specified in a generic framework
for language evaluation that differentiates five types of relationships that may occur
in the bi-directional evaluation of modelling languages against reference
frameworks.

- Construct incompleteness: One or more construct prescribed by the reference
  framework cannot be mapped to any construct of the modelling language as
  illustrated in Fig. 5.1. This is also called deficiency (Recker et al. 2007; Wand
  and Weber 1993).
- Construct excess: Not one construct prescribed by the reference framework can
  be mapped to the one or more construct of the modelling language (0:1 mapping)
  as illustrated in Fig. 5.2. This is also described under the term *overplus* (Recker
  et al. 2007).

Fig. 5.3 Example
of construct overload

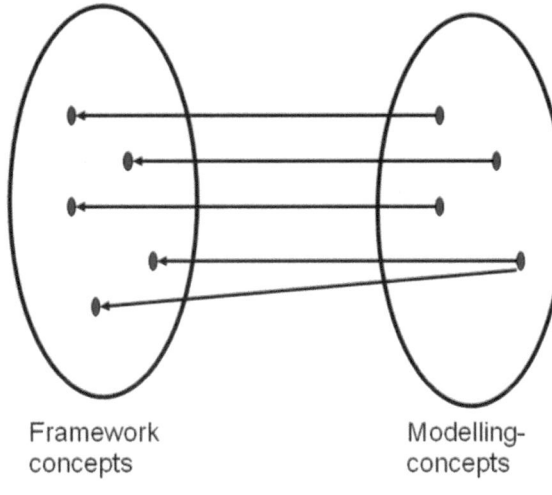

Framework
concepts

Modelling-
concepts

Fig. 5.4 Example
of construct redundancy

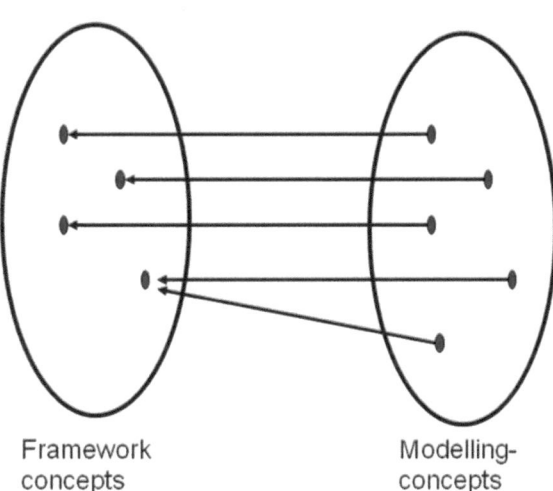

Framework
concepts

Modelling-
concepts

- Construct overload: The construct prescribed by the reference framework can be mapped to more than one construct of the modelling language (1: n mapping) as illustrated in Fig. 5.3. Another term used is *indistinguishability* (Recker et al. 2007).
- Construct redundancy: More than one construct prescribed by the reference framework can be mapped to one and the same construct of the modelling language (n: 1 mapping) as illustrated in Fig. 5.4. This is also described under the term *equivocality* (Recker et al. 2007).

When the construct prescribed by the reference framework can be unequivocally mapped to only one construct of the modelling language (1:1 mapping) (Recker et al. 2007), use the term *equivalence*. The framework for language evaluation presented above draws on previous work in related disciplines. Weber (1997) uses a similar although not identical framework to explain the two situations of ontological completeness and clarity of a language. Guizzardi (2005) argues in a similar fashion in the context of structural specifications, and Gurr (1999) uses similar mapping relations to analyse diagrammatic communication.

One early example of looking upon this more broadly than expressiveness and formality, also taking the individual human modeller and other model stakeholders and their perception into account, was the work of Sindre (1990). He distinguished two main kinds of criteria:

- Criteria for the conceptual basis of the language (what we often call the meta-model)
- Criteria for the external representation of the language (what we often call the notation of the language)

  For each of these kinds, Sindre identified four groups of criteria:
- Perceptibility: How easy is it for human beings to understand the language?
- Expressive power: Is it possible to express in the language (expressiveness)?
- Expressive economy: How efficiently can things be expressed in the language?
- Method/tool potential: How easily does the language lend itself to proper method and tool support?

The original work on language quality in SEQUAL (Krogstie 1995) took these aspects into account, structuring them relative to the sets of the SEQUAL framework. This work has been extended in several rounds after this, and the current version of the language quality aspects of SEQUAL is described in more detail below. As indicated in Chap. 1, models are very useful in connection to communication between people. Going back to Shannon and Weaver (1963), communication entails both encoding by the sender and decoding by the receiver. Encoding has been discussed in detail, e.g. in the work of Bertin (1983). According to Bertin (1983), there are four different effects of encoding:

1. Association: The marks can be perceived as similar
2. Selection: The marks can be perceived as different
3. Order: The marks can be perceived as ordered
4. Quantity: The marks can be perceived as proportional

   Eight different variables are presented to convey one or more of these meanings in diagrams:
- Planar variables: Horizontal position, vertical position
- Retinal variables: Shape (association and selection), size (selection, order and quantity), colour (association and selection), brightness (value) (selection and order), orientation (association), texture (association, selection and order)

  Figure 5.5 (from Gopalakrishnan et al. 2011) illustrates how different retinal variables can be used to differentiate between different locations.

For decoding, Moody (2009) presents a model differentiating between aspects of perception and cognition.

- Perceptual discrimination: Features are detected by specialised feature detectors. Based on this, the model is parsed into its parts.
- Perceptual configuration: Structure and relationship among diagram elements are inferred. In the area of Gestalt psychology, a number of principles on how to

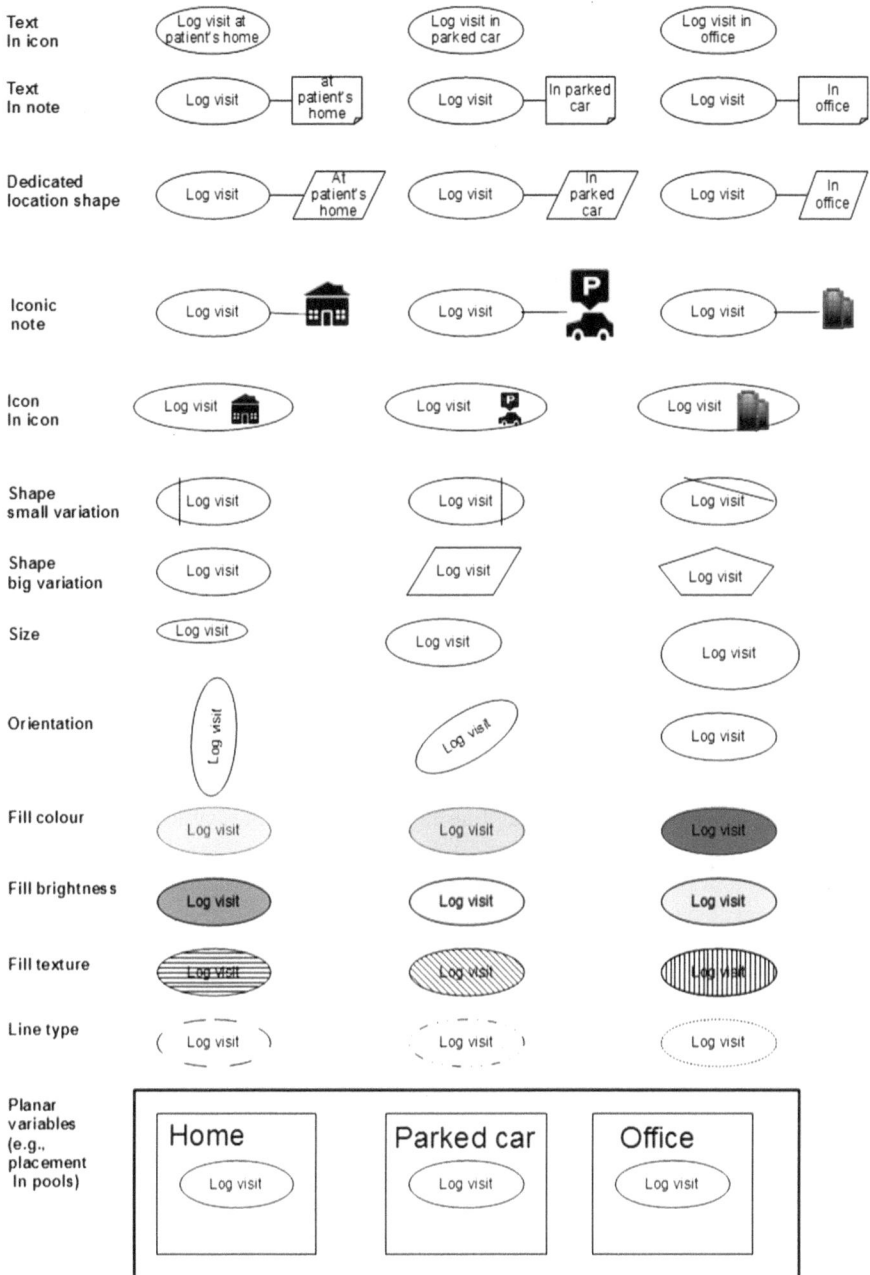

Fig. 5.5 Showing location of activities by retinal variables. In the 'Fill colour' row, node fills are *yellow*, *blue* and *red* (From Gopalakrishnan et al. 2011)

convey meaning through perceptual means are provided (Ware 2000). Most of these are related to the language, although some can also apply on the model level:

- A closed contour in a node-link diagram generally represents a concept of some kind.
- The shape of a closed contour is frequently used to represent a concept type.
- The colour of an enclosed region represents a concept type.
- The size of an enclosed region can be used to represent the magnitude of a concept.
- Lines that partition a region within a closed contour can delineate subparts of a concept (cf. the use of Venn diagrams in set theory).
- Closed-contour regions may be aggregated by overlapping them. The result is readily seen as a composite concept.
- A number of closed-contour regions within a larger closed contour can represent conceptual containment. (An effect often used in decomposition of process models for instance).
- Placing closed contours spatially in an ordered sequence can represent conceptual ordering of some kind (e.g. ordering of processes temporarily from left to right following the reading order or the timing sequence).
- A linking line between concepts represents some kind of relationship between them.
- A line linking closed contours can have different colours, or other graphical qualities such as waviness, and this effectively represents an attribute or type of relationship.
- The thickness of a connecting line can be used to represent the magnitude of a relationship (a scalar attribute).
- A contour can be shaped with tabs and sockets that can indicate which components have particular relationships.
- Proximity of components can represent groups.

- Attention management: All or part of the perceived image is brought into working memory. Working memory has very limited capacity. To be understood, statements in the model must be integrated with prior knowledge in the long-term memory of the interpreter. Differences in prior knowledge (expert-novice differences) greatly affect the speed and accuracy of processing.

Areas such as participant and comprehensible appropriateness build upon this basis and have also been detailed in a later work, e.g. through the work presented in Moody (2009) where nine principles are proposed for modelling notations:

1. *Semiotic clarity* (SC) means that there should be a 1:1 mapping between graphical symbols and concepts. Defects might be symbol redundancy (several symbols for the same concept), symbol overload (the same symbol can refer to several concepts), symbol excess (symbols which do not denote any concept), and symbol deficit (concepts for which there is no symbol). Overload is considered the worst, causing ambiguity and misinterpretation. Deficit may sometimes be a necessity rather than a problem, because the diagram will become too

cluttered if it tries to show everything graphically (Moody 2009). Note that this is related to the aspects described in Fig. 5.1, but are not the same, given that here we compare the conceptual basis and the concrete notation of the language.

2. *Perceptual discriminability* (PD): How easily and accurately can symbols be differentiated from each other? It will be easier for the user to distinguish between shapes that are obviously different from a quick glimpse (e.g. squares, circles, triangles) than between shapes that are different only in subtle details (e.g. rectangles with a varying height/width ratio, with or without rounded corners, or with different border types or textual fonts). The redundant usage of several visual variables together (e.g. both colour and shape) may improve discriminability even further (e.g. green square, yellow circle, red triangle).

3. *Semantic transparency* (ST): How well does a symbol intuitively reflect its meaning? According to Moody, symbols can be either *immediate*, having a nice intuitive relationship with their corresponding concepts; *opaque*, having only an abstract relationship; or even worse, *perverse*, its intuitive interpretation being misleading versus the represented concept.

4. *Complexity management* (CM): What constructs does the diagram notation have for supporting different levels of abstraction, information filtering, etc.? Decomposition is a key word here. It would also be preferable for a notation to avoid an explosion in the number of lines between nodes, since many, long and crossing lines will make a diagram much easier to read than fewer and shorter lines which are not crossing.

5. *Cognitive integration* (CI): Does the notation provide explicit mechanisms to support navigation between different diagrams? This may be navigation between different abstraction levels, or between different types of diagrams, e.g. from an activity diagram to a class diagram, to see the structural properties of the information objects processed in some activity.

6. *Visual expressiveness* (VE): To what extent does the notation utilise the full range of visual variables available (cf. the range of visual variables depicted in Fig. 5.2). As argued in Moody (2009), most notations mainly use shape – plus maybe various line types (e.g. full lines, dotted lines) and textual annotations inside diagrams – whereas colour and texture, e.g. are less used.

7. *Dual coding* (DC): Using text to complement graphics. While the usage of only text could give poor visual discrimination (as indicated in principle 6), the usage of both text and visual cues could be an advantage, as this again gives more redundancy of information and reduces the likelihood for misunderstandings.

8. *Graphic economy* (GE): Avoiding a too large number of different symbols, which would make the notation difficult to learn and understand.

9. *Cognitive fit* (CF): Trying to adapt the notation to the audience, i.e. possibly using different dialects with different stakeholder groups.
These principles are not orthogonal. According to Moody (2009):

- Symbol excess and symbol redundancy increase graphic complexity.
- Symbol overload and symbol deficit reduce graphic complexity.
- Perceptual discriminability increases visual expressiveness and vice versa.

- Increasing visual expressiveness decreases graphic economy, which again limits visual expressiveness.
- Graphic economy and perceptual discriminability co-vary.

As we will discuss later in the chapter, there are also a number of additional trade-offs that come into play when using SEQUAL and similar frameworks for evaluating the quality of modelling languages, or evolving or constructing new modelling languages, examples of concrete usage of SEQUAL that we will return to in Chap. 7.

5.1   Language Quality in SEQUAL

Language quality relates the modelling languages used to the other sets in Fig. 4.1. Six areas for language quality are identified based on this, as illustrated in Fig. 5.6, and these are described further below. The areas are related both to the meta-model (conceptual basis) and the notation (external representation) (cf. the distinction originally introduced by Sindre).

The areas are:

1. Domain appropriateness
2. Comprehensibility appropriateness
3. Participant appropriateness
4. Modeller appropriateness
5. Tool appropriateness
6. Organisational appropriateness

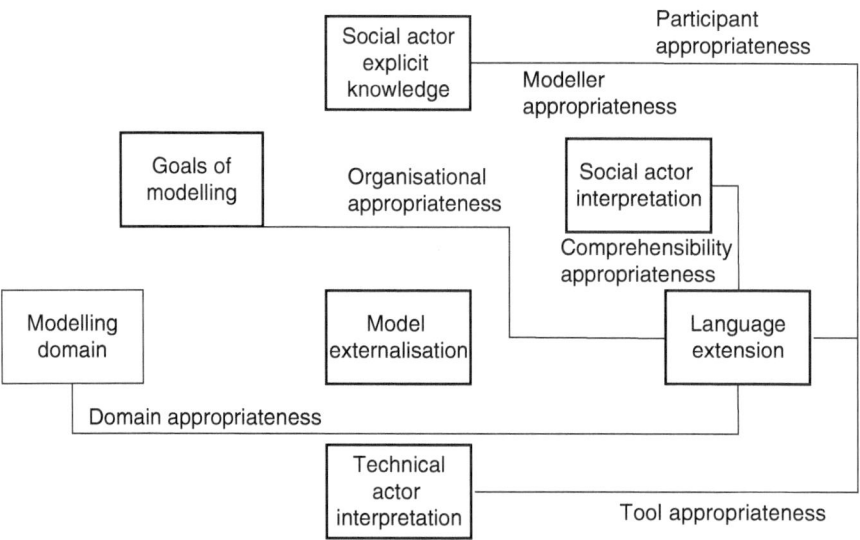

Fig. 5.6 Language quality in the SEQUAL quality framework

5.1.1   Domain Appropriateness

Domain appropriateness relates the modelling language and the domain. Ideally, the *conceptual basis* of a modelling language must be powerful enough to express anything in the domain, not having what (Wand and Weber 1993) is termed *construct incompleteness*. On the other hand, you should not be able to express things that are not in the domain, i.e. what is termed *construct excess* (Wand and Weber 1993).

The only requirement to the external representation is that it does not destroy the conceptual basis. This includes two aspects of what Moody (2009) includes under semiotic clarity: symbol excess and symbol deficit. The two other aspects mentioned by Moody as part of semiotic clarity are included as part of comprehensibility appropriateness discussed below.

One approach to evaluate domain appropriateness relative to the conceptual basis is to look at how the modelling perspectives found useful for the relevant modelling tasks are covered. Eight general modelling perspectives were identified in Sect. 3.3: behavioural, functional, structural, rule-oriented, object-oriented, language-action-oriented (communicational), role- and actor-oriented and topological. More detailed evaluations of languages within these perspectives can be based on more detailed evaluation frameworks used within these perspectives (such as Embley et al. 1995; Iivari 1995; van der Aalst 2003). This is first useful when we know that what we want to represent can be described by this perspective in the first place.

Another approach is to base an evaluation on an ontological theory – see, e.g. Opdahl et al. (1999) that uses the BWW ontology presented by Wand and Weber (1993) (also described in Sect. 3.2).

We will return to more detailed specifications of domain appropriateness in Chap. 7 related to the evaluation of modelling languages for concrete domains.

Domain appropriateness is primarily a mean to achieve semantic quality (i.e. by making it possible to represent the domain using the modelling language).

5.1.2   Comprehensibility Appropriateness

Comprehensibility appropriateness relates the language to the social actor interpretation. The goal is that the participants in the modelling effort using the language understand all the possible statements of the language.

For the conceptual basis, we have the following guidelines in this area:

- The number of concepts should be reasonable. For a generic modelling language, there are an infinite number of statements that we might want to make (vs. domain appropriateness), and these have to be dealt with through a limited number of concepts. This means that:
  - The core (most important) concepts must be general rather than specialised.

- The concepts must be composable, which means that we can group related statements in a natural way.
- The language must be flexible in precision:

  To express precise knowledge one needs precise constructs. This means that the language must be formal and unambiguous. Formality is further discussed in relation to tool appropriateness below.

  At the same time, one needs vague constructs for modelling vague knowledge. To fulfil both requirements, the vagueness must also be formalised (i.e. even vague constructs must have a definite interpretation – the constructs are called vague because their interpretation is wide compared to the more precise constructs).

  If the number of constructs has to be large (due to characteristics of the domain that is to be covered), the phenomena should be organised hierarchically and/or in sub-languages of reasonable size linked to specific modelling tasks, making it possible to approach the modelling language at different levels of abstraction or from different perspectives and usage areas.

UML, for instance, can be argued to be a complex language, with a total of 233 different concepts (Castellani 1999). The quality of UML is discussed in more detail in Chap. 7.

• The concepts of the language should be easily distinguishable from each other (vs. construct redundancy (Wand and Weber 1993)).

The use of concepts should be uniform throughout the whole set of statements that can be expressed within the language. Using the same construct for different phenomena (concept overload) or different constructs for the same function depending on the context will tend to make the language confusing.

• The language must be flexible in the level of detail.
• Statements must be easily extendible with other statement providing more details.
• The language must contain constructs that can represent the intention of the model. In the case of a language with formal semantics, this aspect is discussed as part of tool appropriateness below (i.e. since if the model has operational semantics, it might be executed to show the consequences of the model, whereas if it has a mathematical semantics, formal analysis can be used to the same effect). Neither system nor enterprise modelling languages normally has the possibility of intentional modelling.

Since most of the aspects of 'Physics of Notation' relates to the external representation (language notation) of this area, we will structure the discussion according to the categories provided by Moody (2009). Further examples are provided in Chap. 7 on the application of the framework for the evaluation of different modelling languages.

• Semiotic clarity (SC): Whereas we have included symbol excess and symbol deficit under domain appropriateness, symbol overload (several symbols for the same concept) and symbol redundancy (the same symbol can refer to several concepts) are included as part of comprehensibility appropriateness. In a model any graphical mark in the model is part of, what Goodman (1976) terms syntactic disjointness which of the symbols in a model, any graphical mark in the model, is part of what Goodman (1976) terms syntactic disjointness. For instance, when adornments are provided to indicate cardinalities in a data model, this can be linked to the line directly (as using crow-feet in the IE data modelling language compared to use loose numbers indicating cardinality).

- Perceptual discriminability (PC): Different concepts should be represented in a way so that they can be easily differentiated, e.g. with using symbols of different shapes. The use of dual coding (DC) principle (using text to complement graphics) is also something that can be included. If using colours to mark semantics of the language concepts, one should not use more than 5–6 different colours in a given view (Shneiderman 1992) using the differentiating colours described in Sect. 4.3. The colour of the label-text should depend on the colour of the symbol as discussed in Sect. 4.3, Empirical Quality. One also should have in mind how a model with coloured symbols will look when printed in black and white (i.e. if the semantic differentiation meant to be carried by the colouring is retained in black and white or not). As an example of poor use of colour is the use of blue and violet in ORM to differentiate alethic and deontic constraints (Sect. 3.3.4).

- Semantic transparency (ST): The external representation of different phenomena should be intuitive in the sense that the symbol chosen for a particular phenomenon somehow reflects this better than another symbol would have done. Moody (2009) differentiates three archetypical levels relative to semantic transparency:
    - A symbol is semantically immediate if a novice reader would be able to infer its meaning from its appearance alone (e.g. a stick man to represent a person).
    - A symbol is semantically opaque if there is a purely arbitrary relationship between its appearance and its meaning (e.g. circles in i* representing an actor).
    - A symbol is semantically perverse if a novice reader would be likely to infer a different (or even opposite) meaning from its appearance. Moody highlights UML package merge as an example of this.

This is partly dependent on the concrete participants, even if general guidelines might be devised. For instance, it can be useful to represent areas in a model that are not complete using a specific notation such as the use of wiggly lines (Gause and Weinberg 1989) or amoeba shapes (Sindre 1990). Winn (1990) used diagram elements with meaningless labels in different spatial configurations and asked subjects to describe the relationships between them. He found the four patterns depicted in Fig. 5.7.

The subset relationship is similar to the conceptual containment from cognitive psychology; intersection is related to aggregation by overlap and sequence/causality is an example of a relationship between concepts (Ware 2000). Other relevant aspects from cognitive psychology in this area is to use closed contours for concepts (which are usually done, note that the Location-concept in GEMAL described in Sect. 3.5.3 probably should be improved taking this into account) and alternative ways of splitting up an area by lines within the area. Other examples are the use of

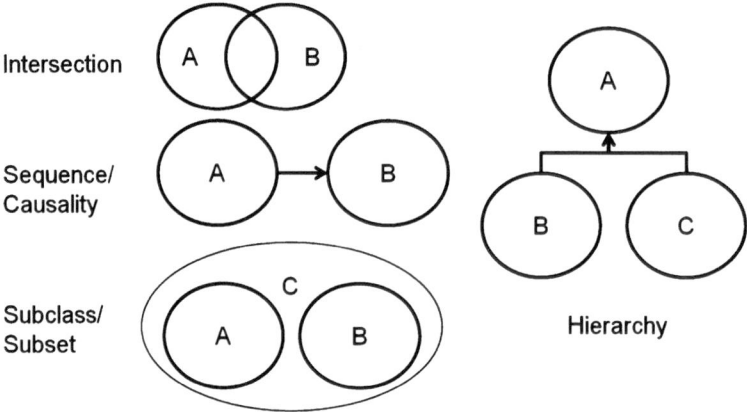

Fig. 5.7 Intuitive visualisations

a trash can to show things that are deleted, and the use of cultural associations such as using red colour to denote danger (red also being the colour most easily spotted).

- Complexity management (CM): This relates to how the language supports the generic mechanisms for decomposition and dealing with different levels of precision discussed as part of the conceptual basis above. It is also important that composition of symbols can be made in an aesthetically pleasing way. Within the area of graph aesthetics, a number of guidelines have been devised as discussed under empirical quality, and aspects of the notation might make it more or less easy to adhere to, e.g. reducing long edges and reduce the number of crossing lines. For instance, contrary to traditional DFDs, several process modelling languages mandate that all inflow enters the same side of the process symbol, and all outflow exits from another side. This often leads to that models written in the language have unnecessarily many crossing or long lines.

- Graphic economy (GE): In addition to avoiding too many symbols, one should also strive for symbolic simplicity – both concerning the primitive symbols of the language and the way they are supposed to be connected. If the symbols themselves are visually complex, models containing a lot of symbols will be even more complex, and thus difficult to comprehend. At the external level, graphic economy is concerned with how many symbols one need to use to express the statements of the model. It will usually be the case that the things easily expressed conceptually will also be easily expressed externally, and the things which are complicated in the underlying basis will also have to be complicated externally. However, the conceptual basis and the external representation of a language should not necessarily be the same. A good external representation should always have an expressive economy better than that of the basis. This is because the external representation has many possibilities that the underlying basis does not have:

– Omission of symbols that are understood in the context.
– Special symbols can be defined for constructs which are frequent (or important).
– Multiple mentioning of the same phenomena is unavoidable at the basis level. At the external level, such multiple mentioning can often be avoided.

Of course, there are some pitfalls to avoid.

- Blank symbols, i.e. symbols that do not contain any information for anyone.
- External redundancy, i.e. showing the same phenomena in different ways in the same external representation.
- Depend too much on textual differentiation between concepts. Textual differentiation is a common but cognitively inefficient way of dealing with graphic complexity. Text in the form of labels is important in distinguishing instances. Moody (2009) argues that text is an effective way of distinguishing between symbol instances, not between symbol (concept) types.

Diagrams have a significantly larger potential for expressive economy than tables or text. On the other hand, it is impossible to convey everything diagrammatically. Thus, the best thing to do to achieve expressive economy is to try to express the frequent and most important statements diagrammatically and the less frequent textually.

Moody's principle of visual expressiveness (VE) (the use of all the retinal variable of Bertin) is by us rather looked upon as a mean to reach the goals for comprehensibility appropriateness rather than a goal in itself (e.g. a simple language such as DFD does not need to use all these variables).

In a language, not all concepts are equally important. The use of *emphasis* (EM) in the notation should be in accordance with the relative importance of the statements in the given model. Factors that have an important impact on visual emphasis are the following:

- Size (the big is more easily noticed than the small given that size ratios are predefined)
- Solidity (e.g. **bold** letters vs. ordinary letters, full lines vs. dotted lines, thick lines vs. thin lines, filled boxes vs. non-filled boxes)
- Difference from ordinary pattern (e.g. *slanted* letters, a rare symbol will attract attention among a large number of ordinary ones)
- Foreground/background differences (if the background is white, things will be easier noticed the darker they are)
- Colour (red attracts the eye more than other colours)
- Change (blinking or moving symbols attract attention)
- Pictures vs. text (pictures usually having a much higher perceptibility, information conveyed in pictures will be emphasised at the cost of information conveyed textually)
- Connectivity (objects able to connect to many others (having a high degree) will attract attention compared to objects making few connections)

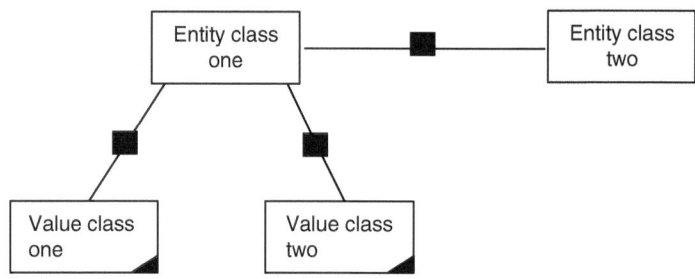

Fig. 5.8 Example of misguided emphasis in ERT

An example of misguided emphasis in the ERT language of Tempora (described in Sect. 3.3.5) is illustrated in Fig. 5.8.

ERT being a structural language should emphasise on the main entity classes, whereas what is highlighted is the relationship classes (in something that is actually a blank symbol) and the value classes (by the black parts).

Finally we look at guidelines when integrating sub-languages of a combined language (such as UML or EEML).

- Cognitive integration (CI): As indicated above, languages often need to be divided into different sub-languages, and work on different abstraction levels. Moody (2009) differentiates between two aspects:
  - Conceptual integration: Mechanisms to help the interpreter assemble information from separate diagrams into a coherent mental representation of the system. High-level diagrams, such as context diagrams in DFDs, Rich Pictures in SSM and the use of top-level models in Enterprise Architecture Frameworks are examples of such structuring mechanisms, also called summary or long-shot diagrams.
  - Perceptual integration: Perceptual cues to simplify navigation and transitions between diagrams. Here one can use knowledge from cartography on wayfinding (Lynch 1960), following four stages:
    Orientation: Where am I?
    Route choice: Where can I go?
    Route monitoring: Am I on the right way?
    Destination recognition: Have I arrived at the destination?

For instance, DFDs and similar languages for process decomposition use a numbering scheme indicating the placement of the model in the process hierarchy. Navigational maps showing the possible navigational routes between diagrams in different sub-languages are so far only supported in a limited degree. In addition to be able to represent navigational links and modelling context, the other aspects described here, e.g. semiotic clarity and perceptual integration, apply also between diagrams.

Comprehensibility appropriateness is primarily a means to achieve empirical and through that pragmatic quality.

5.1.3 Participant Appropriateness

Participant appropriateness relates the participant knowledge to the language. The conceptual basis should correspond as much as possible to the way individuals perceive reality. Moody's principle of semantic transparency relates to this, and we have put this principle (and the principle of cognitive fit) here rather than in the area of comprehensibility appropriateness, since what is intuitive often differs from person to person and from culture to culture according to their previous experience. Thus, this will initially be directly dependent on the participants in a modelling effort. When it comes to the existing use of modelling languages, already in the late 1980s, Senn (1989) reported that the level of awareness of structured methods (i.e. using data and process modelling languages) was high among IS professionals – as many as 90% of all analysts were at that time familiar with these methods, according to some estimates. These kinds of techniques together with object-oriented modelling techniques such as UML are currently taught in most bachelor and master studies in computer science, software engineering and information systems.

On the other hand, the knowledge of the participants is not static, i.e. it is possible to educate persons in the use of a specific language. In that case, one can base the language on experiences with languages for the relevant types of modelling, and languages that have been used successfully earlier in similar tasks. Most experiences in this area are based on the use of systems modelling languages. In connection to this, it is interesting to look at experiments trying to find out which languages or perspectives people find most easy to learn. Few empirical studies of this kind have been performed. Vessey and Conger (1994) reported in empirical investigations among novice analysts that they seemed to have much greater difficulty applying an object-oriented methodology than a data- or process-oriented methodology. Process modelling was found easier to apply than data modelling. In Tempora, the experience was that whereas participants had small problems in learning to use both the process modelling language and the main parts of the data modelling language, the formal textual rule language was difficult for people to comprehend. On the other hand, the phenomenon of rules is generally well-known. As stated by Twining and Miers (1982), 'One reason why the notion of "rule" is such an important one not only in law, but in fields as varied as linguistics, sociology, anthropology, education, psychology and philosophy, is that there is hardly any aspect of human behaviour that is not governed or at least guided by rules'. When it comes to the communication perspective, some experience related to learning speech-acts theory as part of using tools such as the Coordinator (Flores et al. 1988) is presented in Bullen and Bennet (1991). In many cases, the users found the linguistically motivated parts of the language difficult to understand and apply. In other cases, this was not regarded as a problem. When it comes to actors and roles, we believe these phenomena classes to be easy to comprehend based on their widespread use in, e.g. organisational diagrams.

Another important point in this connection is that it should be possible to express inconsistencies and dispute in the language since inconsistency between how people perceive reality is a fact of life that can be useful to represent so that these can be revealed and discussed explicitly as we discussed under the treatment of social quality.

Participant appropriateness is primarily a means to achieve semantic quality (for the modeller) and pragmatic quality (for the model interpreter).

5.1.4 Modeller Appropriateness

This area relates the language to the knowledge of the one doing the modelling. The ideal goal is that there are no statements in the explicit knowledge of the modeller that cannot be expressed in the language.

This focuses on how relevant knowledge may be articulated in the modelling language. This is clearly linked to concepts like 'articulation work' and 'situated action' and the debate in Computer Supported Cooperative Work (CSCW) whether actual work can be captured in a model, or whether such a model always will be a post-hoc rationalisation (Suchman 1987). Although related to the area of participant appropriateness, we can devise the following guidelines in addition:

- The language should help in the externalisation of tacit knowledge. Nonaka and Takeuchi (1995) highlighted how the use of metaphors and analogies is useful to be able to achieve this.
- It should, for dynamic areas, be easy to model as part of actual work, and not only before (planning) or after (post-hoc rationalisation), i.e. supporting interactive models in simple languages as discussed in Sect. 6.6 on active and interactive models.

Although for the modeller this area is related to participant appropriateness, that area looks at the passive knowledge of a modelling language, whereas modeller appropriateness addresses the active use of the language to create new models. As discussed by Moody (2009), the emphasis on different criteria for comprehensibility appropriateness differs between novice and expert modellers.

- Novices have more difficulty discriminating between symbols (Britton and Jones 1999; Koedinger and Anderson 1990).
- Novices are more affected by complexity (Blankenship and Dansereau 2000).
- Novices have to consciously remember what symbols mean (Winn 1993).

Note that optimising the notation for novices might make it less effective for experts (Kalyuga et al. 2003), which could suggest to have two different dialects of a modelling language. We see from practice that only smaller parts of complex languages seem to be used in practice (Erickson and Siau 2007; zur Muehlen and Recker 2008). These dialects could be more consciously developed by having lite-versions focusing specifically on perceptual discriminability, complexity management, semantic transparency, dual coding and graphic economy, probably on the expense of domain appropriateness (Moody 2009). In addition to being used relative to experts and novices, the cognitive fit (CF) principles could be applied in a more fine-grained manner if it is deemed effective.

Modeller appropriateness is primarily a means to achieve semantic quality (completeness) in the sense that you enable the modellers to express all relevant knowledge.

5.1.5 Tool Appropriateness

Tool appropriateness relates the language to the interpretation from the technical audience (tools). Most of the aspects here relate to the conceptual basis of the language. For tool interpretation, it is especially important that the language lends itself to automatic reasoning. This requires formality (i.e. both formal syntax and semantics being operational and/or logical), but formality is not necessarily enough, since the reasoning must also be efficient to be of practical use. This is covered by what we term *analysability* (to be able to efficiently exploit the mathematical semantics) and *executability* (to be able to efficiently exploit the operational semantics).

A trade-off between tool appropriateness and domain appropriateness can often be witnessed. For instance, the OWL language exists in three variants as described also in Sect. 3.3.5.

1. OWL Lite provides a classification hierarchy and limited constraints.
2. OWL DL provides maximum expressiveness while ensuring computational completeness.
3. OWL Full provides maximum syntactic freedom; however, it makes no guarantee about the decidability.

In enterprise modelling, for instance, it is (as discussed in Chap. 2) usual to include different stakeholders in modelling sessions and modelling conferences, using more manual techniques. As discussed in Moody (2009), to be appropriate for use with manual techniques (e.g. on wall-charts, whiteboards, etc.) there might be a need for at least dialects or sub-sets of the language that take this usage into account.

- Need for perceptual discriminability is higher due to variations of drawing styles by different people.
- Semantic transparency: Pictures and icons are more difficult to draw than simple geometric shapes.
- Visual expressiveness: Some visual variables (colour, value and texture) might be more difficult to use.

Usually, the manually drawn models are at some point transferred to data-based modelling tools, where more traditional techniques for tool appropriateness get more important.

Different aspects of tool appropriateness are a means to achieve syntactic, semantic and pragmatic quality (through formal syntax, mathematical semantics and operational semantics, respectively).

When looking at more specific areas and uses of modelling, tool appropriateness can be made more concrete, as will be exemplified in the next chapters.

5.1.6 Organisational Appropriateness

Organisational appropriateness focuses on to what extent the language used is appropriate to reach the organisational goals of the organisation using it, taking into account standardisation on technology, tools and modelling methods within the (relevant parts of) organisation now and in the future, potentially also facilitating cross-organisational usage. This is primarily to support the achievement of deontic quality achieving value from modelling both in the short and the long run.

5.2 Quality of Meta-Models (Language Models)

In addition to aspects related directly to the language as such, one should also look at the quality of the official model of a modelling language (the language model, which is by Prasse (1998) covered under documentation). A modelling language is described, e.g. in a notation guide and a semantic description (vs. how, for instance, UML 2.0 is described by OMG (2006)).

A notation guide typically contains structured text and example models, often in some sort of hypertext-structure. The semantic description contains typically a meta-model (in a given language or set of languages for meta-modelling as discussed in Sect. 3.1.3) and structured text to describe this meta-model in further detail.

Different types of users for these models have very different needs:

- Users (modellers and interpreters) of the language primarily need the language model to make it easier to develop models of their domain and to learn the language to be able to comprehend models made in the language.
- Adapters of the language need to understand the existing language to adapt it to more specific needs through meta-modelling. When making additions, it is often necessary to know which cognitive mechanisms (vs. Bertin 1983; Ware 2000) are already in use so as to not overload existing mechanisms with new semantics.
- Tool developers need to understand the notation and meta-model semantics to support the use of the language by building modelling tools that can incorporate different techniques that are useful to achieve models of high quality as summarised in Table 4.2.

The first user-group is the one that gets the main focus in most cases. Looking upon the language model across the levels of model quality, we have the following (briefly restating the description of the main levels):

Physical Quality

Internalisability: A modelling language is typically described in text and models. The relevant parts of the descriptions should be available for those that need it in an efficient way: For example, all users need the notation guide for those parts of the language they want to use. It is important that the description cover the version of the language that is currently in use (currency). For a meta-modeller, it is important that it is possible to update the language model including the language description in a controlled way, again taking care of necessary versioning mechanisms.

Empirical Quality

For informal textual models, a range of means for readability have been devised, such as a number of different readability indexes (see Chap. 4, Sect. 4.3). Other general guidelines regard not mixing different fonts, colours, etc., in a paragraph being on the same level within the overall text. For graphical models in particular, layout modifications are found to improve the comprehensibility of models. For meta-models and example models, one can judge if these are made aesthetically pleasing.

Syntactic Quality

There is one syntactic goal, syntactical correctness, meaning that all statements in the model are according to the syntax and vocabulary of the language. Syntactic errors are of two kinds: syntactic invalidity, in which words or graphemes not part of the language are used, and syntactic incompleteness, in which the model or text lacks constructs or parts to obey the language's grammar. For the textual part of the language model, one needs to assure that this is according to the language and structure chosen. Similarly, the model examples and meta-model must follow the chosen syntax of the language used.

Semantic Quality

Focus here is on semantic completeness, i.e. all parts of the language are described in text and in the meta-model. Semantic validity of the language model focuses on that the different descriptions are consistent both within and with each other. The language model should only describe the modelling language, and nothing more. Note that in most cases of language models, the domain is to a larger degree 'objectively' given, e.g. in the definition by UML by what has been agreed through the standardisation process performed in OMG.

Pragmatic Quality

It includes means to make it easier to understand and make use of the modelling language through the language model. This can include use of indexes, cross-references and glossaries. It can also be done through tutorials and through linking the model of modelling language to the use of the language in a modelling environment. Have modelling tool support for the meta-model (and meta-model extension) is also useful in this regard.

Social Quality

Social quality is relevant both in connection to the development of a standard language and in connection to meta-modelling extensions. People can obviously dislike the representation of a language and its appropriateness, thus good examples of use in, e.g. the notation guide are very important here. A broad standardisation process can also be useful to ensure agreement on the language.

Deontic Quality

The model of the modelling language helps in the efficient use of the modelling language for those tasks that it is meant to be used for (to minimise training time, etc.).

Language quality of the language used for meta-modelling can be a further point to evaluate according to the six criteria above, e.g. to what extent it is appropriate to use UML Class diagrams for meta-modelling, as discussed under Sect. 4.4.

When using the SEQUAL (or any other quality framework) to do an evaluation of a modelling language, we should keep the following in mind:

- It is possible to make good models in a poor modelling language.
- It is possible to make poor models in a comparatively good modelling language.
- You will always find some deficiencies in any language and tool support. On the other hand, it is useful to know the weak spots to avoid the related potential problems. Such deficiencies should in general be addressed with the use of modelling techniques, and an overall methodology.

Trade-off is both between areas, but also within areas as indicated in the description of the 'Physics of Notation'. It is also worth noting that the perception of language quality is highly dependent on the expectation of the participants on the language. For example, expert modellers might want to have a more formal modelling language to be able to design executable process models. However, such a modelling language might not fit well with novice users and business experts.

5.3   Specialisations of SEQUAL for Language Quality

SEQUAL has been specialised for a number of different types of modelling languages. As an example of this, we will provide a description of the specialisation for enterprise models. Enterprise models (EM) intend to represent all aspects of an organisation, not only the IT systems. Based on SEQUAL and needs identified in the ATHENA A1 project (specifically requirements building further on the UEML project (Knothe et al. 2001; Petit 2002)), a number of detailed criteria for the evaluation of enterprise modelling languages have been identified. These are described in the following sections.

5.3.1   Domain Appropriateness of Enterprise Modelling Languages

A large number of the existing requirements are within this area partly based on the UEML project (Knothe et al. 2001; Petit 2002) and work on BPM (van der Aalst et al. 2003). The numbers relate to codes used in these or other projects, and have been retained to ensure traceability back to these works. The order of requirements within each area is not prioritised:

- UEML_5: EM should help to synchronise several modelling tools (e.g. HLA – high level architecture).

- UEML_12: EM should create a link between processes, purposes and business goals.
- UEML_14: EM has to provide an interlinked standard template set for representation of specific functional, process type and business areas in the companies. Comment: Needs to be specialised, can take as an outset the state of the art in these areas and also look at what is represented in the involved modelling approaches.
- UEML_15: EM should provide connectivity between strategic, engineering, management of operational process and operational processes and their changes – as a basis for process distribution and coordination.
- UEML_16: EM should be useful to improve enterprise processes (such as achieving Six Sigma levels of process performance, and setting measures and targets for future development). Comment: Here judged as the need to represent necessary aspects of processes to do this analysis. If specific (automatic) analysis techniques are to be supported, one needs to add this under semantic quality enhancing tools.
- UEML_18: EM should provide capabilities to model both 'hard' and 'soft' aspects of human participative and resource systems in support of team engineering. Comment: This is related for instance to social network analysis (SNA).
- UEML_22: EM should help to capture and explain business rules. Comment: Might also be a methodological part of this (but it is generally assumed that the methodology should support the capturing of all concepts in the language).
- UEML_23: EM should help to show the relations between process and business and between their rules.
- UEML_31: EM has to be open and therefore use generic concepts to provide flexibility. Comment: Same as SEQ – 8, the concepts must be general rather than specialised.
- UEML_32: EM should include a standard set of meta-model for each class, files and constraints.
- UEML_37: EM should express social and organisational relationships in the enterprise.
- UEML_44: EM should foresee semantics and syntax to support integration in the future (e.g. semantic classes like the periodic element system).
- UEML_50: EM should represent more than one orientation into a model (e.g. include both functional and process orientation).
- IDEAS 6: The language should have capability to model the virtual enterprise, as well as the different kinds of partnerships, and the different related aspects (contractual aspects and roles in the cooperation).
- IDEAS 7: Supporting holistic distributed modelling and use of models.
- S19: Enterprise modelling project definition services: To support effective project portfolio management of the modelling projects, visual modelling should be used. This includes definition of project goals and dependencies between the projects.

In addition, the following general requirements apply:

- SEQ-1: It should not be possible to express things that are not in the domain. Certain, very design-specific concepts found, e.g. in OOD-languages are not appropriate in an EM language.

- SEQ-2: All aspects of the conceptual basis should be possible to represent in the external representation and vice versa.

The following concepts have been identified as necessary/useful for an EM language (Petit 2002):

1. UEML-1: Goals, objectives and norms (strategy, goals, business rules, culture, etc.)
2. Functional aspects:
   (a) UEML-2a: Processes (functions/activities) (including material processing functions, data processing, storage, transfer and input/output functions)
   (b) UEML-2b: Process decomposition (hierarchical)
   (c) Behaviour/dynamics description:
       (i) UEML-2ci: Relationships between activities (sequence, repetition, branch, join, etc.) preconditions, triggering conditions, i.e. control flow operators. These are detailed further below.
       (ii) UEML-2cii: Concurrent processing, communication among processes (rendezvous, synchronous-asynchronous messages, semaphores, etc.), cooperative activities
       (iii) UEML-2ciii: Events
       (iv) UEML-2civ: Exception handling (time-outs, watch-dogs)
       (v) UEML-2cv: Time (process duration, etc.), timing constraints, through-put, communication delays, processing delays, queuing delays, etc.
       (vi) UEML-2cvi: Priorities (attached to activities)
       (vii) UEML-2cvii: Probabilistic behaviour, non-deterministic behaviour (runtime choice, etc.)
3. Resource aspects:
   (a) UEML-3a: Products and services for sale
   (b) UEML-3b: Material, material flow
   (c) UEML-3c: Energy flow
   (d) UEML-3d: Data, relationship between data, constraints (integrity), information flow, relation between data and activities
   (e) UEML-3e: Orders
   (f) Processing resources:
       (i) UEML-3fi: Technology (IT applications, technical infrastructure), information technical systems and manufacturing technical systems, human resources
       (ii) UEML-3fii: Resource capabilities, resource allocation, resource reliability (mean time between failure (MTBF), etc.), capacity, availability, etc.
   (g) UEML-3g: Manufacturing plant layout
   (h) UEML-3h: Business-oriented algorithms
4. Organisational aspects:
   (a) UEML-4a: Organisational units, people, positions and departments
   (b) UEML-4b: Roles and roles structures/task decision and responsibility fields, competencies, skills, experience and qualification
   (c) UEML-4c: Authority
   (d) UEML-4d: Decisions, decisions levels and decision centres

5. Other aspects:
    (a) UEML-5a: Progress in work
    (b) UEML-5b: Performance figures, values for economic figures and cost of processes

Obviously, not all aspects are equally important in all domains and relative to all modelling goals.

Specifically for business process modelling, the following patterns are identified from the BPM literature (van der Aalst et al. 2003).

Process
- BPM-P1: Process start state – to describe conditions that need to be in place before executing a process
- BPM-P2: Process end state – to describe conditions that need to be in place after executing the process
- BPM-P3: Pre-conditions – to describe the conditions that must be satisfied before a process can be called synchronously or asynchronously
- BPM-P4: Post-conditions – to describe the conditions that must be satisfied after a process has returned control

Activity
- BPM-A1: Activity description – to describe the business activity in terms of what it does
- BPM-A2: Pre-conditions – to describe the conditions that must be satisfied before a business activity can be performed
- BPM-A3: Post-conditions – to describe the conditions that must be satisfied after a business activity has been performed
- BPM-A4: State after failure – to describe the expected state in case post-conditions are not satisfied
- BPM-A5: Resource consumption specification – to specify resource consumption information
- BPM-A6: Activity duration specification – to specify the duration of an activity
- BPM-A7: Arrival rate of business documents – to specify the arrival rate of business documents
- BPM-A8: Role assignment – to assign a role that performs the business activity
- BPM-A9: Resource assignment – to assign a resource that is used during performance of a business activity
- BPM-A10: Business document assignment – to assign a business document to an activity

Transition
- BPM-T1: Guard conditions – to specify a guard condition
- BPM-T2: Execution probability – to specify the probability an outgoing transition is taken after a decision point
- BPM-T3: Resource information – to capture and maintain resource specific information

- BPM-T4: Initial state – to describe the state that must be true before the resource is first accessed by an activity
- BPM-T5: State at activity completion – to describe the state that must be true after the activity has completed

Role
- BPM-R1: To describe the roles that perform the activities
- BPM-R2: Organisational role category – to specify that roles within this category are associated with organisations or organisation units, not persons
- BPM-R3: Person role category – to specify that roles within this category are associated with persons, not organisations or organisation units
- BPM-R4: Functional role category – to specify that roles within this category can be either a person or an organisation or organisation unit

Business Document
- BPM-BD1: Business document description – to textually describe a business document
- BPM-BD2: Initial state – to describe the state that must be true before the business document is first accessed by an activity
- BPM-BD3: State at activity completion – To describe the state that must be true after the activity has completed.

Information Exchange
- BPM-IE1: Pre-conditions – to describe the conditions that must be satisfied before an information exchange can be performed
- BPM-IE2: Post-conditions – to describe the conditions that must be satisfied after an information exchange has been performed

Workflow (Control Flow Patterns)
- BPM-WF1: Sequence – an activity in a workflow process is enabled after the completion of another activity in the same process.
- BPM-WF2: Parallel split – a point in the workflow process where a single thread of control splits into multiple threads of control which can be executed in parallel, thus allowing activities to be executed simultaneously or in any order.
- BPM-WF3: Synchronisation – a point in the workflow process where multiple parallel sub-processes/activities converge into one single thread of control, thus synchronising multiple threads. It is an assumption of this pattern that each incoming branch of a synchroniser is executed only once (if this is not the case, then see Patterns 13–15 (multiple instances requiring synchronisation)).
- BPM-WF4: Exclusive choice – a point in the workflow process where, based on a decision or workflow control data, one of several branches is chosen.
- BPM-WF5: Simple merge – a point in the workflow process where two or more alternative branches come together without synchronisation. It is an assumption of this pattern that none of the alternative branches is ever executed in parallel

(if this is not the case, then see pattern 8 (Multiple merge) or pattern 9 (Discriminator)).

- BPM-WF6: Multiple choice – a point in the workflow process where, based on a decision or workflow control data, a number of branches are chosen.
- BPM-WF7: Synchronising merge – a point in the workflow process where multiple paths converge into one single thread. If more than one path is taken, synchronisation of the active threads needs to take place. If only one path is taken, the alternative branches should converge without synchronisation. It is an assumption of this pattern that a branch that has already been activated cannot be activated again while the merge is still waiting for other branches to complete.
- BPM-WF8: Multiple merge – a point in a workflow process where two or more branches converge without synchronisation. If more than one branch gets activated, possibly concurrently, the activity following a merging is started for every activation of every incoming branch.
- BPM-WF9: Discriminator – the discriminator is a point in a workflow process that waits for one of the incoming branches to complete before activating the subsequent activity. From that moment on, it waits for all remaining branches to complete and ignores them. Once all incoming branches have been triggered, it resets itself so that it can be triggered again (which is important otherwise it could not really be used in the context of a loop).
- BPM-WF10: N-out-of-M Join – merge many execution paths, perform partial synchronisation and execute subsequent activity only once.
- BPM-WF11: Arbitrary cycles – execute a point in a workflow process where one or more activities can be done repeatedly.
- BPM-WF12: Implicit termination – a given sub-process should be terminated when there is nothing else to be done. In other words, there are no active activities in the workflow and no other activity can be made active (and at the same time the workflow is not in deadlock).
- BPM-WF13: Multiple instances without synchronisation – within the context of a single case (i.e. workflow instance), multiple instances of an activity can be created, i.e. there is a facility to spawn off new threads of control. Each of these threads of control is independent of other threads. Moreover, there is no need to synchronise these threads.
- BPM-WF14: Multiple instances with a priori known design time knowledge – for one process instance an activity is enabled multiple times. The number of instances of a given activity for a given process instance is known at design time. Once all instances are completed, some other activity needs to be started.
- BPM-WF15: Multiple instances with a priori known runtime knowledge – for one case an activity is enabled multiple times. The number of instances of a given activity for a given case varies and may depend on characteristics of the case or availability of resources, but is known at some stage during runtime, before the instances of that activity have to be created. Once all instances are completed, some other activity needs to be started.
- BPM-WF16: Multiple instances with no a priori runtime knowledge – for one case an activity is enabled multiple times. The number of instances of a given

activity for a given case is not known during design time, nor is it known at any stage during runtime, before the instances of that activity have to be created. Once all instances are completed some other activity needs to be started. The difference with Pattern 15 is that even while some of the instances are being executed or already completed, new ones can be created.

- BPM-WF17: Deferred choice – a point in the workflow process where one of several branches is chosen. In contrast to the XOR-split (pattern 4), the choice is not made explicitly (e.g. based on data or a decision), but several alternatives are offered to the environment. However, in contrast to the AND-split (pattern 2), only one of the alternatives is executed. This means that once the environment activates one of the branches, the other alternative branches are withdrawn. It is important to note that the choice is delayed until the processing in one of the alternative branches is actually started, i.e. the moment of choice is as late as possible.

- BPM-WF18: Interleaved parallel routing – a set of activities is executed in an arbitrary order. Each activity in the set is executed, the order is decided at runtime and no two activities are executed at the same moment (i.e. no two activities are active for the same workflow instance at the same time).

- BPM-WF19: Milestone – the enabling of an activity depends on the case being in a specified state, i.e. the activity is enabled only if a certain milestone has been reached which did not expire yet. Consider three activities named A, B and C. Activity A is only enabled if activity B has been executed and C has not been executed yet, i.e. A is not enabled before the execution of B and A is not enabled after the execution of C.

- BPM-WF20: Cancel activity – an enabled activity is disabled, i.e. a thread waiting for the execution of an activity is removed.

- BPM-WF21: Cancel case – a case, i.e. process instance, is removed completely (i.e. even if parts of the process are instantiated multiple times, all descendants are removed).

The last list on workflow control patterns was triggered by a bottom-up analysis and comparison of workflow management software. Provided during 2000 and 2001, this analysis included the evaluation of 15 workflow management systems, with focus being given to their underlying modelling languages. During the initial investigation 20 *control-flow patterns* (van der Aalst et al. 2003) were derived. This was later extended to 43 patterns that where formalised in coloured Petri-net notation (Russell et al. 2006a). In 2005, the workflow patterns work was extended to also analyse constructs for the data (Russell et al. 2005a) with 40 patterns and the resource perspectives of workflows (Russell et al. 2005b) with 43 patterns. At the same time, the area of workflow exception handling was also investigated, which resulted in the identification of a set of *exception handling patterns* (Russell et al. 2006b) systematising the various mechanisms for dealing with exceptions occurring in the control-flow, the data or the resource perspectives. We have here kept close to the list of the original patterns (see http://www.workflowpatterns.com/ for further details).

5.3.2   Comprehensibility Appropriateness of Enterprise Modelling Languages

- UEML_4: EM should provide capabilities to manage the different degrees of certainty in an enterprise. Comment: Related to SEQ-10, 'the language needs to be flexible in precision'.
- UEML_27: EM should use a clear semantic and clear constructs to improve communication and common understanding. Comment: This can be further made more precise by guidelines from SEQUAL (see below).
- UEML_34: EM need for different users' adequate representation of the underlying concepts and relations. Comment: Could also imply a requirement for viewing mechanisms relative to pragmatic quality.
- UEML_42: EM should use classes of compatible semantics belonging to an underlying semantic domain. Comment: Is it possible to use a reference ontology to link different classes?
- UEML_48: EM should be usable for modelling weak people, i.e. people that are not familiar with graphical modelling languages (novices). Comment: When these people need to also model, this is also relevant for modeller appropriateness.
- UEML_49: EM should be simple, but still have sufficient expressiveness.
- UEML_52: EM should be modular to allow the modeller to be more agile.

The following from the quality framework might overlap and extend the above (SEQ).

- SEQ-8: The concepts of the language should be general.
- SEQ-9: The concepts should be composable.
- SEQ-10: There should be both precise and vague concepts in the language.
- SEQ-11: The concepts of the language should be easy to distinguish from each other.
- SEQ-12: The use of concepts should be uniform.
- SEQ-13: The language must be flexible in the level of detail.
- SEQ-14: The language must be able to represent the intention of the model.
- SEQ-15: Symbolic discrimination should be easy.
- SEQ-16: It should be easy to distinguish which symbol a graphical mark is part of.
- SEQ-17: The use of symbols should be uniform (one symbol is used for one concept).
- SEQ-18: Symbols are as simple as possible.
- SEQ-19: The use of colour is appropriate.
- SEQ-20: The use of emphasis is appropriate.
- SEQ-21: Composition of symbols can be made in an aesthetically pleasing way.

5.3.3   Participant Appropriateness of Enterprise Modelling Languages

- UEML_25: EM should be easy to learn, making an easy training.
- SEQ-3: The language should use concepts familiar to the enterprise users.

- SEQ-4: The notation should be intuitive for the enterprise users.
- SEQ-5: It should be possible to easily show the level of completeness and consistency of a part of a model.

5.3.4 Modeller Appropriateness of Enterprise Modelling Languages

- UEML_30: EM should enable to build a model according to individual situated aspects of different purposes and therefore has to support different approaches.
- SEQ-6: It should be possible to update the models as part of work governed by the models (interactive models).
- SEQ-7: It should be possible to have metaphorical modelling. What are good metaphors in a certain case will be very difficult to foresee; thus, this is rather a requirement to the meta-modelling capabilities of the approach than the core language itself.

5.3.5 Tool Appropriateness of Enterprise Modelling Languages

- UEML_5: EM should help to synchronise several modelling tools. Comment: Judge as the need to support a common format which can map to the internal format of the languages of different tools.
- UEML_35: EM needs an invariant and unique behavioural semantics. This is important for stable exchange and common understanding of enterprise models. Comment: Must clarify what parts of the overall language need to have a behavioural semantics, since this is not necessarily applicable to all parts of the language. In the enterprise modelling area, this is particularly relevant for process modelling.
- SEQ-23: The language has a formal (well-defined) syntax.
- SEQ-24: The language has a formal (well-defined) semantics.

5.3.6 Organisational Appropriateness of Enterprise Modelling Languages

- UEML_28: EM should use fully shared concepts and theories to be understandable and be simple to improve communication between stakeholders; between users of enterprise models; between users, modellers and designers; between modellers; and between designers. Comment: Since fully shared concepts within this area do not exist on a general level, this has to be looked upon and judged within a smaller organisational setting or related to existing standards.

In Sect. 7.3.3, relevant parts of this framework are used in connection to the evaluation or the interchange format developed in the Athena project (POP*).

5.4 Summary

One specific kind of means for creating good models, the use of appropriate languages for the modelling task at hand, has been discussed in this chapter under the banner of language quality, i.e. to what extent a modelling language is appropriate to the organisational context, knowledge of the modellers and other stakeholders, the domain to be modelled and the interpretation of the model by social and technical actors being involved in modelling.

In addition to be used for a framework of understanding, SEQUAL can also be used for the evaluation of conceptual modelling approaches. What we are able to evaluate is the potential for the modelling approaches to support the creation of conceptual models of high quality. The discussion on language quality can be used directly for evaluation purposes. We will return to this in Chap. 7.

Review Questions

1. Describe the six types of language quality in SEQUAL.
2. Describe the nine areas of language quality in Moody's 'Physics of Notation'.
3. Describe how the nine areas of Moody's 'Physics of Notation' relate to the six areas of SEQUAL.
4. Provide guidelines for how colour can be used in conceptual modelling languages.
5. Give an overview of the workflow patterns found in BPM systems.

Problems and Exercises

Individual Exercises
1. Give an overview of Bertin's framework for variables to use to convey meaning.
2. Where are the variables for Bertin relevant relative to quality of modelling languages?
3. Look up the meta-model/language description of BPMN on http://www.omg.org. Evaluate the quality of the meta-model using SEQUAL.
4. Looking at BPMN as an example, give examples of trade-offs between tool appropriateness, domain appropriateness and comprehension appropriateness for a modelling language.
5. When specialising the guidelines in SEQUAL to a specific type of modelling, in what area would you expect most specialisation to be done? Why is this so?

Pair Exercises
1. Discuss experiences with modelling where you think the language used was appropriate. Why was it appropriate? What type of appropriateness was most important?

2. How does the importance of different types of language appropriateness differ when the goal of modelling (cf. Fig. 1.3) differs?

Group Exercises

Use the description of the main course arrangement process in Appendix C as a basis for this task:

1. Model the case using BPMN. Evaluate the appropriateness of BPMN for modelling the case.
2. Model the concrete performance of the course you are currently performing also using BPMN. Evaluate the appropriateness of BPMN for modelling this situation.
3. Compare the appropriateness of BPMN for modelling on the type level (as in task 1) and on the instance level (as in task 2).
4. Model the case with another modelling language of your own choice (Z, Z might be EPC, YAWL (i.e. 'EPC, YAWL, UML activity diagram or similar.') UML activity diagram or similarly). Evaluate the appropriateness of Z for modelling the case.
5. Compare the appropriateness for modelling the case using language BPMN and the modelling language of your own choice. Which language was most appropriate for this case?
6. If BPMN is extended with concept actor from the i* language, would that improve or reduce the appropriateness of BPMN to model the domain in the case study?
7. Identify process patterns that you have made in the process models developed in this task.

References

Bertin, J.: Semiology of Graphics: Diagrams, Networks, Maps. University of Wisconsin Press, Madison (1983)

Blankenship, J., Dansereau, D.F.: The effect of animated node-link displays on information recall. J. Exp. Educ. **68**(4), 293–308 (2000)

Britton, C., Jones, S.: The untrained eye: how languages for software specification support understanding by untrained users. Hum. Comput. Interact. **14**, 191–244 (1999)

Bullen, C.V., Bennett, J.L.: Groupware in practice: an interpretation of work experiences. In: Dunlop, C., Kling, R. (eds.) Computerization and Controversy: Value Conflicts and Social Choices, pp. 257–287. Academic, Boston (1991)

Castellani, X.: Overview of models defined with charts of concepts. In: Falkenberg, E., Lyytinen, K., Verrijn-Stuart, A.A. (eds.) Proceedings of the IFIP8.1 Working Conference on Information Systems Concepts (ISCO4); An Integrated Discipline Emerging September 20–22, Leiden, pp. 235–256 (1999)

Embley, D.W., Jackson, R.B., Woodfield, S.N.: OO system analysis: is it or isn't it? IEEE Softw. **12**(3), 19–33 (1995)

Erickson, J., Siau, K.: Can UML be simplified? Practitioner use of UML in separate domains. In: proceedings EMMSAD 2007. Proceedings of Twelfth International Workshop on Exploring Modeling Methods in System Analysis and Design, Trondheim, Norway, pp. 89–98 (2007)

Flores, F., Graves, M., Hartfield, B., Winograd, T.: Computer systems and the design of organizational interaction. ACM Trans. Off. Inf. Syst. **6**(2), 153–172 (1988)

Gause, D.C., Weinberg, G.M.: Exploring Requirements: Quality BEFORE Design. Dorset House, New York (1989)

Goodman, N.: Languages of Art: An Approach to a Theory of Symbols. Hackett, Indianapolis (1976)

Gopalakrishnan, S., Krogstie, J., Sindre, G.: Extending use and misuse cases to capture mobile applications. NOKOBIT – Norsk konferanse for organisasjoners bruk av informasjonsteknologi s, 1–14 (2011)

Guizzardi, G.: Ontological Foundations for Structural Conceptual Models, vol. 015. Telematica Instituut, Enschede (2005)

Gurr, C.A.: Effective diagrammatic communication: syntactic, semantic and pragmatic issues. J. Vis. Lang. Comput. **10**(4), 317S–342S (1999)

Kalyuga, P., Ayres, S.K., Chang, S.J.: The expertise reversal effect. Educ. Psychol. **38**(1), 23–31 (2003)

Knothe, T., Busselt, C., Böll, D.: Deliverable D2.3 report on UEML (Needs and requirements). UEML, Thematic Network – Contract no: IST – 2001 – 34229, 2003. www.ueml.org (2001)

Koedinger, K., Anderson, J.: Abstract planning and conceptual chunks: elements of expertise in geometry. Cognit. Sci. **14**, 511–550 (1990)

Krogstie, J.: Conceptual modeling for computerized information systems support in organizations. PhD, University of Trondheim, The Norwegian Institute of Technology, Trondheim, Norway (1995)

Lynch, K.: The Image of the City. MIT Press, Cambridge (1960)

Moody, D.L.: The "Physics" of notations: toward a scientific basis for constructing visual notations in software engineering. IEEE Trans. Softw. Eng. **35**, 756–779 (2009)

Nonaka, I., Takeuchi, H.: The Knowledge-Creating Company. Oxford University Press, New York (1995)

Olle, T.W., Sol, H.G., Verrijn-Stuart, A.A.: Information Systems Design Methodologies: A Comparative Review. North-Holland, Amsterdam/New York (1982)

Olle, T.W., Sol, H.G., Tully, C.J.: Information Systems Design Methodologies: A Feature Analysis. North-Holland, Amsterdam/New York (1983)

OMG.: Unified modeling language v 2.0 OMG. Web site http://www.omg.org (2006)

Opdahl, A., Henderson-Sellers, B., Barbier, F.: An ontological evaluation of the OML metamodel. In: Falkenberg, E., Lyytinen, K., Verrijn-Stuart, A. (eds.) Proceedings of the IFIP8.1 Working Conference on Information Systems Concepts (ISCO4); An Integrated Discipline Emerging September 20-22, Leiden, pp. 217–232 (1999)

Petit, M.: Enterprise Modeling Language Comparison Framework: A Proposal, UEML project Deliverable d1.1 IST – 2001 – 34229 (2002)

Prasse, M.: Evaluation of object-oriented modeling languages. A comparison between OML and UML. In: Schader, M., Korthaus, A. (eds.) The Unified Modeling Language – Technical Aspects and Applications, pp. 58–78. Physica-Verlag, Heidelberg (1998)

Recker, J., Rosemann, M., Krogstie, J.: Ontology- versus pattern-based evaluation of process modeling language: a comparison. Commun. Assoc. Inf. Syst. **20**, 774–799 (2007)

Russell, N., ter Hofstede, A.H.M., Edmond, D., van der Aalst, W.M.P.: Workflow data patterns: identification, representation and tool support. In: Proceedings from Conceptual Modeling – ER 2005, pp. 353–368. Springer, Klagenfurt (2005a)

Russell, N., van der Aalst, W.M.P., ter Hofstede, A.H.M., Edmond, D.: Workflow resource patterns: identification, representation and tool support. In: Proceedings from Advanced Information Systems Engineering – CAiSE 2005, pp. 216–232. Springer, Porto (2005b)

Russell, N., ter Hofstede, A.H.M., van der Aalst, W.M.P., Mulyar, N.A.: Workflow control-flow patterns: a revised view. BPM Center Report BPM-06-22, BPMcenter.org (2006a)

Russell, N., van der Aalst, W.M.P., ter Hofstede, A.H.M.: Workflow exception patterns. In: Proceedings from Advanced Information Systems Engineering – CAiSE 2006, pp. 288–302. Springer, Luxembourg, Grand-Duchy of Luxembourg (2006b)

Senn, J.A.: Analysis & Design of Information Systems. McGraw-Hill, New York (1989)

Shneiderman, B.: Designing the User Interface: Strategies for Effective Human-Computer Interaction, 2nd edn. Addison Wesley, Reading (1992)

Shannon, C.E., Weaver, W.: The Mathematical Theory of Communication. University of Illinois Press, Urbana (1963)

Sindre, G.: HICONS: A general diagrammatic framework for hierarchical modelling. PhD thesis, IDT, NTH, Trondheim, Norway, 1990. NTH report 1990:44, IDT report 1990:31 (1990)

Suchman, L.: Plans and Situated Actions. Cambridge University Press, New York (1987)

Twining, W., Miers, D.: How to Do Things with Rules? Weidenfeld and Nicholson, London (1982)

van der Aalst, W.M.P., ter Hofstede, A.H.M., Kiepuszewski, B., Barros, A.P.: Workflow patterns. Distrib. Parallel Databases **14**(3), 5–51 (2003)

Vessey, I., Conger, S.A.: Requirements specification: learning object, process, and data methodologies. Commun. ACM **37**(5), 102–113 (1994)

Wand, Y., Weber, R.: On the ontological expressiveness of information systems analysis and design grammars. J. Inf. Syst. **3**(4), 217–237 (1993)

Ware, C.: Information Visualization: Perception for Design. Morgan Kaufmann, San Francisco (2000)

Weber, R.: *Ontological Foundations of Information Systems*. Melbourne, Australia: Coopers & Lybrand and the Accounting Association of Australia and New Zealand (1997)

Winn, W.D.: Encoding and retrieval of information in maps and diagrams. IEEE Trans. Prof. Commun. **33**(3), 103–107 (1990)

Winn, W.D.: An account of how readers search for information in diagrams. Contemp. Educ. Psychol. **18**, 162–185 (1993)

zur Muehlen, M., Recker, J.C.: How much language is enough? Theoretical and practical use of the business process modeling notation. In: Proceedings CAiSE'08 Montpellier France. Springer, Berlin (2008)

Specialisations of SEQUAL

We have so far in this book described the generic framework (described SEQUAL-Gen in Fig. 6.1) and quality of modelling languages in Chaps. 4 and 5 respectively. As indicate here, a number of specialisations have been made for different types of models.

- SRS – Software requirements specifications
- DM – Data models
- Met – IS Methodologies (methodology models)
- DESIGN – Design models and running system (cf. ISO/IEC 9126)
- DQ – Data quality
- IM – Interactive models
- EM – Enterprise models/modelling languages
- BPM – Business Process Models
- ONT – Ontologies
- SOA – Models used in the area of Service Oriented Architecture
- MDA – Models used in Model-driven Architecture
- UML – UML models
- MAPS – MAPQUAL (not in the figure)

We will present some of these specialisations in the rest of this chapter, including specialisations for business process models, requirements specification models, data models, data quality, ontologies, interactive models, and maps.

6.1 Quality of Business Process Models

Although process modelling in IS-development can be traced back to at least the 1970s, business process modelling is gaining in importance as discussed in Sect. 2.3.4. Process modelling can be done to achieve one or more of the goals of modelling described in Chap. 1. A focus here is on the use of business process models for sense-making, communication, and improvements of business processes, although ways of deploying the model of the new, improved process is also of importance of course.

J. Krogstie, *Model-Based Development and Evolution of Information Systems:* 281
A Quality Approach, DOI 10.1007/978-1-4471-2936-3_6,
© Springer-Verlag London 2012

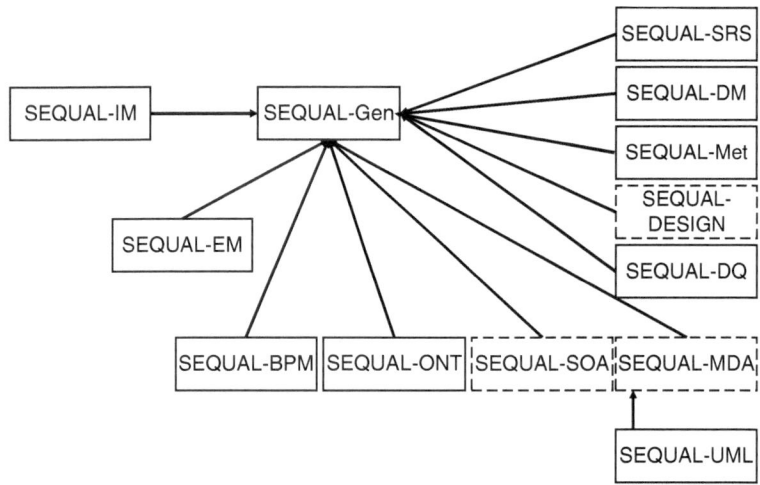

Fig. 6.1 Specialisations of SEQUAL

As described in Sect. 3.4, there is a large number of process modelling languages from many modelling perspectives. Still, in business process modelling, most work has been done relative to languages combining functional and behavioural aspects, such as BPMN, EPC, and UML Activity diagrams. Quality of languages for business process modelling as part of enterprise modelling was discussed in Chap. 5, and we will here look at the quality of business process models in particular.

In an enterprise, different processes are in use. If the enterprise wants to reach its goals and stay in front in the market, every process has to be evaluated and maybe changed to support the goals.

6.1.1 What Is a Good Business Process?

There exist no universal rules for what a good process is. We will here present process aspects that can define if we have a good enough or a 'bad' process.

6.1.1.1 Customer Value and Economic Profit

The main goal for most enterprises is to have economic profit. In addition to this, and also as a way to reach this goal, the business wants to have pleased customers. In Table 6.1, we present dimensions of value that is valid for most customer groups.

A customer will experience improvement in an enterprise process if he/she gets his/her product faster, cheaper, with less resources used, and with better quality or service than before. Improvement in one of these dimensions could involve that your enterprise gets more customers, increases its market share etc.

Table 6.1 Dimensions of value

Component of value	What a customer wants
Time	Fast
Quality	Right
Cost	Cheap
Service	Easy
Resource-usage (including carbon footprint)	Low

6.1.1.2 Employee Well-Being

Every serious business should try to take good care of their employees. It is important that the persons working in the enterprise are pleased with their situation. If the individuals' goals and motivation are in strong contrast to the overlying business goals, a conflict situation will often arise. Based on this, one should also consider the employees' needs and wishes when designing or rethinking business processes. This has to do both with physical aspects like ergonomics, and with psychological aspects such as motivation, needs etc. Both views are important and should be taken into consideration.

6.1.1.3 Focus on Standard Processes

It is suggested to focus on standard processes. If you design processes adapted to all kinds of exceptions, they often become too complicated and therefore unsuited for the normal cases. It is often more effective to adjust the process for normal cases, and have peculiar methods for handling exceptions.

With this in mind, one has to find out what the most effective solution in every special case is. It is important to design a process chain that can handle all exceptions and in the same time treat normal instances efficiently.

6.1.2   How Can Improvement Be Measured?

In order to evaluate whether a new process is better than the existing one, some means of measurement are necessary. Some characteristics to help developing good measures are:

- *Accuracy*: Accuracy will be useful in the evaluation giving the ability to measure how well or to what extent you reached the goal.
- *(Perceived) Objectivity*: Objectivity is important to ensure that you will get the same conclusion independent of which person or persons who did the evaluation.
- *One or more dimensions (e.g. time)*: The main advantage of using more than one dimension in the goals is that it gives the opportunity to evaluate the results against different criteria of success. If the measures focus on just one dimension, there is a danger of sub-optimisation, which means that an improvement in one field entails a poorer result for the total product.

- *Specifying the target*: A specified target will give a better evaluation of the result. A general target like 'We want the process execution to become faster' is not as good as 'We want the process execution to become 75% faster'.
- *Balancing the trade-offs between cost/quality and speed/flexibility*: Unfortunately, lower cost often will entail decreased quality; higher speed will entail decreased flexibility and opposite. When developing goals, one has to consider this to find goals that are possible to reach at the same time.
- *Clear to all involved*: The goals and measures must be clear to all persons involved. To get an effective and productive working process, everyone has to pull in the same direction. Understandable and motivating goals and measures are prerequisite for this.
- *Can be shown to support the organisation's strategies*: If some of the goals and measures are in conflict to the organisation's strategies, it will never be able to reach its main goal.

One always should have to stretch to reach a goal. According to psychology and organisational theory, both too low and too high goals can be demotivating.

6.1.3   Heuristics for Improving Processes

We will in this part present some ideas for improvement of the total process. Most of these are based on Willoch (1994).

H1: Specialising and generalising tasks

If a process consists of sequential tasks performed by many different people with special competence, two problems often arise:
1. The tasks take up too much specialist time.
2. It is difficult to track status of the process because there are many persons involved.

Willoch's suggested solution to this problem is represented in Fig. 6.2. The idea is to give a group or one person the main responsibility for the process. This person or persons can execute smaller tasks between the specialist tasks, and also have customer contact. In this way, the specialists can release time for other more important duties and the customer have one contact point where he or she can have all the desirable information.

H2: Reorganise partial processes

A second solution mentioned by Willoch is to organise sequential partial processes in parallel. If it is possible, this will in most cases decrease the execution time of a process.

Another possibility is to merge two or more partial processes, or split one partial process in various smaller processes. Merging can be an effective tool for improvement, if the processes are tightly bound. Desirable consequences of merging and splitting partial processes are for example better use of resources and faster process accomplishment.

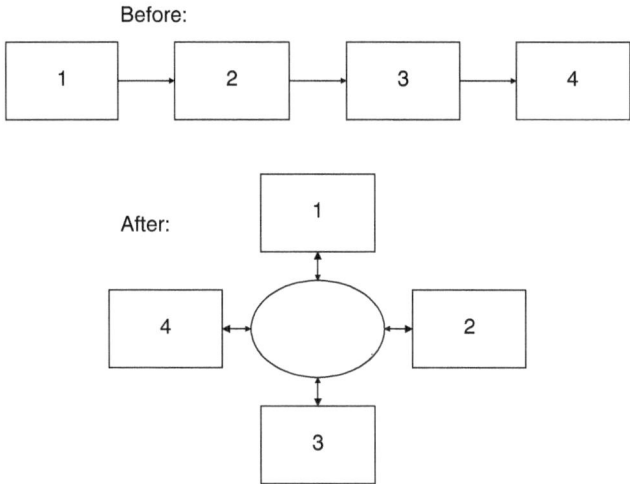

Fig. 6.2 Specialising and generalising tasks

A thorough analysis of the partial processes and their internal dependency can also uncover parts that are useless for the whole process. These parts are only a waste of time and resources, and should therefore be eliminated.

H3: Centralise and decentralise structures
To gain advantage of both the centralising and decentralising structures, Willoch presents a combined model. The centralising principle gives flexibility and customer contact, and the decentralising gives control and efficiency. The principle is best explained by use of a model, see Fig. 6.3.

H4: Reduce inputs and outputs
A high number of input and output flows between different departments and groups within an organisation increase organisational complexity. The chance of misunderstandings and errors is high, and the many flows can also delay the process execution. According to Willoch, it therefore is a good idea to try to reduce the number of input and output flows.

H5: Postpone aggregated control
When individually controlled transactions have a total cost that is higher than the cost of sending them altogether, there is a natural solution to make common control and postpone transactions to save money.

H6: Reallocate processes or process parts
An effort suggested by Willoch is to reallocate. That means to move processes or process parts to the customer or to other external supplies. This can be done to save money or move control to another place.

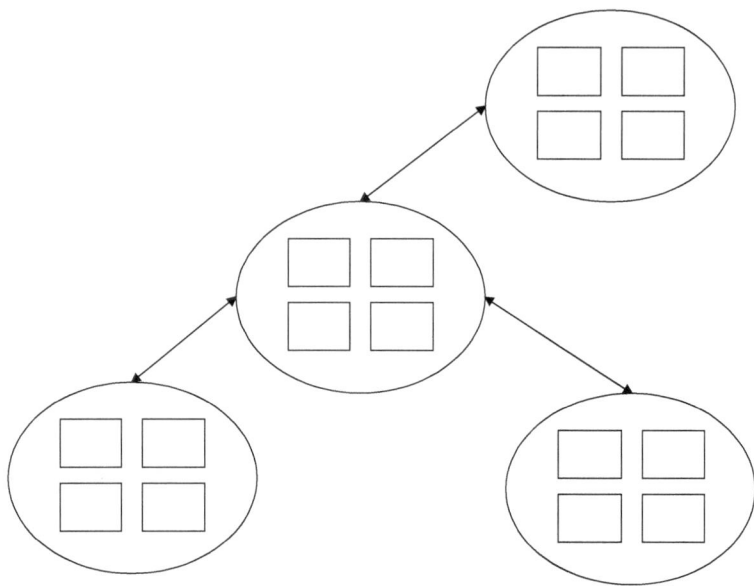

Fig. 6.3 Centralised and decentralised structures

H7: Change the number of alternatives

If the number of alternatives is too big, this can result in complexity and inefficiency. If the selection of alternatives is too small, one risks that none of the solutions are appropriate for the special case. Willoch proposes to evaluate the alternatives to find a suitable number of choices.

H8: Change the decision moment

Earlier decisions will make it easier to continue the process and make it more efficient. Later decisions will give time to evaluate and choose between the alternatives, and therefore give more flexibility.

H9: Introducing new technology

Access to new technology will give opportunities to change and improve the process execution. It is important that the enterprise evaluate the time to do the change, so it matches with e.g. new releases of a software product. Remember that introducing new technology might necessitate other processes that use resources, thus one need to look at the total resource consumption.

In Mendling et al. (2010), the authors suggest seven process modelling (7 PMG) guidelines in an attempt to provide a limited set of easily understandable guidelines.

- G1: Use as few elements in the model as possible. Larger models tend to be more difficult to understand (Mendling et al. 2007a) and have a higher error probability than small models (Mendling et al. 2007a, b).
- G2: Minimise the routing paths per element. The higher the degree of an element in the process model, i.e. the number of input and output arcs together, the harder

it becomes to understand the model (Mendling et al. 2007a). As shown in Mendling et al. (2007b), there is a strong correlation between the number of modelling errors and the average or maximum degree of elements in a model. This is similar to principle H4 above.

- G3: Use one start and one end event. The number of start and end events is positively connected with an increase in error probability (Mendling et al. 2007b). Most workflow engines require a single start and end node (van der Aalst et al. 2003).Moreover, models satisfying this requirement are easier to understand and allow for all kinds or analysis (e.g. soundness checks).Note that this is primarily an issue when wanting to execute the process model.
- G4: Model as structured as possible. A process model is structured if every split connector matches a respective join connector of the same type. Structured models can be seen as formulas with balanced brackets, i.e. every opening bracket has a corresponding closing bracket of the same type. Unstructured models are not only more likely to include errors (Mendling et al. 2007b); people also tend to understand them less easily (Mendling et al. 2007a).
- G5: Avoid OR routing elements. Models that have only AND and XOR connectors are less error-prone (Mendling et al. 2007b). Furthermore, there are some ambiguities in the semantics of the OR-join leading to paradoxes and implementation problems (Kindler 2006).
- G6: Use verb-object activity labels. A wide exploration of labelling styles that are used in actual process models, discloses the existence of two popular styles and a rest category (Recker and Mendling 2006). From these, people consider the verb-object style, like 'Inform complainant', as significantly less ambiguous and more useful than action-noun labels (e.g. 'Complaint analysis') or labels that follow neither of these styles (e.g. 'Incident agenda') (Mendling and Recker 2008). This is similar to the original guidelines for naming of tasks in DFDs.
- G7: Decompose the model if it has more than 50 elements. For models with more than 50 elements, the error probability tends to be higher than 50% (Mendling et al. 2007b). This means that large models should be split up into smaller models. Note that early guidelines for DFD was more restrictive, e.g. to have no more than seven processes at a given decomposition level (based on the 7 ± 2 guideline for human short term memory) (Gane and Sarson 1979).

It should be noticed that the potential interaction effects between the seven proposed guidelines are intricate and diverse. For a given process model, many guidelines can be applicable, at various places in a process model, and conflicting to different degrees. In Mendling et al. (2010), a suggested prioritisation is G4, G7, G1, G6, G2, G3, and G5. This should obviously also be held against other quality types (e.g. model completeness and validity).

6.1.4 Quality of Process Models According to SEQUAL

Quality of business process models are discussed here following the levels of the SEQUAL framework.

6.1.4.1 Physical quality

The physical quality requirements are the same for business process models as for other modelling activities, i.e. the model must be sufficiently persistent, current, and available relative to the goals of modelling and those involved.

6.1.4.2 Empirical quality

Empirical Quality also inherits the standard guidelines for graph layout from Sect. 4.3. In addition, all the 7 PMG guidelines can be positioned at this level, since they can be easily counted. As is normally the case, this will contribute to pragmatic quality. Thus the following specific guidelines apply:

- G1: Use as few elements in the model as possible. This is the same as the general principle on expressive economy.
- G2 and H4: Minimise the routing paths per element.
- G3: Use one start and one end event.
- G4: Model structured by ensuring that every split connector matches a respective join connector of the same type.
- G5: Avoid OR routing elements.
- G6: Use verb-object activity labels.
- G7: Decompose the model if it has too many elements (50 in total, but try to have less than 10 processes in the same diagram).

The guideline on focusing on standard processes (and not include all exception in the main diagram) also applies here, something that is also supported from (Wesenberg 2011).

6.1.4.3 Syntactic quality

This area follows the standard categories described in Sect. 4.4. Since you usually have parts of a process models that at some time should be executable, you would like that the language-model also include a representation of the behavioural semantics, especially if you have a meta-modelling environment where you might want to make updates to the modelling language.

6.1.4.4 Semantic quality

To ensure the possibility of consistency, checking two of the guidelines in 7 PMG is specifically important:

- G3: Use one start and one end event.
- G5: Avoid OR routing elements.

We noted that these where given low priority in the 7PMG report. On the other hand, if consistency and formal analysis (or simulation vs. next area) is important, one might want to prioritise these higher. The same applies for checks of that the decompositions are correctly modelled.

For achieving perceived semantic quality, the suggested model property is *variety*. In enterprise modelling this is of special importance, since there are so many different humans involved. People with different background and knowledge will probably not understand the same types of models.

When working on process improvements, one compares to an improved domain; thus relative to validity of the model, one has the following guidelines:

- H1: Ensure the right level of specialisation of tasks.
- H2: Arrange process in parallel if possible.
- H3: Have the right level of centralisation in the process.
- H4: Reduce the number of inputs and outputs.
- H5: Postpone aggregated control.
- H6: Reallocate process parts of it saves resources.
- H7: Have a reasonable number of alternatives.
- H8: Put the decision moment at the appropriate time.
- H9: Use new technology if appropriate.

The use of these mechanisms relates to evaluating the value for customers and company, as discussed in Sect. 6.1.1 according to measures developed as outlined in Sect. 6.1.2.

It can be argued that the detailed guidelines for this relates to the more precise goal of modelling, thus should be looked upon as part of deontic quality.

6.1.4.5 Pragmatic quality

Guideline G3 might also apply here relative to the possibility for executing the process model e.g. for prototyping, explanation generation, animation or simulation. An executing process model can also be beneficial for audience training. Apart from this, the normal aspects applies.

6.1.4.6 Social quality

As described in Sects. 2.3.5 and 2.4, and in Sect. 6.1.1 in this chapter, agreement both on the measure used to judge process improvement, and the final process are important. Often, a final process is based on a merge of several processes, e.g. different processes form different department, or the existing process merged with the process implied through a procured software system such as an ERP system. In this regard, mechanisms for comparison of different models would be useful. Matching business process models is discussed in (Dijkman et al. 2010; Rittgen 2011). Three aspects of model similarity are identified: Node matching, structural, and behavioural similarity. *Node matching* tries to map nodes from the one model to nodes of the other model by comparing the labels, attributes and types of nodes. Node matching can be effected with semantic or syntactic measures. The latter is based on the string-edit distance, i.e. the number of letters that need to be added, replaced or deleted to transform the label of an activity in one model to that of an activity in the other model. Semantic matching is based on a database of synonyms. Based on the node matching, the two models can be compared now with the help of structural or behavioural similarity. The former uses only structural information on the model, i.e. the way in which activities are connected with 'arrows', but does not look at their meaning in terms of control flow. Two models are considered structurally equivalent if two nodes are always connected in the same way in one model as their matching counterparts in the other.

Behavioural equivalence looks at the actual execution of the processes described by the models. Here, two models are considered equivalent if, at any time during process execution, an activity that can be performed in one process can also be performed in the other, and vice versa. A weakness with these types of similarity measures is that they usually do not focus on which areas of the model where similarity is of most importance.

One should also be able to deal with inconsistencies, in the sense that not all need to follow the same process in all areas. This is discussed more in Sect. 6.6, quality of interactive models.

Not all parts of models have the same importance. If two models were inconsistent, it would have been nice to generate some kind of information on the differences. Are the parts that do not match important parts of the model? How hard is it to change parts of the first or the other process to make them consistent? Are the inconsistent parts automated or manual processes? The tool could, after the analysis, suggest which processes or process parts to change.

6.1.4.7 Deontic quality

As discussed under semantic quality, a goal for this type of model is to improve the process according to improvements relative to time, quality, cost, resource consumption (which can also include aspects such as carbon footprint), and service, and the goals for this will guide the use of guideline H1–H9. For most models, the goal of total validity and completeness is impossible to reach. For enterprise models, this is important to have in mind. If one is trying to include everything in the model or models, the modelling activity will become a never-ending story. To end up with a model with high semantic quality, it is also essential to have a clear understanding of what that single model should contain. We can think of cases where we have reached the state of feasible validity and completeness, but the modelling domain is too big, and therefore we still do not have a really good model. A model that tries to cover too many aspects becomes unusable for all of them, because it does not cover any of them well enough. The preparation, ensuring that the goal of modelling is clear before one starts to make a model, is therefore really important.

6.2   Quality of Requirement Specification Models

In Davis et al. (1993), the work on quality properties for a software requirement specification (SRS) is summarised. The paper also includes proposals for metrics and weights for the different properties. The following long list of unsorted properties is described that are described in more detail throughout the section:

- Unambiguous
- Complete
- Correct
- Understandable
- Verifiable

- Internally Consistent
- Externally Consistent
- Achievable
- Concise
- Design-independent
- Traceable
- Modifiable
- Electronically Stored
- Executable/Interpretable/Prototypable
- Annotated by Relative Importance
- Annotated by Relative Stability
- Annotated by version
- Not Redundant
- At Right Level of Detail
- Precise
- Reusable
- Traced
- Organised
- Cross-referenced

An SRS can be looked upon either as being a model of the perceived future IS as required by someone, or of the perceived future CIS without locking it to one specific implementation (which is the normal case). In either case, the domain also includes already base-lined documents and models created earlier in the development effort (what we have termed the modelling context in Sect. 4.1.5).

In an SRS, one usually use a mix of conceptual models and natural language text, thus it is necessary to include quality means for both kinds of representation types in combination. Thus, in addition to our own work and the work of Davis, we base the overview of work done on quality for textual requirements models (Fabbrini et al. 1998). One important aspect when discussing requirements models is that they are meant to be understood by persons with very varying background (compared to e.g. design models, which are normally only used by persons with detailed software development knowledge).

We discuss means within each quality level in detail, starting with those areas that are specifically mentioned by Davis. We have highlighted these properties in *italic* when positioning them within the quality framework below.

6.2.1 Physical Quality of an SRS

The only property in this area mentioned by Davis is that the SRS should be *electronically stored*. This is subsumed by our persistent mean for addressing the physical quality aspect of internaliseability, and enables availability. Other standard means for physical quality as described in Sect. 4.2 is relevant also for requirements specification.

6.2.2   Empirical Quality of an SRS

Davis partly addresses this area with the property *understandable*: An SRS is under-standable if all classes of SRS readers can easily comprehend the meaning of all requirements with a minimum of explanation. An important factor in achieving this is language quality aspects of the modelling languages that have been used such as comprehensibility and participant appropriateness. The property *concise* (An SRS is concise if it is as short as possible without affecting any other quality of the SRS) is a mean at this level. It can also be linked to overall size limitation of the SRS. To further make Davis' goal more concrete, the same guidelines apply as for diagram-matical and textual models in general when it comes to empirical quality presented in Sect. 4.3.

6.2.3   Syntactic Quality of an SRS

This area is not addressed directly by Davis, although some of the aspects on the semantic level can easily be reduced to syntactic issues by mandating certain aspects to be part of the language used for the modelling of requirements (e.g. priority, version, and stability information, see below). Since Davis does not mention this explicitly as a mean, we will discuss these properties as part of semantic quality. The standard guidelines for syntactic quality that are presented in Sect. 4.4 apply also for an SRS.

6.2.4   Semantic Quality of an SRS

Important means for achieving semantic quality are using modelling languages that are appropriate for the domain and modeller knowledge as discussed under language quality. An important aspect in relation to a requirement specification is that the languages used should not put too strict constraints on the technical solution. Properties in the discussion of Davis that potentially influence this area are *design independent, traceable, annotated by relative importance, annotated by relative stability, annotated by version,* and *precise.* Since these properties are not always covered and mandated as an integral part of the modelling language, we will return to these areas in more detail below as specific means for semantic quality or for deontic quality. In fact, a large number of the properties discussed by Davis concern semantic quality. It is important to notice that these quality properties appear to have been suggested under the assumption of an objectivistic world-view. When comparing them with validity and completeness as we have defined them, we thus do this under the presumption that the modelling domain is inter-subjectively agreed among the involved social actors of the audience.

When looking upon semantic quality relative to the primary domain, we have the property *complete.* According to Davis, an SRS is complete if
1. Everything that the software is supposed to do is included in the SRS.

2. Responses of the software to all realisable classes of input data in all recognisable classes of situations are included.
3. All pages are numbered, all figures and tables are numbered, named, and referenced; all terms are defined; all units of measure are provided; and all referenced material is present.
4. No sections are marked 'To be determined'.

The first point is the same as our measure of completeness, whereas achieving the second can be supported through using for instance the driving question technique. Item three and four on the other hand is a kind of incompleteness that is easier to deal with either by manually checking for such situation after including them as part of a standard document-structure to be followed for the SRS, or by including such aspects as part of the syntax of the modelling language. In this way, one is able to reduce what is presented as a semantic problem into one of checking for syntactic completeness and validity at the potential cost of restricting the freedom in the expression of requirements.

Correct: An SRS is correct if and only if every requirement represent something required of the system to be built. This is the same as what we term 'validity'.

The property *internally consistent* (An SRS is internally consistent if and only if no subset of individual requirements stated therein conflict) is subsumed by the combination of validity and completeness since an inconsistency must be caused by at least one invalid statement or the lack of a statement that are to sort out the inconsistency. To illustrate, consider the case in which you model an organisation's business rules for implementing these in an information system. Suppose the system must account for the following two rules:

- 'If a company has been our customer for more than 10 years, the customer status should be "high priority"'.
- 'If a customer has been late with payments more than three times, the customer status should be "low priority"'.

What then if a company who has been the customer for 12 years is late with payments more than three times? You could decide to change the first rule to rate the customer as 'medium priority' or the second to 'more than four times'. Either of these two actions would mean that the original rules were invalid. On the other hand, you might decide that both rules are valid, and add another rule 'if there are contradictory rules about customer status, the sales manager should resolve the issue', which requires the system simply to notify someone. Adding a rule to resolve a contradiction would mean that the original model was incomplete because it had no such rule.

Davis suggests using languages with formal syntax and semantics to address inconsistency, a mean for semantic quality also proposed in the general SEQUAL framework. Note that semantic consistency checking might only detect an inconsistency, it will be up to humans to judge if the inconsistency is because of invalidity, incompleteness, or both of the model.

Another property being either a matter of incompleteness or invalidity relative to the primary domain is *precise*. (An SRS is precise if and only if (a) numeric quantities are used whenever possible and (b) the appropriate levels of precision are used for all numeric quantities.) The first aspect is covered by completeness. If the granularity of precision is too high, this can also be regarded as incompleteness; whereas if it is too low, there is a case of invalidity.

Properties related to the *model context* are:

- *Traced* (An SRS is traced if and only if the origin of each of its requirements is clear) is subsumed by completeness since such links to other models and/or sources of the requirements should be captured in the model if they are deemed relevant.
- *Externally consistent* (An SRS is externally consistent if and only if no requirement stated therein conflict with any already base-lined project documentation). Statements within such documentation will be part of the modelling context; thus, the same can be said about external consistency as was said about internal consistency above.

Some additional semantic means mentioned as properties by Davis are:

- *Modifiable*: An SRS is modifiable if its structure and style are such that any changes can be made easily, completely, and consistently. To improve the semantic quality of a model, one needs to change the model. This includes both the cases where the model is found invalid or incomplete in relation to a stable domain, or when the domain changes, e.g. when the requirements to the system or its environment change. In connection to requirements or environment change, Davis suggests the property.
- *Not redundant*: An SRS is redundant if the same requirement is stated more than once. Unlike the other properties, redundancy is not necessarily bad. Redundancy can in fact improve pragmatic quality (see below) at the cost of conciseness. The main problem of redundancy hits when the SRS is changed. Thus, avoiding uncontrolled redundancy is a (secondary) mean to ensure modifiability.

6.2.5   Pragmatic Quality of an SRS

Some properties mentioned by Davis that is relevant for pragmatic quality are:

- *Executable/Interpretable/Prototypable*: An SRS is executable, interpretable, or prototypable if and only if there are a software tool capable of inputting the SRS and providing a dynamic behavioural model. To perform the indicated activities, one obviously need tool support for models developed in languages having an operational semantics that can be interpreted by a tool, although the existence of the tool support is not a quality feature of the model itself.
- *Organised*: An SRS is organised if and only if its contents are arranged so that readers can easily locate information and logical relationships among adjacent sections are apparent. One way is to follow any of many SRS standards, e.g. group by type of requirement, class of user, common stimulus, common response, feature, or object.
- *Cross-referenced*: An SRS is cross referenced if and only if cross-references are used in the SRS to relate sections containing requirements to other sections containing identical (i.e. redundant) requirements, more abstract or more detailed descriptions of the same requirements and requirements that depend on them or on which they depend. As discussed earlier, such links are needed to assure the

comprehension of the overall model; thus having them can be classified as a pragmatic mean. They are also related to modifiability. Using e.g. hyperlinks and having advanced browsing capabilities are useful tool support in this area.

6.2.6 Social Quality of an SRS

Davis does not address this area, although it is in practice necessary to achieve agreement among the different participants as for the contents of the requirements model. Techniques discussed in Sect. 4.7 are relevant to take into account in this respect.

6.2.7 Deontic Quality of an SRS

A number of properties suggested by Davis are related to the organisational value of the SRS.

- *Annotated by relative importance*: An SRS is annotated by relative importance if a reader can easily determine which requirements are of most importance, which are next most important etc. Since this is usually needed to be able to allocate resources sensibly, and determine priorities when budgets are insufficient for addressing all requirements, this is part of deontic quality.
- *Annotated by relative stability*: An SRS is annotated by relative stability if a reader can easily determine which requirements are most likely to change, which are next most likely etc. Since this is needed for designers to know where to build in flexibility, an SRS that is not annotated in this way is incomplete relative to achieving the goals of making the SRS.
- *Annotated by version*: An SRS is annotated by version if a reader can easily determine which requirements will be satisfied in which version of the product. When relevant, the lack of this information is also an example of incompleteness relative to the needs from project management.

On the above three aspects, if it is decided that the language for modelling being used should contain such information, the lack of this can rather be looked upon as an example of syntactic incompleteness than deontic incompleteness.

- *Traceable*: An SRS is traceable if and only if it is written in a manner that facilitates the referencing of each individual statement. This indicates requirements to the language to be used for modelling; thus, if the decided language includes these kind of aspects, a requirement specification missing them would be syntactically incomplete. If these aspects are not formally included in the language, one needs to treat them as problems of deontic completeness. Lacking traceability can also influence pragmatic quality.
- *Verifiable*: An SRS is verifiable if there are finite, cost effective techniques that can be used to verify that every requirement stated therein is satisfied by the system to be built. This is partly related to completeness, especially when the requirement is difficult to verify because of ambiguity (see also below). Problems with verifiability because of lack of precision are discussed under the property

'precise'. When verifiability is problematic because of undecidability, this should
be explicitly stated if it is relevant.

- *Achievable*: An SRS is achievable if and only if there could exist at least one
  system design and implementation that correctly implements all the requirements
  stated in the SRS. Since it is part of the purpose of an SRS that it should be transformed (usually manually) into a computerised information system, an SRS that
  is not achievable is invalid from the deontic point of view. This specific kind of
  invalidity calls for particular means such as establishing proof of concept through
  technologically oriented prototyping.
- *Design-independent*: An SRS is design-independent if and only if there are more
  than one system design and implementation that correctly implements all requirements stated in the SRS. This is covered by validity, since if the SRS was not design-
  independent, it would be over-constrained, and these extra constraints can be looked
  upon as invalid statements in an SRS.
- *At right level of detail*: Requirements can be stated at many levels of abstractions. The
  right level of detail is a function of how the SRS is being used. Generally, the SRS
  should be specific enough so that any system built that satisfies the requirements
  in the SRS satisfies all user needs, and abstract enough so that all systems
  that satisfy all user needs also satisfy all requirements. This indicates that the
  requirements specification needs to be complete, and not over-constrained, i.e. valid,
  as discussed earlier, thus no new aspects are really included by this property.
- *Unambiguous*: An SRS is unambiguous if and only if every requirement stated
  therein has only one possible interpretation. On a high level, this can be claimed to
  be subsumed by validity and completeness. If the model is consistent and valid,
  nothing is wrong with having ambiguity, except that you should state explicitly that
  all alternative interpretations are intended. Without this explicit statement, there is
  incompleteness related to the organisational goals. This said, an unambiguous
  specification is obviously better than an ambiguous from the point of view of pragmatic quality, even if every interpretation of the ambiguity in itself is correct. For
  instance, a reader may at some point not recognise the ambiguity and consider one
  interpretation only. Davis suggests the use of formal languages to address ambiguity. Many ambiguities can also be detected on a syntactic level (see e.g. Fabbrini
  et al. 2001), but similarly as for inconsistency, what is the right interpretation must
  be decided on the semantic or deontic levels by individual humans.

6.2.8 Orthogonal Aspects

Finally, there is one of the properties suggested by Davis that can be looked upon
across all the semiotic levels namely *reusable*: An SRS is reusable if and only if its
sentences, paragraphs, and sections can be easily adopted and adapted for use in
subsequent SRS. This is dependent on many factors at different quality levels:

- The model needs to have good physical quality i.e. it must be physically represented
  in a persistent form that is available to those who potentially will want to reuse it.

- For reuse of semi-formal and formal models, Davis do not expect the actual models to be reusable as is, but rather that their presence will cause the next SRS writer to reuse the use of such modelling languages, and do it in a correct way. For this to be successful, the original models should be syntactically correct.
- In cases where one actually wants to reuse the model as is (i.e. were the domains are very similar), the model should have a high semantic quality. For white-box reuse, the model need to be modifiable, and should also be comprehensible and comprehended, thus one need to support techniques for achieving empiric and pragmatic quality. The model should also be annotated with additional statements making it easier to find the sought for model, thus influencing what is an appropriate completeness.
- Where existing models need to be compared with models developed in a separate project, social means and techniques such as model integration and conflict resolution can be useful to investigate to what extent the solutions based on the model to be reused, should actually be reused.
- Successful reuse will influence the cost of modelling in a positive way, addressing aspects of deontic quality.

6.2.9   Overall Comparison

As also discussed in (Lindland et al. 1994), the kind of overviews as those presented by Davis has some weaknesses. We see that the properties are partly overlapping. *Modifiability* is for instance related to *redundancy*, *traceability*, *machine readability*, *tracedness*, and that the specification is *organised* and *cross-referenced*. The problem appears partly because the list mixes goals and means to achieve these goals and because some goals are unrealistic, even impossible to reach. According to the first definition of complete, for example, a specification should include everything that the software is supposed to do. This kind of ideal goals is addressed in our framework with the notion of feasibility (related to the deontic quality). It is indirectly addressed also by Davis by giving suggestions on standards for an SRS through other of his properties, although he is not linking these up to the discussion on completeness.

Other important points when comparing the frameworks are:
- Whereas Davis' work can be classified as objectivistic, built on the belief that it is possible to state true, objective requirements to a CIS, we take into account that the requirements to a CIS are constructed as part of the dialogue between the involved participants. In this light, areas such as consistency and validation become more complex.
- We are able to discuss the relationships between the knowledge, models, and understanding of the individual participants of the modelling effort, and not only the relationships between the abstracted 'need of the customers' and the model in the form of an SRS on an aggregated level.

- The technical areas (physical, empirical, and syntactic quality) are surprisingly poorly covered by Davis. For pragmatic quality, only some of the many possible means described in the modelling literature are mentioned.
- Davis does not discuss social quality and agreement. Reaching agreement is by (Pohl 1994) regarded as one of the three main dimensions of a requirement specification process.
- By including the properties of requirement specifications within the framework as a specialisation of SEQUAL for this specific model type, we get a more detailed overview in the areas of semantic and deontic quality, where the work reported by Davis helps us to develop a much more detailed discussion.

6.3   Quality of Data Models

One type of models that have been used for a long time, are data models. As discussed in Sect. 3.3.4, data models are a type of structural models. Going back to ANSI SPARC (Tsichritzis and Klug 1978), one differentiates between three levels of data models:

- Conceptual model (e.g. ER models as used as example in Chap. 4)
- Logical models (e.g. in the form of relational tables)
- Physical model (e.g. a physical implementation of a relational database)

There is typically well-defined ways of going between these levels, although often automatic mappings are not sufficient in practice to get ideal database performance based on the conceptual and logical models.

When working with conceptual models, we typically concentrate on the conceptual level, although often with the goal of producing logical/physical models as part of running information systems.

Also some of the early work on quality of models focused on data models (Moody and Shanks 1994), a model that was extended (Moody 1998, 2003) based on empirical investigations on its use.

Moody (2003) contain the following wanted characteristics and metrics within the areas:

- Correctness is defined as whether the model conforms to the rules of the data modelling technique (i.e. whether it is a valid data model). This includes diagramming conventions, naming rules, definition rules, rules of composition, and normalisation. Proposed metrics:
  - 1. Number of violations to data modelling standards
  - 2. Number of instances of entity redundancy
  - 3. Number of instances of relationship redundancy
  - 4. Number of instances of attribute redundancy
- Completeness refers to whether the data model contains all information required to support the required functionality of the system.
  - 5. Number of missing requirements (Type I errors)
  - 6. Number of superfluous requirements (Type II errors)

- – 7. Number of inaccurately defined requirements
- – 8. Number of inconsistencies with process model
- Integrity is defined as whether the data model defines all business rules that apply to the data.
  - – 9. Number of missing business rules
  - – 10. Number of incorrect business rules
  - – 11. Number of business rules inconsistent with process model
  - – 12. Number of business rules redundantly defined in process model rules
- Flexibility is defined as the ease with which the data model can cope with business and/or regulatory change.
  - – 13. Number of data model elements which are subject to change
  - – 14. Probability adjusted cost of change
  - – 15. Strategic impact of change
- Understandability is defined as the ease with which the concepts and structures in the data model can be understood.
  - – 16. User rating of understandability
  - – 17. User interpretation errors
  - – 18. Application developer rating of understandability
  - – 19. Subject area-entity ratio
  - – 20. Entity-attribute ratio
- Simplicity means that the data model contains the minimum possible entities and relationships.
  - – 21. Number of entities (E)
  - – 22. System complexity (E+R)
  - – 23. Total complexity (aE+bR+cA)
- Integration is defined as the consistency of the data model with the rest of the organisation's data.
  - – 24. Number of data conflicts with Corporate Data Model
  - – 25. Number of data conflicts with existing systems
  - – 26. Number of data items duplicated in existing systems or projects
  - – 27. Rating of ability to meet corporate needs
- Implementability is defined as the ease with which the data model can be implemented within the time, budget and technology constraints of the project.
  - – 28. Development cost estimate
  - – 29. Technical risk rating

Based on the empirical investigation (which mainly perceived only metric 22, 26, and 28 to be cost beneficial to keep track of in the context of the particular case), two additional metrics were proposed:

- Metric 30. *Reuse Level.* This is the inverse or 'positive' of the level of duplication metric (Metric 26) and measures the number of existing data items reused as part of the new mode
- Metric 31. *Number of Issues by Quality Factor.* Each quality issue raised as a result of quality reviews can be classified by the quality factor it relates to. The number of issues raised and their severity by quality factor gives a 'defect frequency' which can be used for comparison over time

Although one learning from (Moody 2003) is that one might want to limit the number of metrics, it is not from this given what metrics to best include, thus we aim below for a more complete overview of aspects of data model quality, of which not necessarily all are used at the same time.

Another overview of data model (schema) quality is presented in Batini and Scannapieco (2006), containing the following areas:

- Correctness with respect to the model concerns the correct use of the concepts in the language. The negative example is to represent First Name as an entity, and not as an attribute (since First Name do not have unique existence in the real world)
- Correctness with respect to requirements
- Minimalisation – no requirement is represented more than once
- Completeness
- Pertinence that measures many unnecessary conceptual elements are included
- Readability through aesthetics
- Readability through simplicity
- Normalisation

Whereas the last applies first on the logical level, the others apply on the conceptual level and will be included below where we discuss means within each quality level in detail, starting with those areas that are specifically discussed by Moody/Shanks and Batini. These aspects from Moody are highlighted in *italic* with a starting *M-*, and those from Batini are represented in *italic* with a starting *B-* when positioning them within SEQUAL below

6.3.1   Physical Quality of a Data Model

No measures for this are included in the work of Batini and Moody. The normal measures of persistence, currency, and availability applies as with all other models.

6.3.2   Empirical Quality of a Data Model

This area is supported with some of the metrics under *M-understandability* (metric 19 and 20). In addition, it can be argued that the metrics under *M-simplicity* using metric 21, 22, and 23 and *B-readability through conciseness* applies as means at this level (similarly as *concise* is a mean for an SRS as discussed in Sect. 6.2). Traditional guidelines for graph aesthetics covered also by *B-readability through aesthetics* (as discussed in Sect. 4.3) apply in the following way:

- Angles between edges going out from the same node should not be too small. And additional aspects that makes this specifically relevant is, when cardinality constraints are given with annotations (e.g. like in Fig. 1.1) which you find in many data modelling languages.
- Minimise the area occupied by the diagram.
- Balance the diagram with respect to the axis.
- Minimise the number of bends along the edge.

- Minimise the number of crossings between edges.
- Place nodes with high degree in the centre of the drawing. This is typically central entities, whose positioning in the middle also will help to emphasise these.
- Minimise differences among nodes' dimensions (given nodes of the same type). A challenge here can specifically be in languages where attributes is listed as part of the entity-class symbols (e.g. UML class diagrams).
- Minimise the global length of edges.
- Minimise the length of the longest edge.
- Have symmetry of sons in hierarchies. In particular, relevant when you depict generalisation-hierarchies
- Have a uniform density of nodes in the drawing.
- Have verticality of hierarchical structures. This means that in a tree/hierarchy, nodes at the same level in the tree are placed along a horizontal line with a minimum distance between. Also applies in particular to structures such as generalisation hierarchies.

One can also device guidelines for the naming of concepts, depending a bit on the concrete language. For example, for an ER-model, one would have:

- Entity classes should be named with nouns and noun phrases in singular form. If a noun phrase is used, use spaces to divide the words
- Relationship classes should be named with nouns. Note that in languages where the role-name on each side of the relationship class are named, these should be named with verb phrases. For instance in ORM, these are mandated to be in so-called mixfix-notation, to support automatic verbalisation (Halpin and Curland 2006) as a paraphrasing technique to support pragmatic quality.
- Attributes should be named using nouns or adjectives. Should be unique within an entity class (different entity classes can have attributes with the same name).

When developing the logical and physical data models from the conceptual models, there might be additional guidelines, some of which are technology specific (e.g. due to reserved words in the DBMS). It should not be necessary to worry about this at the conceptual level.

6.3.3   Syntactic Quality of a Data Model

Parts of *M-correctness* (metric 1: number of violations to data modelling standard) relates to syntactic quality. Expect that this also include rules for the language used for describing business rules (Business rules being only concretely mentioned under the area *M-integrity*).

6.3.4   Semantic Quality of a Data Model

When looking upon semantic quality relative to the primary domain, we have the following properties: *M-Completeness* (metric 5: Number of missing requirements) and *M-integrity* (metric 9: Number of missing business rules relates to completeness). The same applies to Batini's point on *B-completeness*.

M-Completeness (metric 6: Number of superfluous requirements) and *M-integrity* (metric 10: Number of incorrect business rules) relates to validity. The same applies to Batini's points on *B-correctness* with respect to model and *B-correctness* with respect to respect to requirements.

M-Completeness (metric 7: Number of inaccurately defined requirements) relates to precision, which as discussed in Sect. 6.2 either is a matter of incompleteness or invalidity. Inconsistency within the data model is similarly either an example of incompleteness or invalidity. Given a parallel development of a process model, *M-completeness* (metric 8: Number of inconsistencies with process model) and *M-integrity* (metric 11: Number of business rules inconsistent with the process model) falls into this area. If the process model is rather part of the model context, it can be positioned together with the below areas.

Properties related to the model context are related to the area M-*integration*:
- Metric 24: Number of data conflicts with Corporate Data Model
- Metric 25: Number of data conflicts with existing systems

Some additional semantic means mentioned are related to redundancy. As with an SRS, unlike the other properties, redundancy is not necessarily bad. Redundancy can in fact improve empirical and pragmatic quality (see below) at the cost of conciseness. This relates to *M-correctness* (metrics 1, 2, 3), *M-integrity* (metric 12), *M-integration* (metric 26), and *B-minimalisation* (Batini).

M-Reuse (metric 30) can also be looked upon as a technique that potentially improve completeness (but as indicated in Sect. 6.2, might include issues relative to other aspects).

The main problem of redundancy hits when the SRS is changed, thus redundancy is problematic relative to *M-flexibility*, although the concrete metrics suggested is positioned under deontic quality.

6.3.5   Pragmatic Quality of a Data Model

The following metrics under *M-understandability* is positioned here (and not under empirical quality) due to the concrete mentioning of user ratings and user interpretation. This includes metric 16, 17, and 18. Verbalisation (Halpin and Curland 2006) is an interesting technique for making it easier to understand the data models. The verbalisation language for ORM 2 was architected to meet five main design criteria: Expressiveness, clarity, flexibility, localizability, and formality
- For reasons of expressiveness, both alethic and deontic modalities are supported.
- Localisation concerns as well as support of natural verbalisation for predicates of any arity dictate the use of mixfix predicates (e.g. ... introduced ... to ... on ...).
- For clarity and flexibility reasons, constraint verbalisations may be presented in positive or negative form (showing how to satisfy or violate the constraint), and may use *relational or attribute style* (employing predicate readings or role names) or a mix of the two.

6.3.6 Social Quality of a Data Model

Moody and Batini do not address this area. Techniques discussed in Sect. 4.7 are relevant to take into account in this respect, specifically those being based on schema integration (Francalanci and Pernici 1993).

6.3.7 Deontic Quality of a Data Model

The remaining metrics from Moody belong at this level, in particular
- *M-Flexibility*, in particular as the metrics are phrased
  - Metric 13: Number of data model elements that are subject to change. This relate to the SRS point on *annotated by relative stability*
  - Metric 14: Probability adjusted cost of change
  - Metric 15: Strategic impact of change
- *M-Integration* (metric 27: Rating of ability to meet corporate needs)
- *M-Implementability* (compare with the characteristic *achievable* for an SRS in Sect. 6.2)
  - Metric 28: Development cost estimate
  - Metric 29: Technical risk rating
- *B-Pertinence* relates to the aspects discussed under an SRS relating to *at right level of detail* (in particular the aspect of being over-constrained)
- Other possible relevant aspects taken from the discussion on an SRS in Sect. 6.2 are
  - *Annotated by relative importance*
  - *Annotated by version*
  - *Traceable*
  - *Design-independent*
  - *Unambiguous*

6.3.8 Final Remarks

As with an SRS in the previous section, we see some benefit both for SEQUAL and for a framework for the quality of data models
- The eight areas of Moody are poorly conceptualised, as can be witnessed with that metrics for the same area is positioned at different quality levels in SEQUAL.
- The overview of Moody is weak relative to the physical, empirical, and social level.
- The work of Batini is weak on the physical, syntactic, pragmatic, and social level.
- The work by Moody enrich the areas of semantic and deontic quality for this type of model.

Table 6.2 Dimensions of data quality

Dimension name	Category	Definition
Accuracy	Syntactic	Distance between v (the correct value) and v' (the incorrect value)
	Semantic	
Completeness		Degree to which all values are present in a data collection
Time-related aspects	Currency	Degree to which the data is up-to-date
	Volatility	Frequency with which data vary with time
	Timeliness	How current the data is for the task at hand
Consistency		Coherence of the same datum, represented in multiple copies, or different data to respect integrity constraints and rules
Interpretability		Concerns the documentation including the data model, and other metadata that are available to correctly interpret the meaning of data
Accessibility		Data is accessible for those needing access to the data in a format that can be understood
Quality of information source	Beliveability	Is the data provided true, real and credible?
	Reputation	Is the source normally credible?
	Objectivity	Is the source believed to be objective?

6.4 Data Quality

Traditionally, one have looked at model quality for models on the M1 (type) level (to use the DIF levels presented in Sect. 3.1.3). On the other hand, it is clear especially in enterprise modelling that the relevant models also contain aspects on the M0 or instance level, an area described as containing data (or objects in MOF). Thus, also data quality can be looked upon relative to the SEQUAL framework. Discussions on data quality must be looked upon in concert with discussions on data model (or schema) quality, as discussed above. Here, we will start looking at how the dimensions of data quality fit the levels of the SEQUAL framework, similar to how we mapped the work on requirements specifications and data models above.

There are a number of approaches to the discussion of dimensions of data quality. Different authors use terms in the area somewhat differently. I will base this section on the framework presented in Batini and Scannapieco (2006), where the following aspects are discussed relative to the data values. The examples relates to a data in a relational database, with tables including tuples having attributes of pre-defined values, and in addition include integrity constraints (Table 6.2).

When looking upon the data quality in isolation, the defined data model can be looked upon as part of the context (i.e. a pre-existing model that this model should relate to). Obviously, how the data is meant to be and actually are used influences on the perceived quality of the data. To also capture this, Price and Shanks (2004, 2005) use the term information quality to combine a product-based and service-based view. The product-based perspective, covered by traditional data quality, focuses on the design and internal IS view. From this view, quality is defined in terms of the degree to which the data meets initial requirements specifications or the degree to which the data corresponds to the relevant real-world phenomena that it purports to represent. The limitation with this is that even if data corresponds to requirements specifications or the real-world, there can still be quality deficiencies with respect to actual use-related data requirements, which may differ from the planned uses catered for in the initial specifications. This leads to a service-based perspective of quality, commonly called *information quality*, which focuses on the information consumer's response to their task-based interactions with the IS. Price and Shanks defines this area in the following way, building upon traditional semiotic theory (Morris 1938). Based on empirical evaluations of the original framework presented in 2004, the following quality categories has been defined (Price and Shanks 2005).

Syntactic Criteria (based on rule conformance)
- *Conforming to metadata, i.e. integrity rules.* Data follows specified database integrity rules.

Semantic Criteria (based on external correspondence)
- *Mapped completely.* Every real-world phenomenon is represented.
- *Mapped unambiguously.* Each identifiable data unit represents at most one specific real-world phenomenon.
- *Phenomena mapped correctly.* Each identifiable data unit maps to the correct real-world phenomenon.
- *Properties mapped correctly.* Non-identifying (i.e. non-key) attribute values in an identifiable data unit match the property values for the represented real-world phenomenon.
- *Mapped consistently.* Each real-world phenomenon is either represented by at most one identifiable data unit or by multiple, but consistent identifiable units or by multiple identifiable units whose inconsistencies are resolved within an acceptable time frame.
- *Mapped meaningfully.* Each identifiable data unit represents at least one specific real-world phenomenon.

Pragmatic Criteria (use-based consumer perspective)
- *Accessible (easy, quick).* Data is easy and quick to retrieve.
- *Suitably presented (suitably formatted, precise, and measured in units).* Data is presented in a manner appropriate for its use, with respect to format, precision, and units.
- *Flexibly presented (easily aggregated; format, precision, and units easily converted).* Data can be easily manipulated and the presentation customised as needed, with respect to aggregating data and changing the data format, precision, or units.
- *Timely.* The currency (age) of the data is appropriate to its use.
- *Understandable.* Data is presented in an intelligible manner.
- *Secure.* Data is appropriately protected from damage or abuse (including unauthorised access, use, or distribution).
- *Type-sufficient.* The data includes all of the types of information important for its use.

- *Allowing access to relevant metadata.* Appropriate metadata is available to define, constrain, and document data.
- *Perceptions of the syntactic and semantic criteria defined earlier.*

We discuss means within each quality level in detail, starting with those areas that are specified by Batini et al. and Price et al. These are highlighted in *italic* when positioning them within SEQUAL below.

6.4.1 Physical data quality

Aspects of *persistence*, data being *accessible (Price)* for all *(accessibility (Batini))*, *currency (Batini)* and *security (Price)* cover aspects on the physical level, although this area can be extended with a lot of the standard database-functionality.

6.4.2 Empirical data quality

Is addressed by *understandable (Price)*.

6.4.3 Syntactic data quality

Conforming to metadata (Price) including to the expected data type of the data (as described in the data model/data schema) are the main measures of syntactic data quality.

6.4.4 Semantic data quality

Completeness is covered both with *completeness (Batini) mapped completely (Price)*, and *mapped unambiguously (Price)*.

Validity is covered by *accuracy (Batini)*, both syntactic and semantic, the difference between these is rather to decide on how incorrect the data is, *phenomena mapped correctly (Price), properties mapped correctly (Price)* and *mapped meaningfully (Price)*. Since the rules of representation are formally given, *consistency (Batini)/ mapped consistently (Price)* is normally also related to validity.

6.4.5 Pragmatic data quality

The main aspect at this level is *interpretability (Batini), suitably presented (Price)* and *flexibly presented (Price). Allowing access to relevant metadata (Price)* is an important mean to achieve comprehension.

6.4.6   Social data quality

The area *quality of information source (Batini)* touches important aspect as for the social quality of the data.

6.4.7   Deontic data quality

A number of aspects are on this level. Whereas *currency (Batini)* was put at the physical levels, aspects do decide *volatility (Batini)* and *timeliness (Batini)/ timely (Price)* needs to relate to the goal of having the data. The same is the case for *type-sufficient (Price)*, the inclusion of all the types of information important for its use.

6.5   Quality of Ontologies

Whereas we in Chap. 1, use the term 'ontological' in a philosophical sense, computer science have also adapted a more mundane meaning of the term. An ontology of a domain typically captures essential established facts about a domain, and applies a global logic for reasoning about these facts, for transforming between different data representations etc. Ontology languages are better equipped for representing e.g. product property structures, than conventional software engineering approaches such as ER-modelling or UML class diagrams. However, by demanding a formal, precise, and global representation, ontologies are not well equipped to capture local, heterogeneous product views from different disciplines, or unfolding, incomplete, and incoherent models reflecting the current state of product information during e.g. the early phases of design. Semantic approaches are designed to simplify automatic reasoning, but the critical problems of pragmatic information capture from users, inter-disciplinary sense-making and interpretation of product information, demands more interpretive flexibility and situated, user-controlled analysis, and reasoning. Ontology languages were discussed briefly in Sect. 3.3.4.

In Chandrasekaran et al. (1999), different kinds of ontologies are classified based on the level of generality:

- Top-level ontologies describe very general concepts like space, time, matter, object, event, and action. They are independent of a particular problem or domain. Top-level ontologies in some literature are also called upper-level ontologies.
- Domain ontologies describe the vocabulary related to a generic domain (like medicine, or automobiles).
- Task ontologies describe generic tasks or activities (like diagnosis or selling). Application ontologies describe concepts depending both on a particular domain and task.

In Strasunskas and Tomassen (2008), an overview of existing ontology quality assessment is provided. We will below discuss these relative to the levels of quality in

SEQUAL. The following section is based on their overview. Most existing quality assessments aim at defining a generic quality evaluation framework and, therefore, do not take into account specific application of ontologies. The OntoQA framework (Tartir et al. 2005) is proposed to evaluate ontologies and knowledge bases. There metrics are divided into two categories: Schema metrics and instance metrics (vs. discussion on data model quality and data quality earlier in this chapter). The Ontometric (Lozano-Tello and Gomez-Perez 2004) methodology defines a reference Ontology that consists of metrics to evaluate ontology, methodology, language and tool (used to develop ontology) – 117 metrics in total. T Analysis of the literature shows that ontologies are typically examined according to five aspects: Structure (empirical and partly syntactic quality), population of classes (empirical quality), syntax (syntactic quality), vocabulary (semantic quality), and usage statistics (social quality).

- *Structural evaluation.* Structural evaluation deals with assessment of taxonomical relations vs. other semantic relations, under some presupposition about what is a better structure of the model. This is what is termed taxonomic quality in (Sampson et al. 2011), but what from the point of view of SEQUAL can be positioned as a specialisation of empirical quality. In OntoClean (Guarino and Welty 2004), the authors define the following areas:
  - Essence: A property of an entity is essential to that entity if it must be true in every possible world.
  - Rigidity: A property is rigid if it is essential to all it's possible instances.
  - Identity: Being able to recognise the individual entities of the world being the same.
  - Unity: Being able to recognise all the parts that form an individual entity.

  In OntoSelect (Buitelaar et al. 2004) metric, called *structure*, is used. The value of the structure measure is simply the number of properties relative to the number of classes in the ontology. Similarly, *density measure* defined in (Alani et al. 2006) indicates how well a given concept is defined in the ontology. *Relationship richness* (Tartir et al. 2005) reflects the diversity of relations and placement of relations in the ontology. Looking on the discussion of the variety of needs and specialisations on the core abstraction mechanisms discussed in Chap. 3, it is questionable how useful such metrics are. If the richness is low (i.e. a lot of the syntactical features of the language are not used in the ontology), one might question the domain appropriateness of the ontology language, alternatively the participant appropriateness. Given that these presuppositions on how a good model (ontology) should be structured are typically supported in the ontology modelling language on the other hand, these can be looked upon as a specialisation of syntactic quality.

- *Population of classes.* This quality aspect is based on instance related metrics. We discussed this topic briefly together with structural aspects when describing classification in Sect. 3.1.3 referring to the work of Parsons and Wand (1997a, b). Tartir et al. (2005) define *class richness* that measures how instances are distributed across classes. The amount of classes having instances is compared with the overall number of classes. *Average population* indicates the number of instances compared to the number of classes. It is used to determine how well a knowledge base has been populated, again according to some presumptions on what a good ontology is. One aim for such metrics is to ensure comprehension of the overall model, thus we position this is a specialisation of empirical quality.

- *Evaluation of syntax.* This checks whether an ontology is syntactically correct (syntactic quality). Syntactic quality is a central quality aspect in most quality frameworks (e.g., Burton-Jones et al. 2005; Lozano-Tello and Gomez-Perez 2004).
- *Cohesion to domain and vocabulary.* Correspondence between an ontology and a domain is another important aspect in ontology quality evaluation (semantic quality). There, ontology concepts (including taxonomical relations and properties) are checked against terminology used in the domain. In the OntoKhoj approach (Patel et al. 2003), ontologies are classified into a directory of topics by extracting textual data from the ontology (i.e. names of concepts and relations). Similarly, Brewster et al. (2004) extracted a set of relevant domain-specific terms from documents. The amount of overlap between the domain-specific terms and the terms appearing in the ontology is then used to measure the fit between the ontology and the corpus. Similar lexical approach is taken in EvaLexon (Spyns and Reinberger 2005); here, recall/precision type metrics are used to evaluate how well ontology triples were extracted from a corpus. (Burton-Jones et al. 2005) define a metric called *accuracy* that is measured as a percentage of false statements in an ontology (vs. validity as part of semantic quality).
- *Usage statistics and metadata.* Evaluation of this aspect focuses on the level of annotation of ontologies, i.e. the metadata about an ontology and its elements. There are defined three basic levels of usability profiling in (Gangemi et al. 2006) as follows. *Recognition annotations* take care of user-satisfaction, provenance, and version information; *efficiency annotations* deal with application-history information; and the last level is about *organisational-design information.* These aspects relates partly to social quality (user satisfaction) and partly to deontic quality. Burton-Jones et al. (2005) define similar metrics, namely, *relevance* assesses the amount of statements that involve syntactic features marked as useful or acceptable to the user/agent (deontic quality); *history* accounts for how many times a particular ontology has been accessed relatively to other ontologies (social quality). In Burton-Jones et al. (2005), a metric called *authority* – i.e. how many other ontologies use concepts from this ontology. This is also related to social quality.

We see that aspect relative to physical quality, pragmatic quality, and partly deontic quality is little discussed in the literature. As we have discussed quality of data models in a separate section, when we discuss quality of ontologies, it entails:

- The ontologies are models represented as a logical theory, being hierarchically structured.
- The ontologies are expected to be useful across different organisational settings (since it is expected to represent a shared conceptualisation).

Given the focus on logic, pragmatic quality relative to tool understanding is often implicitly emphasised, and not comprehension of humans, although this might often be of interest for those developing ontologies (ontology engineers) and the domain experts involved in validation ontologies, and should be given more weight. Usage of ontologies over organisational boundaries can be done for different purposes, thus the goal of the ontology (i.e. model) can be varying. Examples of goals are:

- Structure web-content to enable machine-based communication to fulfil the original semantic web vision (Berners-Lee et al. 2001). Related to this is the use of ontologies for service retrieval.
- Use of ontologies to support human information retrieval (Strasunskas and Tomassen 2008).
- The use of ontologies to ensure interoperability: Semantic annotation (Lin et al. 2006; Lin and Krogstie 2010) is based on a reference ontology that is used to construct annotation expressions, aimed at giving a clear, agreed, unambiguous meaning to documental (human oriented) knowledge or to enterprise software elements used in co-operative processes. Semantic annotation can be used to associate a formal meaning to enterprise models and in particular to information structures and business processes in order to realise a semantic interoperability platform.
- The reuse of ontologies: Since an ontology is meant to capture general information about the world, it is expected to be possible to be able to use an existing ontology related to a domain/concept in another application (Hella and Krogstie 2010).

What to discuss as part of quality of ontologies is thus dependent on the overall goal, since it differs a lot if the main user of the result is a system or a person. We will exemplify with the last aspect related to reuse of ontologies for a usage area where formal reasoning with the help of the ontology is attempted.

6.5.1 Quality of Ontologies for Reuse

We view ontologies as models that can be reused or built on, and apply SEQUAL to provide a systematic analysis of the quality of ontologies. The main concepts or sets of the SEQUAL framework and their relationships are described below. For each set, we refer to the ontology to be evaluated in general and specify what the desired qualities are:

- **G** – The goal is reuse as is or as a basis of an existing ontology in the relevant domain (see **D** below) to be able to provide personalised services.
- **K** – The knowledge of the evaluators
- **L** – The language the profile ontology is represented in
- **M** – The model (ontology) to be evaluated
- **D** – The modelling domain covered by the evaluated ontology. We need an ontology that supports the description of a user to be able to receive personalised services
- **T** – All the statements in the ontology represented and interpreted by a tool
- **I** – Social actor interpretation is the set of all statements which the externalised model consists of, here as perceived by the evaluator

The quality categories described next are used for the evaluation:

- *Physical quality*: The ontology should be physically available and it should be possible to make changes to it. An available ontology should be possible to open and update in an ontology editor. In this way it will be possible to view and access the ontology, and further make changes to it if necessary. We decided to use Protégé in the evaluation reported in Sect. 7.2, a free, open source ontology editor with an active community.

- *Empirical quality*: If a visual representation of the ontology is provided, it should be intuitively and easy to understand, following the guidelines of graph aesthetics. The metrics relative to the population of classes and structure (taxonomic quality) would be relevant in this regard as discussed above. High empirical quality will support the achievement of pragmatic quality.
- *Syntactic quality*: The ontology should be represented according to the syntax of a preferred machine readable language. More specifically, we prefer in the evaluation reported in Sect. 7.2 below OWL DL. It is a W3C recommendation, and provides ensured decidability. WonderWeb OWL Ontology Validator has been used for OWL sublanguage specification. As discussed above it is an advantage that the structural (taxonomic) quality of the ontology is good.
- *Semantic quality*: The ontology should cover the area of interest fully or partially so that it is possible to easily extend it to do cover the domain (completeness). It could also be possible to take out a subset of the ontology so that it does not cover more than what is necessary (validity). As part of validity, we have the area accuracy as discussed above. Terms used in the ontology should be congruent with words used in the domain. It is important that there is good correspondence between the concepts needed and the ones provided by the existing ontology. Our goal is not to create a new standard personal profile, but to be able to reuse an already tested and used model. Semantic quality is the most important quality category in the reported case.
- *Pragmatic quality*: It should be possible to understand what the ontology contains, and being able to use it for the meant purpose. The pragmatic quality category also includes provision of necessary documentation. Documentation that is easy to understand is advantageous, and it should be consistent with the actual ontology.
- *Social quality*: The ontology should have a relatively large group of followers and parts should be used by other ontologies (this can be judged through metadata, e.g. recognition annotation, efficiency annotation).
- *Deontic quality*: The ontology should be freely available and accessible through a freely available tool. It should be available in a standard format and it should be probable that it is available and supported for the coming years.

An example of the use of this framework is presented in Sect. 7.2.

6.6   Quality of Interactive Models

Compared with requirements models and data models (discussed in Sects. 6.2 and 6.3, which typically first will get a noticeable effect on the domain a long time after the models are developed), so-called interactive models have a much larger potential for bringing about changes to the domain directly. As described in Sect. 2.3.6, a model is *active* if it directly influences the reality it reflects, i.e. changes to the model also change the way some actors perceive reality. Actors in this context include users as well as software components. Since process models describe – or even prescribe – specific paths of action under specific circumstances, the road from interpretation of the model to action may be very short, especially for interactive models, where changes have potential immediate effect on system behaviour at least for a restricted number of users. This also makes it especially important to understand and be able to evaluate the quality of such models. We will here present a specialisation of SEQUAL for this purpose.

An interactive model is immersed in its usage context. Model articulation and activation take place concurrently, and are mutually dependent upon each other. Agreement among actors is vital for large scale IS development, because it is costly to fix errors late in the project. For an interactive model, the costs of fixing errors can often be diminished. The goal of social quality for interactive models thus becomes to support social learning and construction of shared understanding rather that strict agreement.

Similarly, global semantic and syntactic correctness becomes less important because users can be put in charge of resolving inconsistencies during interactive activation. For learning, the ability to represent inconsistent points of view is crucial. A system should thus not deny articulation of syntactically incomplete model fragments, but instead capture inconsistent views so that they can be negotiated.

Interactive activation implies that the goal of semantic completeness is replaced by a goal of letting the users articulate their reality at the level of detail and specificity that they find useful. Incompleteness can be resolved at the time of activation.

Interactive modelling quality (Krogstie and Jørgensen 2002) demands a more dynamic approach than when we look at e.g. a requirements specification, focusing on how these sets of statements interact and influence each other in the interdependent processes of articulation, activation, and reuse. This perspective is conceptualised below, defining core processes as sequences of activities that transform statement sets in the quality framework model. A focus on core processes rather than static quality parameters emphasise interdependencies and trade-offs which designers of interactive systems must resolve. The rest of this section describes basic concepts in this framework.

- *Articulation ($D \rightarrow M$)*. Articulation is the process where domain features are represented in the model (M) by means of the modelling language (L). It should (but does need to) increase the semantic quality of the model.
- *Manual Articulation ($D \rightarrow K \rightarrow M$)*. Most articulation is manual, involving the external representation of participant knowledge (K) about the domain (D) into the model (M) using a language (L). In addition to empirical, physical, and semantic quality, it depends on the quality of participant knowledge about the domain, and the appropriateness of the language with respect to the domain and participants' knowledge.
- *Automatic Articulation ($D \rightarrow T \rightarrow M$)*. Sensors are computerised components that capture information from the model domain, through interfaces to external information systems or hardware devices.

- *External change ($D(t) \rightarrow D(t+1)$).* Changes in the domain (D) may become known to the participants of the project (K). Known changes may become articulated into the model M.
- *Model Evolution ($M(t) \rightarrow M(t+1)$).* Model evolution may be triggered by change and reflected through articulation, or it is motivated by the need to cause future domain change through activation.
- *Activation ($M \rightarrow D$).* Model activation involves model-guided actions that transform the domain (D).
- *Automatic Activation ($M \rightarrow T \rightarrow D$).* Automatic activation implies that the model is interpreted and acted upon by a computerised component, in our terminology a *model activator*. The *tool appropriateness* of the modelling language reflects its potential for automatic activation.
- *Manual Activation ($M \rightarrow I \rightarrow K \rightarrow D$).* Human actions based on an interpretation (I) of the model (M) constitute a manual activation process. The involved actors may also have created the model themselves (being participants in the modelling). Performing actions involve changing the domain D, and should thus be reflected in the model M. While automatic activation is deducible from the model and thus already captured, manual actions include elements of human model interpretation, which should be captured in the model.
- *Interactive Activation ($M \rightarrow I \leftrightarrow T \rightarrow D$).* Interactive activation exists in different forms. In many workflow systems, it is the technical component that tells the users what to do (e.g. by putting tasks in their inboxes). In other words, the modelled sequence of tasks is automatically interpreted, but the tasks are performed manually ($M \rightarrow T \rightarrow I \rightarrow D$). In graphical user interfaces, the opposite sequence ($I \rightarrow T \rightarrow D$) is more common. Here, it is up to the user to select which operation the system should perform next. If an action is the result of interactive or automatic model activation, its effects should be automatically captured in the model. This scheme increases the semantic quality without extra work for the users, completing the cycle $M \rightarrow I \leftrightarrow T \rightarrow D \rightarrow M$.
- *Learning ($M \rightarrow K$).* The model contributes to an increase in knowledge by the participant of the domain D.
- *Meta-modelling ($K \rightarrow L$).* Meta-modelling involves changing the modelling language. It is typically carried out in order to improve the comprehensibility of the language for human actors, or to make it more suitable in a specific domain. Meta-modelling faces similar problems as reuse, but may also benefit from the immediate domain availability, which characterises interactive models. Local language adaptations can potentially increase the pragmatic and semantic qualities of the resulting models.

As we understand, compared to traditional models used during the early phases of systems development, interactive models are faced with a different set of requirements. We summarise these using the sets in the SEQUAL quality framework, before outlining how these requirements influence the discussion of quality at the different levels within the quality framework.

- **G**, the goals of modelling are more related to have an up to date, tailored model to support the individual users or smaller groups of closely cooperating users in their actual tasks, and is less directly linked to overall goals of an organisation. Note that this is obviously a balance, since one should not be able to change parts of the model that it is defined as very important for the organisation to keep stable (e.g. rules for performing financial transactions that must be adhered to of legal reasons). In addition, the model should support individual and organisational learning.

- *L*, the language extension: The languages used need to be simple enough, and models should be represented in such a way that a large number of people with a diversity of backgrounds are able to use them. The language might be updated either in a preparatory step or as an integrated part of modelling though meta-modelling.
- *D*, the domain is more closely related to the task at hand, and not to a generic, abstract domain. It is also more obvious to see how the modelling quite instantly are able to have organisational effect and change the domain through articulation of new knowledge.
- *M*, the currently externalised model: as normal.
- *A*, K_m and K_s. A wider range of people are actively involved in modelling, amplifying the social, psychological, and organisational aspects. More people (potentially all users) act as modellers and model interpreters, thus the difference between the set of modellers and general social actor at least in the initial articulation is smaller.
- *I*, the social actor interpretation: need to be able to quickly update the interpretation of model changes done by one person that also influences other people.
- *T*, the technical actor interpretation: the model as interpreted by information systems. The models are available at run-time, but might only be partly defined, i.e. the tools used must be made with interaction possibilities in mind, and be able to respond quickly to changes induced by humans.

The main quality types are specialised in the following way:

Physical quality
For active models, the modellers include not only software professionals, but also end users. Hence, stronger requirements to support physical quality are likely, both because one will want to have the models available for all users to be able to update them more frequently due to learning, and this needs to be supported. As will be discussed below, it must be possible to differentiate which parts of the model that can be changed by the user and those that cannot.

Empirical quality
Due to the local nature of use of the extensions of interactive models, the requirements to an aesthetic layout are less than for models acting to present a common picture or a standard process in an organisation.

Syntactic quality
As a result of providing user oriented models, interactive model approaches will have to enhance formal syntax means by providing more functionality in the area of

error detection, prevention and recovery; especially regarding allowing the continued enactment of completed, error-free parts, and the support for filling out missing pieces in the model at the appropriate time.

Semantic quality

Actions often involve changing the domain D, and should thus be reflected back into the model M. If an action is supported by an information system with interactive models, it can be automatically captured, increasing the semantic quality of the interactive model without extra work for the users. The possibility to rapidly update the model (and thus the system) is one of the main advantages with this approach. In systems engineering, new approaches like incremental development and agile methods attempt to shorten the learning and reimplementation cycle, but they are still hampered with a long time-span from learning of the end-user to model and system-change that can benefit the end-user compared to what can be achieved with interactive models. In addition, users are likely to have more in-depth knowledge K of their domain D than software developers and customer representatives who seldom take part in the practice of the domain although might have been involved at a concrete level earlier. Consequently, the potential for high semantic quality at the time of activation is greater. Hence, simplicity, adaptability, and user-orientedness of the modelling language are even more crucial for interactive models than for more traditional models.

Pragmatic quality

The core of active models is how models are *activated*. Activation implies *interpretation* of the model and corresponding *action* by either the social or the technical actors. Technical pragmatic quality demands complete models with an operational semantics, while the social pragmatic quality of the models and the cognitive economy of externalisation ($K \rightarrow M$) often demands more flexible, informal approaches. Interactive model interpretation enables models with user-controlled levels of formality, detail, and preciseness, bridging the gap between theory and practice.

This immediate nature of active models, stemming from the interaction of the real world domain and active model, can also enhance the social pragmatic quality of the models. When both the real world and the model that reflects it are available and adaptable for the users, the connections between them are easier to understand. Simulation and training methods can be developed that utilises this connection. Zuboff's study of industrial control rooms (Zuboff 1988) shows great benefits for users that are able to work both with the conceptual tools of the computer and the physical environment of the work place side by side.

Social quality

In traditional systems development, agreement among participants about the requirements is crucial since they form the basis for a lot of detailed technical work that cannot easily be redone. Active models have a more immediate connection to the system and the environment it represents than traditional analysis and design models, so users have access also to the domain when negotiating a shared understanding. Social quality in the sense of agreement is thus perhaps not as important when assumptions readily can be tested immediately in the real world, at least when being used among a limited number of people.

If an active model is to be reused in another setting, agreement on semantics is more important. Social quality of interactive models influences the processes of negotiating meaning and domesticating reusable model fragments into the local situation and work practice (Voss et al. 2000). In these processes, the ability to represent conflicting interpretations and make local modifications is just as important as the ability to represent agreement (the end result) in an unambiguous way. Also, since people learn through their work and use of the models, agreement is likely to be partial and temporary.

Deontic quality

When using interactive models, the models are more a work tool for the individual and group, utilising models on the instance level. Thus the primary goals for the model to fulfil are those of the user and group in their situated action. When reusing models that of some reason are not to be changed (for instance because they decode a procedure that need to be done in a certain way to be legally correct), these organisational rules have to be enforced by the support-system, thus it must be possible to differentiate which parts of the model that can be changed by the user and those that cannot, and potentially having this controlled by the role of the user. Tracking of model elements back to organisational goals or earlier baseline models are general means for supporting the deontic quality.

Interactive models should be coupled to organisational learning. At the organisational level, process models are particular knowledge representations resembling organisational images (Argyris and Schön 1973). An organisation's theory of action is embedded in a behavioural world that shapes and constrains its theory-in-use. To achieve double-loop learning – i.e. 'doing the right things' instead of 'doing the things right' – models must include links to intentional aspects (Carlsen and Gjersvik 1997). The gap between real and modelled processes has been highlighted as a major inhibiting factor of process support systems and organisational learning (Argyris and Schön 1973) alike. Thus, interactive models have a great potential for flexibly supporting knowledge management and business process improvement. At the group level, organisational learning and social reality construction influence how we view the creation, update, and enactment of process fragments. Organisations are socially constructed through joint action by involved social actors. Here, interactive models as an articulation of work play the role of boundary objects for supporting perspective making and perspective taking (Boland and Tenkasi 1995). By giving users control over the models, we empower them to externalise and share knowledge.

Modelling as an action impacts as we have seen above the different sets in the quality framework. We briefly describe these impacts here, summarising potential aspects of pragmatics seen in this light:

- Change in goal G: Based on the modelling, you might realise that the overall goal for your process should be updated, i.e. supporting double-loop learning.

- Change in language L: It might be found that the chosen language is not appropriate for modelling the current domain by the involved participants, and has to be enhanced or replaced, i.e. meta-modelling takes place. One can look upon meta-modelling as a kind of triple-loop learning. In single-loop learning, you adjust to the existing model, in double-loop learning you adjust the model (i.e. explicit knowledge about what is right), whereas in meta-modelling you adjust the way of representing the model.
- Change in domain D: The model makes one realise problems with the existing process, thus leading to business process improvement.
- Change in knowledge K: Learning by the participants through modelling and activation of models.
- Change in interpretation I: Through validation tasks, one often changes the understanding of the model.
- Change in tool interpretation T: For instance, by developing new or changing existing model activators.

6.7   Quality of Maps

As discussed in Sect. 3.3.9, the modelling of location is of increasing importance. The modelling of space has a long history in the realm of cartography, and it is interesting to see how SEQUAL can be applied on other types of visual knowledge representations than traditional node and edge diagrams, and how the quality of combined conceptual and topographic models (maps) can be supported.

6.7.1   Characteristics of Maps

Maps have a long history related to the making, studying and use of this type of knowledge representation. A map is commonly a reference to a depiction of the world. We have defined maps as an abstract representation that preserves the geographical topological information. The definition thus also includes more unusual maps (e.g. diagrams such as metro-maps) as well as preserving the common understanding of maps. Although the history of map-making is much longer than the history of conceptual modelling, guidelines for quality of maps is less structured than guidelines for quality of models. On the other hand, since the main purpose of a map is communication of meaning using signs (just as conceptual models), one would expect many of the same issues to be relevant.

In cartography, the notion of map communication has been recognised (MacEachren 1995) and methods towards understanding this have been developed. Human interpretation relates directly to this notion and one could argue that the communication models developed, including the 'map use cube' (MacEachren 1995), are enabling methods for increasing the comprehension of the map.

Related to comprehension is the work by (Bertin 1983) on visual variables described in Chap. 5. In addition to the visual variables, attention towards classification of symbols has been suggested (Robinson et al. 1995). The foundation is the notion of the graphic primitives *point*, *line* and *area*, which is considered to be main elements for constructing a map (the meta-meta model). Emphasising these primitives can thus affect the empirical quality, such as for instance emphasising of points and areas to increase attention towards concept of these types. Another field that has been influential for discussion of empirical quality of maps is Gestalt psychology (Ware 2000) also described in Chap. 5.

6.7.2 MAPQUAL

In Nossum (2008), guidelines for quality of maps following the categories of SEQUAL have been developed, which we here term MAPQUAL. Although MAPQUAL to a large extend is a specialisation of SEQUAL, there are also some distinct differences that makes it more natural to look upon these as two related frameworks (i.e. the variants of the generic SEQUAL framework is not a strict hierarchy, although we can use the same categories for both SEQUAL and MAPQUAL).

This section aims at investigating the most significant differences between the two frameworks. The results from the investigation will provide a basis for identifying problem areas when combining conceptual models and cartographic maps and thus pose as a basis for developing new guidelines with respect to this kind of combined models.

The discussion is structured by each quality facet for both map/model quality and language quality highlighting the differences.

6.7.2.1 Language Quality

The differentiation between language and model (map) are not common to find in cartography. There exists no tradition of defining languages in a strict manner for making maps, although standardisations towards both symbol sets and rules for applying them exist. MAPQUAL recognise this and aims at investigating how existing cartographic research can be structured following the SEQUAL structure of language quality. The discussion will first go into some foundational differences on the meta-meta level and then investigate each quality facet, and shed light on whether there are differences between the two frameworks or not.

Cartography revolves, generally, around geographical information, which is strongly reflected in the visualisation used. Generally, the visualisation method can be said to comprise three graphic primitives point, line and area and relations between these (Points being within an area, lines crossing an area etc.). This is inherently different from meta-meta models in conceptual modelling which usually comprise of nodes and edges between nodes (alternatively edges to other edges in addition), in addition to containment.

- Domain appropriateness: Due to the lack of discussion and formal separation of domain and language in cartography, MAPQUAL is similar to SEQUAL with respect to domain appropriateness. It is believed that most of the rational in

SEQUAL holds true for a cartographic context even when a formal separation and definition of cartographic domain and language occurs.

- Participant appropriateness: As mentioned by Nossum (2008), cartography has a tradition of exploiting the 'natural' or cognitive knowledge of participants to a large extent. For example, the use of colour for type of areas in a map reflect colour in the real world. In conceptual modelling, the tradition of creating a new language and thus disseminate this knowledge is more common. While of course both approaches consider the fundamental human perception research, they approach it slightly differently. Although they have different approaches to participant appropriateness, the understanding and discussion of participant appropriateness of a language is fairly similar in both MAPQUAL and SEQUAL.

- Modeller (cartographer) appropriateness: Similar to participant appropriateness, MAPQUAL and SEQUAL are similar with respect to modeller appropriateness. Although it should be mentioned that there seems to be less emphasis in cartography towards this quality facet than in conceptual modelling.

- Comprehensibility appropriateness: Comprehensibility is divided into two discussions: Conceptual basis and external representation. Conceptual basis comprise the discussion on which concepts that are included in the language. SEQUAL provides several concrete guidelines for the conceptual basis as will be discussed in the next chapter. These guidelines have validity in cartography as well as for conceptual modelling. Thus MAPQUAL and SEQUAL are similar in this respect. External representation focus on how the notation of the language is formed, i.e. the graphical aspects of the language. In this facet, there are significant differences between MAPQUAL and SEQUAL. Cartography has a strong tradition of investigating graphic design principles and especially mentioned are so-called visual variables (Bertin 1983). SEQUAL also draw on the visual variables; however, MAPQUAL and cartography are more geared towards extensive use of these properties. Traditionally, maps have a heavier focus on the use of colours and the use of texture as a visual technique, and then use colours that are intuitive (E.g. green for forest, blue for oceans, lakes and rivers etc.). SEQUAL encourage to be able to support a free approach to composition of symbols. Such free composition of symbols cannot be a general guideline in cartography as the geographical attributes often are constraining this freedom. Thus, one can argue that achieving high aesthetics in cartography is more complex than in conceptual modelling, where graph aesthetics can support the achievement of aesthetics. Concrete guidelines where SEQUAL differs from MAPQUAL are:
  - *Composition of symbols in aesthetically pleasing way (i.e. crossing lines, long lines etc.).* Generally not applicable in cartography in this sense (but for other purposes e.g. to overlay different areas with different visual variables).
  - *A linking line between concepts indicates relationship.* Semantics of lines are generally different in cartography.
  - *A line linking closed contours can have different colours or other graphical attributes – indicating an attribute or type of relationship.* Semi-valid for cartography, however not in the context of relationship.

- Tool appropriateness: Tool appropriateness is traditionally not considered in cartography. Thus, MAPQUAL is similar to SEQUAL on the discussion of tool appropriateness, although with less focus on executional semantics.
- Organisational appropriateness: MAPQUAL is fairly similar to SEQUAL with respect to organisational appropriateness, although MAPQUAL focus more on a cartographic context and the current standardisation efforts in this area.

6.7.3   Comparing Quality of Maps and Quality of Models

We here discuss the different levels of quality.
- Physical quality: MAPQUAL is fairly similar to SEQUAL with respect to physical quality. Cartography is traditionally more geared towards making tangible representation of maps (i.e. printed maps) – although this is shifting towards more intangible representations for instance in a software environment (i.e. web mapping tools). SEQUAL focuses much on guidelines for a modelling environment and different functionalities that it should provide. It should be noted that these guidelines are adapted to an information systems context; however, the guidelines should hold true for a cartographic environment as well – especially for navigational functionality.
- Empirical quality: MAPQUAL shows significant differences from SEQUAL in this area. This is mainly due to the differences between conceptual modelling and cartography and their inherent differences when it comes to abstraction of the information visualised. Colours are heavily used in cartography to separate different concepts from each other. In conceptual modelling, the use of colours has been sparse and avoided to a large degree. Gopalakrishnan et al. (2011), Moody (2009) suggest to incorporate colours more in conceptual models, but to limit the numbers of different colours used. The inherent geographical attributes of cartographic concepts often restricts the freedom of layout modifications, such as choosing where a concept should be placed on a map. In more 'radical' maps (such as a metro map), this freedom exists to some extent. There the freedom of layout is restrained mostly by the geographical topology posed by the concepts, which is clearly more similar to conceptual modelling. The restriction of layout freedom induces quite strict possibilities of aesthetic changes to the map. Guidelines for increasing empirical quality of conceptual models base themselves, mostly, on the freedom of layout, supported by guidelines for graph aesthetics. These guidelines can thus not be directly applied to a map. In cartography, one could see the aesthetics and geographical attributes as orthogonal dimensions. Empirical quality is the facet of map/model quality where MAPQUAL and SEQUAL are most different. In cartography, the domain is (mostly) concrete and physical of some sort. The visualisation method conforms to this and attempts to preserve most of the concreteness of the information, for instance by restraining visualisation by geographical attributes (i.e. location). Conceptual modelling, on the other hand, is much more geared

towards information as such, showing relations among different information. An abstract representation of this information is thus preferred as a visualisation method, for instance by keeping only core information and relations. Conceptual modelling and cartography shares the background for the guidelines for empirical quality. Shared roots can be found in gestalt psychology and graphic design principles as well as the general field of aesthetics.

- Syntactical quality: In cartography, there is a lack of definition of formal languages in designing maps; thus, the guidelines for syntactical quality in MAPQUAL are solely based on the syntactical quality presented in SEQUAL.
- Semantic and perceived semantic quality: It is the relation between the domain, map/model and social actor knowledge and interpretation. Thus, this facet is assumed to be generally applicable for cartography as well as for conceptual modelling. In cartography, the quality of the data, in terms of measure errors and similar, is quite common to use as a semantic quality measure. In relation to this, we can also look at data quality in Sect. 6.4 in general. It should be noted that such metrics does not necessarily cover all aspects of semantic quality as semantic and perceived semantic quality concentrates more on the statements made in the map versus the statements in the domain and their human perception and interpretation.
- Pragmatic quality: MAPQUAL has generally the same understanding of pragmatic quality as the understanding in SEQUAL. Human interpretation is probably the best covered aspect of pragmatic quality in cartography. It should be noted that MAPQUAL does not include an extensive investigation in the research of human interpretation of maps (i.e. map communication) in cartography, but recognise that there are significant similarities between this and SEQUAL's understanding of human interpretation. MAPQUAL and SEQUAL are thus more or less equal with respect to pragmatic quality. It should, however, not be neglected to take this quality facet into account when investigating quality properties of maps and models as pragmatic quality is recognised to be one of the most important quality facets for maps.
- Social quality: MAPQUAL base the discussion of social quality of cartographic maps solely on the discussion of social quality in SEQUAL.
- Deontic quality: Similar to social quality, deontic quality in MAPQUAL is similar to organisational quality in SEQUAL. Emphasis is put into the potential benefits that cartography could receive by more applications of the understanding of organisational quality of maps.

An evaluation of MAPQUAL, reported in (Nossum 2008), was performed consisting of using one cartographic expert to evaluate the quality of a set of maps without using the framework. We then evaluated two maps in the same set using MAPQUAL as the guiding framework. Juxtaposing the overall results from these two evaluations provides an overview of differences and similarities. We found that most of the findings from the cartographic expert evaluation are recognised. Additionally, the evaluation using MAPQUAL is more structured and covering all facets of the framework.

6.7.4   Quality of Integrated Conceptual and Topological Models

So far, we have defined maps to be a kind of models. An underlying assumption has been that cartographic maps represent, primarily, geographic space-oriented concepts. However, cartographic maps can easily represent also non-geographic concepts. Some research has been put into applying cartographic visualisation techniques on general non-geographic information as also discussed in Chap. 5 (Moody 2009; Skupin and Fabrikant 2003) and the opposite, applying general information visualisation techniques on geographic information. However, little work has looked on the possibilities of combining conceptual models with cartographic maps. When investigating and comparing MAPQUAL and SEQUAL, we found the largest difference being rooted in the difference of the underlying meta-meta model of maps and conceptual models, and how this influences guidelines for language design to achieve comprehensibility appropriateness of the combined language and thus potentially empirical and pragmatic quality of the model. Some important aspects are:

1. Clearly discriminate between geographical oriented lines and conceptual lines (relationships as links).
2. Clearly differentiate between nodes (concept) which are often depicted by a geometric shape, and geographic areas (by texture or colour for instance, or by using icons for the conceptual aspects).
3. Indicate topological information by positioning of conceptual nodes according to the topology where relevant.
4. Position concepts according to their temporal nearness.
5. Conceptualise geographical position when the conceptual structures are the most important (e.g. as a location-concept).

6.8   Summary

We have in this chapter looked upon a number of special types of models, both models on a type level and instance level. Concretely we have looked at

- Quality of business process models
- Quality of requirements models
- Quality of data models
- Quality of data
- Quality of ontologies
- Quality of interactive models
- Quality of maps

We see that the seven quality levels of SEQUAL can be used relative to all the different types of models, but that existing work on these types of models (e.g. quality of process models or data models) enrich the depth of discussion and concrete metrics compared to the generic framework provided in Chap. 4. On the other hand, we find that in most areas, we get a more thorough discussion by including all the levels of SEQUAL, which in all cases can be seen to have relevance.

Compared to Fig. 6.1, we see that we have not discussed all possible specialisations. We also see that we within the different fields can come up with a more fine-grained discussion (e.g. quality of data models on a conceptual level vs. quality of data models on a logical level). In addition, combinations e.g. discussing quality of data models and data quality together should be pursued.

Review Questions

1. What differentiate maps and conceptual models, and how does this influence the discussion of quality of combined topological and conceptual models?
2. Describe the important aspects of quality of data models.
3. Describe the important aspects of quality of data.
4. How do the work of Batini et al. and the work on Price et al. on quality of data differ?
5. Describe the important aspect of quality of business process models.
6. How is an ontology different from a data model?
7. Describe the important aspects of quality of an ontology.
8. Describe the important aspects of quality of interactive models.
9. How is the discussion of quality of interactive models different from the discussion of quality of business process models?
10. Describe the important aspects of quality of a software requirements specification (SRS).

Problems and Exercises

Individual Exercises
1. Evaluate the quality of a data model you have made (e.g. as part of exercises in connection to Chap. 3) both accordance with the standard SEQUAL framework, and then relative the specialisation presented in this chapter.
2. Evaluate the quality of a business process model you have made (e.g. as part of exercises in connection to Chap. 3) both accordance with the standard SEQUAL framework, and then relative the specialisation presented in this chapter.

Pair Exercises
1. Discuss the differences of quality of a data model on the conceptual level and a quality of a data model on the logical level.
2. Discuss the differences of quality of a data model on the physical level and a quality of a data model on the logical level.

Group Exercises
1. Newer languages combine a number of perspectives. Provide a suggested specialisation of SEQUAL for approaches combining data and process models.
2. Develop a basis for a framework for quality of UML-models used to create CIMs (Computationally independent models).

3. Develop a basis for a framework for quality of UML-models used to create PIMs (Platform independent models).
4. As described in the beginning of Chap. 4, there are specific guidelines for design quality. Based on these, develop a specialisation of SEQUAL for the quality of design-models.
5. Develop a common framework for assessing the combined quality of data models and data.

References

Alani, H., Brewster, C., Shadbolt, N.: Ranking ontologies with AKTiveRank. In: Cruz, I., Decker, S., Allemang, D., Preist, C., Schwab, D., Mika, P., Uschold, M., Aroyo, L. (eds.) ISWC 2006. LNCS, vol. 4273, pp. 1–15. Springer, Heidelberg (2006)

Argyris, C., Schön, D.: Organisational Learning: A Theory of Action Perspective. Addison Wesley, Reading (1973)

Batini, C., Scannapieco, M.: Data Quality: Concepts, Methodologies and Techniques. Springer, Berlin/New York (2006)

Berners-Lee, T., Handler, J., Lassila, O.: The semantic web. Sci. Am. **284**(5), 34–43 (2001)

Bertin, J.: Semiology of Graphics: Diagrams, Networks, Maps. University of Wisconsin Press, Madison (1983)

Boland, R.J., Tenkasi, R.V.: Perspective making and perspective taking in communities of knowing. Organ. Sci. **6**(4), 350–372 (1995)

Brewster, C., Alani, H., Dasmahapatra, S., Wilks, Y.: Data driven ontology evaluation. In: International Conference on Language Resources and Evaluation, Lisbon, Portugal (2004)

Buitelaar, P., Eigner, T., Declerck, T.: OntoSelect: a dynamic ontology library with support for ontology selection. In: Proceedings of the Demo Session at ISWC 2004, Hiroshima, Japan (2004)

Burton-Jones, A., Storey, V., Sugumaran, V., Ahluwalia, P.: A semiotic metrics suite for assessing the quality of ontologies. Data Knowl. Eng. **55**(1), 84–102 (2005)

Carlsen, S., Gjersvik, R.: Organizational metaphors as lenses for analyzing workflow technology. Paper presented at the GROUP '97 conference, Phoenix, 16–19 Nov 1997

Chandrasekaran, B., John, R.J., Benjamins, V.R.: What are ontologies, and why do we need them? IEEE Intell. Syst. **14**, 20–26 (1999)

Davis, A.M., Overmeyer, S., Jordan, K., Caruso, J., Dandashi, F., Dinh, A., Kincaid, G., Ledeboer, G., Reynolds, P., Sitaram, P., Ta, A., Theofanos, M.: Identifying and measuring quality in a software requirements specification. In: Proceedings of the First International Software Metrics Symposium, Baltimore, pp. 141–152 (1993)

Dijkman, R., Dumas, M., van Dongen, B., Käärik, R., Mendling, J.: Similarity of business process models: metrics and evaluation. Inf. Syst. **36**, 498–516 (2010)

Fabbrini, F., Fusani, M., Gervasi, V., Gnesi, S., Ruggieri, S.: Achieving quality in natural language requirements. In: Proceedings of the 11th International Software Quality Week (QW'98) San Francisco, 26–29 May 1998

Fabbrini, F., Fusani, M., Gnesi, S., Lami, G.: An automatic quality evaluation for natural language requirements. In: Proceedings of REFSQ'01, Interlaken, Switzerland, 4–5 June 2001

Francalanci, C., Pernici, B.: View integration: a survey of current developments. Technical Report 93–053, Politecnico de Milano, Milan (1993)

Gane, C., Sarson, T.: Structured Systems Analysis: Tools and Techniques. Prentice Hall, Englewood Cliffs (1979)

Gangemi, A., Catenacci, C., Ciaramita, M., Lehmann, J.: Modelling ontology evaluation and validation. In: Sure, Y., Domingue, J. (eds.) ESWC 2006. LNCS, vol. 4011, pp. 140–154. Springer, Heidelberg (2006)

Gopalakrishnan, S., Krogstie, J., Sindre, G.: Extending use and misuse cases to capture mobile applications. NOKOBIT – Norsk konferanse for organisasjoners bruk av informasjonsteknologi, pp. s. 1–s. 14 (2011)

Guarino, N., Welty, C.: An overview of OntoClean. In: Handbook on Ontologies, pp. 151–172. Springer, Berlin (2004)

Halpin, T., Curland, M.: Automated verbalization for ORM 2. In: Meersman, R., Tari, Z., Herrero, P. (eds.) Proceedings of OTM Workshop. LNCS, vol. 4278, pp. 1181–1190. Springer, Heidelberg (2006)

Hella, L., Krogstie, J.: A structured evaluation to assess the reusability of models of user profiles. Paper presented at the EMMSAD – conference on evaluating modeling methods in systems analysis and design, Hammamet, Tunis, 7–8/6 2010

Kindler, E.: On the semantics of EPCs: resolving the vicious circle. Data Knowl. Eng. **56**(1), 23–40 (2006)

Krogstie, J., Jørgensen, H.D.: Quality of interactive models. In: First International Workshop on Conceptual Modelling Quality (IWCMQ'02). 11 Oct 2002. Tampere, Finland. Springer, Berlin (2002)

Lin, Y., Krogstie, J.: Semantic annotation of process models for facilitating process knowledge management. Int. J. Inf. Syst. Model. Des. **1**(3), 45–67 (2010)

Lin, Y., Strasunskas, D., Hakkarainen, S., Krogstie, J., Sølvberg, A.: Semantic annotation framework to manage semantic heterogeneity of process models. Paper presented at the CAiSE'2006, Luxembourg (2006)

Lindland, O.I., Sindre, G., Sølvberg, A.: Understanding quality in conceptual modeling. IEEE Softw. **11**(2), 42–49 (1994)

Lozano-Tello, A., Gomez-Perez, A.: Ontometric: a method to choose appropriate ontology. J. Database Manag. **15**(2), 1–18 (2004)

MacEachren, A.: How Maps Work. Guilford Press New York (1995)

Mendling, J., Reijers, H., Cardoso, J.: What makes process models understandable? In: Alonso, G., Dadam, P., Rosemann, M. (eds.) Business Process Management, 5th International Conference, BPM 2007, Brisbane, Australia, September 24–28, 2007, Proceedings. Lecture Notes in Computer Science, vol. 4714, pp. 48–63. Springer, Brisbane (2007a)

Mendling, J., Neumann, G., van der Aalst, W.M.P.: Understanding the occurrence of errors in process models based on metrics. In: Meersman, T., Tari, Z. (eds.) OTM Conference 2007, Proceedings, Part I. Lecture Notes in Computer Science, vol. 4803, pp. 113–130. Springer, Berlin (2007b)

Mendling, J., Reijers, H.A., van der Aalst, W.M.P.: Seven process modeling guidelines (7PMG). Inf. Softw. Technol. (IST) **52**(2), 127–136 (2010)

Moody, D.L., Shanks, G.G.: What makes a good data model? Evaluating the quality of entity relationship models, in Proceedings of the 13th International Conference on the Entity-Relationship Approach (ER'94), pp. 94-111, Manchester, England (1994)

Moody, D.L.: Metrics for evaluating the quality of entity relationship models. In: Proceedings of the Seventeenth International Conference on Conceptual Modelling (ER '98), Singapore, November 16–19. Elsevier Lecture Notes in Computer Science (1998)

Moody, D.L.: The method evaluation model: a theoretical model for validating information systems design methods. In: Proceedings of the 11th European Conference on Information Systems, ECIS 2003, Naples, 16–21 June 2003

Moody, D.L.: The "physics" of notations: toward a scientific basis for constructing visual notations in software engineering. IEEE Trans. Softw. Eng. **35**, 756–779 (2009)

Morris, C.: Foundations of the theory of signs. In: International Encyclopedia of Unified Science, vol. 1. University of Chicago Press, London (1938)

Nossum, A.: MAPQUAL: understanding quality in cartographic maps. Technical report, Norwegian Technical University of Science and Technology (2008)

Parsons, J., Wand, Y.: Choosing classes in conceptual modeling. Commun. ACM **40**(6), 63–69 (1997a)

Parsons, J., Wand, Y.: Using objects for systems analysis. Commun. ACM **40**(12), 104–110 (1997b)

Patel, C., Supekar, K., Lee, Y., Park, E.: OntoKhoj: a semantic web portal for ontology searching, ranking and classification. In: Proceedings of the Workshop on Web Information and Data Management, pp. 58–61. ACM Press, New York (2003)

Pohl, K.: The three dimensions of requirements engineering: a framework and its applications. Inf. Syst. **19**(3), 243–258 (1994)

Price, R., Shanks, G.: A semiotic information quality framework. IFIP WG8.3 International Conference on Decision Support Systems (DSS2004), pp. 658–672, Prato, Italy, 1–3 July 2004

Price, R., Shanks, G.: A semiotic information quality framework: development and comparative analysis. J. Inf. Technol. **20**(2), 88–102 (2005)

Recker, J., Mendling, J.: On the translation between BPMN and BPEL: conceptual mismatch between process modeling languages. In: Latour, T., Petit, M. (eds.) Proceedings of the CAiSE Workshops at the 18th Conference on Advanced Information Systems Engineering (CAiSE 2006), Luxembourg, Luxembourg, pp. 521–532. Presses Universitaries de Namur, Belgique (2006)

Rittgen, P.: Business process model similarity as a proxy for group consensus POEM 2011, Oslo, 2–3 Nov (2011)

Robinson, A., Sale, R., Morrison, J.: Elements of Cartography. Wiley, New York (1995)

Sampson, J., Krogstie, J., Veres, C.: Ontology alignment quality: a framework and tool for validation – International Journal on Information Systems Modeling and Design, *2*(3) (2011)

Skupin, A., Fabrikant, S.: Spatialisation methods: a cartographic research agenda for non-geographic information visualization. Cartogr. Geogr. Inf. Sci. **30**(2), 99–119 (2003)

Spyns, P., Reinberger, M.L.: Lexically evaluating ontology triples generated automatically from texts. In: Proceedings of ESWC 2005. LNCS 3532, pp. 563–577. Springer, Heidelberg (2005)

Strasunskas, D., Tomassen, S.L.: Empirical insights on a value of ontology quality in ontology-driven web search. Lecture Notes in Computer Science = Lecture notes in artificial intelligence, vol. 5332, pp. s. 1318–1336

Tartir, S., Arpinar, I., Moore, M., Sheth, A., Aleman-Meza, B.: OntoQA: metric-based ontology quality analysis. In: IEEE Workshop on Knowledge Acquisition from Distributed, Autonomous, Semantically Heterogeneous Data and Knowledge Sources, Houston, IEEE Computer Society, pp. 45–53 (2005)

Tsichritzis, D., Klug, A.: The ANSI/X3/SPARC DBMS framework. Inf. Syst. **3**, 173–191 (1978)

van der Aalst, W.M.P., ter Hofstede, A.H.M., Kiepuszewski, B., Barros, A.P.: Workflow patterns. Distrib. Parallel Databases **14**(3), 5–51 (2003)

Voss, A., Procter, R., Williams, R.: Innovation in use: interleaving day-to-day operation and systems development. In: Proceedings of the CPSR/IFIP WG 9.1 Participatory Design Conference, Nov 28–Dec 1, New York (2000)

Ware, C.: Information Visualization. Morgan Kaufmann, San Francisco (2000)

Wesenberg, H.: Enterprise modeling in an agile world. In: Proceedings of the 4th Conference on Practice of Enterprise Modeling, Oslo, 2–3 Nov (2011)

Willoch, B.E.: Business Process Reengineering – En praktisk innføring og veiledning. Fagbokforlaget Vigmostad og Bjorke AS, Bergen (1994)

Zuboff, S.: In the Age of the Smart Machine. Basic Books, New York (1988)

Applications of SEQUAL

Different parts of SEQUAL can be used in a number of different ways, including:
1. Guide the modelling process to achieve models of high quality
2. Evaluate the quality of existing models
3. Evaluate the quality of modelling languages:
   - To choose between different languages
   - To guide further development of a modelling language
4. Guide meta-modelling when developing new languages for specific situations (related to above point)
5. Evaluate the appropriateness of tools to support the development of models of high quality
   We present in this chapter examples of these different usage areas.

7.1 Process Heuristics for Information Systems Modelling

We will here give an overview of an approach for using SEQUAL to guide the modelling process. The example used is a requirements engineering process where the goal is to come up with a requirements specification model. The modelling task follows the SPEC-cycle (see Fig. 7.1), as originally described in (Sindre and Krogstie 1995). The steps related to requirements engineering (RE) (using terminology from RE-processes (Loucopoulos and Karakostas 1995)) can be described as follows:
- P – preparation: In this state, the organisation is performing actions in preparation of creating the requirements specification, such as:
  - Deciding on the scope of the project or sub-project, including a clarification of what is the domain of interest.
  - Identification of stakeholders based on the domain and deciding on which stakeholders are the most important.
  - Selection of participation strategy and participants from the identified stakeholder group.

J. Krogstie, *Model-Based Development and Evolution of Information Systems:*
A Quality Approach, DOI 10.1007/978-1-4471-2936-3_7,
© Springer-Verlag London 2012

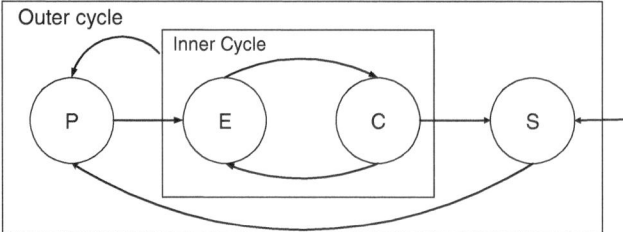

Fig. 7.1 The SPEC-cycle of modelling

- Deciding on the format of the SRS, and (parts of) modelling languages to be used (vs. those aspects indicated as being transferable from deontic quality and semantic quality to syntactic quality in Sect. 6.2, e.g. annotated by relative importance).
- Make ready for the use of different supporting tools and techniques.
- Training of participants in the use of the selected modelling languages and tools.
- Knowledge elicitation (for the modeller to get more knowledge on the primary domain and to establish the modelling domain). This often includes the development of problem domain models. This can be looked upon as a modelling task following its own SPEC-cycle that is performed in parallel with the development of the SRS (Loucopoulos and Karakostas 1995).
- Planning of the subsequent RE-tasks (based on the goals of modelling).
- E – expansion: Requirements are stated, hence the model M is growing. During expansion, statements may be made more or less uncritically, i.e. thorough validation is not undertaken, and there might be errors introduced in M. Still, as long as some valid statements are made, the model's degree of completeness will grow. This task in relation to requirements engineering is often termed 'specification' (Loucopoulos and Karakostas 1995).
- C – consolidation: The model statements (especially those captured in the previous expansion phase) are consolidated with respect to perceived validity, comprehension, and agreement. This task in relation to requirements engineering is often termed 'validation' (Loucopoulos and Karakostas 1995).
- S – suspension: The modelling activity is suspended for instance due to that the SRS have been agreed upon and baselined (to start design), or the project may have been aborted (Fig. 7.2).

This diagram consists of an inner cycle of expansion and consolidation, and an outer cycle including preparation and suspension. The starting state has been defined as suspension (S), i.e. before you do anything, you are in a state of suspension. The fact that there is no accepting state reflects the view that a computerised information system is never finished, although the SRS might temporally be regarded as baselined

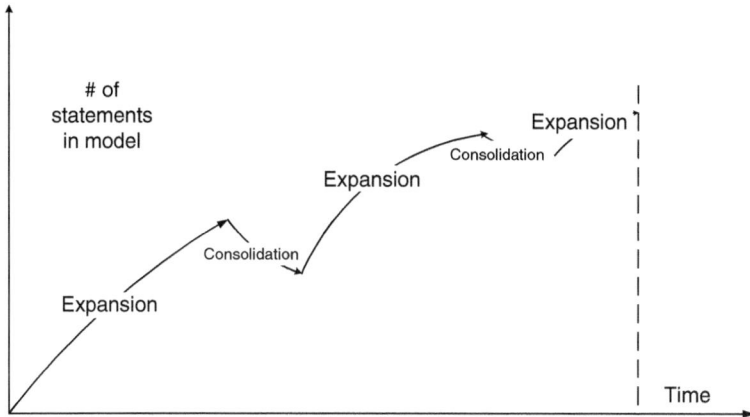

Fig. 7.2 Growth of an SRS over time

for the current release or project. When the work on a new release starts, the requirements specification is unfrozen, starting a new preparation phase.

In practice, the requirements specification process is often a time-boxed process, and organisational goals limiting the process are very often linked to calendar-time and cost. The process (in particular, when being done as part of developing a new system) usually have a relatively large P-phase, and 3–4 inner cycles of expansion and consolidation as indicated in Fig. 7.2 below, before a model is baselined. Later in a project, changes to the baselined are controlled and added one by one, alternatively a new iteration with its separate SPEC-cycle is started if the domain is extended as part of an incremental or agile development approach. In the projects we have studied, the first expansion-phase is the one with most statements added, and the number of new statements decreases in later phases. It might also be necessary to return to the preparation phase as discussed in more detail below. A similar pattern within requirements specification work is reported in (Nguyen and Swatman 2001).

The focus of the heuristics to be discussed here will mostly be on the inner cycle, in particular the switching between E and C.

This switch can be based on:
- Resource limit: You are supposed to use a certain amount of time or work force for E, then go to C, and vice versa, and similarly for E and C together vs. S.
- Chunk size: The number of statements made at one visit in E. When this size has been reached, there may be a policy to switch to C.
- Progress: You observe the progress made at E or C and switch when this has fallen below a certain threshold. The progress will decrease when the process has been in the same state for a while because the most evident statements will be stated first, and the most evident errors found first. Moreover, staying too long in E will yield a big chunk, for which incomprehension and disagreement is likely to hinder further growth of the specification.

To determine the progress of modelling and the extent, to which feasible quality has been reached, it is useful to know the point estimates for the quality goals, and their corresponding ratios (vs. resource consumption). In addition, model size has been included because it is important in the management of expansion, and model value because it is important in considerations about feasibility.

1. Perceived validity (PV), and ratio of perceived validity (PVR)
2. Perceived completeness (PC), and ratio of perceived completeness (PCR)
3. Perceived pragmatic quality (PP), and ratio of perceived pragmatic quality (PPR), focusing here on human understanding
4. Perceived social quality (PS), and ratio of perceived social quality (PSR)
5. Model size (MS), and ratio of model size (MSR)
6. Model value (MV), and ration of model value (MVR)

The model size (e.g. number of requirements) should be possible to obtain automatically through the modelling tool. For the other data, one needs to register:

1. For all parts of the requirements specification, which part has been perceived as complete (within the decided scope), which part has been perceived as incomplete, and how big this incompletion is estimated to be.
2. For all requirements, which have been acknowledged as comprehended, which have been turned out to be incomprehensible, and which have not yet been assessed.
3. For all requirements, which have been agreed upon and by whom, which have been disagreed upon and by whom, and which have not yet been checked?
4. For each activity (here: each visit at E or C), how much resources are spent.
5. For each activity, what is the perceived value increment to the model?

The most complicated numbers to obtain are perceived completeness and model value. Even if these are dropped, it will be possible to provide some useful heuristics, as will be shown below.

7.1.1   Expansion Heuristics

The heuristics are based on recognising certain symptoms:

- Symptom E1: Resource consumption approaching limit
- Symptom E2: MS increment approaching recommended chunk size
  - Action (E1 or E2): Switch to consolidation
- Symptom E3: MSR < minimum threshold (expansion is getting unproductive)
- Symptom E4: MVR < 1 (growth of model value is less than resources being spent, i.e. work currently being done is perceived to yield deficit)
  - Possible actions (E3 or E4):
    - Switch to consolidation (if the problem is due to significant incomprehension or disagreement). If the chunk is well within the recommended size, it may also be sensible to lower the recommended chunk size.
    - Switch to other techniques (if the problem is due to exhaustive use of some techniques and there are others that can be tried). For example, one can switch from an ad hoc suggestion of model statements, into using for instance the driving question technique.

- Involve new participants (if the problem is due to exhaustive use of some participants and there are others, which are perceived to possess relevant knowledge that has not been involved yet).

7.1.2   Consolidation Heuristics

Consolidation heuristics are more complex than expansion heuristics, since there are more goals and measures involved. We will avoid listing the most obvious heuristics. Hence, it is normally sensible to first address physical quality (i.e. that the model is available for those involved in consolidation). If relevant tool-support is available, empirical and syntactic quality could be addressed early. Note that in the first cycle, the emphasis on empirical and syntactic quality might be lower, since at this stage, it is important to get the ideas out in the open (i.e. rather focus on increasing semantic quality). In the last cycle, empirical and syntactic quality will typically have a higher importance, since one is then often preparing the final RE-models and documents which are the ones that are to be officially accepted, signed and baselined, often by management personnel not directly involved in the detailed development of the SRS.

As for the validation, one would normally address pragmatic quality before validity, completeness, and agreement because comprehension of the model is necessary to achieve anything else with some certainty. Further, it is sensible to address validity and agreement before completeness. Guidance for this sequencing can be done by heuristics investigating the values PP, PV, PS, and PC. This will not be discussed below. Instead, we will look at symptoms indicating problems with the consolidation being done.

- Symptom C1: Resource consumption approaches the limit.
  - Action: Switch to expansion (if resources available) or to suspension (if out of resources, and/or the last cycle produced very few new consolidated requirements). If one or more of the values for PV, PC, PP, or PS is not good, one might also consider extending the amount of resources to be used for this task.
- Symptom C2: PVR, PPR, PSR < min. threshold (i.e. consolidation is being exhausted).
- Symptom C3: MVR < 1 (i.e. perceived value being added to the SRS by consolidation is less than resources being spent).
  Possible actions (C2 and C3):
- Conclude that feasible quality has been reached (if the values for PV, PC, PP, PS are sufficiently good).
- End this part of the project as hopeless, postpone the area to a later iteration, or at least backtrack to some previous decision (if the values for PV, PC, PP, and PS are bad and it is impossible to see any way out).
- Switch to expansion (if the value for PC is regarded as worse than PV, PP, and PS).
- Switch to preparation to start using other techniques or undertake additional language training (if one or more of the values PV, PP, PS are unacceptable; concentrate on

techniques applicable for the quality aspect which is most pressing. For example if comprehension is unsatisfactory, one might consider extending the model with statements giving it an operational semantics, thus enabling execution of the model).

- Involve other participants (if one or more of the values PV, PP, PS is unacceptable).

7.1.3 Heuristics to Guide Method Evolution

Whereas the above guidelines relate to the development of one model, learning from one such task can be used also to guide the evolution of the modelling method by aggregating collected information over several projects.

- What modelling languages, techniques, tools etc. are good for various categories of problems in the organisation?
- What is the optimal chunk size (in first, second, third cycle)?
- What is the optimal statement growth ration for various kinds of problems?
- What team constellations are good for various kinds of problems (e.g. what combination of skills and knowledge)?
- What kind of knowledge seems to be in shortage in the organisation?

In addition, post-project evaluations can be taken into concern here. In this type of work, one should be aware of intrinsic differences between different types of problems. The development and refinement of methodological processes has been discussed a lot in software engineering, through the use of different types of maturity models. We will not go in detail on this area in this book, but just note that further research must be done on a modelling process to get high-quality models, which can take into account newer work (Nelson et al. 2011).

7.2   Evaluating Ontology-Models for Reuse

The example application for evaluation of model quality relates to the reuse of ontologies related to 'Persons' to support the provision of personalisation of application services. The main goal with personalisation is to improve the user's experience of a service. Personalisation is often needed to overcome information overflow and is important for service providers to acquire better knowledge of their end-users and for achieving improved business results (Bonnet 2003). Personalisation usually requires the user to directly interact with a service, and any preferences are usually kept by the service provider and not the user. However, it is essential for the decision on personalisation to refocus from the service provider to the user if the personal preferences of the user depend on context and one wants to protect the privacy of the user (Kofod-Petersen et al. 2010). One of the main challenges for future personalised support lies in the combination of public and private information, and the combination of personalisation and contextualisation (Zimmerman et al. 2005). To provide personalised mobile services, different types of information are useful.

Here we focus on users' personal profiles. The profile contains all the information related to a person as an actor, its goals etc., and follows the user everywhere independently of the context. Then, we have information about the capabilities of the mobile device (as described in W3C Delivery context ontology (W3C 2009)). The environment of the person using the device will term the context of use. We note that many that work on mobile applications include parts of the information we have in the personal and device profiles in the term context (e.g. in relation to the definition of context by Dey and Abowd 2000), but we find it fruitful to more clearly distinguish these terms, since the profile information follows the user as he change context.

In the work leading up to the need for ontology reuse, we have looked in particular on a case of personalised information support for food shopping. Even though we have focused on a specific domain, with personas and scenarios with characteristics related to this, the concept of a personal profile concerning how it is to be communicated with the world is what we want to evaluate. The information that is to be captured in the personal profile can be divided in three main parts.

1. *Personal information.* This consists of type of information that is common for all users. This changes very seldom. Typical examples are name, birth date and address.
2. *Stable interests.* These are called stable because the type of information does not change frequently, due to importance and relevance for the person. Once a user has an interest, he is likely to have this interest for a longer time span, e.g. favour a specific producer of jam, finding it positive that food is ecologically produced or that price is not considered crucial. Because of the personal value of expressing this and keeping this type of information updated, a user would typically be motivated to do this by himself if it would change.
3. *Temporary interests.* For a limited time, a user could be interested in for example buying a new digital compact camera. In our case, the daily shopping list represents the temporary interests, so it should be possible to create a shopping list. As soon as the goal is fulfilled, it is no longer part of the personal profile.

We have considered both upper and domain ontologies. We have only looked into ontologies that are publicly available and referenced in papers. Ontologies only mentioned in papers without being directly available (Gandon and Sadeh 2004; Ghosh and Dekhil 2008; Mendis 2007; Stan et al. 2008) are not considered. In the following sections, we will describe the ontologies assessed.

7.2.1   FOAF

The Friend Of A Friend (FOAF) (FOAF 2010) ontology has a simple vocabulary for describing people, what they do and their relations to other people. Hence, it is often used for describing people's social connections and networks. FOAF is represented using RDFS and OWL. FOAF is a popular, much used, and discussed use of semantic Web technology (Goldbeck and Rothstein 2008). Its popularity is evident from related activities. A set of communities and projects are mentioned at their project

Web page, but are not described in detail and not linked to. In addition, FOAF related news is available at delicious. Other communication channels are IRC and mailing lists.

The terms defined are categorised as *FOAF basics, Personal info, Online accounts/IM, Projects and Groups,* and *Documents* and *Images.* FOAF is situated around the class *Person.* The FOAF vocabulary is intended to be uncomplicated, pragmatic, and designed to allow simultaneous deployment and extension. FOAF is intended for wide scale use. Personal information is made accessible by having people publishing information about them in the FOAF format. When the person information is published, machines will be able to use it. FOAF core is considered stable.

7.2.2   OpenCyc

Cycorp provides the Cyc technology, for intelligence and reasoning. Cycorp has an open source version of the knowledge base, called OpenCyc (OpenCyc 2011). It consists of hundreds of thousands of terms, together with millions of assertions that relate terms to each other. The OpenCyc upper ontology covers the domain of all of human consensus reality. Since it tries to cover everything in the world, the ontology is large.

The formal language CycL is used to represent the original version. Its syntax and semantics derives from first-order predicate calculus. The knowledge base consists of modules that are called microtheories. Such microtheories are a kind of sub-ontologies. This knowledge base is possible to download, and accessed through a Web browser. However, OpenCyc is now also represented in an ontology language and OWL versions of the OpenCyc ontology can be downloaded.

Online concept browsers as illustrated in Fig. 7.3 below are available. Concepts are separated into collections and predicates. A search result is a written definition, of the term, together with its unique tag and aliases. In addition, super concepts, sub concepts, and instance of concepts are listed. The concept browsers have no tree structure to view the relation between concepts. There is also a more general OpenCyc blog.

7.2.3   SUMO

The Suggested Upper Merged Ontology (SUMO 2003) was created as part of the IEEE Standard Upper Ontology Working Group (SUO WG). SUMO consists of definitions that are intended for general-purpose terms and wants to be a basis for domain ontologies that are more specific. The original SUMO is specified using SUO-KIF, Standard Upper Ontology – Knowledge Interchange Format, and is a simplified form of the knowledge representation language KIF. Later, SUMO has been translated into OWL. SUMO has been referenced in many papers independent of its funders.

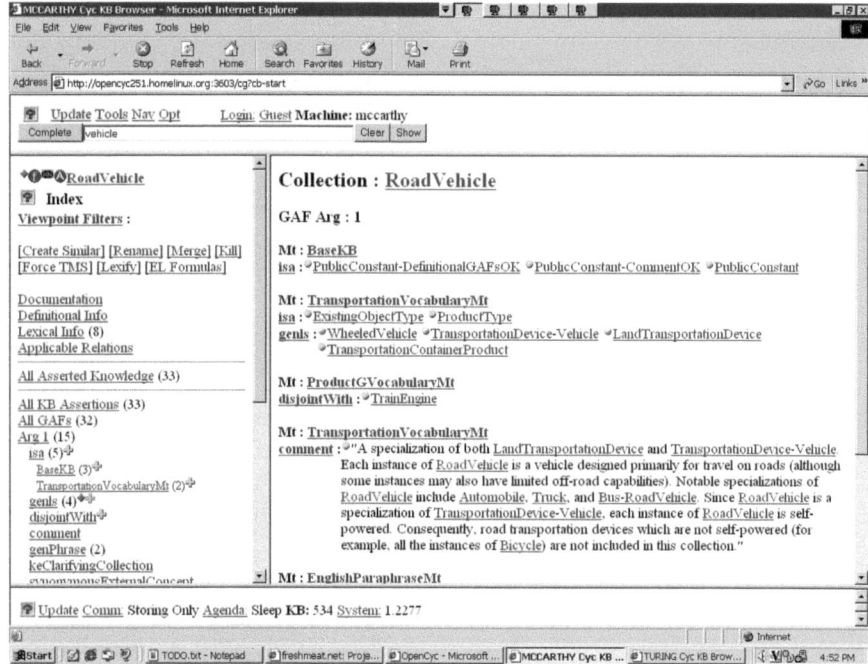

Fig. 7.3 Screenshot from OpenCyc online browser

SUMO's initial goal was to construct a single, consistent, and comprehensive ontology. Now, SUMO has been put together with Mid-level Ontology (MILO) and several domain ontologies. Domain ontologies that are included are, for example, the ontology of Communications, Countries and Regions, Economy, Finance, and Geography.

It is possible to browse the content of the knowledge base in their online browser. SUMO is connected to the WordNet lexicon (Miller 1995). In the SUMO online browser, one can navigate from a SUMO concept to the corresponding WordNet term. In SUMO, a person is modelled as class *Human* that is equivalent to WordNet's person as a human being or a human body.

SUMO consists of around 1,000 well-defined and well-documented concepts. The concepts are interconnected into a semantic network together with a number of axioms. An overview is depicted in Fig. 7.4. The axioms are common-sense notions that are generally recognised among the concepts. Open source toolset for browsing and inference can be downloaded with KIF knowledge engineering environment.

7.2.4   GUMO + UbisWorld

GUMO (General User Model Ontology) (Heckmann et al. 2005a), developed in OWL, is made for the 'uniform interpretation of distributed user models in intelligent

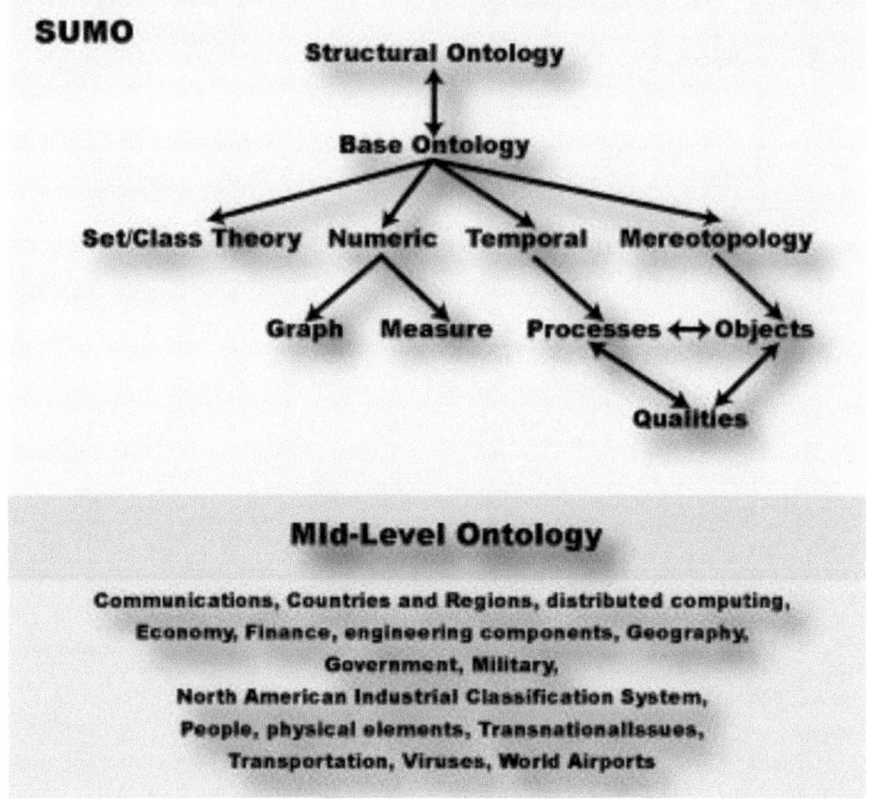

Fig. 7.4 SUMO overview from http://www.ontologyportal.org/1201

Semantic Web enriched environments'. GUMO is related to UserML (User Model Markup Language), which is a RDF-based exchange language for user modelling between decentralised systems (Heckmann et al. 2005a). The GUMO ontology can be integrated with ubiquitous applications with the UbisWorld user model service.

The focus of the (UbisWorld 2009) approach lays on research issues of user modelling, ubiquitous computing, and semantic Web. UbisWorld can also be used for simulation, inspection, and control of the real world. UbisWorld is a version of GUMO that includes additions that can be used for the ubiquitous computing area.

GUMO + UbisWorld have the following basic user dimensions with differing time span: *Emotional state, characteristics,* and *personality.* A user model service manages the information about users and gives more advantages than a user model server would do. GUMO and UserML together focus on creating a common language and ontology for communication of user models (Heckmann et al. 2005b).

gumo.org and ubisworld.org share a common interface. To get access to provided features, it is necessary to sign up as a member. The ontologies in different versions, among them static and dynamic versions, exist. The Ontology Bowser presents a set of ontologies that can be viewed as foldable class trees. External ones (e.g. SUMO, GUMO, OpenCyc) can also be viewed.

7.2.5   Ontology Evaluation

In the next sections, the evaluation is presented. It is a result of a comparison of what the ontologies are and represent, and the expectations for the different quality categories according to the desired personal profile ontology specified according to SEQUAL above.

7.2.5.1 Evaluation of FOAF for Reuse

Physical quality: FOAF is available with a vocabulary specification and an OWL-file. The OWL file opens in Protégé, and changes can be made to update these files.

Empirical quality: FOAF is not presented visually in the information found, and there is no overview figure provided. Even though FOAF is a small ontology with relatively few classes and relationships, it would be advantageous with a graphical representation of how the concepts relate. Classes and properties are described in writing and with some practical examples. Access to much related information is available from main Web page.

Syntactic quality: The OWL validator classifies FOAF to OWL Full.

Semantic quality: FOAF covers the class Person that is disjoint with Project, Document and Organisation. The Person class has the following properties: currentProject, family_name, firstName, geekCode, img, interest, knows, myersBriggs, pastProject, plan, publications, schoolHomepage, surname, topic_interest, workInfoHomepage, workplaceHomepage, aimChatID, based_near, birthday, depiction, dnaChecksum, fundedBy, gender, givenname, holdsAccount, homepage, irqChatID, isPrimaryTopicOf, jabberID, logo, made, maker, mbox, mbox_sha1sum, membershipClass, msnChatID, name, nick, openid, page, phone, theme, tipjar, weblog, yahooChatID, term_status, assurance, src_assurance.

Most of the properties are related to the online world of a user, and not the life as a physical actor. Some are also not relevant, e.g. the property *interest* that in FOAF implies a person's interest in a document. Parts of the basic types of information correspond to our definition of personal information. However, it is not complete. Little of FOAF is superfluous. For example, in relation to recommendation solutions, information or relations to other persons could be relevant. There are several aspects from the person domain that are missing though.

Pragmatic quality: Documentation of FOAF terms is provided. Classes and properties are described in relation to what they are used for. There is documentation for the decisions that has been taken and explanations to the created ontology. Examples for each class are available, and make it easier to understand what a class or concept is intended for. The reference to the OWL file could be more visible. Some of the names of the properties are not very intuitive.

Social quality: FOAF has a relatively large group of followers. It is possible to chat about FOAF related subjects at an IRC channel '#foaf'. FOAF also has a mailing list and is used in many social networks and projects. FOAF is included as a part of GUMO.

Deontic quality: FOAF is freely available. It is available in a standard format, and will probably be available and supported for the coming years.

7.2.5.2 Evaluation of OpenCyc for Reuse

Physical quality: OWL-files are freely available in a downloadable zip-file. The OpenCyc ontology is very big, and was too large to open in Protégé. The online concept browsers made it possible to search and view concepts.

Empirical quality: OpenCyc does not have any visual representation, hence it is difficult to get an understanding of the content of the ontology. Concepts are described in writing, but the relation to other concepts cannot intuitively be discovered other than through direct relations to other concepts.

Syntactic quality: The OWL sublanguage used has not been detectable because of the file size.

Semantic quality: Difficult with a more detailed analysis because it could not be viewed in Protégé, the concept browser does not show the information hierarchically, and manual inspection is difficult. Thus, this evaluation is based on the written documentation and the concept browser. The initial impression of the concept *person* is that there could be an overlap with our needs. However, as only class and axioms and not attributes are included in the concept browser, its completeness is hard to assess. In addition, it is difficult to understand the model based on the OWL file itself.

In general, it seems like OpenCyc describes more about the world than we need, e.g. OWL constructs (e.g. owl class, owl datatype property) and CycL terms have been specified in the same way as other OpenCyc concepts. Hence, it seems like concepts are modelled at a very low level. In addition, it would be difficult to extract the parts that were needed because of all the dependencies and the size of OpenCyc. Hence, validity is poor.

Pragmatic quality: There is limited documentation for how to use and understand OpenCyc. Documentation about the original OpenCyc model is available, but it would take great efforts to become familiar with it. It is not clear whether the information is intended for the original version, the OWL version, or both. Training material exists, but is for the use of the original version only. Parts of a handbook are not available (e.g. Section 7), and the last update was done in 2002. The concept browsers do not give much insight into the model, other than very long written descriptions that only give an overview. Missing hierarchical representation is a drawback, as one cannot view the entire structure. The separation of concept in collections and predicates in (Opencyc 2011) is not explained, and what kinds of concepts belong to which term is not clear. All these factors, and the lack of user manual intended for the OWL version, makes it difficult to start using OpenCyc.

Social quality: It is difficult to know how many followers there are and to what degree the OpenCyc ontology is used in other projects. They have a discussion forum. However, this is a forum with little activity. OpenCyc also have an IRC Channel and a blog with little activity. Last update was November 2008. However, it seems like the original OpenCyc has higher priority than the OWL version. All these social forums are mostly intended for the original version and the OWL version is seldom explicitly mentioned or referenced.

Deontic quality: The OpenCyc ontology is freely available in a standard format, and will probably be available and supported for the coming years. Might be stable, but updates are probable.

7.2.5.3 Evaluation of SUMO for Reuse

Physical quality: SUMO has been translated into OWL, and a selection of domain ontologies is included. It is possible to open and adapt SUMO in Protégé.

Empirical quality: The visual overview does not separate SUMO, MILO, and domain ontologies. The complete class hierarchy makes it possible to view all the relations between classes. Because of its size, crossing lines in the figure are inevitable. The figure is still readable, and ok to navigate even though scrolling is necessary.

Syntactic quality: The OWL validator classifies SUMO as OWL Full.

Semantic quality: The figure depicted in the description about SUMO and the class hierarchy does not correspond with the classes found in the OWL file. SUMO is detailed enough to include the class *Human* that corresponds to our concept of a person. Other classes that could be relevant are also included. Human is a subclass of both Hominid and CognitiveAgent, and has subclasses Man and Woman. These classes have the properties named: age, ancestor, attribute, authors, BackFn, believes, bottom citizen, completelyFills, component, connected, considers, contains, cooccur, copy, crosses, date, desires, developmentalForm, diameter, documentation, editor, element, equal, exactlyLocated, exploits, faces, familyRelation, father, fills, FrontFn, grasps, hasPurpose, height, home, ImmediateFamilyFn, immediateInstance, inhabits, inList, inScopeOfInterest, instance, interiorPart, knows, larger, leader, legalRelation, length, located, measure, meetsSpatially, member, monetaryValue, mother, needs, Overlaps-Partially, overlapsSpatially, parent, part, partiallyFills, partlyLocated, penetrates, possesses, properlyFills, properPart, property, PropertyFn, refers, relatedInternalConcept, represents, Sibling, side, smaller, spouse, stays, superficialPart, surface, time, top, traverses, uniqueIdentifier, uses, wants, WealthFn, wears, WhenFn, width, son/daughter, brother/sister, and husband/wife. Large parts of the ontology are irrelevant (poor validity). The same applies to attributes. Neither personal information, stable interests, nor temporary interests are fully supported. More constructs are necessary to be able to cover our domain fully. In general, the most visible overlap is in connection to the leaf nodes we have mentioned, and not so much on the higher-level concepts.

Pragmatic quality: In the Protégé tree structure there are two other classes on the same level as the class Entity, which are left out of overview figures. Papers referencing to SUMO give a comprehensible overview of the upper levels of SUMO. The specific domain ontologies that have been included are not described, but seem to be an integrated part of SUMO. No tutorial or user manual is found for the ontology. Material found relates only to the KIF version of SUMO and tools. Several of the attribute names are not intuitive, and do not indicate which classes or types the relation connects. In addition, they say little about the direction of the relationship (e.g. whether a man IS a son, or HAS a son).

Social quality: SUMO is assumed mature since there is little activity related to it. We have not found documentation covering how much used it is in other projects.

Deontic quality: SUMO is freely available. It is available in a standard format, and will probably be available and supported for the coming years.

7.2.5.4 Evaluation of GUMO + UbisWorld for Reuse

Physical quality: Different versions of OWL-files are available. This can be opened and updated in Protégé.

Empirical quality: A visualisation as foldable trees in online browser is available. The full ontologies cannot be viewed, as only smaller parts can be viewed at a time.

Syntactic quality: The OWL validator classifies GUMO + UbisWorld to OWL Full.

Semantic quality: Considering the general description, we would expect several similarities with what we need in relation to a person profile. However, concepts we would think of as relations are modelled as classes, independently of the person class. In GUMO, classes that describe a person and his surroundings are modelled, e.g. *DomainDependentDimensions* with subclass *Interest*, and *BasicUserDimensions* with the subclass *Demographics* and *DomainDependentDimensions* with subclass *Interest*. In the UbisWorld extension, a *Person* class is included. Hundreds of Person instances are defined, but do not have properties. Few properties are modelled, and none are relevant for us. From this, we find that there is a mismatch in how the domain and the related concepts are modelled. Therefore, personal information, stable interests, and temporary interests cannot be fully modelled.

Pragmatic quality: Several OWL versions of GUMO and UbisWorld exist, but when to use which one is not specified. The Web sites do not provide any tutorial or user manual. The online ontology browser provides foldable trees of selected parts, together with elements and statements about them in a separate window. It is unfortunate that the browser in the tree structure includes symbols that are not explained (e.g. grey/orange squares, auxiliaries, ranges), and that the assumed corresponding concepts in the OWL versions are modelled as classes. Information presented in the browser contains different, sometimes more, knowledge, and different representation of concepts than the OWL versions. For example, the person Boris from browser which has different properties (e.g. hasProperty Gender, hasProperty Age, hasProperty SpatialLocation, hasProperty Heartbeat), but these are not represented in the OWL version. Such inconsistencies between browser and OWL versions are confusing. It would be advantageous with more information to clarify how information in the online browser is connected to the OWL versions. Specifically, how attributes relate to a person, or if it is not supposed to be directly related to a person in the OWL version should be specified.

Social quality: GUMO is still under development. It is difficult to know how many followers there are, but several papers about GUMO and the environment have been published from a group of people related to its development.

Deontic quality: One needs a user profile and password to access available files, but these are freely available once logged in. The ontology is available in a standard format, and will probably be available and supported the coming years. It might not be stable though.

7.2.6 Summary of Evaluation

The result of the evaluation is summarised in Table 7.1. We see that for physical quality all providers have available OWL files for download. Even the knowledge bases that have not initially been created as OWL-ontologies have been translated into OWL. All can be viewed and edited in Protégé except OpenCyc.

Only SUMO provides a visual view of the structure of the ontology, hence giving an idea of content and class relationships. Empirical quality for FOAF is also regarded to ok satisfactory given it is the smallest ontology, and therefore has a structure that can be understood without visualisations. Even though GUMO + UbisWorld provide a foldable tree structure, it only gives a partial view and is inconvenient to use. OpenCyc and concept browsers do not give much insight on overall structure.

When it comes to semantic quality, we find differences. The large ontologies have a broader view on a person than what is useful for our purpose. We view a person as a physical actor that needs to be described so that he can act in the world. The personal information category of the profile has been best covered by FOAF and SUMO. Stable and temporary interests have not been covered completely by any of the ontologies. GUMO + UbisWorld have modelled many relevant aspects of a person, but they are not connected to a person class, therefore causing a semantic mismatch relative to our specification. In addition, FOAF and GUMO + UbisWorld have irrelevant elements, but not to the same extent as the large ontologies.

Table 7.1 Summary of evaluation

Quality category	FOAF	OpenCyc	SUMO	GUMO + UbisWorld
Physical	Available	Available, but too big to open	Available	Available
Empirical	Ok	Less satisfactory	Ok	Less satisfactory
Syntactic	OWL Full	Not decidable	OWL Full	OWL Full
Semantic	Partial overlap but not complete, ok validity	Difficult to decide completeness, poor validity	Partial overlap but not complete, poor validity	Overlap, but modelling mismatch
Pragmatic	Ok	Not satisfactory	Not satisfactory	Not satisfactory
Social	Mature and widely used	Assumed mature, not specified how much it is used	Assumed mature, not specified how much used it is	Not mature, but referenced
Deontic	Free, accessible, and stable	Free, not accessible, and probably stable	Free, accessible, and probably stable	Free, accessible, and not stable

Unfortunately, it is difficult to understand the logic behind the structure of the ontologies. In general, the models are difficult to read and there are few practical examples where they are used. Hence, the pragmatic quality for particularly OpenCyc, SUMO, and GUMO + UbisWorld is poor. Browsers that describe separate concepts are not sufficient to understand the model as a whole, and how the different fragments are connected. More documentation directly related to the ontologies and explanations would be advantageous. FOAF has the best pragmatic quality.

The social quality also differs. FOAF is the only ontology explicitly stated as stable, while OpenCyc and SUMO are based on stable knowledge bases. However, whether the OWL versions themselves are prone to changes is not mentioned. FOAF is the most mature ontology, based on its use and number of adaptors. There are small variances regarding the organisational quality of the ontologies. All ontologies are freely available and are likely to be available in the future. However, with differing indications for how stable they will be.

The result of the evaluation is that reuse of these ontologies will not be straightforward. None of the ontologies satisfy the majority of quality requirements. Therefore, it will also be time consuming if parts of any of the ontologies were to be used as a basis for further development.

In addition to being useful for evaluating ontologies for a particular domain (here profile ontology), the approach gives general insight and information about the evaluated ontologies and about reuse of ontologies in general. It seems like the evaluated ontologies are not made to be easily reusable. Particularly, the creation of ontological versions in OWL of existing knowledge bases seems not well thought-through. In the first place, they are created in OWL Full, which gives no computational guarantee. Second, little documentation is available for the modelling decisions and how to use and understand the ontologies.

Our evaluation of reuse of these ontologies is in accordance with the two 'rules of three' in software development introduced by Glass (2003) 'It is three times as difficult to build reusable components as single use components, and a reusable component should be tried out in three different applications before it will be sufficiently general to accept into a reuse library'. This contradicts the purpose of ontologies enabling understanding and reuse. When an ontology has been created for a specific purpose by a set of modellers, it is shared between them. A different set of modellers would probably have a different view of the world. For an ontology to be reusable, more effort is needed in the construction, and it should be used in several applications.

7.3 Evaluating the Quality of Modelling Languages

Evaluation of quality of a modelling language can be done purely analytically (as the first example below), empirically, or a combination of the two (as in the two industrial cases presented later in the section).

7.3.1 Analytical Evaluation of the Quality of UML

An overview of UML was given in Sect. 3.5.1. In this section, we give an updated assessment of UML (version 2.0) highlighting both the positive aspects and the areas where improvement is needed. Earlier we have also looked at how UML in combination with the modelling techniques found in the UML-tool Rational Rose, could support the development of models of high quality (Krogstie 2001). Before presenting the evaluation, we will position UML in relation to the sets of SEQUAL.

D – Domain: According to OMG (2006), UML is a language for specifying, visualising, constructing, and documenting the artefacts of software systems, as well as for business modelling and other non-software systems. In other words, UML is meant to be used in analysis of business and information, requirement specification and design. UML is meant to support the modelling of (object-oriented) transaction systems, real-time and safety critical systems. In addition, UML is used for meta-modelling of UML itself. For those areas being directly related to the modelling domain, we will differentiate the discussion according to the different domains.

Language: We have based the evaluation on UML (version 2.0) (OMG 2006). We have not looked at any defined profiles (extensions), but concentrated on the core language. We have neither performed any detailed evaluation of OCL (Object Constraint Language). The language model we have evaluated is the official OMG-standard, in its textual form, including pictures of the different views of the meta-model and example models. Although there exist a lot of UML-books and tutorials linked to the different available UML-tools that can improve the understanding and use of the language, we have only looked specifically at the OMG standard in this evaluation.

The sets' 'Knowledge', 'Model', 'Goals', and 'Interpretation' must be judged from case to case in the practical application of a modelling language and tools. Also when it comes to weighting the different criteria against each other, this must be done in the light of the specific modelling task to be supported by the language, such as has been done by Krogstie and Arnesen (2004) and Nysetvold and Krogstie (2006), which is presented below.

The primary aim of this evaluation is to help people using UML to recognise the existing weaknesses, to be able to address these using appropriate methods and tools. It has also been used to give input to areas that should be addressed in later versions of the standard language.

The basis for the evaluation is in addition to SEQUAL

- UML 2.0 language specification (OMG 2006)
- Practical experience using UML both by the author and by other people interviewed by the author in both an industrial and an academic setting.
- Other evaluations found in the literature.

7.3.2 Language Quality of UML

The UML semantics (based on the meta-model) is the basis for evaluating the conceptual basis, whereas the notation guide is used as a basis for the evaluation of the external representation.

7.3.2.1 Domain Appropriateness

Looking a bit more in detail than what we did in Sect. 3.5.1 on the coverage of the eight main modelling-perspectives in information systems modelling, we find:

- The object-oriented perspective is primarily relevant during analysis of information and design (Davis 1995). UML has (not surprisingly) a very good support for modelling according to an object-oriented perspective, although with a limited modelling capability regarding responsibilities.
- The structural perspective is primarily relevant during analysis of information and design. This perspective is also well supported, although not as well as in languages made specifically for this purpose such as ORM (Halpin 2001). Traditional abstraction-mechanisms such as aggregation, classification, and generalisation are provided, but other OO-modelling languages and different languages for semantic data modelling have a more precise representation of these abstraction mechanisms (Barbier et al. 2001). Volumetrics is only partly supported.
- The behavioural perspective can be useful in all domains, but is particularly used in systems design. UML supports the behavioural perspective using Statecharts, but does not support the refinement of Statecharts in a satisfactory way according to (Hitz and Kappel 1998).

- The functional (process) perspective is supported on a high level through Use Case modelling (aka. 0-level DFD), a language that has been highly criticised for not being well-defined (Hitz and Kappel 1998; Génova et al. 2002). Whereas Use-cases are meant for requirements modelling, activity diagrams can be used for simple procedural description by showing control flow and the production of data or objects in a process flow. Changes to the activity diagrams are introduced in UML2.0 to improve the modelling of business processes and for supporting process simulation. The lack of traditional dataflow in activity diagrams has been noted as a problem. Note that another standard in this area, BPMN (OMG 2011) has been taken over by OMG, although there are no immediate plans for including BPMN in UML.
- The actor-role perspective can be relevant in analysis of business and design. It is partly covered using the Collaboration Diagrams. Using roles in Sequence Diagrams or 'swimlanes' in Activity Diagrams, we also get a role-oriented view, but there is no intuitive way to represent organisational and group-structures and how they interact in UML, something which is very useful for the analysis of organisations and organisational structures.
- Single rules can be used in all domains. It is possible to formulate single static rules in OCL. There are some general problems with constraints expressed in an OO modelling framework in particular rules applying to several objects (Høydalsvik and Sindre 1993). Temporal and deontic constraints are hard to express. Whereas these kinds of concepts are not included in UML, another OMG initiative, SVBR described briefly in Sect. 3.3.5 includes e.g. deontic operators. For the moment, there are no plans for including SVBR in UML. There are also problems expressing non-functional requirements, such as QoS (Aagedal and Ecklund 2002), performance (Pllana and Fahringer 2002), reliability, or security requirements (Lodderstedt et al. 2002). There are also technical problems with visibility of e.g. private attributes used in constraints. There is no support for goal-hierarchies (Mylopoulos et al. 1999), a technique primarily used in analysis of businesses and requirements specification.
- The language-action perspective, which is most useful for the analysis of businesses, is not supported.
- The topological perspective is not supported

Although comprehensive, UML cannot be used to model complete applications. It lacks some constructs for e.g. architecture (Hilliard 1999), user-interfaces (Kovacevic 1998), hypermedia (Baumeister et al. 1999), and web-development (Hennicker and Koch 2001). Also for emerging areas, such as mobile agents (Klein 2001) and mobile information systems (Kosiuczenko 2002) several extensions have been suggested.

A meta-model of UML is defined (using parts of UML itself), and there exist extension mechanisms to make the language more applicable in specific domains. UML extensions have focused on lightweight extension mechanisms, such as stereotypes, constraints and tagged values (compared to meta-classes, which is regarded as a heavyweight extension mechanism).

Most of UML is first useful during design. These language mechanisms should not be used in analysis and requirements specification, even in areas where the transition from analysis to design is 'seamless'. (There are quite some evidence that especially for business systems, this transition is far from seamless even when using object-oriented modelling in all domains (Davis 1995; Høydalsvik and Sindre 1993; Lauesen 1998)). Proper guidelines for avoiding this are not consistently provided, and there is no support for avoiding using analysis and design concepts in the same model. It is generally believed that a good method should help you to keep information about what a system should do, separated from how that functionality should be implemented in a specific implementation environment. The connections between such models should also be possible to express. UML gives limited support in this regard.

There are also mismatches between underlying basis and external representation. In sequence diagrams, for instance, the following characters are semantically vacant (Morris and Spanoudakis 2001) giving examples of symbol excess.

- Time axis
- Swimlanes
- Sequence number labelling an arrow
- Lifeline
- Lifeline split into two or more concurrent lifelines
- Activation box
- Construction marks
- Slanted downward arrow
- Arrows leaving a single point labelled with guard conditions which are not mutually exclusive

We also find examples of concrete constructs in the meta-model, with no representation in the notation, i.e. symbol deficit (e.g. 'namespace' and 'model').

7.3.2.2 Comprehensibility Appropriateness

Some main observations on this area:

- UML can be argued to be overly complex, with 233 different concepts (in UML 1.x) (Castellani 1999). In (Siau and Cao 2001) a detailed comparison using the complexity metrics devised by (Rossi and Brinkkemper 1994) is presented. The various diagrams in UML are found to not be distinctly different from the diagrams in other OO methods. Although UML has more diagramming techniques than other OO methods, each of the diagramming techniques in isolation is no more complex than techniques found in other OO methods. In fact, for most of the metrics, most UML diagrams rank in the middle, except class diagrams, which are more complex than similar diagrams in other approaches. On the overall method level on the other hand, UML stands out noticeably, being most complex according to most of the metrics. Compared to other OO-method, UML consist of 3–19 times more object types, 2–27 more relationship types, and 2–9 times more property types. As a result, UML is 2–11 times more complex than other OO methods. On the other hand, Erickson and Siau (2007) point to that the actual usage of a large number of the concepts within UML is limited, making the problem in practice less acute.

- With so many concepts, it is not surprising that some redundancy and overlap is witnessed, introducing symbol overload. Some examples:
  - The concepts Signal and Operation call are almost identical.
  - How to differentiate between the use of types and the use of classes is poorly defined.
  - Guards, Preconditions, Postconditions, Constraints, Multiplicity, and Invariants are all different types of rules. On the other hand, these terms might be so well established in the usage of different diagrams that it causes few problems in practice.
- Symbol redundancy: Several examples of this can be found. For instance, a transition in an activity diagram represents a flow of control, whereas a transition in a Statechart diagram symbolises a change of state.
- Perceptual discrimination:
  - Both classes and objects are shown using rectangles.
  - Slightly slanted arrows may not be differentiable from horizontal arrows in sequence diagrams.
  - There is nothing in the sequence diagram notation to distinguish between the name of a signal and the name of an operation.
  - Use-cases, States in Statecharts and Activities in Activity Diagrams are all shaped more or less like an ellipse.
  - The same symbol is used for choice in Activity diagram, aggregation, and n-ary associations.
- UML contains many possibilities of adding (often small) adornments to the models. In addition to that such adornments often are difficult to see and comprehend, when sensed, they are found to often be difficult to link to the right concept (syntactic disjointness). Morris and Spanoudakis (2001) for instance, have identified the following problems in relation to syntactic disjointness in sequence diagrams alone:
  - Name of arrow/timing label
  - Sequence number labelling an arrow/timing label/name of error
  - Text label next to activation box or in the left margin/timing label/name of error/sequence number labelling an arrow
  - Guard condition attached to x-arrow/name of arrow/timing label
  - Iteration condition attached to arrow-x/name of arrow/timing label
- Uniform use of symbols: The predecessor of the structural model in UML, OMT had many deficiencies in this area, some of which have been addressed in UML:
  - Contrary to OMT, there is in UML a uniform way of showing cardinality (what is called 'multiplicity' In UML).
  - Associations are shown in two ways, compared to the four ways of showing associations in OMT (see Fig. 7.5).
  - Different symbols are used for a role if it is external to the system (pin-man) or internal (rectangle).
  - An interface is shown in two different ways (as a circle, or as a class-symbol).

Fig. 7.5 Different symbols
for depicting associations
in UML

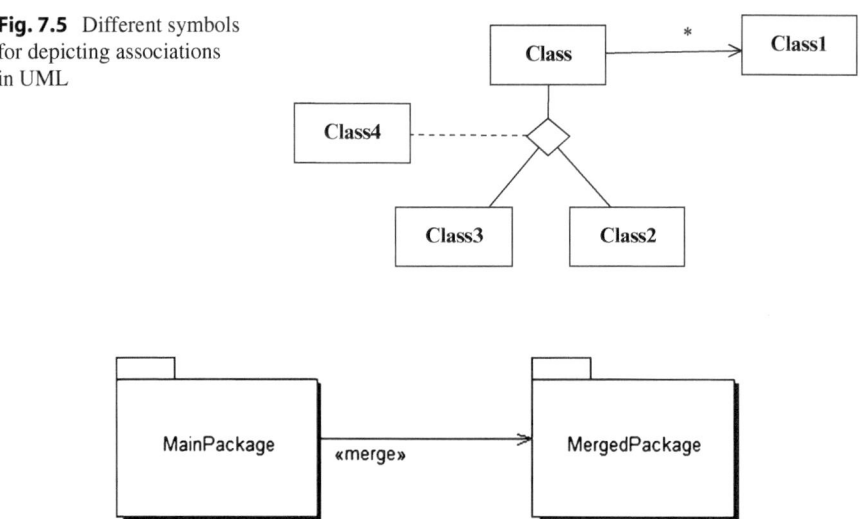

Fig. 7.6 Semantically perverse notation in UML

Many of these deficiencies are relatively unproblematic, since different aspects
are focussed on in the different models. On the other hand, having too many issues
like this makes it more difficult to learn to use the overall the language and comprehend models made in the language. This is specifically important in models used to
analyse business and information, and requirement specification, which are potentially
meant to be comprehended by many people with different backgrounds.

- Semantic transparency: According to Moody (2009), some UML conventions
  (e.g. package merge) are semantically perverse. A package merge is a directed
  relationship between two packages that indicates that the contents of the two
  packages are to be combined, illustrated in Fig. 7.6. There are no differentiation
  between a sub-language for novices and a language for experts, although
  investigations (Erickson and Siau 2007) indicates that different sub-sets of the
  modelling language and different diagrams are used for the modelling of different
  types of systems.
- Complexity management: According to Moody (2009), UML lacks a consistent
  approach to complexity management, in that different diagram types have different
  ways of dealing with complexity, while some diagram types such as class
  diagrams have none at all.
- Graphic economy: Some symbols are unnecessarily complex, e.g. the components in Components Diagrams. There are historical reasons for the use of this
  symbol, to make it easier for people used to the Booch notation to recognise
  these. For those unfamiliar with the Booch-notation on the other hand, this is
  negative. As illustrated in Moody (2009), Textual differentiations is used to a
  large degree in UML e.g. by using text and typographic characteristics (bold,
  italics, and underlining) to distinguish between concepts.

- Use of emphasis: In the structural model, emphasis is set on classes and objects through the size of the symbols, which appears to be sensible. Most of the usage of filled symbols found in OMT is removed, with the exception of full aggregation, which can be argued to be an intuitive use of this effect. That the class-symbols get different size and shape dependant on the number of attributes and operations that are defined makes these potentially more visually complex. This is out-weighted by the fact that the diagrams get much simpler than if attributes and operations should be represented separately, as done in many languages for structural modelling. The same positive remark can be made on the onion-notation inherited through adopting Harel's Statecharts. The possibility of grouping classes/objects in packages and composite classes and objects is also potentially a positive aspect in this connection, which is an improvement over its predecessors.
- Cognitive integration: UML lacks a summary diagram, and the relationships between different diagram types are unclear.

7.3.2.3 Participant and Modeller Appropriateness

It can be argued that for those being familiar with the main OO-modelling concepts and main OO modelling-languages, the core of UML should not represent a too steep learning curve. We should also note that almost all Computer Science and Information Systems-degrees now include a course or more where parts of UML is lectured and used. On the other hand, we have noted the complexity of the language above. The large number of constructs in UML is partly due to its diverse diagramming techniques coming from a number of approaches (Siau and Cao 2001). Constructs in use case diagrams are very different from constructs in class diagrams. Class diagrams are also very different from activity diagrams or Statecharts. This diversity causes problems. First, there are more constructs to learn. Second, the knowledge and experience gained in using one diagramming technique cannot be easily transferred to another diagramming technique in UML. Sometimes, as indicated above, one concept can have different semantics in different diagrams. This can be very confusing for a novice user.

7.3.2.4 Tool Appropriateness

The UML-syntax is rigorously defined, and the language is described through a meta-model made in the structural model of UML with accompanying OCL-rules and natural language descriptions of the semantics. Using UML to model UML means that some of the definitions are circular, and this leaves UML (formally speaking) undefined. This would be unproblematic if most practitioners already understood and agreed on the meaning of the concepts (e.g. classes, inheritance, and associations) that are involved. To illustrate that this can be problematic, we can point to that the concept 'inheritance' is used in three different ways in the OO-literature (Taivalsaari 1996). UML supports one of these. There are significant improvements in the meta-model of UML 1.4 and UML 2.0 compared with the first version of the language, although it falls short of a strict meta-modelling approach (Kobryn 1999). UML 1.4 had neither a formal mathematical nor an operational semantics, and there is no support for the generation of design models from analysis models, or implementation models from design models. OCL also give the potential for some of the analysis and consistency checking that a formally defined mathematical semantics would provide. In UML 2.0, a formal (operational) action language have been included to support a wider repertoire of modelling techniques. In addition, transformations are supported in more rigour. Only some parts of UML have been provided a formal (operational) semantics. So-called semantic variation points are included in UML 2.0 to clearly indicate where the semantics is not rigorously defined. In any case, the UML meta-model only describe the structural aspects of the language, and not the behavioural aspects.

7.3.3 Quality of the UML Language Model

As indicated above, we base this on the standard-document from OMG. This is a textual document with inline, static models. For UML 2.0, there also exist models for browsing using a UML-tool. As indicated in the preface of the standards document, the intended audience of the document is OMG, standards organisations, book authors, trainers and tool builders, and not modellers themselves, which are referred to a reference manual. The relevant parts of the document are several hundred pages long, and we will here only presents some highlights of the evaluation.

7.3.3.1 Physical Quality
OMG's specification of UML 2.0 is primarily externalised as a several hundred page document that includes example models and a meta-model in UML itself. It is available for anyone on the OMG-web site in PDF, thus is not easily available for update in case of need to develop extensions. New versions are made available as they are developed, although it often takes a lot of time from the standard is finalised to that it is published due to the quality control process of the large document.

7.3.3.2 Empirical Quality
Since the model is not available in e.g. Word, we have not done a detailed evaluation of the readability of the text. Looking at samples of text though, this seems to be reasonably good. The meta-models and example models also seem to be of good empirical quality from the point of view of graph aesthetics.

7.3.3.3 Syntactic Quality
The main parts of the document have detailed structuring and typographic guidelines that are largely followed. The text is written in correct American English. Model examples and meta-models appear to be according to the UML-syntax.

7.3.3.4 Semantic Quality
The description of the notation and semantics is fairly complete. On the other hand, several inconsistencies exist in the language, partly because the way the meta-model is made has resulted in the inheritance of sometimes meaningless (or at least undefined) properties.

7.3.3.5 Pragmatic Quality

The pragmatic quality of the model is somewhat poor, since to understand the meaning of a given concept, you often need to look in three to four different places. In a flat text, with limited direct references, this is cumbersome to work with. Some help is given through the consistent structuring, the index, table of contents and glossary; but, here a lot of additional support would be possible to provide if one had had the language model available e.g. in a hypertext structure, or linked to a modelling tool.

7.3.3.6 Social Quality

The model is developed using the OMG-standardisation process. The membership roster of OMG, about 800 strong, includes virtually every large company in the computer industry, and hundreds of smaller ones. Most of the companies that shape enterprise and Internet computing today are represented on the Board of Directors. Any company may join OMG and participate in the standards-setting process. The one-company-one-vote policy ensures that every company has an effective voice in the process, and thus makes it possible to achieve good backing of standards that has been developed using the process. The standardisation process is fairly rigorous, but well established and thus relatively easy to follow for those who have an interest in following and contribute to the process.

7.3.3.7 Deontic Quality

The goal of the language and language model is described in the introductory chapters, where these goals are partly also linked to specific concepts in the language. On the other hand, it is difficult to track all the different parts of the modelling language back to the goals. This again would only be possible if a more hypertext or model-oriented way of representing the language model was chosen.

7.3.4 Evaluating Domain Appropriateness of BPMN

In the above evaluation of UML, the area of domain appropriateness of the conceptual basis is dealt with on a relatively high level. A more detailed evaluation on this area can be performed. We exemplify this here relative to an evaluation of BPMN using BWW (described in Sect. 3.2.1) and workflow patterns (as included in the specification of generic requirements to an enterprise modelling language in Sect. 5.3). A combination of these approaches is used in Recker et al. (2007). The numbering on workflow patterns are from Sect. 5.3.1. The findings were structured relative to the error-classes depicted in Figs. 5.1, 5.2, 5.3, and 5.4 and is summarised here

7.3.4.1 Construct Incompleteness

BPMN lack capabilities to model state-related aspects of business processes. BPMN is incapable of modelling states assumed by things and state-based patterns, respectively. Here, BWW and workflow patterns complement each other and together make a strong case for a potential revision and extension of the BPMN language in order to advance BPMN in its capability of modelling state-related semantics.

Another interesting incompleteness of BPMN is the lack of means to describe some of the data patterns. In particular, data interaction to and from multiple instances tasks cannot comprehensively be described, which is to a large extent credited to the lack of attributes in the specification of the language constructs. This finding aligns with the BWW finding that BPMN lacks mechanisms to describe properties, especially property types that *emerge* or are *mutual* due to couplings of things, or those that characterise a component thing of a composite thing (*hereditary*).

Furthermore, the Workflow Pattern analysis reveals incompleteness in BPMN's support for the majority of the resource patterns. This finding can also be supported by the BWW-based analysis as it was found that the constructs in BPMN dedicated to modelling an organisational perspective, *viz.*, Lane and Pool, are very unclearly specified (see below). Hence, it appears that a language specification containing unclear definitions on a construct level lead to incompleteness in composing these constructs to meaningful combinations of constructs.

7.3.4.2 Construct Excess

The perspective of construct excess proposes that the Workflow Patterns framework can be used as a means of reasoning for explaining why a particular language contains some constructs that, from a BWW-perspective, seem to be unnecessary for capturing domain semantics. In particular, control flow mechanisms such as logical connectors, selectors, gateways, and the like are repeatedly proposed as construct excess as they do not map to any construct of the BWW model. However, the Workflow Patterns framework suggests that these constructs nevertheless are central to control-flow modelling based on the understanding that these mechanisms essentially support the notion of being 'in between' states or activities (van der Aalst 2003).

7.3.4.3 Construct Overload

The Workflow Pattern-based evaluation reveals that while BPMN is capable of expressing all basic control-flow patterns (BPM-WF1-5), it contains multiple representations for them, thereby potentially causing confusion as to which representation for a pattern is most appropriate in a given situation. This aligns with the finding below that BPMN contains a relatively high degree of construct redundancy. Especially, in terms of modelling essential concepts, such as things, events and transformation, it appears that BPMN contains a relatively large number of redundant constructs (different forms of activity and event constructs in particular) – which complements the finding that the modelling of the most basic workflow patterns is doubled and thereby unnecessarily complex.

7.3.4.4 Construct Redundancy

The notion of construct redundancy reveals an interesting facet in the comparison of the two reference frameworks in that the findings from each framework do not seem to match with each other. As an example, the control flow patterns BPM-WF 9, 12, 13, and 14 were found to use the same graphical notation, with the differences between the solutions for these patterns only readable from the attribute settings. From the graphical model itself, it is thus impossible to identify which distinct process pattern is being represented. This in turn may result in user confusion.

The BWW analysis reveals that the Lane and Pool constructs as well as a number of event types are extensively overloaded. These constructs allow for the representation of various domain aspects, in the case of the Lane construct for example things, classes of things, systems, kinds of things etc.

These findings are not supported by the Workflow Pattern-based analysis. The patterns BPM-WF4, 6, 9, 12, 13 and 14 that were found to have equivocal representations in BPMN do not rely on the Event, Pool, or Lane constructs. Here, it would appear that the findings from the two analyses contradict each other.

7.3.4.5 Equivalence

From a BWW-perspective, there is not a single language construct in BPMN that is unambiguously and unequivocally specified. While this finding per se is problematic as the usage of any given construct potentially causes confusion in the interpretation of the resulting model (Recker et al. 2006), the Workflow Patterns framework shows that the atomic constructs provided in BPMN can nevertheless be arranged in a meaningful, unambiguous manner to arrange a series of control-flow, data, and resource patterns. This indicates that it is not sufficient to analyse languages solely on a construct level, but it is moreover required to assess the modelling context in which the language constructs are used to compose 'chunks' of model semantics. In this matter, the Workflow Patterns framework appears to be an extension in the level of analysis offered by BWW, which look at individual concepts.

7.3.5   Evaluating Quality of Enterprise Modelling Languages

SEQUAL has been used in several organisations to support the selection of a modelling language. We will present two of these, being done for an oil company (Krogstie and Arnesen 2004), and for an insurance company (Nysetvold and Krogstie 2006), respectively.

7.3.5.1 Business Process Modelling in an Oil Company

The company is one of the largest companies in Norway. It is primarily in the energy sector, specifically within upstream and downstream of oil and gas. Although the main work of the company is connected to Norway and the North Sea, the company also has an increasing international presence.

7.3.5.2 Requirements

The detailed requirements to the modelling language were established in discussion with company representatives. The main contact for this area at the company, being responsible e.g. for methodological issues in the company, had both a long-time background in connection to several enterprise modelling tasks within different parts of the company, and a good overview of modelling and modelling techniques in general, with a PhD-degree within the area. Our discussions were primarily with him, and he communicated further with different parties within the company.

The main requirements were the following:

- The process modelling language should be a language for sense-making and communication (category 1 and 2 in the overview in Chap. 1).
- The language should be usable by leaders on top and medium levels, and others that are not used to model with graphical languages.
- The language should be simple, but still have sufficient expressiveness.
- The language should be independent of any specific modelling domain.
- It should be possible to use the language to describe work-processes across organisational areas.
- It should be possible to use the modelling language both for modelling routine and non-routine work.
- It should be possible to model processes both on a type and on an instance level.

The following concepts were regarded as mandatory to be able to model:

1. Processes – including decomposition of the process
2. Activities – indicating the lowest level of a process model
3. Roles
4. Decisions and decision-points
5. Flow between processes, activities, and decision points

The following concepts were regarded as recommended (but not mandatory) to be able to model:

1. Deliverables (process results e.g. in the form of documents)
2. System resources (here with a focus on computerised information systems as the main type of resources)

It was not a requirement that all the concepts should be expressed with a separate symbol.

It should be possible to develop the model incrementally. More concretely, this meant:

- It should be possible to model only processes and flows and independently model these concepts.
- It should be possible to model activities and flows and independently model these concepts.
- It should be possible to model roles, decision points, system resources, and deliverables independently.

A general set of requirements to a modelling language based on the version of SEQUAL has been developed. This amounts to around 70 requirements. These were looked at relative to the requirements of the company, and their importance was evaluated as indicated in Table 7.2.

Table 7.2 Grading of language quality requirements

Grade	Explanation
0–3	Requirement has no or very limited relevance
4–6	Generally relevant requirements, but not specifically important for the case
7–9	Specifically relevant requirements for the specific needs of the case
10 (mandatory)	An absolutely necessary requirement

Only requirements given a grade of seven or more were included to be used in the evaluation. In addition, requirements on domain appropriateness were detailed further compared to the general framework, including the mandatory and recommended concepts mentioned above. This resulted in the evaluation-criteria listed in Table 7.3.

The company was in this connection not interested in automatic reasoning and execution/simulation, and did not want requirements on tool appropriateness to decide on the choice. It was mandatory that the syntax of the language was well-defined though.

7.3.5.3 Evaluation

The approach to the evaluation was the following: First, a short-list of relevant languages was identified by us and the client in co-operation. The chosen languages were then evaluated according to the selected criteria. To look upon this in more detail, all languages were used for the modelling of several real cases (including both models on an instance and a type level) using an 'independent' modelling tool, i.e. a tool that could be used for modelling with all notations, without being particularly made for one of them. The tool used in this case was Microsoft Visio. By showing the resulting models and evaluation results to the persons from the company, we got feedback and corrections both on the models and the grading. The overall result identified two candidates, where aspects such as available tool support in connection to supporting all aspects of model quality (i.e. organisational quality) were instrumental to come up with a final choice.

Based on discussions with the company and experts on Enterprise Modelling, five languages were selected on a short-list of relevant languages. One that was an internal variant of a flow-charting technique, and four externally made languages. These will be briefly described.

Language Used in the Modelling Conference Technique (Gjersvik et al. 2004)

Gjersvik has developed a very simple process modelling language to use in so-called participatory modelling conferences, which had been used in the company earlier. The language has only three symbols: Process, Products (intermediate and final), and Flow between processes and products. This language and the technique was described in Sect. 2.4.1.

Table 7.3 Selected requirements to modelling language

No	Requirement	Type of req.
1	The language should be independent of business domain	Domain appropriateness, underlying basis
2	The language should be able to express the following concepts:	
2.1	Processes: A process can consist of several sub-processes or activities, i.e. process decomposition	"
2.2	Activities: The lowest level of a process model	"
2.3	Roles (of persons involved in the process)	"
2.4	Decision points/decision rules	"
2.5	Flow between processes, activities, and decision points.	"
2.6(r)	Deliverables (results)	"
2.7(r)	System resources (information-systems used in the process).	"
3	It must be possible to decompose processes in as many levels as necessary	"
4	Also the process-symbols should be decomposable	Domain appropriateness, external representation
5	The terms used for concepts must be same as terms used for these concepts in the company	Participant appropriateness conceptual basis
6	It must be easy to learn the language	" "
7	The external representation must be intuitive, meaning that the symbol represents the concept better than another symbol would	Participant appropriateness external representation
8	The different concepts must be easily distinguishable	Comprehensibility appropriateness conceptual basis
9	The number of concepts must be at a reasonable level	"
10	The language must be flexible in the level of detail	"
11	Perceptual discriminability should be easy	Comprehensibility appropriateness external representation
12	The use of symbols should be uniform	"
13	One should strive for symbolic simplicity, both in the individual symbols, and for how they are related.	"
14	The use of emphasis in the notation should be in accordance with the relative importance of the concept	"

EEML (Extended Enterprise Modelling Language) (Krogstie and Jørgensen 2004)

EEML (Extended Enterprise Modelling Language) was originally developed in the EU-project EXTERNAL. EEML was described in Sect. 3.5.2.

UML Activity Diagrams (from UML 1.4) (Booch et al. 1999)

This is described earlier in Sect. 3.5.1

Table 7.4   Grading of modelling languages relative to requirements

Grade	Explanation
0–3	There is no, or very limited, support of the requirement
4–6	The requirement is partly supported
7–9	There is satisfactory support of the requirement
10	The requirement is very well supported

IDEF-0 (Integration Definition Language 0) (IDEF-0 1993)

IDEF-0-diagrams have two main symbols: Functions (boxes), Flow (arrows) of different types between functions, and different types of ports on the functions (input, output, control, and mechanisms)

7.3.5.4   The Current Language for Enterprise Modelling in the Company

Through earlier enterprise modelling and reengineering-projects, the company had developed a language that is similar to role-oriented process flow-languages. The following concepts are provided:

1. Role
2. Input (Start)
3. Output (Product)
4. Process
5. Activity
6. Decision point
7. Delivery flow
8. Internal connector
9. External connector
10. QA check point
11. Document
12. Information system

A work-process can be decomposed in several sub-processes, which can be decomposed further. On the lowest level, one has activities, which cannot be decomposed.

7.3.5.5   Overview of Evaluation Results

Below the main result of the evaluation is summarised. For every language, every requirement is scored according to Table 7.4.

The grading for each language is found in Table 7.5. The two last rows summarise the results.

Based on the evaluation, two of the languages where clearly inferior: IDEF-0 and Gjersvik's language. The internal language developed/adapted by the company itself has the highest sum taking into account also the recommended requirements, whereas UML activity diagrams got slightly ahead when only including the mandatory requirements. EEML comes third using both summations. EEML was regarded as too complex when only looking at the support of modelling category one and two (which is not surprising, since it is meant to be used across all categories), with too many concepts, symbols and constraints for inexperienced modellers. Thus, looking

Table 7.5 Grading per requirement per language

No	Requirement	Gjersvik	EEML	Company internal	UML – AD	IDEF-0
1	Domain independence	10	10	10	10	10
2	Expressiveness					
2.1	Processes	10	10	10	10	10
2.2	Activities	6	6	10	6	6
2.3	Roles	0	10	10	10	0
2.4	Decision points	0	7	7	7	0
2.5	Flow	5	10	10	10	10
2.6	Deliverables (results)	8	10	10	5	10
2.7	System resources	0	8	7	0	0
3	Decomposable processes	0	10	7	7	10
4	Decomposable symbols	0	10	7	7	10
5	Equal naming of concepts and domains	9	6	8	9	7
6	Language easy to learn	10	6	7	8	6
7	Intuitive external representation	7	8	9	9	10
8	Easy to separate symbols	10	6	10	10	10
9	Reasonable number of concepts	4	5	7	9	4
10	Flexible in precision	4	10	10	5	0
11	Easy to differentiate different symbols	10	5	7	9	10
12	Consistent notation	5	10	7	10	3
13	Symbolic simplicity	9	5	10	10	10
14	Use of emphasis	7	7	9	10	10
	Sum including recommended requirements 2.6 and 2.7	114	159	172	161	136
	Sum excluding recommended requirements 2.6 and 2.7	106	141	155	156	126

only at the language quality, two languages were found as candidates for further investigation. Based on earlier critique of UML activity diagrams (in UML version 1.4), it was somewhat surprising that this language scored as high as it did. On the other hand, when using this only for sense-making and communication, one could ignore the somewhat alienating official state-oriented semantics defined in UML 1.4, and use the activity diagram more or less as a traditional flow-chart. When looking at these languages in connection to other aspects in SEQUAL, e.g. including tool support, it appeared that for instance even if activity diagrams as defined in UML 1.4 do have decomposition, the available UML-tool in the company at the time (Rational Rose) did not support decomposition of activities very well at the time. It neither supported the more intuitive semantics of activity-diagrams (which was introduced in UML2.0), but rather the official semantics at the time.

The final choice was done by the company, which in this case decided to keep and extend their existing language, differentiating between two versions of the language and provide further tool and organisational support for using these variants. The choice was based on both the language appropriateness, and the availability and cost of wide tool support for the language. Note that at the time this evaluation was done, BPMN had not yet been standardised. At a later stage, the company has decided to switch to use BPMN as the official modelling notation for process models.

7.3.5.6 Selecting a Business Process Modelling Language in an Insurance Company

The insurance company in our second case has a large number of life insurance and pension insurance customers. The insurances are managed by a large number of systems of different age being based on different technology. The business processes of the company go across systems, products and business areas, and the work pattern is dependent on the system being used. The company has modernised its IT architecture. The new IT architecture is service-oriented, based on a common communication bus and an EAI-system to integrate the different existing system. To be able to support end-to-end business processes in this architecture, there is a need for tools for development and evolution and enactment of business processes.

7.3.5.7 Company Requirements

The general requirements on language quality were looked at relative to the requirements of the case organisation, and their importance was evaluated. The analysis together with the case organisation resulted in the requirements found in Table 7.6.

The overall approach to the evaluation was quite similar to the one presented above. First, a short-list of relevant languages was identified by us and the case organisation in co-operation. The chosen languages were then evaluated according to the selected criteria on a 0–3 scale (compared to the 0–10 scale used in the case reported above). To look upon this in more detail, all languages were used for the modelling of several real cases from the insurance domain using a modelling tool that could accommodate all the selected languages (which in this case was METIS, now called Troux Architect). By showing the resulting models and evaluation results to persons from the company, we got feedback and corrections both on the models and our grading. The models were also used specifically to judge the participant appropriateness.

Based on discussions with persons in the case-organisation and experts on business process modelling, three languages were selected on a short-list of relevant languages.

EEML (Extended Enterprise Modelling Language)
See the description in Sect. 3.5.2

UML 2.0 Activity Diagrams
See the description in Sect. 3.5.1

BPMN (OMG 2011)
See the description in Sect. 3.3.3

Table 7.6 Requirements for process modelling language in insurance company

No	Requirement	Type of req.
1.1	The language should support the following concepts	Domain appropriateness
	(a) Processes, that must be possible to decompose	
	(b) Activities	
	(c) Actors/roles	
	(d) Decision points	
	(e) Flow between activities, tasks and decision points	
1.2	The language should support	"
	(a) System resources	
	(b) States	
1.3	The language should support basic process control patterns (van der Aalst 2003)	"
1.4	The language should support advanced branching and synchronisation patterns	"
1.5	The language should support structural patterns	"
1.6	The language should support patterns involving multiple instances	"
1.7	The language should support state based flow patterns	"
1.8	The language should support cancellation patterns	"
1.9	The language must include extension mechanisms to fit the domain	"
1.10	Elements in the process model must be possible to link to a data/information model	"
1.11	It must be possible to make hierarchical models	"
2.1	The language must be easy to learn, preferably being based on a language already being used in the organisation	Participant appropriateness
2.2	The language should have an appropriate level of abstraction	"
2.3	Concepts should be named similarly as it is in the domain where relevant	"
2.4	The external representation of concepts should be intuitive to the stakeholders	"
2.5	It should exist good guidelines for the use of the language	"
4.1	It must be easy to differentiate between different concepts	Comprehensibility appropriateness
4.2	The number of concepts should be reasonable	"
4.3	The language should be flexible in precision	"
4.4	It must be easy to differentiate between the different symbols in the language	"
4.5	The language must be consistent, not having one symbol to represent several concepts, or more symbols that express the same concept.	"
4.6	One should strive for graphical simplicity	"
4.7	It should be possible to group related statements	"
5.1	The language should have a formal syntax	Tool appropriateness
5.2	The language should have a formal semantics	"
5.3	It must be possible to generate BPEL – documents from the model	"

(continued)

Table 7.6 (continued)

No	Requirement	Type of req.
5.4	It must be possible to represent web-services in the model	ʺ
5.5	The language should lend itself to automatic execution and testing	ʺ
6.1	The language must be supported by tools that are either already available or can be made easily available in the organisation	Organisational appropriateness
6.2	The language should support traceability between the process model and any automated process support system	ʺ
6.3	The language should support the development of models that can improve the quality of the process	ʺ
6.4	The language should support the development of models that help in the follow-up of separate cases	ʺ

Table 7.7 Grading of requirements fulfilment

Grade	Explanation
0	There is no support of the requirement
1	The requirement is partly supported
2	There is satisfactory support of the requirement
3	The requirement is very well supported

7.3.5.8 Overview of Evaluation Results

Below, the main result of the evaluation is summarised. For every language, every requirement is scored according to the below scale on 0–3 (Table 7.7).

The grading is found in Table 7.8. The three last rows summarise the results.

None of the languages satisfies all the requirements, but BPMN is markedly better overall. With 77 points, BPMN scores 78% of maximum score, whereas the others score between 65% and 70%.

BPMN has the highest score in all categories, except for domain appropriateness, which is the category with highest weight, due to the importance of being able to express the relevant business process structures. EEML is found to have the best domain appropriateness, but loses to BPMN on tool appropriateness and participant appropriateness.

Comprehensibility appropriateness is the category that has the second highest weight (number of criteria), since the organisation regards it to be very important that it is possible to use the language across the different areas of the organisation, to improve communication between the IT-department and the business departments. In this category, BPMN and UML Activity Diagrams scores the same, which is not surprising given that they use the same kind of swimlane-metaphor as a basic structuring mechanism. EEML got a lower score, primarily due to the graphical complexity of the visualisation of some of the concepts, combined with the fact that EEML has a larger number of concepts than the others.

Table 7.8 Grading of requirements in insurance company

No.	Requirement description	UML AD	BPMN	EEML
1.1	The language should support the listed concepts	3	3	3
1.2	The language should support the listed concepts	2	2	3
1.3	The language should support basic control patterns	3	3	3
1.4	The language should support advanced branching and synchronisation patterns	2	3	3
1.5	The language should support structural patterns	2	3	1,5
1.6	The language should support patterns involving multiple instances	2	2	2
1.7	The language must support state based flow patterns	1	1	2
1.8	The language must support cancellation patterns	3	3	3
1.9	The language must include extension mechanisms to fit the domain	3	1	1
1.10	Elements in the process model must be possible to link to a data/information model	3	1	3
1.11	It must be possible to make hierarchical models	3	3	3
2.1	The language must be easy to learn, preferably being based on a language already being used in the organisation	2	3	1
2.2	The language should have an appropriate level of abstraction	3	3	3
2.3	Concepts should be named similarly as it is in the domain	1	3	2
2.4	The external representation of concepts should be intuitive to the stakeholders	2	2	2
2.5	It should exist good guidelines for the use of the language	2	2	1
4.1	It must be easy to differentiate between different concepts	3	3	2
4.2	The number of concepts should be reasonable	3	3	1
4.3	The language should be flexible in precision	1	2	3
4.4	It must be easy to differentiate between the different symbols in the language	2	2	1
4.5	The language must be consistent, not having one symbol to represent several concepts, or more symbols that express the same concept	3	3	3
4.6	One should strive for graphical simplicity	3	2	1
4.7	It should be possible to group related statements	1	1	2
5.1	The language should have a formal syntax	3	3	3
5.2	The language should have a formal semantics	1	3	2
5.3	It must be possible to generate BPEL documents from the model	2	3	0
5.4	It must be possible to represent web-services in the model	1	3	1
5.5	The language should lend itself to automatic execution and testing	1	3	2
6.1	The language must be supported by tools that are either already available or can be made easily available in the organisation	3	3	1

(continued)

Table 7.8 (continued)

No.	Requirement description	UML AD	BPMN	EEML
6.2	The language should support traceability between the process model and any automated process support system	2	3	1
6.3	The language should support the development of models that can improvement the quality of the process	1	1	1
6.4	The language should support the development of models that help in the follow-up of separate cases	1	1	2
	Sum	67.5	77	63.5
	Sum without tool appropriateness	59.5	62	55.5
	Sum without participant appropriateness	57.5	64	53.5

Participant appropriateness and tool appropriateness was scored equally high, and BPMN score somewhat surprisingly high on both areas. When looking at the evaluation not considering tool appropriateness, we see that the three languages score at a similar level. Thus, it is in this case, the focus towards the relevant implementation platforms (BPEL and web services) that in this case is putting BPMN on top. On the other hand, we see that this focus on technical aspects appears not to destroy for the language as a communication tool between people, at least not as it is regarded in the evaluation in this case.

In the category of organisational appropriateness, BPMN and UML Activity Diagrams score almost the same. The organisation had for some time used UML Activity Diagrams, but it also appeared that tools supporting BPMN were available for the organisation. The organisation concluded that it wanted to go forward using BPMN for this kind of modelling in the future.

We have in this section described the use of a general framework for discussing the quality of models and modelling languages in concrete cases of evaluating business process modelling languages.

The case illustrates how the generic SEQUAL framework can (and must) be specialised to a specific organisation and type of modelling to be useful in a concrete evaluation task, which it was also found to be by the people responsible for these aspects in the case organisations. In the first case, with a different emphasis than in the second, UML activity diagrams got a much higher score than EEML, whereas in the second, they scored almost equally high.

It can be argued that the actually valuation is relatively simplistic (flat grades on a 0–3 scale (or 0–10 scale in the first case) that is summarised). On the other hand, different kinds of requirements are weighted taking into account the number of criteria in the different categories. An alternative to flat grading is to use pair wise comparison and AHP (Analytical Hierarchy Process) on the alternatives (Krogstie 1999). The weighting between expressiveness, tool appropriateness, organisational appropriateness, and human understanding can also be discussed. For later evaluations of this sort, we would like to use several variants of grading schemes to investigate if and to what extent this would affect the result.

This said, we should not forget that language quality properties are never more than means for supporting the model quality (where the modelling task typically has specific goals on its own). Thus instead of only evaluating modelling languages 'objectively' on the generic language quality properties of expressiveness and comprehension, it is very important that these language quality goals are linked to model quality goals to more easily adapt such a generic frameworks to the task at hand. This is partly achieved by the inclusion of the area of organisational appropriateness. The evaluation results are also useful when a choice has been made, since those areas where the chosen language does not score high can be supported through appropriate tools and modelling methodologies.

7.3.6   Quality of Enterprise Modelling Interchange Format

We present here an evaluation of POP*, a meta-model for supporting interchange of enterprise models written in different modelling languages. The following subsection is based on the description of POP* in (Ziemann et al. 2006).

7.3.6.1 The POP* Meta-model

The main goal of the POP* methodology is to provide a 'standard' *model exchange device*, a common format containing a set of basic modelling constructs. By creating mappings from individual enterprise modelling languages (EMLs) to this common format, enterprises will be able to exchange models in those EMLs.

The exchange device looked at here is the *POP* methodology*, and consists of the POP* meta-model together with guidelines and scenarios for its management and use. The work is inspired by existing initiatives and standards, most notably the process oriented BPDM (OMG 2004), BPMN 1.0 (BPMI 2004), UEML 1.0 (Berio et al. 2003), and ISO/DIS19440 (ISO 2004). Although some overlap may be found between POP* and the mentioned initiatives, the ambition was for POP* to take a holistic approach, covering all relevant aspects of collaborating enterprises.

7.3.6.2 Structure of the POP* Meta-model

An enterprise is complex, and is correspondingly hard to capture completely in a model. The approach is to decompose the concept of enterprise into several dimensions/perspectives, each representing a certain aspect of an enterprise, or a perspective from which to consider the enterprise in question. This has also been termed *knowledge dimensions*. Five dimensions are included in POP*, namely the Process, Organisation, Product, Decision and Infrastructure dimensions, in addition to a set of general concepts (POP* Core) applicable by all dimensions.

The dimensions are described as follows:
1. The *Product dimension* is used to model product architectures or product structures.
2. The *Organisation dimension* focuses on organisational structures, human beings, and their interaction.

3. The *Process dimension* includes constructs related to activities, tasks and processes going on in the enterprise or between enterprises. This is shown in more detail below.
4. The *Decision dimension* is used to model the decision-making structure in terms of decision centres and decision activities.
5. The *Infrastructure dimension* includes constructs to support modelling of infrastructures and the services they provide.

7.3.6.3 The Process Dimension Meta-model

The process dimension includes modelling constructs related to activities, tasks and processes going on in an enterprise or between enterprises.

The main components in a POP* compliant process model are *connect points* connected by *flows*. Any connect point may have zero or more flows coming in to or going out from it, and the logical behaviour in each case is denoted by its properties *in-flow logic* and *out-flow logic*, respectively.

A connect point may be either a *process* or a *gateway*. The decomposable concept of Process is used to represent any kind of activity or work, at any level of abstraction. Gateways have the same (flow) logical capabilities as Process, but are empty in the sense that it does not represent any work, and is used mainly to represent control flow. Various types of resources and actors may be connected to the process by any of the relationships *has input, has output, has control* and *has resource,* indicating the resources' and actors' participation in the process. Note that the relationships mentioned relates objects directly to the process in which they take part. Their respective parts in the process are expressed by attaching *roles* to the relationships. In this context, roles may be one of the subtypes Input, Output, Control or Resource (inspired by IDEF0), which are to be attached to the task has input, has output, has control and has resource relationships, respectively.

7.3.6.4 Evaluation Results

Based on the criteria defined in Sect. 5.3 we have performed an analytical evaluation of the POP* language (ATHENA 2006). In the overall list of criteria, we looked upon criteria in all these areas for both the conceptual basis and the notation. Given that POP* is not supposed to have a notation per se, only criteria relevant for the conceptual basis have been evaluated. Of these, we have also regarded some to be out of scope for the POP* work. In addition, for a general evaluation, aspect related to the needs of specific people and organisations are not included. Thus, the criteria used are primarily within the areas of domain appropriateness, comprehensibility appropriateness and tool appropriateness. The selection process ended up with 103 criteria, the majority of criteria being related to domain appropriateness (i.e. that POP* can represent/express major enterprise modelling concepts). It is especially on this area specific needs have been identified (building further on the work done on this in the UEML-project (Knothe et al. (2001); Petit 2002). For domain appropriateness, there are a large number of areas defined. Obviously, not all aspects are equally important in all domains and relative to all modelling goals, and in some cases some of these concept might even bring negative value. On the other hand, for a generic model exchange environment, it is important to be able to capture a large number of concepts.

For the selected criteria, for both version 1 and version 2 of POP*, we evaluated these according to the following scale

- 3: Covers the criteria
- 2: Covers most of the criteria
- 1: Covers limited parts of the criteria
- 0: Do not address the criteria at all

No further prioritisation of criteria has been performed (i.e. all selected criteria have been given the same weight).

Below, we summarise how well POP* cover the main modelling in areas within enterprise modelling as outlined in Chap. 1:

- 1 + 2 Human-sense making and communication: Well covered
- 3 Computer-assisted analysis: Limited coverage
- 4 Quality assurance: Limited coverage
- 5 Model deployment and activation:
    - 5.1 Manually through people: Well covered
    - 5.2 Automatically: Somewhat limited coverage
    - 5.3 Interactively: Well covered
- 6 The model is a basis and gives the context for a traditional system development project, without being directly implemented: Some limitations

Especially areas 1, 2, and 5.3 (for supporting model-generated workplaces as described in Sect. 2.3.6) are regarded as specifically relevant for POP*. These are also those areas where the coverage is best. In addition, there are usages within IT-development (area 6) and evolution and interoperability that are specifically relevant.

Table 7.9 contains the results from evaluating the language quality aspects for version one and version two of POP*.

Summing up the results of the individual criteria as, we got the following overall results:

- POP* version 1: 57%
- POP* version 2 : 71%

That is we can say that at least as the solution as described, we surpass the KPIs defined in the project of covering 60% of the requirements. In addition, practical experiments have been performed to interchange models between three different tools, using three different process modelling languages.

In the first version, we did not reach the goal. The following limitations were identified mostly related to domain appropriateness:

- Major limitation as for the modelling of all sorts of goals, rules, and conditions. This area was partly addressed in version 2.
- Need for a typology of objects. This was addressed in version 2.
- Limitation as for the modelling of states (of things in general, including processes, documents etc.). This was addressed in version 2.
- Limitations as for the modelling of aspects related to time and time-dependant behaviour. This was partly addressed in version 2.

Table 7.9 Evaluation of POP* version 1 and version 2

Criteria	Short description (see Sect. 5.3 for further description)	POP* v1	POP* v2
UEML_12	Link between processes purposes and business goals	0	2
UEML_15	Connectivity between strategic, engineering, management of operational process	1	2
UEML_16	EM should be useful to improve enterprise processes	1	1
UEML_18	Model 'hard' and 'soft' aspects of human participative and resource systems	1	2
UEML_22	Capture and explain business rules	0	2
UEML_23	Relations between process and business and between their rules	1	1
UEML_31	Use generic concepts to provide flexibility	2	2
UEML_32	Meta-data possibilities for each construct	0	0
UEML_37	Capture social and organisational relationships	3	3
UEML_44	Foresee semantics and syntax to support integration in the future	3	3
UEML_50	More than one orientation in a model	3	3
IDEAS_6	Model the virtual enterprise	2	2
IDEAS 7	Holistic Distributed modelling and use of models	3	3
S19	Project definition services	2	2
SEQ-1	Not be possible to express things that are not in the domain	3	3
UEML-1	Goals	0	2
UEML-2a	Functional aspects	3	3
UEML-2b	Process decomposition	3	3
UEML-2ci	Relationships between activities	2	2
UEML-2cii	Concurrent processing	2	2
UEML-2ciii	Events	2	2
UEML-2civ	Exception handling	1	1
UEML-2cv	Time	1	2
UEML-2cvi	Priorities	1	1
UEML-2cvii	Probabilistic behaviour	1	1
UEML-3a	Products and services for sale	3	3
UEML-3b	Material, material flow	1	3
UEML-3c	Energy flow	0	0
UEML-3d	Data, relationship between data	1	2
UEML-3e	Orders	2	3
UEML-3fi	Technology	2	3
UEML-3ii	Resource capabilities	2	2
UEML-3g	Manufacturing plant layout	0	2
UEML-3h	Business algorithms	2	2
UEML-4a	Organisational units, people, positions, departments	3	3
UEML-4b	Roles and roles structures	3	3
UEML-4c	Authority	3	3
UEML-4d	Decisions, decisions levels and decision centres	2	3

(continued)

Table 7.9 (continued)

Criteria	Short description (see Sect. 5.3 for further description)	POP* v1	POP* v2
UEML-5a	Progress in work	2	3
UEML-5b	Performance figures	1	2
BPM-P1	Process start state	1	2
BPM-P2	Process end state	1	2
BPM-P3	Pre-conditions	1	2
BPM-P3	Post-conditions	1	2
BPM-A1	Activity description	3	3
BPM-A2	Pre-conditions	1	2
BPM-A3	Post-conditions	1	2
BPM-A4	State after failure	1	2
BPM-A5	Resource consumption specification	1	1
BPM-A6	Activity duration specification	3	3
BPM-A7	Arrival rate of business documents	1	1
BPM-A8	Role assignment	3	3
BPM-A9	Resource assignment	3	3
BPM-A10	Business document assignment	2	3
BPM-T1	Guard conditions	1	2
BPM-T2	Execution probability	0	0
BPM-T3	Resource information	1	2
BPM-T4	Initial state	0	2
BPM-T5	State at activity completion	0	2
BPM-R1	Role-related information	3	3
BPM-R4	Functional role category	3	3
BPM-BD1	Business document description	3	3
BPM-BD2	Initial state	0	2
BPM-BD3	State at activity completion	0	2
BPM-IE1	Pre-conditions	1	2
BPM-IE2	Post-conditions	1	2
BPM-WF1	Sequence	3	3
BPM-WF2	Parallel split	3	3
BPM-WF3	Synchronisation	3	3
BPM-WF4	Exclusive choice	3	3
BPM-WF5	Simple merge	3	3
BPM-WF6	Multiple choice	3	3
BPM-WF7	Synchronising merge	3	3
BPM-WF8	Multiple merge	3	3
BPM-WF9	Discriminator	3	3
BPM-WF10	N-out-of-M join	0	0
BPM-WF11	Arbitrary cycles	3	3
BPM-WF12	Implicit termination	0	0
BPM-WF13	MI without synchronisation	0	0

(continued)

Table 7.9 (continued)

Criteria	Short description (see Sect. 5.3 for further description)	POP* v1	POP* v2
BPM-WF14	MI with a priori known design time knowledge	0	0
BPM-WF15	MI with a priori known runtime knowledge	0	0
BPM-WF16	MI with no a priori runtime knowledge	0	0
BPM-WF17	Deferred choice	0	0
BPM-WF18	Interleaved parallel routing	1	1
BPM-WF19	Milestone	0	1
BPM-WF20	Cancel activity	3	3
BPM-WF21	Cancel case	3	3
UEML_30	Build a model according to individual situated aspects	3	3
SEQ-7	Metaphorical modelling	3	3
UEML_4	Manage the different degrees of certainty	1	1
UEML_27	Clear semantic and clear constructs	1	2
UEML_42	Classes of compatible semantic	1	1
UEML_49	EM should be simple, but still have sufficient expressiveness	2	2
UEML_52	EM should be modular	3	3
SEQ-8	The concepts of the language should be general	3	3
SEQ-9	The concepts should be composable	3	3
SEQ-10	Both precise and vague concepts	2	2
SEQ-11	Concepts should be easy to distinguish from each other	2	2
SEQ-12	Use of concepts should be uniform	3	3
SEQ-13	The language must be flexible in the level of detail	3	3
SEQ-14	Represent the intention of the model elements	1	1
UEML_5	Help to synchronise several modelling tools	2	2
UEML_35	Invariant and unique behavioural semantic	1	1
SEQ-23	Formal (well-defined) syntax	3	3
	Coverage	178	219
		0.57	0.71

- Limitations related to advanced control-flow and aspects related to type/instances of e.g. processes as found applicable in automated workflow. This continues to be a limitation.
- Limitations as for physical layout. This was partly addressed in version 2.

Relative to tool appropriateness we identified a limitation as for the definition of behavioural semantics. This continues to be a limitation. There are also certain issues relative to comprehensibility appropriateness, e.g. as for how simple it is to keep different concepts apart. Although conscious about the problem, we realise that it is difficult to address all issues on this area, and at the same time addressing all areas related to domain appropriateness.

7.4   Developing Domain Specific Languages

In Sect. 2.3.3, we briefly discussed domain specific modelling (DSM) and domain specific modelling languages (DSL). Just as aspects of quality of modelling language are essential when developing new modelling languages, this is important when adapting, limiting, or extending existing modelling languages. We will here describe two approached to modelling language development.
1. Analytical and empirical evaluation of minor extensions to an existing modelling language to support an acknowledge limitation of the modelling language
2. A methodology based on the SEQUAL framework for full-fledge meta-modelling

7.4.1   Developing Minor Extension of Existing Languages

There are a number of examples on where people want to extend an existing language in one direction, typically because of a need to express certain concepts that is of particular relevance. Examples of this are in particular found in the use of profiles in UML some of which we mention below, a mechanism that is particularly made to support the extension of the meta-model. A limitation of the profile mechanism is that it does not discuss such extensions when they are related to updating the notation. We present here ways of thinking relative to this, both for the analytical treatment to decide candidates for extensions, and ways to perform empirical evaluations of such extension. There have been several efforts presenting adaptations of standard diagram notations. In Mendling et al. (2010), the authors propose to insert small icons inside each business process activity. Baumeister et al. (2003) propose some extensions to UML activity diagrams specifically targeting the modelling of mobile systems. Decker (2009) also proposes an adapted notation of UML activity diagrams, specifically targeting access control for mobile workflow. Kosiuczenko (2002) proposes an adaptation of UML sequence diagram that uses a location centred notation similar to that of Baumeister et al. (2003). Baumeister et al. (2003) also proposes an extension to UML class diagrams for mobility, plus some related extensions for modelling security aspects. Several other papers have proposed extensions of UML activity diagrams, but on a more technical level, addressing execution level behaviour or formal examples, e.g. Latella et al. (2005) makes a similar formal extension of state-charts for mobility.

The case relates to extending a modelling language in a way so that it covers an additional modelling perspective. The case was briefly introduced in Sect. 3.3.9 on the topological perspective, in how to introduce the notion of geographical place in a traditional process modelling notation. This section, based on material found in Gopalakrishnan et al. (2010, 2011a, b, c), is extended to take into account the latest work on quality of modelling languages reported in this book.

As discussed in Sect. 3.3.9, location is not much used in traditional modelling notations. As illustrated there, in particular for mobile and multi-channel information systems it is often relevant to model where something is supposed to take place, location being a central context-variable. It is interesting in this area to investigate the possibility of capturing the location in process models. The work reported in this paper has focused on how to best achieve this in diagram notations that slightly adapt mainstream notations. UML activity diagrams have been used as an example in concrete investigations (e.g. experiments), but the notational remedies applied could equally well have been used in BPMN or other similar process notations. The choice to focus on small adaptations is because there is a lot of investment embedded in existing notations, in terms of developers who have learnt to use them and tools available to support them. Suggesting a radically different notation would disregard this investment, and although the new notation might be theoretically optimal for mobile work processes, likelihood of industrial adoption would be smaller, especially where there exist well-established, standard notations such as UML and BPMN with advanced tool support.

The overall approach for the addressing the task have been:

1. To use analytical and descriptive evaluation on a wide range of notation alternatives. Figure 5.5 illustrates the range of possibilities for representing location using different retinal variables.
2. To use controlled experiments on the notations that appear as most promising from step 1.
3. In case findings in step 2 contradict the results of the evaluation in step 1, there is likely something wrong with the criteria used in the analytical/descriptive evaluation, which might therefore have to be redone, i.e. repeating again from step 1.

The first evaluation has taken as outset the main areas of comprehensibility appropriateness of the notation, following the nine areas described by Moody, but adding EM – Emphasis discussed in Sect. 5.1.2. Since we regard location as an important aspect, it should be emphasised in particular. Other important concepts in UML Activity diagrams are, in particular, the activity and the swim-lane for the role. Not all of Moody's nine principles (Moody 2009) are equally relevant to us. Three of the principles are excluded, namely *cognitive integration*, because it concerns relationships between several diagrams or diagram types while we are only considering activity diagrams at this point, *dual coding*, because this concerns the combination of text and visual means – which can be done fairly independent of what visual trick we use for location, and *cognitive fit*, which concerns the usage of different dialects for different stakeholder groups (where, if anything, we would need representatives from these various groups to perform the evaluations rather than doing it ourselves). This leaves us with six of Moody's principles in addition to emphasis; on the other hand, we add one additional criterion that is not in Moody's list, namely support for *multiple locations*. In our examples, in Fig. 5.3, each activity is shows as taking place in one particular location. However, for a mobile information system some activities must be supported in many different locations, so that it is up to the user's preference where to perform it (e.g. either in the office or in the car). Some activities might even take place in several places at once, for instance if performed by two collaborating persons in different locations. The need to attach several locations to some activities might obviously cause additional challenges to our notation alternatives.

Table 7.10 Evaluation of notations, responsibility-centred alternatives above grey line, location-centred alternatives below (Adapted from Gopalakrishnan et al. 2011b)

Show location by...	SC	PD	ST	CM	VE	GE	EM	ML	Sum
Text in activity node	–	–			--	++	--		−3
Text in note	–	–		--	--	++	–	+	−4
Dedicated location shape				--	--	–	++	++	−1
Iconic note	+	++	++	–	–	--	+	++	+4
Icon in icon	+	++	++	+	–	--			+3
Shape, small variation	+	–		+	--		–	–	−3
Shape, big variation	+	+		+	--	--		--	−3
Fill colour	+	++	–	+	+	+	+		+6
Fill brightness	+	+	–	+	+	+		–	+3
Fill texture	+	+		+	+	+		–	+4
Planar, responsibility by									
Iconic note	+	++	++	–	–	--	+	--	0
Icon in icon	+	++	++	+	–	--		--	+1
Fill colour	+	++		+	+	+	+	--	+5
Fill brightness	+	+		+	+	+		--	+3
Fill texture	+	+	+	+	+	+		--	+4

The rows in Table 7.10 are various notation alternatives for location; for space reasons, we omitted some that were obviously poor. The columns are the criteria used (SC = semiotic clarity, PD = perceptual discriminability, ST = semantic transparency, CM = complexity management, VE = visual expressiveness, GE = graphical economy, EM = Emphasis, and ML = multiple locations. The scores range from very poor (--), through poor, neutral, good, to very good (++). The rows above the grey line are for notation with small adaptation, i.e. planar variables used for responsibility so location must use retinal variables. Below the grey lines are alternatives using planar variables for location, so that responsibility must be shown by retinal variables. Here, we only included the five best alternatives from the upper half, since the relative merits of the various alternatives will be pretty much the same whether the retinal variables are supposed to depict location or responsibility.

We do not explain all the 120 marks in this table in detail, more information can be found in a technical report (Gopalakrishnan and Sindre 2011b). The analytical evaluation was performed by two researchers independently, then going through a consensus process afterwards, to reduce the threat of scoring error and arbitrary interpretation of evaluation criteria. However, both evaluators – although having different cultural backgrounds – came from the same university, and having a 4 year scientific relationship (supervisor and Ph.D. student), so the results must be taken with caution.

The alternatives using fills (either colour, grey-tones or patterns) generally scored well in the evaluations, because they do not introduce new nodes or links (i.e. good for complexity management), put to use visual variables that are not used for any other purposes in the notation in question (i.e. good for visual expressiveness), and are fairly easy to discriminate visually (i.e. good for perceptual discriminability). This is especially true for colour (except for colour-blind users), but brightness and texture will also be fine as long as each diagram has a limit of four to five different actors or locations that must be distinguished. Another good alternative is the use of meaningful icons inside the activity nodes ('icon in icon'). These have a big advantage where colour-fills and similar alternatives were not impressive, namely in being intuitively understandable, i.e. good for semantic transparency.

As for the choice between the radical, location centred notations using planar variables for location (lower part of Table 7.10), or the less radical responsibility centred notations using retinal variables for location (upper part), the planar alternatives might be slightly better for semantic transparency, but have problems with multiple locations, in which case activity nodes might have to be duplicated in several swim-lanes. For multiple locations, the dedicated location shape or iconic note will be the best, since an activity node can trivially be connected to a number of location nodes. Icon in icon or colour fills is not too bad either, since one can put several icons or colours inside the same node.

In Gopalakrishnan et al. (2010, 2011a) several experiment comparing two and two of the best candidates are reported. Here, we will just describe the research method used for this type of research and the main results, and refer to the original papers for the detailed results.

The first experiment was to compare a colour notation with a notation using notes. The second experiment then compared the colour notation with a similar notation using pattern-fills. Both these experiments were designed in exactly the same way, with the following experimental tasks: (1) Testing the participants' understanding of a case provided in the written experiment materials, measured by their score in answering a number of true/false questions, and (2) Testing the participants' problem solving abilities using the notation, measured by their ability to detect errors in a diagram – this, investigated by providing a textual case description declared to be correct and a diagram assumed to capture this, but deliberately seeded with some errors. In addition, we elicited the participant's opinion about the notations through a post-task questionnaire. We, thus, had three main variables to measure for each participant about each notation:

- *Understanding*: the fraction of correct answers to the true/false questions
- *Error detection*: the fraction of correctly detected errors to the total number of errors in the deficient diagram
- *Average opinion*: the average score on 14 questionnaire items about the notation

We chose the within-subjects alternative (Field and Hole 2003) for both our experiments, using a Latin Squares design to control for factors of technique and case order. We conducted two experiments using exactly the same design:

- The first experiment, performed in March 2010, compared the colour notation (X) and annotation by UML notes (Y), using cases dealing with home care (1) and traffic control (2), as reported in more detail in Gopalakrishnan et al. (2010).

- The second experiment, performed in February 2011, compared the colour notation (X) and pattern-fills (Y), using cases dealing with home care (1) and flight check-in (2), as reported in more detail in Gopalakrishnan and Sindre (2011a, b). The cases were somewhat more complex than those used in the first experiment were.

None of the participants from the first experiment were used again in the second experiment, since reuse of participants might have introduced a learning factor from the first to second experiment, thus making it more difficult to control the results. In both cases, participants were third year computer science students, 46 for the first experiment, 57 for the second experiment – but belonging to different classes since the second experiment took place a year after the first. In both cases, the students participated in the experiments voluntarily, not as part of any course, but the class received some money in reward for the participation of the students to support an excursion that the class were planning some months later. All the participants had received an introduction to UML and UML Activity Diagrams in their second year, in a compulsory course in software engineering.

Given that the colour notation came out as the most promising alternative in the analytical evaluation, we had the following key hypotheses for our experiments:

- **H1x,y**: Understanding for notation X will be better than for notation Y
- **H2x,y**: Error detection for notation X will be better than for notation Y
- **H3x,y**: Average opinion for notation X will be better than for notation Y

Also, there could be more detailed hypotheses relating to different question groups investigated in the post-task survey, i.e. five questions related to Perceived Ease of Use, five to Perceived Usefulness, and four to Intention to Use. These hypotheses would be similar to H3, i.e. assuming that the colour notation would score better than the pattern notation.

Both experiments were run according to the same scheme. The participants were randomly distributed to the four experiment groups in a Latin Squares design. They then performed the following tasks:

1. Answering a pre-experiment questionnaire: Questions investigated previous knowledge on modelling, UML, activity diagrams, specifications, IT work experience and knowledge about the domains the cases were taken from (home care and flight check-in), in total eight questions that were to be answered within 5 min. The purpose of these questions was to control for selection bias.
2. Reading a tutorial about the first diagram notation to be used (notation X or Y, depending on the person's group assignment).
3. Being presented with experimental textual case description (case 1 or 2), together with a diagram (in notation X or Y), and at the end of this, participants must answer 12 true/false questions related to that particular case.
4. Answering a post-task questionnaire about the notation just used, containing 14 questions investigating Perceived Ease of Use (PEOU), Perceived Usefulness (PU), and Intention to Use (ITU) as inspired by the TAM model (Davis 1989).
5. Repeating steps 2–4 using the other notation on a different case. Totally, 54 min were allotted to complete steps 2–5 and return the booklet.

6. A separate booklet with textual description and notations on both cases deliberately seeded with errors was distributed again and now the task was to find the errors, i.e. discrepancies between the diagram and the natural language case description. The errors (five errors per diagram) were the same both for the pattern and coloured variants of a case, and the allotted time 10 min.

In the first experiment, the colour notation excelled for the performance-based variables, yet opinion-based variables appeared equal between treatments. In the second experiment, there was no significant advantage in performance, but instead the colour notation had a strongly significant advantage for opinion. Normally, one might think that a strong preference for one notation should also be accompanied by a strong advantage in performance, and vice versa. However, other experiments have also shown that this is not necessarily the case. In (Opdahl and Sindre 2009) one technique had a significant performance advantage, yet no such advantage was found for opinion, indeed, there was no notable correlation between the participants' performance with a technique and opinion about that technique. So, a natural conclusion here seems to be that the participants have generally found the colour notation more visually appealing than the pattern notation, but they were still able to perform equally well with the b/w patterns, which given the limited number of locations might not be so surprising after all, since they could still be distinguished. For the colour vs. annotation experiment the situation might have been the opposite: Both notations may have felt visually appealing to the participants, but the increased diagrammatic complexity of the annotated notation still reduced their performance.

7.4.1.1 Threats to Validity

Wohlin et al. (2000) suggest four categories for threats to validity in experiments:
1. Conclusion validity
2. Construct validity
3. Internal validity
4. External validity

Conclusion validity concerns the relationship between the treatment given and the outcome in measured variables. One important question is whether the sample size is big enough to justify the conclusions, which can be investigated by means of the calculated effect size (ES). Accepted hypotheses were $H1_{color,annot}$ about better understanding (ES=0.51), $H2_{color,annot}$ about better error detection (ES=0.45, or with outliers removed, ES=0.77), and $H3_{color,pattern}$ about better participant opinion (ES=1.60). Denoting the Type I error probability by α (accepting a relationship that really is not there) and the Type II error probability by β (overlooking a relationship that really was there), the following holds:

$$N = \frac{4(u_{\alpha/2} + u_\beta)^2}{ES^2}$$

If we use α=0.05 (our threshold for accepting a relationship as significant) and β=0.20, we get $N=32/(ES)^2$ (Hopkins 2001) as a required sample size. This means that we should have had a sample size of 123 for understanding and 158 for error detection (or 54 for the ES achieved when outliers were removed). Our sample size was only 46 (or 43 with outliers removed). The fact that our sample size is smaller than the required ones means that our results for hypotheses $\mathbf{H1}_{color,annot}$ and $\mathbf{H2}_{color,annot}$ have to be interpreted with caution, although the difference clearly came out as significant. On the other hand, for $\mathbf{H3}_{color, pattern}$ the much bigger effect size needs only 25 participants while having 57.

Construct validity is concerned with the inference from the measures made in the experiment to the theoretical constructs to be observed (understanding, problem solving effectiveness). Of course, there are other ways to explore understanding than true/false questions, and other ways to explore effectiveness than asking participants to identify errors (e.g. to use the knowledge conveyed in the model to solve additional tasks (Gemino and Wand 2003). However, identification of errors is an important task in system development, and answering questions is one relevant way of testing understanding.

Internal validity means that the observed outcomes were due to the treatment, not to other factors. Participants were randomly assigned to treatment groups, and a Latin-Squares experimental design was used to further eliminate selection bias, and to control for any learning effects. In addition, we used a pre-experiment questionnaire to test whether other factors such as previous relevant experience could explain the differences between the various groups, but not finding any such effects. The use of students at the same level of study typically limits issues of internal validity.

External validity questions whether it is possible to generalise from the experimental setting to other situations. One question is whether one can generalise to other process notations than UML activity diagrams, e.g. BPMN? This is impossible to answer from the experimental data, but intuitively there is no particular reason why the situation should be different for BPMN or other similar process diagrams. Another and perhaps more difficult question is whether one can generalise from the experimental setting to industrial systems development. The use of students instead of practitioners is a notable threat here. However, this threat is reduced by the fact that we are only trying to compare two notations in relative terms, not evaluate their merits in more absolute terms. Adapted notations would be new also to practitioners, thus reducing the advantage they might otherwise have had over students. However, there are other simplifications also made in the experiment versus industrial practice. Modelling in industrial projects is often a group activity, where several stakeholders with different roles and backgrounds build and discuss a model together to get a joint understanding of the situation. In our experiments, participants each worked with the models individually, and the participant group was quite homogeneous, namely technology students. Hence, the experiments have not investigated the full range of challenges for the modelling notations, and an advantage that was present for individual usage of a model with technically competent users might not be the same with group usage involving less technically skilled persons.

Furthermore, models used in experiments often have to be simple compared to the models used in practice. The diagrams used in our experimental tasks typically distinguished between three and five different locations. In some practical situations, it might be necessary to distinguish between more locations, although the number of relevant places to distinguish is usually limited. Black/white patterns would be likely to break down if having to distinguish with much more than five locations. Colour would go a little longer, but would also end up with too subtle differences if the number of locations becomes high. In such case, approaches using icons or text might be better for distinguishing a higher number of locations. Hence, experiments with a higher number of locations in the diagrams would also be interesting. As for the analytical part of the evaluation, human error and researcher subjectivity are the main threats. These were partly mitigated by having two researchers perform the evaluation independently, and mainly using criteria found in the literature rather than self-made criteria. Still, this mitigation was only partial. Although the two researchers have different cultural backgrounds they currently belong to the same institution, and are both computer scientists, so using other evaluators with other work backgrounds could have given different results. More empirical data would be needed to make sure that the notation alternatives discarded as inferior from the analytical evaluation would indeed be poor in practice.

7.4.2 Supporting Comprehensive Meta-modelling

Whereas a lot of work has been done on abstractly defining new modelling languages, going back to the 1970s with DFD and ER-modelling, relatively little work is reported on methodologies for developing modelling languages to be used in a specific organisational setting. Although meta-modelling tools and approaches for language and method engineering have been available for a number of years, it is first over the last 10 years tools and approaches making meta-modelling comparatively easy to do have become mainstream. This supports a shift in focus from technical implementation of the tool support for the modelling language to specifying the requirements to the new modelling language. On the one side, within UML for instance, extension mechanisms have been defined within the language itself, starting with profiles in UML 1.X, and many UML tools provide these possibilities to their developers. Full meta-modelling has been made available in tools for domain specific modelling (DSM) such as MetaEdit (Kelly and Tolvanen 2008) and in enterprise modelling, such as METIS (Lillehagen and Krogstie 2008). Here, a case study is presented where we present a methodology for doing this based on the thinking of the SEQUAL-framework.

The organisation of the case study is an international organisation with around 300 offices around the world. The business area of the specific project we have been studying has grown over the last decades, allowing the different units to more or less carry out their back office work in their own preferred ways. A few years back they decided to try to increase the efficiency through harmonisation of the work processes across the international units. With the term *harmonised* they mean *standardised*, but with the possibilities of some local adaptations and differences. The harmonised work processes were decided to be supported through a new specially designed and developed in-house software application.

At an early point of the project, the company decided to use modelling as an approach for developing and documenting the existing and the harmonised work processes. The high-level processes were modelled using the tool Visio, using the language IDEF-0. These were among others used for communication, involvement of management, gap analysis in the units, and as an input to software development. At some point a need for more detailed models were recognised and very detailed so-called swimlane-models using Excel. These models combine text and graphical work descriptions with roles, systematised and clearly viewed through a spreadsheet. Parallel to this, descriptions of the processes was written in text documents (Word). Thus, at this point, the harmonised work processes were documented in three different places, with no mechanisms for supporting the integration and concerted evolution of the models. It was difficult to keep them updated, and the need of having the information about, the description of, and the models of the harmonised work processes in one tool became obvious. The company decided to use a specific tool (METIS) and an enterprise modelling language offering the IDEF-0 language together with a number of other sub-languages, in order to model the harmonised work processes. The case study is further described in Krogstie et al. (2004).

The chosen enterprise modelling language was seen as too comprehensive and complex for the needs of the organisation, covering much more than needed, and not covering some important issues for this project and organisation. At this point, we joined in with an activity of creating a specially adapted modelling language, implementing this language in the chosen modelling tool, and re-modelling the existing VISIO-models, excel-swimlanes, supplemented with the word text descriptions in the tool, using the tailored language. Our goal was to make the resulting language more user-friendly and to satisfy the needs within this particular organisation. In order to establish the requirements for the new language, workshops with the modellers within the project were held, we studied the existing documentation and models, and followed the thinking in SEQUAL as outlined below, identifying the relevant sets to be involved in modelling. Parts of the template were removed, while some new features had to be developed. When the requirements of the new language were implemented in the template and tool, we re-modelled the old models, swimlanes, and text descriptions in the new tool, using the new specially adapted and extended modelling language.

A base hypothesis for this work was that 'It is necessary to adapt existing standard enterprise modelling languages to support the diverse modelling needs of the project in an optimal way'. The work started out looking at the sets defined in SEQUAL. First, we identified the goals of the projects, and based on that, identifying the goals of modelling within the project, developing a goal hierarchy. This and the rest of the results from the requirements process were modelled in EEML. The overall approach can be described relative to Fig. 7.7, which is a screenshot of the top-level containers of this model. Looking back at Fig. 4.1, we see that the top-

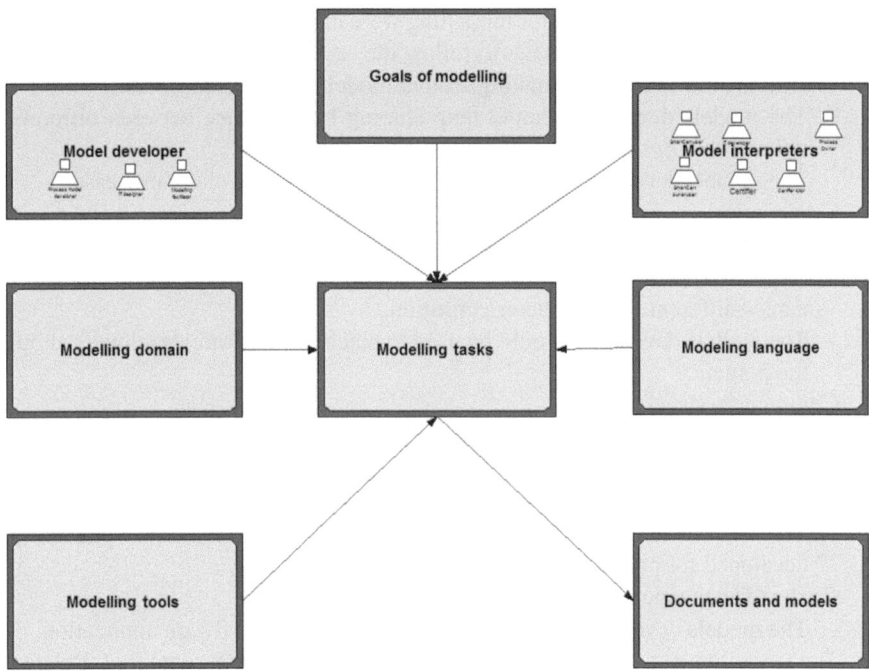

Fig. 7.7 Overall structuring of language RE-approach

level containers (including different sub-models) largely correspond to the sets in SEQUAL:

- Goals of modelling corresponds to **G**.
- The model developers have the knowledge **K**.
- The model interpreters perform model interpretation **I**.
- Modelling task to fulfil the modelling goals use modelling language enabling the required language extension (**L**), to model a modelling domain (**D**) creating models and documentation (**M**).
- Modelling tools are used in connection to this, also interpreting the model as needed based on the goals of modelling (**T**).

The goals of the overall project are structured and linked to the goals of modelling to support the fulfilling of these goals. The goals of modelling are in turn linked to relevant modelling tasks, taking into account the modelling domain. Roles and concrete people in these roles are identified for each modelling task, both relative to model developers and model interpreters. Representatives of these roles were then involved in more detailed specification of needed modelling tasks, and an appropriate modelling language for representing relevant knowledge in a comprehensible way. In addition, requirements to a modelling tool was elicited and linked to the identified modelling tasks. Based on the implementation of the language in a tool, models were made to elicit further requirements to what needed to be represented.

A number of different goals for modelling were identified (also listed in Sect. 4.1 but reiterated here to make it easier to follow the case study):

- Communication and sense-making around models of the current state
  - The models developed should help sharing best practice between different units of the organisation.
  - The models developed should be helpful in the refining of the processes.
- Communication around models of the future state
  - The new work process should be documented through the models.
  - The models developed should help harmonise the current work processes across different parts of the organisation.
  - The models developed should be used to teach the software developers about the domain.
- Computer-assisted analysis
  - The models developed should help analyse the current work processes
- Model deployment
  - The models developed should be used as a procedural tool in everyday work.
  - The models developed should support the use of the software application developed for process-support.
- Context for change
  - The models developed should define the scope of the software application.

The modelling activities to support the main goals were then identified. Related to the taxonomy of the modelling tasks presented in the introduction, this gives the following overview (we have here further differentiated between the model developers and the model interpreters (those only reading/commenting the model) since they have very different needs for functionality). The tasks that it was chosen to give priority are highlighted in boldface (Table 7.11).

7.4.2.1 Identify Requirements to the Modelling Language

The work related to defining the new modelling language was specifically based on workshops and interviews with people in the different relevant roles (as identified in the table above) in connection to the development, use, and evolution of the existing models, in addition to the re-modelling of the existing harmonised models using METIS ITM (a generic modelling language used within IT management and Enterprise Architecture). METIS ITM has later (2008) been renamed to Troux Semantics in the latest version of the tool (Troux Architect). METIS was a main candidate to act as a basis for a new modelling approach since other parts of the organisation had started trying out the tool.

First, we identified a number of concepts and relationships in different modelling domains based on the existing models. This was then matched to existing domains in METIS ITM. The needed changes and additions to this were then described.

7.4.2.2 Process Modelling

In connection to process modelling, it was recognised that two views of the model were important to support the functional IPO-view (ala IDEF-0) and the role-oriented RAD-view (ala UML activity diagrams). Different concepts are

Table 7.11 Goals for modelling, modelling tasks and modelling stakeholders in the case study

Modelling task		Model developers	Model interpreter
1. Visualise processes for communication	**1.1 Model harmonised process**	Process modeller Process owner	Worker Tool user Tool super user Process owner Software designer
	1.2 Model local process for comparison	Process owner, Process developer Local worker	Process owner Local user
2. Analyse processes for improvements		Corporate process owner Local operating manager	Process owner
4. Manual Activation of model	4.1 Learning the job		'Doers' Worker training
	4.2 Assisting job performance		Doers (a) Workers (b) Managers (c) Planners (d) Admin
	4.3 Learning the tool	Tool super user	Tool super user Tool user
	4.4 Assistance in the use of the tool		
5. Use model as basis for tool development		Process modeller	Software designer

shown in these views in different ways. Only models on the type level were regarded as obligatory.

Using ITM as a basis, one could address this by taking a subset of the Process Logic Domain of ITM (a sub-language within ITM which is an implementation of IDEF-0), and add some properties to the main modelling types as illustrated in Fig. 7.8. Processes can as in IDEF-0 be decomposed, and it is possible to indicate input, output, control (e.g. KPIs – Key Performance Indicators), and resources. Input and output can be linked to information objects or information groups (see below) and examples of mechanisms are the performer of process (possible to link to a role) and documents and information objects linked to a process.

7.4.2.3 Information Modelling

Although more traditional data modelling (e.g. using UML class diagrams) was perceived to be useful in the future, for the first version, it was chosen to use simple information modelling, as illustrated in Fig. 7.9, where it is shown how information objects can be decomposed, and grouped into information-groups. Information attributes can be specified for information objects. In addition, relationships to processes and other parts of the language were included as indicated above.

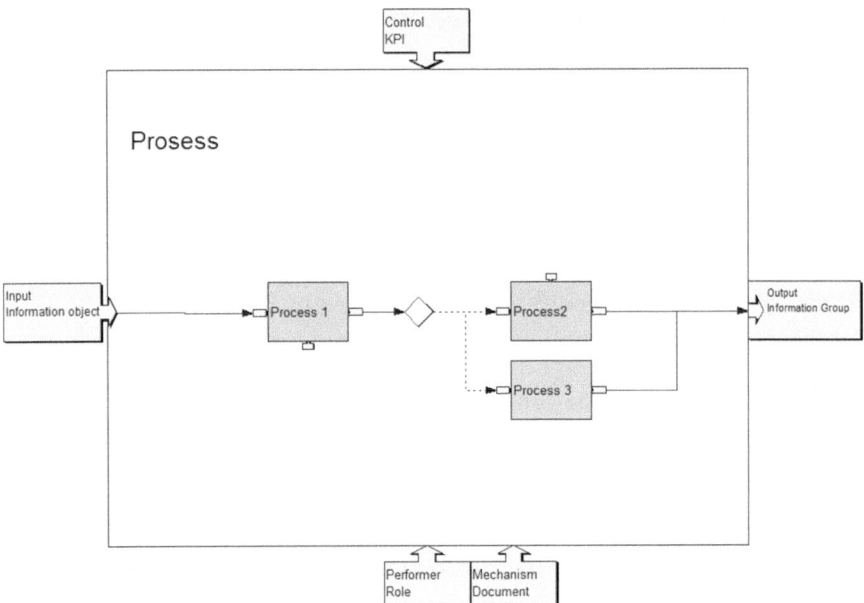

Fig. 7.8 Main part of process modelling language

7.4.2.4 Modelling of People and Organisation

Finally, there was a need for organisational modelling, also with relationships from this to the process models. Main parts of the language for organisational modelling are found in Fig. 7.10. Here we see the possibility of an organisational structure, and linking roles to organisational units. Persons can be members of organisations and fill roles in the organisation.

The full ITM contains 26 domains (sub-languages), compared to the three domains indicated above as a basis for the language, of which only some parts were necessary from each of these domains. Thus, a special sub-language of ITM needed to be provided and extended. These extensions were not too complicated to do in the chosen tool (METIS), at least not for a METIS meta-modelling expert. This specialised modelling language have then been used and further adapted according to needs found in practical use.

Compared to the process described in relation to the use of MetaEdit in Sect. 2.3.3, the differentiation between concept development and notation development is less clear-cut, which often will be the case when there are some previous experiences with modelling in the community to use the new modelling approach. Thus, even if one ideally should decide on concepts and the meta-model before dealing with notation, there will usually be an interplay between these two both due to cognitive baggage, and through the need to experiment with the usage of the new language to evolve this into a stable state.

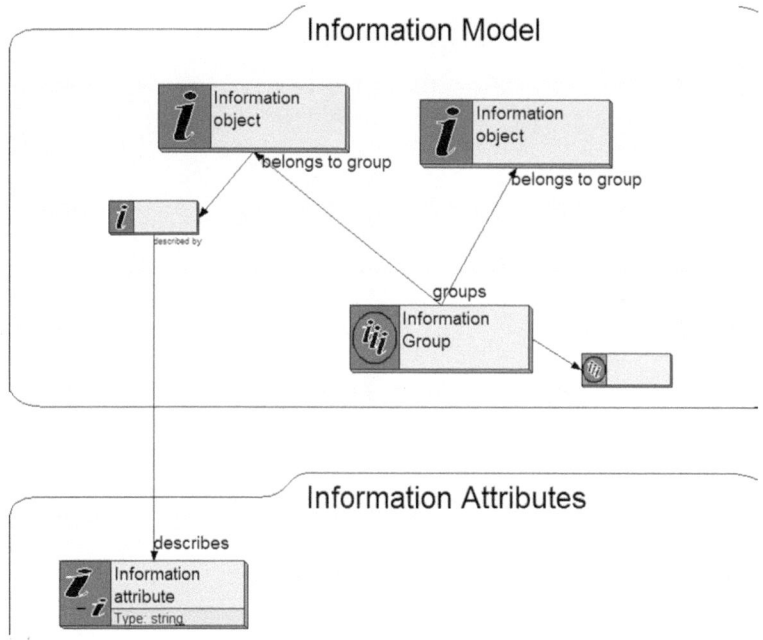

Fig. 7.9 Main parts of information modelling

We evaluate the language as developed using the modelling language quality aspects of SEQUAL.

7.4.2.5 Overview of Language Quality Evaluation

1. *Domain appropriateness.* The language has been developed precisely to cater for the domain of user, and to exclude concepts not in the domain. The domain appropriateness was validated through re-modelling information found in the existing models, and further developing these based on current needs in the organisation. Extensions to the language are possible to do in the tool if new needs arise in the future. This necessitates that the organisation understands the need to have someone responsible for meta-model management, and invest in the necessary knowledge and tools to do this.

2. *Comprehensibility appropriateness.* The language has been made with quite few modelling concepts. More expressiveness has been put into relationship classes and object properties. Using traditional complexity metrics such as (Rossi and Brinkkemper 1994), to put expressiveness in relationships and properties does not necessarily result in a less complex language. On the other hand, due to the specific functionalities of the modelling tool that could enforce the allowed relationships between two concepts (a kind of error prevention), the complexity of

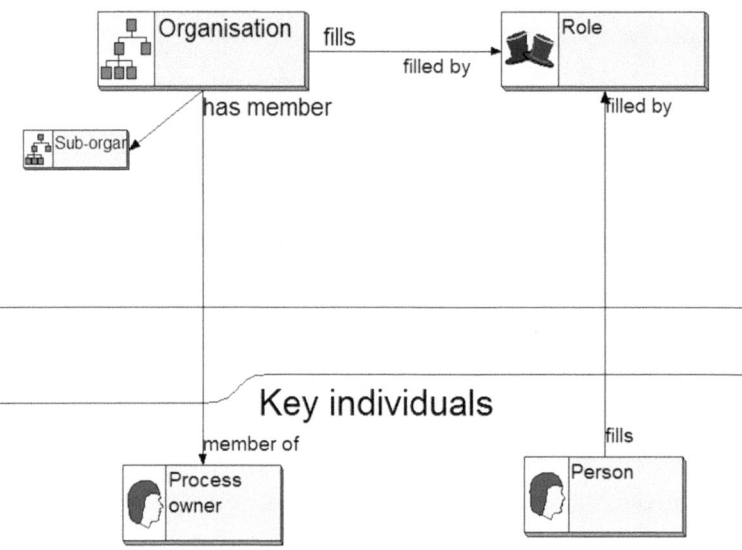

Fig. 7.10 Concepts for organisational modelling

many relationship classes is easier to handle than complexity induced by many object classes. Note that this will put less visual emphasis on these aspects; thus, there is a trade-off on how much to represent as nodes, and how much as edges, putting the most central concepts as nodes, cf. the discussion on textual differentiation in Sect. 5.1.2.

3. *Participant appropriateness.* The language was based on the concepts already in use in the organisation, and should thus be easy to learn. In practice, it turned out that although some people in the organisation were used to think in this way, for others not originally being involved in modelling there was a learning curve.

4. *Modeller appropriateness.* As indicated above, the language was made using familiar concepts. In addition, some of the graphical notation was made to specifically fit the current organisation.

5. *Tool appropriateness.* The language we developed had a formally defined syntax, and syntax checks could thus be provided by the modelling tool. Since the need for automated model analysis and model activation was not focused on in the first version of the language, no formal semantics was provided for the language.

6. *Organisational appropriateness*. The language is a further development of a language used in other parts of the organisation. The extensions of the language are created in such a way that it is possible to use the models written in this language by others in the organisation using standard METIS ITM.

7.4.2.6 Tool Requirements
The following summarises the identified needs within the project for modelling tool support, indicating to what extent the modelling tool could address the requirements. The structure of the presentation is according to the quality levels of SEQUAL presented in Sects. 4.2, 4.3, 4.4, 4.5, 4.6, 4.7, and 4.8.

7.4.2.7 Physical Quality
- Support a model repository with versioning: METIS team server includes this, but this was not bought by the organisation.
- Possible to see differences between versions of models: Only indirectly supported in METIS team server.
- Models available for annotation by many: Possible using the METIS annotator.
- Models available for browsing on web by all users: Possible using the METIS model browser, or alternatively by creating web-reports. The tool had to go through a technical approval process before the browser could be installed and used.
- English single language interface to the models was regarded as sufficient, since English is the official language of the whole organisation.
- There were no requirements for import/export of models to other tools.

7.4.2.8 Empirical Quality
- Possible to differentiate different types of relationships (with text, colour etc.): METIS can provide different colours, text etc. on the relationships. This was not exploited in the language developed.
- Role (swimlane-view) available on process model: Included in METIS and adopted for the language developed, although not in the same way as the project had used previously (Excel spreadsheets).

7.4.2.9 Syntactic Quality
- Support syntax check of the model: METIS enable both the possibility of syntax error prevention and syntax error detection.

7.4.2.10 Semantic Quality
- As the requirements to the modelling language above illustrates, it is necessary that the tool provides meta-modelling facilities, both to be able to choose only limited parts of a language in order not to be able to model things that are not included in the domain, and to add additional object types, concepts, relationship types, and properties to be able to model what actually is in the domain.

- Support consistency checking when doing changes to models: METIS have some possibilities to support validation, although limited possibilities to define new rules of consistency.
- Support constructivity (e.g. to be able to model a detailed process, and then get the outer properties of a collection of detailed processes automatically derived). Minimally to be able to check for constructivity in the decomposition structures: Partly supported in the IDEF-0 implementation of METIS.

7.4.2.11 Pragmatic Quality
- Support views according to user group
    - Model views: Only the relevant parts of the overall model are shown, based on criteria related to model or language. METIS support this well, and model views can be made persistent. The main model and the views can be updated in a coordinated manner. On the other hand, it was experienced as very difficult to use this functionality by normal users.
    - Language view: Only relevant parts of the modelling language used are available for a given task. METIS can support this using the concept of viewstyles. This was not exploited in the language we developed.
- Scenario-views: Since the models are on a type level (and not on the instance level), it is difficult to support scenario-views with the current modelling language. Quite large changes need to be done to also support models on an instance level, but it is possible to implement.
- It should be possible to look at the model at different levels of abstraction: METIS supports this through different types of hierarchical modelling constructs. In the language developed, this is witnessed both in process-decomposition mechanisms and organisational breakdown structure.

7.4.2.12 Social Quality
- Support differentiating between harmonised and local process: METIS can support this, e.g. by having specific properties indicating if a process is global or local. This was not implemented in the language developed.
- Support the modelling of exceptions: METIS can support this, but the chosen modelling language then needs to be further extended.
- Support argumentation-process relating to getting agreement on new versions of the harmonised process. Not specifically supported in METIS, although the annotation mechanism in METIS annotator can support this process.

7.4.2.13 Deontic Quality
- The tool should be aligned with company standard: METIS has been tested in other parts of the organisation, and partly taken into use.
- Cost/benefit of tool should be favourable: METIS is an expensive tools; thus, this was an issue all along, since it is often difficult to quantify the value of introducing a new technique or tool.

- Need available training of users to be able to get up to speed locally: METIS is delivered including both canned and human provided courses on different levels, although especially human provided courses were experienced as quite expensive.
- The tool should be available for the next 5 years: METIS has a substantial user base, and has been around in different version for the last 15 years.

7.5 Summary

SEQUAL can be used in a number of different ways:
1. Guide the modelling process to achieve models of high quality
2. Evaluate the quality of existing models
3. Evaluate the quality of modelling languages
   (a) To guide further development
   (b) To choose between different languages
4. Guide meta-modelling when adapting or developing new modelling languages
5. Evaluate the appropriateness of tools to support the development of models of high quality

We have in particular looked upon the area 1, 3 and 4 in this chapter. An example of area 2 (in Sect. 7.2) and of area 5 is provided in Sect. 7.4.2.

Review Questions

1. Give an overview of different ways to use SEQUAL in practice.
2. Describe the SPEC-cycle of modelling.
3. What characterises ontologies compared to a traditional structural model?
4. Describe a methodology for developing a new modelling language.
5. Describe negative aspects relative to comprehensibility appropriateness of UML.
6. Describe aspects of threat to validity when doing an experiment comparing modelling languages.

Problems and Exercises

Individual Exercises
1. What is the main difference between testing a modelling approach with real users and with students?
2. What are the main differences between doing analytical and empirical evaluations of modelling languages using SEQUAL?
3. Evaluate the quality of BPMN for process modelling.
4. Evaluate the quality of SVBR for goal and rule modelling.

Pair Exercises

1. When adapting the language quality framework for a particular situation, which part of the framework is adapted most? Why is this?

Group Exercises

1. You want to compare BPMN and UML activity diagrams for modelling for communication in a given domain (you can choose domain, or use the domain described in Appendix C). Describe how you would design an experiment to investigate which language was best in this setting.
2. Compare the language quality of BPMN 1 and BPMN 2.
3. Select a domain, use a modelling language that all are familiar with and model the domain in iterations according to the inner part of the SPEC-cycle. Count the number of new statements added in each iteration and see if a similar pattern of growth and loss in Expansion and Consolidation is witnessed as depicted in Fig. 7.2.
4. Choose a modelling environment that you are using regularly. Evaluate the tool/environment using SEQUAL.

References

Aagedal, J.Ø., Ecklund, E.F.: Modeling QoS: towards a UML profile. In: Proceedings UML 2002, Dresden (2002)

ATHENA: Deliverable DA1.6.1 Evaluation and Benefits Assessment. Krogstie, J., Knothe, T., Anastasio, M., Ohren, O. SINTEF, Oslo (2006)

Barbier, F., Henderson-Sellers, B., Opdahl, A.L., Gogolla, M.: The whole-part relationship in the unified modeling language: a new approach. In: Siau, K., Halpin, T. (eds.) Unified Modeling Language: System Analysis, Design and Development Issues. IDEA Group, Hershey (2001)

Baumeister, H., Koch, N., Mandel, L.: Towards a UML extension for hypermedia design. In: France, R., Rumpe, B. (eds.) UML'99 – The Unified Modeling Language. Beyond the Standard: Second International Conference, pp. 614–629, Fort Collins, CO, October 28–30 (1999)

Baumeister, H., Koch, N., Kosiuczenko, P., Stevens, P., Wirsing, M.: UML for global computing. In: Priami, C. (ed.) Global Computing. Programming Environments, Languages, Security, and Analysis of Systems. LNCS, vol. 2874, pp. 1–24. Springer, Berlin/Heidelberg (2003)

Berio, G., et al.: Deliverable D 3.1; Requirements analysis: initial core constructs and architecture. (UEML v. 1.0). In: Thematic Network – IST-2001-34229. Torino (2003)

Bonnet, S.: Model Driven Software Personalization. Smart Objects Conference (SOC2003), Grenoble, France (2003)

Booch, G., Rumbaugh, J., Jacobson, I.: The Unified Modeling Language: User Guide. Addison-Wesley, Reading (1999)

BPMI: Business Process Modeling Notation (BPMN) Version 1. www.bpmi.org/downloads/BPMN-V1.0.pdf (2004)

Davis, A.: Object-oriented requirements to object-oriented design: An easy transition? J. Syst. Softw. **30**(1/2), 151–159 (1995)

Castellani, X.: Overview of models defined with charts of concepts. In: Falkenberg, E., Lyytinen, K., Verrijn-Stuart, A. (eds.) Proceedings of the IFIP8.1 Working Conference on Information Systems Concepts (ISCO4); An Integrated Discipline Emerging, September 20–22, Leiden, The Netherlands, pp. 235–256 (1999)

Davis, F.D.: Perceived usefulness, perceived ease of use and user acceptance of information technology. MIS Q. **13**(3), 319–340 (1989)

Decker, M.: Modelling location-aware access control constraints for mobile workflows with UML Activity Diagrams. In: Proceedings of 3rd International Conference on Mobile Ubiquitous Computing, Systems, Services and Technologies, Sliema, Malta (2009)

Dey, A.K., Abowd, G.D.: Towards a better understanding of context and context-awareness. In: Workshop on The What, Who, Where, When, and How of Context-Awareness, as Part of the 2000 Conference on Human Factors in Computing Systems (CHI 2000), The Hague (2000)

Erickson, J., Siau, K.: Can UML be simplified? Practitioner use of UML in separate domains In: proceedings EMMSAD 2007. Proceedings of Twelfth International Workshop on Exploring Modeling Methods in System Analysis and Design, Trondheim, Norway, pp. 89–98 (2007)

Field, A., Hole, G.: How to Design and Report Experiments. SAGE Publications, London (2003)

FOAF.: FOAF project web page. http://xmlns.com/foaf/spec (2010). Last accessed Dec 2011

Gandon, F.L., Sadeh, N.M.: Semantic web technologies to reconcile privacy and context awareness. J. Web Semant. 1, 27 (2004)

Gemino, A., Wand, Y.: Evaluating modeling techniques based on models of learning. CACM 46(10), 79–84 (2003)

Génova, G., Llorens, J., Quintana, V.: Digging into Use Case Relationships. In: Proceedings UML 2002, Dresden (2002)

Ghosh, R., Dekhil, M.: Mashups for semantic user profiles. In: Proceeding of the 17th International Conference on World Wide Web. ACM, Beijing (2008)

Gjersvik, R., Krogstie, J., Følstad, A.: Participatory development of enterprise process models. In: Krogstie, J., Siau, K., Halpin, T. (eds.) Information Modelling Methods and Methodologies. Idea Group, Hershey (2004)

Glass, R.L.: Facts and Fallacies of Software Engineering. Addison-Wesley, Boston (2003)

Golbeck, J., Rothstein, M.: Linking social networks on the web with FOAF. In: Proceedings of the Twenty-Third Conference on Artificial Intelligence AAAI'08, Chicago (2008)

Gopalakrishnan, S., Sindre, G.: Diagram Notations for Mobile Work Processes Presented at PoEM 2011, Oslo, Norway, 2–3 Nov (2011a)

Gopalakrishnan, S., Sindre, G.: Analytical Evaluation of Notational Adaptations to Capture Location of Activities in Process Models. Technical report M3W-1. Norwegian University of Science and Technology (NTNU), Trondheim. http://www.idi.ntnu.no/~guttors/m3w1.pdf (2011b)

Gopalakrishnan, S., Krogstie, J., Sindre, G.: Adapted UML activity diagrams for mobile work processes: experimental comparison of colour and pattern fills. In: Proceedings of 16th International Conference on Exploring Modeling Methods in Systems Analysis and Design (EMMSAD'11). Springer, London (2011c)

Gopalakrishnan, S., Krogstie, J., Sindre, G.: Adapting UML Activity Diagrams for Mobile Work Process Modelling: Experimental Comparison of Two Notation Alternatives Proceedings PoEM 2010. Springer, Delft, the Netherlands (2010)

Gopalakrishnan, S., Krogstie, J., Sindre, G.: Extending Use and Misuse Cases to Capture Mobile Applications. NOKOBIT – Norsk konferanse for organisasjoners bruk av informasjonsteknologi s, pp. 1–14 (2011b)

Halpin, T.: Supplementing UML with concepts from ORM. In: Siau, K., Halpin, T. (eds.) Unified Modeling Language: System Analysis, Design and Development Issues. IDEA Group, Hershey (2001)

Heckmann, D., Schwartz, T., Brandherm, B., Kröner, A.: Decentralized user modeling with UserML and GUMO Heckmann05.pdf. In: Proceedings of DASUM 2005, Edinburgh, Scotland (2005a)

Heckmann, D., Schwartz, T., Brandherm, B., Schmitz, M., Wilamowitz-Moellendorff, M.: GUMO – the general user model ontology. In: Proceedings of UM 2005: International Conference on User Modeling. Springer, Berlin/Heidelberg/Edinburgh (2005b)

Hennicker, R., Koch, N.: Systematic design of web applications with UML. In: Siau, K., Halpin, T. (eds.) Unified Modeling Language: System Analysis, Design and Development Issues. IDEA Group, Hershey (2001)

Hilliard, R.: Using the UML for architectural description. In: France, R., Rumpe, B. (eds.) UML'99 – The Unified Modeling Language. Beyond the Standard: Second International Conference, Fort Collins, CO, pp. 614–629, 28–30 Oct (1999)

Hitz, M., Kappel, G.: Developing with UML – some pitfalls and workarounds. In: Proceeding UML'98, pp. 9–20. Springer, Mulhouse (1998)

Hopkins, W.G.: A New View of Statistics (Technical Report). University of Queensland, Australia, Brisbane (2001)

Høydalsvik, G.M., Sindre, G.: On the purpose of object-oriented analysis. In: Paepcke, A. (ed.) Proceedings of the Conference on Object-Oriented Programming Systems, Languages, and Applications (OOPSLA'93) September, pp. 240–255. ACM Press, New York (1993)

IDEF-0: Federal Information Processing Standards Publication 183, December 21, Announcing the Standard for Integration Definition for Function Modeling (IDEF-0). http://www.idef.com/pdf/idef0.pdf (1993)

ISO.: International organization for standardization. Enterprise integration – constructs for enterprise modeling (ISO/DIS 19440). Prepared by CEN TC 310 and ISO/TC 184, Geneva (2004)

Kelly, S., Tolvanen, J.-P.: Domain Specific Modeling. Wiley, Hoboken (2008)

Klein, C.: Extension of the unified modeling language for mobile agents. In: Siau, K., Halpin, T. (eds.) Unified Modeling Language: System Analysis, Design and Development Issues. IDEA Group, Hershey (2001)

Knothe, T., Busselt, C., Böll, D.: Deliverable D2.3 Report on UEML (Needs and Requirements). UEML, Thematic Network – Contract n°: IST – 2001–34229, 2003. www.ueml.org (2001)

Kobryn, C.: UML 2001. A standardization odyssey. Commun. ACM **42**(10), 29–37 (1999)

Kofod-Petersen, A., Gransæther, P.A., Krogstie, J.: An empirical investigation of attitude towards location-aware social network service. Int. J. Mob. Commun. **8**(1), 53–70 (2010)

Kosiuczenko, P.: Sequence Diagrams for Mobility. Workshop Proceedings ER'2002. Springer, Tampere (2002)

Kovacevic, S.: UML and user interface modeling. In: Proceedings UML'98, pp. 253–266. Springer, Mulhouse (1998)

Krogstie, J.: Using quality function deployment in software requirements specification. Paper presented at the fifth international workshop on requirements engineering: Foundations for Software Quality (REFSQ'99), Heidelberg, 14–15 June 1999

Krogstie, J.: Using a semiotic framework to evaluate UML for the development of models of high quality. In: Siau, K., Halpin, T. (eds.) Unified Modelling Language: Systems Analysis, Design, and Development Issues, pp. 89–106. IDEA Group, Hershey (2001)

Krogstie, J., Arnesen, S.: Assessing enterprise modeling languages using a generic quality framework. In: Krogstie, J., Siau, K., Halpin, T. (eds.) Information Modeling Methods and Methodologies. Idea Group, Hershey (2004)

Krogstie, J., Jørgensen, H.D.: Interactive models for supporting networked organisations. In: 16th Conference on Advanced Information Systems Engineering. Springer, Riga (2004)

Krogstie, J., Dalberg, V., Jensen, S.M.: Harmonising Business Processes of Collaborative Networked Organization Using Process Modelling in PROVE'04 Toulouse, France (2004)

Latella, D., Massink, M., Baumeister, H., Wirsing, M.: Mobile UML statecharts with localities. In: Priami, C., Quaglia, P. (eds.) Global Computing. LNCS, vol. 3267, pp. 34–58. Springer, Berlin/Heidelberg (2005)

Lauesen, S.: Real-life object-oriented systems. IEEE Softw. **15**(2), 76–83 (1998)

Lillehagen, F., Krogstie, J.: Active Knowledge Modeling of Enterprises. Springer, Berlin (2008)

Lodderstedt, T., Basin, D., Doser, J.: SecureUML: a UML-based modeling language for model-driven security. In: Proceedings UML 2002. Springer, New York (2002)

Loucopoulos, P., Karakostas, V.: System Requirements Engineering. McGraw-Hill, London/New York (1995)

Mendis, V.: RDF user profiles – bringing semantic web capabilities to next generation networks and services. In: Proceedings of the ICIN Conference. Bordeaux France, 8–11 Oct (2007)

Mendling, J., Recker, J., Reijers, H.A.: On the usage of labels and icons in business process models. Int. J. Inform. Syst. Model. Des. **1**(2), 40–58 (2010)

Miller, G.A.: WordNet: a lexical database for English. Commun. ACM **38**, 39–41 (1995)

Moody, D.L.: The "physics" of notations: toward a scientific basis for constructing visual notations in software engineering. IEEE Trans. Softw. Eng. **35**, 756–779 (2009)

Morris, S., Spanoudakis, G.: 34th Annual Hawaii International Conference on System Sciences (HICSS-34)-Volume 3 Maui, Hawaii IEEE CS Press (2001)

Mylopoulos, J., Chung, L., Tu, E.: From object-oriented to goal-oriented requirements analysis. Commun. ACM **42**(1), 31–37 (1999)

Nelson, H.J., Poels, G., Genero, M., Piattini, M.: A conceptual modeling quality framework. Softw. Qual. J. **20**(1), 1–28 (2011)

Nguyen, L., Swatman, P.A.: Managing the Requirements Engineering Process REFSQ 2001, Interlaken, Switzerland (2001)

Nysetvold, A.G., Krogstie, J.: Assessing business process modeling languages using a generic quality framework. In: Siau, K. (ed.) Advanced Topics in Database Research Series, vol. 5, pp. 79–93. Idea Group, Hershey (2006)

OMG: Object Management Group, Business Process Definition Metamodel. http://www.omg.org/spec/BPDM/ (2004)

OMG: Unified Modeling Language v 2.0 OMG Web site. http://www.omg.org (2006)

OMG: BPMN v2 Specification. Technical report, OMG. (http://www.omg.org/), http://www.omg.org/spec/BPMN/2.0/, Jan (2011)

Opdahl, A.L., Sindre, G.: Experimental comparison of attack trees and misuse cases for security threat identification. Inf. Softw. Technol. **51**(5), 916–932 (2009)

OpenCyc: OpenCyc Web page. http://opencyc.org/. Last accessed Dec 2011 (2011)

Petit, M.: Enterprise Modeling Language Comparison Framework: A Proposal, UEML, Europena Commission. http://cordis.europa.eu/projects/rcn/64694_en.html (2002)

Pllana, S., Fahringer, T.: On Customizing the UML for Modeling Performance-Oriented Applications. In: Proceedings UML 2002. Springer, Berlin/New York. (2002)

Recker, J., Indulska, M., Rosemann, M., Green, P.: How good is BPMN really? Insights from theory and practice. In: 14th European Conference on Information Systems, Goeteborg, Sweden, pp. 1582–1593 (2006)

Recker, J., Rosemann, M., Krogstie, J.: Ontology- versus pattern-based evaluation of process modeling language: a comparison. Commun. Assoc. Inf. Syst. **20**, 774–799 (2007)

Rossi, M., Brinkkemper, S.: Complexity metrics for system development methods and techniques. Inf. Syst. **21**(2), 209–227 (1994)

Siau, K., Cao, Q.: Unified Modeling Language (UML) – a complexity analysis. J. Database Manag. **12**, 26–34 (2001)

Sindre, G., Krogstie, J.: Process heuristics to achieve requirements specification of feasible quality. In: Pohl, K., Peters, P. (eds.) Second International Workshop on Requirements Engineering: Foundations for Software Quality (REFSQ'95), Jyväskylä, Finland, pp. 92–103 (1995)

Stan, J., Egyed-Zsigmond, E., Joly, A., Maret, P.: A user profile ontology for situation-aware social networking. In: 3rd Workshop on Artificial Intelligence Techniques for Ambient Intelligence. Patras, Greece, 21–22 July 2008

SUMO: SUMO Web Page. http://suo.ieee.org/SUO/SUMO/index.html (2003). Last accessed Dec 2011

Taivalsaari, A.: On the notion of inheritance. ACM Comput. Surv. **28**(3), 438–479 (1996)

Ubisworld: http://www.ubisworld.org/ (2009). Last accessed Dec 2011

van der Aalst, W.M.P.: Don't go with the flow: web services composition standards exposed. IEEE Intell. Syst. **18**(1), 72–76 (2003)

W3C: Delivery Context Ontology W3C Working Draft 16 June 2009. http://www.w3.org/TR/dcontology/ (2009)

Wohlin, C., Runeson, P., Höst, M., Ohlsson, M.C., Regnell, B., Wesslén, A.: Experimentation in Software Engineering: An Introduction. Kluwer, Norwell (2000)

Ziemann, J., Ohren, O., Jaekel, F.W., Kahl, T., Knothe, T.: Achieving Enterprise Model Interoperability Applying a Common Enterprise Metamodel. Accepted at INTEROP-ESA 2005, March, Bordeaux, France (2006)

Zimmermann, A., Specht, M., Lorenz, A.: Personalization and Context Management. User Modeling and User-Adapted Interaction. Springer, Dordrecht (2005)

Summary and Outlook

Modelling as a technique has been around in theory since the 1960s and in practice since the 1970s. Although the steady use of such techniques has been witnessed, in particular in some domains, future developments for IT-supporting organisations means new challenges where the role of modelling is so far unclear. Whereas we in Chap. 2 in particular looked into the history of methodologies for information systems support and evaluation and the use of modelling in these methodologies, we will here end the book with a description of some trends for future technological development, and how the role of modelling can be envisaged in this landscape.

8.1 Future Technological Developments

The future business environment must take into account a stronger integration across traditional organisational borders and countries. In the FiNES position paper (Li et al. 2011), a number of organisational trends are highlighted:

- *The disappearing boundaries of the enterprise*: Virtual teams, extended value chains, dynamic value networks and a range of digital ecologies (Vyatkin et al. 2010) such as digital ecosystems will change the contours of the business world.
- *Everybody is an enterprise*: The role of SMEs and especially micro enterprises and start-ups is expected to become even more important.
- *The what-you-sense-is-what-you-get (WYSIWYG) enterprise*: With massive quantities of real-time information becoming available, one can get new real-time enterprise applications.
- *A knowledge commons for enterprises:* There is a need for an open and accessible 'Knowledge Commons' facilitated by the Internet for all to freely, responsibly and legitimately exploit.
- *The advent of intelligent virtual reality*: With increasing dematerialisation blurring the physical with the virtual, enterprises are not only becoming digital, they are acquiring multiple roles, cyber presences and distinctive virtual identities.

J. Krogstie, *Model-Based Development and Evolution of Information Systems:*
A Quality Approach, DOI 10.1007/978-1-4471-2936-3_8,
© Springer-Verlag London 2012

Combined with societal trends (e.g. demographic, legislative, financial, geo-political and environmental) that demand change in current practice, there is a number of issues that must be addressed in future business information systems to support these organisational and societal needs:

- The support of end-to-end design and engineering process (including full life-cycle support of products)
- Integration across organisations and nations
- Systems being provided by ecosystems of providers and prosumers rather than by individual providers
- Event-oriented systems utilising the Internet of things

We will give an overview of each of these areas in the next section, discussing in particular the application of modelling techniques that support developments in these areas.

8.1.1   The Support of End-to-End Design and Engineering Process

Even with an apparent shift to a service-oriented economy, manufacturing and engineering remain important for the economy. We also witness new trends and paradigms, such as sustainable manufacturing and mass customisation. Consequently, the manufacturing industry is facing significant structural changes.

The key enabler for coping with these changes will be IT, due to its strong impact on innovation and productivity. The current IT for the manufacturing landscape is characterised by scattered data formats, tools and processes dedicated to different phases in the product life cycle. In the concept phase of a product, often simple tools like MS PowerPoint are used, whereas later on it may be specialised CAx solutions, PLM and ERP systems. Moreover, the flow of information is closely aligned to the product life cycle (i.e. information from the design phase goes into the manufacturing phase, but not in the opposite direction). In addition, user feedback is often neglected in design. Given the diversity of tools and data formats, manufacturing struggles to cope with new trends in this area. For example, both the trend to mass customisation and the demand for increased sustainability require a tight integration of the design, manufacturing and usage phases of a product, which is currently not in place. What is missing is an integrated, holistic view on data, persons and processes across the full product life cycle. As experiences of the past show, a tight integration of all tools used throughout a product lifetime is not feasible. A model-based approach to address this in a more federated manner, which has been briefly described earlier in this book, is the application of AKM (Active Knowledge Modeling) (Lillehagen and Krogstie 2008).

AKM requires a new way of representing knowledge as visual models, where complex, rigid, software-oriented languages are replaced by simple and agile domain concepts. A model is a representation of some aspects of the real-world entities and phenomena, as interpreted by some actor(s). A model is active if it also influences the reality that it represents. Knowledge is held by people, so knowledge modelling languages should be based on human communication, sense-making and learning rather than on computer and software concepts.

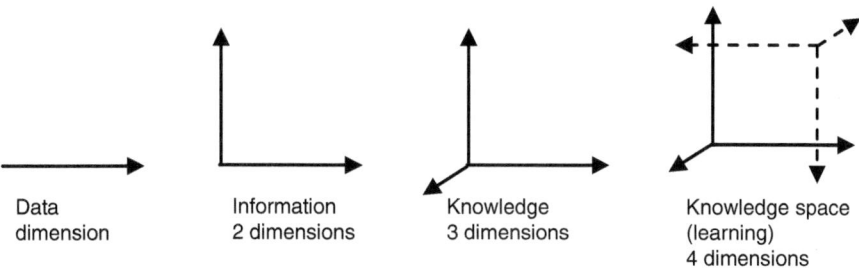

Fig. 8.1 Dimensions in modelling (From Lillehagen and Krogstie 2008)

Activation cannot be solely based on automated execution. Instead, users must be supported by flexibly interpreting the models and acting upon them in the situations that arise. The more precise and detailed a model is, the more automatic execution it supports. However, exception handling requires that the users be allowed to 'open up' the model and change the default, automatic interpretation of it.

Knowledge architectures consist of knowledge explicitly represented in structured models, and of the mental views of the people involved in creating and using these models. Knowledge is explicitly represented as information and data structures. As illustrated in Fig. 8.1, data consists of symbols used for conveying information and knowledge. Data becomes information when its meaning is interpreted by some actor. We thus see data as a one-dimensional representation, a stream of symbols. Information adds a second dimension that reflects the meaning of the original data, often called meta-data. Knowledge implies a justification of the information or that the information guides action. Knowledge establishes structures and relationships between information elements, and uses them to manage dependencies. Knowledge representations must thus possess at least three dimensions: data, its meaning and the structure; justifications; and actions that the knowledge results in. In order to support reflection on knowledge, a fourth dimension is needed. Reflection on knowledge is required in, e.g. learning, knowledge management, design, innovation, collaboration, creation of shared understanding and other creative tasks. We refer to representations that contain four reflective dimensions as knowledge spaces.

In software systems, the second dimension is typically represented as program code that defines how the data is manipulated, stored and presented to the user. Among humans, the second dimension can be illustrated by the capability to understand a certain language, such as English. If you do not understand the language, speech becomes incomprehensible data.

Few computerised systems are really knowledge-based. Their data structures and program code are fixed. By using the system, humans can bring in the extra dimensions of interpretation and reflection needed for knowledge and learning. However, these additional dimensions cannot be reflected back into the computerised system as updated data structures or program logic. There is no easy way to affect the behaviour of the system other than manually changing the code. Thus, reflection, knowledge and learning cannot be shared among the people using the system. What a user can learn from the system is limited to the two dimensions that were coded

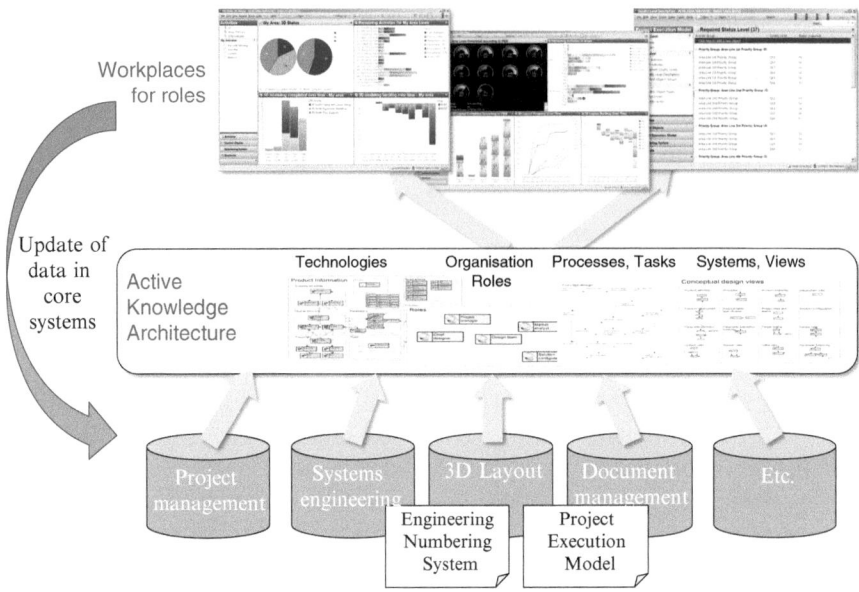

Fig. 8.2 Operational view of a model-generated workplace (Adapted from Krogstie 2011)

into the system from the start. The knowledge space of software consists of two explicit dimensions (data and code) and two mental views possessed by different roles (programmers and users).

The concept of model-generated workplaces (MGWP; see Fig. 8.2 for an example) can be used to make the models available in a tailorable way. MGWP is a working environment for the business users (including designers and engineers) involved in running the business operations of the enterprise. It is a user platform that provides the graphical front-end for human users to interact with software services supporting their day-to-day business activities. The workplace can be tailored to meet the specific requirements of different roles or persons within an enterprise, providing customised presentation and operation views based on data in the enterprise systems.

An overall solution will benefit from a combination of this type of approach with semantic web-oriented approaches when formalisation of the knowledge representations is beneficial. This can be more or less formal (cf. the ontology spectrum depicted in Fig. 3.23), e.g. represented using linked data or some variant of OWL.

8.1.2   Cross-Organisational Integration

Over the last 10–15 years, the number of varying organisational forms has increased a lot, from strictly structured supply chains to loosely structured communities of interest. Cooperation across traditional organisational boundaries is increasing, as outsourcing and electronic business is enabled by the Internet and IS in general. When such cooperation moves beyond the buying and selling of goods and well-defined services, there is a need for a flexible infrastructure that supports not only information exchange, but also knowledge creation and sharing.

An extended enterprise (EE) (also often termed *virtual enterprise*) is defined as a dynamic networked organisation, being developed ad hoc to reach a certain goal based on the resources of several existing cooperating enterprises. The EE partners often come from different countries, using different languages and having different cultural backgrounds. The EE partners want to harvest knowledge from the EE to be reused in the originating organisation or in other EEs. An approach that needs to be extended to support this situation is process-support environment like workflow modelling and BPM. Based on globalisation trends, other challenges also pop up. The case described in Sect. 7.4.2 is an example of the needs when a multi-national company needs to coordinate its local business units in order to serve other multinational companies in an integrated fashion. As reported in Krogstie et al. (2004, 2008), there was in this case a need to standardise the processes of the company's national branches in order to build a common image of the organisation (both inwards and outwards) and to support the certification of the cross-national processes of their multinational customers, but at the same time adhere to national and cultural rules and expectations for how to do business. Similar examples from other businesses (e.g. car rental industry) are presented in van der Aalst (2011).

Such aspects are not only of importance in business, but also in the public administration area. Public administrations and service providers face growing challenges linked to the application of new IT solutions in the knowledge-intensive society and are forced to rethink traditional administrative structures and functions and adapt their services to meet new societal demands with reduced budgets. In the public sector, there is an increasing emphasis, in particular in Europe, on cross-department and cross-national applications to increase reuse of solutions across traditional borders (Aagesen et al. 2011), as described for instance in the last EU Ministerial Declaration on eGovernment (EU 2009). For instance, even in small countries like Norway and the Netherlands, there are around 430 local municipalities which in principle execute variants of the same processes (van der Aalst 2011; Aagesen et al. 2011), which are different due to political and demographic reasons.

In connection to using BPM for future integration, one can point to four important trends (Houy et al. 2010):

1. Processes are increasingly interconnected also across traditional organisational and national borders.
2. The number of processes an organisation wants to cope with is rapidly increasing.
3. Modern technology is generating potentially enormous amounts of event data (also called big data) representing the states of different processes and products (described further in Sect. 8.1.4).
4. A large spectre of end-user devices are used to access enterprise system in different situations necessitating a flexible multi-channel support influencing which parts of the workflow are available in which manner depending on the context of use.

The handling of this complexity which is generated by many thousands of process types, process instances and process events is a new challenge in BPM, and thus also for the modelling of business processes, where one needs to address 'BPM-in-the-large'. Some characteristics of BPM-in-the-large are (Houy et al. 2011):

- The need for more flexible process structures that can be adapted to the situation
- Increasing number of processes with potentially increasing number of dependencies between them
- Loosely coupled BPM services, organised in a decentralised way
- Usage of many different process modelling languages
- Focus on comprehensive business networks and ecosystems

Digital ecosystems also relate to another side of the coin, the future landscape of providers of IT services, which we discuss in the next section.

8.1.3   Ecosystems of Providers and Prosumers of IT Systems

As indicated in Chap. 2, the trend for a long time has been that systems are being developed and evolved further and further away from the core users of the system. Rather than being provided by distinct entities, we see a development in the direction of systems to a larger degree being supported by *virtual communities* of human/organisational *actors*, co-working on partially shared digital artefacts (Ali Babar et al. 2009). The term '*digital ecosystem*' has recently been used to generalise such communities, emphasising that their actors constantly interact and cooperate with other actors in both local and remote ecosystems. Such systems are characterised by self-organisation, scalability and sustainability, providing both economic and social value as a specialisation of the more generic concept of digital ecologies. Examples are communities for Open Source (OSS) and Creative Commons, Knowledge Commons, social media networks as in Facebook, blogs and computer games, or voluntary groups of citizens or academics.

However, the existing digital ecosystems have limited scope, various degrees of transparency, insufficient capabilities for search and evaluation of useful, high-quality artefacts from the huge and ever-evolving Internet, and none does fully support a wide range of shared artefacts from a wide range of actors. There are two main variants of digital ecosystems: *content ecosystems* and *software ecosystems*.

Content ecosystems are networks that deal with creation and sharing of artistic and intellectual artefacts. The impact of IT on participative and democratic processes and on creativity is already here, and will continue to grow with the increasing diffusion of web-based social networking and user-generated content and services. Internet already allows visual and multi-modal interactions, and these interactions will become richer.

Software ecosystems are 'a set of businesses functioning as a unit and interacting with a shared market for software and services, together with relationships among them. These relationships are frequently underpinned by a common technological platform and operate through the exchange of information, resources, and artefacts' (Jansen et al. 2009), as briefly discussed in Chap. 2.

To address combined digital content and software ecosystems, there must be concerted improvements of the state of the art in three traditionally unrelated research areas:

1. Enterprise architecture and enterprise modelling
2. New business models
3. Data management

The kind of modelling we are looking on in this book applies in particular to the first two areas and we will further discuss these below. Within many organisations, it has become customary to develop enterprise architectures as described in Sects. 2.2.9 and 2.3.5. An ecosystem architecture takes the ideas of enterprise architecture to a higher level of abstraction, looking upon the support of a more fluid landscape of business actors providing and consuming services for information systems support in an organisational setting. In this way, it extends the process perspective in BPM-in-the-large to a wider set of modelling perspectives. This demands a new approach to enterprise integration. User-initiated software applications and enterprise mash-ups should be based on flexible approaches such as AKM and support learning (Lillehagen and Krogstie 2008) and process knowledge management (Jørgensen 2004).

For this to function, one must support more open business models. In these business models, one must consider financial success, sustainability, competition, copyright and licensing, and the impact on work processes, leadership, internal coordination, work processes, strategy and planning. The open innovation approach (Chesbrough 2003, 2011) is often chosen as a basic cooperation mechanism. Companies should allow more free import and export of ideas and knowledge concerning products, processes and business models that flow between organisation and their environments. However, the problems connected to IP and revenue sharing must be considered. Furthermore, an open innovation strategy must be reflected not only in the business models, but also by revised behaviour. The cooperating organisations contribute to a complex value network, whose success criteria go beyond traditional value chain analysis, in order to capture the complex interdependencies between companies and between technological architectures and business models. The SEM language (Jansen et al. 2009) attempts to analyse the business along customer-supplier lines. The e^3 value model, also covered in Sect. 3.3.8 (Gordijn et al. 2006), describes value-generation among partners in a value network and might be extended to cater for digital ecosystems.

8.1.4   Event-Oriented Systems Utilising the Internet of Things

During the last decade, large changes have taken place in the IT arena. What previously was termed convergence (between the telecommunications world, IT, media and later also the power systems in what is now popularly called smart grids) is now emerging in practice, propelled by several simultaneous trends.

1. The continuing miniaturisation of computing resources making it possible to perform computing at some level everywhere, by any device.

2. The availability of high-bandwidth access to computing resources in an increasing number of places.
3. The infrastructure being built up for utilising remote computing resources (these days often presented under the term '*cloud computing*'; see Sect. 2.1.7 for an introduction to cloud computing).
4. More power-efficient solutions. Many battery-operated devices can last more than a year, and passive solutions used by RFID and NFC (Near Field Communication) are powered by the readers. Parasitic energy harvesting devices that extract small amounts of energy from the environment can power sensors where normal power solutions are not available.

The emergence of the IoT will lead to a world in which countless everyday objects are interconnected and have their own computational power. These active and interactive objects will be able to monitor and change their environment via sensors and actuators and to interact and collaborate with each other and with the people around them. Although more accessible, to quickly produce innovative applications and services for this setting is not an easy task. Information systems need to change from transaction orientation to event orientation, using event-driven architectures (EDA) (Chandy and Schulte 2009) reflecting the nature of IoT applications. These applications are characterised by being:

- Collaborative, that is, including numerous active components that behave concurrently, running on distributed devices, and collaborates to provide a desired functionality.
- Event-driven and reactive, that is, continuously reacting on a large number of events from the physical environment, from users and from other parts of the system.
- Dynamic and adaptive, meaning that the applications, associations and collaborations are dynamically established and configured depending on the current context at runtime. The information gathered is often used to support human decision-making rather than to only automate a predefined process. Interaction with human users is essential both to use the systems efficiently and to effectively improve the systems over time through capturing the experiences from the use of the system.

This brings a need for supporting

1. Rapid application development
2. Rapid application deployment
3. End-user tailoring of application and services
4. Collaborative IoT applications

We will here look at the last of these areas in particular. As an example, we here in particular look on mobile, collaborative applications and services for application in the health sector (Hadzic and Chang 2010). Any healthcare system aims to monitor the health of the population and to mitigate its threats by collecting and analysing data about health problems, and subsequently reacting on them. As such, a healthcare system can be described as a distributed, event-driven, reactive problem-solving machinery. Having, as its base, a set of interconnected, semi-autonomous care providing units, one of the most crucial functions of a healthcare system is the mechanism for distributing health problems to the most appropriate problem solver. From assisted self-help groups to nursing homes, from the local doctor to the more distant, technologically advanced university hospital, cost-effective care requires an efficient mechanism for shuffling medical problems to the most appropriate problems solvers.

What is the most appropriate level of problem solving might be a matter of healthcare policy, but mostly is dictated by technological advances and decisions to bring these to work. As new technologies tend to come with at a high price, some medical technology investments must be accompanied by a redirection of the flow of patients to the care unit that decided to implement the technology. Other medical technologies establish a window of opportunities for new patient groups.

Hence, the establishing of new healthcare technologies bring about profound changes in the flow of problems and patients within the system, changes that has brought today's information exchange and communication system to the limit and must be addressed by event-driven rather than transaction-driven systems.

Clinicians face data processing challenges in decision-making situations. Of these, there are two types:

1. *Deciding on medical acts – what to do with the patient.*
2. *Deciding on coordination acts – which patient to work on next.* Knowing what has been going on in the clinical process enables clinicians to adapt their plans and coordinate their work with that of others. In addition to patient data, these decisions are informed by data about what other personnel are doing and which resources (rooms and equipment) are in use.

In the ongoing COSTT project (www.costt.no), one focuses on the question of how the second challenge can be supported by IT. The digital information infrastructure that is now emerging in many hospitals will become a vast resource. To be able to utilise this large collection of data, there will be an increased need for data filtering, processing and visualising techniques and for systems that assist upon the decisions of clinicians and coordinators by providing useful data visualisations. Another relevant area is the efficient monitoring of persons outside the hospital in potential need of care, but with no interest in surveillance.

Traditional information systems often try to automate as much as possible based on static knowledge of the situation to be supported. Already in the 1980s it was realised that for many processes it was better to use IT for informing humans rather than for automating their work (Zuboff 1988), and one has since then described a number of archetypical process types that can be reasonably supported by IT as also discussed in Sect. 1.3. The different process types decide the extent to which the underlying technology can be based on hard-coded, predefined, evolving or implicit process models.

Workflow traditionally focuses on static process support where one generally separates process definition (articulation, modelling) from process enactment (practice, activation). These activities are supported by different tool components and performed by different roles. As the process is enacted, the roles are filled with individual people (process participants), and they seldom have knowledge outside their own responsibilities.

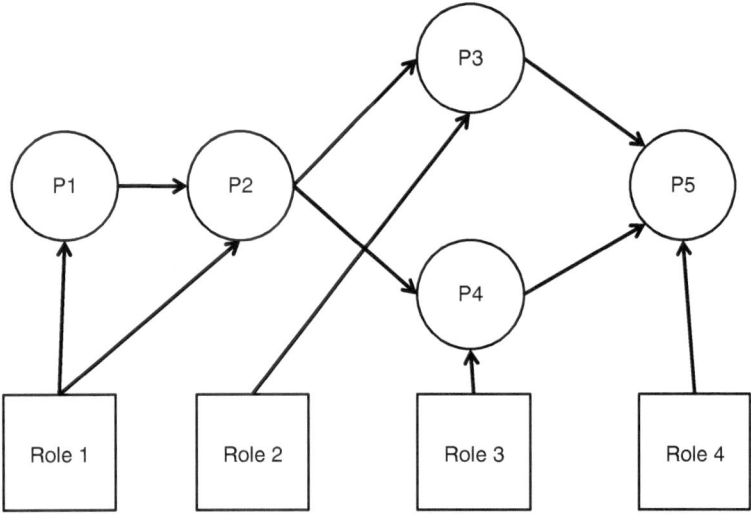

Fig. 8.3 Role-restricted scope of information access (Adapted from Krogstie 2011)

This is illustrated in Fig. 8.3 where those in Role1 have overview of the task necessary for P1 and P2, Role2 for P3, etc. A more resilient solution would be to let those in a role (e.g. Role3 which do P4) also have access to information relevant for P3 (parallel task), P2 (prior task) and P5 (dependant task), at least when there are irregularities from normal procedures.

To reiterate from Sect. 2.3.5, the limited success of WfMS in supporting knowledge intensive and cooperative work has partly been attributed to lack of flexibility. Most work within this area looks at how conventional systems can be extended and enhanced, how static workflow systems can be made *adaptive*. Some also investigate more far-reaching adaptability including late modelling during enactment and local adaptation of particular workflow instances. Most researchers in this area recognise that change is a way of life in organisations, but a basic premise is still that work is repetitive and can be relatively completely prescribed. Within the community, an understanding seems to have emerged that change requires process definition and process enactment to be intertwined.

8.2 Modelling in Future Technological Development from a Quality Perspective

As we saw in the previous section, there are a number of new challenges and opportunities for modelling due to the new technological and organisational developments. We will end the book by analysing this in more detail, again turning to the levels in the SEQUAL framework.

There are two main development scenarios. What we term the *steady-state scenario*, where modelling is a somewhat esoteric activity for a limited number of experts is of course one possibility, but not very interesting for us to discuss here. The more positive view in the light of the above is that abstraction techniques such as modelling are taken into use in an increasing number of areas, to make it possible to at all be able to manage the development. Looking at this scenario, one striking aspect is that the number and variety of stakeholders that will need to relate to models of some sort will increase. Given the increased educational level in most countries, with an increasing group of people with master degrees, it is not unlikely that more people will also be able to relate to these types of abstractions, given that one of the things that you are exposed to in a master study of most types is training to deal with abstractions. Looking at the sets in SEQUAL, we can thus foresee the following under this scenario:

- G: The same list of goals of modelling that is found in Chap. 1 will still be relevant, but emphasis on less formal, interactive formats will increase to be able to support the increasingly federated landscape needed to address future IT-driven environments. Thus, a number of aspects relating to quality of interactive models discussed in Sect. 6.6 will apply to a larger extent. On the other hand, since the work on quality of interactive models is originally developed for the support of smaller groups, this must be contrasted to the large-scale federated use of models envisaged above that span both organisational and geographical boundaries. Main consequences of this will be discussed below.
- D: The range of relevant domains is increasing further, also within what can be classified as the 'same' system, given that systems to an increasing degree range across, and are expected to integrate, a number of areas.
- K: In many areas one needs to deal with a more varied set of stakeholders, with a more varied set of skills and knowledge. Not only do you need to align IT-experts with 'business' – experts. Also people across a large range of business areas, being used to express their knowledge in a wide variety of notations and knowledge systems needs to be aligned.
- L: As we have seen relative to domain-specific modelling, the possibilities of tailoring the language to fit the domain and the knowledge of the stakeholders have increased. To bring more people into (semi-)formal modelling, these possibilities will have to be exploited to a larger degree. Thus, rather than having a consolidation of modelling languages like the one we saw in object-oriented design with UML, there will be an increasing number of variants of modelling languages. We will also see a mix of richer media components being integrated with the more traditional 'box and arrow'-conceptual modelling notations, thus supporting richer meta-meta models defining the type of constructs to include in models in the first place. Some of these developments are described in Lillehagen and Krogstie (2008). New approaches, such as value modelling, will complement more traditional enterprise modelling languages, although we expect most approaches will be possible to position relative to one of the eight modelling perspectives described in Sect. 3.3.
- T: An increasing number of tools will be available to extract model information from raw data, e.g. in the area of process mining (van der Aalst 2011). In addition, tools for meta-meta modelling and meta-modelling will be more common.

• M: Models will be pervasively available being coordinated in a federated manner. Models will be across meta-levels in an increasing degree (compared to the models in traditional software engineering being primarily on the type level. Whereas one also deals with some models on the instance level, it is currently not common to combine both type and instance level, except in some flavours of enterprise modelling). Models, in particular active models, will have a larger value in themselves, acting to a larger extent as knowledge commons and open models (http://www.openmodels.at/).

We believe the core dimensions and aspects of SEQUAL as described in Chap. 4 will be relevant also for models as used for future systems. On the other hand, as illustrated in Chap. 6, a number of specialisations might be envisaged. We will briefly discuss some main aspects here.

• Physical quality: Rather than being based on central repositories, more distributed, federated storage of model fragments must be available, utilising standard interchange formats.

• Empirical quality: Support for empirical quality will be more built in, e.g. in tools that build up models from raw data, e.g. in process mining, thus integrating information visualisation tools in modelling tools utilising generic knowledge on good visualisation tactics to a larger degree. The same generic mechanisms that are discussed in Chap. 4 applies, at least when keeping within the same meta-meta model. Note that different meta-meta models can induce the need for rethinking guidelines for achieving empirical quality (cf. the discussion on quality of maps in Sect. 6.7).

• Syntactic quality: Syntactic quality can be looked upon as trivial in a sense, since adherence can be enforced. On the other hand, one often sees that one extends languages with new aspects in an (not always conscious) attempt to turn semantic problems into syntactic problems. New tools based on meta-modelling make this easier to do, and then make it even more important to do right in the sense that one does not end up with too restricted languages for the different islands of modelling to evolve in a way best for their goals.

• Semantic quality: The federated approach needed for modelling will bring new challenges as for how we look upon the semantic quality of the overall model. Whereas semantic quality in smaller domains would be followed up much as before (i.e. looking at the feasible (perceived) completeness and validity), one would to a larger degree need to be able to live with inconsistencies across federations. In connection to this, it would be important to be able to clearly identify those aspects of the models across domains that need to be consistent. The areas of consistency are in some areas obvious (e.g. in process modelling, one needs consistency in the interfaces). In other areas, e.g. in data models, these needs are less clear-cut.

• Pragmatic quality: Given that more stakeholders are involved, this is of increasing importance. Different techniques can be used for different types of stakeholders, supporting multiple views for different stakeholder types on the same model to ensure individual comprehension.

- Social quality: This will be important in smaller communities, and in interfaces between communities, but less needed across federation. Note on the other hand that since different stakeholder groups might see different views of the overall model, possibly visualised in radically different ways, the effort to assure that they comprehend the models equally will potentially have to increase.
- Deontic quality: Models will be more important, in particular in organised conduct across traditional organisational boundaries and needs to be followed up in a more professional manner (Wesenberg 2011).

8.3 Final Words

One can easily be blinded by the speed of the technological development. When one started to see widespread impact of pervasive and ubiquitous technology, where 'The most profound technologies are those that disappear. They weave themselves into the fabric of everyday life until they are indistinguishable from it' (Weiser 1991), I asked myself to what extent there was a need for modelling in this landscape. When returning to research in 2000, I turned to focus in particular on mobile information systems in the light of this. Although that journey is another book, the conclusion so far is that although technology is changing fast, conceptual issues are much more sticky, which is especially clear when looking upon IS in the large. Although we are struggling with many of the same conceptual issues, new technologies have accentuated different aspects, e.g. the improved importance of space and place. As indicated in this chapter, the same is envisaged for the future. Although there are large technological changes expected, there is a need to represent and transfer knowledge in an appropriate way. Many of the deep conceptual aspects and challenges are similar to before, and have to be mastered by new generations.

References

Aagesen, G., van Veenstra, A.F., Janssen, M., Krogstie, J.: The entanglement of enterprise architecture and IT-governance: the cases of Norway and the Netherlands. Paper presented at the HICCS. IEEE CS Press (2011)

Ali Babar, M., Dingsøyr, T., Lago, P., van Vliet, H. (eds.): Software Architecture Knowledge Management – Theory and Practice. Springer, Berlin (2009)

Chandy, K., Schulte, W.: Event Processing: Designing IT Systems for Agile Companies. McGraw-Hill, New York (2009)

Chesbrough, H.: Open Innovation. The new Imperative for Creating and Profiting from Technology. Harvard Business School Press, Boston (2003)

Chesbrough, H.: Open Services Innovation. Rethinking Your Business to Growth and Compete in a New Era. Jossey-Bass, San Francisco (2011)

EU: Ministerial Declaration on eGovernment. In: 5th Ministerial eGovernment Conference, Malmø, Sweden, 18–20 Nov 2009

Gordijn, J., Yu, E., van der Raadt, B.: E-service design using i* and e³value modeling. IEEE Softw. 23(3), 26–33 (2006)

Hadzic, M., Chang, E.: Application of digital ecosystem design methodology within the health domain. Trans. Syst. Man Cybernet. A Syst. Hum. 40(4), 779–788 (2010)

Houy, C., Fettke, P., Loos, P., van der Aalst, W.M.P., Krogstie, J.: BPM-in-the-Large – towards a higher level of abstraction in business process management. Paper presented at GISP under WCC, Brisbane, Australia, Sept 2010

Houy, C., Fettke, P., Loos, P., van der Aalst, W.M.P., Krogstie, J.: Business process management in the large. Bus. Inf. Syst. Eng. **3**(6), 385–388 (2011)

Jansen, S., Finkelstein, A., Brinkkemper, S.: A sense of community: a research agenda for software ecosystems. In: Proceedings of the 31st International Conference on Software Engineering (ICSE), New and Emerging Research Track – Companion Volume, 16–24 May 2009, Vancouver, Canada, pp. 187–190 (2009)

Jørgensen, HD.: Interactive process models. PhD thesis, IDI, NTNU (2004)

Krogstie, J.: Business information systems utilizing the future internet. Presented at BIR, Riga, Latvia, Oct 2011

Krogstie, J., Dalberg, V., Jensen, S.M.: Harmonising business processes of collaborative networked organisations using process modelling. In: Virtual Enterprises and Collaborative Networks. IFIP, vol. 149, pp. 81–88. Springer, Boston (2004)

Krogstie, J., Dalberg, V., Jensen, S.M.: Process modeling value framework. In: Manolopoulos, Y., Filipe, J., Constantopoulos, P., Cordeiro, J. (eds.) ICEIS 2006. LNBIP, vol. 3, pp. 309–321. Springer, Berlin (2008)

Li, M.-S., et al. (eds.): Position paper on orientations for FP8 a European innovation partnership for European enterprises, version 3.0, 21 Jan 2011. Future Internet Enterprise Systems (FInES) (2011)

Lillehagen, F., Krogstie, J.: Active Knowledge Modeling of Enterprises. Springer, Berlin (2008)

van der Aalst, W.M.P.: Intra and inter-organizational process mining: discovering processes within and between organizations. In: PoEM 2011, Oslo, Norway, 2–3 Nov 2011

Vyatkin, V., Zhabelova, G., Ulieru, M., McComas, D.: Toward digital ecologies: intelligent agent networks controlling interdependent infrastructure. In: IEEE Conference on Smart Grid Communications, Gaithersburg, Oct 2010

Weiser, M.: The computer for the twenty-first century. Sci. Am. **265**(3), 94–104 (1991)

Wesenberg, H.: Enterprise modeling in an agile world PoEM 2011. In: Proceedings of the 4th Conference on Practice of Enterprise Modeling, Oslo, Norway, 2–3 Nov 2011

Zuboff, S.: In the Age of the Smart Machine. Basic Books, New York (1988)

Appendix A: Terminology

We give in this appendix a comprehensive overview of the terminology used in the book. We have also included some of the abbreviations being used. Terms will be written in italic type when first defined, and will be written in italics when they are used as part of other definitions. The terminology is influenced by our philosophical stance of social construction. This appears especially in the definitions of the basic terms, although the definitions themselves are written in a categorical style for us to be able to use the terms consistently. A constructivistic view is also followed in FRISCO, which has provided what is arguably the most comprehensive framework for information systems terminology. Similarly, to FRISCO, we have used a set-theoretic approach, although a set-theoretic formalisation is not emphasised here. Terms are grouped in the following areas:

1. Time
2. Phenomena
3. State and rules
4. Data, information and knowledge
5. Language and models
6. Actors and activities
7. Systems
8. Social construction
9. Methodology

In some cases, the definition of a term is found after it has been used in another definition.

A.1 Time

The definitions in this area are to a large extent pragmatic, to be able to use them in a consistent manner in the later definitions. Thus, we are not entering into philosophical or quantum mechanical aspects of the nature of time.

Time points. Time can be represented by time points such that the only relation between time points other than identity is that one time point precedes the other.

Time interval. A time interval is the ordered pair of time points (the begin- and end-point of the interval) such that the first precedes the other.

Time scale. A time scale divides time into coherent time intervals.

Time unit. The smallest time interval that can be represented on a given time scale is termed the time unit.

Duration. The duration of a time interval is the number of consecutive time units between the one after the one in which the begin-point of the time interval occurs, until and including the time unit in which the end-point of the time interval occurs. A *time point* has no *duration*.

A.2   Phenomena

A phenomenon is used as the elementary unit of the terminology. In other similar terminologies, the term 'thing' is used in this respect. Others use the term 'concept' as the elementary unit.

Phenomenon. A phenomenon is something as it appears in the mind of a person. The world is perceived by persons to consist of phenomena. A phenomenon can be perceived to exist independently of the perceiving person, or be perceived to be purely mental. With the phrase 'something which is perceived to exist independent of the perceiver', we mean something that the person in question regards as existing external to him, for instance another person. An idea of a new *CIS* that only appears in someone's mind though have no such 'real-world' equivalence, at least not until it is externalised.

Relevance. A phenomenon is of relevance to a non-empty set of persons in a time interval if it is of interest to all members of the set in the time interval.

Potential relevance. A phenomenon is of potential relevance to a non-empty set of persons in a time interval if it is of interest to at least one of the persons in the set in the time interval.

Relevance is socially and temporally constrained which are as expected taking social construction into account. Relevance needs the notion of shared explicit knowledge (see below) to be meaningful, i.e. if there are no phenomena that are perceived equally by two persons, no phenomena will be relevant.

Domain. A domain is defined as the source of any kind of mapping. 'Domain' includes the meaning known from algebra, but the term 'mapping' is used in a slightly more general sense than usual. Not only sets can be mapped into sets as in mathematics, but also areas into areas. When used in the mathematical sense, a domain will be a finite or infinite set of values.

Property. A property is an aspect of a phenomenon that can be described and given a value. A phenomenon will have a set of potentially relevant properties. The values for the properties are members of the domains for these properties. All phenomena have at least one property, namely, its perceived individual existence or lack thereof.

Type. A non-empty set of properties that together characterise certain phenomena.

Subtype. A subtype S of a type T is a set of properties such that T is a proper subset of S.

Supertype. A subset of a type.

Class. The set of all phenomena of a certain type. These phenomena are called the members of the class.

Subclass. The subclass S of a class T is the proper subset of the class T such that the phenomenon in S has a type that is a subtype of the type of the phenomena of T. When having several sub-classes of a class, you can have different cases based on coverage and disjointness.
- A set of subclasses of a class cover the class if all members of the class are members of at least one of the subclasses.
- A set of subclasses of a class are disjoint if no members of a subclass are members of any of the other subclasses of the class.
- A set of subclasses that are both disjoint and cover the class is called a partition of the class.

Environment. The environment of a phenomenon is the set of actors which act upon it.

A.3   State and Rules

State. The state of a phenomenon is the set of mappings of all properties of the phenomenon into values from the domain of the properties. A phenomenon can only be in one state within a time unit. Note that different persons might perceive the state of a phenomenon differently.

State space. The state space of a phenomenon is the set of all possible states of the phenomenon. All subsystems of a system have their own state space.

Transition. A transition is a mapping from a domain comprising states to a co-domain comprising states.

Event. An event is a change of state of a phenomena. It is effected through a transition. An event happens within a time unit (i.e. it has a zero duration).

Trigger. A trigger is a relationship between an event and one or more activities and expresses the perceived cause for an actor to carry out the activities.

History. The history of a phenomenon is the chronologically ordered states of the phenomenon.

Rule. A rule is something that influences the actions of a set of actors. A rule is either a rule of necessity (alethic rule) or a deontic rule.

The term *rule* is used to cover more situations than what is usually found in so-called rule-based systems, since it also includes what is often referred to as goals, guidelines or instrumental rules.

Rule of necessity. A rule of necessity is a rule that must always be satisfied. It is either analytic or empirical (see below).

Analytic rule. A rule of necessity that cannot be broken by an intersubjectively agreed definition of the terms used in the rule is called analytic. For example, 'The age of a person is never below 0'.

Empirical rule. A rule of necessity that cannot be broken according to present shared explicit knowledge is called empirical. Although not as strongly necessary as an analytic rule, these kind of rules are rules that can be treated as if they are rules of necessity, and one would not expect them to be broken. For example, 'Nothing can travel faster than the speed of light'.

Deontic rule. A rule that is only socially agreed among a set of persons. A deontic rule can thus be violated without redefining the terms in the rule. A deontic rule can be classified as being an obligation, a recommendation, a permission, a discouragement or a prohibition. The inclusion of recommended and discouraged above is novel compared to traditional deontic logic, but has been included in newer frameworks for deontic logic and deontic operators.

Constitutive rule. A deontic rule that applies to phenomena that exist only because the rule exist. Generally, this kind of rule can be written: A counts as B in context C. When using a general rule-format, the context is included in the precondition.

Static rule. A rule restricting the allowable states of a phenomenon is called static.

Dynamic rule. A rule restricting the allowable state transitions of a phenomenon is called dynamic.

Temporal rule. A rule referring to the situation of more than one state Both rules of necessity and deontic rules can be classified as being static or dynamic.

Lawful transition. A transition is lawful if it obeys the dynamic rules of necessity regarding the phenomenon.

Deontic transition. A transition is deontic if it is lawful and also obeys the dynamic deontic rules regarding the phenomenon.

Lawful state space. The set of states of a phenomenon that comply with the static rules of necessity concerning the phenomenon is termed the *lawful state space*.

Deontic state space. The set of states of a phenomenon that are lawful and in addition comply with the static deontic rules concerning the phenomenon is termed the deontic state space.

Internal event. An event that arises in a phenomenon by virtue of a lawful or deontic transition in the phenomenon is called internal.

External event. An external event is an event that arises in a phenomenon by virtue of the act of an actor in the environment of the phenomenon.

Stable state. A state in which a phenomenon will remain unless forced to change by virtue of an external event.

Unstable state. A state that will change into another state by virtue of an internal event is called unstable.

A.4   Data, Information and Knowledge

Knowledge. Knowledge is the justified true belief of a person. Knowledge is by definition linked to the individual person. It can be divided into explicit and tacit knowledge.

Explicit knowledge. The awareness of a person of properties and values of properties of phenomena. This indicates that it is both explicit knowledge to be aware of a person's height in cm, and that 'height' is a relevant property of a person. Since also a person is a phenomenon, the explicit knowledge he or she has can be looked upon as part of the state of this phenomenon since a potential relevant property of a person can be that he is able to know something, and what he or she knows. Through infinite introspection, this could indicate that the knowledge of a person is infinite, but since it is seldom relevant with this kind of introspection, this is not found problematic. Explicit knowledge can be more or less precise, certain and complete.

Example on precision: That someone knows that a city has 2,433,775 inhabitants at a certain time is more precise explicit knowledge than if the same person knows that a city has around 2.5 million inhabitants.

Example on completeness: That someone knows that Oslo is the capital of Norway is less complete knowledge of Oslo than to also know that Oslo is located in the southern part of Norway.

Example on certainty: A poor farmer in Kuala Lipis who once has heard about the city of Bombay and that it lies in India has less certain explicit knowledge than someone who has been there himself. If you hear something several times from several different people, your certainty of some explicit knowledge will usually increase. If you have only read it once in a tabloid newspaper, your certainty of the 'fact' is usually lower.

In FRISCO, explicit knowledge is termed *information*. We define the term 'information' differently below.

Shared explicit knowledge. Shared explicit knowledge is an inter-subjectively agreed identical awareness of some properties and values of properties of phenomena by two or more persons that have been achieved through a process of social construction.

Tacit knowledge. Tacit knowledge is knowledge that cannot be represented externally to the person and only shows up in the actions of the person having the knowledge. It is possible to differentiate between two kinds of tacit knowledge. That which could have been represented externally, but which one either choose not to, or cannot find the appropriate symbols for, and so-called true tacit knowledge which cannot in principle be externally represented fully.

Information. Information is externalised explicit knowledge, which is not already known by the person who receives it, i.e. a state transition for a person's knowledge appears when he receives information, and thus receiving information can be looked upon as an event. This means that information is socially and temporally constrained. If you already know something (and know that you know it), you do not perceive to receive information if you are told the same thing again (even if the certainty of the knowledge might increase). Thus, our definition is hopefully close to the one used in everyday language as illustrated by the statement: 'Information is what you get or may get if you ask certain kinds of questions.... Answers to such questions are often provided at some information desk.'

Symbol. The explicit knowledge of a person can be externalised in a persistent form using symbols.

Message. A set of related symbols expressed in a language transmitted by an actor intended for a non-empty set of actands. The set of actands that ultimately receives the message can be empty.

Communication. The exchange of messages between actors.

Sign. A sign is the triplet (symbol, person, phenomenon), i.e. a sign is symbol that represent a phenomenon for a person.

Data. Data are symbols that can be preserved, transformed and transported by a computer. Data and other symbols can be internalised as knowledge by persons.

A.5   Language and Model

Language. A set of symbols, the graphemes of the language being the smallest units in the writing system capable of causing a contrast in meaning, a set of words being a set of related symbols constituting the vocabulary of the language, rules to form sentences being a set of related words (syntax), and some inter-subjectively agreed definitions of what the different sentences mean (language semantics). In a natural language, e.g. English, the symbols and words will be ordered linearly, whereas in a two-dimensional modelling language, symbols are ordered spatially. In addition to the aspects described above, one also often talks about the pragmatics when discussing languages, being the relationship between symbols, words and sentences and the effect these have on persons.

Statement. A sentence representing a single property of a certain phenomenon.

Language extension. The set of all statements that can be made according to the graphemes, vocabulary and syntax of a language.

Natural language. A natural language is the language of a cultural society (for instance a tribe or a nation). It is usually learned and applied from childhood by the set of persons belonging to the society.

Professional language. A professional language is a language used by a set of persons working in a certain kind of area or in a scientific discipline. Usually such a language is not learned before the person has been active in the area for a while.

Formalism. A formalism is a formal language, i.e. a language with a precisely defined vocabulary, syntax and semantics. The semantics can be operational and/or logical. If the semantics is based on mathematical logic, we use the term *logical formalism*. If it is possible to execute a set of sentences in the language on a computer, the language is said to have an operational semantics. All formalisms are professional languages.

Semi-formal language. A semi-formal language is a language with a precisely defined vocabulary and syntax, but without a precisely defined semantics. In addition, semi-formal languages (e.g. DFD) are professional languages.

Informal language. An informal language is neither formal nor semi-formal. Natural languages are of this category, and also a professional language can be informal.

Abstraction. An abstraction is the phenomenon of a set of phenomena and its properties at some level of approximation. The abstraction contains incomplete explicit knowledge about the phenomena, i.e. there are more that can be known about the phenomena than is covered in the abstraction. This does not mean that the abstraction cannot contain all relevant knowledge in a given time interval.

Classification. The abstraction where individual phenomena are grouped together in a class based on perceived common properties. Example: 'Rod Stewart' and 'Mick Jagger' can be grouped together in the class 'singers'.

Aggregation. An abstraction that is a Cartesian product of classes. For example, a bicycle being built up from wheels, a seat, a frame, handlebars, etc.

Generalisation. An abstraction that is a subset of the union of a set of classes. For example, both employees and customers are persons.

Association. An abstraction that is a set of classes. For example, the classes 'Men' and 'Women' are members of the set 'sex-groups'.

Model. A model is an abstraction externalised in a professional language. A model is assumed to be simpler than, resemble, and have the same structure and way of functioning as the phenomena it represents.

Conceptual model. A model of a domain made in a formal or semi-formal language with a limited vocabulary.

Comment: Many conceptual modelling languages are partly diagrammatic, in which case they are combination of logographic and iconographic symbols, but this is not looked upon as a requirement. Some conceptual modelling languages also have aspects that are pictographic.

Language model. The model of a language. Within conceptual modelling, this is often termed 'meta-model', which is only a proper term when looking upon it from the point of view of repository-management for a modelling tool where the instantiation of the model is another model in the same or a different modelling language.

System model. A model of a system.

A.6   Actors and Activities

A phenomenon is acted upon by another phenomenon if its history is different from what it would have been if the other phenomenon did not influence it.

Actor. An actor is a phenomenon that acts upon another phenomenon, the *actand.*

Acquaintances. The acquaintances of an actor are the set of actors that either acts upon or is acted upon by the actor.

Social actor. A social actor is an actor that includes at least one person. Social actors might be individual or organisational (see below).

Technical actor. A technical actor is an actor that does not include any persons. Technical actors can be computational and temporal. Other subtypes of actors might for instance be production actors, but these will not be discussed here. Whereas temporal actors are some time-measuring device (i.e. a clock of some sort), computational actors are either hardware actors or software actors. Computational actors are either atomic or systemic including atomic and systemic subsystems. Computational actors can be said to be compatible in the following meanings:
- Hardware compatibility: Stating which hardware actors that can act upon each other.
- Executional compatibility: Describe which software actors that can be executed on which hardware actors.
- Software compatibility: Stating which software actors that can act upon each other.

Software actors can be versions of 0:N other software actors, i.e. a software actor can be recreated by performing a set of state changes to the actor it is a version of. A set of state changes in this meaning are called a delta. The original actor is called a predecessor of the version actor, whereas this is called a successor of the original actor. Software actors might have several predecessors and successors. These relations are transitive. Two or more software actors that have the same immediate predecessor are termed variants.

Internal actor. Actors being internal to an organisation are actors being part of the organisational system of the organisation in one or more of the relevant roles they are currently filling.

External actor. Actors being external to an organisation are actors not being part of the organisational system of the organisation in any of the relevant roles they are currently filling.

Individual social actor. A person interacting with his environment is termed an individual social actor. We will use the term *person* synonymously with the term *individual social actor.*

Organisational social actor. An organisational actor is a social actor that consists of a set of more than one person performing goal-oriented and co-ordinated action. An organisational actor can also include technical actors, but this is not mandatory.

Permanent organisational actor. An organisational actor for which a begin time-point of its existence can be perceived, but normally not the future end time-point.

Temporary organisational actor. An organisational actor for which both the begin time-point and the possibly future end time-point of its existence can be perceived.

Periodic organisational actor. An organisational actor for which a set of begin time-points and (possibly future) end time-points of its existence can be perceived, and where there is normally the same time-interval between the different begin time-points. The duration of this time-interval is longer than the individual lifetime of the organisational actor.

Action. An action is the phenomenon of one phenomenon acting upon other phenomena.

Activity. An activity is a system of actions.

Stakeholder. The stakeholders of an activity are the set of persons who perceive or are perceived by other persons to potentially lose or gain from the activity.

Participant. The participants of an activity are the set of persons who act upon the actands of the activity as part of the activity.

Process. A process is an activity that takes a set of phenomena and transforms them into a possibly empty set of phenomena.

Role. Actions that can be expected by an actor or by other actors.

Agent. An actor acting in a particular role.

Formal role. A role where part of the expected actions of an actor filling the role is institutionalised by an organisational actor. A typical example of a formal role is a position such as a professor. All roles usually also have two additional aspects:
- The informal part of the role. Expectations to an actor filling the role that are not institutionalised. For example, 'a professor is absent-minded'.
- The expectation to an agent, because of the particular actor filling the role.

Role conflict. Inconsistent expectations to an actor because of filling two or more roles in the same time interval or because of differing expectations to a role that the actor fill from two or more other actors.

A.7   Systems

System. A system is a set of correlated phenomena, which itself is a phenomenon. Each phenomenon that is contained in the system is part of the system. To be a system, it has at least one (systemic) property not possessed by any of its parts. The following example indicates the necessity of the requirement of a systemic property: If you buy some eggs from a farmer and use two of them for breakfast, then the correlated phenomena: You, the farmer, the farmer's hen that laid the eggs, the frying pan you used to prepare the eggs, and the two eggs now in your stomach could fit as a system using a definition not including a systemic property.

System viewer. A person who perceives the system as a phenomenon.

Subsystem. A subsystem of a system is a system that is part of another system, the set of phenomena being part of the subsystem is a proper subset of the set of phenomena being part of the whole system.

Subsystem structure. A partition of a system into a set of subsystems together with a set of correlations among the subsystems.

Active system. A system where at least one of the subsystems is an activity is called an active system.

Passive system. If there is no subsystem in the system that is an activity, it is called a passive system.

Open system. A system is open if it has an environment that can influence the system.

Information system (IS). An information system is a system for the dissemination of data between persons, i.e. to potentially increase their knowledge.

Data system. A data system is a system to preserve, transform and transport data. A data system is usually a sub-system of an information system. Both data systems and information systems may be contained in the domain they convey data about.

Organisation. An organisation is defined as a non-empty set of persons, and other phenomena that is a phenomenon where goal-oriented and co-ordinated action is aimed at. An organisation is an organisational (social) actor when interacting with other actors. The term *enterprise* is often used synonymously to organisation.

Organisational system. An organisational system is a system having the actors and activities of an organisation as subsystems.

Organisational information system (OIS). An OIS is the information system for the dissemination of data within an organisation. The OIS is a sub-system of an organisational system.

Computerised information system (CIS). A CIS is an information system that is based on the use of computers for the dissemination of data.

User (of a CIS). A user of a CIS is someone who potentially increases his or her knowledge about some phenomena other than the CIS with the support of the CIS. An end-user increases his and her knowledge in areas which are relevant to him or her independently of the actual CIS by interacting with the CIS. Indirect users of a CIS increase their knowledge by getting results from the CIS without directly interacting with the actual CIS.

Computerised organisational information system (COIS). A COIS is a system for the dissemination of data within an organisation that are based on the use of computers. This is a subsystem of the OIS of the organisation. The COIS contains the set of internal software actors which support the internal social actors of the organisation, and the hardware actors these software actors are executed on.

Application systems. An application system is a subsystem of the COIS being adapted to the goals of the organisation. When an application system interacts with its environment, it is an applicative actor.

(Application system) portfolio. The portfolio of an organisation is the set of application systems in the COIS of the organisation.

Dynamic system. A system that always is in a state from which there exists a lawful transition.

Static system. A system that is not dynamic is called static.

A.8   Social Construction

Definitions of terms from social construction theory as they are used in the book are given here.

Local reality. The local reality of a person is the way the person perceives the world that he or she acts in. In addition to the person's explicit and tacit knowledge, this also includes feelings and values of the person.

Externalisation. Making part of the local reality of a person available for others. The most important ways social actors externalise their local reality are to speak and to construct languages, artefacts such as models, and institutions such as rules.

Organisational reality. That which guides and controls a person's actions in an organisation.

Internalisation. Making sense out of the actions, institutions, artefacts etc. in the organisation and making this organisational reality part of the individual local reality of a person.

Organisational closure. A process of social construction where the actors keep reproducing the same organisational reality.

A.9   Methodology

The terms below are defined here in the context of conceptual modelling for IS support in organisations.

Conceptual modelling. The activity of developing conceptual models.

Audience. The actors that need to relate to the conceptual models developed during conceptual modelling.

(Modelling) method. A method is a set of rules for creating models with a language.

(Modelling) approach. An approach consists of a non-empty set of semi-formal or formal languages and a number of rules for using these languages to construct models.

(Model) verification. The process of assuring whether a model, created according to a certain approach, conforms to the rules of necessity of the language used, and has the expected semantic.

(Model) validation. The process of assuring that a model corresponds to the explicit knowledge of those social actors that are the source of the model. Whereas verification is potentially decidable, validation is not so, one can never be 100% certain that the externalisation in the form of a conceptual model correspond to the local reality of an individual. Even though validation is a useful activity, in particular due to the possibility for falsification, i.e. one can say that a model do not correspond to one's internal reality.

(Model) transformation. A process where a model written in a language is transformed into another model in the same language.

Statement insertion. A transformation where the resulting model contains statements that are not contained in the original model.

Statement deletion. A transformation where the resulting model do not contain all statements that are contained in the original model.

Syntactically valid statement deletion. A statement deletion resulting in a model being conformant to the syntax of the language the model is written in.

(Model) layout modification. Transforming a model into another model containing the same statements laid out differently in two dimensions.

(Model) filtering. Transforming a model into another model containing a subset of the statements of the original model. A model filtering consists of a set of statement deletions.

Syntactically valid (model) filtering. Model filtering resulting in a model being conformant to the syntax of the language of the model.

(Model) translation. A process where a model written in a language is transformed into another model written in a (set of) different language(s).

Rephrasing. A transformation where some of the implicit statements of a model are made explicit.

Paraphrasing. A translation where the involved languages are textual.

Visualisation. A translation where the source language is textual, and the target language is diagrammatic.

Code-generation. A computer-supported translation where the target language has an executional semantics for which there exist tools for automatic execution.

Complete translation. A translation where all statements in the source model are also contained in the target model.

Valid translation. A translation in which all statements in the target model are also contained in the source model.

Development of an application system in an organisation. The process of producing a new application system in the organisation based on the current OIS and the knowledge of internal and potentially external actors.

Development is divided into two categories.
- Development of replacement systems being application systems that replace existing application systems, and offer the same functionality as already existing application systems.
- Development of application systems covering functional areas that are not currently supported by the existing COIS.

Maintenance of an application system in an organisation. The process of creating an updated version of an application system used in the organisation through a temporally ordered set of lawful transitions based on an existing application system and the knowledge of internal and potentially external actors.

Corrective maintenance. Maintenance performed to identify and correct processing failures, performance failures and implementation failures in an application system.

Adaptive maintenance. Maintenance performed to adapt application systems to the changes among the supporting technical actors of the application system.

Perfective maintenance. Maintenance performed to improve the performance, maintainability, or other attributes of a computer program. Perfective maintenance has been divided into enhancive maintenance and non-functional perfective maintenance. Enhancive maintenance implies changes and additions to the functionality offered to the users by the system. Non-functional perfective maintenance implies improvements to the quality and other features being important for the developer and maintainer of the system, such as modifiability. Non-functional perfective maintenance thus includes what is often termed preventive maintenance, but also such things as improving the performance and security of the system.

Application portfolio evolution. Development or maintenance where changes in the application system increase the functional coverage of the portfolio of the organisation. This includes development of new application systems which covers areas which are not covered by the existing COIS, and also includes enhancive maintenance.

Application portfolio upkeep. Work made to sustain the functional coverage of the portfolio of the organisation. This includes the three other types of maintenance, but also includes the development of replacement systems.

Methodology. A system of rules, approaches and computational actors to aid development and/or maintenance of application systems.

Appendix B: List of Abbreviations

7PMG	Seven Process Modelling Guidelines
ABC	Actor Bank Channel
ACL	Agent Communication Language
ADM	Actor Dependency Model
AKM	Active Knowledge Modelling http://activeknowledgemodeling.com/
AM	Agile Modelling http://www.agilemodeling.com/
API	Application Programming Interface
Archimate	http://www3.opengroup.org/subjectareas/enterprise/archimate
ARIS	Architecture of Integrated Information System
ASD	Adaptive Software Development
BIM	Business Integration Methodology
BPEL	Business Process Execution Language
BPM	Business Process Modelling/Management
BPMN	Business Process Modelling Notation http://www.omg.org/spec/BPMN/2.0/
BPR	Business Process Reengineering
C3S3P	Concept, Scaffolding, Scenario, Solution, Platform Configuration, Platform Delivery, Performance
CIM	Computational Independent Model (in MDA)
CIS	Computerised Information System
COIS	Computerised Organisational Information System
CONFORM	Configuration Management Formalisation for Maintenance
CPC	Configurable Product Components
CPPD	Collaborative Product and Process Design
CRAI	Competence, Resource, Aspect, Individual
CVW	Configurable Visual Workplaces
DAG	Directed Acyclic Graph
DBMS	Database Management System
DEMO	Design and Engineering, Methods and Organisation http://www.demo.nl/
DFD	Data Flow Diagram

DSL	Domain-Specific Language
DSM	Domain-Specific Model/Modelling
e3Value	http://e3value.few.vu.nl/
EDA	Event-Driven Architecture
EE	Extended Enterprise
EEML	Extended Enterprise Modelling Language
EIS	Existing Information System
EKD	Enterprise Knowledge Development
EPC	Event Process Chain
EPML	Event-Driven Process Chain Markup Language
ER	Entity Relationship
ERP	Enterprise Resource Planning
EXTERNAL	
FCIS	Future Computerised Information System
FDD	Feature-Driven Development
FIPA	Foundation for Intelligent Physical Agents
FIS	Future Information System
FOAF	Friend of a Friend http://xmlns.com/foaf/spec
FRISCO	Framework for Information Systems Concepts http://home.dei. polimi.it/pernici/ifip81/documents/1998-Lindgreen-FRISCO.pdf
FSM	Finite State Machine
GEMAL	Generic Enterprise Modelling and Activation Language
GERAM	Generalised Enterprise Reference Architecture and Methodology
GOPRR	Graph, Object, Property, Role, Relationship
GRL	Goal-Oriented Requirements Engineering
GUMO	General User Model Ontology http://gumo.org/
HCI	Human Computing Interaction
HLA	High Level Architecture
IBIS	Issue-Based Information Systems
IoT	Internet of Things
IS	Information System
ISD	Internet-Speed Development
ITIL	IT Infrastructure Library
KQML	Knowledge Query and Manipulation Language
MBSD	Model-Based Software Development
MDA	Model-Driven Architecture
MDSD	Model-Driven Software Development
MGWP	Model-Generated Workplaces
MOF	Meta Object Facility
NFC	Near Field Communication
NIAM	Natural Language Information Analysis Method
OIS	Organisational Information System
OMG	Object Management Group http://www.omg.org/
OOA	Object-Oriented Analysis
OOD	Object-Oriented Design
OOR	Object-Oriented Requirements

OOSE	Object-Oriented Software Engineering
ORM	Object Role Modelling http://www.orm.net
OSS	Open Source Software
OWL	Ontology Web Language
PIM	Platform Independent Model (in MDA)
PLM	Product Lifecycle Management
PMBOK	Project Management Book of Knowledge
PML	Process Modelling Language
PP	Pragmatic Programmer
PSM	Platform Specific Model (in MDA)
RAD	Role Activity Diagrams
RDF	Resource Description Framework
RE	Requirements Specification
RFID	Radio Frequency Identification
RIN	Role Interaction Nets
RUP	Rational Unified Process
S-BPM	Subject-Oriented Business Process Management
SBVR	Semantics of Business Vocabulary and Rules http://www.omg.org/spec/ SBVR/1.0/
SCRUM	
SDL	Specification and Description Language
SEQUAL	Semantic Quality Framework
SMM	Software Maintenance Model
SNA	Social Network Analysis
SPEC	Suspension, Preparation, Expansion, Consolidation
SRS	Software Requirements Specification
SSM	Soft Systems Methodology
STD	State Transition Diagrams
STM	State Transition Matrices
SUMO	Suggested Upper Merged Ontology
TDD	Test-Driven Development
TOGAF	The Open Group Architecture Framework http://www.opengroup.org/ togaf/
UCM	Use Case Maps
UEML	Unified Enterprise Modelling Language http://www.uemlwiki.org/
UML	Unified Modelling Language http://www.uml.org/
URN	User Requirements Notation (include i*/GRL) http://jucmnav. softwareengineering.ca/ucm/bin/view/UCM/DraftZ151Standard
W3C	World Wide Web Consortium http://www.w3.org
WfMS	Workflow Management System
WS-CDL	Web Services Choreography Description Language
XML	Extended Mark-up Language
XP	Extreme Programming
YAWL	Yet Another Workflow Language http://www.yawlfoundation.org/
ZIFA	Zachman Institute for Framework Architecture http://www.zachman. com/

Appendix C: Cases

In this appendix, we present the cases used throughout the book. The cases include aspects relative to both type level modelling and instance level modelling. The description in the book on the instance level is related to courses and conference arrangements that we have been involved in ourselves. For other scholars, it should be easy to change this to include your own courses or arrangements.

C.1 Teaching at the University (Both on the Study-Program and Course Level)

A number of tasks are performed in connection to carry through courses at a university. The case to be used throughout the exercises is related to the administration of university courses. We will look at this both generally (on the type level) and specifically (where the specific instance will be the courses TDT4250 and TDT4252 given in the years 2012–2013).

The process can be divided in three main parts:
1. Course preparation
2. Course performance
3. Course evaluation as a basis for the course preparation for the following year, realising the cyclic nature of this process

We will describe the main parts below.

C.1.1 Course Preparation

In connection to each course at the university, certain tasks are to be done relative to planning the teaching and evaluation of a course before the course starts.

The goal of the plan is to ensure that the course is well prepared before the course starts. The planning normally takes the learning goals of the subject description as an outset. The planning is meant to cover factual, pedagogical and practical matters to ensure that the students have the appropriate learning environment to achieve the set learning goals. Courses are included in one or more study programs given by the different faculties of the university. The university has both national and international study programs. The international study programs are taught in English; thus, if a course is included in at least one international study program, it will be taught in English. If not it is normally taught in the official language in the country of the university.

All courses are provided by an institute. The leader of the institute formally assigns the responsible teacher for each topic for each semester. This is based on a proposal by the research group being responsible for the course. The responsible teacher has the responsibility for planning the course in the semester, and for coordinating the teaching activities. Based on the course description and previous experiences, the responsible teacher makes the learning goals and the ways to achieve these goals, through lectures and exercises, more concrete.

The course responsible must report the need for resources necessary to perform the teaching and to ensure the learning among the students. This includes the need for rooms and AV equipment for teaching assistants. These needs are communicated to the institute. The need for course material is given to the local bookstore together with a suggestion for the number of students. This is done sufficiently early so that all resources can be made available at the start of the semester.

The preparation is summarised in a plan for the semester, to be of assistance to students and other teachers and teaching assistants in the topic. The semester plan is published on It's Learning (the local LMS) or by other means (e.g. on the web), or a combination of the two.

C.1.2 Course Performance

Courses are normally a mix of curricula that is wholly or partly lectured, and exercises for practical work on topics within the course. Some exercises might be mandatory, and might be included as a basis for part of the evaluation/grading of the course (portfolio evaluation).

The plan developed in the course preparation typically contains details for this process, including when different parts of the curricula are to be lectured, when the lectures are, and when the different exercises are to be done. The teachers and/or teaching assistants prepare the exercise in detail before making it available. The students are then assigned to do the exercises, and must work on this, preparing an answer to be delivered before the deadline provided. When the exercises are delivered, they are graded by the teaching staff (if part of the grade) and feedback is provided.

C.1.3 Course Evaluation

Evaluation of the students is usually done through a final exam, potentially in combination with other evaluation types as indicated above. Exams can be written or oral. In case of a written exam, the questions need to be prepared a number of days before the exam. The administration makes sure to administer the exam, and provides the environment to control that the exam is done according to regulations. After the exam, the answers are returned to the teacher, who makes sure that they are graded (either by himself or by an external examiner or both). When all results are in (but within three working weeks from the date of the exam), the combined results are given to the administration, which makes sure that they are made available for the students. The students can then (a) be satisfied with the result, (b) ask for additional feedback behind the grading, or (c) complain on the exam-results (either directly or after the feedback asked for in point b) has been returned. In case of a complaint, a new examiner not being involved in the first grading will be appointed, and a new grade will be issued independent of the first grading. If the grades are not delivered in time, the institute is fined by the university.

C.2   Arrangement of International Conferences and Events

Parts from this case are used for examples throughout the book.

C.2.1   Overall Setting (Basis for Type-Level Model)

An international group is involved in running a conference series, trying to take into account all the needs, both of those arranging a conference in the series and those participating in the conference in the series. In addition to supporting both conference organisers and conference participants, it aims to support the integration with the systems of travel service providers, conference locations, publishers of conference proceedings, tourist boards and professional societies (e.g. IEEE, ACM and IFIP).

Organisations such as universities and research organisations arrange irregularly international scientific conferences within a specific theme. The conference is usually part of an annual or bi-annual series of similar conferences. A conference can consist of presentation of accepted articles and invited presentations, poster sessions and demonstrations/stands, panels, workshops and tutorials. Accepted articles shall be available to the conference participants at the start of the conference in the form of a so-called conference proceedings developed by a professional publisher.

Who will be the organiser of the conference in a series in a particular year is decided by the conference board at annual meetings, based on applications from interested research groups.

In connection to a particular conference, an organisation committee and a program committee is established. The program committee consists of a number of researchers working within the theme of the conference that are normally distributed across the world. To get good papers, the program committee of the conference announces a Call for Papers. Potential authors receive this, and some of them decide to send in one or more paper for review. The paper can be written by one or more persons. The paper must be sent to the program chair (the leader of the program committee) within an announced deadline. The article cannot at the same time be submitted to another conference. An article that has previously been published cannot be submitted to a new event.

One of the authors functions as a contact person to the program chair. When the article is received by the program chair, the contact person gets a receipt, and the article is sent to between three and five persons of the program committee for review. The reviews have to be returned by a certain date. Based on the returned reviews, a number of the articles are selected on a program committee meeting, which can be a physical or a virtual meeting. Papers that have fewer than three reviews or very varying reviews will be given an additional review during the meeting. Papers can be accepted either as full papers, short papers, posters or be rejected. Accepted papers are bundled into sessions in the conference program, usually consisting of between two and four papers within the same sub-theme.

After the decision on selection has been made, this is announced to the contact persons of each paper. Authors of accepted papers (full or short) must create a final version of their article, a so-called camera-ready copy (CRC), within a predefined deadline. The CRC must follow the size limitations and layout rules of the publisher of the proceedings. In addition to this, the authors are expected to take into account the comments by the reviewers when they are preparing the CRC. For certain papers one might use so-called shepherds to follow-up that requested changes are actually performed or there is a proper argumentation if this is not the case. At least one of the authors must register for the conference and present the paper in the allotted slot in the conference program. Up until the point of acceptance of the article, the author is free to withdraw the paper, but this is not possible after the final version is submitted, and the copyright transfer form is sent to the publisher of the pro-ceedings. Note that when you submit a paper in the first place, there is already pending obligations on you (or one of the co-authors) to go to the conference and present the paper if it is accepted (note also that presenters at such conferences normally pay the registration fee).

Those with invited presentations, tutorials, panels or posters must also send in a description of their presentation to the program chair within the CRC deadline, but their work does not undergo the same thorough review process.

Within research, you can find different research communities, i.e. collection of researchers interested in a certain research area or research theme. In general, it is obligatory for a research community to spread scientific results, either through arranging scientific conferences or by publishing journals. One thing that charac-terises a scientific conference is that the papers to be presented are selected through a detailed review process as described above. The same community would thus need to arrange conferences within their research field. It is quite a lot of work arranging conferences of this type, thus it is normal that a conference series moves between different locations each year, being arranged by one of the organisations that are part of the community. Since there is a certain economic risk in arranging a conference, it is important that the conference is successful in the sense that it attracts a sufficient number of paying participants. One way to achieve this is to attract a number of good papers to the conference and to create a good program. Parts of a good program might be panels, tutorials, workshops, poster/demo sessions and invited presenters (so-called keynote speakers that are famous within their research field). In addition, the social program of the conference might be important in this respect given the opening for building the common history of the research community.

An organisation arranging a scientific conference depends on a number of other people and organisations for the practical arrangement of the conference. Whereas the organising and program committees are typically recruited from the research community and do the work relating to securing the quality of the scientific program for free, there need to be facilities for holding the conference, housing the participants, supporting their trip to the conference, taking care of payments and money matters, publishing information on the web, arranging social events part of the social program, perform registration at the start of the conference and publish proceedings. Many of these tasks can be supported by a conference arrangement organisation, whereas others are supported by organisations such as travel arrangers, local tourist offices, conference venues, hotels and publishers (for the proceedings). All these services cost money, which have to be balanced by the income mainly through the participant fee and from sponsors. Thus, a budget needs to be developed to guide the choices of the organising committee.

In connection to a scientific conference, it is as stated above important that the best papers are accepted. The authors are those with primary interest in getting the papers published, and should not be able to influence the review process in a subjective way. On the other hand, people in the program committee are usually allowed to submit papers to a conference. For smaller conferences/workshops, even the organising committee might be allowed to submit papers. To improve the objectivity, it is normal that the review process is so-called double blind, i.e. that you do not know who has written the paper you review, and the authors do not know who has performed the review. The overall review process is normally managed through a web-based paper management system. This system can be configured to follow a number of variants of the review process described above.

To make registration and payment easy, it is usually possible to do this using credit card over the Internet. This also applies for booking hotel rooms and for travel arrangements in general.

C.2.2 Basis for Instance-Level Model (Most Information Found on the Web)

One of the first scientific conferences of this type to be supported by the system was the CAiSE conference series. CAiSE'07 was held in Trondheim 11–15 June 2007 (see http://caise07.idi.ntnu.no). CAiSE'08 was held in Montpellier, France. CAiSE'07 was arranged at Britannia Hotel (http://www.britannia.no) with the support of NTNU Videre (http://www.ntnu.no/videre/konferanser.html) for the practical arrangements.

Index

J. Krogstie, *Model-Based Development and Evolution of Information Systems:*
A Quality Approach, DOI 10.1007/978-1-4471-2936-3,
© Springer-Verlag London 2012